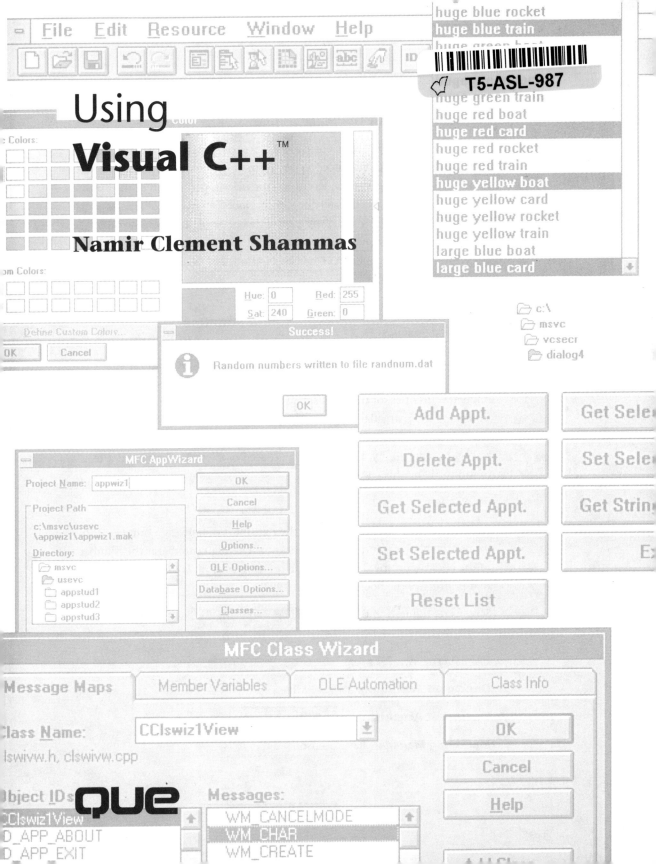

Using

Visual C++™

Namir Clement Shammas

T5-ASL-987

que

Using Visual C++

Copyright© 1994 by Que® Corporation.

Library of Congress Catalog No.: 94-65145

ISBN: 1-56529-626-5

96 95 94   4 3 2

Interpretation of the printing code: the rightmost double-digit number is the year of the book's printing; the rightmost single-digit number is the number of the book's printing. For example, a printing code of 94-1 shows that the first printing of the book occurred in 1994.

Screens reproduced in this book were created using Collage Plus from Inner Media, Inc., Hollis, NH.

Publisher: David P. Ewing

Director of Publishing: Michael Miller

Director of Acquisitions and Editing: Corinne Walls

Marketing Manager: Ray Robinson

Dedication

To TATOLA: Tania, Tony, and Lara Shammas

Credits

Publishing Manager
Joseph Wikert

Product Director
Bryan Gambrel

Production Editor
Jodi Jensen

Editor
Alice Martina Smith

Technical Editors
Robert L. Bogue
Salvatore Mangano
James Shields
Bob Zigon

Book Designer
Amy Peppler-Adams

Cover Designer
Jay Corpus

Production Team

Gary Adair	Angela Bannan
Danielle Bird	Karen Dodson
Brook Farling	Carla Hall
Bob LaRoche	Beth Lewis
Wendy Ott	Nanci Sears Perry
Linda Quigley	Kris Simmons
Amy L. Steed	Becky Tapley
Michael Thomas	Jennifer Willis
Donna Winter	Michelle Worthington
Lillian Yates	

Indexer
Michael Hughes

Editorial Assistants
Michelle Williams
Jill Stanley

Composed in *Stone Serif* and *MCPdigital* by Que Corporation

About the Author

Namir C. Shammas is a professional writer specializing in programming language and object-oriented technology. He is the author or coauthor of more than 30 books dealing with Pascal, BASIC, C, and C++. Prior to writing books, he worked as a chemical engineer in water treatment where he used computers to analyze data and to design water treatment equipment.

His most recent writing projects include *Using Borland C++ 4,* Special Edition, by Que Corporation (coauthor), and *Windows Programmer's Guide to Microsoft Foundation Class Libraries*, by Sams Publishing.

Acknowledgments

A book of this size requires the collective efforts of many people. I would like to thank Joe Wikert, publishing manager, for his vision of what this project should be. I also want to thank Bryan Gambrel, product director, and Jodi Jensen and Alice Martina Smith, editors, for their patience and consistent efforts in smoothing out the text. In addition, I want to thank the technical editors, Salvatore Mangano, Robert L. Bogue, James Shields, and Bob Zigon, for their valuable feedback. Finally, I want to extend my appreciation to all the folks at Prentice Hall who worked hard to put this book in your hands.

Trademarks

All terms mentioned in this book that are known to be trademarks or service marks have been appropriately capitalized. Que cannot attest to the accuracy of this information. Use of a term in this book should not be regarded as affecting the validity of any trademark or service mark.

Microsoft Visual C++ and Microsoft Windows are trademarks of Microsoft Corporation.

Using Visual C++

Introduction to Visual C++

Visual C++ Programming

Advanced Programming

Advanced Utilities

Appendixes

We'd Like to Hear from You!

In its continuing effort to produce the highest-quality books, Que would like to hear your comments. As radical as this may sound coming from a publishing company, we really want you, the reader and user, to let us know what you like and dislike about this book and how we can improve future books.

In order to better serve you, Prentice Hall Computer Publishing now has a forum on CompuServe through which our staff and authors are available for questions and comments (type **GO QUEBOOKS** at any prompt). In addition to visiting our forum, feel free to contact me personally on CompuServe at 70714,1516. You can also send your comments, ideas, or corrections to me by fax at (317) 581-4663 or write to me at the address below. Your comments will help us to continue publishing the best computer books on the market.

Bryan Gambrel
Product Director
Que Corporation
201 W. 103rd Street
Indianapolis, IN 46290

Contents

III Advanced Visual C++ Programming   541

11 Using the Toolbar and Status Bar   543

12 Using MDI Windows   587

16 Using the Workbench Browse Window   773

17 Using the Workbench Debugger   797

IV Advanced Visual C++ Utilities   825

18 Using the Spy Utility   827

19 Using the Stress Application   843

A ASCII and Extended ASCII Codes   857

B Controls Resource Script   867

Introduction

Windows offers a sophisticated graphical user interface (GUI) that is superior to the text-based user interface of MS-DOS. The price we must pay for this refined GUI interface is a dramatic increase in the programming effort required.

Windows programs are more complicated and larger in size than similar MS-DOS programs. This added complexity means that programmers like yourself must withstand a formidable learning curve to program Windows applications. To make matters worse, many programmers feel that they are aiming at a moving target. No sooner do you become familiar and somewhat comfortable with your new Windows programming skills, than Microsoft adds new features and introduces new Windows variants (such as Windows NT and Windows for Workgroups). To help Windows programmers, Microsoft has made its C/C++ compiler package more sophisticated. Visual C++ version 1.0 and 1.5 offer interesting programming tools, such as AppWizard and Class-Wizard, that make it easy to create Windows programs quickly.

Is This Book for You?

This book is aimed at readers who are already familiar with C++, Windows, and the basics of Windows programming. Prior knowledge of the Microsoft Foundation Classes (MFC) is a plus but not a requirement. This book covers many programming topics that use C++ and the MFC class. If you only use the C compiler portion of the Visual C++ product, this book is not for you! Because of the huge amount of available information, covering every aspect of Visual C++ and the MFC library in any one book is impossible. I cover most of the MFC library using a hands-on approach.

What's in This Book?

This book contains 19 chapters and four appendixes. The following paragraphs provide a brief description of what you will find in each of these elements.

Part I, "Introduction to Visual C++," includes Chapters 1 through 5. This first part offers the basic information you need to work with the Visual Workbench, AppWizard, ClassWizard, and App Studio utilities. In addition, this part of the book introduces you to the classes in the MFC library.

Chapter 1, "Overview of the Visual C++ Workbench," discusses the Visual Workbench and its various options. These options enable you to manage files, edit text, view various information, manage program project files, browse through declarations and definitions, conduct debugging sessions, invoke programming tools, fine-tune the various Workbench components (including the compiler, linker, and resource compiler), manage the Workbench windows, and obtain on-line help.

Chapter 2, "Overview of the MFC Hierarchy," discusses managing Windows messages in Visual C++, offers you an overview of the MFC hierarchy, and presents a set of simple programming examples. The bulk of the chapter deals with presenting the various groups of MFC classes. (The more advanced MFC classes are discussed in Appendix C).

Chapter 3, "Using the AppWizard Utility," shows you how you can use the AppWizard utility to generate skeleton programs. The chapter presents the various kinds of programs the AppWizard can generate, and these programs include support for SDI or MDI windows, the toolbar and status bar, and the print and print preview features.

Chapter 4, "Using the ClassWizard Utility," presents the ClassWizard utility and discusses invoking it and using its various options. The chapter illustrates how to add new member functions to manage the message maps of an application you generated using AppWizard.

Chapter 5, "Using the App Studio Utility," focuses on using the App Studio utility to create, edit, and remove various kinds of resources. These resources include menus, dialog boxes, icons, bitmaps, and string tables. The chapter shows you how to use the App Studio utility to modify an existing menu resource, add a new dialog box resource, and create a new form view.

Part II, "Visual C++ Programming," includes Chapters 6 through 10. This part presents the classes in the MFC library that support the various common visual controls, such as pushbuttons, edit boxes, and list boxes.

Chapter 6, "Working with the Static Text, Pushbutton, and Edit Controls," discusses these most fundamental visual controls. The chapter discusses the relevant member functions for the classes supporting these controls, presents the control styles, and also offers programming examples using these controls.

Chapter 7, "Working with the Grouped Controls," presents the grouped controls that include the check box, radio button, and group (also called *frame*) controls. The chapter discusses the relevant member functions for the classes supporting these controls, presents the control styles, and offers programming examples using these controls.

Chapter 8, "Working with the Scrollable Controls," focuses on the scrollable controls including the scroll bar, list box, and combo box. The chapter discusses the relevant member functions for the classes supporting the scrollable controls, presents the control styles, and offers programming examples that use these controls. The chapter also discusses handling single-selection and multiple-selection list boxes.

Chapter 9, "Working with Dialog Boxes," discusses dialog boxes and the use of the Microsoft Foundation Class (MFC) library to create both modal and modeless dialog boxes. The chapter also presents an example of creating a dialog box as a non-child window. In addition, the chapter discusses the techniques for transferring data between the controls of a dialog box and its parent window.

Chapter 10, "Using the Common Dialog Boxes," presents the common dialog boxes that enable you to select colors, select fonts, print, open files, save files, search for text, and replace text. The chapter presents the various common dialog box classes and their supporting structures. The examples illustrate how to invoke the various common dialog boxes and how to use the helper member functions to obtain user input.

Part III, "Advanced Visual C++ Programming," includes Chapters 11 through 17. This part presents more advanced aspects of the MFC library, such as programming Visual Basic controls, working with the toolbar and status bar, and managing run-time errors.

Chapter 11, "Using the Toolbar and Status Bar," focuses on MFC classes that support the toolbar and status bar windows. The chapter presents the CToolBar class, guidelines for using this class, and offers a sample program you can use to program the toolbar. The chapter also presents the CStatusBar class, guidelines for using this class, and offers another sample program you can use to program the status bar.

Chapter 12, "Using MDI Windows," discusses MDI Windows and presents the MFC classes CMDIFrameWnd and CMDIChildWnd. The chapter covers how to manage MDI messages and offers two sample MDI-compliant programs.

Chapter 13, "Using Visual Basic Controls," focuses on the Visual Basic (VBX) controls. The text introduces you to the VBX control properties, methods, and events, and presents the CVbControl class. The chapter discusses using the AppWizard, ClassWizard, and App Studio utilities to create programs with VBX controls. The chapter offers an example using the VBX grid control— a spreadsheet-like control containing columns and rows of text.

Chapter 14, "Using the *CString* and Collections Classes," focuses on the CString and collections classes that model strings, arrays, lists, and maps. The chapter offers programs to test several CString member functions, to test arrays of CString objects, to test lists of CString objects, and to test maps of CString objects.

Chapter 15, "Using the Exceptions Classes," discusses the Visual C++ exception mechanism and the exception MFC classes. These classes support general exceptions as well as those related to memory, file, archive, resource, user, unsupported features, OLE, and ODBC operations.

Chapter 16, "Using the Workbench Browse Window," focuses on using the Browse window to examine macros, data types, variables, data members, function calls, and class hierarchies. The chapter discusses special features that enable you to view the calls between various functions and the hierarchy of targeted classes.

Chapter 17, "Using the Workbench Debugger," presents the Visual C++ Workbench Debugger and discusses hard and soft debugging modes, setting breakpoints, and the use of conditional and unconditional breakpoints. In addition, the chapter looks at using the function call stack, mixing assembly code with C++ statements, and managing the Watch window.

Part IV, "Advanced Visual C++ Utilities," includes Chapters 18 and 19. This final part of the book presents stand-alone utilities that enable you to examine and test your Windows applications.

Chapter 18, "Using the Spy Utility," focuses on using The Spy Utility to monitor window messages. The chapter discusses the various message-monitoring options that enable you to select specific windows or messages to monitor.

Chapter 19, "Using the Stress Application," presents the utility that performs limited-resource stress on your applications. The chapter discusses the various stress testing options and presents several examples for different levels of stress testing.

Appendix A, "ASCII and Extended ASCII Codes," provides a convenient chart of the 256 characters defined by the American Standard Code for Information Interchange (ASCII).

Appendix B, "Controls Resource Script," discusses the resource scripts for menus and for the various controls that appear in dialog boxes.

Appendix C, "Advanced MFC Classes," examines advanced MFC classes, such as common dialog boxes and exceptions.

Appendix D, "Moving from OWL2 to MFC2," discusses the topic of moving OWL2-based programs to MFC 2.x. This appendix presents general translation comments and then discusses translating classes and message map macros. The text also presents two examples: a minimal Windows program and a command-line oriented calculator.

Conventions Used in This Book

To make this book easier to use, the following typographical conventions have been implemented:

- Words or phrases defined for the first time appear in *italics*. Words or phrases that you are asked to type appear in **bold**. Screen displays and on-screen messages appear in a special monospace typeface.

- Names of classes, functions, variables, messages, macros, and so on appear in monospace type.

■ A code continuation character (➡) has been used when a code line is too long to fit within the margins of this book. This symbol simply indicates that due to page constraints, a code line has been broken that normally would appear on a single line.

■ In several chapters, certain code lines have been highlighted with a gray screen. This screen indicates code that is discussed specifically in the surrounding text. In many cases (particularly in Chapters 4 and 5), these highlighted lines indicate code that I added to code originally generated by a utility (such as ClassWizard). In other cases, the gray screen is provided to draw your focus to code that is central to the discussion.

I hope this book helps you in working with Visual C++ to build MFC-based Windows applications.

Happy Programming!

Namir Clement Shammas
January 20, 1994

Part I

Introduction to Visual C++

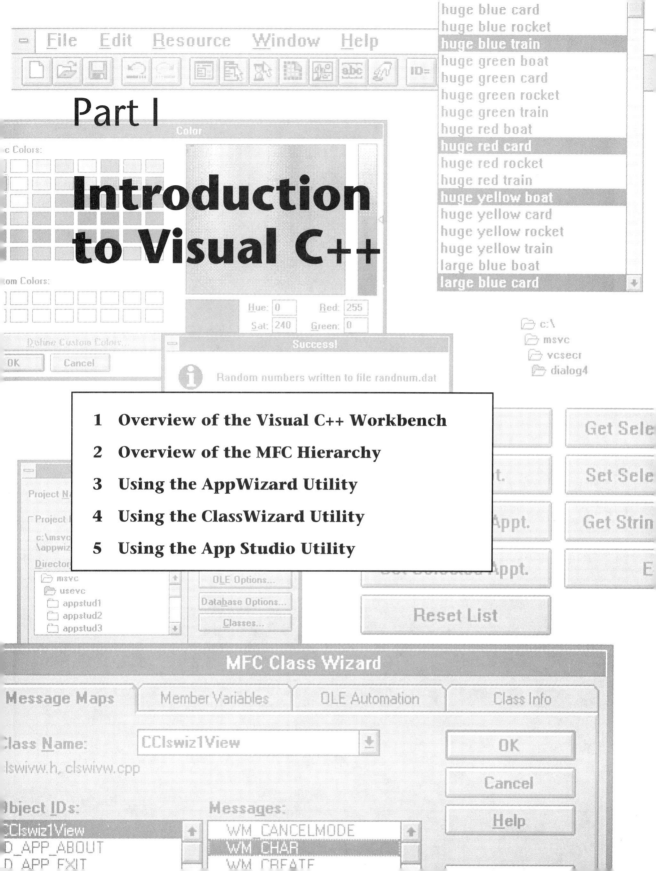

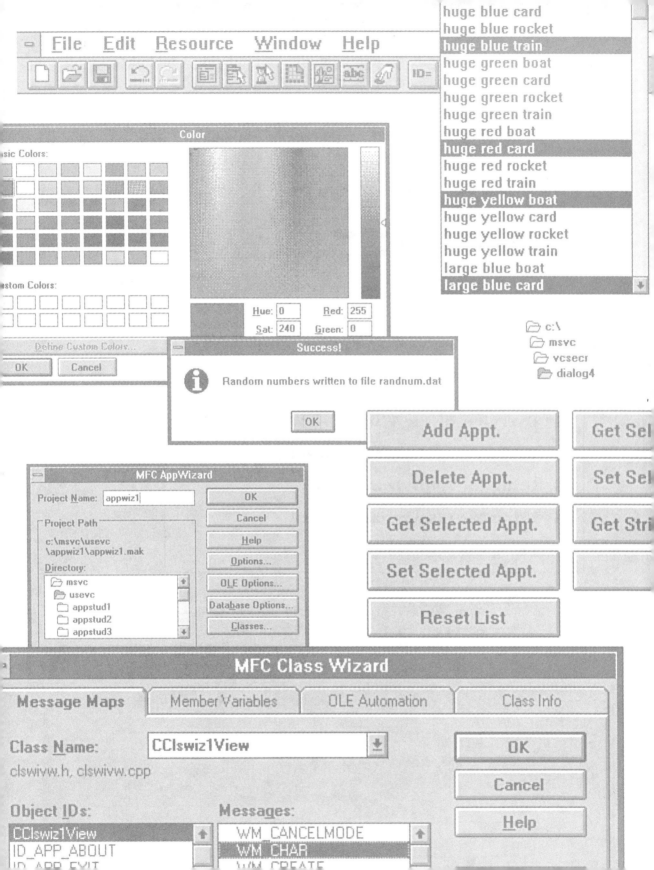

Chapter 1

Overview of the Visual C++ Workbench

To work with Visual C++, you begin by loading the Visual C++ Workbench. It seems fitting, therefore, to first introduce you to the Visual C++ Workbench program development environment. Keep in mind that the Visual Workbench offers commands of various sophistication. Some commands perform general tasks, such as file management. Others perform more advanced programming tasks, such as debugging. In this chapter, you learn how to load the Visual Workbench, and you also learn about the following Visual Workbench menus:

- The File menu

- The Edit menu

- The View menu

- The Project menu

- The Browse menu

- The Debug menu

- The Tools menu

- The Options menu

- The Window menu

- The Help menu

The discussion of the advanced Workbench commands includes simple examples that should give you a feel for how these commands work and also help you become familiar with them. Some of the advanced commands are discussed in more detail later in this book.

Loading the Visual Workbench

Loading the Visual Workbench is easy. You can use a mouse and double-click the Visual C++ icon, usually found in the Microsoft Visual C++ folder. Alternatively, you can access the Windows File Manager, pull down the File menu, choose the Run command, and then enter the following command:

    C:\MSVC\BIN\MSVC.EXE

This command assumes that you have installed Visual C++ in the default drive C: and in the default directory \MSVC. (No command-line switches are available for loading the Visual Workbench.) Figure 1.1 shows the Visual Workbench.

Figure 1.1
The Visual
Workbench.

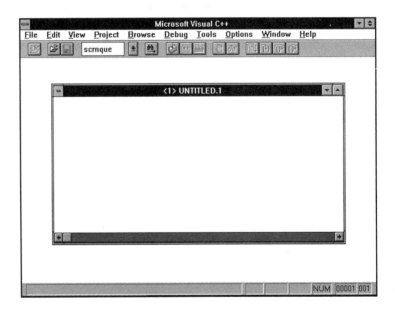

The File Menu

The File menu commands let you manage the various kinds of source files that are involved in creating a program. The File menu includes the following commands, which are summarized in Table 1.1: New, Open, Close, Save, Save As, Save All, Print, Page Setup, and Exit.

Command	Shortcut Key	Purpose
Table 1.1 File Menu Commands		
New	Ctrl+N	Creates an empty and unnamed source code window.
Open...	Ctrl+O	Opens an existing source file.
Close		Closes the currently selected window.
Save	Ctrl+S	Writes the currently selected window to its associated file. In the case of a new window, this command invokes the Save As dialog box to request the name of the associated file.
Save As...		Renames the file associated with the currently selected window. If the window is new, this command invokes the Save As dialog box to request the name of the associated file.
Save All		Saves all currently opened windows to their associated files.
Print...		Prints the currently selected window. Invokes the Print dialog box.
Page Setup...		Sets up the printer by invoking the Page Setup dialog box.
Exit		Exits the Visual Workbench.

The New Command

The New command opens a new source window. Each window in the Visual Workbench includes a title consisting of the window's number (enclosed in angle brackets) followed by the name of the associated file. When you create

the first new source window, Visual Workbench uses the temporary name
UNTITLED.1. The second new source window is named UNTITLED.2, and so on.
When assigning a number to a source window, Visual Workbench uses the
first available window number. For example, suppose that you have five new
source windows open in the Visual Workbench, and you delete window
number 3. The next window you open will be given the number 3 because
that is the first available window number. Source windows are numbered
beginning with 1 and going up from there.

The Open Command

The Open command lets you open a source code file for viewing or editing
and invokes the Open File dialog box, shown in Figure 1.2. In the File Name
text box, you can type the name of a file located on any existing drive and
directory, and you can use wild-card characters as necessary. Beneath the File
Name text box is a list box which displays all files (in the currently selected
path) that match the filename wild card that was entered. The Open File
dialog box also has drop-down list boxes that display the available drives,
directories, and predefined file types. If you want to open a source file for
viewing only, click the Read-Only check box control.

Figure 1.2

The Open File
dialog box.

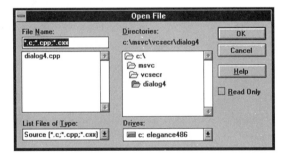

The Open command remembers the last selection you made. The next time
you open a file, the Open File dialog box displays the drive and directory of
the most recently selected file. Another feature of the Open command is that
it does not enable you to open a file that is already open. Instead, the command generates a beep and displays a message in the status line at the bottom of the Visual Workbench.

You can press the shortcut key combination Ctrl+O to access the Open File
dialog box. Alternatively, you can access the dialog box by clicking the
bitmapped open folder icon on the toolbar (the second icon from the left).

The Close Command

Use the Close command to close the currently selected window (also called the *active* window). If that window has been updated and the update not yet saved, you are prompted to save the contents of the window. You can close all open windows without exiting the Visual Workbench by choosing the Close All command from the Window menu.

The Save Command

The Save command writes the contents of the currently selected window to the file associated with it. If the active window is new, this command invokes the Save As dialog box to request the name of the associated file.

You can save the active window by pressing the shortcut key combination Ctrl+S or by clicking the bitmapped disk icon on the toolbar (the third icon from the left).

The Save As Command

The Save As command lets you specify a new filename for the active source window. This command invokes the Save As dialog box, shown in Figure 1.3, to prompt you for the output source filename. The Save As dialog box is very similar to the Open File dialog box and enables you to select the drive, directory, and name for the output filename.

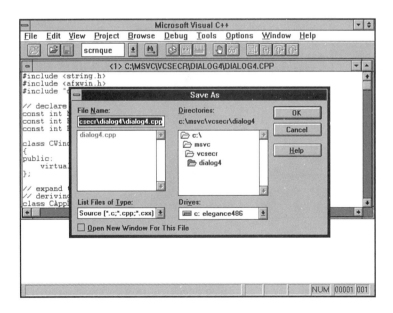

Figure 1.3
The Save As dialog box.

The Save All Command

The Save All command provides a convenient and systematic way for you to save all the source windows in the Visual Workbench. This command ensures that all windows are updated with a minimum of effort. You especially appreciate this convenient command when you have to frequently save the contents of all your windows because of possible power interruptions.

The Print Command

The Print command enables you to produce a hard copy of the source code in the active widow. This command invokes the Print dialog box, shown in Figure 1.4. The dialog box contains a frame control with two radio buttons that are labeled All and Selection. These buttons let you choose between printing the entire contents of a source window or printing only the selected text. In addition, the Print dialog box contains a drop-down list box that displays the list of currently available printers. You can manipulate the setup of the currently selected printer by clicking the command button labeled Setup.

Figure 1.4

The Print
dialog box.

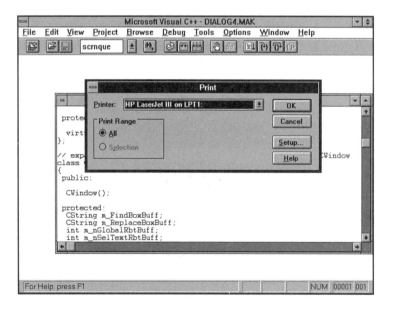

The Setup button invokes the Setup dialog box, shown in Figure 1.5. This dialog box (which may look different than the one you see if you have another kind of printer) enables you to select printing parameters, such as the paper size, paper source, graphics resolution, number of copies, memory, output orientation, font cartridges, and fonts.

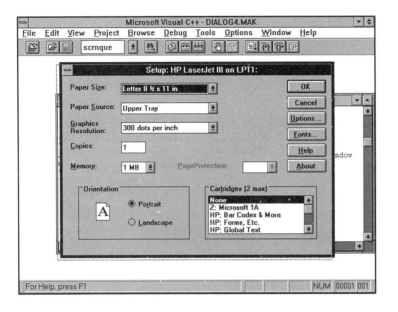

Figure 1.5
The Setup
dialog box.

The Page Setup Command

You can use the Page Setup command to specify how the printed output
looks. This command invokes the Page Setup dialog box, shown in Figure 1.6.
As you can see in this figure, the dialog box contains edit controls that allow
you to specify a header and footer, as well as the left, right, top, and bottom
margins.

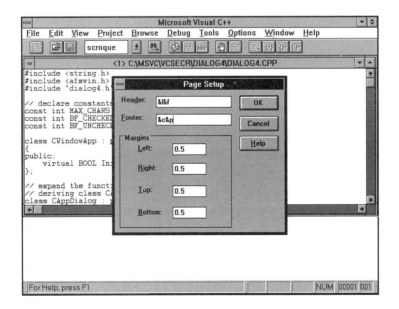

Figure 1.6
The Page Setup
dialog box.

Table 1.2 shows the special codes you can use to format the header and footer. For example, if you enter the string **&l&f** for the header and the string **&c&p** for the footer, the output page displays a left justified filename in the header and a centered page number in the footer.

Table 1.2 Header and Footer Formatting Codes	
Format Code	**Function**
&f	Filename
&p	Page number
&t	Current system time
&d	Current system date
&l	Left-justified
&c	Centered
&r	Right-justified

Note: The format codes are case-insensitive.

The Exit Command

The last command in the File menu is Exit. This command closes all the source windows and then closes the Visual Workbench. If any source windows open in the Workbench have not been updated, the Visual Workbench prompts you to save them before it closes them.

The Edit Menu

The Edit menu commands support text editing and searching. The Edit menu contains the following commands, which are summarized in Table 1.3: Undo, Redo, Cut, Copy, Paste, Delete, Find, Replace, Find Matching Brace, and Read-Only.

Table 1.3 Edit Menu Commands		
Command	**Shortcut Key**	**Purpose**
Undo	Ctrl+Z	Undoes the most recent editing actions.

Command	Shortcut Key	Purpose
Redo	Ctrl+A	Reverses the last undo action.
Cut	Ctrl+X	Deletes selected text and writes it to the Clipboard. The previous contents of the Clipboard are overwritten.
Copy	Ctrl+C	Copies the currently selected text to the Clipboard. The previous contents of the Clipboard are lost.
Paste	Ctrl+V	Pastes text from the Clipboard at the insertion point. Any selected text is overwritten by the pasted text.
Delete	Del	Deletes text without saving it to the Clipboard.
Find...	Alt+F3	Searches for text using the Find dialog box.
Replace...		Replaces text using the Replace dialog box.
Find Matching Brace	Ctrl+]	Moves to the corresponding brace.
Read Only		Toggles read-only mode to protect the contents of a source window from accidental changes.

The Undo Command

You can use the Undo command to reverse the effect of your most recent editing actions. The actual number of editing actions you can undo depends on the size of your undo buffer. This buffer has the default size of 4K, but you can set it from 0K to 64K. (You can alter the size of the undo buffer by choosing the Editor command from the Options menu. The Editor command displays an edit box in which you can enter the new size of the undo buffer.) The shortcut keys for the Undo command are Ctrl+Z and Alt+Backspace.

The Redo Command

The Redo command enables you to counteract the effects of the Undo command. You can use Redo to restore the results of the editing actions that you just reversed with Undo. (This command should be particularly useful to programmers who get bleary eyed from long hours in front of the computer). The Redo shortcut key combinations are Ctrl+A and Ctrl+Backspace.

The Cut Command

The Cut command enables you to delete a block of selected text and write it to the Clipboard (which overwrites the previous contents of the Clipboard). You can then use the Paste command to insert the deleted text in one or more locations in a source window. The Cut and Paste commands are useful to move text from one location to another—both within a single source window and between source windows. The shortcut key combination for Cut is Ctrl+X.

The Copy Command

Use the Copy command to copy a block of selected text into the Clipboard (which overwrites the previous contents of the Clipboard). You can then insert the copied text in one or more locations in the same source window or in other windows by using the Paste command. The shortcut key combination for the Copy command is Ctrl+C.

The Paste Command

The Paste command lets you insert the contents of the Clipboard at the current cursor location. This action overwrites any text that is highlighted. You can use the Paste command with the Cut and Copy commands to move and copy text, respectively. The shortcut key combination for Copy is Ctrl+V.

The Delete Command

The Delete command deletes text without copying it to the Clipboard. If text is selected, Delete removes the selected text. If no text is selected, Delete removes the character located to the right of the edit cursor.

> **Note**
>
> Use the Undo command to reverse the action of the Delete command. Undo is available in this situation because Delete copies the deleted characters into the undo buffer.

The Find Command

You can use the Find command to perform versatile text searches ranging from simple text to sophisticated text patterns, known as *regular expressions* (see sidebar "Regular Expressions"). You can also use Find to locate text and then set a bookmark on the line containing the matching text. The shortcut key combination for Find is Alt+F3. Figure 1.7 shows the Find dialog box. In the Find What combo box, you enter the text or text pattern for which you want to search. You can recall previous text or a text pattern by choosing the appropriate item from the Find What drop-down list.

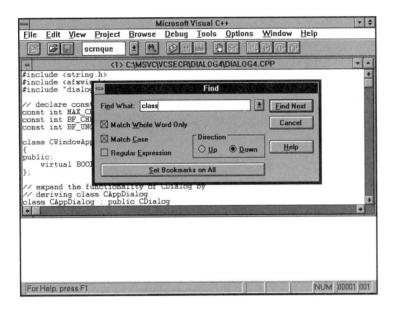

Figure 1.7
The Find
dialog box.

Use the following controls to fine-tune the operation of the Find dialog box:

- The Match Whole Word Only check box determines whether or not the matching text should match an entire word.

- The Match Case check box specifies whether or not the search is case-sensitive.

- The Regular Expression check box determines whether the selected text in the Find What combo box is treated as a regular expression (see the sidebar "Regular Expressions").

- The Direction frame control contains the Up and Down radio buttons, which determine the search direction.

The Find dialog box has two buttons that trigger different kinds of searches. The Find Next command button searches for the next matching text or text pattern. The Set Bookmarks on All command button searches all the matching text or text patterns and sets bookmarks on the matching lines. The View menu in the Visual Workbench offers commands that enable you to view the next and previous bookmarks. More about those commands in the next section.

You can use the toolbar to quickly search for new text or for the next occurrence of specified text. The toolbar contains a combo box that enables you to recall a previous search string or to enter a new one. To conduct another text search, click the bitmapped binocular icon on the toolbar (fifth icon from the left). The Visual Workbench performs the text search based on the most recent settings in the Find dialog box.

Regular Expressions

Regular expressions are special strings that contain text patterns. These patterns are used in searching for a range of strings. Regular expressions use special characters to specify the text pattern. The Visual Workbench supports the following characters:

.	Represents any individual character. For example, the pattern m..t matches *meat, meet, ment*, and any other four-character word that starts with *m* and ends with *t*.
*	Matches zero or more of the characters or the expression preceding the asterisk. For example, the pattern Robin*son matches *Robinson* and *Robison*.
+	Matches one or more of the characters or the expression preceding the plus character. For example, the pattern Sham+as matches *Shammas* and *Shamas*.
^	Matches a pattern at the beginning of a line. For example, the pattern ^if only matches a code line that starts with the characters *i* and *f*.
$	Matches a pattern at the end of a line. For example, the pattern -1)$ matches any line that ends with the string *-1)*.
[]	Matches any of the characters appearing in the brackets or any range of ASCII characters delimited by a hyphen. For example, the pattern 199[0-9] matches *1990* through *1999*. The pattern me[aen]t matches *meat, meet, and ment*, but not *melt*.
\{\}	Matches any sequence of characters between the escaped braces. For example, the text pattern \{ba\}*by matches *by, baby, bababy, babababy,* in the word *babababy*.
\	Specifies that the preceding character be treated as a normal character and not as part of the pattern characters. For example, the pattern \[i\] matches the string *[i]*.

Let's look at some examples of how you can use the Find command. Listing 1.1 shows the line-numbered source code for the file LINREG.CPP. The line numbers assist in specifying the location of matching text.

Listing 1.1 Line-Numbered Source Code for LINREG.CPP

```
 1:  // Program which performs linear regression
 2:
 3:  #include <iostream.h>
 4:  #include <math.h>
 5:
 6:  // declare linear regression class
 7:  class regRec {
 8:
 9:   public:
10:    regRec()
11:      { initSums(); }
12:
13:    void initSums();
14:    void updateSums(double* x, double* y, unsigned count);
15:    void calcMean();
16:    void calcSdev();
17:    void calcLR();
18:    void showResults();
19:
20:
21:   protected:
22:    double sum;
23:    double sumx;
24:    double sumxx;
25:    double sumy;
26:    double sumyy;
27:    double sumxy;
28:    double meanx;
29:    double meany;
30:    double sdevx;
31:    double sdevy;
32:    double slope;
33:    double intercept;
34:    double rsqr;
35:  };
36:
37:
38:  inline double sqr(double x)
39:  {
40:    return x * x;
41:  }
42:
43:  void regRec::initSums()
44:  {
45:    sum = 0;
46:    sumx = 0;
47:    sumxx = 0;
48:    sumy = 0;
```

(continues)

Listing 1.1 Continued

```
49:    sumyy = 0;
50:    sumxy = 0;
51:  }
52:
53:  void regRec::updateSums(double* x, double* y, unsigned count)
54:  {
55:    sum = double(count);
56:    for (unsigned i = 0; i < count; i++) {
57:      sumx += x[i];
58:      sumxx += sqr(x[i]);
59:      sumy += y[i];
60:      sumyy += sqr(y[i]);
61:      sumxy += x[i] * y[i];
62:    }
63:  }
64:
65:  void regRec::calcMean()
66:  {
67:    meanx = sumx / sum;
68:    meany = sumy / sum;
69:  }
70:
71:  void regRec::calcSdev()
72:  {
73:    sdevx = sqrt((sumxx - sqr(sumx) / sum)/(sum - 1));
74:    sdevy = sqrt((sumyy - sqr(sumy) / sum)/(sum - 1));
75:  }
76:
77:  void regRec::calcLR()
78:  {
79:    slope = (sumxy - meanx * meany * sum) /
80:            sqr(sdevx) / (sum - 1);
81:    intercept = meany - slope * meanx;
82:    rsqr = sqr(sdevx / sdevy * slope);
83:  }
84:
85:  void regRec::showResults()
86:  {
87:    cout << "\n\n"
88:         << "Data size = " << sum       << "\n"
89:         << "R-square  = " << rsqr       << "\n"
90:         << "Slope     = " << slope      << "\n"
91:         << "Intercept = " << intercept  << "\n"
92:         << "Mean X    = " << meanx      << "\n"
93:         << "Mean Y    = " << meany      << "\n"
94:         << "Sdev X    = " << sdevx      << "\n"
95:         << "Sdev Y    = " << sdevy      << "\n";
96:  }
97:
98:  main()
99:  {
100:    const unsigned MAX = 100;
101:    regRec LR;
102:    double x[MAX];
103:    double y[MAX];
```

```
104:    unsigned n;
105:
106:    do {
107:      cout << "Enter number of points (at least 2) : ";
108:      cin >> n;
109:      cout << "\n";
110:    } while (n < 2 ¦¦ n >= MAX);
111:
112:    for (unsigned i = 0; i < n; i++) {
113:      cout << "Enter x[" << i << "] ? ";
114:      cin >> x[i];
115:      cout << "Enter y[" << i << "] ? ";
116:      cin >> y[i];
117:    }
118:
119:    LR.updateSums(x, y, n);
120:    LR.calcMean();
121:    LR.calcSdev();
122:    LR.calcLR();
123:    LR.showResults();
124:
125:    return 0;
126:  }
```

Let's first look at using regular expressions in a text search. Load the file LINREG.CPP (located in the directory \MSVC\USEVC) and perform the following tasks:

1. Select the window containing the source code for the file LINREG.CPP.

2. Invoke the Find command.

3. Enter the string **sumx*** in the Find What combo box.

4. Click the Regular Expression check box to mark an X, which causes the dialog box to disable the Match Whole Word Only check box.

5. Click the Match Case check box to mark an X.

6. Click the Find Next command button. The search matches the member sum in line number 22 and highlights it. At the same time, the Find dialog box relocates itself and alters its shape to become a Find dialog bar.

7. Click the Find Next command button in the Find dialog bar. The Visual Workbench now matches the search pattern with the member sumx in line 23. Repeat this step to find the other matches. You will notice that the pattern sumx+ ends up matching all the members of the structure regRec that begin with *sum*.

Now move the cursor back to the beginning of the listing and reinvoke the Find command. Enter the text pattern **sumx+** and repeat steps 6 and 7. What is the difference in the matching text now? Using the text pattern sumx+ ends up matching with the members sumx, sumxx, and sumxy throughout the listing.

Next, test the bookmark feature. Move the cursor back to the beginning of the file. Invoke the Find command. Make sure that the text pattern is sumx+, and then click the Set Bookmarks on All command button. The Visual Workbench marks all the source code lines containing the members sumx, sumxx, and sumxy. To view the next line with a bookmark, press the F2 key (more about managing bookmarks in the next section). To clear the bookmarks (at least for now) simply close the window containing the source code of file LINREG.CPP and then open it again.

Note

The Set Bookmarks on All command button adds a new set of bookmarks to any existing bookmarks. To clear the current set of bookmarks, choose Clear All Bookmarks from the View menu before you invoke the Find command.

The Replace Command

You can use the Replace command to replace both simple text and text patterns with simple text. This command invokes the Replace dialog box, shown in Figure 1.8. The Replace dialog box has two combo boxes labeled Find What and Replace With. These controls, as their names suggest, contain the search and replacement text. The Replace dialog box has the same check box controls as the Find dialog box. In addition, the Replace dialog box has two replacement command buttons, labeled Find Next and Replace All. The first command button enables you to locate matching text before you determine whether you want to replace it. The second command button lets you find and replace text in one swoop.

Caution

Use the Find Next command button when you are replacing text that matches a text pattern. This approach lets you view the matching text before you replace it. To be doubly safe, work on a *copy* of the source code and not the original. By using this precaution, you have the luxury of resorting to the original document, if necessary, with little effort.

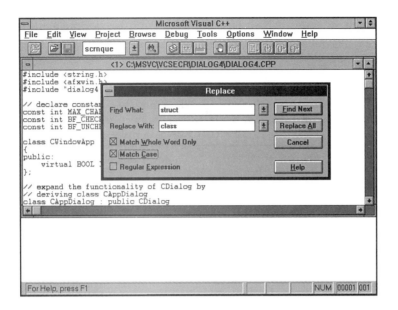

Figure 1.8

The Replace dialog box.

The Find Matching Brace Command

The Find Matching Brace command enables you to check for the correct pairing of open and close braces by jumping to a matching brace. The shortcut key combination for Find Matching Brace is Ctrl+]. To locate the matching brace, move the cursor to the left of the open or close brace you want to match. Then invoke this command, and the cursor jumps to the matching brace. If the brace you are checking has no counterpart, the Visual Workbench beeps.

The Read-Only Command

The Edit menu's final command is Read-Only, which enables you to protect the source code in a window from accidentally being altered. The command toggles the read-only mode of the source code. When the read-only mode is on, the Visual Workbench displays a check mark after this command, and the status bar displays the word READ.

The View Menu

The View menu offers several commands that let you view various aspects of your source code and different windows in the Visual Workbench. The View menu includes the following commands, which are summarized in Table 1.4:

Line, Mixed Source/Asm, Next Error, Previous Error, Toggle Bookmark, Next Bookmark, Previous Bookmark, Clear All Bookmarks, Toolbar, Status Bar, and Syntax Coloring.

Table 1.4 View Menu Commands		
Command	**Shortcut Key**	**Purpose**
Line...		Moves to a specified line.
Mixed Source/Asm	Ctrl+F7	Displays assembly code.
Next Error	F4	Moves to the next program build error.
Previous Error	Shift+F4	Moves to the previous program build error.
Toggle Bookmark	Ctrl+F2	Turns on or off the bookmark that highlights a line of code.
Next Bookmark	F2	Moves to the next bookmark.
Previous Bookmark	Alt+F3	Moves to the previous bookmark.
Clear All Bookmarks		Turns off the bookmark that highlights the marked code lines.
Toolbar		Toggles the visibility of the toolbar.
Status Bar		Toggles the visibility of the status bar.
Syntax Coloring		Selects whether to color the source code; also gives you the choice to color your code as either C or a C++ source code.

The Line Command

Use the Line command to jump to a source code line by specifying its number. The Line command invokes a simple dialog box that contains a line number edit control. The line number you type must be in the range of 1 to 32000. If you enter a number that is greater than the number of lines in the source code (and smaller than 32001), Visual Workbench moves the cursor to the last line.

The Mixed Source/Asm Command

The Mixed Source/Asm command enables you to view your source code along with its equivalent assembly code during a debugging session. Figure 1.9 shows a sample display (from the LINREG.EXE program) that I generated when I invoked the Mixed Source/Asm command while single-stepping through the program. The shortcut key combination for this command is Ctrl+F7.

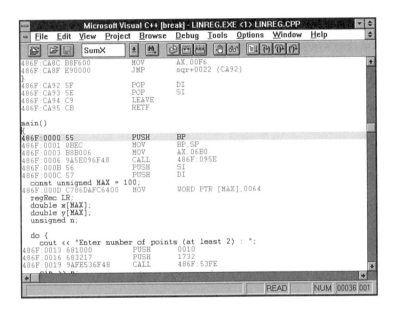

Figure 1.9
Sample display generated by the Mixed Source/Asm command.

The Next Error Command

The Next Error command helps you locate the next error generated by building a program. The Visual Workbench highlights the line containing the offending code and displays the associated error message in the status line. The shortcut key for this command is F4.

The Previous Error Command

The Previous Error command enables you to visit the previous error generated by building a program. The Visual Workbench highlights the line containing the offending code and displays the associated error message in the status line. The shortcut key combination for this command is Shift+F4.

The Toggle Bookmark Command

The Toggle Bookmark command enables you to toggle a bookmark. You can use this command to manually mark specific lines of code and perhaps show these lines to a colleague. You can also use this command in conjunction with the Find dialog box. The Find dialog box first sets the bookmarks for the lines containing matching text. Then you examine the lines and decide which ones you want to unmark. The shortcut key combination for this command is Ctrl+F2.

The Next Bookmark Command

The Next Bookmark command moves the cursor to the next line containing a bookmark. The shortcut key for this command is F2.

The Previous Bookmark Command

The Previous Bookmark command moves the cursor to the previous line containing a book. The shortcut key combination for this command is Shift+F2.

The Clear All Bookmarks Command

The Clear All Bookmarks command clears all bookmarks in one swoop. Use this command to clear the current set of bookmarks before assigning a new set of bookmarks using the Find dialog box. If you do not use this command, the Find dialog box simply adds additional bookmarks to your existing ones.

> **Note**
>
> The Find dialog box adds bookmarks and does not automatically remove existing ones.

The Toolbar Command

The Toolbar command toggles the visibility of the toolbar. The Visual Workbench marks this command with a check mark when the toolbar is visible. Hiding the toolbar offers more vertical space for the source windows.

The Status Bar Command

The Status Bar command toggles the visibility of the status bar. The Visual Workbench marks this command with a check mark when the status bar is visible. Hiding the status bar offers more vertical space for the source windows.

The Syntax Coloring Command

The last command in the View menu, Syntax Coloring, enables the editor to display colored keywords. This command contains a nested menu that lets you choose among C syntax coloring, C++ syntax coloring, and no coloring. With syntax coloring, you can quickly detect misspelled keywords because they do not change color after you finish typing them. In addition, syntax coloring enables you to quickly detect commented statements.

The Project Menu

The Project menu offers commands that let you create applications and then manage the process. Visual C++, like other Windows and DOS C/C++ compilers, uses project files to create a wide variety of applications. Such applications range from DOS .COM files to Windows DLLs. Visual C++ project files use the .MAK file extension. The Project menu includes the following commands, which are summarized in Table 1.5: AppWizard, New, Open, Edit, Close, Compile File, Build, Rebuild All, Stop Build, Execute, Scan Dependencies, Scan All Dependencies, Load Workspace, and Save Workspace.

Table 1.5 Project Menu Commands

Command	Shortcut Key	Purpose
AppWizard...		Generates a Windows application using AppWizard.
New...		Creates a new project using the New Project dialog box.
Open...		Opens an existing project and automatically closes the currently opened project.
Edit... *PRJ*.MAK		Adds or deletes files from a project file.
Close		Closes the current project file.
Compile File *name*	Ctrl+F8	Compiles the source file associated with the active source window.
Build *target*	Shift+F8	Builds all the files in the project while observing the dependency rules.
Rebuild All *target*	Alt+F8	Builds all the files in the project without observing the dependency rules.
Stop Build		Halts the build as soon as the currently used tool terminates its task.

(continues)

Table 1.5 Continued		
Command	**Shortcut Key**	**Purpose**
Execute *target*	Ctrl+F5	Runs the project's program.
Scan Dependencies *filename*		Updates the dependency list for the file in the active source window.
Scan All Dependencies		Updates the dependency list for the entire project.
Load Workspace *PRJ*.WSP		Loads one of three previously saved workspaces associated with the current project.
Save Workspace *PRJ*.WSP		Saves one of three workspaces associated with the current project.

The AppWizard Command

The AppWizard command provides you with a powerful tool for creating a Windows application. The AppWizard tool simplifies the process involved in creating such applications. Chapter 3 focuses on using this command to invoke the AppWizard tool.

The New Command

The New command lets you create a new .MAK project file. The command first invokes the New Project dialog box, which enables you to specify the following:

- The name of the project.

- The kind of compiled file to generate (see the sidebar "Compiled Files").

- Whether the application uses the Microsoft Foundation Classes.

- The directory that will contain the project file.

Compiled Files

Visual C++ enables you to generate the following kinds of programs and libraries:

- Window applications (.EXE)

- Windows dynamic-link libraries (.DLL)

- Visual Basic custom controls (.VBX)

- QuickWin applications (.EXE)

- Static libraries (.LIB)

- Windows P-Code applications (.EXE)

- MS-DOS applications (.EXE)

- MS-DOS P-code applications (.EXE)

- MS-DOS overlaid applications (.EXE)

- MS-DOS COM applications (.COM)

QuickWin applications emulate MS-DOS in Windows. The emulation is not complete and excludes cursor control and keyboard scanning techniques. Nevertheless, you can write short DOS-like C and C++ programs on the fly and compile them into QuickWin applications. You can use the C++ stream I/O and the standard C I/O library with QuickWin applications.

Visual C++ enables you to generate P-code Windows and MS-DOS applications. P-code applications contain pseudo-code, which is executed at run time by an interpreter (the C/C++ compilers include the run-time interpreter in the .EXE file). Consequently, P-code .EXE files are smaller and slower than equivalent fully compiled .EXE files.

Visual C++ lets you include MFC classes in your MS-DOS programs. These programs can use auxiliary MFC classes, such as the collections classes and the string class.

Clicking the OK button of the New Project dialog box invokes the Edit - *Projectname* dialog box, shown in Figure 1.10. This dialog box includes controls that list the current drives, directories, wild cards, and files that match the currently selected wild card. In addition, the dialog box contains a list box that shows the project's files. To add a file to the project, select a file and then click the Add command button. This action inserts a new file in the Files in Project list box. To remove a file from the project, select that file and click the Delete command button. The Edit - *Projectname* dialog box does not let you add .H files, because they should be included in .RC and .CPP files.

Typically, you add .DEF, .RC, and .CPP files when you are creating a program using the C++ compiler. To add all the matching files to the list of project files, click the Add All command button.

Figure 1.10

The Edit-*Projectname* dialog box

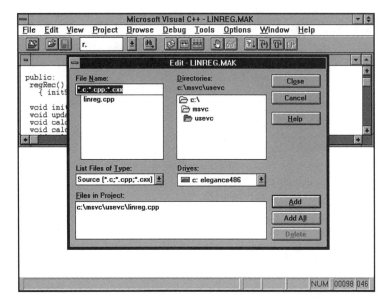

The Open Command

The Open command permits you to open an existing project file. The command invokes the Open Project dialog box, shown in Figure 1.11. The dialog box contains list boxes and combo boxes that enable you to select any existing drive and directory in order to locate the project file you want. The dialog box also contains a check box that allows you to read *external* project files—files that were not created by Visual Workbench. When the Visual Workbench loads a .MAK project file, it also reads the accompanying .VCW status file. The information in the status file enables Visual Workbench to restore the status of the project, including source windows and preferences.

> **Note**
>
> After you are finished creating a new project or loading an existing one, the list of the project's files becomes available by clicking the leftmost bitmapped icon on the toolbar. This action causes the list of files, including header files, to appear. You can open any project file by selecting that file and then clicking the mouse.

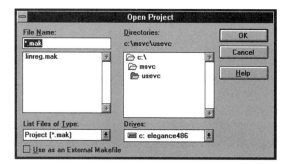

Figure 1.11
The Open Project
dialog box.

I

Introduction to Visual C++

Let's look at an example of an existing project being loaded. Using the
Open command, load the project file LINREG.MAK located in the directory
C:\MSVC\USEVC (this path assumes that you installed Visual C++ on
the default drive C: and in the default directory \MSVC). The project
LINREG.MAK generates a QuickWin application. Now click the leftmost
bitmapped icon on the toolbar to view the list of files in the project
LINREG.MAK. The list contains the single entry LINREG.CPP. To simplify
the example and reduce the number of files, I placed all the source code in
the file LINREG.CPP, which is included on the disk that accompanies this
book. Select that file and click the mouse to open it. Later in this section,
you compile, link, and run this QuickWin application.

The Edit Command

The Edit command (which is only available if you have loaded a project or
created a new one) invokes the Edit - *Projectname* dialog box so that you can
add files to the project or delete files from the project.

> **Note**
>
> The Edit command does not let you alter the kind of compiled file that is generated.
> For this kind of change, you must select the Project command from the Options
> menu.

The Close Command

The Close command closes the current project. The process involves writing
the updated project data to the .MAK file and the Workbench status to the
associated .VCW file.

The Compile File Command

The Compile File command compiles the file in the active source window. The Visual Workbench displays the progress and outcome of the compilation in the read-only Output Window. If the compilation process results in any warnings or errors, you can use the Next Error and Previous Error commands from the View menu to inspect the offending statements in the compiled source file. The shortcut key combination for Compile File is Ctrl+F8.

The Build Command

Use the Build command to build a source file (and the files included in that file). You can build a source file in either debug mode or in release mode. To select the mode, choose the Project command from the Options menu. Use the debug mode while you are developing your applications, and the compiler and linker will include debugging information in the compiled program. Use the release mode after you have finished testing your program. The Visual Workbench displays the progress and outcome of the file build in the read-only Output Window. If the compilation or linking processes result in any warnings or errors, you can use the Next Error and Previous Error commands from the View menu to inspect the offending statements in the compiled source file. The shortcut key combination for Build is Shift+F8.

The Rebuild All Command

The ReBuild All command enables you to build all the source files for the current project, regardless of their dependencies. You can rebuild the source files in either debug mode or in release mode, just as you could with the Build command. The Visual Workbench displays in the read-only Output Window the progress and outcome as the files are built. If the compilation or linking processes result in any warnings or errors, you can use the Next Error and Previous Error commands from the View menu to inspect the offending statements in the compiled source file. The shortcut key combination for ReBuild is Alt+F8.

The Stop Build Command

The Stop Build command enables you to interrupt a build or a rebuild operation. Typically, you elect to stop building a program when you remember that you need to make at least one more change in the source code before compiling the program.

The Execute Command

The Execute command runs the program at normal speed (as opposed to single-stepping through it). If your project generates an MS-DOS .EXE application, the Visual Workbench invokes a copy of DOS and then runs your MS-DOS program. If your project generates a Windows or Windows NT .EXE program, the run-time system launches it as an ordinary Windows or Windows NT application.

Remember the project LINREG.MAK that you opened earlier in this section? Choose the Execute command to compile, link, and run the QuickWin application. The Visual Workbench prompts you to compile and build the project files in a series of message dialog boxes. After the Workbench generates the QuickWin application, press Ctrl+F5 to launch the program. The QuickWin program runs in a special window. Here is a sample session with the LINREG.EXE program (user input appears in bold):

```
Enter number of points (at least 2) : 4
Enter x[0] ? 10
Enter y[0] ? 50
Enter x[1] ? 25
Enter y[1] ? 77
Enter x[2] ? 30
Enter y[2] ? 86
Enter x[3] ? 35
Enter y[3] ? 95

Data size = 4
R-square  = 1
Slope     = 1.8
Intercept = 32
Mean X    = 25
Mean Y    = 77
Sdev X    = 10.8012
Sdev Y    = 19.4422
```

When a QuickWin program ends its execution, the status line of the QuickWin window displays a short message to that effect. Close the QuickWin window by pressing Ctrl+C or by choosing the Exit command from the File menu of the QuickWin window.

Introduction to Visual C++

The Scan Dependencies Command

Typical Windows applications involve multiple source code files, header files, and resource files. The Visual Workbench builds and maintains the list of files that are involved in a project. The Workbench first generates this list when you create a new project. The list includes source files (typically with .C, .CPP, and .CXX extensions), resource script files (with the .RC extension), and the include files (which can have .H, .HPP, .HXX, .INC, .FON, .CUR, .BMP, .ICO, and .DLG extensions). The Visual Workbench maintains the interdependencies of the files in a project. You can view the list of project files by clicking the Project Files toolbar icon (the leftmost bitmapped icon on the toolbar).

The Scan Dependencies command reconstructs the include file dependencies for the file in the active source window. When you pull down the Project menu, you see the name of the active file appended to this command. Use the Scan Dependencies command after you add one or more include files to the source code of the active window, and it reconstructs the list of include files.

The Scan All Dependencies Command

The Scan All Dependencies command reconstructs the include file dependencies for all the files in the current project. Use this command after you add new include files to the source code of several project source files. This command offers the convenience of updating the dependencies for the entire project in one swoop.

The Load Workspace Command

You can use the Load Workspace command to select loading one of the three workspaces you have previously saved. None of these three workspaces have default values. Therefore, if you attempt to load a nonexistent workspace, the Visual Workbench displays an error message. The three workspaces have the default names Edit, Debug, and Custom and have the shortcut key combinations Ctrl+1, Ctrl+2, and Ctrl+3, respectively.

The Save Workspace Command

The Visual Workbench enables you to store the state of the Workbench, its source windows, and its settings in three workspaces. In addition, the Visual Workbench automatically saves the current workspace (which becomes the Last Workspace Used). Each project has its own set of workspaces. The information describing these workspaces is stored in the file with the same project name and the extension .WSP. The final command in the Project menu, the Save Workspace command, enables you to save the current workspace in any one of the three available workspaces. The command invokes a nested menu, which presents the names of the workspaces. The three workspaces have the default names Edit, Debug, and Custom and have the shortcut key combinations Ctrl+Shift+1, Ctrl+Shift+2, and Ctrl+Shift+3, respectively. These names essentially are factory set, but you can alter them using the Workspace command from the Options menu.

The Browse Menu

The Browse menu provides a versatile set of commands that enables you to browse through symbols (such as data types, variables, constants, and functions), to create new classes, and to manage the Windows messages to which these classes respond. The Browse menu includes the following commands, which are summarized in Table 1.6: Go to Definition, Go to Reference, Next, Previous, Pop Context, Open, and ClassWizard. Chapter 15 covers the Browse menu in more detail.

Table 1.6 Browse Menu Commands

Command	Shortcut Key	Purpose
Go to Definition	F11	Jumps to the start of the symbol definition.
Go to Reference	Shift+F11	Jumps to the first location where the symbol is referenced.
Next	Ctrl+NumPad+	Jumps to the next location where the symbol is referenced.
Previous	Ctrl+NumPad–	Jumps to the previous location where the symbol is referenced.
Pop Context	Ctrl+NumPad*	Jumps to the location of the selected symbol.
Open PRJ.BSC		Opens the Browse window.
ClassWizard...	Ctrl+W	Generates a new class or maps a Windows message to a member function.

Note: The NumPad *designation that precedes the characters +, –, and * in the second column indicates that you must access these characters by using the numeric keypad.*

When you build a program, the Visual Workbench generates a database for the various symbols. The database contains sophisticated information that tracks where a symbol is defined and referenced. This information is valuable in studying and debugging complex applications.

The Go to Definition Command

The Go to Definition command locates the definition of a symbol. To use this command, place the cursor to the left of, or anywhere on, the symbol's name. Then invoke the command by selecting it or by pressing its shortcut key, F11. The Visual Workbench responds by locating the definition of the targeted symbol.

Let's experiment with finding three kinds of symbols in the program LINREG.CCPP, shown in Listing 1.1. Load the program, if you haven't already, and perform the following tasks:

1. Move the cursor to line 120 at which point the function main sends a calcMean message (which is not a Windows message) to the object LR (in structured programming language, this action refers to the calling by instance LR of the calcMean member function). Place the cursor anywhere over the symbol calcMean. Now press the F11 function key. The Visual Workbench moves the cursor to the beginning of line 66, right after the definition of the member function calcMean.

2. Move the cursor back to line 120 and place the cursor anywhere on the instance LR and then press F11. The Visual Workbench moves the insertion cursor to the declaration of instance LR, located on line 101.

3. Move the cursor to the regRec class name on line 101 and press F11. The Visual Workbench moves the insertion cursor to the declaration of class regRec, located on line 7.

These tasks give you an idea of how to use the Go to Definition command to locate the definitions of data types, variables, and member functions.

The Go to Reference Command

The Go to Reference command moves the insertion cursor to the first location where the selected symbol is referenced. The shortcut key for this command is Shift+F11. Use the Next and Previous commands to navigate through the references of a symbol in a project.

The Next Command

The Next command moves the insertion cursor to the next location where the selected symbol is referenced. The shortcut key for this command is Ctrl+Numpad+.

The Previous Command

The Previous command moves the insertion cursor to the previous location where the selected symbol was referenced. The shortcut key for this command is Ctrl+Numpad–.

The Pop Context Command

The Pop Context command moves back to the last symbol used before the last Go to Definition or Go to Reference command was applied.

The Open *PRJ*.BSC Command

The Open*PRJ*.BSC command opens the Browse window (shown in Figure 1.12) with the database listed. If no database is listed, the Visual Workbench invokes the Open File dialog box so that you can select a .BSC database file. The Browse window enables you to view various kinds of information, such as data types, class definitions, declarations of class instance, and function calls. Figure 1.12 shows the Browse window while the declaration of class regRec from Listing 1.1 is being viewed. Chapter 16 discusses using the Browse window in more detail and also discusses viewing more complex Windows applications.

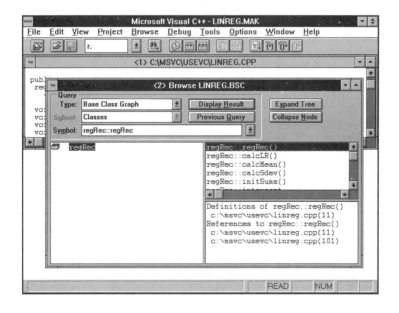

Figure 1.12
The Browse window.

The ClassWizard Command

The ClassWizard is the final command in the Browse menu. Together with the AppWizard, the ClassWizard command provides a powerful programming tool. The command enables you to declare a new MFC-based class or to add new message-response member functions to an existing MFC-based class. You learn more about using the AppWizard and ClassWizard programming tools in Chapters 3 and 4, respectively.

The Debug Menu

The Debug menu offers various commands that enable you to manage program debugging from within the Visual Workbench. The Debug menu includes the following commands, which are summarized in Table 1.7: Go, Restart, Stop Debugging, Step Into, Step Over, Step Out, Step to Cursor, Show Call Stack, Breakpoints, and QuickWatch. As you can tell from these commands, the Debug menu offers several methods to control single-stepping through a program in a debugging session. In addition, the Debug menu commands let you use various data watch windows to view the values in local variables, global variables, and the CPU registers. Chapter 17 discusses the debugging commands in more detail and shows you how to use the debugger windows with different applications.

Table 1.7 Debug Menu Commands

Command	Shortcut Key	Purpose
Go	F5	Runs the program associated with the current project.
Restart	Shift+F5	Reloads the program and starts again.
Stop Debugging	Alt+F5	Ends the debugging session.
Step Into	F8	Single-steps through each program line.
Step Over	F10	Single-steps through each program line but executes functions without entering them.
Step Out	Shift+F7	Runs the program to the first statement after the current function call.

Command	Shortcut Key	Purpose
Step to Cursor	F7	Runs the program until it reaches the place of the insertion point.
Show Call Stack...		Displays the call stack.
Breakpoints...		Clears and sets a breakpoint.
QuickWatch	Shift+F9	Opens the QuickWatch window to add, view the value of, or alter the value of a watched variable.

The Go Command

The Go command enables you to run a program until it either reaches a breakpoint or reaches the end. The command triggers full-speed execution either from the start of the program, from a breakpoint, or to terminate single-stepping through a program. The shortcut key for this command is F5. Alternatively, you can click the fourth bitmapped icon from the right on the toolbar, which shows a document with a downward-pointing arrow to the document's right.

The Restart Command

The Restart command reloads the program into memory and discards the previous values in the program's variables; in other words, this command enables you to start the program with a clean slate. If the program was built with the Debug mode command, the Restart command runs the program until it reaches either the function `main` or `WinMain`. The shortcut key combination for this command is Alt+F5.

The Stop Debugging Command

The Stop Debugging command ends the debugging session while the program is at a breakpoint or is between steps.

The Step Into Command

The Step Into command enables you to single-step through the next statement and trace any available function calls in that statement. Use this command to investigate the action of called functions and member functions. The shortcut key for this command is F8. Alternatively, you can click the third bitmapped icon from the right on the toolbar, which shows a set of braces with an arrow pointing to the space between them.

Introduction to Visual C++

The Step Over Command

The Step Over command permits you to single-step through the next statement without tracing the execution of any existing function calls. Use this command when you feel certain that the called functions do not need to be traced. The shortcut key combination for this command is Shift+F7. You can also click the second bitmapped icon from the right on the toolbar, which shows an arrow pointing over and around a set of braces.

The Step Out Command

The Step Out command offers a valuable addition to the other single-step commands. The Step Out command enables you to skip single-stepping the remaining statements in a function and resume at the next statement that called that function. This command eases the frustrations of single-stepping through nested function calls. Now you can just as easily get out of single-stepping a called function as you got into it. The shortcut key for this command is F10, or click the rightmost bitmapped icon on the toolbar, which shows an arrow pointing outward from the space between a set of braces.

The Step to Cursor Command

The Step to Cursor command, in effect, assigns a temporary breakpoint and executes the program until it reaches that breakpoint. The command uses the current cursor location as the place for the temporary breakpoint. The shortcut key for this command is F7.

The Show Call Stack Command

The Show Call Stack command invokes the Call Stack dialog box, shown in Figure 1.13, to list all the functions that have been called to reach the current statement. The most recently called function is located at the top of the list. The dialog box contains the check box labeled Show Function Parameters, which makes the Call Stack dialog box display the address of the parameters.

The Breakpoints Command

The Breakpoints command invokes the Breakpoints dialog box, shown in Figure 1.14, which enables you to manage the breakpoints in your source code. The dialog box contains command buttons to add, remove, disable, and clear all of the breakpoints. The Visual Workbench supports nontrivial kinds of breakpoints, which stop program execution under the following conditions:

■ At a specific location if an expression is true

■ At a specific location if an expression has changed

■ At the current statement if an expression is true

■ At the current statement if an expression has changed

■ At WndProc if a specific message is received

The Breakpoints dialog box lets you specify the type of breakpoint, its location (file or line number), and the tested expression.

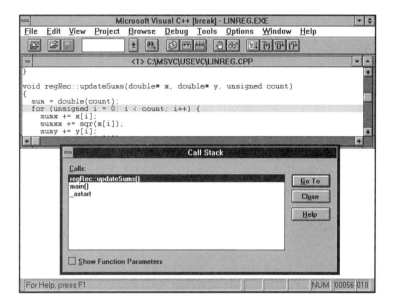

Figure 1.13
The Call Stack dialog box.

Figure 1.14
The Breakpoints dialog box.

The QuickWatch Command

The final command in the Debug menu, the QuickWatch command, enables you to inspect and modify variables and members of class instances. The command invokes the QuickWatch dialog box, shown in Figure 1.15. The dialog box shows the value for the selected variables by placing the cursor over the value. The dialog box displays structures and class instances in an outline form. You can expand or collapse the members of a structure or class instance by using the Zoom command button. When the dialog box displays a collapsed structure or class instance, it places a + sign to the left of the data item. By contrast, the dialog box places a - sign to the left of an expanded structure or class instance. The Add to Watch Window command button enables you to add the symbol selected in the Subject list to the Watch window. The Modify command button invokes a dialog box that displays the current value in the selected item and then lets you enter a new value.

Figure 1.15
The QuickWatch
dialog box.

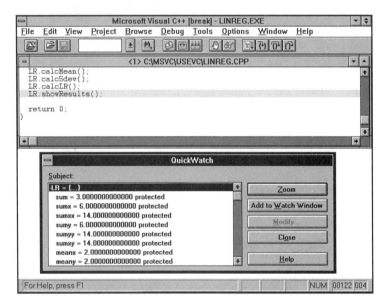

The Tools Menu

The Tools menu enables you to invoke programming and debugging tools from within the Visual Workbench. The Tools menu includes the default initial commands AppStudio and CodeView for Windows, which are summarized in Table 1.8. To add or delete commands in the Tools menu, use the Tools command from the Options menu.

Table 1.8 Tools Menu Commands

Command	Shortcut Key	Purpose
AppStudio		Generates resources using the App Studio tool.
CodeView		Runs CodeView for Windows.

The Options Menu

The Options menu offers commands that let you fine-tune the Visual Workbench itself and fine-tune your program development. The Options menu includes the following commands, which are summarized in Table 1.9: Project, Debug, Directories, Editor, Workspace, Tools, Color, and Font. Each of these commands invokes a dialog box, and some invoke nested dialog boxes.

Table 1.9 Options Menu Commands

Command	Shortcut Key	Purpose
Project...		Customizes the settings of the compiler and linker, sets the build mode, and sets the project type.
Debug...		Specifies an .EXE or .DLL file to debug, sets hard or soft debug mode, and toggles hexadecimal display.
Directories...		Designates the directories for the include files, libraries, executable files, MFC source files, and help files.
Editor...		Specifies miscellaneous commands for the editor.
Workspace...		Sets the workspace commands.
Tools...		Adds and removes tools from the Tools menu.
Color...		Customizes the syntax coloring.
Font...		Alters the font in a source window.

The Project Command

The Project command enables you to specify how the compiler, linker, and resource linker work. This command invokes the Project Commands dialog box, in which you can perform the following steps:

1. Reselect the kind of compiled file generated when the project is built.

2. Specify whether the project uses the MFC library.

3. Select the compiler commands. This process involves the C/C++ Compiler Options dialog box. This dialog box enables you to determine how the compiler works. The dialog box offers a list of categories that includes code generation, custom options, custom options (C++), debug options, listing files, memory models, optimization, P-code generation, precompiled headers, preprocessor, segment names, and Windows Prolog/Epilog code. When you select a category, the dialog box alters the category frame control to show controls that assist in customizing that category. Figure 1.16 shows the C/C++ Compiler Options dialog box while the Memory Model category is selected.

Figure 1.16

The C/C++ Compiler Options dialog box while the Memory Model category is selected.

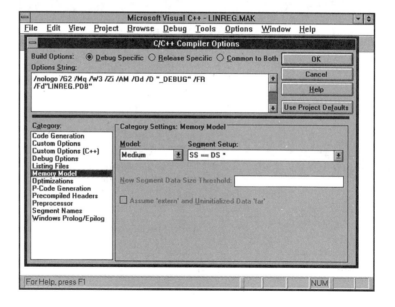

4. Select the linker options. This process involves the Linker Options dialog box, which enables you to determine how the linker works. The dialog box offers a list of categories that includes input, memory image, output, Windows libraries, and miscellaneous options.

Figure 1.17 shows the Linker Options dialog box while the Memory Image category is selected.

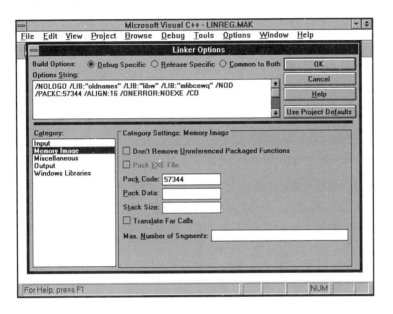

Figure 1.17
The Linker Options dialog box while the Memory Image category is selected.

Introduction to Visual C++

The Debug Command

The Debug command enables you to fine-tune the debugging operations. This command invokes the Debug dialog box, where you can make the following choices:

- Choose between soft mode or hard mode debugging. In hard mode, the debugger traps all the messages from the system queue. Consequently, the hard mode captures all the keyboard and mouse input and effectively disables all other applications.

- Select the host .EXE program to debug a .DLL dynamic link library.

- Specify whether the Watch and Locals windows display the values of variables in hexadecimal or decimal formats.

The Directories Command

The Directories command enables you to specify the paths for the executable files, include files, library files, help files, and MFC files. This command invokes the Directories dialog box, which contains three combo boxes and two edit controls. The combo boxes handle specifying the first three types of files I just mentioned. The edit controls are for specifying the paths for the help and MFC files.

The Editor Command

The Editor command enables you to fine-tune the operations of the Visual Workbench editor. It is important to point out that this option does *not* let you reassign the tasks of the keys. Instead, this option performs rather minor customization. The option invokes the Editor dialog box, in which you can customize the following options:

- *Tab settings*. You can specify the tab stops and whether to keep the tab characters or to insert spaces.

- *Scroll bar configuration*. You can specify whether the source windows should have vertical and/or horizontal scroll bars.

- *Source files*. You can make choices about the following: saving files before running tools, being prompted before files are saved, or having .RC resource files opened using the App Studio tool.

- *Undo buffer*. You can specify the size (in kilobytes) of the undo buffer. Your input can range from 0 to 64K.

The Workspace Command

The Workspace command lets you alter the current names of the three workspaces used to store the state of the Visual Workbench. The option invokes the Workspace dialog box, shown in Figure 1.18, which lets you specify the current names of the workspaces. In addition, you can indicate the name of the workspace you want to load when you open the current project. The Workspace dialog box enables you to specify whether to close all windows that are not related to the workspace being loaded.

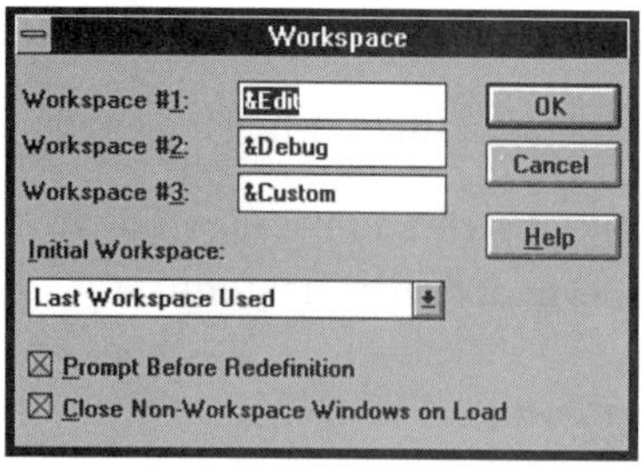

Figure 1.18

The Workspace dialog box.

The Tools Command

You can use the Tools command to add, remove, and reorganize the commands in the Tools menu. This command invokes the Tools dialog box shown in Figure 1.19. The dialog box shows the commands currently in the Tools menu and provides a family of command buttons to help you perform the following tasks:

- Add a new tool to the Tools menu. When you choose the Add button, the Add Tool dialog box appears and enables you to locate the file for the tool you want to add.

- Remove a new tool from the Tools menu.

- Move a command upward in the list of tools.

- Move a command downward in the list of tools.

The last two tasks enable you to specify exactly where each command should appear in the Tools menu.

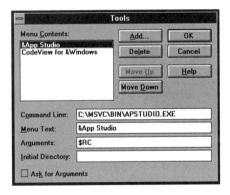

Figure 1.19
The Tools
dialog box.

The Tools dialog box also contains edit controls you can use to supply the following information for each newly added tool:

- The command line needed to invoke the tool

- The menu text

- The argument for the tool

- The initial directory

The Tools dialog box contains a check box you can use to make the Visual Workbench prompt you for arguments each time it invokes the tool.

The Color Command

You can use the Color command to customize the colors used to highlight C or C++ keywords. This command invokes the Color dialog box, shown in Figure 1.20, which lists the items whose colors you can customize. The dialog box shows a sample of the currently selected item. In addition, the dialog box offers two 16-color palettes to select the background and foreground colors of the currently selected item. The two command buttons enable you to restore the default colors for the currently selected item or to restore the default colors for all items.

Figure 1.20

The Color dialog box.

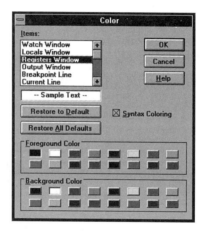

The Font Command

You can use the final command in the Options menu, the Font command, to select the font type and size that is used in a Visual Workbench source window. The command invokes the Font dialog box (shown in Figure 1.21) in which you can select the font, the font style, and the font size. Sample text for the currently selected font is displayed in the dialog box. To make the current font the default font (used to display the text from all loaded files) click the Use as Default Font command button.

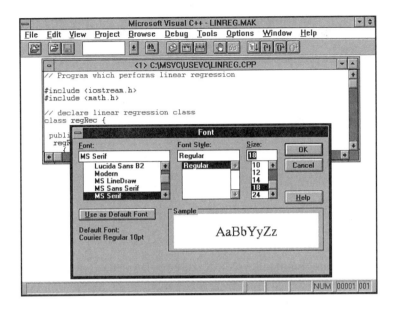

Figure 1.21
The Fonts
dialog box.

The Window Menu

The Window menu offers commands to arrange and manage the windows in the Visual Workbench. The Window menu includes the following commands, which are summarized in Table 1.10: Cascade, Tile, Duplicate, Close All, Watch, Locals, Registers, and Output.

Table 1.10 The Window Menu Commands		
Command	**Shortcut Key**	**Purpose**
Cascade		Arranges the source windows in an overlapped fashion.
Tile		Arranges the source windows by placing them side by side.
Duplicate		Opens another copy of an existing source window.
Close All		Closes all open source windows.
Watch		Opens or brings to the top the Watch window, which you can use to view the values of variables in a debugging session.

(continues)

Table 1.10 Continued		
Command	**Shortcut Key**	**Purpose**
Locals		Opens or brings to the top the Locals window, which you can use to view the local variables and their values.
Registers		Opens the Register window, which shows the CPU registers and flags.
Output		Opens the Output window, which shows the output from the build utilities. This output includes warning and error messages.

The Cascade Command

With the Cascade command, you can arrange the windows in the Visual Workbench in a cascaded fashion. This command arranges the windows by their Z-order (that is, the order in which they overlay each other).

The Tile Command

The Tile command lets you arrange the windows in the Visual Workbench side by side.

The Duplicate Command

The Duplicate command creates a duplicate source window for an existing one. Each duplicated window adds a colon to its title, followed by the copy number of that window. For example, if you have the file LINREG.CPP open as the only source window, its initial title is `<1> C:\MSVC\USEVC\LINREG.CPP`. When you invoke the Duplicate command, you create a second source window. One of the two windows has the title `<1> C:\MSVC\USEVC\LINREG.CPP:1`, and the other window has the title `<1> C:\MSVC\USEVC\LINREG.CPP:2`.

The Close All Command

The Close All command closes all the windows currently in the Visual Workbench client area. The command prompts you to save the modified contents of any window that has not been saved.

The Watch Command

The Watch command brings up the Watch window, which you can use to view the values of variables during a debugging session. Typically, you add watched variables using the QuickWatch dialog box. You can also type the names of the variables you want to watch. Each watched variable must be typed on a separate line, and you can delete only an entire line or an entire structured variable or class instance. The Watch window does not allow partial deletion of watched items.

The Locals Command

The Locals command offers the convenience of watching the values of variables that are local to the currently executing function or member function. The command automatically includes the local variables of the currently executing function and displays their values. All you have to do is invoke the Locals command. Moreover, when the current function returns to the caller function, the Locals window updates its contents to show the local variables of the caller function.

The Registers Command

The Registers command displays the Registers window, which shows you the values of the CPU registers and flags. The Registers window lets you monitor the values of the CPU registers when you perform the kind of debugging that involves examining the output assembly language. The Registers window is a read-only window.

The Output Command

The Output command displays the Output window. This window displays the progress of compiling and linking source files, building a project, and all the warnings and error messages associated with these processes. The Output window is a read-only window.

The Help Menu

The Help menu provides on-line help for a variety of topics. The Help menu includes the following commands, which are summarized in Table 1.11: working with the Visual Workbench itself, using the build tools, the C and C++ programming languages, the MFC library, the Windows 3.1 API functions, and technical support. The Visual Workbench uses the Microsoft Help engine, which, as a Windows user, you should be accustomed to using.

Table 1.11 The Help Menu Commands		
Command	**Shortcut Key**	**Purpose**
Visual WorkBench		Offers how-to help information regarding the Visual Workbench.
Build Tools		Provides help on particular compiler and linker commands.
C/C++ Language		Displays help on the C and C++ languages and their functions.
Foundation Classes		Presents help on the Microsoft Foundation Class (MFC) Library.
Window 3.1 SDK		Offers help on Windows 3.1 API functions.
Search for Help On...		Locates a keyword in Help.
Obtaining Technical Support		Offers product support.
About Visual C++		Provides information about Visual C++, including the registered owner of the package in use.

Summary

This chapter offered an overview of the Visual Workbench. You learned about the following aspects of working with the Workbench:

- Loading the Visual Workbench involves clicking the Visual C++ icon or typing a simple command from the File Manager.

- The File menu commands manage opening, closing, saving, and printing files.

- The Edit menu commands support basic text editing, text search, text replacement, and braces matching.

- The View menu commands provide for managing bookmarks, toggling the toolbar and the status bar, moving to specific lines, and displaying colored syntax.

- The Project menu commands support generating and building applications, compiling and linking files, and managing the Visual Workbench workspace.

- The Browse menu commands provide the means to locate the definitions and reference of symbols, create new classes, and add new member functions that respond to Windows messages.

- The Debug menu commands offer the ability to single-step through the execution of a program, view the function call stack, manage breakpoints, and manage watched variables.

- The Tools menu commands launch programming tools from within the Visual Workbench.

- The Options menu commands let you customize the project, the debug mode, the paths of project files, the editor, the workspace, the Tools menu, the syntax color, and the fonts used by the source windows.

- The Window menu commands manage the windows in the client area of the Visual Workbench, and display the Watch, Locals, Registers, and Output windows.

- The Help commands supply you with various kinds of on-line help and documentation.

Introduction to Visual C++

Chapter 2

Overview of the MFC Hierarchy

Visual C++ includes the Microsoft Foundation Class (MFC) library as an important tool for building Windows applications using C++. The MFC library significantly shortens the source code for Windows applications. Moreover, the Visual Workbench includes the AppWizard and ClassWizard programming tools, which automate the creation of MFC-based Windows applications. This chapter presents an overview of the MFC library and discusses how MFC-based Windows programs handle Windows messages. You learn about the following topics:

- How to manage Windows messages and the message table macros

- Overview of the class categories in the MFC library

- The document and application classes

- The window support class

- The control classes

- The dialog box classes

- The frame window classes

- The view classes

- The control bar classes

- The menus class

- The graphical drawing objects classes

- The graphical drawing classes

- The file services classes

- The exception classes

- The collections classes

- The OLE 2.0 support classes

- The ODBC support classes

- The miscellaneous classes

- Simple MFC examples

This chapter also includes the declarations of many classes in the MFC library. These declarations give you a feel for the specialized operations implemented in each class. In addition, the declarations listed in this chapter offer you a hard copy that you can use as a reference (especially when you do not have access to a computer).

Managing Windows Messages

Managing Windows messages involves sending them and responding to them. Sending messages involves a rather simple mechanism that involves calling one of a few member functions of an MFC class. Responding to messages is more complex. In addition, sending messages using the appropriate MFC class resembles sending messages C-style using Windows API functions. By contrast, responding to messages using C++ and MFC is very different from responding to messages using C functions. Let's first look at responding to Windows messages.

Responding to Messages

The Microsoft Foundation Class library uses a special mechanism to determine how an application responds to particular messages. This mechanism involves a few macros. The macro afx_msg enables you to declare (or mark, if you prefer) the message response member functions by placing the macro name afx_msg before the return type of the function. The class that contains at least one message-response function must declare the macro DECLARE_MESSAGE_MAP(). This macro initializes the message map that is defined in the implementation part of the program. A typical example of declaring message response functions is shown in the following code:

```
class CAppWindow : CFrameWnd {
public:
    CAppWindow();
protected:
    // handle painting
    afx_msg void OnPaint();
    // handle resizing a window
    afx_msg void OnSize(UINT nType, int cx, int cy);
    // handle closing the window
    afx_msg void OnClose();
    DECLARE_MESSAGE_MAP();
};
```

The OnPaint, OnSize, and OnClose member functions respond to the pre-defined messages WM_PAINT, WM_SIZE, and WM_CLOSE. The class implementation includes the definitions of these member functions as well as the special message map macros START_MESSAGE_MAP() and END_MESSAGE_MAP(). These special macros contain other macros that map the individual member functions and the messages they respond to. The message map macros for the above class are as follows:

```
BEGIN_MESSAGE_MAP(CAppWindow, CFrameWnd)
    ON_WM_PAINT()
    ON_WM_SIZE()
    ON_WM_CLOSE()
END_MESSAGE_MAP()
```

Notice that the BEGIN_MESSAGE_MAP contains two arguments: the application window class and its parent MFC class. Stating the classes involved is required. Notice the three ON_WM_*XXXX* macros. The first one, ON_WM_PAINT(), specifies that the default member function, OnPaint, responds to the message WM_PAINT. In fact, the Microsoft Foundation Class library has a large set of predefined message-mapping macros that relate various class member functions with WM_*XXXX* messages. The ON_WM_SIZE() and ON_WM_CLOSE() macros are but two additional examples. The ON_WM_SIZE() macro tells the OnSize member function to respond to the WM_SIZE message. Likewise, the ON_WM_CLOSE() macro ties the OnClose member function to the WM_CLOSE message.

Sending Messages

Windows enables your applications to send messages to themselves, to other applications, or to Windows itself. The Windows API functions SendMessage, PostMessage, and SendDlgItemMessage provide important tools for sending messages. The SendMessage function sends a message to a window and requires that window to handle the transmitted message. The SendMessage function is declared as follows:

```
DWORD SendMessage(HWND hWnd, WORD wMsg, WORD wParam, LONG lParam);
```

The parameter hWnd is the handle of the window receiving the message. The parameter wMsg specifies the message sent. The parameters wParam and lParam provide information that is based on the message wMsg. You can use the SendMessage function to communicate with other windows and controls.

The PostMessage function is similar to SendMessage, except that it lacks the sense of urgency. The message is posted in the Windows message queue, and the message is handled later by the targeted window when it is convenient for that window. The declaration of the Boolean PostMessage function is shown in the following:

```
BOOL PostMessage(HWND hWnd, UINT wMsg,
                 WPARAM wParam, LPARAM lParam);
```

The parameter hWnd is the handle of the window receiving the message. The parameter wMsg specifies the message being sent. The parameters wParam and lParam provide information that is based on the message wMsg.

The SendDlgItemMessage function sends a message to a particular item in a dialog box. The declaration of the SendDlgItemMessage function is posted next:

```
LRESULT SendDlgItemMessage(HWND hwndDlg, int idDlgItem,
                           UINT uMsg, WPARAM wParam, LPARAM lParam);
```

The parameter hwndDlg is the handle of the dialog box that contains the targeted control. The parameter idDlgItem indicates the integer identifier of the dialog box item that receives the message. The parameter wMsg specifies the message sent. The parameters wParam and lParam provide information that is based on the message wMsg.

The class CWnd declares the SendMessage, PostMessage, and SendDlgItemMessage member functions to send messages to a host window. These member functions are declared as follows:

```
LRESULT SendMessage(UINT message, WPARAM wParam = 0,
                    LPARAM lParam = 0);

BOOL PostMessage(UINT message, WPARAM wParam = 0,
                 LPARAM lParam = 0);

LRESULT SendDlgItemMessage(int nID, UINT message,
                           WPARAM wParam = 0, LPARAM lParam = 0);
```

User-Defined Messages

The MFC library lets you define your own messages. The constant WM_USER (see Table 2.1) is associated with the number of the first message. You have to declare constants that represent the offset values for your custom messages. For example, you can use the `#define` directive to define your own messages:

```
#define WM_USER1 (WM_USER + 0)
#define WM_USER2 (WM_USER + 1)
#define WM_USER3 (WM_USER + 2)
```

Table 2.1 shows the ranges of Windows messages for Windows 3.1.

Table 2.1 The Ranges of Windows 3.1 Messages			
Constant	**Value**	**Message Range**	**Meaning**
WM_USER	0x0400	0x0000-0x03FF	Windows messages
		0x0400-0x7FFF	Programmer-defined window messages
		0x8000-0xBFFF	Reserved for use by Windows
		0xC000-0xFFFF	String messages for use by applications

The user-defined messages specify the commands sent by menu items or keyboard input. The message mapping macro `ON_COMMAND` is used to associate the user-defined command with its response member function. The general form for the `ON_COMMAND` macro is

```
ON_COMMAND(command, command_function)
```

To illustrate how to employ user-defined messages, consider the following messages, `CM_CALC` and `CM_STORE`, declared in the header file USRMSG.H:

```
#define CM_CALC (WM_USER + 0)
#define CM_STORE (WM_USER + 1)
```

The declaration of the window class that responds to these messages is as follows:

```
#include <afxwin.h>
#include "usrmsg.h"
class CAppWindow : CFrameWnd
{
public:
    CAppWindow();
protected:
    // handle painting
    afx_msg void OnPaint();
    // handle calculation command
    afx_msg void CMCalc();
```

```
        // handle store command
        afx_msg void CMStore();
        // handle closing the window
        afx_msg void OnClose();
        DECLARE_MESSAGE_MAP();
};
```

Here is the corresponding message map:

```
BEGIN_MESSAGE_MAP(CAppWindow, CFrameWnd)
    ON_WM_PAINT()
    ON_COMMAND(CM_CALC, CMCalc)
    ON_COMMAND(CM_STORE, CMStore)
    ON_WM_CLOSE()
END_MESSAGE_MAP()
```

The first ON_COMMAND macro specifies that the CMCalc member function will respond to the CM_CALC command message. The second ON_COMMAND macro indicates that the CMStore member function will respond to the CM_STORE command message.

Overview of the MFC Library

The MFC library contains several groups of classes that offer specific operations. These operations include aspects such as application management, data structures, visual controls, dialog boxes, graphics, and error handling. The category of classes in the MFC library includes the following:

- The document and application classes manage Windows documents and applications.

- The control classes deal with the visual controls, such as the edit control, command button, list box, and combo box.

- The dialog box classes handle custom dialog boxes and the common dialog boxes (the File, Color Selection, Font Selection, Print, Find/ Replace dialog boxes).

- The frame window classes manage both single-document frame windows and multiple-document frame and child windows.

- The view classes handle views, scrollable views, form views, and edit views, which are involved in sophisticated forms of data input and output.

- The control bar classes deal with the toolbar, status bar, dialog bar of an application, along with splitter windows (such as the one used by the Windows File manager to display the directory tree and the files in the currently selected directory).

- The menus class deals with managing menus and manipulating menu items.

- The graphical drawing objects classes deal with drawing bitmaps, font selection and use, and palette management.

- The graphical drawing classes handle drawing points, lines, circular shapes, rectangles, polygons, and other shapes.

- The file services classes manage binary and text files.

- The exception classes deal with raising and trapping run-time errors. These errors may be caused by bad operations related to files, memory, resources, and OLE.

- The collections classes offer three sets of classes that manage arrays, lists, and maps (that is, hash tables) of various kinds of data types and classes.

- The OLE support classes manage OLE transactions.

- The miscellaneous classes handle run-time object model support, simple value types (strings, date/time, points, rectangles, and sizes), structures (file state, creation context, printer information, and memory state), and support classes.

The classes in the MFC library, except for the miscellaneous classes, are derived from the class CObject. Here is the declaration of this class:

```
class CObject
{
public:
// Object model (types, destruction, allocation)
    virtual CRuntimeClass* GetRuntimeClass() const;
    virtual ~CObject();  // virtual destructors are necessary
    // Diagnostic allocations
    void* operator new(size_t, void* p);
    void* operator new(size_t nSize);
    void operator delete(void* p);

// Disable the copy constructor and assignment by default so you
// will get compiler errors instead of unexpected behaviour if you pass
// objects by value or assign objects.
protected:
```

```
        CObject();
    private:
        CObject(const CObject& objectSrc);          // no implementation
        void operator=(const CObject& objectSrc);   // no implementation
    // Attributes
    public:
        BOOL IsSerializable() const;
        BOOL IsKindOf(const CRuntimeClass* pClass) const;
    // Overridables
        virtual void Serialize(CArchive& ar);
        // Diagnostic Support
        virtual void AssertValid() const;
        virtual void Dump(CDumpContext& dc) const;
    // Implementation
    public:
        static CRuntimeClass AFXAPI_DATA classCObject;
    };
```

The declaration of class `CObject` shows that the class is not merely an empty shell. Instead, `CObject` contains member functions that support operations such as dynamic allocation, serialization query, object assignment, and dynamic object identification.

The Document and Application Classes

The document and application classes own and maintain all other windows in an application. These classes are in charge of shaping the Windows application. The following outline shows the subhierarchy of document and application classes:

```
+ CCmdTarget
    - CWinApp
    + CDocTemplate
        - CSingleDocTemplate
        - CMultiDocTemplate
    + CDocument
        + COleDocument
            + COleLinkingDoc
        - COleServerDoc
```

The class `CCmdTarget` serves as the root for this subhierarchy and implements operations and data members that are common to all its descendant classes. These operations mainly involve receiving and responding to Windows messages. The class `CDocTemplate` offers important refinements that relate to document templates: these refinements manage the creation of documents, views, and frame windows. The operations of class `CDocTemplate` are further refined by the classes `CSingleDocTemplate` and `CMultiDocTemplate`. These classes offer templates for the single document interface (SDI) and the multiple document interface (MDI).

The class `CDocument` begins another set of refinements to class `CCmdTarget`. The `CDocument` class offers the basic operations and data members for your custom document classes and for the OLE document classes. The latter classes include the `COleLinkingDoc` and `COleServerDoc`. The class `COleLinkingDoc` is a client document that manages the client items in an OLE compliant application. The class `COleServerDoc` is a server document class that builds and manages server items.

For your initial work with the MFC library, the next section focuses on the class `CWinApp`, which represents an MFC-based Windows application. The class encapsulates the operations involved in initializing, running, and terminating a Windows program.

The *CWinApp* Class

The class `CWinApp`, a descendant of class `CCmdTarget`, manages the operations required to initialize, run, and end an MFC-based Windows application. The following code shows the declaration of class `CWinApp`:

```
class CWinApp : public CCmdTarget
{
     DECLARE_DYNAMIC(CWinApp)
public:
// Constructor
     CWinApp(const char* pszAppName = NULL); // app name defaults to
                                             // EXE name
// Attributes
     // Startup args (do not change)
     HINSTANCE m_hInstance;
     HINSTANCE m_hPrevInstance;
     LPSTR m_lpCmdLine;
     int m_nCmdShow;
     // Running args (can be changed in InitInstance)
     CWnd* m_pMainWnd;              // main window (optional)
     const char* m_pszAppName;   // human readable name
                            // (from constructor or
                            //  AFX_IDS_APP_TITLE)
     // Support for Shift+F1 help mode.
     BOOL m_bHelpMode;                // are we in Shift+F1 mode?
public:  // set in constructor to override default
     const char* m_pszExeName;      // executable name (no spaces)
     const char* m_pszHelpFilePath; // default based on module path
     const char* m_pszProfileName;  // default based on app name
// Initialization Operations - should be done in InitInstance
protected:
     void LoadStdProfileSettings(); // load MRU file list and last
                                    // preview state
```

```
                    void EnableVBX();
                    void EnableShellOpen();
                    void SetDialogBkColor(COLORREF clrCtlBk = RGB(192, 192, 192),
                                    COLORREF clrCtlText = RGB(0, 0, 0));
                            // set dialog box and message box background color
                    void RegisterShellFileTypes();  // call after all doc
                                                    // templates are registered
            // Helper Operations - usually done in InitInstance
            public:
                    // Cursors
                    HCURSOR LoadCursor(LPCSTR lpszResourceName) const;
                    HCURSOR LoadCursor(UINT nIDResource) const;
                    // for IDC_ values
                     HCURSOR LoadStandardCursor(LPCSTR lpszCursorName) const;
                    // for OCR_ values
                    HCURSOR LoadOEMCursor(UINT nIDCursor) const;
                    // Icons
                    HICON LoadIcon(LPCSTR lpszResourceName) const;
                    HICON LoadIcon(UINT nIDResource) const;
                      // for IDI_ values
                    HICON LoadStandardIcon(LPCSTR lpszIconName) const;
                    // for OIC_ values
                    HICON LoadOEMIcon(UINT nIDIcon) const;
                    // Profile settings (to the app specific .INI file)
                    UINT GetProfileInt(LPCSTR lpszSection, LPCSTR lpszEntry,
                                    int nDefault);
                    BOOL WriteProfileInt(LPCSTR lpszSection, LPCSTR lpszEntry,
                                    int nValue);
                    CString GetProfileString(LPCSTR lpszSection, LPCSTR lpszEntry,
                                    LPCSTR lpszDefault = NULL);
                    BOOL WriteProfileString(LPCSTR lpszSection, LPCSTR lpszEntry,
                                    LPCSTR lpszValue);
            // Running Operations - to be done on a running application
                    // Dealing with document templates
                    void AddDocTemplate(CDocTemplate* pTemplate);
                    // Dealing with files
                    // open named file
                    virtual CDocument* OpenDocumentFile(LPCSTR lpszFileName);
                    // add to MRU
                    virtual void AddToRecentFileList(const char* pszPathName);
                    // Printer DC Setup routine, 'struct tagPD' is a PRINTDLG
                    // structure
                    BOOL GetPrinterDeviceDefaults(struct tagPD FAR* pPrintDlg);
                    // Preloading/Unloading VBX files and checking for existance
                    HMODULE LoadVBXFile(LPCSTR lpszFileName);
                    BOOL UnloadVBXFile(LPCSTR lpszFileName);
            // Overridables
                    // hooks for your initialization code
                    virtual BOOL InitApplication();
                    virtual BOOL InitInstance();
                    // running and idle processing
                    virtual int Run();
                    virtual BOOL PreTranslateMessage(MSG* pMsg);
                    virtual BOOL OnIdle(LONG lCount); // return TRUE if more idle
                                                    // processing
                    // exiting
                    virtual BOOL SaveAllModified(); // save before exit
```

```
    virtual int ExitInstance(); // return app exit code
    // Advanced: to override message boxes and other hooks
    virtual int DoMessageBox(LPCSTR lpszPrompt, UINT nType,
                     UINT nIDPrompt);
    virtual BOOL ProcessMessageFilter(int code, LPMSG lpMsg);
    virtual LRESULT ProcessWndProcException(CException* e,
                                 const MSG* pMsg);
    virtual void DoWaitCursor(int nCode); // 0  => restore,
                                          // 1  => begin,
                                          // -1 => end
    // Advanced: process async DDE request
    virtual BOOL OnDDECommand(char* pszCommand);
    // Help support (overriding is advanced)
    // general
    virtual void WinHelp(DWORD dwData, UINT nCmd = HELP_CONTEXT);
// Command Handlers
protected:
    // map to the following for file new/open
    afx_msg void OnFileNew();
    afx_msg void OnFileOpen();
    // map to the following to enable print setup
    afx_msg void OnFilePrintSetup();
    // map to the following to enable help
    afx_msg void OnContextHelp();    // shift-F1
    afx_msg void OnHelp();           // F1 (uses current context)
    afx_msg void OnHelpIndex();      // ID_HELP_INDEX, ID_DEFAULT_HELP
    afx_msg void OnHelpUsing();      // ID_HELP_USING
// Implementation
protected:
    MSG m_msgCur;                        // current message
    CPtrList m_templateList;             // list of templates
    HGLOBAL m_hDevMode;                  // printer Dev Mode
    HGLOBAL m_hDevNames;                 // printer Device Names
    DWORD m_dwPromptContext;             // help context override for
                                         // message box
    int m_nWaitCursorCount;              // for wait cursor (>0 => waiting)
    HCURSOR m_hcurWaitCursorRestore;     // old cursor to restore after
                                         // wait cursor
    CString m_strRecentFiles[_AFX_MRU_COUNT]; // default MRU
                                              // implementation
    void (CALLBACK* m_lpfnCleanupVBXFiles)();
    void UpdatePrinterSelection(BOOL bForceDefaults);
    void SaveStdProfileSettings();  // save options to .INI file
    BOOL ProcessHelpMsg(MSG& msg, DWORD* pContext);
    HWND SetHelpCapture(POINT ptCursor);
public: // public for implementation access
    ATOM m_atomApp, m_atomSystemTopic;   // for DDE open
    HCURSOR m_hcurHelp;       // always loaded if m_bHelpMode == TRUE
    UINT m_nNumPreviewPages;  // number of default printed pages
    // memory safety pool
    size_t  m_nSafetyPoolSize;      // ideal size
    void*   m_pSafetyPoolBuffer;    // current buffer
    void SetCurrentHandles();
    BOOL PumpMessage();       // low level message pump
    int GetOpenDocumentCount();
    // helpers for standard commdlg dialogs
    BOOL DoPromptFileName(CString& fileName, UINT nIDSTitle,
```

```
            DWORD lFlags, BOOL bOpenFileDialog,
            CDocTemplate* pTemplate);
        int DoPrintDialog(CPrintDialog* pPD);
public:
        virtual ~CWinApp();
#ifdef _AFXDLL
        // force linkage to AFXDLL startup code and special stack segment
        // for applications linking with AFXDLL
        virtual void _ForceLinkage();
#endif //_AFXDLL
protected: // standard commands
        //{{AFX_MSG(CWinApp)
        afx_msg void OnAppExit();
        afx_msg void OnUpdateRecentFileMenu(CCmdUI* pCmdUI);
        afx_msg BOOL OnOpenRecentFile(UINT nID);
        //}}AFX_MSG
        DECLARE_MESSAGE_MAP()
};
```

The class CWinApp (and its descendants) use the constructor to create an instance of a Windows application. The class contains member functions that enable you to load the standard or custom cursor, load a standard or custom icon, load the profile settings from an .INI file, and write the profile settings to an .INI file. The member functions InitApplication and InitInstance let you initialize the application and each instance, respectively. The member function Run causes the program to run after it is initialized. The class CWinApp also contains message-handling member functions that handle messages generated by a few common menu options, such as opening a new or an existing file.

The Window Support Class

The MFC library declares the class CWnd, a descendant of class CCmdTarget, to implement common support for different kinds of windows, such as visual controls, dialog boxes, and views. The class CWnd contains a large number of member functions. You never declare instances of class CWnd in your Windows applications; however, you may derive descendant classes from class CWnd if you want to build a new category of visual windows. The declaration of class CWnd is as follows:

```
class CWnd : public CCmdTarget
{
        DECLARE_DYNCREATE(CWnd)
protected:
        static const MSG* PASCAL GetCurrentMessage();
// Attributes
public:
```

```
    HWND m_hWnd;                // must be first data member
    HWND GetSafeHwnd() const;
    DWORD GetStyle() const;
    DWORD GetExStyle() const;
// Constructors and other creations
    CWnd();
    static CWnd* PASCAL FromHandle(HWND hWnd);
     // INTERNAL USE
    static CWnd* PASCAL FromHandlePermanent(HWND hWnd);
    static void PASCAL DeleteTempMap();
    BOOL Attach(HWND hWndNew);
    HWND Detach();
    BOOL SubclassWindow(HWND hWnd);
    BOOL SubclassDlgItem(UINT nID, CWnd* pParent);
               // for dynamic subclassing of windows control
protected: // This CreateEx() wraps CreateWindowEx - dangerous
          // to use directly
    BOOL CreateEx(DWORD dwExStyle, LPCSTR lpszClassName,
        LPCSTR lpszWindowName, DWORD dwStyle,
        int x, int y, int nWidth, int nHeight,
        HWND hWndParent, HMENU nIDorHMenu, LPSTR lpParam = NULL);
private:
    CWnd(HWND hWnd);      // just for special initialization
public:
    // for child windows, views, panes etc
    virtual BOOL Create(LPCSTR lpszClassName,
        LPCSTR lpszWindowName, DWORD dwStyle,
        const RECT& rect,
        CWnd* pParentWnd, UINT nID,
        CCreateContext* pContext = NULL);
    virtual BOOL DestroyWindow();
    // special pre-creation and window rect adjustment hooks
    virtual BOOL PreCreateWindow(CREATESTRUCT& cs);
    // virtual AdjustWindowRect
    virtual void CalcWindowRect(LPRECT lpClientRect);
// Window tree access
    int GetDlgCtrlID() const;
        // return window ID, for child windows only
    CWnd* GetDlgItem(int nID) const;
        // get immediate child with given ID
    CWnd* GetDescendantWindow(int nID) const;
        // like GetDlgItem but recursive
    void SendMessageToDescendants(UINT message,
        WPARAM wParam = 0, LPARAM lParam = 0, BOOL bDeep = TRUE);
    CFrameWnd* GetParentFrame() const;
// Message Functions
    LRESULT SendMessage(UINT message, WPARAM wParam = 0,
               LPARAM lParam = 0);
    BOOL PostMessage(UINT message, WPARAM wParam = 0,
               LPARAM lParam = 0);
// Window Text Functions
    void SetWindowText(LPCSTR lpszString);
    int GetWindowText(LPSTR lpszStringBuf, int nMaxCount) const;
    int GetWindowTextLength() const;
    void GetWindowText(CString& rString) const;
    void SetFont(CFont* pFont, BOOL bRedraw = TRUE);
    CFont* GetFont() const;
```

```
// CMenu Functions - non-Child windows only
    CMenu* GetMenu() const;
    BOOL SetMenu(CMenu* pMenu);
    void DrawMenuBar();
    CMenu* GetSystemMenu(BOOL bRevert) const;
    BOOL HiliteMenuItem(CMenu* pMenu, UINT nIDHiliteItem,
                    UINT nHilite);
// Window Size and Position Functions
    BOOL IsIconic() const;
    BOOL IsZoomed() const;
    void MoveWindow(int x, int y, int nWidth, int nHeight,
                    BOOL bRepaint = TRUE);
    void MoveWindow(LPCRECT lpRect, BOOL bRepaint = TRUE);
    // SetWindowPos's pWndInsertAfter
    static const CWnd AFXAPI_DATA wndTop;
    // SetWindowPos's pWndInsertAfter
    static const CWnd AFXAPI_DATA wndBottom;
#if (WINVER >= 0x030a)
    // SetWindowPos pWndInsertAfter
    static const CWnd AFXAPI_DATA wndTopMost;
    // SetWindowPos pWndInsertAfter
    static const CWnd AFXAPI_DATA wndNoTopMost;
#endif
    BOOL SetWindowPos(const CWnd* pWndInsertAfter, int x, int y,
                    int cx, int cy, UINT nFlags);
    UINT ArrangeIconicWindows();
    void BringWindowToTop();
    void GetWindowRect(LPRECT lpRect) const;
    void GetClientRect(LPRECT lpRect) const;
#if (WINVER >= 0x030a)
    BOOL GetWindowPlacement(WINDOWPLACEMENT FAR* lpwndpl) const;
    BOOL SetWindowPlacement(const WINDOWPLACEMENT FAR* lpwndpl);
#endif
// Coordinate Mapping Functions
    void ClientToScreen(LPPOINT lpPoint) const;
    void ClientToScreen(LPRECT lpRect) const;
    void ScreenToClient(LPPOINT lpPoint) const;
    void ScreenToClient(LPRECT lpRect) const;
#if (WINVER >= 0x030a)
    void MapWindowPoints(CWnd* pwndTo, LPPOINT lpPoint,
                        UINT nCount) const;
    void MapWindowPoints(CWnd* pwndTo, LPRECT lpRect) const;
#endif
// Update/Painting Functions
    CDC* BeginPaint(LPPAINTSTRUCT lpPaint);
    void EndPaint(LPPAINTSTRUCT lpPaint);
    CDC* GetDC();
    CDC* GetWindowDC();
    int ReleaseDC(CDC* pDC);
    void UpdateWindow();
    void SetRedraw(BOOL bRedraw = TRUE);
    BOOL GetUpdateRect(LPRECT lpRect, BOOL bErase = FALSE);
    int GetUpdateRgn(CRgn* pRgn, BOOL bErase = FALSE);
    void Invalidate(BOOL bErase = TRUE);
    void InvalidateRect(LPCRECT lpRect, BOOL bErase = TRUE);
    void InvalidateRgn(CRgn* pRgn, BOOL bErase = TRUE);
    void ValidateRect(LPCRECT lpRect);
```

```
    void ValidateRgn(CRgn* pRgn);
    BOOL ShowWindow(int nCmdShow);
    BOOL IsWindowVisible() const;
    void ShowOwnedPopups(BOOL bShow = TRUE);
#if (WINVER >= 0x030a)
    CDC* GetDCEx(CRgn* prgnClip, DWORD flags);
    BOOL LockWindowUpdate();
    BOOL RedrawWindow(LPCRECT lpRectUpdate = NULL,
        CRgn* prgnUpdate = NULL,
        UINT flags = RDW_INVALIDATE | RDW_UPDATENOW | RDW_ERASE);
    BOOL EnableScrollBar(int nSBFlags,
                UINT nArrowFlags = ESB_ENABLE_BOTH);
#endif
// Timer Functions
    UINT SetTimer(UINT nIDEvent, UINT nElapse,
        void (CALLBACK EXPORT* lpfnTimer)(HWND, UINT, UINT, DWORD));
    BOOL KillTimer(int nIDEvent);
// Window State Functions
    BOOL IsWindowEnabled() const;
    BOOL EnableWindow(BOOL bEnable = TRUE);
    // This active window applies only to top-most (i.e. Frame
    // windows)
    static CWnd* PASCAL GetActiveWindow();
    CWnd* SetActiveWindow();
    // Capture and Focus apply to all windows
    static CWnd* PASCAL GetCapture();
    CWnd* SetCapture();
    static CWnd* PASCAL GetFocus();
    CWnd* SetFocus();
    static CWnd* PASCAL GetDesktopWindow();
// Obsolete and non-portable APIs - not recommended for new code
    void CloseWindow();
    BOOL OpenIcon();
    CWnd* SetSysModalWindow();
    static CWnd* PASCAL GetSysModalWindow();
// Dialog-Box Item Functions
// (NOTE: Dialog-Box Items/Controls are not necessarily in dialog boxes!)
    void CheckDlgButton(int nIDButton, UINT nCheck);
    void CheckRadioButton(int nIDFirstButton, int nIDLastButton,
                    int nIDCheckButton);
    int GetCheckedRadioButton(int nIDFirstButton, int nIDLastButton);
    int DlgDirList(LPSTR lpPathSpec, int nIDListBox,
                    int nIDStaticPath, UINT nFileType);
    int DlgDirListComboBox(LPSTR lpPathSpec, int nIDComboBox,
                    int nIDStaticPath, UINT nFileType);
    BOOL DlgDirSelect(LPSTR lpString, int nIDListBox);
    BOOL DlgDirSelectComboBox(LPSTR lpString, int nIDComboBox);
    UINT GetDlgItemInt(int nID, BOOL* lpTrans = NULL,
                    BOOL bSigned = TRUE) const;
    int GetDlgItemText(int nID, LPSTR lpStr, int nMaxCount) const;
    CWnd* GetNextDlgGroupItem(CWnd* pWndCtl,
                    BOOL bPrevious = FALSE) const;
    CWnd* GetNextDlgTabItem(CWnd* pWndCtl,
                    BOOL bPrevious = FALSE) const;
    UINT IsDlgButtonChecked(int nIDButton) const;
    LRESULT SendDlgItemMessage(int nID, UINT message,
                    WPARAM wParam = 0, LPARAM lParam = 0);
```

```
        void SetDlgItemInt(int nID, UINT nValue, BOOL bSigned = TRUE);
        void SetDlgItemText(int nID, LPCSTR lpszString);
// Scrolling Functions
    int GetScrollPos(int nBar) const;
    void GetScrollRange(int nBar, LPINT lpMinPos,
                        LPINT lpMaxPos) const;
    void ScrollWindow(int xAmount, int yAmount,
                        LPCRECT lpRect = NULL,
                        LPCRECT lpClipRect = NULL);
    int SetScrollPos(int nBar, int nPos, BOOL bRedraw = TRUE);
    void SetScrollRange(int nBar, int nMinPos, int nMaxPos,
            BOOL bRedraw = TRUE);
    void ShowScrollBar(UINT nBar, BOOL bShow = TRUE);
    void EnableScrollBarCtrl(int nBar, BOOL bEnable = TRUE);
    virtual CScrollBar* GetScrollBarCtrl(int nBar) const;
                // return sibling scrollbar control (or NULL if none)
#if (WINVER >= 0x030a)
    int ScrollWindowEx(int dx, int dy,
                    LPCRECT lpRectScroll, LPCRECT lpRectClip,
                    CRgn* prgnUpdate, LPRECT lpRectUpdate, UINT flags);
#endif

// Window Access Functions
    CWnd* ChildWindowFromPoint(POINT point) const;
    static CWnd* PASCAL FindWindow(LPCSTR lpszClassName,
                    LPCSTR lpszWindowName);
    CWnd* GetNextWindow(UINT nFlag = GW_HWNDNEXT) const;
    CWnd* GetTopWindow() const;
    CWnd* GetWindow(UINT nCmd) const;
    CWnd* GetLastActivePopup() const;
    BOOL IsChild(const CWnd* pWnd) const;
    CWnd* GetParent() const;
    CWnd* SetParent(CWnd* pWndNewParent);
    static CWnd* PASCAL WindowFromPoint(POINT point);
// Alert Functions
    BOOL FlashWindow(BOOL bInvert);
    int MessageBox(LPCSTR lpszText, LPCSTR lpszCaption = NULL,
            UINT nType = MB_OK);
// Clipboard Functions
    BOOL ChangeClipboardChain(HWND hWndNext);
    HWND SetClipboardViewer();
    BOOL OpenClipboard();
    static CWnd* PASCAL GetClipboardOwner();
    static CWnd* PASCAL GetClipboardViewer();
#if (WINVER >= 0x030a)
    static CWnd* PASCAL GetOpenClipboardWindow();
#endif
// Caret Functions
    void CreateCaret(CBitmap* pBitmap);
    void CreateSolidCaret(int nWidth, int nHeight);
    void CreateGrayCaret(int nWidth, int nHeight);
    static CPoint PASCAL GetCaretPos();
    static void PASCAL SetCaretPos(POINT point);
    void HideCaret();
    void ShowCaret();
```

```
// Drag-Drop Functions
#if (WINVER >= 0x030a)
    void DragAcceptFiles(BOOL bAccept = TRUE);
#endif
// Dialog Data support
public:
    BOOL UpdateData(BOOL bSaveAndValidate = TRUE);
                // data wnd must be same type as this
// Layout and other functions
public:
    void RepositionBars(UINT nIDFirst, UINT nIDLast,
                    UINT nIDLeftOver);
    void UpdateDialogControls(CCmdTarget* pTarget,
                    BOOL bDisableIfNoHndler);
// Window-Management message handler member functions
protected:
    virtual BOOL OnCommand(WPARAM wParam, LPARAM lParam);
    afx_msg void OnActivate(UINT nState, CWnd* pWndOther,
                    BOOL bMinimized);
    afx_msg void OnActivateApp(BOOL bActive, HTASK hTask);
    afx_msg void OnCancelMode();
    afx_msg void OnChildActivate();
    afx_msg void OnClose();
    afx_msg int OnCreate(LPCREATESTRUCT lpCreateStruct);
    afx_msg HBRUSH OnCtlColor(CDC* pDC, CWnd* pWnd, UINT nCtlColor);
    afx_msg void OnDestroy();
    afx_msg void OnEnable(BOOL bEnable);
    afx_msg void OnEndSession(BOOL bEnding);
    afx_msg void OnEnterIdle(UINT nWhy, CWnd* pWho);
    afx_msg BOOL OnEraseBkgnd(CDC* pDC);
    afx_msg void OnGetMinMaxInfo(MINMAXINFO FAR* lpMMI);
    afx_msg void OnIconEraseBkgnd(CDC* pDC);
    afx_msg void OnKillFocus(CWnd* pNewWnd);
    afx_msg LRESULT OnMenuChar(UINT nChar, UINT nFlags, CMenu* pMenu);
    afx_msg void OnMenuSelect(UINT nItemID, UINT nFlags,
                        HMENU hSysMenu);
    afx_msg void OnMove(int x, int y);
    afx_msg void OnPaint();
    afx_msg void OnParentNotify(UINT message, LPARAM lParam);
    afx_msg HCURSOR OnQueryDragIcon();
    afx_msg BOOL OnQueryEndSession();
    afx_msg BOOL OnQueryNewPalette();
    afx_msg BOOL OnQueryOpen();
    afx_msg void OnSetFocus(CWnd* pOldWnd);
    afx_msg void OnShowWindow(BOOL bShow, UINT nStatus);
    afx_msg void OnSize(UINT nType, int cx, int cy);
#if (WINVER >= 0x030a)
    afx_msg void OnWindowPosChanging(WINDOWPOS FAR* lpwndpos);
    afx_msg void OnWindowPosChanged(WINDOWPOS FAR* lpwndpos);
#endif
// Nonclient-Area message handler member functions
    afx_msg BOOL OnNcActivate(BOOL bActive);
    afx_msg void OnNcCalcSize(BOOL bCalcValidRects,
                    NCCALCSIZE_PARAMS FAR* lpncsp);
    afx_msg BOOL OnNcCreate(LPCREATESTRUCT lpCreateStruct);
    afx_msg void OnNcDestroy();
    afx_msg UINT OnNcHitTest(CPoint point);
```

```
        afx_msg void OnNcLButtonDblClk(UINT nHitTest, CPoint point);
        afx_msg void OnNcLButtonDown(UINT nHitTest, CPoint point);
        afx_msg void OnNcLButtonUp(UINT nHitTest, CPoint point);
        afx_msg void OnNcMButtonDblClk(UINT nHitTest, CPoint point);
        afx_msg void OnNcMButtonDown(UINT nHitTest, CPoint point);
        afx_msg void OnNcMButtonUp(UINT nHitTest, CPoint point);
        afx_msg void OnNcMouseMove(UINT nHitTest, CPoint point);
        afx_msg void OnNcPaint();
        afx_msg void OnNcRButtonDblClk(UINT nHitTest, CPoint point);
        afx_msg void OnNcRButtonDown(UINT nHitTest, CPoint point);
        afx_msg void OnNcRButtonUp(UINT nHitTest, CPoint point);
// System message handler member functions
#if (WINVER >= 0x030a)
        afx_msg void OnDropFiles(HDROP hDropInfo);
        afx_msg void OnPaletteIsChanging(CWnd* pRealizeWnd);
#endif
        afx_msg void OnSysChar(UINT nChar, UINT nRepCnt, UINT nFlags);
        afx_msg void OnSysCommand(UINT nID, LPARAM lParam);
        afx_msg void OnSysDeadChar(UINT nChar, UINT nRepCnt, UINT nFlags);
        afx_msg void OnSysKeyDown(UINT nChar, UINT nRepCnt, UINT nFlags);
        afx_msg void OnSysKeyUp(UINT nChar, UINT nRepCnt, UINT nFlags);
        afx_msg void OnCompacting(UINT nCpuTime);
        afx_msg void OnDevModeChange(LPSTR lpDeviceName);
        afx_msg void OnFontChange();
        afx_msg void OnPaletteChanged(CWnd* pFocusWnd);
        afx_msg void OnSpoolerStatus(UINT nStatus, UINT nJobs);
        afx_msg void OnSysColorChange();
        afx_msg void OnTimeChange();
        afx_msg void OnWinIniChange(LPCSTR lpszSection);
// Input message handler member functions
        afx_msg void OnChar(UINT nChar, UINT nRepCnt, UINT nFlags);
        afx_msg void OnDeadChar(UINT nChar, UINT nRepCnt, UINT nFlags);
        afx_msg void OnHScroll(UINT nSBCode, UINT nPos,
                        CScrollBar* pScrollBar);
        afx_msg void OnVScroll(UINT nSBCode, UINT nPos,
                        CScrollBar* pScrollBar);
        afx_msg void OnKeyDown(UINT nChar, UINT nRepCnt, UINT nFlags);
        afx_msg void OnKeyUp(UINT nChar, UINT nRepCnt, UINT nFlags);
        afx_msg void OnLButtonDblClk(UINT nFlags, CPoint point);
        afx_msg void OnLButtonDown(UINT nFlags, CPoint point);
        afx_msg void OnLButtonUp(UINT nFlags, CPoint point);
        afx_msg void OnMButtonDblClk(UINT nFlags, CPoint point);
        afx_msg void OnMButtonDown(UINT nFlags, CPoint point);
        afx_msg void OnMButtonUp(UINT nFlags, CPoint point);
        afx_msg int OnMouseActivate(CWnd* pDesktopWnd, UINT nHitTest,
                                UINT message);
        afx_msg void OnMouseMove(UINT nFlags, CPoint point);
        afx_msg void OnRButtonDblClk(UINT nFlags, CPoint point);
        afx_msg void OnRButtonDown(UINT nFlags, CPoint point);
        afx_msg void OnRButtonUp(UINT nFlags, CPoint point);
        afx_msg BOOL OnSetCursor(CWnd* pWnd, UINT nHitTest, UINT message);
        afx_msg void OnTimer(UINT nIDEvent);
// Initialization message handler member functions
        afx_msg void OnInitMenu(CMenu* pMenu);
        afx_msg void OnInitMenuPopup(CMenu* pPopupMenu, UINT nIndex,
                                BOOL bSysMenu);
// Clipboard message handler member functions
```

```
     afx_msg void OnAskCbFormatName(UINT nMaxCount, LPSTR lpszString);
     afx_msg void OnChangeCbChain(HWND hWndRemove, HWND hWndAfter);
     afx_msg void OnDestroyClipboard();
     afx_msg void OnDrawClipboard();
     afx_msg void OnHScrollClipboard(CWnd* pClipAppWnd,
                          UINT nSBCode, UINT nPos);
     afx_msg void OnPaintClipboard(CWnd* pClipAppWnd,
                          HGLOBAL hPaintStruct);
     afx_msg void OnRenderAllFormats();
     afx_msg void OnRenderFormat(UINT nFormat);
     afx_msg void OnSizeClipboard(CWnd* pClipAppWnd, HGLOBAL hRect);
     afx_msg void OnVScrollClipboard(CWnd* pClipAppWnd, UINT nSBCode,
                          UINT nPos);
// Control message handler member functions
     afx_msg int OnCompareItem(int nIDCtl,
                     LPCOMPAREITEMSTRUCT lpCompareItemStruct);
     afx_msg void OnDeleteItem(int nIDCtl,
                     LPDELETEITEMSTRUCT lpDeleteItemStruct);
     afx_msg void OnDrawItem(int nIDCtl,
                     LPDRAWITEMSTRUCT lpDrawItemStruct);
     afx_msg UINT OnGetDlgCode();
     afx_msg void OnMeasureItem(int nIDCtl,
                     LPMEASUREITEMSTRUCT lpMeasureItemStruct);
     afx_msg int OnCharToItem(UINT nChar, CListBox* pListBox,
                     UINT nIndex);
     afx_msg int OnVKeyToItem(UINT nKey, CListBox* pListBox,
                     UINT nIndex);
// MDI message handler member functions
     afx_msg void OnMDIActivate(BOOL bActivate,
               CWnd* pActivateWnd, CWnd* pDeactivateWnd);
// Overridables and other helpers (for implementation of derived
// classes)
protected:
     // for deriving from a standard control
     virtual WNDPROC* GetSuperWndProcAddr();
     // for dialog data exchange and validation
     virtual void DoDataExchange(CDataExchange* pDX);
public:
     // for translating Windows messages in main message pump
     virtual BOOL PreTranslateMessage(MSG* pMsg);
protected:
     // for processing Windows messages
     virtual LRESULT WindowProc(UINT message, WPARAM wParam,
                          LPARAM lParam);
     // for handling default processing
     LRESULT Default();
     virtual LRESULT DefWindowProc(UINT message, WPARAM wParam,
                          LPARAM lParam);
     // for custom cleanup after WM_NCDESTROY
     virtual void PostNcDestroy();
     // for notifications from parent
     virtual BOOL OnChildNotify(UINT message, WPARAM wParam,
                        LPARAM lParam, LRESULT* pLResult);
     // return TRUE if parent should not process this message
// Implementation
public:
     virtual ~CWnd();
     // helper routines for implementation
```

```
        BOOL SendChildNotifyLastMsg(LRESULT* pLResult = NULL);
        BOOL ExecuteDlgInit(LPCSTR lpszResourceName);
        static BOOL PASCAL GrayCtlColor(HDC hDC, HWND hWnd,
                 UINT nCtlColor, HBRUSH hbrGray, COLORREF clrText);
        void CenterWindow(CWnd* pAlternateOwner = NULL);
        // implementation message handlers for private messages
        afx_msg LRESULT OnVBXEvent(WPARAM wParam, LPARAM lParam);
protected:
        // implementation of message routing
        friend LRESULT CALLBACK AFX_EXPORT _AfxSendMsgHook(int,
                                          WPARAM, LPARAM);
        friend LRESULT PASCAL _AfxCallWndProc(CWnd*, HWND, UINT,
                                          WPARAM, LPARAM);

        //{{AFX_MSG(CWnd)
        //}}AFX_MSG
        DECLARE_MESSAGE_MAP()
};
```

The descendants of class CWnd inherit the numerous operations supported by the member functions of the class. These operations include the following:

- Creating and initializing a window

- Manipulating and querying the state of a window

- Managing the size and location of a window

- Accessing a window and its components

- Mapping the coordinates of a window

- Manipulating the text in a window or the caption of a window

- Managing the scrolling of a window

- Performing drag-and-drop operations

- Manipulating the editing caret of a window

- Managing the controls in a dialog box

- Controlling the items of a menu window

- Installing and removing a system timer

- Alerting the application user

- Managing Windows messages

- Accessing the Clipboard and manipulating its contents

- Exchanging data with the controls of a dialog box

- Handling a wide range of Windows messages generated by user input (both keyboard and mouse button clicks) and other Windows messages

The Control Classes

The control classes represent a subhierarchy in the MFC library that represents visual controls. The following outline lists the controls classes and shows how they are derived from each other:

```
- CStatic
+ CButton
      - CBitmapButton
+ CEdit
      + CHEdit
            - CBEdit
- CListBox
- CComboBox
- CScrollBar
- CVBControl
```

The *CStatic* Class

The class CStatic, a descendant of class CWnd, models the static text controls. This control represents text that is either completely fixed or text that can be changed by using the inherited member function SetWindowText. The declaration of class CStatic is as follows:

```
class CStatic : public CWnd
{
    DECLARE_DYNAMIC(CStatic)
// Constructors
public:
    CStatic();
    BOOL Create(LPCSTR lpszText, DWORD dwStyle,
                const RECT& rect, CWnd* pParentWnd,
                UINT nID = 0xffff);
#if (WINVER >= 0x030a)
    HICON SetIcon(HICON hIcon);
    HICON GetIcon() const;
#endif
// Implementation
public:
    virtual ~CStatic();
protected:
    virtual WNDPROC* GetSuperWndProcAddr();
};
```

The class declares a public constructor, which enables you to specify the control's text, style, size, parent window, and optional ID. The style parameter enables you to specify whether or not the text is permanently fixed.

The *CButton* Class

The class CButton models the command button, the check box, and the radio button controls. Here is the declaration of the CButton class:

```
class CButton : public CWnd
{
    DECLARE_DYNAMIC(CButton)
// Constructors
public:
    CButton();
    BOOL Create(LPCSTR lpszCaption, DWORD dwStyle,
                const RECT& rect, CWnd* pParentWnd, UINT nID);
// Attributes
    UINT GetState() const;
    void SetState(BOOL bHighlight);
    int GetCheck() const;
    void SetCheck(int nCheck);
    UINT GetButtonStyle() const;
    void SetButtonStyle(UINT nStyle, BOOL bRedraw = TRUE);
// Overridables (for owner draw only)
    virtual void DrawItem(LPDRAWITEMSTRUCT lpDrawItemStruct);
// Implementation
public:
    virtual ~CButton();
protected:
    virtual WNDPROC* GetSuperWndProcAddr();
    virtual BOOL OnChildNotify(UINT, WPARAM, LPARAM, LRESULT*);
};
```

The class declares a default constructor that creates an invisible empty control object. The member function Create defines the control further by specifying the caption, style (which indicates whether the control is a command button, a check box, or a radio button), size, location, parent window, and unique ID. The class offers member functions to set and clear the check state (used for check box and radio button controls).

The *CBitmapButton* Class

The class CBitmapButton, a descendant of class CButton, supports bitmapped buttons that add, to dialog boxes and other windows, controls with a special look. The following code shows the declaration of class CBitmapButton:

```
class CBitmapButton : public CButton
{
    DECLARE_DYNAMIC(CBitmapButton)
public:
// Construction
    CBitmapButton();
```

```
          BOOL LoadBitmaps(LPCSTR lpszBitmapResource,
                  LPCSTR lpszBitmapResourceSel = NULL,
                  LPCSTR lpszBitmapResourceFocus = NULL,
                  LPCSTR lpszBitmapResourceDisabled = NULL);
          BOOL AutoLoad(UINT nID, CWnd* pParent);
     // Operations
          void SizeToContent();
     // Implementation:
     protected:
          // all bitmaps must be the same size
          CBitmap m_bitmap;            // normal image (REQUIRED)
          CBitmap m_bitmapSel;         // selected image (OPTIONAL)
          CBitmap m_bitmapFocus;       // focused but not selected
     (OPTIONAL)
          CBitmap m_bitmapDisabled;    // disabled bitmap (OPTIONAL)
          virtual void DrawItem(LPDRAWITEMSTRUCT lpDIS);
     };
```

The CBitmapButton class declares a constructor, which creates an invisible,
empty, bitmapped button object. The member function LoadBitmaps lets you
specify the bitmap resources that represent the button's normal, selected,
focused, and disabled states. These bitmap images work in concert with the
other member functions inherited from classes CButton and CWnd. Other member functions enable you to associate a bitmapped button to a dialog box or
parent window and to resize the bitmapped button to the size of the bitmap.

The *CEdit* Class

The class CEdit models the single-line and multi-line edit controls. The edit
controls support the cut, copy, and paste text processing operations, text
selection, and cursor movement. You can use multi-line edit controls with
vertical and horizontal scroll bars to support versatile editing in a dialog box
or window. The declaration of the class CEdit is as follows:

```
     class CEdit : public CWnd
     {
          DECLARE_DYNAMIC(CEdit)
     // Constructors
     public:
          CEdit();
          BOOL Create(DWORD dwStyle, const RECT& rect,
                  CWnd* pParentWnd, UINT nID);
     // Attributes
          BOOL CanUndo() const;
          int GetLineCount() const;
          BOOL GetModify() const;
          void SetModify(BOOL bModified = TRUE);
          void GetRect(LPRECT lpRect) const;
          DWORD GetSel() const;
          void GetSel(int& nStartChar, int& nEndChar) const;
          HLOCAL GetHandle() const;
          void SetHandle(HLOCAL hBuffer);
```

```
                    // NOTE: first word in lpszBuffer must contain the size of
                    // the buffer!
                    int GetLine(int nIndex, LPSTR lpszBuffer) const;
                    int GetLine(int nIndex, LPSTR lpszBuffer, int nMaxLength) const;
        // Operations
                    void EmptyUndoBuffer();
                    BOOL FmtLines(BOOL bAddEOL);
                    void LimitText(int nChars = 0);
                    int LineFromChar(int nIndex = -1) const;
                    int LineIndex(int nLine = -1) const;
                    int LineLength(int nLine = -1) const;
                    void LineScroll(int nLines, int nChars = 0);
                    void ReplaceSel(LPCSTR lpszNewText);
                    void SetPasswordChar(char ch);
                    void SetRect(LPCRECT lpRect);
                    void SetRectNP(LPCRECT lpRect);
                    void SetSel(DWORD dwSelection, BOOL bNoScroll = FALSE);
                    void SetSel(int nStartChar, int nEndChar, BOOL bNoScroll = FALSE);
                    BOOL SetTabStops(int nTabStops, LPINT rgTabStops);
                    void SetTabStops();
                    BOOL SetTabStops(const int& cxEachStop);    // takes an 'int'
                    // Clipboard operations
                    BOOL Undo();
                    void Clear();
                    void Copy();
                    void Cut();
                    void Paste();
        #if (WINVER >= 0x030a)
                    BOOL SetReadOnly(BOOL bReadOnly = TRUE);
                    int GetFirstVisibleLine() const;
                    char GetPasswordChar() const;
        #endif
        // Implementation
        public:
                    virtual ~CEdit();
        protected:
                    virtual WNDPROC* GetSuperWndProcAddr();
        };
```

The class CEdit provides the default constructor and the member function
Create to create an edit control. The Create function lets you specify the style
of the control. This style provides the choice between single-line and multi-
line control forms, automatic case character conversion to either lowercase or
uppercase, the appearance of scroll bars (in the case of the multi-line form),
and the appearance of a frame around the edit control. In addition, the function Create specifies the size, location, parent window, and unique ID of the
edit control. The class supplies a set of member functions to support nontrivial editing-related operations, such as cut, copy, clear, and paste text,
undoing the last editing operation, setting a selection, replacing a selection
with new text, scrolling text lines, and querying line-related information.

The *CHEdit* Class

The CHEdit class, a descendant of class CEdit, supports the operation of a handwriting edit control used in Pen Computing. The class uses the default constructor and the member function Create to build a handwriting edit control. With the function Create, you can specify the size, location, parent window, and unique ID of the edit control. The member functions of class CHEdit offer operations that manage aspects of handwriting, such as the handwriting "ink" and the area of text recognition.

The *CBEdit* Class

The CBEdit class, a descendant of class CHEdit, supports boxed handwriting edit controls. The CHEdit controls support the input and editing of text using standard pen editing gestures. These controls display a *comb*, which points out to the user the location of the next input character. Consequently, the comb offers better character recognition because it supplies the text recognizer with data regarding the position of the input text.

The *CScrollBar* Class

The class CScrollBar models vertical and horizontal scroll bars, which enable application users to view information that does not entirely fit in a window or a view. The declaration of the class CScrollBar is shown in the following code:

```
class CScrollBar : public CWnd
{
    DECLARE_DYNAMIC(CScrollBar)
// Constructors
public:
    CScrollBar();
    BOOL Create(DWORD dwStyle, const RECT& rect,
            CWnd* pParentWnd, UINT nID);
// Attributes
    int GetScrollPos() const;
    int SetScrollPos(int nPos, BOOL bRedraw = TRUE);
    void GetScrollRange(LPINT lpMinPos, LPINT lpMaxPos) const;
    void SetScrollRange(int nMinPos, int nMaxPos,
                BOOL bRedraw = TRUE);
    void ShowScrollBar(BOOL bShow = TRUE);
#if (WINVER >= 0x030a)
    BOOL EnableScrollBar(UINT nArrowFlags = ESB_ENABLE_BOTH);
#endif
// Implementation
public:
    virtual ~CScrollBar();
protected:
    virtual WNDPROC* GetSuperWndProcAddr();
};
```

The class enables you to create scroll bar controls using the default constructor and the member function Create. The Create function enables you to specify the control style, size, location, parent window, and unique ID. The style lets you select between a vertical and horizontal scroll bar and also lets you fine-tune the alignment of the various visual components of the scroll bar. The class offers a family of member functions to toggle the visibility of the control, enable or disable the control, set and query the scrolling range, and set and query the scroll box position.

The *CListBox* Class

The class CListBox models the single-selection and multi-selection list box controls. List boxes enable application users to select input from a set of items, instead of the user having to remember and then type the item of choice. Here is the declaration of class CListBox:

```
class CListBox : public CWnd
{
    DECLARE_DYNAMIC(CListBox)
// Constructors
public:
    CListBox();
    BOOL Create(DWORD dwStyle, const RECT& rect,
            CWnd* pParentWnd, UINT nID);
// Attributes
    // for entire listbox
    int GetCount() const;
    int GetHorizontalExtent() const;
    void SetHorizontalExtent(int cxExtent);
    int GetTopIndex() const;
    int SetTopIndex(int nIndex);
    // for single-selection list boxes
    int GetCurSel() const;
    int SetCurSel(int nSelect);
    // for multiple-selection list boxes
    int GetSel(int nIndex) const; // also works for single-selection
    int SetSel(int nIndex, BOOL bSelect = TRUE);
    int GetSelCount() const;
    int GetSelItems(int nMaxItems, LPINT rgIndex) const;
    // for list box items
    DWORD GetItemData(int nIndex) const;
    int SetItemData(int nIndex, DWORD dwItemData);
    void* GetItemDataPtr(int nIndex) const;
    int SetItemDataPtr(int nIndex, void* pData);
    int GetItemRect(int nIndex, LPRECT lpRect) const;
    int GetText(int nIndex, LPSTR lpszBuffer) const;
    int GetTextLen(int nIndex) const;
    void GetText(int nIndex, CString& rString) const;
    // Settable only attributes
    void SetColumnWidth(int cxWidth);
    BOOL SetTabStops(int nTabStops, LPINT rgTabStops);
    void SetTabStops();
```

```
        BOOL SetTabStops(const int& cxEachStop);      // takes an 'int'
#if (WINVER >= 0x030a)
        int SetItemHeight(int nIndex, UINT cyItemHeight);
        int GetItemHeight(int nIndex) const;
        int FindStringExact(int nIndexStart, LPCSTR lpszFind) const;
        int GetCaretIndex() const;
        int SetCaretIndex(int nIndex, BOOL bScroll = TRUE);
#endif
// Operations
        // manipulating list box items
        int AddString(LPCSTR lpszItem);
        int DeleteString(UINT nIndex);
        int InsertString(int nIndex, LPCSTR lpszItem);
        void ResetContent();
        int Dir(UINT attr, LPCSTR lpszWildCard);
        // selection helpers
        int FindString(int nStartAfter, LPCSTR lpszItem) const;
        int SelectString(int nStartAfter, LPCSTR lpszItem);
        int SelItemRange(BOOL bSelect, int nFirstItem, int nLastItem);
// Overridables (must override draw, measure and compare for owner draw)
        virtual void DrawItem(LPDRAWITEMSTRUCT lpDrawItemStruct);
        virtual void MeasureItem(LPMEASUREITEMSTRUCT lpMeasureItemStruct);
        virtual int CompareItem(LPCOMPAREITEMSTRUCT lpCompareItemStruct);
        virtual void DeleteItem(LPDELETEITEMSTRUCT lpDeleteItemStruct);
// Implementation
public:
        virtual ~CListBox();
protected:
        virtual WNDPROC* GetSuperWndProcAddr();
        virtual BOOL OnChildNotify(UINT, WPARAM, LPARAM, LRESULT*);
};
```

The class CListBox enables you to build a list box control by using the default constructor and the member function Create. The Create function permits you to specify the style, size, location, parent window, and unique ID of the list box control. The style parameter permits you to determine the appearance and operation of the list box by making certain choices, including the following:

- Whether to include a vertical or a horizontal scroll bar

- Whether to allow tabbing to the list box control

- Whether the user can select between single-selection and multiple-selection control versions

- Whether to sort alphabetically, in ascending order, the items in the list box control

- Whether to allow multiple items to be selected when the user holds down the Shift key and clicks the left mouse button

The class also declares several groups of member functions, which perform the following operations:

- *General operations*. Set and query various control parameters, statistics, and text items.

- *Single-selection operations*. Set and retrieve the selected string.

- *Multiple-selection operations*. Set and retrieve the selected strings, obtain the number of selections, and manipulate a range of items in a list box.

- *String operations*. Include adding, deleting, inserting, selecting, and searching for strings in the list box.

- *Owner-draw operations*. Offer the parent window more control over drawing a list box.

The *CComboBox* Class

The class CComboBox supports the combo box control, which typically combines the operations of the edit box and list box controls. The combo box usually enables a user either to select an item from the list box or to type a new item in the edit box. There are three kinds of combo boxes: simple, drop-down, and drop-down list. The simple combo box includes the edit box and the list box that is always displayed. The drop-down combo box differs from the simple combo box in that the list box appears only when you click the down arrow. The third kind of combo box—the drop-down list combo box— also provides a list box only when you click the down arrow, but this combo box contains no edit box. The declaration of the class CComboBox is as follows:

```
class CComboBox : public CWnd
{
    DECLARE_DYNAMIC(CComboBox)
// Constructors
public:
    CComboBox();
    BOOL Create(DWORD dwStyle, const RECT& rect, CWnd* pParentWnd,
            UINT nID);
// Attributes
    // for entire combo box
    int GetCount() const;
    int GetCurSel() const;
    int SetCurSel(int nSelect);
    // for edit control
    DWORD GetEditSel() const;
    BOOL LimitText(int nMaxChars);
    BOOL SetEditSel(int nStartChar, int nEndChar);
    // for combobox item
    DWORD GetItemData(int nIndex) const;
```

```
        int SetItemData(int nIndex, DWORD dwItemData);
        void* GetItemDataPtr(int nIndex) const;
        int SetItemDataPtr(int nIndex, void* pData);
        int GetLBText(int nIndex, LPSTR lpszText) const;
        int GetLBTextLen(int nIndex) const;
        void GetLBText(int nIndex, CString& rString) const;
#if (WINVER >= 0x030a)
        int SetItemHeight(int nIndex, UINT cyItemHeight);
        int GetItemHeight(int nIndex) const;
        int FindStringExact(int nIndexStart, LPCSTR lpszFind) const;
        int SetExtendedUI(BOOL bExtended = TRUE);
        BOOL GetExtendedUI() const;
        void GetDroppedControlRect(LPRECT lprect) const;
        BOOL GetDroppedState() const;
#endif
// Operations
        // for drop-down combo boxes
        void ShowDropDown(BOOL bShowIt = TRUE);
        // manipulating listbox items
        int AddString(LPCSTR lpszString);
        int DeleteString(UINT nIndex);
        int InsertString(int nIndex, LPCSTR lpszString);
        void ResetContent();
        int Dir(UINT attr, LPCSTR lpszWildCard);
        // selection helpers
        int FindString(int nStartAfter, LPCSTR lpszString) const;
        int SelectString(int nStartAfter, LPCSTR lpszString);
        // Clipboard operations
        void Clear();
        void Copy();
        void Cut();
        void Paste();
// Overridables (must override draw, measure and compare for owner draw)
        virtual void DrawItem(LPDRAWITEMSTRUCT lpDrawItemStruct);
        virtual void MeasureItem(LPMEASUREITEMSTRUCT lpMeasureItemStruct);
        virtual int CompareItem(LPCOMPAREITEMSTRUCT lpCompareItemStruct);
        virtual void DeleteItem(LPDELETEITEMSTRUCT lpDeleteItemStruct);
// Implementation
public:
        virtual ~CComboBox();
protected:
        virtual WNDPROC* GetSuperWndProcAddr();
        virtual BOOL OnChildNotify(UINT, WPARAM, LPARAM, LRESULT*);
};
```

The class CComboBox enables you to build a combo box control by using the default constructor and the member function Create. The Create function permits you to specify the style, size, location, parent window, and unique ID of the combo box control. The style parameter lets you determine the appearance and operation of the combo box by making certain choices, including the following:

■ The kind of combo box control that is used: simple, drop-down, or drop-down list

- Whether to allow tabbing to the control

- Whether to allow automatic horizontal scrolling in the edit control portion

- Whether the items in the list box portion of the control are sorted alphabetically, in ascending order

The class also declares several groups of member functions, which perform the following operations:

- *General operations.* Set and query various control parameters, statistics, and text items.

- *Edit control operations.* Perform text editing, such as clear, cut, copy, and paste.

- *String operations.* Include adding, deleting, inserting, selecting, and searching for strings in the combo box.

- *Owner-draw operations.* Offer the parent window more control over drawing a combo box.

The *CVBControl* Class

The class CVBControl supports creating Visual Basic controls and enables you to use them in both Visual Basic and in Visual C++ programs. This class permits you to perform a variety of operations, such as loading VB controls, obtaining their properties, setting their properties, and altering their position on-screen. The declaration of the class CVBControl is shown in the following code:

```
class CVBControl : public CWnd
{
    DECLARE_DYNAMIC(CVBControl)
// Constructors
public:
    CVBControl();
    BOOL Create(LPCSTR lpszWindowName, DWORD dwStyle,
        const RECT& rect, CWnd* pParentWnd, UINT nID,
        CFile* pFile = NULL, BOOL bAutoDelete = FALSE);
// Attributes
    // Property Access Routines
    BOOL SetNumProperty(int nPropIndex, LONG lValue, int index = 0);
    BOOL SetNumProperty(LPCSTR lpszPropName, LONG lValue,
                int index = 0);
    BOOL SetFloatProperty(int nPropIndex, float value, int index = 0);
    BOOL SetFloatProperty(LPCSTR lpszPropName, float value,
                int index = 0);
```

```
        BOOL SetStrProperty(int nPropIndex, LPCSTR lpszValue,
                        int index = 0);
        BOOL SetStrProperty(LPCSTR lpszPropName, LPCSTR lpszValue,
                        int index = 0);
        BOOL SetPictureProperty(int nPropIndex, HPIC hPic, int index = 0);
        BOOL SetPictureProperty(LPCSTR lpszPropName, HPIC hPic,
                        int index = 0);
        LONG GetNumProperty(int nPropIndex, int index = 0);
        LONG GetNumProperty(LPCSTR lpszPropName, int index = 0);
        float GetFloatProperty(int nPropIndex, int index = 0);
        float GetFloatProperty(LPCSTR lpszPropName, int index = 0);
        CString GetStrProperty(int nPropIndex, int index = 0);
        CString GetStrProperty(LPCSTR lpszPropName, int index = 0);
        HPIC GetPictureProperty(int nPropIndex, int index = 0);
        HPIC GetPictureProperty(LPCSTR lpszPropName, int index = 0);
        // Get the index of a property
        int GetPropIndex(LPCSTR lpszPropName) const;
        LPCSTR GetPropName(int nIndex) const;
        // Get the index of an Event
        int GetEventIndex(LPCSTR lpszEventName) const;
        LPCSTR GetEventName(int nIndex) const;
        // Class name of control
        LPCSTR GetVBXClass() const;
        // Class information
        int GetNumProps() const;
        int GetNumEvents() const;
        BOOL IsPropArray(int nIndex) const;
        UINT GetPropType(int nIndex) const;
        DWORD GetPropFlags(int nIndex) const;
        // Error reporting variable
        // Contains the VB error code returned by a control
        int m_nError;
// Operations
        // BASIC file number (channel) to CFile association
        static void PASCAL OpenChannel(CFile* pFile, WORD wChannel);
        static BOOL PASCAL CloseChannel(WORD wChannel);
        static CFile* PASCAL GetChannel(WORD wChannel);
        static void BeginNewVBHeap();
        void AddItem(LPCSTR lpszItem, LONG lIndex);
        void RemoveItem(LONG lIndex);
        void Refresh();
        void Move(RECT& rect);
// Implementation
public:
        virtual ~CVBControl();
        DWORD GetModelFlags();
        DWORD GetModelStyles();
        void ReferenceFile(BOOL bReference);
        static void EnableVBXFloat();
        static BOOL ParseWindowText(LPCSTR lpszWindowName,
            CString& strFileName, CString& strClassName,
            CString& strCaption);
        HCTL GetHCTL();
        // Control Defined Structure -- Dangerous to use directly
        BYTE FAR* GetUserSpace();
        struct CRecreateStruct  // Implementation structure
        {
```

```
            char* pText;
            DWORD dwStyle;
            CRect rect;
            HWND hWndParent;
            UINT nControlID;
        };
        enum
        {
            TYPE_FROMVBX,     // Coming from VBX, assume proper type
            TYPE_INTEGER,     // int or LONG
            TYPE_REAL,        // float
            TYPE_STRING,
            TYPE_PICTURE
        };
        virtual LRESULT DefControlProc(UINT message, WPARAM wParam,
                             LPARAM lParam);
        void Recreate(CRecreateStruct& rs);
        CVBControlModel* GetModel();
public:
        int GetStdPropIndex(int nStdID) const;
        BOOL SetPropertyWithType(int nPropIndex, WORD wType,
                             LONG lValue, int index);
        LONG GetNumPropertyWithType(int nPropIndex, UINT nType,
                             int index);
        HSZ GetStrProperty(int nPropIndex, int index, BOOL& bTemp);
        CString m_ctlName;          // Read only at run-time
        // Trace routine to allow one library version
        static void CDECL Trace(BOOL bFatal, UINT nFormatIndex, ...);
        void VBXAssertValid() const;    // non-virtual helper
        static BOOL EnableMemoryTracking(BOOL bTracking);
protected:
        static CVBControl* NEW();
        void DELETE();
        virtual BOOL OnChildNotify(UINT, WPARAM, LPARAM, LRESULT*);
        LRESULT CallControlProc(UINT message, WPARAM wParam,
                             LPARAM lParam);
        BOOL CommonInit();
        void SetDefaultValue(int nPropIndex, BOOL bPreHwnd);
        BOOL SetStdProp(WORD wPropId, WORD wType, LONG lValue);
        LONG GetStdNumProp(WORD wPropId);
        CString GetStdStrProp(WORD wPropId);
        BOOL SetFontProperty(WORD wPropId, LONG lData);
        void BuildCurFont(HDC hDC, HFONT hCurFont, LOGFONT& logFont);
        LONG GetNumFontProperty(WORD wPropId);
        WORD GetCharSet(HDC hDC, LPCSTR lpFaceName);
        virtual LRESULT DefWindowProc(UINT message, WPARAM wParam,
                             LPARAM lParam);
        virtual void PostNcDestroy();
        void FireMouseEvent(WORD event, WORD wButton,
                         WPARAM wParam, LPARAM lParam);
        BOOL CreateAndSetFont(LPLOGFONT lplf);
        BOOL LoadProperties(CFile* pFile, BOOL bPreHwnd);
        BOOL LoadProp(int nPropIndex, CFile* pFile);
        BOOL LoadPropData(int nPropIndex, CFile* pFile);
        BOOL IsPropDefault(int nPropIndex);
        CVBControlModel* LoadControl(LPCSTR lpszFileName,
                             LPCSTR lpszControlName);
```

```
        afx_msg void OnVBXLoaded();
        void AllocateHCTL(size_t nSize);
        void DeallocateHCTL();
        static int ConvertFontSizeToTwips(LONG lFontSize);
        // This actually returns a float masquerading as a long
        static LONG ConvertTwipsToFontSize(int nTwips);
protected:
    CVBControlModel* m_pModel;
    BOOL m_bRecreating;             // Do not destroy on this NCDestroy
    BOOL m_bAutoDelete;             // TRUE if automatically created
    BOOL m_bInPostNcDestroy;        // TRUE if deleting from Destroy
    BOOL m_bLoading;                // TRUE if loading properties from
                                    // formfile
    int m_nCursorID;
    // variables for stack overrun protection
    UINT m_nInitialStack;          // SP when control recieved first
                                    // message
    UINT m_nRecursionLevel;        // Level of control proc recursion
    BOOL m_bStackFault;            // TRUE if stack fault hit
    UINT m_nFaultRecurse;          // level at which stack faulted
    HBRUSH m_hbrBkgnd;             // brush used in WM_CTLCOLOR
    HFONT m_hFontCreated;          // Font created by control
    HCURSOR m_hcurMouse;
    HCTL m_hCtl;                    // Control handle
    COLORREF m_clrBkgnd;
    COLORREF m_clrFore;
    CRect m_rectCreate;             // Created Size
    CString m_strTag;
    friend LRESULT CALLBACK AFX_EXPORT _AfxVBWndProc(HWND hWnd,
            UINT msg, WPARAM wParam, LPARAM lParam);
    friend LRESULT CALLBACK AFX_EXPORT _AfxVBProxyProc(HWND hWnd,
            UINT msg, WPARAM wParam, LPARAM lParam);
    friend WORD CALLBACK AFX_EXPORT _AfxVBFireEvent(HCTL hControl,
            WORD idEvent, LPVOID lpParams);
    friend WORD CALLBACK AFX_EXPORT _AfxVBRecreateControlHwnd(
            HCTL hControl);
    // Friends required for VB API access
    //{{AFX_MSG(CVBControl)
    //}}AFX_MSG
    DECLARE_MESSAGE_MAP()
    ///////////////////////
    // Implementation
    // These APIs can not be referenced by applications
public:
    DWORD Save(CFile* pFile);
    BOOL Load(CFile* pData);
protected:
    BOOL m_bCreatedInDesignMode;
    BOOL m_bVisible;
    friend class CVBPopupWnd;
    BOOL SaveProperties(CFile* pFile, BOOL bPreHwnd);
    BOOL SaveProp(int nPropIndex, CFile* pFile);
    BOOL SavePropData(int nPropIndex, CFile* pFile);
    LONG InitPropPopup(WPARAM wParam, LPARAM lParam);
    void DoPictureDlg(int m_nPropId);
    void DoColorDlg(int m_nPropId);
    void DoFontDlg(int m_nPropId);
    void FillList(CListBox* pLB, LPCSTR lpszEnumList);
};
```

The declaration of class CVBControl indicates that it offers a substantial number of operations to support Visual Basic controls. The class enables you to build a VBX control using the default constructor and the member function Create. This function permits you to specify the VBX data string (which includes the name of the .VBX file, the control name, and the VBX window text) along with the style, size, location, parent window, unique ID, pointer to the associated control-attribute file, and auto deletion flag of the VBX control. The CVBControl class offers several groups of member functions to support the following kinds of operations:

- Accessing the properties of the VBX control

- Accessing the attributes of the VBX control; these operations include the query of events handled by the VBX control

- Methods-related operations used to add, move, refresh, and remove from a list managed by the VBX control

- Performing run-time operations, which include creating heap space for the VBX control, as well as opening, accessing, and closing the file buffer used by the VBX control (in a manner similar to Visual Basic file I/O)

The Dialog Box Classes

The MFC library provides the dialog box classes to support both custom and common dialog boxes. Common dialog boxes are the standard dialog boxes available in Windows 3.1 and later. Refer to Appendix C for an overview of the dialog box classes.

The Frame Window Classes

The frame window classes consist of three classes and support windows enclosed in frames. The following outline shows the subhierarchy of the frame window classes:

```
+ CFrameWnd
        - CMDIFrameWnd
        - CMDIChildWnd
```

In the case of applications with single-document windows, you derive the window classes from class CFrameWnd. In the case of multiple-document windows, you derive the frame window classes from CMDIFrameWnd and the child window classes from CMDIChildWnd.

The *CFrameWnd* Class

The class CFrameWnd, a descendant of class CWnd, supports single-document interface (SDI) overlapped or pop-up frame windows. The descendants of CFrameWnd, which you derive, may contain views and any combination of the visual controls. The declaration of class CFrameWnd is shown in the following code:

```
class CFrameWnd : public CWnd
{
    DECLARE_DYNCREATE(CFrameWnd)
// Constructors
public:
    static const CRect AFXAPI_DATA rectDefault;
    CFrameWnd();
    BOOL LoadAccelTable(LPCSTR lpszResourceName);
    BOOL Create(LPCSTR lpszClassName,
                LPCSTR lpszWindowName,
                DWORD dwStyle = WS_OVERLAPPEDWINDOW,
                const RECT& rect = rectDefault,
                CWnd* pParentWnd = NULL,  // != NULL for popups
                LPCSTR lpszMenuName = NULL,
                DWORD dwExStyle = 0,
                CCreateContext* pContext = NULL);
    // dynamic creation - load frame and associated resources
    virtual BOOL LoadFrame(UINT nIDResource,
                DWORD dwDefaultStyle = WS_OVERLAPPEDWINDOW |
                                               FWS_ADDTOTITLE,
                CWnd* pParentWnd = NULL,
                CCreateContext* pContext = NULL);
// Attributes
    virtual CDocument* GetActiveDocument();
    // Active child view maintenance
    CView* GetActiveView() const;          // active view or NULL
    void SetActiveView(CView* pViewNew);   // active view or NULL
    BOOL m_bAutoMenuEnable;
    // TRUE => menu items without handlers will be disabled
// Operations
    virtual void RecalcLayout();
    virtual void ActivateFrame(int nCmdShow = -1);
// Overridables
    virtual void OnSetPreviewMode(BOOL bPreview,
                        CPrintPreviewState* pState);
protected:
    virtual BOOL OnCreateClient(LPCREATESTRUCT lpcs,
                        CCreateContext* pContext);
// Implementation
```

```
public:
    int m_nWindow;  // general purpose window number - display as ":n"
        // -1 => unknown, 0 => only window viewing document
        // 1 => first of many windows viewing document, 2=> second
protected:
    UINT m_nIDHelp;                 // Help ID (0 for none, see
                                    // HID_BASE_RESOURCE)
    HACCEL m_hAccelTable;           // accelerator table
    UINT m_nIDTracking;             // tracking command ID or string IDS
    UINT m_nIDLastMessage;          // last displayed message string IDS
    CView* m_pViewActive;           // current active view
    BOOL (CALLBACK* m_lpfnCloseProc)(CFrameWnd* pFrameWnd);
public:
    BOOL IsTracking() const;
    virtual BOOL OnCmdMsg(UINT nID, int nCode, void* pExtra,
        AFX_CMDHANDLERINFO* pHandlerInfo);
    virtual CWnd* GetMessageBar();
    virtual void OnUpdateFrameTitle(BOOL bAddToTitle);
protected:
    LPCSTR GetIconWndClass(DWORD dwDefaultStyle, UINT nIDResource);
    void UpdateFrameTitleForDocument(const char* pszDocName);
    virtual BOOL PreCreateWindow(CREATESTRUCT& cs);
    virtual BOOL PreTranslateMessage(MSG* pMsg);
    virtual BOOL OnCommand(WPARAM wParam, LPARAM lParam);
    virtual void PostNcDestroy();   // default to delete this.
    int OnCreateHelper(LPCREATESTRUCT lpcs, CCreateContext* pContext);
    //{{AFX_MSG(CFrameWnd)
    // Windows messages
    afx_msg int OnCreate(LPCREATESTRUCT lpCreateStruct);
    afx_msg void OnDestroy();
    afx_msg void OnNcDestroy();
    afx_msg void OnClose();
    afx_msg void OnInitMenuPopup(CMenu*, UINT, BOOL);
    afx_msg void OnMenuSelect(UINT nItemID, UINT nFlags,
                              HMENU hSysMenu);
    afx_msg LRESULT OnSetMessageString(WPARAM wParam, LPARAM lParam);
    afx_msg void OnEnterIdle(UINT nWhy, CWnd* pWho);
    afx_msg void OnSetFocus(CWnd* pOldWnd);
    afx_msg void OnHScroll(UINT nSBCode, UINT nPos,
                           CScrollBar* pScrollBar);
    afx_msg void OnVScroll(UINT nSBCode, UINT nPos,
                           CScrollBar* pScrollBar);
    afx_msg void OnSize(UINT nType, int cx, int cy);
    afx_msg BOOL OnEraseBkgnd(CDC* pDC);
    afx_msg void OnActivate(UINT nState, CWnd* pWndOther,
                            BOOL bMinimized);
    afx_msg void OnActivateApp(BOOL bActive, HTASK hTask);
    afx_msg void OnSysCommand(UINT nID, LONG lParam);
    afx_msg BOOL OnQueryEndSession();
    afx_msg void OnDropFiles(HDROP hDropInfo);
    afx_msg BOOL OnSetCursor(CWnd* pWnd, UINT nHitTest, UINT message);
    afx_msg LRESULT OnCommandHelp(WPARAM wParam, LPARAM lParam);
    afx_msg LRESULT OnHelpHitTest(WPARAM wParam, LPARAM lParam);
    afx_msg LRESULT OnDDEInitiate(WPARAM wParam, LPARAM lParam);
    afx_msg LRESULT OnDDEExecute(WPARAM wParam, LPARAM lParam);
    afx_msg LRESULT OnDDETerminate(WPARAM wParam, LPARAM lParam);
    afx_msg void OnSysColorChange();
    // standard commands
```

```
        afx_msg void OnUpdateControlBarMenu(CCmdUI* pCmdUI);
        afx_msg BOOL OnBarCheck(UINT nID);
        afx_msg void OnUpdateKeyIndicator(CCmdUI* pCmdUI);
        //}}AFX_MSG
        DECLARE_MESSAGE_MAP()
};
```

The member functions of class CFrameWnd enable the descendant classes to create frame windows using the constructor followed by either the member function Create or LoadFrame. You also can create a frame window using a document template, which involves class CSingleDocTemplate. The member function Create has parameters that specify the Windows class registration name, window name, style, location, size, parent window, optional associated menu, extended style attributes, and context creation data. The member function LoadFrame has parameters that specify the ID of shared resources connected with the frame window, the style, parent window, and context-creation data.

The class CFrameWnd offers a good number of member functions to support various operations and to override the message handling declared in class CWnd. Among the operations supported by the class are the ones that set and query the active view, query the active document, toggle the print preview mode, and create a client window for the frame.

The *CMDIFrameWnd* Class

The class CMDIFrameWnd, a descendant of class CFrameWnd, provides the support for the multiple-document interface (MDI) frame window. The MDI frame window manages multiple MDI child windows. The declaration of class CMDIFrameWnd is shown in the following code:

```
    class CMDIFrameWnd : public CFrameWnd
    {
        DECLARE_DYNCREATE(CMDIFrameWnd)
    public:
    // Constructors
        CMDIFrameWnd();
    // Operations
        void MDIActivate(CWnd* pWndActivate);
        CMDIChildWnd* MDIGetActive(BOOL* pbMaximized = NULL) const;
        void MDIIconArrange();
        void MDIMaximize(CWnd* pWnd);
        void MDINext();
        void MDIRestore(CWnd* pWnd);
        CMenu* MDISetMenu(CMenu* pFrameMenu, CMenu* pWindowMenu);
        void MDITile();
        void MDICascade();
    #if (WINVER >= 0x030a)
        void MDITile(int nType);
        void MDICascade(int nType);
```

```
        #endif
        // Overridables
            // MFC V1 backward compatible CreateClient hook (called by
            // OnCreateClient)
            virtual BOOL CreateClient(LPCREATESTRUCT lpCreateStruct,
                                      CMenu* pWindowMenu);
            // customize if using a 'Window' menu with non-standard IDs
            virtual HMENU GetWindowMenuPopup(HMENU hMenuBar);
        // Implementation
        public:
            HWND m_hWndMDIClient;       // MDI Client window handle
            HMENU m_hMenuDefault;        // menu when no active child (owned)
            virtual BOOL PreCreateWindow(CREATESTRUCT& cs);
            virtual BOOL LoadFrame(UINT nIDResource,
                          DWORD dwDefaultStyle = WS_OVERLAPPEDWINDOW |
                                                 FWS_ADDTOTITLE,
                          CWnd* pParentWnd = NULL,
                          CCreateContext* pContext = NULL);
            virtual BOOL OnCreateClient(LPCREATESTRUCT lpcs,
                                        CCreateContext* pContext);
            virtual BOOL PreTranslateMessage(MSG* pMsg);
            virtual void OnUpdateFrameTitle(BOOL bAddToTitle);
            virtual BOOL OnCmdMsg(UINT nID, int nCode, void* pExtra,
                AFX_CMDHANDLERINFO* pHandlerInfo);
        protected:
            virtual LRESULT DefWindowProc(UINT nMsg, WPARAM wParam,
                                          LPARAM lParam);
            virtual BOOL OnCommand(WPARAM wParam, LPARAM lParam);
            //{{AFX_MSG(CMDIFrameWnd)
            afx_msg void OnDestroy();
            afx_msg void OnSize(UINT nType, int cx, int cy);
            afx_msg void OnActivate(UINT nState, CWnd* pWndOther,
                            BOOL bMinimized);
            afx_msg void OnUpdateMDIWindowCmd(CCmdUI* pCmdUI);
            afx_msg BOOL OnMDIWindowCmd(UINT nID);
            afx_msg void OnWindowNew();
            afx_msg LRESULT OnCommandHelp(WPARAM wParam, LPARAM lParam);
            //}}AFX_MSG
            DECLARE_MESSAGE_MAP()
        };
```

The class CMDIFrameWnd enables its descendant classes to create MDI frame
windows using the constructor with either the member function Create
or LoadFrame (which are both inherited from class CFrameWnd). The class
CMDIFrameWnd provides a set of member functions to create the client window
area and to manage MDI child windows. Managing these windows includes
setting and querying the active MDI child window, selecting the next MDI
child window, arranging the minimized MDI child windows, maximizing
MDI child windows, restoring an MDI child window from a minimized or
maximized state, arranging the MDI child windows in a tiled format, and
arranging the MDI child windows in a cascaded format.

The *CMDIChildWnd* Class

The class CMDIChildWnd, a descendant of class CFrameWnd, supports MDI child windows. Typically, the descendants of this class work with the descendants of class CMDIFrameWnd in your applications. Here is the declaration of class CMDIChildWnd:

```
class CMDIChildWnd : public CFrameWnd
{
    DECLARE_DYNCREATE(CMDIChildWnd)
// Constructors
public:
    CMDIChildWnd();
    BOOL Create(LPCSTR lpszClassName,
                LPCSTR lpszWindowName,
                DWORD dwStyle = WS_CHILD | WS_VISIBLE |
                                WS_OVERLAPPEDWINDOW,
                const RECT& rect = rectDefault,
                CMDIFrameWnd* pParentWnd = NULL,
                CCreateContext* pContext = NULL);
// Attributes
    CMDIFrameWnd* GetMDIFrame();
// Operations
    void MDIDestroy();
    void MDIActivate();
    void MDIMaximize();
    void MDIRestore();
// Implementation
protected:
    HMENU m_hMenuShared;          // menu when we are active
public:
    virtual BOOL PreCreateWindow(CREATESTRUCT& cs);
    virtual BOOL LoadFrame(UINT nIDResource, DWORD dwDefaultStyle,
                        CWnd* pParentWnd,
                        CCreateContext* pContext = NULL);
            // 'pParentWnd' parameter is required for MDI Child
    virtual BOOL DestroyWindow();
    virtual BOOL PreTranslateMessage(MSG* pMsg);
    virtual void ActivateFrame(int nCmdShow = -1);
protected:
    virtual CWnd* GetMessageBar();
    virtual void OnUpdateFrameTitle(BOOL bAddToTitle);
    virtual LRESULT DefWindowProc(UINT nMsg, WPARAM wParam,
                        LPARAM lParam);
    //{{AFX_MSG(CMDIChildWnd)
    afx_msg void OnMDIActivate(BOOL bActivate, CWnd*, CWnd*);
    afx_msg int OnCreate(LPCREATESTRUCT lpCreateStruct);
    afx_msg void OnSize(UINT nType, int cx, int cy);
    //}}AFX_MSG
    DECLARE_MESSAGE_MAP()
};
```

The class CMDIChildWnd lets its descendant classes create MDI child windows using the constructor with either the member function Create or LoadFrame (which is inherited from class CFrameWnd). The function Create has parameters that specify the Windows class registration name, window name, style, location, size, parent MDI frame window, and creation-context data.

The class CMDIFrameWnd offers a set of member functions to access the parent MDI frame window, as well as to activate, maximize, restore, and destroy an MDI child window.

The Views Classes

The views classes are descendants of class CWnd and offer a sophisticated interface between the end user and the Windows application. Views enable end users to view and print data, in addition to accepting keyboard or mouse input from the user. The various classes in this group provide different levels of sophistication in data input and output. Views are attached to documents that store the views' data. A document can have multiple views, but a view can only belong to one document. The views in a document can display similar or different kinds of data. For example, one set of views may let you browse through a group of text files; another set of views may let you browse through both text and graphics files. Turn to Appendix C for an overview of the views classes.

The Control Bar Classes

The control bar classes support a special category of controls that mostly appear as bars either at the top or bottom of a window. These bars let you quickly select operations and bypass the use of the menu or view the status of a window. See Appendix C for an overview of the control bar classes.

The Menus Class

The MFC library supports menus using the class CMenu, which is a descendant of class CObject. This class enables you to load, manipulate, and manage entire menus, as well as menu selections and options. The declaration of class CMenu is shown in the following code:

```
class CMenu : public CObject
{
    DECLARE_DYNCREATE(CMenu)
public:
```

```
// Constructors
    CMenu();
    BOOL CreateMenu();
    BOOL CreatePopupMenu();
    BOOL LoadMenu(LPCSTR lpszResourceName);
    BOOL LoadMenu(UINT nIDResource);
    BOOL LoadMenuIndirect(const void FAR* lpMenuTemplate);
    BOOL DestroyMenu();
// Attributes
    HMENU m_hMenu;               // must be first data member
    HMENU GetSafeHmenu() const;
    static CMenu* PASCAL FromHandle(HMENU hMenu);
    static void PASCAL DeleteTempMap();
    BOOL Attach(HMENU hMenu);
    HMENU Detach();
// CMenu Operations
    BOOL DeleteMenu(UINT nPosition, UINT nFlags);
    BOOL TrackPopupMenu(UINT nFlags, int x, int y,
                             CWnd* pWnd, LPCRECT lpRect = 0);
// CMenuItem Operations
    BOOL AppendMenu(UINT nFlags, UINT nIDNewItem = 0,
                    LPCSTR lpszNewItem = NULL);
    BOOL AppendMenu(UINT nFlags, UINT nIDNewItem,
                    const CBitmap* pBmp);
    UINT CheckMenuItem(UINT nIDCheckItem, UINT nCheck);
    UINT EnableMenuItem(UINT nIDEnableItem, UINT nEnable);
    UINT GetMenuItemCount() const;
    UINT GetMenuItemID(int nPos) const;
    UINT GetMenuState(UINT nID, UINT nFlags) const;
    int GetMenuString(UINT nIDItem, LPSTR lpString, int nMaxCount,
                    UINT nFlags) const;
    CMenu* GetSubMenu(int nPos) const;
    BOOL InsertMenu(UINT nPosition, UINT nFlags, UINT nIDNewItem = 0,
                    LPCSTR lpszNewItem = NULL);
    BOOL InsertMenu(UINT nPosition, UINT nFlags, UINT nIDNewItem,
                    const CBitmap* pBmp);
    BOOL ModifyMenu(UINT nPosition, UINT nFlags, UINT nIDNewItem = 0,
                    LPCSTR lpszNewItem = NULL);
    BOOL ModifyMenu(UINT nPosition, UINT nFlags, UINT nIDNewItem,
                    const CBitmap* pBmp);
    BOOL RemoveMenu(UINT nPosition, UINT nFlags);
    BOOL SetMenuItemBitmaps(UINT nPosition, UINT nFlags,
                    const CBitmap* pBmpUnchecked,
                    const CBitmap* pBmpChecked);
// Overridables (must override draw and measure for owner-draw menu
// items)
    virtual void DrawItem(LPDRAWITEMSTRUCT lpDrawItemStruct);
    virtual void MeasureItem(LPMEASUREITEMSTRUCT lpMeasureItemStruct);
// Implementation
public:
    virtual ~CMenu();
};
```

The class CMenu creates an empty menu object by using the default constructor. The member functions CreateMenu, CreatePopupMenu, LoadMenu,
LoadMenuIndirect, and Attach enable you to create, load, and attach menus to

existing `CMenu` objects. The function `LoadMenu` loads a menu resource from the program file and attaches it to a `CMenu` object. The function `LoadMenuIndirect` loads a menu from a memory-resident menu template and attaches it to a `CMenu` object. The function `CreateMenu` creates an empty menu and attaches it to a `CMenu` object. The `CreatePopupMenu` creates an empty pop-up menu and attaches it to a `CMenu` object. The function `Attach` attaches the handle of an existing Windows menu to a `CMenu` object.

The class `CMenu` offers groups of member functions that support operations such as adding, inserting, removing, modifying, enabling (and disabling), and checking (and unchecking) menu items. The class also provides a set of member functions to manipulate submenus and to delete, detach, and destroy various components of a menu.

The Graphical Drawing Objects Classes

The graphical drawing objects classes encapsulate GDI (Graphical Drawing Interface) Windows API functions to support drawing objects, such as pens, brushes, fonts, bitmaps, palettes, and regions. The following outline shows the subhierarchy of the graphical drawing objects:

```
+ CGdiObject
     - CPen
     - CBrush
     - CFont
     - CBitmap
     - CPalette
     - CRgn
```

The root of the graphical drawing objects classes is class `CGdiObject`, a descendant of class `CObject`. The classes offer member functions that enable you to select drawing objects to be used in drawing device context (represented by the `CDC` class and its descendants). The MFC library supports default selections for the various drawing objects. The typical programming style stores the default drawing objects before using custom ones. Then the program restores these default drawing objects after the program is done with the custom drawing objects.

The Graphical Drawing Classes

The graphical drawing classes, which are descendants of class CObject, support various graphical device contexts. The operations provided by these classes enable Windows programs to draw points, lines, rectangles, circular shapes, polygons, and other sophisticated shapes. The following outline shows the subhierarchy for the graphical drawing classes:

```
+ CDC
        - CClientDC
        - CWindowDC
        - CPaintDC
        - CMetaFileDC
```

The classes CClientDC and CPaintDC display graphics in the client area. The class CPaintDC is used by the OnPaint message handling function of a class. Other member functions that update the client area must use instances of class CClientDC. The class CWindowDC enables a class to draw on the entire window (both the client and frame areas). The class CMetaFileDC supports a device context for a Windows metafile (which contains a series of graphics device interface commands used to redraw an image).

The File Services Classes

The file services classes encapsulate the data and operations of binary and text files. The following outline shows the subhierarchy of the file services classes:

```
+ CFile
        - CStdioFile
        - CMemFile
```

The class CFile encapsulates the data and operations of binary files. The class CStdioFile supports the operations of a buffered stream file, typically used to handle text file I/O. The class CMemFile encapsulates the data and operations of in-memory binary files.

The Exception Classes

Visual C++ supports a macro-based mechanism for setting, intercepting, and handling exceptions at run-time. The MFC library offers the set of exceptions classes to model the various kinds of run-time errors. The following outline shows the subhierarchy of the exceptions classes:

```
+ CException
      - CMemoryException
      - CFileException
      - CArchiveException
      - CNotSupportedException
      - CResourceException
      - CUserException
      - COleException
      - CDBException
```

The class CException, a descendant of class CObject, serves two purposes: first, it is the base for the other exception classes; second, it represents a general exception. The class CMemoryException handles out-of-memory errors that occur in dynamic allocations. The class CFileException deals with file I/O errors and declares a nested enumerated type, which lists the kinds of file I/O errors. The class CArchiveException manages archive errors (special object file I/O). Like the file exception, this class declares a nested enumerated type that lists the kinds of archive I/O errors. The class CNotSupportedException handles errors generated by unsupported features. The class CResourceException deals with errors raised by failing to locate a specified resource. The class CUserException manages user errors (errors raised by logical conditions). The class COleException handles errors associated with bad OLE operations. The class CDBException handles run-time errors related to the new ODBC feature.

The Collections Classes

The MFC library is a software tool with the caliber of a commercial third-party package. You cannot build such an extensive library without the support of fundamental data structures, such as arrays, lists, and hash tables. The collections classes offer these structures to be used by the other classes in the MFC library and directly in your applications (including MS-DOS programs). Refer to Appendix C for an overview of the collections classes.

The OLE Support Classes

The OLE support classes sustain OLE 2.0 operations in OLE-aware documents. Visual C++ 1.5 has altered a few OLE classes found in version 1.0 (which supported OLE 1.0) and introduced many new classes to support embedded and linked objects, the drag and drop of OLE objects, and OLE-related dialog boxes. The OLE classes are scattered over various subhierarchies, based on what they contribute to the support of OLE 2's versatile features.

The ODBC Classes

Visual C++ 1.5 has added a new set of classes to support the ODBC (Open Database Connectivity). The ODBC classes are CDatabase, CRecordset, CFieldExchange, CLongBinary, CRecordView, and CDBException.

The class CDatabase, a descendant of class CObject, provides the bridge to access a data source (located in a database file). The class provides members to open, close, and fine-tune the modes of operating on the data source. For example, the class provides member functions to start and end a series of reversible transactions, to reverse the transactions, and to execute SQL (pronounced *sequel*) statements.

The class CRecordset, a descendant of class CObject, models a collection of database records known as *recordsets*. The instances of class CRecordset support two kinds of recordsets: *snapshots* and *dynasets*. A snapshot is a static recordset that represents the state of the database at the instance the snapshot was created. The dynaset is a dynamic recordset that remains updated by the transactions of the database users. The class CRecordset supports the following kinds of operations:

Scrolling through records

Updating (adding, deleting, and editing) records and designating a locking mode

Filtering the recordset to pick specific records

Sorting the records in the recordset

Parameterizing the recordset to customize its selection with data only available at run time

The class CFieldExchange provides member functions to assist the record field exchange (RFX) process involving the other MFC database classes. The CFieldExchange class supports swapping data between the field data members or the parameter data members of a recordset instance and the associated table columns on the data source.

The CRecordView, a descendant of class CFormView, models a view that shows the fields of database records with visual controls. An instance of class CRecordView is a special form view that is attached to a CRecordSet instance.

The record view automatically exchanges data with the recordset using the dialog box exchange (DDX) and record field exchange (RFX) mechanisms. The class CRecordView also provides member functions to move to the first, last, next, and previous records, as well as to query if the current record is either the first or last in the recordset.

The class CLongBinary, a descendant of class CObject, assists in handling sizable binary data objects, called BLOBs (Binary Large Objects), which exist in a database. A bitmap is a good example of a BLOB.

The class CDBException (which I also introduced earlier with the exception classes), a descendant of class CException, models the exception raised by a database class.

The Miscellaneous Classes

The miscellaneous classes represent stand-alone auxiliary classes that are part of the MFC library but are not descendants of class CObject. Table 2.2 lists the classes and their roles.

Table 2.2 Miscellaneous Classes in the MFC Library	
Class	**Role**
CArchive	Encapsulates file archiving operations that involve class instances
CDumpContext	Offers a destination for diagnostic dumps
CRuntimeClass	Determines the exact class of an object at run-time
CString	Encapsulates ASCIIZ string operations including functions and operators
CTime	Models the absolute time and date
CTimeSpan	Represents the relative time and date
CRect	Encapsulates the data and operations for rectangular areas
CPoint	Encapsulates the data and operations for an (X, Y) point
CSize	Manages the distance, relative locations, or paired values
CFileStatus	Offers a structure to keep track of the size, attributes, and date/time stamps of a file

Class	Role
CCreateContext	Supplies a structure passed by a document template to a function that creates windows
CPrintInfo	Offers a structure representing print and print preview information
CMemoryState	Offers snapshots of memory utilization
CDataExchange	Supports the data exchange between the controls of a dialog box and the parent window
CCmdUI	Encapsulates the data and operations for updating user-interface objects

Simple MFC Examples

Let's look at two examples of MFC-based Windows programs. The first example shows a minimal MFC-based Windows program. The second shows an MFC-based program that has a minimally functioning menu and responds to the left and right mouse buttons being pressed.

The Minimal MFC Program

The first program is MINWINAP.EXE and is a minimal Windows application. You can move, resize, minimize, and maximize the program's window using either a mouse or the menu selections available in the system menu. To close the window, you have to choose the Close command from the system menu. Other than these operations, the program does nothing! For example, if you click the mouse, nothing visual happens. Figure 2.1 shows a sample session with the MINWINAP.EXE program.

To create any Windows application you must have a .DEF file. Listing 2.1 shows the contents of the MINWINAP.DEF file. This file has information that includes the application's name, title, modes of operations, and heap size. Listing 2.2 shows the source code for the MINWINAP.CPP program.

To create the MINWINAP.EXE program, create the MINWINAP directory as a child of the \MSVC\USEVC directory. Store the files MINWINAP.CPP and MINWINAP.DEF in the \MSVC\USEVC\MINWINAP directory. Also use the latter directory to store the MINWINAP.MAK file, which is created by the Visual Workbench.

Figure 2.1

A sample session with the MINWINAP.EXE program.

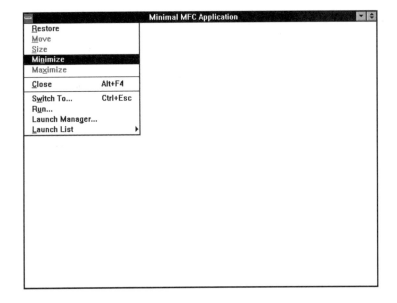

Listing 2.1 The MINWINAP.DEF Definition File

```
NAME         MinWinAp
DESCRIPTION  'Minimal MFC Windows Application'
EXETYPE      WINDOWS
CODE         PRELOAD MOVEABLE DISCARDABLE
DATA         PRELOAD MOVEABLE MULTIPLE
HEAPSIZE     1024
```

Listing 2.2 Source Code for the MINWINAP.CPP Program

```cpp
#include <afxwin.h>
// Define a window class derived from CFrameWnd
class CAppWindow : public CFrameWnd
{
public:
   CAppWindow()
   { Create(NULL, "Minimal MFC Application",
               WS_OVERLAPPEDWINDOW, rectDefault); }
};
// Define an application class derived from CWinApp
class CWindowApp : public CWinApp
{
public:
    virtual BOOL InitInstance();
};
// Construct the CWindowApp's m_pMainWnd data member
BOOL CWindowApp::InitInstance()
{
  m_pMainWnd = new CAppWindow();
  m_pMainWnd->ShowWindow(m_nCmdShow);
```

```
        m_pMainWnd->UpdateWindow();
        return TRUE;
    }
    // application's constructor initializes and runs the app
    CWindowApp WindowApp;
```

The source code provided in Listing 2.2 shows a minimal MFC-based Windows application that uses the template presented earlier in this chapter. The program contains the declaration of an application class `CWindowApp` (a descendant of `CWinApp`) and a window class `CAppWindow` (a descendant of `CWnd`).

The listing contains the directive to include the header file AFXWIN.H. This file ensures that all the required Windows and Microsoft Foundation Class declarations are available to the compiler.

The source code also contains the declaration of class `CWindowApp`, which only contains the member function `InitInstance`. This function creates an instance of `CAppWindow`, which is accessed by the inherited pointer-typed data member `m_pMainWnd`.

The program contains the declaration of the window class `CAppWindow`. This class only declares a class constructor to create the class instances using the `CFrameWnd::Create` member function. The member function `CFrameWnd::Create` has the following declaration:

```
    BOOL Create(
        const char FAR* lpClassName,        // Windows class
                                            // registration name
        const char FAR* lpWindowName,       // title
        DWORD dwStyle = WS_OVERLAPPEDWINDOW, // style attribute
        const RECT& rect = recDefault,      // location and size
        const CWnd* pParentWnd = NULL,      // parent window
        const char FAR* lpMenuName = NULL); // ID of menu
```

The `lpClassName` is the Windows registration class name. This non-OOP name specifies the window category name. The `lpWindowName` parameter specifies the caption or title of the window. The `dwStyle` parameter specifies the style of the created window and contains the default value of `WS_OVERLAPPEDWINDOW`. The `rect` parameter defines the location and size of the window and contains the default value for `rectDefault`. The `pParentWnd` parameter is the pointer to the parent window and contains the default value of `NULL`. The `lpMenuName` parameter defines the name of the menu resource attached to the window. Some menu resources have a numeric ID associated with a constant. To use this kind of menu resource, invoke the macro `MAKEINTRESOURCE` and supply it with the numeric ID of the sought menu. This macro translates the numeric ID into a string.

The last program statement declares an application instance. This declaration results in the execution of the MFC program.

The Simple MFC Program

After building a minimal MFC-based application, let's write a new application that adds a few operations to the application. The next program performs the following main tasks:

- Responds to the left button mouse click (when the mouse is inside the application window) by displaying a message box with an OK button.

- Responds to the right button mouse click by displaying a message box that asks you whether you want to close the window.

- Supports a menu that includes nested-menu selections. The menu items, except for Exit, are dummy ones.

Most Windows applications include menus. The MINWINAP.EXE application has only the system menu. This section shows you how to use a resource file to build a menu that can be attached to the application's window. This section also provides an example that loads a menu from a menu resource while creating a window. Figure 2.2 shows a sample session with the MINWINAP.EXE program.

Figure 2.2
A sample session with the SECWINAP.EXE program.

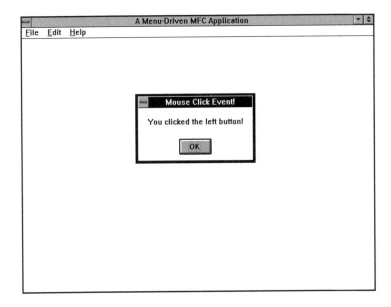

Listing 2.3 shows the contents of the SECWINAP.DEF definition file.

Listing 2.3 The SECWINAP.DEF Definition File

```
NAME          SecWinAp
DESCRIPTION   'An MFC Windows Application'
EXETYPE       WINDOWS
CODE          PRELOAD MOVEABLE DISCARDABLE
DATA          PRELOAD MOVEABLE MULTIPLE
HEAPSIZE      1024
```

The various MENUITEM statements contain CM_*xxxx* constants that define the result of selecting the menu items. The CM_*xxxx* constants are defined in the SECWINAP.H header file, shown in Listing 2.4. Listing 2.5 shows the source code for the SECWINAP.CPP program.

Note

Appendix B describes the syntax for the menu and dialog box resource scripts. After you read the first section, which discusses the menu resources, you can move on to examine the contents of the menu resource file SECWINAP.RC, shown in Listing 2.4. This resource file contains a single menu definition with the OPTIONS name ID. The menu contains three main menu items: File, Edit, and Help. The File and Edit menu items are pull-down menus. The Edit menu commands include Delete, which is also a pop-up menu. The menus contain horizontal separator bars, and all the menus use the ampersand (&) character to define corresponding hot keys.

Create the directory SECWINAP as a subdirectory of \MSVC\USEVC and store all the project's files in the new directory. The project's .MAK file should contain the files SECWINAP.CPP, SECWINAP.RC, and SECWINAP.DEF.

Listing 2.4 Script of the SECWINAP.RC Resource File

```
#include <windows.h>
#include <afxres.h>
#include "secwinap.h"
OPTIONS MENU LOADONCALL MOVEABLE PURE DISCARDABLE
BEGIN
  POPUP "&File"
  BEGIN
    MENUITEM "&New", CM_FILENEW
    MENUITEM "&Open", CM_FILEOPEN
    MENUITEM "&Save", CM_FILESAVE
    MENUITEM "Save&As", CM_FILESAVEAS
    MENUITEM SEPARATOR
```

(continues)

Listing 2.4 Continued

```
    MENUITEM "E&xit", CM_EXIT
    END
    POPUP "&Edit"
    BEGIN
      MENUITEM "&Undo", CM_EDITUNDO
      MENUITEM SEPARATOR
      MENUITEM "C&ut", CM_EDITCUT
      MENUITEM "C&opy", CM_EDITCOPY
      MENUITEM "&Paste", CM_EDITPASTE
      POPUP "&Delete"
      BEGIN
        MENUITEM "&Line", CM_EDITDELETE
        MENUITEM "&Block", CM_EDITDELETE_BLOCK
      END
      MENUITEM "&Clear", CM_EDITCLEAR
    END
    MENUITEM "&Help", CM_HELP
END
```

Listing 2.5 Source Code for the SECWINAP.CPP Program

```
#include <afxwin.h>
#include "secwinap.h"
// Define a window class derived from CFrameWnd
class CAppWindow : public CFrameWnd
{
public:
  CAppWindow()
  { Create(NULL, "A Menu-Driven MFC Application",
           WS_OVERLAPPEDWINDOW, rectDefault, NULL, "OPTIONS"); }

protected:
  // handle the left mouse button click
  afx_msg void OnLButtonDown(UINT nFlags, CPoint point);
  // handle the right mouse button click
  afx_msg void OnRButtonDown(UINT nFlags, CPoint point);
  // handle the Exit menu option
  afx_msg void OnExit();

  // message map macro
  DECLARE_MESSAGE_MAP()
};
// Define an application class derived from CWinApp
class CWindowApp : public CWinApp
{
public:
  virtual BOOL InitInstance();
};
void CAppWindow::OnLButtonDown(UINT nFlags, CPoint point)
{
  MessageBox("You clicked the left button!",
             "Mouse Click Event!", MB_OK);
```

```
  }
  void CAppWindow::OnRButtonDown(UINT nFlags, CPoint point)
  {
    MessageBeep(0); // beep
    // prompt user if he or she want to close the application
    if (MessageBox("Want to close this application", "Query",
                   MB_YESNO | MB_ICONQUESTION) == IDYES)
      SendMessage(WM_CLOSE);
  }
  void CAppWindow::OnExit()
  { SendMessage(WM_CLOSE); }
  BEGIN_MESSAGE_MAP(CAppWindow, CFrameWnd)
      ON_WM_LBUTTONDOWN()
      ON_WM_RBUTTONDOWN()
      ON_COMMAND(CM_EXIT, OnExit)
  END_MESSAGE_MAP()
  // Construct the CWindowApp's m_pMainWnd data member
  BOOL CWindowApp::InitInstance()
  {
    m_pMainWnd = new CAppWindow();
    m_pMainWnd->ShowWindow(m_nCmdShow);
    m_pMainWnd->UpdateWindow();
    return TRUE;
  }
  // application's constructor initializes and runs the app
  CWindowApp WindowApp;
```

The program in Listing 2.5 declares class CAppWindow as a descendant of
CFrameWnd to implement the desired options. This descendant class declares a constructor, three message response member functions, and the
DECLARE_MESSAGE_MAP macro. The CAppWindow constructor works in a manner
similar to that in the program MINWINAP.CPP. Notice that the call to function
Create has a list of arguments that ends with the string OPTIONS. This string
specifies the name of the menu resource to load, and the menu resource
name matches the one in Listing 2.3. The member functions OnLButtonDown
and OnRButtonDown respond to the Windows messages WM_LBUTTONDOWN
and WM_RBUTTONDOWN, respectively. This response is also echoed in the
BEGIN_MESSAGE_MAP macro that specifies the messages handled by the various
member functions. The CAppWindow class also declares the member function
OnExit to respond to the Exit menu command.

The source code defines the member function OnLButtonDown. This function
merely calls the inherited CWnd::MessageBox member function to display the
string You clicked the left button! in a message box with the caption Mouse
Click Event!. The message box contains an OK button that you can click to
resume program execution.

Introduction to Visual C++

The program also defines the member function OnExit. This function responds to the CM_EXIT command generated when Exit is chosen from the menu. The CM_EXIT command is associated with the Windows message command WM_COMMAND.

The source code defines the member function OnRButtonDown. The function first invokes the MessageBeep Windows API function to sound a beep. The function then calls the CWnd::MessageBox function to display a box with the caption Query, the message Want to close this application, Yes and No buttons, and a question mark icon. The if statement compares the result of the MessageBox function with the predefined constant IDYES. When the two values match, the function calls the CWnd::SendMessage member function to close the window using the WM_CLOSE message.

The program defines the macros BEGIN_MESSAGE_MAP and END_MESSAGE_MAP. These macros contain the message mapping macros ON_WM_LBUTTONDOWN, ON_WM_RBUTTONDOWN, and ON_COMMAND. The first two macros have no arguments and, therefore, resort to the default mapping. Consequently, the OnLButtonDown and OnRButtonDown member functions respond to the WM_LBUTTONDOWN and WM_RBUTTONDOWN messages, respectively. The ON_COMMAND macro traps the CM_EXIT menu command and invokes the member function OnExit to handle it.

Summary

This chapter provided an overview of the MFC library and included the declarations of many of its classes. You learned about the following topics:

- Managing Windows messages involves using macros that map the message handled and the responding member functions. The MFC library has a specific scheme for naming the responding member functions.

- The document and application classes manage the Windows application and the document templates. These classes are responsible for initializing, running, and ending a Windows application. In addition, these classes provide templates for documents that manage views and frame windows.

- The window support class, CWnd, offers a rich set of operations that are common to its descendant classes. The descendant classes model visual controls, dialog boxes, views, control bars, and frame windows.

- The controls classes model the visual controls, including the static text, various kinds of command buttons, list boxes, combo boxes, different kinds of edit controls, the scroll bars, and the VBX controls.

- The MFC library provides the dialog box classes to support both custom and common dialog boxes.

- The frame window classes provide applications with both SDI and MDI frame windows. In the case of MDI windows, these classes offer support for the frame and child windows.

- The views classes offer versatile data input and output windows. Views enable application users to input data using the keyboard and the mouse and to view and print information.

- The control bar classes support special controls that mostly appear as bars either at the top or bottom of a window.

- The menus class, CMenu, encapsulates the operations involved in loading, building, managing, and removing menus and menu items.

- The graphical drawing objects classes model pens, brushes, fonts, bitmaps, palettes, and regions. All these drawing objects are used by the graphical drawing classes to implement sophisticated graphics images.

- The graphical drawing classes support drawing points, lines, circular objects, rectangles, polygons, and other graphics shapes.

- The file services classes model binary and text files.

- The exception classes permit your applications to raise and handle various kinds of run-time errors. These errors include ones related to file, archive, memory, resource, OLE, and unsupported feature operations. The classes even provide for a user-exception.

- The collections classes offer valuable data structure classes that model dynamic arrays, lists, and maps (that is hash tables).

- The OLE support classes provide support for the OLE 2.0 client and server documents and items.

■ The ODBC classes, new in Visual C++ 1.5, add a new set of classes to support the Open Database Connectivity.

■ The miscellaneous classes present a set of auxiliary classes and data structures that contribute to the operations of the MFC library. Among these classes are ones that handle time/date, string, point, rectangle-data, archive, and print information.

Chapter 3

Using the AppWizard Utility

The Visual Workbench contains the versatile AppWizard utility, which assists you in creating MFC-based Windows applications. In fact, Microsoft uses AppWizard, along with the ClassWizard and App Studio utilities, as a strong selling point for Visual C++. This chapter shows you how to use AppWizard and examines some of the different kinds of listings AppWizard can generate. You learn about:

- Working with AppWizard to create a minimal MFC Windows program

- Creating a minimal MFC Windows program with a toolbar and status bar

- Generating a minimal MFC Windows program with print and print preview features

- Building a minimal MFC Windows program that supports MDI windows.

- Generating a minimal MFC Windows program that combines the preceding three features

> **Note**
>
> The AppWizard utility generates a number of files, most of which are source code files. This output can be overwhelming for some readers who are novice Visual C++ programmers. Therefore, this chapter studies the output of AppWizard for the kinds of minimally functioning programs mentioned earlier. *The primary goal of this chapter is to make you familiar and comfortable with the source code files generated by AppWizard.* This familiarity will help you in reading and understanding the output source files in the upcoming chapters. I recommend that you print and then compare the source files generated for each project in this chapter.

The Minimal Program

This section serves two purposes: it introduces you to AppWizard (one of the easiest tasks in the world!) and shows you how to create a minimal MFC-based Windows program generated by AppWizard. The following discussion incorporates these two purposes.

To invoke the AppWizard, choose the AppWizard command from the Project menu. Figure 3.1 shows the MFC AppWizard dialog box that appears when you choose AppWizard.

Figure 3.1
The MFC
AppWizard
dialog box.

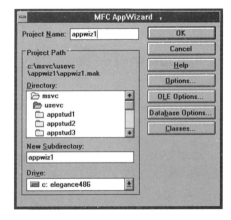

The AppWizard dialog box contains the following controls:

- *Project Name edit control.* Accepts the name of the project.

- *Project Path list box.* Shows you where the new project subdirectory will be located. You can select the directory that becomes the parent of the new project subdirectory.

- *Directory list box.* Enables you to select an existing directory to which the AppWizard will attach the new project directory.

- *New Subdirectory edit control.* Enables you to use a name that is different from the default subdirectory name (which is based on the project name).

- *Drive drop-down list box.* Permits you to access any other on-line drive.

- *Classes... pushbutton.* Enables you to view and edit the names of the classes involved in the project.

- *Options... pushbutton.* Permits you to fine-tune how the source code is generated in project files.

- *OLE Options... pushbutton.* Permits you to generate an OLE-aware application.

- *Database Options... pushbutton.* Permits you to support ODBC (Open Database Connectivity) in your Windows programs.

- *Help pushbutton.* Offers on-line help.

- *Cancel pushbutton.* Cancels the creation of a new project.

- *OK pushbutton.* Starts the process of creating a new subdirectory project, all the related source code files, and the related subdirectories.

Let's use AppWizard to create a minimal MFC program (this version is more sophisticated than the MINWINAP.CPP program presented in Chapter 2). Perform the following steps:

1. Choose the AppWizard command from the Project menu. In the Project Name box, type **appwiz1**; then select the directory \MSVC\USEVC as the parent for the new project.

2. Click the Options... button. The Options dialog box pops up, which is similar to the one shown in Figure 3.2. By default, the top three and the bottom check boxes are marked. To generate a minimal MFC program, uncheck the first three check boxes (the resulting dialog box should match the one in Figure 3.2).

Figure 3.2
The Options
dialog box as the
APPWIZ1 project
is being created.

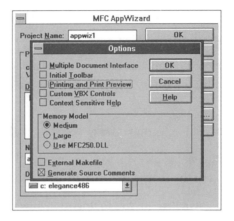

3. Click the OK button in the Options dialog box. Now you're back to the
   MFC AppWizard dialog box.

4. Click the Classes... button. The Classes dialog box pops up, as shown in
   Figure 3.3, and lists the following project classes:

   ■ The class CAppwiz1App, which models the MFC application.

   ■ The class CMainFrame, which supports the SDI frame window.

   ■ The class CAppwiz1Doc, which models the application's document.

   ■ The class CAppwiz1View, which represents the application's view.

Figure 3.3
The Classes
dialog box as the
APPWIZ1 project
is being created.

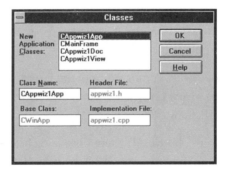

> **Note**
>
> The classes listed in the Classes dialog box indicate that, by default, the AppWizard utility builds applications with documents and views. These applications are versatile in many ways (for one, they support printing), but they are not the only way to create MFC Windows applications. The other method, which does not utilize AppWizard, bypasses the use of document and view classes in a Windows program.

The Classes dialog box contains edit boxes that display the names of the currently selected class, its header file, its implementation file, and its base class. If you select the document class, the dialog box also shows you the file extension and type for the documents created by your application.

5. Click the OK button in the Classes dialog box. You are back to the MFC AppWizard dialog box.

6. Click the OK button to view a summary of the classes and features and to start generating the source code files. The click action causes the New Application Information dialog box to pop up (see Figure 3.4). This dialog box shows the classes and the features of the project you are about to create.

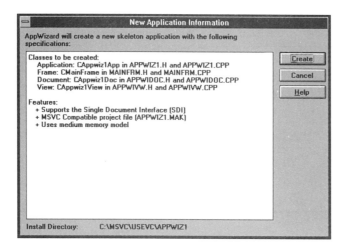

Figure 3.4
The New Application Information dialog box displays information about the classes and features of the APPWIZ1 project.

7. Click the Create button to generate the source code files for the
APPWIZ1 project. The Visual Workbench displays a few message dialog
boxes that report the progress as the files are created.

After completing all these steps, you can list the files by clicking the project
files button on the toolbar (the first icon from the left). Table 3.1 shows the
source code files generated in the \MSVC\USEVC\APPWIZ1 directory. The
AppWizard utility also generates the directory \MSVC\USEVC\APPWIZ1\RES
and places the resource files and resource script files in that directory.

Table 3.1 Source Code Files Generated in the Directory \MSVC\USEVC\APPWIZ1		
Filename	**Size**	**Contents**
APPWIZ1.DEF	353	Project definition file
APPWIZ1.MAK	3384	Project make file
RESOURCE.H	361	Header for standard resources
APPWIZ1.RC	6471	Project resource file
APPWIDOC.H	943	Header file for document class
APPWIDOC.CPP	1741	Implementation file for document class
APPWIVW.H	1077	Header file for view class
APPWIVW.CPP	1687	Implementation file for view class
APPWIZ1.H	821	Header file for application class
APPWIZ1.CPP	3287	Implementation file for application class
MAINFRM.H	825	Header file for window frame class
MAINFRM.CPP	1262	Implementation file for window frame class
STDAFX.H	283	Header file for standard MFC *include* files
STDAFX.CPP	204	Implementation file for standard MFC *include* files

Thus, the AppWizard generates files for the application, frame window, document, and views classes, along with resource (including icon and bitmap files), definition, and project make files.

> **Note**
>
> Some of the source code listings generated by AppWizard have been edited here to fit the page margins and to shorten their lengths.

Running the Program APPWIZ1.EXE

To build and run the APPWIZ1.EXE program file, you choose the Execute command from the Project menu. The menu bar in APPWIZ1.EXE includes these pull-down menus: File, Edit, and Help. Figure 3.5 shows the About dialog box, which appears when you choose the About command from the Help menu.

Figure 3.5
The About box for the APPWIZ1.EXE program.

In the Edit menu, the commands Undo, Cut, Copy, and Paste are disabled because they lack associated message-handling member functions. The File menu contains the commands New, Open, Save, Save As, and Exit, which are shown in Figure 3.6. Only the Exit command is fully functioning; the other commands are partially operational. For example, if you choose the Open command, the File Open dialog box pops up so that you can select a file. However, nothing actually happens with the file, except that it becomes part of the window title!

Figure 3.6

The File menu of the APPWIZ1.EXE program.

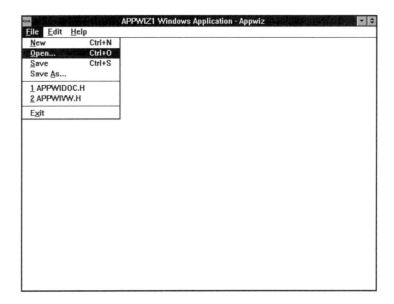

In the following sections, I discuss the various source code files generated by the AppWizard utility.

The APPWIZ1.DEF File

Listing 3.1 shows the contents of the APPWIZ1.DEF definition file. The NAME and DESCRIPTION clauses include the APPWIZ1 project name. Comment lines are indicated by a semicolon character as the first non-space character on a line.

Listing 3.1 The APPWIZ1.DEF Definition File

```
; appwiz1.def : Declares the module parameters for the application.
NAME         APPWIZ1
DESCRIPTION  'APPWIZ1 Windows Application'
EXETYPE      WINDOWS
CODE         PRELOAD MOVEABLE DISCARDABLE
DATA         PRELOAD MOVEABLE MULTIPLE
HEAPSIZE     1024   ; initial heap size
; Stack size is passed as argument to linker's /STACK option
```

The RESOURCE.H File

The header file RESOURCE.H, shown in Listing 3.2, contains a set of #define statements that define the IDs for the About dialog box (the identifier IDD_ABOUTBOX) and the main menu (using the identifier IDR_MAINFRAME). The other _APS_NEXT_XXXX constants are not directly used in the other source code files.

Listing 3.2 Source Code for the RESOURCE.H Header File

```
//{{NO_DEPENDENCIES}}
// App Studio generated include file.
// Used by APPWIZ1.RC
//
#define IDR_MAINFRAME               2
#define IDD_ABOUTBOX                100
#define _APS_NEXT_RESOURCE_VALUE    101
#define _APS_NEXT_CONTROL_VALUE     101
#define _APS_NEXT_SYMED_VALUE       101
#define _APS_NEXT_COMMAND_VALUE     32768
```

The APPWIZ1.H File

The header file APPWIZ1.H, shown in Listing 3.3, contains the declaration of the application class `CAppWiz1App`. This class is a descendant of class `CWinApp` and declares the constructor, the overridden member function `InitInstance`, and the member function `OnAppAbout`. The AppWizard includes `OnAppAbout` in a special comment it uses to generate the message response table.

Listing 3.3 The APPWIZ1.H Header File

```
// appwiz1.h : main header file for the APPWIZ1 application
//
#ifndef __AFXWIN_H__
    #error include 'stdafx.h' before including this file for PCH
#endif
#include "resource.h"        // main symbols
/////////////////////////////////////////////////////////////////
// CAppwiz1App:
// See appwiz1.cpp for the implementation of this class
//
class CAppwiz1App : public CWinApp
{
public:
    CAppwiz1App();
// Overrides
    virtual BOOL InitInstance();
// Implementation
    //{{AFX_MSG(CAppwiz1App)
    afx_msg void OnAppAbout();
// NOTE - the ClassWizard will add and remove member functions here.
//    DO NOT EDIT what you see in these blocks of generated code !
    //}}AFX_MSG
    DECLARE_MESSAGE_MAP()
};


/////////////////////////////////////////////////////////////////
```

The STDAFX.H File

The header file STDAFX.H, whose contents appear in Listing 3.4, merely includes the MFC header files AFXWIN.H and AFXEXT.H. These statements ensure that the application can use the classes for both the standard and extended MFC operations.

Listing 3.4 Source Code for the STDAFX.H Header File

```
// stdafx.h : include file for standard system include files,
//  or project specific include files that are used frequently, but
//        are changed infrequently
//
#include <afxwin.h>           // MFC core and standard components
#include <afxext.h>           // MFC extensions (including VB)
```

The MAINFRM.H File

The header file MAINFRM.H, shown in Listing 3.5, contains the declaration of the frame window class, CMainFrame. The file declares this class as a descendant of CFrameWnd because the application is SDI-compliant. The class CMainFrame declares a protected constructor, a public destructor, and the debug-related functions AssertValid and Dump. The class also declares a message map, and the listing contains comments that act as placeholders for message-response member functions that you may elect to add using the ClassWizard. (More about ClassWizard in Chapter 4.)

Listing 3.5 Source Code for the MAINFRM.H Header File

```
// mainfrm.h : interface of the CMainFrame class
//
/////////////////////////////////////////////////////////////////////
class CMainFrame : public CFrameWnd
{
protected: // create from serialization only
    CMainFrame();
    DECLARE_DYNCREATE(CMainFrame)
// Attributes
public:
// Operations
public:
// Implementation
public:
    virtual ~CMainFrame();
#ifdef _DEBUG
    virtual    void AssertValid() const;
    virtual    void Dump(CDumpContext& dc) const;
#endif
```

```
// Generated message map functions
protected:
    //{{AFX_MSG(CMainFrame)
// NOTE - the ClassWizard will add and remove member functions here.
//    DO NOT EDIT what you see in these blocks of generated code !
    //}}AFX_MSG
    DECLARE_MESSAGE_MAP()
};
//////////////////////////////////////////////////////////////////////
```

The APPWIVW.H File

The header file APPWIVW.H, shown in Listing 3.6, contains the declaration of the view class CAppwiz1View. The listing declares this class as a descendant of class CView and includes a protected constructor, a public destructor, the public member function GetDocument, the member function OnDraw, and the debug-related functions Assert and Dump. The listing declares the message map and contains a comment-based placeholder that can include any added message-handling member functions. The listings contains an inline implementation of function GetDocument enclosed in an #ifndef compiler directive.

Listing 3.6 Source Code for the APPWIVW.H Header File

```
// appwivw.h : interface of the CAppwiz1View class
//
//////////////////////////////////////////////////////////////////////
class CAppwiz1View : public CView
{
protected: // create from serialization only
    CAppwiz1View();
    DECLARE_DYNCREATE(CAppwiz1View)
// Attributes
public:
    CAppwiz1Doc* GetDocument();
// Operations
public:
// Implementation
public:
    virtual ~CAppwiz1View();
    virtual void OnDraw(CDC* pDC);  // overridden to draw this view
#ifdef _DEBUG
    virtual void AssertValid() const;
    virtual void Dump(CDumpContext& dc) const;
#endif

// Generated message map functions
protected:
    //{{AFX_MSG(CAppwiz1View)
// NOTE - the ClassWizard will add and remove member functions here.
//    DO NOT EDIT what you see in these blocks of generated code !
```

(continues)

Listing 3.6 Continued

```
     //}}AFX_MSG
     DECLARE_MESSAGE_MAP()
};
#ifndef _DEBUG // debug version in appwivw.cpp
inline CAppwiz1Doc* CAppwiz1View::GetDocument()
   { return (CAppwiz1Doc*) m_pDocument; }
#endif
/////////////////////////////////////////////////////////////////////
```

The APPWIDOC.H File

The header file APPWIDOC.H, shown in Listing 3.7, declares the document class CAppwiz1Doc as a descendant of class CDocument. The derived class includes a protected constructor, a public destructor, the public member function Serialize, the message-handling function OnNewDocument, and the debug-related functions AssertValid and Dump.

Listing 3.7 Source Code for the APPWIDOC.H Header File

```
// appwidoc.h : interface of the CAppwiz1Doc class
//
/////////////////////////////////////////////////////////////////////
class CAppwiz1Doc : public CDocument
{
protected: // create from serialization only
     CAppwiz1Doc();
     DECLARE_DYNCREATE(CAppwiz1Doc)
// Attributes
public:
// Operations
public:
// Implementation
public:
     virtual ~CAppwiz1Doc();
     virtual void Serialize(CArchive& ar); // overridden for document i/o
#ifdef _DEBUG
     virtual     void AssertValid() const;
     virtual     void Dump(CDumpContext& dc) const;
#endif
protected:
     virtual     BOOL  OnNewDocument();
// Generated message map functions
protected:
     //{{AFX_MSG(CAppwiz1Doc)
// NOTE - the ClassWizard will add and remove member functions here.
//    DO NOT EDIT what you see in these blocks of generated code !
     //}}AFX_MSG
     DECLARE_MESSAGE_MAP()
};
/////////////////////////////////////////////////////////////////////
```

The APPWIZ1.RC File

The resource file APPWIZ1.RC, whose contents appear in Listing 3.8, shows the resource script used in building program APPWIZ1.EXE. The resource file contains resources for strings, the program menus, menu commands, accelerators (that is, the hot keys and shortcut keys), and the About APPWIZ1 dialog box.

Listing 3.8 Script for the APPWIZ1.RC Resource File

```
//Microsoft App Studio generated resource script.
//
#include "resource.h"
#define APSTUDIO_READONLY_SYMBOLS
/////////////////////////////////////////////////////////////////////
//
// From TEXTINCLUDE 2
//
#include "afxres.h"
/////////////////////////////////////////////////////////////////////
#undef APSTUDIO_READONLY_SYMBOLS
#ifdef APSTUDIO_INVOKED
/////////////////////////////////////////////////////////////////////
//
// TEXTINCLUDE
//
1 TEXTINCLUDE DISCARDABLE
BEGIN
    "resource.h\0"
END
2 TEXTINCLUDE DISCARDABLE
BEGIN
    "#include ""afxres.h""\r\n"
    "\0"
END
3 TEXTINCLUDE DISCARDABLE
BEGIN

    "#include ""res\\appwiz1.rc2""  // non-App Studio
                                    // edited resources\r\n"
    "\r\n"
    "#include ""afxres.rc""  // Standard components\r\n"
    "\0"
END
/////////////////////////////////////////////////////////////////////
#endif    // APSTUDIO_INVOKED
/////////////////////////////////////////////////////////////////////
//
// Icon
//
IDR_MAINFRAME           ICON    DISCARDABLE     res\appwiz1.ico
/////////////////////////////////////////////////////////////////////
//
// Menu
```

(continues)

Listing 3.8 Continued

```
//
IDR_MAINFRAME MENU PRELOAD DISCARDABLE
BEGIN
    POPUP "&File"
    BEGIN
        MENUITEM "&New\tCtrl+N",             ID_FILE_NEW
        MENUITEM "&Open...\tCtrl+O",         ID_FILE_OPEN
        MENUITEM "&Save\tCtrl+S",            ID_FILE_SAVE
        MENUITEM "Save &As...",              ID_FILE_SAVE_AS
        MENUITEM SEPARATOR
        MENUITEM "Recent File",              ID_FILE_MRU_FILE1,GRAYED
        MENUITEM SEPARATOR
        MENUITEM "E&xit",                    ID_APP_EXIT
    END
    POPUP "&Edit"
    BEGIN
        MENUITEM "&Undo\tCtrl+Z",            ID_EDIT_UNDO
        MENUITEM SEPARATOR
        MENUITEM "Cu&t\tCtrl+X",             ID_EDIT_CUT
        MENUITEM "&Copy\tCtrl+C",            ID_EDIT_COPY
        MENUITEM "&Paste\tCtrl+V",           ID_EDIT_PASTE
    END
    POPUP "&Help"
    BEGIN
        MENUITEM "&About APPWIZ1...",        ID_APP_ABOUT
    END
END
/////////////////////////////////////////////////////////////////////////
//
// Accelerator
//
IDR_MAINFRAME ACCELERATORS PRELOAD MOVEABLE
BEGIN
    "N",            ID_FILE_NEW,            VIRTKEY,CONTROL
    "O",            ID_FILE_OPEN,           VIRTKEY,CONTROL
    "S",            ID_FILE_SAVE,           VIRTKEY,CONTROL
    "Z",            ID_EDIT_UNDO,           VIRTKEY,CONTROL
    "X",            ID_EDIT_CUT,            VIRTKEY,CONTROL
    "C",            ID_EDIT_COPY,           VIRTKEY,CONTROL
    "V",            ID_EDIT_PASTE,          VIRTKEY,CONTROL
    VK_BACK,        ID_EDIT_UNDO,           VIRTKEY,ALT
    VK_DELETE,      ID_EDIT_CUT,            VIRTKEY,SHIFT
    VK_INSERT,      ID_EDIT_COPY,           VIRTKEY,CONTROL
    VK_INSERT,      ID_EDIT_PASTE,          VIRTKEY,SHIFT
    VK_F6,          ID_NEXT_PANE,           VIRTKEY
    VK_F6,          ID_PREV_PANE,           VIRTKEY,SHIFT
END
/////////////////////////////////////////////////////////////////////////
//
// Dialog
//
IDD_ABOUTBOX DIALOG DISCARDABLE  34, 22, 217, 55
CAPTION "About APPWIZ1"
STYLE DS_MODALFRAME ¦ WS_POPUP ¦ WS_CAPTION ¦ WS_SYSMENU
```

```
FONT 8, "MS Sans Serif"
BEGIN
    ICON            IDR_MAINFRAME,IDC_STATIC,11,17,20,20
    LTEXT           "APPWIZ1 Application Version 1.0",IDC_STATIC,40,10,119,8
    LTEXT           "Copyright \251 1993",IDC_STATIC,40,25,119,8
    DEFPUSHBUTTON   "OK",IDOK,176,6,32,14,WS_GROUP
END
/////////////////////////////////////////////////////////////////////////////
//
// String Table
//
STRINGTABLE PRELOAD DISCARDABLE
BEGIN
    IDR_MAINFRAME           "APPWIZ1 Windows Application\nAppwiz\nAPPWIZ
➥Document"
END
STRINGTABLE PRELOAD DISCARDABLE
BEGIN
    AFX_IDS_APP_TITLE       "APPWIZ1 Windows Application"
    AFX_IDS_IDLEMESSAGE     "Ready"
END
STRINGTABLE DISCARDABLE
BEGIN
    ID_INDICATOR_EXT        "EXT"
    ID_INDICATOR_CAPS       "CAP"
    ID_INDICATOR_NUM        "NUM"
    ID_INDICATOR_SCRL       "SCRL"
    ID_INDICATOR_OVR        "OVR"
    ID_INDICATOR_REC        "REC"
END
STRINGTABLE DISCARDABLE
BEGIN
    ID_FILE_NEW             "Create a new document"
    ID_FILE_OPEN            "Open an existing document"
    ID_FILE_CLOSE           "Close the active document"
    ID_FILE_SAVE            "Save the active document"
    ID_FILE_SAVE_AS         "Save the active document with a new name"
    ID_APP_ABOUT            "Display program information, version number
➥and copyright"
    ID_APP_EXIT             "Quit the application; prompts to save documents"
    ID_FILE_MRU_FILE1       "Open this document"
    ID_FILE_MRU_FILE2       "Open this document"
    ID_FILE_MRU_FILE3       "Open this document"
    ID_FILE_MRU_FILE4       "Open this document"
    ID_NEXT_PANE            "Switch to the next window pane"
    ID_PREV_PANE            "Switch back to the previous window pane"
    ID_EDIT_CLEAR           "Erase the selection"
    ID_EDIT_CLEAR_ALL       "Erase everything"
    ID_EDIT_COPY            "Copy the selection and put it on the Clipboard"
    ID_EDIT_CUT             "Cut the selection and put it on the Clipboard"
    ID_EDIT_FIND            "Find the specified text"
    ID_EDIT_PASTE           "Insert Clipboard contents"
    ID_EDIT_REPEAT          "Repeat the last action"
    ID_EDIT_REPLACE         "Replace specific text with different text"
    ID_EDIT_SELECT_ALL      "Select the entire document"
    ID_EDIT_UNDO            "Undo the last action"
```

Introduction to Visual C++

(continues)

Listing 3.8 Continued

```
        ID_EDIT_REDO              "Redo the previously undone action"
END
STRINGTABLE DISCARDABLE
BEGIN
        AFX_IDS_SCSIZE            "Change the window size"
        AFX_IDS_SCMOVE            "Change the window position"
        AFX_IDS_SCMINIMIZE        "Reduce the window to an icon"
        AFX_IDS_SCMAXIMIZE        "Enlarge the window to full size"
        AFX_IDS_SCNEXTWINDOW      "Switch to the next document window"
        AFX_IDS_SCPREVWINDOW      "Switch to the previous document window"
        AFX_IDS_SCCLOSE           "Close the active window and prompts to save
➥the documents"
        AFX_IDS_SCRESTORE         "Restore the window to normal size"
        AFX_IDS_SCTASKLIST        "Activate Task List"
END
#ifndef APSTUDIO_INVOKED
/////////////////////////////////////////////////////////////////////////
//
// From TEXTINCLUDE 3
//
#include "res\appwiz1.rc2"  // non-App Studio edited resources
#include "afxres.rc"  // Standard components
/////////////////////////////////////////////////////////////////////////
#endif     // not APSTUDIO_INVOKED
```

The APPWIZ1.RC2 File

The directory \MSVC\USEVC\APPWIZ1\RES contains the additional resource file APPWIZ1.RC2, shown in Listing 3.9. This resource file, which is not modified by App Studio, contains resources related to the program version.

Listing 3.9 Script for the APPWIZ1.RC2 Resource File

```
//
// APPWIZ1.RC2 - resources App Studio does not edit directly
//
#ifdef APSTUDIO_INVOKED
    #error this file is not editable by App Studio
#endif //APSTUDIO_INVOKED
/////////////////////////////////////////////////////////////////////////
// Version stamp for this .EXE
#include "ver.h"
VS_VERSION_INFO     VERSIONINFO
  FILEVERSION       1,0,0,1
  PRODUCTVERSION    1,0,0,1
  FILEFLAGSMASK     VS_FFI_FILEFLAGSMASK
#ifdef _DEBUG
  FILEFLAGS         VS_FF_DEBUG¦VS_FF_PRIVATEBUILD¦VS_FF_PRERELEASE
#else
  FILEFLAGS         0 // final version
```

```
#endif
  FILEOS            VOS_DOS_WINDOWS16
  FILETYPE          VFT_APP
  FILESUBTYPE       0   // not used
BEGIN
    BLOCK "StringFileInfo"
    BEGIN
        BLOCK "040904E4" // Lang=US English, CharSet=Windows Multilingual
        BEGIN
            VALUE "CompanyName",      "\0"
            VALUE "FileDescription", "APPWIZ1 MFC Application\0"
            VALUE "FileVersion",      "1.0.001\0"
            VALUE "InternalName",     "APPWIZ1\0"
            VALUE "LegalCopyright",   "\0"
            VALUE "LegalTrademarks", "\0"
            VALUE "OriginalFilename","APPWIZ1.EXE\0"
            VALUE "ProductName",      "APPWIZ1\0"
            VALUE "ProductVersion",   "1.0.001\0"
        END
    END
    BLOCK "VarFileInfo"
    BEGIN
        VALUE "Translation", 0x409, 1252
        // English language (0x409) and the Windows ANSI codepage (1252)
    END
END
/////////////////////////////////////////////////////////////////////
// Add additional manually edited resources here...
/////////////////////////////////////////////////////////////////////
```

The APPWIZ1.CPP File

The implementation file APPWIZ1.CPP, shown in Listing 3.10, contains the implementation and message map for the application class CAppwiz1. In addition, the listing includes the declaration, implementation, and message map for the About dialog box class, CAboutDlg.

The APPWIZ1.CPP listing contains the message map for class CAppwiz1App, which links the following member functions and Windows messages:

■ Links the message ID_APP_ABOUT with the member function OnAppAbout. This message map enables the program to respond to the About APPWIZ1 command on the Help menu.

■ Links the message ID_FILE_NEW with the member function CWinApp::OnFileNew. This message map permits the program to respond to the New command in the File menu. As you can see, the program actually relies on the member function OnFileNew in the parent class for a response.

- Links the message `ID_FILE_OPEN` with the member function `CWinApp::OnFileOpen`. This message map permits the program to respond to the Open command in the File menu. Again, the program depends on the member function `OnFileOpen` in the parent class for a response.

The source file APPWIZ1.CPP contains implementations for the following class members:

- The constructor. This member has no statements; instead, it contains comments that indicate the location of any constructor code you want to include.

- The member function `InitInstance`. This function initializes the instances of class `CAppwiz1App` by carrying out the following tasks:

  - Loads the options from the standard .INI file.

  - Registers the application, window frame, and view classes in the application's document template.

  - Creates a new document that is empty. This task involves sending the C++ message `OnFileNew` (as opposed to a Windows message) to the class instance.

  - Offers minimal code to process command-line arguments.

- The member function `OnAppAbout`. This function contains two statements and invokes the About dialog box. The first statement declares the instance of class `CAboutDlg`, `aboutDlg`. The second statement sends the C++ message `DoModal` to the object `aboutDlg`.

The implementation file declares the dialog box class `CAboutDlg` as a descendant of class `CDialog`. The dialog box class declares the local untagged enumerated type with the single value `IDD` (which is initialized with the dialog box resource ID of `IDD_ABOUTBOX`). The class also declares a constructor and the member function `DoDataExchange`. The constructor `CAboutDlg` merely invokes the constructor of the parent class and passes the enumerated value IDD to invoke the dialog box resource `IDD_ABOUTBOX`. The code contains comments that define a placeholder for additional code you may want to insert. The function `DoDataExchange` simply calls the function `CDialog::DoDataExchange` and offers a comment-based placeholder for possible additional code.

The listing file defines the message map for the dialog box class. This map is empty and uses a comment-based placeholder for any possible map entries you may add.

Listing 3.10 Source Code for the APPWIZ1.CPP Implementation File

```
// appwiz1.cpp : Defines the class behaviors for the application.
//
#include "stdafx.h"
#include "appwiz1.h"
#include "mainfrm.h"
#include "appwidoc.h"
#include "appwivw.h"
#ifdef _DEBUG
#undef THIS_FILE
static char BASED_CODE THIS_FILE[] = __FILE__;
#endif
/////////////////////////////////////////////////////////////////////
// CAppwiz1App
BEGIN_MESSAGE_MAP(CAppwiz1App, CWinApp)
    //{{AFX_MSG_MAP(CAppwiz1App)
    ON_COMMAND(ID_APP_ABOUT, OnAppAbout)
// NOTE - the ClassWizard will add and remove mapping macros here.
//    DO NOT EDIT what you see in these blocks of generated code !
    //}}AFX_MSG_MAP
    // Standard file based document commands
    ON_COMMAND(ID_FILE_NEW, CWinApp::OnFileNew)
    ON_COMMAND(ID_FILE_OPEN, CWinApp::OnFileOpen)
END_MESSAGE_MAP()
/////////////////////////////////////////////////////////////////////
// CAppwiz1App construction
CAppwiz1App::CAppwiz1App()
{
    // TODO: add construction code here,
    // Place all significant initialization in InitInstance
}
/////////////////////////////////////////////////////////////////////
// The one and only CAppwiz1App object
CAppwiz1App NEAR theApp;
/////////////////////////////////////////////////////////////////////
// CAppwiz1App initialization
BOOL CAppwiz1App::InitInstance()
{
    // Standard initialization
    // If you are not using these features and wish to reduce the size
    //  of your final executable, you should remove from the following
    //  the specific initialization routines you do not need.
    SetDialogBkColor();        // set dialog background color to gray
    LoadStdProfileSettings();  // Load standard INI file
                               // options (including MRU)
// Register the application's document templates.  Document templates
//   serve as the connection between documents, frame windows and views.
```

(continues)

```
             AddDocTemplate(new CSingleDocTemplate(IDR_MAINFRAME,
                     RUNTIME_CLASS(CAppwiz1Doc),
                     RUNTIME_CLASS(CMainFrame),   // main SDI frame window
                     RUNTIME_CLASS(CAppwiz1View)));

        // create a new (empty) document
        OnFileNew();
        if (m_lpCmdLine[0] != '\0')
        {
             // TODO: add command line processing here
        }
        return TRUE;
}
/////////////////////////////////////////////////////////////////////
// CAboutDlg dialog used for App About
class CAboutDlg : public CDialog
{
public:
        CAboutDlg();
// Dialog Data
        //{{AFX_DATA(CAboutDlg)
        enum { IDD = IDD_ABOUTBOX };
        //}}AFX_DATA
// Implementation
protected:
        virtual void DoDataExchange(CDataExchange* pDX);// DDX/DDV support
        //{{AFX_MSG(CAboutDlg)
             // No message handlers
        //}}AFX_MSG
        DECLARE_MESSAGE_MAP()
};
CAboutDlg::CAboutDlg() : CDialog(CAboutDlg::IDD)
{
        //{{AFX_DATA_INIT(CAboutDlg)
        //}}AFX_DATA_INIT
}
void CAboutDlg::DoDataExchange(CDataExchange* pDX)
{
        CDialog::DoDataExchange(pDX);
        //{{AFX_DATA_MAP(CAboutDlg)
        //}}AFX_DATA_MAP
}
BEGIN_MESSAGE_MAP(CAboutDlg, CDialog)
        //{{AFX_MSG_MAP(CAboutDlg)
             // No message handlers
        //}}AFX_MSG_MAP
END_MESSAGE_MAP()
// App command to run the dialog
void CAppwiz1App::OnAppAbout()
{
        CAboutDlg aboutDlg;
        aboutDlg.DoModal();
}
/////////////////////////////////////////////////////////////////////
// CAppwiz1App commands
```

The STDAFX.CPP File

The implementation file STDAFX.CPP, shown in Listing 3.11, merely contains a single `#include` directive to include the header file STDAFX.H.

Listing 3.11 Source Code for the STDAFX.CPP Implementation File

```
// stdafx.cpp : source file that includes just the standard includes
//      stdafx.pch will be the pre-compiled header
//      stdafx.obj will contain the pre-compiled type information
#include "stdafx.h"
```

The MAINFRM.CPP File

The file MAINFRM.CPP, shown in Listing 3.12, contains the implementation (albeit a minimal one) of the window frame class `CMainFrame`. The listing shows a message map with no map entries—only a comment-based placeholder for possible map entries. The class offers a dummy implementation of the constructor and destructor. I say *dummy* because neither member has any statements. The MAINFRM.CPP listing offers implementations for the member functions `AssertValid` and `Dump`. Each of these functions invokes the version of the function defined in the parent class.

Listing 3.12 Source Code for the MAINFRM.CPP Implementation File

```
// mainfrm.cpp : implementation of the CMainFrame class
//
#include "stdafx.h"
#include "appwiz1.h"
#include "mainfrm.h"
#ifdef _DEBUG
#undef THIS_FILE
static char BASED_CODE THIS_FILE[] = __FILE__;
#endif
/////////////////////////////////////////////////////////////////////
// CMainFrame
IMPLEMENT_DYNCREATE(CMainFrame, CFrameWnd)
BEGIN_MESSAGE_MAP(CMainFrame, CFrameWnd)
    //{{AFX_MSG_MAP(CMainFrame)
// NOTE - the ClassWizard will add and remove mapping macros here.
//    DO NOT EDIT what you see in these blocks of generated code !
    //}}AFX_MSG_MAP
END_MESSAGE_MAP()

/////////////////////////////////////////////////////////////////////
// CMainFrame construction/destruction
CMainFrame::CMainFrame()
```

(continues)

Listing 3.12 Continued

```
{
     // TODO: add member initialization code here
}
CMainFrame::~CMainFrame()
{
}


////////////////////////////////////////////////////////////////////
// CMainFrame diagnostics
#ifdef _DEBUG
void CMainFrame::AssertValid() const
{
     CFrameWnd::AssertValid();
}
void CMainFrame::Dump(CDumpContext& dc) const
{
     CFrameWnd::Dump(dc);
}
#endif //_DEBUG
////////////////////////////////////////////////////////////////////
// CMainFrame message handlers
```

The APPWIVW.CPP File

The file APPWIVW.CPP, whose contents appear in Listing 3.13, offers the implementation of the view class CAppWiz1View. The listing shows a message map with no map entries—only a comment-based placeholder for possible map entries. The class offers a dummy implementation of the constructor and destructor (neither member has any statements). The listing offers a minimal implementation for the member function OnDraw. The function declares the instance pDoc as a pointer to the application's document. The listing also offers implementations for the member functions AssertValid and Dump. Each of these functions invokes the version of the function declared in the parent class.

Listing 3.13 Source Code for the APPWIVW.CPP
Implementation File

```
// appwivw.cpp : implementation of the CAppwiz1View class
//
#include "stdafx.h"
#include "appwiz1.h"
#include "appwidoc.h"
#include "appwivw.h"
#ifdef _DEBUG
#undef THIS_FILE
```

```
static char BASED_CODE THIS_FILE[] = __FILE__;
#endif
/////////////////////////////////////////////////////////////////////////
// CAppwiz1View
IMPLEMENT_DYNCREATE(CAppwiz1View, CView)
BEGIN_MESSAGE_MAP(CAppwiz1View, CView)
    //{{AFX_MSG_MAP(CAppwiz1View)
// NOTE - the ClassWizard will add and remove mapping macros here.
//    DO NOT EDIT what you see in these blocks of generated code !
    //}}AFX_MSG_MAP
END_MESSAGE_MAP()
/////////////////////////////////////////////////////////////////////////
// CAppwiz1View construction/destruction
CAppwiz1View::CAppwiz1View()
{
    // TODO: add construction code here
}
CAppwiz1View::~CAppwiz1View()
{
}
/////////////////////////////////////////////////////////////////////////
// CAppwiz1View drawing
void CAppwiz1View::OnDraw(CDC* pDC)
{
    CAppwiz1Doc* pDoc = GetDocument();
    // TODO: add draw code here
}


/////////////////////////////////////////////////////////////////////////
// CAppwiz1View diagnostics
#ifdef _DEBUG
void CAppwiz1View::AssertValid() const
{
    CView::AssertValid();
}
void CAppwiz1View::Dump(CDumpContext& dc) const
{
    CView::Dump(dc);
}
CAppwiz1Doc* CAppwiz1View::GetDocument() // non-debug version is inline
{
    ASSERT(m_pDocument->IsKindOf(RUNTIME_CLASS(CAppwiz1Doc)));
    return (CAppwiz1Doc*) m_pDocument;
}
#endif //_DEBUG
/////////////////////////////////////////////////////////////////////////
// CAppwiz1View message handlers
```

The APPWIDOC.CPP File

The file APPWIDOC.CPP, shown in Listing 3.14, provides the implementation for the document class CAppwiz1Doc. The listing shows a message map with no map entries—only a comment-based placeholder for possible map entries. The class offers a dummy implementation of the constructor and destructor (neither member has any statements). The APPWIDOC.CPP listing offers implementations for the following member functions:

- The OnNewDocument function. This function invokes the parent's OnNewDocument function and ends up returning the Boolean value of the invoked function. The function has comment-based placeholders for additional code.

- The Serialize function. This minimal function supports persistent objects.

- The AssertValid function. This debug-related function simply invokes the parent's version.

- The Dump function. This debug-related function merely calls the parent's version.

Listing 3.14 Source Code for the APPWIDOC.CPP Implementation File

```
// appwidoc.cpp : implementation of the CAppwiz1Doc class
//
#include "stdafx.h"
#include "appwiz1.h"
#include "appwidoc.h"
#ifdef _DEBUG
#undef THIS_FILE
static char BASED_CODE THIS_FILE[] = __FILE__;
#endif
/////////////////////////////////////////////////////////////////////
// CAppwiz1Doc
IMPLEMENT_DYNCREATE(CAppwiz1Doc, CDocument)
BEGIN_MESSAGE_MAP(CAppwiz1Doc, CDocument)
    //{{AFX_MSG_MAP(CAppwiz1Doc)
// NOTE - the ClassWizard will add and remove mapping macros here.
//    DO NOT EDIT what you see in these blocks of generated code !
    //}}AFX_MSG_MAP
END_MESSAGE_MAP()
/////////////////////////////////////////////////////////////////////
// CAppwiz1Doc construction/destruction
CAppwiz1Doc::CAppwiz1Doc()
{
    // TODO: add one-time construction code here
}
CAppwiz1Doc::~CAppwiz1Doc()
{
}
BOOL CAppwiz1Doc::OnNewDocument()
```

```
{
    if (!CDocument::OnNewDocument())
        return FALSE;
    // TODO: add reinitialization code here
    // (SDI documents will reuse this document)
    return TRUE;
}
/////////////////////////////////////////////////////////////////
// CAppwiz1Doc serialization
void CAppwiz1Doc::Serialize(CArchive& ar)
{
    if (ar.IsStoring())
    {
        // TODO: add storing code here
    }
    else
    {
        // TODO: add loading code here
    }
}

/////////////////////////////////////////////////////////////////
// CAppwiz1Doc diagnostics
#ifdef _DEBUG
void CAppwiz1Doc::AssertValid() const
{
    CDocument::AssertValid();
}
void CAppwiz1Doc::Dump(CDumpContext& dc) const
{
    CDocument::Dump(dc);
}
#endif //_DEBUG
/////////////////////////////////////////////////////////////////
// CAppwiz1Doc commands
```

Adding the ToolBar and the Status Bar

Let's use AppWizard to add both the toolbar and the status bar to the minimal MFC program. Perform the following steps:

1. Choose the AppWizard command from the Project menu.

    Type **appwiz2** as the name of the project and select the directory \MSVC\USEVC as the parent for the new project. Figure 3.7 shows the MFC AppWizard dialog box as the APPWIZ2 project is being created.

Figure 3.7
The MFC
AppWizard
dialog box as the
APPWIZ2 project is
being created.

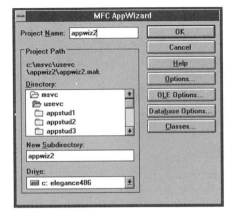

2. Click the Options... button to pop up the Options dialog box. Click the Multiple Document Interface and the Printing and Print Preview check boxes to unmark them, but retain the check mark in the Initial Toolbar box. Figure 3.8 shows the Options dialog box at this stage.

Figure 3.8
The Options
dialog box as the
APPWIZ2 project
is being created.

3. Click the OK button in the Options dialog box. Now you're back to the MFC AppWizard dialog box.

4. Click the OK button to view a summary of the classes and features. The click action causes the New Application Information dialog box to pop up, shown in Figure 3.9. This dialog box states the classes and the features of the project you are about to create.

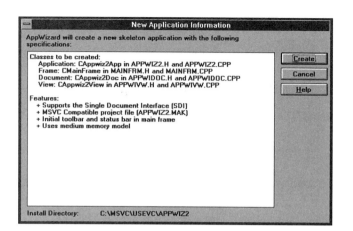

Figure 3.9
The New Application Information dialog box as the APPWIZ2 project is being created.

5. Click the Create button to generate the source code files for the APPWIZ2 project. The Visual Workbench displays message dialog boxes that report the progress as the files are created.

Running the APPWIZ2.EXE Program

Compile and run the APPWIZ2 project by choosing the Execute command from the Project menu. The resulting program is similar to the minimal MFC application you built in the preceding section. Figure 3.10 shows a sample session with the APPWIZ2.EXE program. The APPWIZ2.EXE program has the following enhancements:

- The frame window includes a toolbar. Some of the toolbar buttons are disabled because they correspond to features unavailable in the program.

- The frame window contains a status bar.

- The menu bar includes the View menu, which contains commands to toggle the visibility of the toolbar and the status bar.

Aside from these enhancements, the APPWIZ1.EXE and APPWIZ2.EXE programs are similar in their support (or partial support, to be more exact) of the various menu commands.

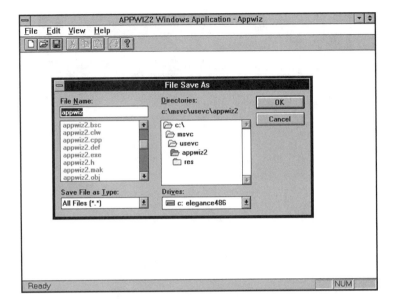

The APPWIZ2 Source Files

How do the source files in the APPWIZ2 project compare with those in
APPWIZ1? The answer to this question is that most of the source files are very
similar, especially in the files that *do not* deal with supporting the toolbar and
status bar. The main difference between the source files of the two projects is
in the names of the classes and other symbols whose names are derived from
the project name. Listing 3.15 shows the contents of the APPWIZ2.DEF definition file. Notice that it greatly resembles the contents of the APPWIZ1.DEF
file in Listing 3.1. The difference is that the APPWIZ2.DEF file makes reference to APPWIZ2 instead of APPWIZ1.

The following sections present the APPWIZ2 project files that have different
statements and so differ from their counterparts in the APPWIZ1 project.

Listing 3.15 The APPWIZ2.DEF Definition File

```
; appwiz2.def : Declares the module parameters for the application.
NAME            APPWIZ2
DESCRIPTION     'APPWIZ2 Windows Application'
EXETYPE         WINDOWS
CODE            PRELOAD MOVEABLE DISCARDABLE
DATA            PRELOAD MOVEABLE MULTIPLE
HEAPSIZE        1024    ; initial heap size
; Stack size is passed as argument to linker's /STACK option
```

The MAINFRM.H File

The header file MAINFRM.H, shown in Listing 3.16, has a new declaration for the frame window class CMainFrame. Here are the new declared members:

- The data member m_wndStatusBar, which is an instance of class CStatusBar. This member represents the status bar owned by the frame window.

- The data member m_wndToolBar, which is an instance of class CToolBar. This member supports the toolbar owned by the frame window.

- The member function OnCreate, which assists in creating instances of class CMainFrame.

Listing 3.16 Source Code for the MAINFRM.H Header File

```
// mainfrm.h : interface of the CMainFrame class
//
/////////////////////////////////////////////////////////////////////
class CMainFrame : public CFrameWnd
{
protected: // create from serialization only
    CMainFrame();
    DECLARE_DYNCREATE(CMainFrame)
// Attributes
public:
// Operations
public:
// Implementation
public:
    virtual ~CMainFrame();
#ifdef _DEBUG
    virtual     void AssertValid() const;
    virtual     void Dump(CDumpContext& dc) const;
#endif

protected:      // control bar embedded members
    CStatusBar      m_wndStatusBar;
    CToolBar      m_wndToolBar;
// Generated message map functions
protected:
    //{{AFX_MSG(CMainFrame)
    afx_msg int OnCreate(LPCREATESTRUCT lpCreateStruct);
// NOTE - the ClassWizard will add and remove member functions here.
//     DO NOT EDIT what you see in these blocks of generated code !
    //}}AFX_MSG
    DECLARE_MESSAGE_MAP()
};
/////////////////////////////////////////////////////////////////////
```

The APPWIZ2.RC File

The resource file APPWIZ2.RC, shown in Listing 3.17, declares the various kinds of resources used by program APPWIZ2.EXE. The APPWIZ2.RC resource file differs from APPWIZ1.RC primarily in the following ways:

- The file APPWIZ2.RC has the resource for the View menu, which contains the menu commands Toolbar and Status Bar.

- The file APPWIZ2.RC has additional ID_*xxxx* identifiers that map strings related to the toolbar and the status bar.

Listing 3.17 Script for the APPWIZ12.RC Resource File

```
//Microsoft App Studio generated resource script.
//
#include "resource.h"
#define APSTUDIO_READONLY_SYMBOLS
/////////////////////////////////////////////////////////////////////////////
//
// From TEXTINCLUDE 2
//
#include "afxres.h"
/////////////////////////////////////////////////////////////////////////////
#undef APSTUDIO_READONLY_SYMBOLS
#ifdef APSTUDIO_INVOKED
/////////////////////////////////////////////////////////////////////////////
//
// TEXTINCLUDE
//
1 TEXTINCLUDE DISCARDABLE
BEGIN
     "resource.h\0"
END
2 TEXTINCLUDE DISCARDABLE
BEGIN
     "#include ""afxres.h""\r\n"
     "\0"
END
3 TEXTINCLUDE DISCARDABLE
BEGIN
     "#include ""res\\appwiz2.rc2""  // non-App Studio edited resources\r\n"
     "\r\n"
     "#include ""afxres.rc""  // Standard components\r\n"
     "\0"
END
/////////////////////////////////////////////////////////////////////////////
#endif    // APSTUDIO_INVOKED
/////////////////////////////////////////////////////////////////////////////
//
// Icon
//
IDR_MAINFRAME          ICON    DISCARDABLE     res\appwiz2.ico
```

```
/////////////////////////////////////////////////////////////////
//
// Bitmap
//
IDR_MAINFRAME           BITMAP   MOVEABLE      res\toolbar.bmp
/////////////////////////////////////////////////////////////////
//
// Menu
//
IDR_MAINFRAME MENU PRELOAD DISCARDABLE
BEGIN
    POPUP "&File"
    BEGIN
        MENUITEM "&New\tCtrl+N",               ID_FILE_NEW
        MENUITEM "&Open...\tCtrl+O",           ID_FILE_OPEN
        MENUITEM "&Save\tCtrl+S",              ID_FILE_SAVE
        MENUITEM "Save &As...",                ID_FILE_SAVE_AS
        MENUITEM SEPARATOR
        MENUITEM "Recent File",                ID_FILE_MRU_FILE1,GRAYED
        MENUITEM SEPARATOR
        MENUITEM "E&xit",                      ID_APP_EXIT
    END
    POPUP "&Edit"
    BEGIN
        MENUITEM "&Undo\tCtrl+Z",              ID_EDIT_UNDO
        MENUITEM SEPARATOR
        MENUITEM "Cu&t\tCtrl+X",               ID_EDIT_CUT
        MENUITEM "&Copy\tCtrl+C",              ID_EDIT_COPY
        MENUITEM "&Paste\tCtrl+V",             ID_EDIT_PASTE
    END
    POPUP "&View"
    BEGIN
        MENUITEM "&Toolbar",                   ID_VIEW_TOOLBAR
        MENUITEM "&Status Bar",                ID_VIEW_STATUS_BAR
    END
    POPUP "&Help"
    BEGIN
        MENUITEM "&About APPWIZ2...",          ID_APP_ABOUT
    END
END
/////////////////////////////////////////////////////////////////
//
// Accelerator
//
IDR_MAINFRAME ACCELERATORS PRELOAD MOVEABLE
BEGIN
    "N",            ID_FILE_NEW,            VIRTKEY,CONTROL
    "O",            ID_FILE_OPEN,           VIRTKEY,CONTROL
    "S",            ID_FILE_SAVE,           VIRTKEY,CONTROL
    "Z",            ID_EDIT_UNDO,           VIRTKEY,CONTROL
    "X",            ID_EDIT_CUT,            VIRTKEY,CONTROL
    "C",            ID_EDIT_COPY,           VIRTKEY,CONTROL
    "V",            ID_EDIT_PASTE,          VIRTKEY,CONTROL
    VK_BACK,        ID_EDIT_UNDO,           VIRTKEY,ALT
```

(continues)

Listing 3.17 Continued

```
        VK_DELETE,       ID_EDIT_CUT,            VIRTKEY,SHIFT
        VK_INSERT,       ID_EDIT_COPY,           VIRTKEY,CONTROL
        VK_INSERT,       ID_EDIT_PASTE,          VIRTKEY,SHIFT
        VK_F6,           ID_NEXT_PANE,           VIRTKEY
        VK_F6,           ID_PREV_PANE,           VIRTKEY,SHIFT
END
/////////////////////////////////////////////////////////////////////////////
//
// Dialog
//
IDD_ABOUTBOX DIALOG DISCARDABLE  34, 22, 217, 55
CAPTION "About APPWIZ2"
STYLE DS_MODALFRAME ¦ WS_POPUP ¦ WS_CAPTION ¦ WS_SYSMENU
FONT 8, "MS Sans Serif"
BEGIN
        ICON            IDR_MAINFRAME,IDC_STATIC,11,17,20,20
        LTEXT           "APPWIZ2 Application Version 1.0",IDC_STATIC,40,10,119,8
        LTEXT           "Copyright \251 1993",IDC_STATIC,40,25,119,8
        DEFPUSHBUTTON   "OK",IDOK,176,6,32,14,WS_GROUP
END
/////////////////////////////////////////////////////////////////////////////
//
// String Table
//
STRINGTABLE PRELOAD DISCARDABLE
BEGIN
        IDR_MAINFRAME           "APPWIZ2 Windows Application\nAppwiz\nAPPWIZ
➥Document"
END
STRINGTABLE PRELOAD DISCARDABLE
BEGIN
        AFX_IDS_APP_TITLE       "APPWIZ2 Windows Application"
        AFX_IDS_IDLEMESSAGE     "Ready"
END
STRINGTABLE DISCARDABLE
BEGIN
        ID_INDICATOR_EXT        "EXT"
        ID_INDICATOR_CAPS       "CAP"
        ID_INDICATOR_NUM        "NUM"
        ID_INDICATOR_SCRL       "SCRL"
        ID_INDICATOR_OVR        "OVR"
        ID_INDICATOR_REC        "REC"
END
STRINGTABLE DISCARDABLE
BEGIN
        ID_FILE_NEW             "Create a new document"
        ID_FILE_OPEN            "Open an existing document"
        ID_FILE_CLOSE           "Close the active document"
        ID_FILE_SAVE            "Save the active document"
        ID_FILE_SAVE_AS         "Save the active document with a new name"
        ID_APP_ABOUT            "Display program information, version
➥number and copyright"
        ID_APP_EXIT             "Quit the application; prompts to save
➥documents"
        ID_FILE_MRU_FILE1       "Open this document"
```

```
        ID_FILE_MRU_FILE2        "Open this document"
        ID_FILE_MRU_FILE3        "Open this document"
        ID_FILE_MRU_FILE4        "Open this document"
        ID_NEXT_PANE             "Switch to the next window pane"
        ID_PREV_PANE             "Switch back to the previous window pane"
        ID_EDIT_CLEAR            "Erase the selection"
        ID_EDIT_CLEAR_ALL        "Erase everything"
        ID_EDIT_COPY             "Copy the selection and put it on the Clipboard"
        ID_EDIT_CUT              "Cut the selection and put it on the Clipboard"
        ID_EDIT_FIND             "Find the specified text"
        ID_EDIT_PASTE            "Insert Clipboard contents"
        ID_EDIT_REPEAT           "Repeat the last action"
        ID_EDIT_REPLACE          "Replace specific text with different text"
        ID_EDIT_SELECT_ALL       "Select the entire document"
        ID_EDIT_UNDO             "Undo the last action"
        ID_EDIT_REDO             "Redo the previously undone action"
        ID_VIEW_TOOLBAR          "Show or hide the toolbar"
        ID_VIEW_STATUS_BAR       "Show or hide the status bar"
END
STRINGTABLE DISCARDABLE
BEGIN
        AFX_IDS_SCSIZE           "Change the window size"
        AFX_IDS_SCMOVE           "Change the window position"
        AFX_IDS_SCMINIMIZE       "Reduce the window to an icon"
        AFX_IDS_SCMAXIMIZE       "Enlarge the window to full size"
        AFX_IDS_SCNEXTWINDOW     "Switch to the next document window"
        AFX_IDS_SCPREVWINDOW     "Switch to the previous document window"
        AFX_IDS_SCCLOSE          "Close the active window and prompts to save
➥the documents"
        AFX_IDS_SCRESTORE        "Restore the window to normal size"
        AFX_IDS_SCTASKLIST       "Activate Task List"
END
#ifndef APSTUDIO_INVOKED
/////////////////////////////////////////////////////////////////////////
//
// From TEXTINCLUDE 3
//
#include "res\appwiz2.rc2"  // non-App Studio edited resources
#include "afxres.rc"  // Standard components
/////////////////////////////////////////////////////////////////////////
#endif     // not APSTUDIO_INVOKED
```

The MAINFRM.CPP File

The file MAINFRM.CPP, shown in Listing 3.18, contains the implementation of the frame window class CMainFrame. This implementation of class CMainFrame differs from the implementation in Listing 3.12 as follows:

■ The new implementation in Listing 3.18 has the map entry ON_WM_CREATE in the table response map. Thus, the class invokes the member function OnCreate in response to the Windows message ON_WM_CREATE.

■ Listing 3.18 declares the static array of unsigned integers, `buttons`. This array stores the IDs of the commands generated by the toolbar buttons.

■ Listing 3.18 declares the static array of unsigned integers, `indicators`. This array stores the IDs for the status line indicators.

■ Listing 13.8 declares the implementation of the member function `OnCreate`. The function invokes the parent's `OnCreate` function and then sends the following C++ messages to the object `m_wndToolBar`:

- Sends the C++ message `Create`.

- Sends the C++ message `LoadBitmap`. This message loads the bitmap resources.

- Sends the C++ message `SetButtons`. This message sets the toolbar buttons.

If any of these C++ messages returns 0, the function exits and returns –1. Otherwise, the function sends the following C++ messages to the object `m_wndStatusBar`:

- The C++ message `Create`, to create the status bar.

- The C++ message `SetIndicators`, to set the indicators in the status bar.

If either of the preceding two C++ messages returns 0, the function exits and returns –1. Otherwise, the function returns 0.

Listing 3.18 Source Code for the MAINFRM.CPP Implementation File

```
// mainfrm.cpp : implementation of the CMainFrame class
//
#include "stdafx.h"
#include "appwiz2.h"
#include "mainfrm.h"
#ifdef _DEBUG
#undef THIS_FILE
static char BASED_CODE THIS_FILE[] = __FILE__;
#endif
/////////////////////////////////////////////////////////////////////////////
// CMainFrame
IMPLEMENT_DYNCREATE(CMainFrame, CFrameWnd)
BEGIN_MESSAGE_MAP(CMainFrame, CFrameWnd)
    //{{AFX_MSG_MAP(CMainFrame)
// NOTE - the ClassWizard will add and remove mapping macros here.
//    DO NOT EDIT what you see in these blocks of generated code !
```

```
      ON_WM_CREATE()
      //}}AFX_MSG_MAP
END_MESSAGE_MAP()
///////////////////////////////////////////////////////////////////
// arrays of IDs used to initialize control bars
// toolbar buttons - IDs are command buttons
static UINT BASED_CODE buttons[] =
{
      // same order as in the bitmap 'toolbar.bmp'
      ID_FILE_NEW,
      ID_FILE_OPEN,
      ID_FILE_SAVE,
      ID_SEPARATOR,
      ID_EDIT_CUT,
      ID_EDIT_COPY,
      ID_EDIT_PASTE,
      ID_SEPARATOR,
      ID_FILE_PRINT,
      ID_APP_ABOUT,
};
static UINT BASED_CODE indicators[] =
{
      ID_SEPARATOR,                  // status line indicator
      ID_INDICATOR_CAPS,
      ID_INDICATOR_NUM,
      ID_INDICATOR_SCRL,
};
///////////////////////////////////////////////////////////////////
// CMainFrame construction/destruction
CMainFrame::CMainFrame()
{
      // TODO: add member initialization code here
}
CMainFrame::~CMainFrame()
{
}
int CMainFrame::OnCreate(LPCREATESTRUCT lpCreateStruct)
{
      if (CFrameWnd::OnCreate(lpCreateStruct) == -1)
          return -1;
      if (!m_wndToolBar.Create(this) ||
          !m_wndToolBar.LoadBitmap(IDR_MAINFRAME) ||
          !m_wndToolBar.SetButtons(buttons,
            sizeof(buttons)/sizeof(UINT)))
      {
          TRACE("Failed to create toolbar\n");
          return -1;            // fail to create
      }
      if (!m_wndStatusBar.Create(this) ||
          !m_wndStatusBar.SetIndicators(indicators,
            sizeof(indicators)/sizeof(UINT)))
      {
          TRACE("Failed to create status bar\n");
          return -1;            // fail to create
      }
      return 0;
}
```

(continues)

Listing 3.18 Continued

```
/////////////////////////////////////////////////////////////////
// CMainFrame diagnostics
#ifdef _DEBUG
void CMainFrame::AssertValid() const
{
    CFrameWnd::AssertValid();
}
void CMainFrame::Dump(CDumpContext& dc) const
{
    CFrameWnd::Dump(dc);
}
#endif //_DEBUG
/////////////////////////////////////////////////////////////////
// CMainFrame message handlers
```

Adding Print Support

Let's use AppWizard to add the print and print preview features to the minimal MFC program. Perform the following steps:

1. Choose the AppWizard... command from the Project menu. Type **appwiz3** as the name of the project and select the directory \MSVC\USEVC as the parent for the new project.

2. Click the Options... button, and the Options dialog box pops up. Click the Multiple Document Interface and the Initial Toolbar check boxes to unmark them, but retain the check mark in the Printing and Print Preview box. Figure 3.11 shows the Options dialog box at this stage.

Figure 3.11
The Options dialog box as the APPWIZ3 project is being created.

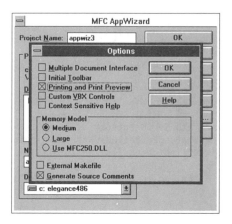

3. Click the OK button in the Options dialog box. Now you're back to the MFC AppWizard dialog box.

4. Click the OK button to view a summary of the classes and features. The click action causes the New Application Information dialog box to pop up (see Figure 3.12). This dialog box lists the classes and features of the project you are about to create.

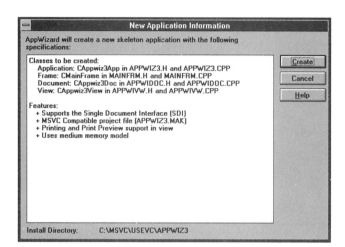

Figure 3.12
The New Application Information dialog box as the APPWIZ3 project is being created.

5. Click the Create button to create the source code files for the APPWIZ3 project. The Visual Workbench displays message dialog boxes that report the progress as the files are created.

Running the APPWIZ3.EXE Program

Compile and run the APPWIZ3 project. The resulting program is similar to the minimal MFC application you built in the first section. Figure 3.13 shows the commands in the File menu for the APPWIZ3.EXE program. Figure 3.14 shows the print preview feature at work. The APPWIZ3.EXE program has the following enhancements:

■ The File menu contains the Print, Print Preview, and Print Setup menu commands.

■ The printing-related commands are operational. However, because the program does not actually read a file, it prints an empty page.

Aside from these enhancements, the programs APPWIZ1.EXE and APPWIZ3.EXE are similar in their partial support of the various menu commands.

Figure 3.13

The File menu commands for the APPWIZ3.EXE program.

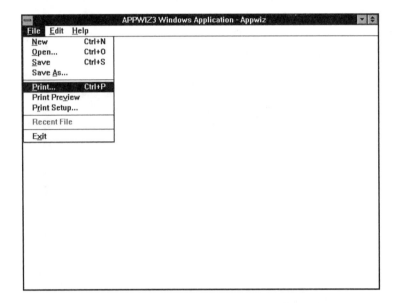

Figure 3.14

The print preview feature in the APPWIZ3.EXE program.

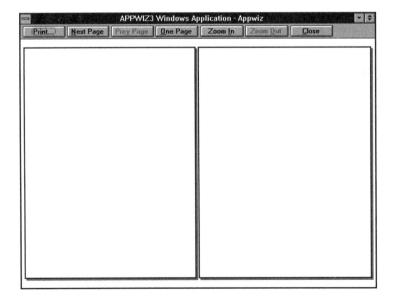

The APPWIZ3 Source Files

Once again, you may ask how the source files in the APPWIZ3 project compare with those in APPWIZ1? And, once again, the answer to this question is that most of the source files are very similar, especially in the files that *do not* deal with supporting the printing-related features. The main difference between the source files of the two projects is in the names of the classes and other symbols whose names are derived from the project name. Listing 3.19 shows the contents of the APPWIZ3.DEF definition file. Notice that it greatly resembles the contents of the APPWIZ1.DEF file in Listing 3.1. The difference is that the APPWIZ3.DEF file makes reference to APPWIZ3 rather than APPWIZ1.

The following sections offer the APPWIZ3 project files, which have different statements and so differ from their counterparts in the APPWIZ1 project.

Listing 3.19 The APPWIZ3.DEF Definition File

```
; appwiz3.def : Declares the module parameters for the application.
NAME            APPWIZ3
DESCRIPTION     'APPWIZ3 Windows Application'
EXETYPE         WINDOWS
CODE            PRELOAD MOVEABLE DISCARDABLE
DATA            PRELOAD MOVEABLE MULTIPLE
HEAPSIZE        1024   ; initial heap size
; Stack size is passed as argument to linker's /STACK option
```

The APPWIVW.H File

The header file APPWIVW.H, shown in Listing 3.20, declares the view class CAppWiz3View and adds the three protected member functions to support the printing operation. The member functions OnPreparePrinting, OnBeginPrinting, and OnEndPrinting prepare, start, and finish the printing process, respectively. These functions have parameters that are pointers to a device context and to the print information.

Listing 3.20 Source Code for the APPWIVW.H Header File

```
// appwivw.h : interface of the CAppwiz3View class
//
/////////////////////////////////////////////////////////////////////
class CAppwiz3View : public CView
{
protected: // create from serialization only
    CAppwiz3View();
    DECLARE_DYNCREATE(CAppwiz3View)
```

(continues)

Listing 3.20 Continued

```
// Attributes
public:
    CAppwiz3Doc* GetDocument();
// Operations
public:
// Implementation
public:
    virtual ~CAppwiz3View();
    virtual void OnDraw(CDC* pDC);  // overridden to draw this view
#ifdef _DEBUG
    virtual void AssertValid() const;
    virtual void Dump(CDumpContext& dc) const;
#endif
    // Printing support
protected:
    virtual BOOL OnPreparePrinting(CPrintInfo* pInfo);
    virtual void OnBeginPrinting(CDC* pDC, CPrintInfo* pInfo);
    virtual void OnEndPrinting(CDC* pDC, CPrintInfo* pInfo);
// Generated message map functions
protected:
    //{{AFX_MSG(CAppwiz3View)
// NOTE - the ClassWizard will add and remove member functions here.
//    DO NOT EDIT what you see in these blocks of generated code !
    //}}AFX_MSG
    DECLARE_MESSAGE_MAP()
};
#ifndef _DEBUG     // debug version in appwivw.cpp
inline CAppwiz3Doc* CAppwiz3View::GetDocument()
    { return (CAppwiz3Doc*) m_pDocument; }
#endif
/////////////////////////////////////////////////////////////////////
```

The APPWIZ3.RC File

The resource file APPWIZ3.RC, shown in Listing 3.21, contains the menu resources to support the printing-related options. These resources include both MENUITEM resources in the POPUP "&File" section, accelerator resources in the IDR_MAINFRAME section, and string resources.

Listing 3.21 Script for the APPWIZ3.RC Resource File

```
//Microsoft App Studio generated resource script.
//
#include "resource.h"
#define APSTUDIO_READONLY_SYMBOLS
/////////////////////////////////////////////////////////////////////
//
// From TEXTINCLUDE 2
//
#include "afxres.h"
```

```
/////////////////////////////////////////////////////////////////////////
#undef APSTUDIO_READONLY_SYMBOLS
#ifdef APSTUDIO_INVOKED
/////////////////////////////////////////////////////////////////////////
//
// TEXTINCLUDE
//
1 TEXTINCLUDE DISCARDABLE
BEGIN
    "resource.h\0"
END
2 TEXTINCLUDE DISCARDABLE
BEGIN
    "#include ""afxres.h""\r\n"
    "\0"
END
3 TEXTINCLUDE DISCARDABLE
BEGIN
    "#include ""res\\appwiz3.rc2""  // non-App Studio edited resources\r\n"
    "\r\n"
    "#include ""afxres.rc""  // Standard components\r\n"
    "#include ""afxprint.rc""  // printing/print preview resources\r\n"
    "\0"
END
/////////////////////////////////////////////////////////////////////////
#endif    // APSTUDIO_INVOKED
/////////////////////////////////////////////////////////////////////////
//
// Icon
//
IDR_MAINFRAME           ICON    DISCARDABLE     res\appwiz3.ico
/////////////////////////////////////////////////////////////////////////
//
// Menu
//
IDR_MAINFRAME MENU PRELOAD DISCARDABLE
BEGIN
    POPUP "&File"
    BEGIN
        MENUITEM "&New\tCtrl+N",              ID_FILE_NEW
        MENUITEM "&Open...\tCtrl+O",          ID_FILE_OPEN
        MENUITEM "&Save\tCtrl+S",             ID_FILE_SAVE
        MENUITEM "Save &As...",               ID_FILE_SAVE_AS
        MENUITEM SEPARATOR
        MENUITEM "&Print...\tCtrl+P",         ID_FILE_PRINT
        MENUITEM "Print Pre&view",            ID_FILE_PRINT_PREVIEW
        MENUITEM "P&rint Setup...",           ID_FILE_PRINT_SETUP
        MENUITEM SEPARATOR
        MENUITEM "Recent File",               ID_FILE_MRU_FILE1,GRAYED
        MENUITEM SEPARATOR
        MENUITEM "E&xit",                     ID_APP_EXIT
    END
    POPUP "&Edit"
    BEGIN
        MENUITEM "&Undo\tCtrl+Z",             ID_EDIT_UNDO
        MENUITEM SEPARATOR
```

(continues)

Listing 3.21 Continued

```
            MENUITEM "Cu&t\tCtrl+X",              ID_EDIT_CUT
            MENUITEM "&Copy\tCtrl+C",             ID_EDIT_COPY
            MENUITEM "&Paste\tCtrl+V",            ID_EDIT_PASTE
        END
        POPUP "&Help"
        BEGIN
            MENUITEM "&About APPWIZ3...",         ID_APP_ABOUT
        END
END
/////////////////////////////////////////////////////////////////////
//
// Accelerator
//
IDR_MAINFRAME ACCELERATORS PRELOAD MOVEABLE
BEGIN
    "N",            ID_FILE_NEW,            VIRTKEY,CONTROL
    "O",            ID_FILE_OPEN,           VIRTKEY,CONTROL
    "S",            ID_FILE_SAVE,           VIRTKEY,CONTROL
    "P",            ID_FILE_PRINT,          VIRTKEY,CONTROL
    "Z",            ID_EDIT_UNDO,           VIRTKEY,CONTROL
    "X",            ID_EDIT_CUT,            VIRTKEY,CONTROL
    "C",            ID_EDIT_COPY,           VIRTKEY,CONTROL
    "V",            ID_EDIT_PASTE,          VIRTKEY,CONTROL
    VK_BACK,        ID_EDIT_UNDO,           VIRTKEY,ALT
    VK_DELETE,      ID_EDIT_CUT,            VIRTKEY,SHIFT
    VK_INSERT,      ID_EDIT_COPY,           VIRTKEY,CONTROL
    VK_INSERT,      ID_EDIT_PASTE,          VIRTKEY,SHIFT
    VK_F6,          ID_NEXT_PANE,           VIRTKEY
    VK_F6,          ID_PREV_PANE,           VIRTKEY,SHIFT
END
/////////////////////////////////////////////////////////////////////
//
// Dialog
//
IDD_ABOUTBOX DIALOG DISCARDABLE  34, 22, 217, 55
CAPTION "About APPWIZ3"
STYLE DS_MODALFRAME ¦ WS_POPUP ¦ WS_CAPTION ¦ WS_SYSMENU
FONT 8, "MS Sans Serif"
BEGIN
    ICON            IDR_MAINFRAME,IDC_STATIC,11,17,20,20
    LTEXT           "APPWIZ3 Application Version 1.0",
                    IDC_STATIC,40,10,119,8
    LTEXT           "Copyright \251 1993",IDC_STATIC,40,25,119,8
    DEFPUSHBUTTON   "OK",IDOK,176,6,32,14,WS_GROUP
END
/////////////////////////////////////////////////////////////////////
//
// String Table
//
STRINGTABLE PRELOAD DISCARDABLE
BEGIN
    IDR_MAINFRAME              "APPWIZ3 Windows Application\nAppwiz\nAPPWIZ
➥Document"
END
```

```
STRINGTABLE PRELOAD DISCARDABLE
BEGIN
     AFX_IDS_APP_TITLE          "APPWIZ3 Windows Application"
     AFX_IDS_IDLEMESSAGE        "Ready"
END
STRINGTABLE DISCARDABLE
BEGIN
     ID_INDICATOR_EXT           "EXT"
     ID_INDICATOR_CAPS          "CAP"
     ID_INDICATOR_NUM           "NUM"
     ID_INDICATOR_SCRL          "SCRL"
     ID_INDICATOR_OVR           "OVR"
     ID_INDICATOR_REC           "REC"
END
STRINGTABLE DISCARDABLE
BEGIN
     ID_FILE_NEW                "Create a new document"
     ID_FILE_OPEN               "Open an existing document"
     ID_FILE_CLOSE              "Close the active document"
     ID_FILE_SAVE               "Save the active document"
     ID_FILE_SAVE_AS            "Save the active document with a new name"
     ID_FILE_PAGE_SETUP         "Change the printing options"
     ID_FILE_PRINT_SETUP        "Change the printer and printing options"
     ID_FILE_PRINT              "Print the active document"
     ID_FILE_PRINT_PREVIEW      "Display full pages"
     ID_APP_ABOUT               "Display program information, version number
➥and copyright"
     ID_APP_EXIT                "Quit the application; prompts to save documents"
     ID_FILE_MRU_FILE1          "Open this document"
     ID_FILE_MRU_FILE2          "Open this document"
     ID_FILE_MRU_FILE3          "Open this document"
     ID_FILE_MRU_FILE4          "Open this document"
     ID_NEXT_PANE               "Switch to the next window pane"
     ID_PREV_PANE               "Switch back to the previous window pane"
     ID_EDIT_CLEAR              "Erase the selection"
     ID_EDIT_CLEAR_ALL          "Erase everything"
     ID_EDIT_COPY               "Copy the selection and put it on the Clipboard"
     ID_EDIT_CUT                "Cut the selection and put it on the Clipboard"
     ID_EDIT_FIND               "Find the specified text"
     ID_EDIT_PASTE              "Insert Clipboard contents"
     ID_EDIT_REPEAT             "Repeat the last action"
     ID_EDIT_REPLACE            "Replace specific text with different text"
     ID_EDIT_SELECT_ALL         "Select the entire document"
     ID_EDIT_UNDO               "Undo the last action"
     ID_EDIT_REDO               "Redo the previously undone action"
END
STRINGTABLE DISCARDABLE
BEGIN
     AFX_IDS_SCSIZE             "Change the window size"
     AFX_IDS_SCMOVE             "Change the window position"
     AFX_IDS_SCMINIMIZE         "Reduce the window to an icon"
     AFX_IDS_SCMAXIMIZE         "Enlarge the window to full size"
     AFX_IDS_SCNEXTWINDOW       "Switch to the next document window"
     AFX_IDS_SCPREVWINDOW       "Switch to the previous document window"
     AFX_IDS_SCCLOSE            "Close the active window and prompts to save
➥the documents"
```

(continues)

Listing 3.21 Continued

```
        AFX_IDS_SCRESTORE        "Restore the window to normal size"
        AFX_IDS_SCTASKLIST       "Activate Task List"
END
#ifndef APSTUDIO_INVOKED
/////////////////////////////////////////////////////////////////////
//
// From TEXTINCLUDE 3
//
#include "res\appwiz3.rc2"  // non-App Studio edited resources
#include "afxres.rc"  // Standard components
#include "afxprint.rc"  // printing/print preview resources
/////////////////////////////////////////////////////////////////////
#endif     // not APSTUDIO_INVOKED
```

The APPWIZ3.CPP File

The file APPWIZ3.CPP contains the implementation of the application
class CAppWiz3App. This implementation differs from its counterpart in the
APPWIZ1.CPP file (see Listing 3.10) in that the table response map has an
additional map entry to handle the Print Setup command. Listing 3.22 shows
just the table response map in the APPWIZ3.CPP file. The rest of the listing is
identical to that in the APPWIZ1.CPP file.

**Listing 3.22 Partial Source Code for the APPWIZ3.CPP
Implementation File**

```
/////////////////////////////////////////////////////////////////////
// CAppwiz3App
BEGIN_MESSAGE_MAP(CAppwiz3App, CWinApp)
    //{{AFX_MSG_MAP(CAppwiz3App)
    ON_COMMAND(ID_APP_ABOUT, OnAppAbout)
// NOTE - the ClassWizard will add and remove mapping macros here.
//    DO NOT EDIT what you see in these blocks of generated code !
    //}}AFX_MSG_MAP
    // Standard file based document commands
    ON_COMMAND(ID_FILE_NEW, CWinApp::OnFileNew)
    ON_COMMAND(ID_FILE_OPEN, CWinApp::OnFileOpen)
    // Standard print setup command
    ON_COMMAND(ID_FILE_PRINT_SETUP, CWinApp::OnFilePrintSetup)
END_MESSAGE_MAP()
```

The APPWIVW.CPP File

The file APPWIVW.CPP, shown in Listing 3.23, contains the implementation
of the view class CAppWiz3View. The implementation holds the definition of
the following printing-related member functions:

■ The member function OnPreparePrinting has a single statement that returns the Boolean value of the inherited function DoPreparePrinting.

■ The member function OnBeginPrinting has no statements. It offers a comment-based placeholder for the statements you have to add to perform any additional initialization before printing.

■ The member function OnEndPrinting has no statements. It offers a comment-based placeholder for the statements you have to add to perform any additional cleanup after printing.

In addition, the APPWIVW.CPP file contains a table response map with entries that deal with the Print and Print Preview commands. These entries map the messages ID_FILE_PRINT and ID_FILE_PRINT_PREVIEW to the inherited member functions OnFilePrint and OnFilePrintPreview, respectively.

Listing 3.23 Source Code for the APPWIVW.CPP Implementation File

```
// appwivw.cpp : implementation of the CAppwiz3View class
//
#include "stdafx.h"
#include "appwiz3.h"
#include "appwidoc.h"
#include "appwivw.h"
#ifdef _DEBUG
#undef THIS_FILE
static char BASED_CODE THIS_FILE[] = __FILE__;
#endif
/////////////////////////////////////////////////////////////////////////
// CAppwiz3View
IMPLEMENT_DYNCREATE(CAppwiz3View, CView)
BEGIN_MESSAGE_MAP(CAppwiz3View, CView)
    //{{AFX_MSG_MAP(CAppwiz3View)
    // NOTE - the ClassWizard will add and remove mapping macros here.
    //    DO NOT EDIT what you see in these blocks of generated code !
    //}}AFX_MSG_MAP
    // Standard printing commands
    ON_COMMAND(ID_FILE_PRINT, CView::OnFilePrint)
    ON_COMMAND(ID_FILE_PRINT_PREVIEW, CView::OnFilePrintPreview)
END_MESSAGE_MAP()
/////////////////////////////////////////////////////////////////////////
// CAppwiz3View construction/destruction
CAppwiz3View::CAppwiz3View()
{
    // TODO: add construction code here
}
CAppwiz3View::~CAppwiz3View()
{
}
```

(continues)

Listing 3.23 Continued

```
/////////////////////////////////////////////////////////////////////
// CAppwiz3View drawing
void CAppwiz3View::OnDraw(CDC* pDC)
{
    CAppwiz3Doc* pDoc = GetDocument();
    // TODO: add draw code here
}
/////////////////////////////////////////////////////////////////////
// CAppwiz3View printing
BOOL CAppwiz3View::OnPreparePrinting(CPrintInfo* pInfo)
{
    // default preparation
    return DoPreparePrinting(pInfo);
}
void CAppwiz3View::OnBeginPrinting(CDC* /*pDC*/, CPrintInfo* /*pInfo*/)
{
    // TODO: add extra initialization before printing
}
void CAppwiz3View::OnEndPrinting(CDC* /*pDC*/, CPrintInfo* /*pInfo*/)
{
    // TODO: add cleanup after printing
}
/////////////////////////////////////////////////////////////////////
// CAppwiz3View diagnostics
#ifdef _DEBUG
void CAppwiz3View::AssertValid() const
{
    CView::AssertValid();
}
void CAppwiz3View::Dump(CDumpContext& dc) const
{
    CView::Dump(dc);
}
CAppwiz3Doc* CAppwiz3View::GetDocument() // non-debug version is inline
{
    ASSERT(m_pDocument->IsKindOf(RUNTIME_CLASS(CAppwiz3Doc)));
    return (CAppwiz3Doc*) m_pDocument;
}
#endif //_DEBUG
/////////////////////////////////////////////////////////////////////
// CAppwiz3View message handlers
```

Adding MDI Support

Let's use AppWizard once more to make a minimal MFC program that supports MDI frame and child windows. Perform the following steps:

1. Choose the AppWizard command from the Project menu. Type **appwiz4** as the name of the project and select the directory \MSVC\USEVC as the parent for the new project.

2. Click the Options... button, and the Options dialog box pops up. Click the Initial Toolbar check box and the Printing and Print Preview check box to unmark them, but retain the check mark in the Multiple Document Interface box. Figure 3.15 shows the Options dialog box at this stage.

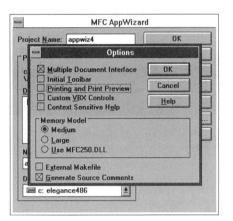

Figure 3.15
The Options dialog box as the APPWIZ4 project is being created.

3. Click the OK button in the Options dialog box. Now you're back to the MFC AppWizard dialog box.

4. Click the OK button to view a summary of the classes and features. The click action causes the New Application Information dialog box to pop up (see Figure 3.16). This dialog box states the classes and the features of the project you are about to create.

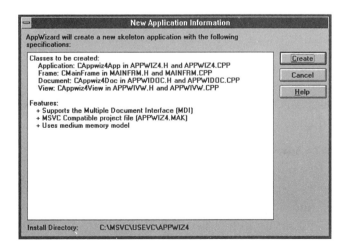

Figure 3.16
The New Application Information dialog box as the APPWIZ2 project is being created.

I

Introduction to Visual C++

5. Click the Create button to generate the source code files for the
APPWIZ4 project. The Visual Workbench displays message dialog
boxes that report the progress as the files are created.

Running the APPWIZ4.EXE Program

Compile and run the APPWIZ4 project. The resulting program is somewhat
similar to the minimal MFC application you built in the first section.
Figure 3.17 shows a sample session with the APPWIZ4.EXE program.

Figure 3.17
A sample
session with the
APPWIZ4.EXE
program.

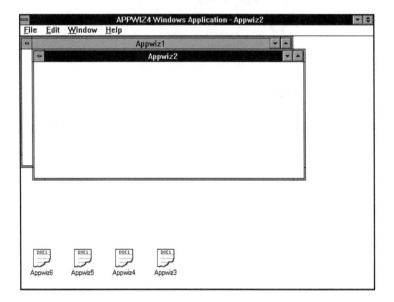

The APPWIZ4.EXE program has the following enhancements:

■ The ability to create and manage one or more MDI child windows.

■ The menu system contains an enhanced Window menu with
commands that enable you to duplicate MDI child windows, tile and
cascade MDI child windows, and arrange the icons of minimized
MDI child windows.

The APPWIZ4 Source Files

The source files in the APPWIZ4 project are very similar to those in the
APPWIZ1 project, especially in the files that *do not* deal with supporting the
MDI child windows. The main difference between the source files of the two
projects is in the names of the classes and other symbols whose names are
derived from the project name. Listing 3.24 shows the contents of the

APPWIZ4.DEF definition file. This file strongly resembles the contents of the APPWIZ1.DEF file in Listing 3.1. The difference is that the APPWIZ4.DEF file makes reference to APPWIZ4 rather than APPWIZ1.

The next sections present the APPWIZ4 project files, which have different statements and so differ from their counterparts in the APPWIZ1 project.

Listing 3.24 The APPWIZ4.DEF Definition File

```
; appwiz4.def : Declares the module parameters for the application.
NAME          APPWIZ4
DESCRIPTION   'APPWIZ4 Windows Application'
EXETYPE       WINDOWS
CODE          PRELOAD MOVEABLE DISCARDABLE
DATA          PRELOAD MOVEABLE MULTIPLE
HEAPSIZE      1024   ; initial heap size
; Stack size is passed as argument to linker's /STACK option
```

The MAINFRM.H File

The header file MAINFRM.H, shown in Listing 3.25, declares the frame window class `CMainFrame`. This declaration makes class `CMainFrame` a child of the MDI frame window class `CMDIFrameWnd`, rather than the SDI frame window class `CFrameWnd`. Consequently, class `CMainFrame` in the MAINFRM.H file has quite a different set of attributes and operations than the ones declared in the APPWIZ1 project (as well as in the APPWIZ2 and APPWIZ3 projects). The other aspects of the class declaration in Listing 3.25 resemble those in Listing 3.5.

Listing 3.25 Source Code for the MAINFRM.H Header File

```
// mainfrm.h : interface of the CMainFrame class
//
/////////////////////////////////////////////////////////////////////
class CMainFrame : public CMDIFrameWnd
{
    DECLARE_DYNAMIC(CMainFrame)
public:
    CMainFrame();
// Attributes
public:
// Operations
public:
// Implementation
public:
    virtual ~CMainFrame();
#ifdef _DEBUG
    virtual     void AssertValid() const;
    virtual     void Dump(CDumpContext& dc) const;
#endif
```

(continues)

Listing 3.25 Continued

```
// Generated message map functions
protected:
     //{{AFX_MSG(CMainFrame)
// NOTE - the ClassWizard will add and remove member functions here.
//    DO NOT EDIT what you see in these blocks of generated code !
     //}}AFX_MSG
     DECLARE_MESSAGE_MAP()
};
/////////////////////////////////////////////////////////////////////
```

The APPWIZ4.RC File

The resource file APPWIZ4.RC, shown in Listing 3.26, shows the various resources used to build the APPWIZ4.EXE program. The resources include ones that support MDI child windows, such as the MENUITEM resource statement in the POPUP "&Window" section and string resources. The program comments on the various menu commands by using string resources to display strings in the status bar.

Notice that the resource file has two sets of menu resources: a short menu version and a long menu version. The program uses the short menu version when there are no MDI child windows.

Listing 3.26 Script for the APPWIZ4.RC Resource File

```
//Microsoft App Studio generated resource script.
//
#include "resource.h"
#define APSTUDIO_READONLY_SYMBOLS
/////////////////////////////////////////////////////////////////////////////
//
// From TEXTINCLUDE 2
//
#include "afxres.h"
/////////////////////////////////////////////////////////////////////////////
#undef APSTUDIO_READONLY_SYMBOLS
#ifdef APSTUDIO_INVOKED
/////////////////////////////////////////////////////////////////////////////
//
// TEXTINCLUDE
//
1 TEXTINCLUDE DISCARDABLE
BEGIN
     "resource.h\0"
END
2 TEXTINCLUDE DISCARDABLE
BEGIN
     "#include ""afxres.h""\r\n"
     "\0"
```

```
END
3 TEXTINCLUDE DISCARDABLE
BEGIN
    "#include ""res\\appwiz4.rc2""  // non-App Studio edited resources\r\n"
    "\r\n"
    "#include ""afxres.rc""  // Standard components\r\n"
    "\0"
END
/////////////////////////////////////////////////////////////////////////
#endif    // APSTUDIO_INVOKED
/////////////////////////////////////////////////////////////////////////
//
// Icon
//
IDR_MAINFRAME           ICON    DISCARDABLE     res\appwiz4.ico
IDR_APPWIZTYPE          ICON    DISCARDABLE     res\appwidoc.ico
/////////////////////////////////////////////////////////////////////////
//
// Menu
//
IDR_MAINFRAME MENU PRELOAD DISCARDABLE
BEGIN
    POPUP "&File"
    BEGIN
        MENUITEM "&New\tCtrl+N",                ID_FILE_NEW
        MENUITEM "&Open...\tCtrl+O",            ID_FILE_OPEN
        MENUITEM SEPARATOR
        MENUITEM "Recent File",                 ID_FILE_MRU_FILE1,GRAYED
        MENUITEM SEPARATOR
        MENUITEM "E&xit",                       ID_APP_EXIT
    END
    POPUP "&Help"
    BEGIN
        MENUITEM "&About APPWIZ4...",           ID_APP_ABOUT
    END
END
IDR_APPWIZTYPE MENU PRELOAD DISCARDABLE
BEGIN
    POPUP "&File"
    BEGIN
        MENUITEM "&New\tCtrl+N",                ID_FILE_NEW
        MENUITEM "&Open...\tCtrl+O",            ID_FILE_OPEN
        MENUITEM "&Close",                      ID_FILE_CLOSE
        MENUITEM "&Save\tCtrl+S",               ID_FILE_SAVE
        MENUITEM "Save &As...",                 ID_FILE_SAVE_AS
        MENUITEM SEPARATOR
        MENUITEM "Recent File",                 ID_FILE_MRU_FILE1,GRAYED
        MENUITEM SEPARATOR
        MENUITEM "E&xit",                       ID_APP_EXIT
    END
    POPUP "&Edit"
    BEGIN
        MENUITEM "&Undo\tCtrl+Z",               ID_EDIT_UNDO
        MENUITEM SEPARATOR
        MENUITEM "Cu&t\tCtrl+X",                ID_EDIT_CUT
        MENUITEM "&Copy\tCtrl+C",               ID_EDIT_COPY
        MENUITEM "&Paste\tCtrl+V",              ID_EDIT_PASTE
```

(continues)

Listing 3.26 Continued

```
        END
        POPUP "&Window"
        BEGIN
                MENUITEM "&New Window",                  ID_WINDOW_NEW
                MENUITEM "&Cascade",                     ID_WINDOW_CASCADE
                MENUITEM "&Tile",                        ID_WINDOW_TILE_HORZ
                MENUITEM "&Arrange Icons",               ID_WINDOW_ARRANGE
        END
        POPUP "&Help"
        BEGIN
                MENUITEM "&About APPWIZ4...",            ID_APP_ABOUT
        END
END
/////////////////////////////////////////////////////////////////////////
//
// Accelerator
//
IDR_MAINFRAME ACCELERATORS PRELOAD MOVEABLE
BEGIN
        "N",            ID_FILE_NEW,            VIRTKEY,CONTROL
        "O",            ID_FILE_OPEN,           VIRTKEY,CONTROL
        "S",            ID_FILE_SAVE,           VIRTKEY,CONTROL
        "Z",            ID_EDIT_UNDO,           VIRTKEY,CONTROL
        "X",            ID_EDIT_CUT,            VIRTKEY,CONTROL
        "C",            ID_EDIT_COPY,           VIRTKEY,CONTROL
        "V",            ID_EDIT_PASTE,          VIRTKEY,CONTROL
        VK_BACK,        ID_EDIT_UNDO,           VIRTKEY,ALT
        VK_DELETE,      ID_EDIT_CUT,            VIRTKEY,SHIFT
        VK_INSERT,      ID_EDIT_COPY,           VIRTKEY,CONTROL
        VK_INSERT,      ID_EDIT_PASTE,          VIRTKEY,SHIFT
        VK_F6,          ID_NEXT_PANE,           VIRTKEY
        VK_F6,          ID_PREV_PANE,           VIRTKEY,SHIFT
END
/////////////////////////////////////////////////////////////////////////
//
// Dialog
//
IDD_ABOUTBOX DIALOG DISCARDABLE  34, 22, 217, 55
CAPTION "About APPWIZ4"
STYLE DS_MODALFRAME ¦ WS_POPUP ¦ WS_CAPTION ¦ WS_SYSMENU
FONT 8, "MS Sans Serif"
BEGIN
        ICON            IDR_MAINFRAME,IDC_STATIC,11,17,20,20
        LTEXT           "APPWIZ4 Application Version 1.0",
                        IDC_STATIC,40,10,119,8
        LTEXT           "Copyright \251 1993",IDC_STATIC,40,25,119,8
        DEFPUSHBUTTON   "OK",IDOK,176,6,32,14,WS_GROUP
END
/////////////////////////////////////////////////////////////////////////
//
// String Table
//
STRINGTABLE PRELOAD DISCARDABLE
BEGIN
```

```
        IDR_MAINFRAME                "APPWIZ4 Windows Application"
        IDR_APPWIZTYPE               "\nAppwiz\nAPPWIZ Document"
END
STRINGTABLE PRELOAD DISCARDABLE
BEGIN
        AFX_IDS_APP_TITLE            "APPWIZ4 Windows Application"
        AFX_IDS_IDLEMESSAGE          "Ready"
END
STRINGTABLE DISCARDABLE
BEGIN
        ID_INDICATOR_EXT             "EXT"
        ID_INDICATOR_CAPS            "CAP"
        ID_INDICATOR_NUM             "NUM"
        ID_INDICATOR_SCRL            "SCRL"
        ID_INDICATOR_OVR             "OVR"
        ID_INDICATOR_REC             "REC"
END
STRINGTABLE DISCARDABLE
BEGIN
        ID_FILE_NEW                  "Create a new document"
        ID_FILE_OPEN                 "Open an existing document"
        ID_FILE_CLOSE                "Close the active document"
        ID_FILE_SAVE                 "Save the active document"
        ID_FILE_SAVE_AS              "Save the active document with a new name"
        ID_APP_ABOUT                 "Display program information, version number
➥and copyright"
        ID_APP_EXIT                  "Quit the application; prompts to save documents"
        ID_FILE_MRU_FILE1            "Open this document"
        ID_FILE_MRU_FILE2            "Open this document"
        ID_FILE_MRU_FILE3            "Open this document"
        ID_FILE_MRU_FILE4            "Open this document"
        ID_NEXT_PANE                 "Switch to the next window pane"
        ID_PREV_PANE                 "Switch back to the previous window pane"
        ID_WINDOW_NEW                "Open another window for the active document"
        ID_WINDOW_ARRANGE            "Arrange icons at the bottom of the window"
        ID_WINDOW_CASCADE            "Arrange windows so they overlap"
        ID_WINDOW_TILE_HORZ          "Arrange windows as non-overlapping tiles"
        ID_WINDOW_TILE_VERT          "Arrange windows as non-overlapping tiles"
        ID_WINDOW_SPLIT              "Split the active window into panes"
        ID_EDIT_CLEAR                "Erase the selection"
        ID_EDIT_CLEAR_ALL            "Erase everything"
        ID_EDIT_COPY                 "Copy the selection and put it on the Clipboard"
        ID_EDIT_CUT                  "Cut the selection and put it on the Clipboard"
        ID_EDIT_FIND                 "Find the specified text"
        ID_EDIT_PASTE                "Insert Clipboard contents"
        ID_EDIT_REPEAT               "Repeat the last action"
        ID_EDIT_REPLACE              "Replace specific text with different text"
        ID_EDIT_SELECT_ALL           "Select the entire document"
        ID_EDIT_UNDO                 "Undo the last action"
        ID_EDIT_REDO                 "Redo the previously undone action"
END
STRINGTABLE DISCARDABLE
BEGIN
        AFX_IDS_SCSIZE               "Change the window size"
        AFX_IDS_SCMOVE               "Change the window position"
        AFX_IDS_SCMINIMIZE           "Reduce the window to an icon"
```

I

Introduction to Visual C++

(continues)

Listing 3.26 Continued

```
        AFX_IDS_SCMAXIMIZE      "Enlarge the window to full size"
        AFX_IDS_SCNEXTWINDOW    "Switch to the next document window"
        AFX_IDS_SCPREVWINDOW    "Switch to the previous document window"
        AFX_IDS_SCCLOSE         "Close the active window and prompts to save
➥the documents"
        AFX_IDS_SCRESTORE       "Restore the window to normal size"
        AFX_IDS_SCTASKLIST      "Activate Task List"
        AFX_IDS_MDICHILD        "Activate this window"
END
#ifndef APSTUDIO_INVOKED
///////////////////////////////////////////////////////////////////////////
//
// From TEXTINCLUDE 3
//
#include "res\appwiz4.rc2"  // non-App Studio edited resources
#include "afxres.rc"  // Standard components
///////////////////////////////////////////////////////////////////////////
#endif      // not APSTUDIO_INVOKED
```

The APPWIZ4.CPP File

The file APPWIZ4.CPP, shown in Listing 3.27, contains the implementation of the application class CAppWiz4App. The highlight of the listing is the definition of the member function InitInstance, which performs the following tasks:

- Sets the background color of the dialog boxes to gray.

- Loads the commands from the standard .INI file.

- Registers the document, MDI child frame, and view classes in the application's document template.

- Creates the main MDI frame window. The function exits, returning a FALSE value, if this task fails.

- Makes the main MDI frame window visible.

- Updates the main MDI frame window.

- Assigns the pointer to the main MDI frame window to the data member m_pMainWnd.

- Creates a new and empty document.

- Offers minimal code to process command-line arguments.

The other statements in APPWIZ4.CPP are very similar to those in the
APPWIZ1.CPP file, found in Listing 3.10.

Listing 3.27 Source Code for the APPWIZ4.CPP Implementation File

```
// appwiz4.cpp : Defines the class behaviors for the application.
//
#include "stdafx.h"
#include "appwiz4.h"
#include "mainfrm.h"
#include "appwidoc.h"
#include "appwivw.h"
#ifdef _DEBUG
#undef THIS_FILE
static char BASED_CODE THIS_FILE[] = __FILE__;
#endif
/////////////////////////////////////////////////////////////////
// CAppwiz4App
BEGIN_MESSAGE_MAP(CAppwiz4App, CWinApp)
    //{{AFX_MSG_MAP(CAppwiz4App)
    ON_COMMAND(ID_APP_ABOUT, OnAppAbout)
// NOTE - the ClassWizard will add and remove mapping macros here.
//    DO NOT EDIT what you see in these blocks of generated code !
    //}}AFX_MSG_MAP
    // Standard file based document commands
    ON_COMMAND(ID_FILE_NEW, CWinApp::OnFileNew)
    ON_COMMAND(ID_FILE_OPEN, CWinApp::OnFileOpen)
END_MESSAGE_MAP()
/////////////////////////////////////////////////////////////////
// CAppwiz4App construction
CAppwiz4App::CAppwiz4App()
{
    // TODO: add construction code here,
    // Place all significant initialization in InitInstance
}
/////////////////////////////////////////////////////////////////
// The one and only CAppwiz4App object
CAppwiz4App NEAR theApp;
/////////////////////////////////////////////////////////////////
// CAppwiz4App initialization
BOOL CAppwiz4App::InitInstance()
{
    // Standard initialization
    // If you are not using these features and wish to reduce the size
    //  of your final executable, you should remove from the following
    //  the specific initialization routines you do not need.
    SetDialogBkColor();        // set dialog background color to gray
    LoadStdProfileSettings();  // Load standard INI file options
                               // (including MRU)
// Register the application's document templates.  Document templates
//  serve as the connection between documents, frame windows and views.
    AddDocTemplate(new CMultiDocTemplate(IDR_APPWIZTYPE,
            RUNTIME_CLASS(CAppwiz4Doc),
```

(continues)

Listing 3.27 Continued

```
                    // standard MDI child frame
                    RUNTIME_CLASS(CMDIChildWnd),
                    RUNTIME_CLASS(CAppwiz4View)));
    // create main MDI Frame window
    CMainFrame* pMainFrame = new CMainFrame;
    if (!pMainFrame->LoadFrame(IDR_MAINFRAME))
        return FALSE;
    pMainFrame->ShowWindow(m_nCmdShow);
    pMainFrame->UpdateWindow();
    m_pMainWnd = pMainFrame;
    // create a new (empty) document
    OnFileNew();
    if (m_lpCmdLine[0] != '\0')
    {
        // TODO: add command line processing here
    }
    return TRUE;
}
/////////////////////////////////////////////////////////////////////
// CAboutDlg dialog used for App About
class CAboutDlg : public CDialog
{
public:
    CAboutDlg();
// Dialog Data
    //{{AFX_DATA(CAboutDlg)
    enum { IDD = IDD_ABOUTBOX };
    //}}AFX_DATA
// Implementation
protected:
    virtual void DoDataExchange(CDataExchange* pDX);
    // DDX/DDV support
    //{{AFX_MSG(CAboutDlg)
        // No message handlers
    //}}AFX_MSG
    DECLARE_MESSAGE_MAP()
};
CAboutDlg::CAboutDlg() : CDialog(CAboutDlg::IDD)
{
    //{{AFX_DATA_INIT(CAboutDlg)
    //}}AFX_DATA_INIT
}
void CAboutDlg::DoDataExchange(CDataExchange* pDX)
{
    CDialog::DoDataExchange(pDX);
    //{{AFX_DATA_MAP(CAboutDlg)
    //}}AFX_DATA_MAP
}
BEGIN_MESSAGE_MAP(CAboutDlg, CDialog)
    //{{AFX_MSG_MAP(CAboutDlg)
        // No message handlers
    //}}AFX_MSG_MAP
END_MESSAGE_MAP()
// App command to run the dialog
void CAppwiz4App::OnAppAbout()
```

```
{
    CAboutDlg aboutDlg;
    aboutDlg.DoModal();
}
///////////////////////////////////////////////////////////////////
// CAppwiz4App commands
```

Combining the Features

Let's use AppWizard to create an MFC Windows program that combines the features described in the previous three sections. Perform the following steps:

1. Choose the AppWizard command from the Project menu. Type **appwiz5** as the name of the project and select the directory \MSVC\USEVC as the parent for the new project.

2. Click the Options... button. By default, the dialog box marks the first three check boxes and the last check box. To generate this particular program, leave these controls marked. Figure 3.18 shows the Options dialog box at this stage.

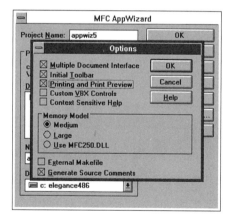

Figure 3.18
The Options dialog box as the APPWIZ5 project is being created.

3. Click the OK button in the Options dialog box. Now you're back to the MFC AppWizard dialog box.

4. Click the OK button to view a summary of the classes and features. The click action causes the New Application Information dialog box to pop up, as shown in Figure 3.19. This dialog box states the classes and the features of the project you are about to create.

Figure 3.19

The New Application Information dialog box as the APPWIZ5 project is being created.

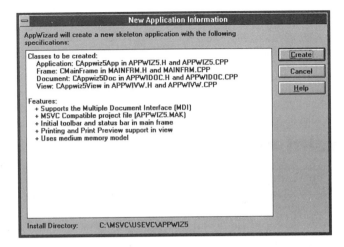

5. Click the Create button to generate the source code files for the APPWIZ5 project. The Visual Workbench displays message dialog boxes that report the progress as the files are created.

Running the APPWIZ5.EXE Program

Build and run the APPWIZ5.EXE program, which contains the toolbar, the status bar, support for printing-related features, and also manages MDI child windows. Figure 3.20 shows a sample session with the APPWIZ5.EXE program. This program combines all the features that have been discussed individually in this chapter. As an exercise, I leave it to you to study the source code listings for the APPWIZ5 project.

Figure 3.20

A sample session with the APPWIZ5.EXE program.

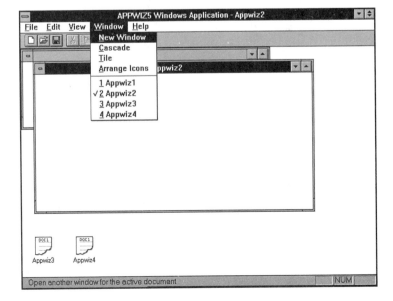

Summary

This chapter showed you how to use the AppWizard tool to generate various kinds of minimal or partially functioning MFC programs. You learned about the following topics:

- How to work with AppWizard to create a minimal Windows program that uses classes in the MFC library. The menu system for this program includes the Exit command as the only fully functioning command.

- How to create a minimal MFC Windows program with a toolbar and a status bar. This program supports the bitmapped toolbar that appears under the menu. Moreover, it displays the status bar at the bottom of the window.

- How to generate a minimal MFC Windows program with print and print preview features. This program offers print preview (of a blank page), prints a blank page, and enables you to set up your printer.

- How to build a minimal MFC Windows program that supports MDI windows. This program supports the creation and management of MDI child windows. You can minimize, maximize, and arrange the MDI child windows.

- How to generate a minimal MFC Windows program that combines the preceding four features.

Besides these topics, this chapter also presented the source code listings for the minimal MFC Windows program created by AppWizard. In addition, the listings were provided for the other minimal programs that were variations of that first program.

Chapter 4

Using the ClassWizard Utility

The last chapter presented the AppWizard utility, which gives you the
capability to quickly create Windows applications that use the document
and view classes. This chapter looks at the ClassWizard utility, which complements the AppWizard. The ClassWizard utility, as the name might suggest,
lets you customize, edit, and even expand the classes generated by the
AppWizard utility. This chapter provides a hands-on approach to using the
ClassWizard, and you learn about the following topics:

- How to invoke the ClassWizard utility

- The Message Maps options

- The Member Variables options

- The Class Info options

- How to add member functions to a view

- How to use the document and view architecture

How to Invoke the ClassWizard Utility

You can invoke the ClassWizard utility from the Visual Workshop by pulling
down the Browse menu and then choosing the ClassWizard command (the
shortcut key combination for the ClassWizard command is Ctrl+W). The
Visual Workshop displays the MFC Class Wizard dialog box. The dialog box

has a visual interface that resembles a file folder (this new Microsoft dialog box interface is now being used in various Microsoft products). The ClassWizard file folder interface offers the following tabs:

■ *Message Maps*. Manages the binding of messages to member functions

■ *Member Variables*. Enables you to add data members to swap information with controls.

■ *OLE Automation*. Offers features to support OLE 2.0.

■ *Class Info*. Enables you to create new classes that support dialog boxes and form views.

The Message Maps Options

By default, the MFC Class Wizard dialog box selects the Message Maps options. These options enable you to add a member function to handle a message, delete a member function, and edit a member function. The Message Maps options display the following controls (see Figure 4.1):

■ *Class Name combo box*. Lets you select a class in the current project.

■ *Objects IDs list box*. Lists the name of the currently selected class, as well as the IDs of the menu options—in other words, all the objects that can receive messages.

■ *Messages list box*. Lists the available messages for the item currently selected in the Objects IDs list box. The list box shows a hand icon to the left of a message that has an associated member function.

■ *Member Functions list box*. Lists the current set of member functions for the item currently selected in the Class Name combo box.

■ *Description text*. Explains the task of the item currently selected in the Messages list box.

■ *Add Class... pushbutton*. Enables you to add a new class to the project.

- *Add Function pushbutton.* Adds a new message handling member function to the Member Functions list box. This new member function corresponds to the message currently selected in the Messages list box.

- *Delete Function pushbutton.* Deletes the item currently selected in the Member Functions list box.

- *Edit Code pushbutton.* Edits the item currently selected in the Member Functions list box. This control causes the Visual Workbench to close the MFC Class Wizard dialog box and to open the source code window containing the targeted member function. In addition, the Visual Workbench highlights the name of that member function.

- *OK, Cancel, and Help pushbuttons.*

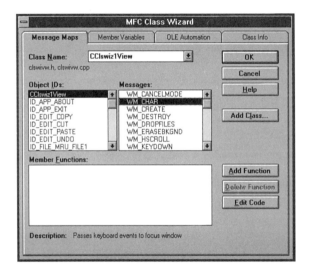

Figure 4.1

A sample session with the MFC Class Wizard dialog box showing the options on the Message Maps tab.

The Member Variables Options

The Members Variables Options, shown in Figure 4.2, let you add data members that parallel the controls of dialog boxes and form views. The program uses these data members to swap information with the controls of the dialog boxes or form views.

Figure 4.2
The MFC Class
Wizard dialog
box showing the
Member Variables
options.

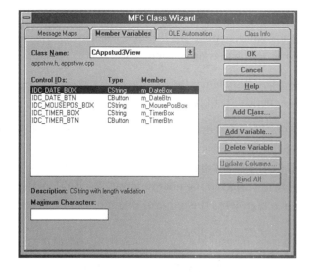

The Class Info Options

The Class Info options, shown in Figure 4.3, enable you to view information about a class in the current project and also permit you to create a new class. The dialog box lets you select the parent of the new class. The new class typically supports a dialog box or form view resource created using the App Studio utility.

In Chapter 5, you learn how ClassWizard works with App Studio to add the resources and code for a new class.

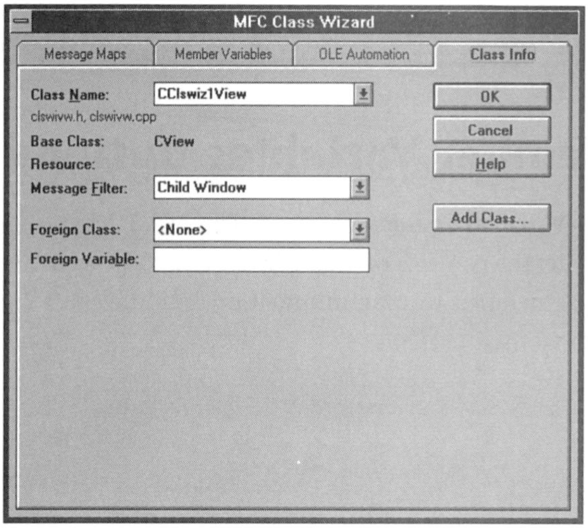

Figure 4.3
The MFC Class
Wizard dialog box
showing the Class
Info options.

How to Add Member Functions to the View Class

Let's look at a simple example that uses the ClassWizard utility to add member functions to the view class of an application generated by AppWizard.

Using the AppWizard Utility

The first step is to create the application's files using the AppWizard utility as follows:

1. Invoke the AppWizard utility by choosing the AppWizard command from the Project menu.

2. Type **clswiz1** as the name of the project that should be created in a directory attached to the directory \MSVC.

3. Click the Options... button to view the Options dialog box.

4. Clear the check boxes for the Multiple Document Interface, Initial Toolbar, and Printing and Print Preview features. Click the OK button in the Options dialog box.

5. Click the OK button of the MFC AppWizard dialog box.

6. Click the Create button of the New Application Information dialog box.

These steps lead to the creation of a minimal MFC-based Windows viewer application. The files for this project are very similar to those of the APPWIZ1 project, which I presented in the last chapter. Because these files are so similar, I can forgo presenting and discussing the various files generated by AppWizard. However, Listings 4.1 and 4.2 do provide the header and implementation files, respectively, for the view class, CClswiz1View.

Listing 4.1 Source Code for the Header File CLSWIVW.H as Generated by AppWizard

```
// clswivw.h : interface of the CClswiz1View class
//
/////////////////////////////////////////////////////////////////////

class CClswiz1View : public CView
{
protected: // create from serialization only
    CClswiz1View();
    DECLARE_DYNCREATE(CClswiz1View)
```

(continues)

Listing 4.1 Continued

```
// Attributes
public:
    CClswiz1Doc* GetDocument();

// Operations
public:

// Implementation
public:
    virtual ~CClswiz1View();
    virtual void OnDraw(CDC* pDC);  // overridden to draw this view
#ifdef _DEBUG
    virtual void AssertValid() const;
    virtual void Dump(CDumpContext& dc) const;
#endif

protected:

// Generated message map functions
protected:
    //{{AFX_MSG(CClswiz1View)
        // NOTE - the ClassWizard will add and remove member functions here.
        //    DO NOT EDIT what you see in these blocks of generated code !
    //}}AFX_MSG
        DECLARE_MESSAGE_MAP()
    };

    #ifndef _DEBUG  // debug version in clswivw.cpp
    inline CClswiz1Doc* CClswiz1View::GetDocument()
      { return (CClswiz1Doc*)m_pDocument; }
    #endif

    ////////////////////////////////////////////////////////////////////////
```

The header file CLSWIVW.H contains the declaration of the view class
CClswiz1View. The listing declares this class as a descendant of class CView and
includes a protected constructor, a public destructor, the public member
function GetDocument, the member function OnDraw, and the debug-related
functions Assert and Dump. The listing declares the message map and contains
a comment-based placeholder that can include any added message-handling
member functions. The listings contain an inline implementation of function
GetDocument, enclosed in an #ifndef compiler directive.

Listing 4.2 Source Code for the Implementation File CLSWIVW.CPP as Generated by AppWizard

```cpp
// clswivw.cpp : implementation of the CClswiz1View class
//

#include "stdafx.h"
#include "clswiz1.h"

#include "clswidoc.h"
#include "clswivw.h"

#ifdef _DEBUG
#undef THIS_FILE
static char BASED_CODE THIS_FILE[] = __FILE__;
#endif

/////////////////////////////////////////////////////////////////////
// CClswiz1View

IMPLEMENT_DYNCREATE(CClswiz1View, CView)

BEGIN_MESSAGE_MAP(CClswiz1View, CView)
    //{{AFX_MSG_MAP(CClswiz1View)
    // NOTE - the ClassWizard will add and remove mapping macros here.
    //    DO NOT EDIT what you see in these blocks of generated code!
    //}}AFX_MSG_MAP
END_MESSAGE_MAP()

/////////////////////////////////////////////////////////////////////
// CClswiz1View construction/destruction

CClswiz1View::CClswiz1View()
{
    // TODO: add construction code here
}

CClswiz1View::~CClswiz1View()
{
}

/////////////////////////////////////////////////////////////////////
// CClswiz1View drawing

void CClswiz1View::OnDraw(CDC* pDC)
{
    CClswiz1Doc* pDoc = GetDocument();
    ASSERT_VALID(pDoc);

    // TODO: add draw code for native data here
}

/////////////////////////////////////////////////////////////////////
// CClswiz1View diagnostics
```

(continues)

Listing 4.2 Continued

```
#ifdef _DEBUG
void CClswiz1View::AssertValid() const
{
    CView::AssertValid();
}

void CClswiz1View::Dump(CDumpContext& dc) const
{
    CView::Dump(dc);
}

CClswiz1Doc* CClswiz1View::GetDocument() // non-debug version is inline
{
    ASSERT(m_pDocument->IsKindOf(RUNTIME_CLASS(CClswiz1Doc)));
    return (CClswiz1Doc*)m_pDocument;
}
#endif //_DEBUG

/////////////////////////////////////////////////////////////////////////
// CClswiz1View message handlers
```

The file CLSWIVW.CPP offers the implementation of the view class
CClsWiz1View. The listing shows a message map with no map entries—only a
comment-based placeholder for possible map entries. The class offers dummy
implementations for the constructor and destructor—neither member has
any statements and neither member calls the corresponding member of the
parent class. The listing offers a minimal implementation for the member
function OnDraw. The function declares the instance pDoc as a pointer to the
application's document. The listing also offers the implementation for the
member functions AssertValid and Dump. Each of these functions invokes the
version of that function declared in the parent class.

Adding the Member Functions

Let's add four member functions to handle the following features supported
by the view class:

■ The view window tracks the current mouse location and displays the
mouse coordinates in the top-left corner of the view. This feature requires handling the Windows message WM_MOUSEMOVE using the member
function OnMouseMove.

■ The view window responds to the left mouse button being clicked by starting and stopping a simple timer. The first time you click the left mouse button, the view displays a message dialog box informing you that you started the timer. The second time you click the left mouse button, the view displays a message dialog box showing the number of seconds that have elapsed since you triggered the timer. The second mouse click also resets the timer—in other words, the timer is not progressive. The timer feature requires handling the Windows message WM_LBUTTONDOWN using the member function OnLButtonDown.

■ The view window responds to the right mouse button being clicked by displaying the current system date and time in a message dialog box. This feature requires handling the Windows message WM_RBUTTONDOWN using the member function OnRButtonDown.

■ The view window reads the characters you type from the keyboard and displays them. When you reach a predefined limit, the view displays any additional characters you type at the beginning of the same line. This feature requires handling the Windows message WM_CHAR using the member function OnChar.

Invoke the ClassWizard utility and select the class CClswiz1View from the Class Name combo box. Now select the ID CClswiz1View from the Object IDs list box. This action displays the set of possible messages that can be handled by the view class. Select the message WM_MOUSEMOVE from the Messages list box and then click the Add Function button. This action causes the name OnMouseMove to be displayed in the Member Functions list box. Repeat the message selection and function addition steps for the messages WM_LBUTTONDOWN, WM_RBUTTONDOWN, and WM_CHAR. Figure 4.4 shows the MFC ClassWizard dialog box after the four targeted member functions have been added. Click the OK button to close the MFC Class Wizard dialog box; then inspect the changes made to the files CLSWIVW.H and CLSWIVW.CPP. Listing 4.3 shows the source code for the header file CLSWIVW.H after it was modified by the ClassWizard utility.

Figure 4.4

The MFC
ClassWizard dialog
box after the four
targeted member
functions were
added.

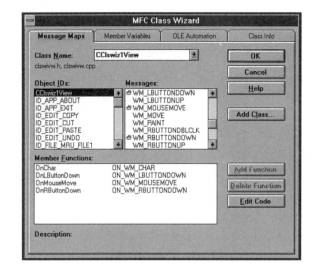

Listing 4.3 Source Code for the Header File CLSWIVW.H after Modification by ClassWizard

```
// clswivw.h : interface of the CClswiz1View class
//
/////////////////////////////////////////////////////////////////
class CClswiz1View : public CView
{
protected: // create from serialization only
    CClswiz1View();
    DECLARE_DYNCREATE(CClswiz1View)

// Attributes
public:
    CClswiz1Doc* GetDocument();

// Operations
public:

// Implementation
public:
    virtual ~CClswiz1View();
    virtual void OnDraw(CDC* pDC);  // overridden to draw this view
#ifdef _DEBUG
    virtual void AssertValid() const;
    virtual void Dump(CDumpContext& dc) const;
#endif

protected:

// Generated message map functions
protected:
    //{{AFX_MSG(CClswiz1View)
    afx_msg void OnChar(UINT nChar, UINT nRepCnt, UINT nFlags);
```

```
        afx_msg void OnLButtonDown(UINT nFlags, CPoint point);
        afx_msg void OnMouseMove(UINT nFlags, CPoint point);
        afx_msg void OnRButtonDown(UINT nFlags, CPoint point);
    //}}AFX_MSG
    DECLARE_MESSAGE_MAP()
};

#ifndef _DEBUG  // debug version in clswivw.cpp
inline CClswiz1Doc* CClswiz1View::GetDocument()
    { return (CClswiz1Doc*)m_pDocument; }
#endif

/////////////////////////////////////////////////////////////////////
```

The ClassWizard has inserted the protected member functions OnChar,
OnLButtonDown, OnMouseMove, and OnRButtonDown in the CLSWIVW.H header
file. These member functions handle the messages you selected in the MFC
ClassWizard dialog box.

Listing 4.4 shows the source code for the implementation file CLSWIVW.CPP
after it was modified by the ClassWizard utility. Examine Listing 4.4, and
then review my comments that follow the listing.

Listing 4.4 Source Code for the Implementation File CLSWIVW.CPP after Modification by ClassWizard

```
// clswivw.cpp : implementation of the CClswiz1View class
//

#include "stdafx.h"
#include "clswiz1.h"

#include "clswidoc.h"
#include "clswivw.h"

#ifdef _DEBUG
#undef THIS_FILE
static char BASED_CODE THIS_FILE[] = __FILE__;
#endif

/////////////////////////////////////////////////////////////////////
// CClswiz1View

IMPLEMENT_DYNCREATE(CClswiz1View, CView)

BEGIN_MESSAGE_MAP(CClswiz1View, CView)
    //{{AFX_MSG_MAP(CClswiz1View)
    ON_WM_CHAR()
    ON_WM_LBUTTONDOWN()
    ON_WM_MOUSEMOVE()
```

(continues)

Listing 4.4 Continued

```
        ON_WM_RBUTTONDOWN()
    //}}AFX_MSG_MAP
END_MESSAGE_MAP()

/////////////////////////////////////////////////////////////////

// CClswiz1View construction/destruction

CClswiz1View::CClswiz1View()
{
    // TODO: add construction code here
}

CClswiz1View::~CClswiz1View()
{
}

/////////////////////////////////////////////////////////////////
// CClswiz1View drawing

void CClswiz1View::OnDraw(CDC* pDC)
{
    CClswiz1Doc* pDoc = GetDocument();
    ASSERT_VALID(pDoc);

    // TODO: add draw code for native data here
}

/////////////////////////////////////////////////////////////////
// CClswiz1View diagnostics

#ifdef _DEBUG
void CClswiz1View::AssertValid() const
{
    CView::AssertValid();
}

void CClswiz1View::Dump(CDumpContext& dc) const
{
    CView::Dump(dc);
}

CClswiz1Doc* CClswiz1View::GetDocument() // non-debug version is inline
{
    ASSERT(m_pDocument->IsKindOf(RUNTIME_CLASS(CClswiz1Doc)));
    return (CClswiz1Doc*)m_pDocument;
}
#endif //_DEBUG

/////////////////////////////////////////////////////////////////
// CClswiz1View message handlers
```

```
void CClswiz1View::OnChar(UINT nChar, UINT nRepCnt, UINT nFlags)
{
    // TODO: Add your message handler code here and/or call default

    CView::OnChar(nChar, nRepCnt, nFlags);
}

void CClswiz1View::OnLButtonDown(UINT nFlags, CPoint point)
{
    // TODO: Add your message handler code here and/or call default

    CView::OnLButtonDown(nFlags, point);
}

void CClswiz1View::OnMouseMove(UINT nFlags, CPoint point)
{
    // TODO: Add your message handler code here and/or call default

    CView::OnMouseMove(nFlags, point);
}

void CClswiz1View::OnRButtonDown(UINT nFlags, CPoint point)
{
    // TODO: Add your message handler code here and/or call default

    CView::OnRButtonDown(nFlags, point);
}
```

The ClassWizard has added the entries ON_WM_CHAR(), ON_WM_LBUTTONDOWN(),
ON_WM_MOUSEMOVE(), and ON_WM_RBUTTONDOWN() to the message map macros.
These entries permit the added member functions to handle the targeted Windows messages sent to the view window. In addition, the ClassWizard utility has added the *minimal* definitions of the new member functions. Each member function offers a default response by invoking the corresponding member function of the parent class. For example, the member function OnChar responds by simply invoking the function CView::OnChar.

Customizing the Code

The last stage of developing the program is to customize the code of the member functions OnChar, OnMouseMove, OnLButtonDown, and OnRButtonDown. You can edit the code directly either by accessing the source code window for the CLSWIVW.CPP file or by using the Edit Code button in the MFC Class Wizard. I used the first method because I also wanted to add #include statements and global constants. Listing 4.5 shows the source code for the implementation file CLSWIVW.CPP after customizing the code for the added member functions. Study the listing, and then read my comments that follow the listing.

**Listing 4.5 Source Code for the Implementation File
CLSWIVW.CPP with the Code for the Added
Member Functions Incorporated**

```cpp
// clswivw.cpp : implementation of the CClswiz1View class
//

#include "stdafx.h"
#include "clswiz1.h"

#include "clswidoc.h"
#include "clswivw.h"

// include additional header files needed to customize the program
#include <stdio.h>
#include <string.h>

#ifdef _DEBUG
#undef THIS_FILE
static char BASED_CODE THIS_FILE[] = __FILE__;
#endif

// define new constants
const MaxStringLen = 40;
const X0 = 10;
const Y0 = 10;
const Y1 = 30;

/////////////////////////////////////////////////////////////////
// CClswiz1View

IMPLEMENT_DYNCREATE(CClswiz1View, CView)

BEGIN_MESSAGE_MAP(CClswiz1View, CView)
    //{{AFX_MSG_MAP(CClswiz1View)
    ON_WM_CHAR()
    ON_WM_LBUTTONDOWN()
    ON_WM_RBUTTONDOWN()
    ON_WM_MOUSEMOVE()
    //}}AFX_MSG_MAP
END_MESSAGE_MAP()

/////////////////////////////////////////////////////////////////
// CClswiz1View construction/destruction

CClswiz1View::CClswiz1View()
{
    // TODO: add construction code here
}

CClswiz1View::~CClswiz1View()
{
}
```

```
/////////////////////////////////////////////////////////////////
// CClswiz1View drawing

void CClswiz1View::OnDraw(CDC* pDC)
{
    CClswiz1Doc* pDoc = GetDocument();

    // TODO: add draw code here
}


/////////////////////////////////////////////////////////////////
// CClswiz1View diagnostics

#ifdef _DEBUG
void CClswiz1View::AssertValid() const
{
    CView::AssertValid();
}

void CClswiz1View::Dump(CDumpContext& dc) const
{
    CView::Dump(dc);
}

CClswiz1Doc* CClswiz1View::GetDocument() // non-debug version is inline
{
    ASSERT(m_pDocument->IsKindOf(RUNTIME_CLASS(CClswiz1Doc)));
    return (CClswiz1Doc*) m_pDocument;
}

#endif //_DEBUG

/////////////////////////////////////////////////////////////////
// CClswiz1View message handlers
```

```
void CClswiz1View::OnChar(UINT nChar, UINT nRepCnt, UINT nFlags)
{
  static char szStr[MaxStringLen+1] = "";
  static int i = 0;
  static BOOL bNew = TRUE;
  CClientDC dc(this);

  if (i < MaxStringLen) {
    szStr[i++] = char(nChar);
    if (bNew) // append null terminator when typing a new string
      szStr[i] = '\0';
  }
  else { // reached the end
    i = 0;
    bNew = FALSE;
    szStr[i++] = char(nChar);
  }
  dc.TextOut(X0, Y1, szStr, strlen(szStr));
}
```

(continues)

Listing 4.5 Continued

```
void CClswiz1View::OnLButtonDown(UINT nFlags, CPoint point)
{
  static bTimerOn = FALSE;
  static long nInitTickCount;
  char szStr[MaxStringLen+1];

  if (bTimerOn) {
    bTimerOn = FALSE;
    sprintf(szStr, "%3.3lf seconds elapsed",
            (GetTickCount() - nInitTickCount) / 1000.0);
    MessageBox(szStr, "Timer Event",
              MB_OK | MB_ICONINFORMATION);
  }
  else {
    bTimerOn = TRUE;
    nInitTickCount = GetTickCount();
    MessageBox("Timer is now On!", "Timer Event",
              MB_OK | MB_ICONEXCLAMATION);
  }
}

void CClswiz1View::OnRButtonDown(UINT nFlags, CPoint point)
{
  char szStr[MaxStringLen+1];
  CTime tm = CTime::GetCurrentTime();

  sprintf(szStr, "Date is %02d/%02d/%4d, Time is %02d:%02d:%02d",
                  tm.GetMonth(), tm.GetDay(), tm.GetYear(),
                  tm.GetHour(), tm.GetMinute(), tm.GetSecond());
  MessageBox(szStr, "Current Date/Time",
            MB_OK | MB_ICONINFORMATION);
}


void CClswiz1View::OnMouseMove(UINT nFlags, CPoint point)
{
  char szStr[MaxStringLen+1];
  CClientDC dc(this);

  sprintf(szStr, "[%03d, %03d]", point.x, point.y);
  dc.TextOut(X0, Y0, szStr, strlen(szStr));
}
```

I manually added the following statements to the implementation file:

- The `#include <stdio.h>` statement so that I could use the function `sprintf`.

- The `#include <string.h>` statement so that I could use the string function `strlen`.

■ The global constant MaxStringLen, which specifies the maximum size of a string (excluding the null terminator).

■ The global constants X0, Y0, and Y1, which specify the coordinates for the mouse location and for the viewed string.

I customized the member function OnChar to intercept the characters you type and to display them in the view window. The function performs the following tasks:

■ Declares a set of static local variables. These variables include the string szStr, the integer variable i, and the Boolean variable bNew.

■ Declares the device context object dc as an instance of CClientDC.

■ Determines whether the value in the static variable i is less than that of the global constant MaxStringLen. If this condition is true, the function performs the following subtasks:

- Assigns the input character to the element i of the static string variable szStr, and then increments the variable i.

- If the static variable bNew is nonzero, assigns the null terminator character to the element i of the variable szStr. This task stores a null terminator in the next character before the output starts to wrap.

The else clause of the if statement performs the following subtasks:

- Assigns 0 to the static variable i. This assignment helps the view window display additional keyboard input at the beginning of the same line.

- Assigns FALSE to the static variable bNew. This flag helps the program determine when further keyboard input should appear at the start of the line.

- Assigns the input character to the element i of the static string variable szStr and then increments the variable i.

- Displays the contents of the variable szStr by sending the C++ message TextOut to the object dc. The arguments for this message specify the coordinates (X0, Y1), the string szStr, and the number of characters strlen(szStr).

I customized the member function OnLButtonDown to toggle an internal timer.
The function performs the following tasks:

■ Declares a set of static local variables. These variables include the Boolean variable bTimerOn (which is initialized to FALSE because the timer
initially is off) and the long integer nInitTickCount.

■ Declares the local string variable szStr.

■ If the variable bTimerOn stores TRUE, the function performs the following subtasks:

• Assigns FALSE to the variable bTimerOn.

• Creates a formatted string image that contains the number of
elapsed seconds. The function calculates this number by taking
the difference between the value of the function GetTickCount (a
Windows API function which returns the number of milliseconds
that Windows has been running) and the static variable
nInitTickCount, and then dividing the number by 1,000.

• Displays the formatted string in a message dialog box.

The else clause of the if statement performs the following subtasks:

• Assigns TRUE to the static variable bTimerOn.

• Assigns the result of the function GetTickCount to the static variable nInitTickCount.

• Displays a message dialog box telling you that the timer is
now on.

I customized the member function OnRButtonDown to display the current
system date and time in a message dialog box. The function performs the
following tasks:

■ Declares the object tm as an instance of class CTime. This declaration
also initializes the object tm with the result of the C++ message
CTime::GetCurrentTime. This message assigns the current system date
and time to the object tm.

- Creates a formatted string image for the date and time. This task sends the C++ messages `GetMonth()`, `GetDay()`, `GetYear()`, `GetHour()`, `GetMinute()`, and `GetSecond()` to the object `tm`. Each message obtains a component of the date or time.

- Displays the formatted string in a message dialog box.

I customized the member function `OnMouseMove` to display the current mouse coordinates in the upper-left corner of the view window. The function performs the following tasks:

- Declares the device context object `dc` as an instance of `CClientDC`.

- Creates a formatted string image for the mouse location. This task involves accessing the members `x` and `y` in the `CPoint`-type parameter `point`.

- Displays the formatted string in a message dialog box.

Compile and run the program. Experiment with the four custom features. Move the mouse around the view window and observe how the displayed coordinates change accordingly. Click the right mouse button to obtain the current system date and time. Then click the left mouse button a few times to start and stop the time. Finally, type characters from the keyboard and notice how the view window echoes them. Also notice that after every 40th character, the view wraps additional characters to the beginning of the same line. Figure 4.5 shows a sample session with the CLSWIZ1.EXE program.

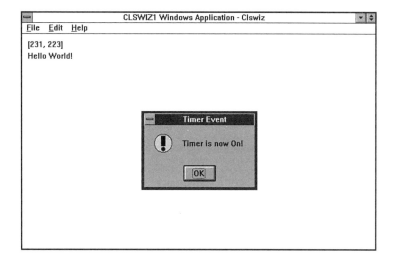

Figure 4.5
A sample session with the CLSWIZ1.EXE program showing mouse coordinates, an input string, and the timer start features.

Figure 4.6 shows the elapsed time feature in a sample session with the CLSWIZ1.EXE program.

Figure 4.6

A sample session with the CLSWIZ1.EXE program that illustrates the elapsed time feature.

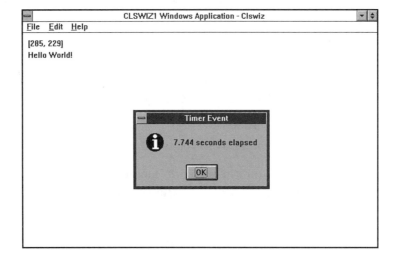

Figure 4.7 shows a sample session with the CLSWIZ1.EXE program in which the system date and time is displayed in a message dialog box.

Figure 4.7

The CLSWIZ1.EXE program showing the system date and time.

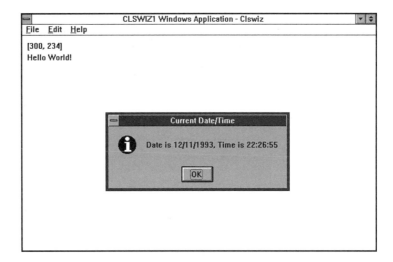

The Document and View Architecture

The CLSWIZ1 project did not take advantage of the document and view architecture. The member functions that I added to the view class relied heavily on local variables (especially static variables) to store the data for the view. This simplified approach works when the application has one view. In the case of multiple views, you have to use the document class to store the data that appears in the view.

Let's look at the CLSWIZ2 project, which is a version of the CLSWIZ1 project that uses the document and view architecture in managing data. Here are the basic ingredients for this simple example:

- The document class has public data members that store the data.

- The document class constructor initializes the public data members.

- The member functions of the view class access the document's public members using the view function GetDocument. This function returns a pointer to the document class instance and enables the various member functions in the view class to access the public data members of the document.

Use the AppWizard utility to create the files for the CLSWIZ2 project in a manner similar to that for the CLSWIZ1 project. Use the Message Map options in ClassWizard to add the four member functions OnChar, OnMouseMove, OnLButtonDown, and OnRButtonDown to the view class.

To customize the code for the CLSWIZ2 project, you have to follow these somewhat different steps:

1. Insert the declaration for the global constant MaxStringLen in the file STDAFX.H. Listing 4.6 shows the source code for the header file STDAFX.H with the customized code incorporated. Inserting the declaration in the STDAFX.H header file enables the document and view class files to use the constant MaxStringLen because these files include the STDAFX.H header file.

Listing 4.6 Customized Source Code for the Header File STDAFX.H

```
// stdafx.h : include file for standard system include files,
// or project specific include files that are used frequently,
// but are changed infrequently
//

#include <afxwin.h>         // MFC core and standard components
#include <afxext.h>         // MFC extensions (including VB)
```

```
// define project constants
const MaxStringLen = 40;
```

2. Declare the following public members in the document class CClswiz2Doc:

- The member tm, which is an instance of class CTime. This member holds the current time and displays it in a message dialog box when you click the right mouse button.

- The member szStr, which is the string that stores the characters you type. The number of characters in the string is MaxStringLen + 1.

- The member nInitTickCount, which stores the tick count value when you start the timer by clicking the left mouse button.

- The member nCharIndex, which stores the index of the member szStr (that receives the input character).

- The Boolean member bNew, which stores the new string state.

- The Boolean member bTimerOn, which stores the timer state.

Listing 4.7 shows the source code for the header file CLSWIDOC.H after the customized code has been incorporated. The header file contains the public members just listed.

Listing 4.7 Customized Source Code for the Header File CLSWIDOC.H

```
// clswidoc.h : interface of the CClswiz2Doc class
//
/////////////////////////////////////////////////////////////////////
/////

class CClswiz2Doc : public CDocument
{
protected: // create from serialization only
    CClswiz2Doc();
    DECLARE_DYNCREATE(CClswiz2Doc)

// Attributes
public:

  CTime tm;
  char szStr[MaxStringLen + 1];
  long nInitTickCount;
  int nCharIndex;
  BOOL bNew;
  BOOL bTimerOn;

// Operations
public:

// Implementation
public:
    virtual ~CClswiz2Doc();
    virtual void Serialize(CArchive& ar);    // overridden for document i/o
#ifdef _DEBUG
    virtual void AssertValid() const;
    virtual void Dump(CDumpContext& dc) const;
#endif

protected:
    virtual BOOL OnNewDocument();

// Generated message map functions
protected:
    //{{AFX_MSG(CClswiz2Doc)
    // NOTE - the ClassWizard will add and remove member functions here.
    //    DO NOT EDIT what you see in these blocks of generated code !
    //}}AFX_MSG
    DECLARE_MESSAGE_MAP()
};

/////////////////////////////////////////////////////////////////////
```

3. Initialize the public members nCharIndex, bNew, bTimerOn, and the string szStr in the constructor of class CClswiz2Doc. Listing 4.8 shows the source code for the implementation file CLSWIDOC.CPP after the code has been customized. The constructor sets the member nCharIndex to 0, the member bNew to TRUE, the member bTimerOn to FALSE, and assigns the null character to the first element of the member szStr.

Listing 4.8 Customized Source Code for the Implementation File CLSWIDOC.CPP

```cpp
// clswidoc.cpp : implementation of the CClswiz2Doc class
//

#include "stdafx.h"
#include "clswiz2.h"

#include "clswidoc.h"

#ifdef _DEBUG
#undef THIS_FILE
static char BASED_CODE THIS_FILE[] = __FILE__;
#endif

/////////////////////////////////////////////////////////////////////////
// CClswiz2Doc

IMPLEMENT_DYNCREATE(CClswiz2Doc, CDocument)

BEGIN_MESSAGE_MAP(CClswiz2Doc, CDocument)
    //{{AFX_MSG_MAP(CClswiz2Doc)
        // NOTE - the ClassWizard will add and remove mapping macros here.
        //    DO NOT EDIT what you see in these blocks of generated code!
    //}}AFX_MSG_MAP
END_MESSAGE_MAP()

/////////////////////////////////////////////////////////////////////////
// CClswiz2Doc construction/destruction

CClswiz2Doc::CClswiz2Doc()
{
    // initialize public data members
    nCharIndex = 0;
    bNew = TRUE;
    bTimerOn = FALSE;
    szStr[0] = '\0';
}

CClswiz2Doc::~CClswiz2Doc()
{
}

BOOL CClswiz2Doc::OnNewDocument()
{
```

```
    if (!CDocument::OnNewDocument())
        return FALSE;

    // TODO: add reinitialization code here
    // (SDI documents will reuse this document)

    return TRUE;
}

/////////////////////////////////////////////////////////////////////
//////////
// CClswiz2Doc serialization

void CClswiz2Doc::Serialize(CArchive& ar)
{
    if (ar.IsStoring())
    {
        // TODO: add storing code here
    }
    else
    {
        // TODO: add loading code here
    }
}

/////////////////////////////////////////////////////////////////////
//////////
// CClswiz2Doc diagnostics

#ifdef _DEBUG
void CClswiz2Doc::AssertValid() const
{
    CDocument::AssertValid();
}

void CClswiz2Doc::Dump(CDumpContext& dc) const
{
    CDocument::Dump(dc);
}
#endif //_DEBUG

/////////////////////////////////////////////////////////////////////
/////
// CClswiz2Doc commands
```

4. Customize the code for the implementation file CLSWIVW.CPP, which includes the following tasks:

   ■ Inserting the #include statements to include the header files STDIO.H and STRING.H.

■ Inserting the declaration of constants X0, Y0, and Y1.

■ Inserting the custom code for the member function
  OnLButtonDown. The statements for this version of the function
  resemble those in the CLSWIZ1 project. There are two main differences. First, the function declares the local document pointer,
  pDoc, to access the public member of the document. Second, the
  function uses the local pointer, pDoc, to access the document's
  members bTimerOn and nInitTickCount. The function still uses a
  local string variable to display the text of the message dialog box.

■ Inserting the custom code for the member function OnMouseMove.
  The statements for this version are identical to those in the
  CLSWIZ1 project.

■ Inserting the custom code for the member function
  OnRButtonDown. The statements for this version of the function
  resemble those in the CLSWIZ1 project. Again, there are two
  main differences. First, the function declares the local document
  pointer, pDoc, to access the public member of the document.
  Second, the function uses the local pointer, pDoc, to access the
  document's members tm and the member functions of class CTime,
  GetMonth, GetDay, GetYear, GetHour, GetMinute, and GetSecond. The
  function also uses a local string variable to display the text of the
  message dialog box.

■ Inserting the custom code for the member function OnChar.
  The statements for this version of the function resemble those in
  the CLSWIZ1 project. The function declares the local document
  pointer, pDoc, to access the public member of the document.
  The function uses this pointer to access the document's members
  CharIndex, bNew, and szStr.

Listing 4.9 shows the source code for the implementation file
CLSWIVW.CPP after the code has been customized for the added
member functions.

Listing 4.9 Source Code for the Implementation File CLSWIVW.CPP with Code for the Added Member Functions Incorporated

```
// clswivw.cpp : implementation of the CClswiz2View class
//

#include "stdafx.h"
#include "clswiz2.h"

#include "clswidoc.h"
#include "clswivw.h"

// include additional header files needed to customize the program
#include <stdio.h>
#include <string.h>

#ifdef _DEBUG
#undef THIS_FILE
static char BASED_CODE THIS_FILE[] = __FILE__;
#endif

// define new constants
const X0 = 10;
const Y0 = 10;
const Y1 = 30;

/////////////////////////////////////////////////////////////////////////
// CClswiz2View

IMPLEMENT_DYNCREATE(CClswiz2View, CView)

BEGIN_MESSAGE_MAP(CClswiz2View, CView)
    //{{AFX_MSG_MAP(CClswiz2View)
    ON_WM_LBUTTONDOWN()
    ON_WM_MOUSEMOVE()
    ON_WM_RBUTTONDOWN()
    ON_WM_CHAR()
    //}}AFX_MSG_MAP
END_MESSAGE_MAP()

/////////////////////////////////////////////////////////////////////////
// CClswiz2View construction/destruction

CClswiz2View::CClswiz2View()
{
    // TODO: add construction code here
}

CClswiz2View::~CClswiz2View()
{
}

/////////////////////////////////////////////////////////////////////////
// CClswiz2View drawing
```

(continues)

Listing 4.9 Continued

```
void CClswiz2View::OnDraw(CDC* pDC)
{
    CClswiz2Doc* pDoc = GetDocument();
    ASSERT_VALID(pDoc);

    // TODO: add draw code for native data here
}

///////////////////////////////////////////////////////////////////////
// CClswiz2View diagnostics

#ifdef _DEBUG
void CClswiz2View::AssertValid() const
{
    CView::AssertValid();
}

void CClswiz2View::Dump(CDumpContext& dc) const
{
    CView::Dump(dc);
}

CClswiz2Doc* CClswiz2View::GetDocument() // non-debug version is inline
{
    ASSERT(m_pDocument->IsKindOf(RUNTIME_CLASS(CClswiz2Doc)));
    return (CClswiz2Doc*)m_pDocument;
}
#endif //_DEBUG

///////////////////////////////////////////////////////////////////////
// CClswiz2View message handlers
```

```
void CClswiz2View::OnLButtonDown(UINT nFlags, CPoint point)
{
  CClswiz2Doc* pDoc = GetDocument();
  char szStr[MaxStringLen+1];

  if (pDoc->bTimerOn) {
    pDoc->bTimerOn = FALSE;
    sprintf(szStr, "%3.3lf seconds elapsed",
            (GetTickCount() - pDoc->nInitTickCount) / 1000.0);
    MessageBox(szStr, "Timer Event",
               MB_OK | MB_ICONINFORMATION);
  }
  else {
    pDoc->bTimerOn = TRUE;
    pDoc->nInitTickCount = GetTickCount();
    MessageBox("Timer is now On!", "Timer Event",
               MB_OK | MB_ICONEXCLAMATION);
  }
}
```

```
void CClswiz2View::OnMouseMove(UINT nFlags, CPoint point)
{
  char szStr[MaxStringLen+1];
  CClientDC dc(this);

  sprintf(szStr, "[%03d, %03d]", point.x, point.y);
  dc.TextOut(X0, Y0, szStr, strlen(szStr));
}

void CClswiz2View::OnRButtonDown(UINT nFlags, CPoint point)
{
  CClswiz2Doc* pDoc = GetDocument();
  char szStr[MaxStringLen+1];
  pDoc->tm = CTime::GetCurrentTime();

  sprintf(szStr, "Date is %02d/%02d/%4d, Time is %02d:%02d:%02d",
                 pDoc->tm.GetMonth(), pDoc->tm.GetDay(),
                 pDoc->tm.GetYear(),  pDoc->tm.GetHour(),
                 pDoc->tm.GetMinute(), pDoc->tm.GetSecond());
  MessageBox(szStr, "Current Date/Time",
             MB_OK | MB_ICONINFORMATION);
}

void CClswiz2View::OnChar(UINT nChar, UINT nRepCnt, UINT nFlags)
{
  CClswiz2Doc* pDoc = GetDocument();
  CClientDC dc(this);

  if (pDoc->nCharIndex < MaxStringLen) {
    pDoc->szStr[pDoc->nCharIndex++] = char(nChar);
    if (pDoc->bNew) // append null terminator when typing a new
string
      pDoc->szStr[pDoc->nCharIndex] = '\0';
  }
  else { // reached the end
    pDoc->nCharIndex = 0;
    pDoc->bNew = FALSE;
    pDoc->szStr[pDoc->nCharIndex++] = char(nChar);
  }
  dc.TextOut(X0, Y1, pDoc->szStr, strlen(pDoc->szStr));
}
```

Compile and run the program for the CLSWIZ2 project. The program operates just like that of the CLSWIZ1 project. Both programs support the same features but use different methods to organize their data.

Summary

This chapter discussed the basics of using the ClassWizard utility and using the document and view architecture. You learned about the following topics:

- How to invoke the ClassWizard utility from the Tools menu. ClassWizard displays the MFC Class Wizard dialog box, which contains Microsoft's new folder interface. This interface enables you to access the Message Maps, Member Variables, OLE Automation, and Class Info options.

- How to use the Message Maps options to select a class or a control and then select a related message to handle. The ClassWizard handles creating the declarations and (minimal) definitions for the new message handler member functions.

- How to use the Member Variables options to add new data members that can handle transferring data between the controls of a dialog box and the document, and between the controls of a form view and the document.

- How to use the Class Info options to view information related to existing classes and to add new classes.

- How to use the document and view architecture to store the relevant data in the document class and to give the view class access to that information.

- How to use the ClassWizard to add member functions to a view created by AppWizard. The example provided in this chapter shows you how to handle the Windows messages related to moving the mouse, clicking the left and right mouse buttons, and typing characters from the keyboard.

Chapter 5

Using the App Studio Utility

The App Studio is a powerful utility that supports visual programming. Using the App Studio, especially in conjunction with AppWizard and ClassWizard, you can develop Windows applications much more easily than in the traditional *manual* fashion. This chapter uses a hands-on approach to present the App Studio. You learn about the following topics:

- Invoking the App Studio utility

- Using the App Studio options

- Using App Studio to modify a menu resource of an application generated by AppWizard

- Using App Studio to add a new dialog box resource to an application generated by AppWizard

- Using App Studio to add new controls to a form view in an application generated by AppWizard

Invoking App Studio

You invoke App Studio by choosing the App Studio command from the Tools menu in the Visual Workshop. With App Studio, you can create and edit accelerator, dialog box, icon, menu, and string table resources. You can invoke App Studio either independently or to work with the resources of the current project. In the latter case, App Studio loads the current project resources and displays them in an MFC Resource Script window. Figure 5.1 shows a sample MFC Resource Script window.

Figure 5.1

A sample session with App Studio showing the MFC Script Resource window.

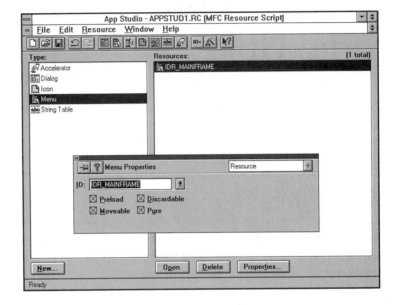

The MFC Script Resource window contains the Type pane and the Resources pane. The Type pane lists the currently available resource types. The Resources pane lists the currently available resources for the resource type that is selected. As Figure 5.1 illustrates, the MFC Resource Script window contains several command buttons across the bottom of the window: New..., Open, Delete, and Properties.... The New... button enables you to create a new resource that corresponds to the resource type currently selected, the Open button opens the resource currently selected in the Resources pane, the Delete button deletes the resource currently selected in the Resources pane, and the Properties... button displays the properties dialog box. (Figure 5.1 shows a sample properties dialog box.) The properties dialog box enables you to fine-tune the properties of a resource or a resource component.

The following sections provide examples of App Studio in use. These examples use App Studio to

■ Modify an existing menu and add accompanying accelerators.

■ Add a new dialog box resource to replace the standard message dialog box. This addition involves drawing the controls in the custom dialog box resource.

■ Draw the controls on a form view.

These examples present a hands-on approach for working with App Studio; it is not my intention, however, to cover every aspect of App Studio or to rewrite its manual.

Modifying a Menu Resource

This section presents a simple application that supports the following features:

■ The display of the current system date and time

■ The start and stop of a simple timer

■ The continuous display of the current mouse location

■ The echoing of keyboard input in the view

The application supports the first two features through both mouse clicks and menu options. Clicking the right mouse button displays the current system date and time in a message dialog box. Clicking the left mouse button toggles the start and stop of the timer. When you start the timer, the application displays a message dialog box telling you that you started the timer. When you stop the timer, the application displays a message dialog box showing the elapsed time. This action also resets the timer. The application supports these features by using menu options to display the date and time, to start the timer, and to stop the timer.

Now that I've described the application, let's generate it using AppWizard. This process has four phases. The first phase uses AppWizard to create an application by checking the boxes for these options: Multiple Document Interface, Initial Toolbar, and Printing and Print Preview. In other words, create a minimal Windows application that uses the document and view classes. The application's view is a descendant of class CView.

The second phase in creating the application involves loading the App Studio to edit the menu resource as generated by AppWizard. This menu resource requires extensive editing. Follow these steps:

1. Load App Studio and maximize the MFC Script Resource window (as shown in Figure 5.1).

2. Select the menu resource type.

3. Select the IDR_MAINFRAME menu resource and then click the Open button.

4. App Studio loads the IDR_MAINFRAME menu resource. Edit the current menu bar by deleting menus and menu commands and adding new ones until you end up with the menu resource shown in Figure 5.2. To delete a menu command, click the command and then press the Delete key. To insert a command, select the empty menu item place-holder and then either press Enter or double-click that item. App Studio responds by displaying a properties dialog box for the new item. The dialog box enables you to enter the caption and identifier for the menu item and to fine-tune its properties. Use the identifiers CM_DATE_TIME, CM_START_TIMER, and CM_STOP_TIMER for the Date/Time, Start Timer, and Stop Timer commands, respectively. In addition, insert a separator menu item after the first command.

Figure 5.2
The edited menu resource for the APPSTUD1 project.

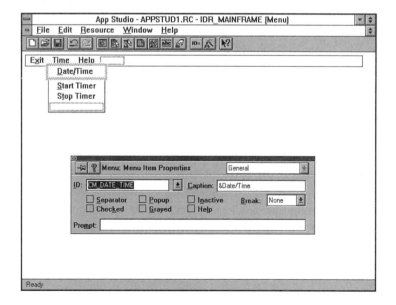

5. Save the edited resource and close it.

6. Select the accelerators resource type and then choose the IDR_MAINFRAME accelerators resource. App Studio displays the list of accelerators in the IDR_MAINFRAME accelerator resource.

7. Delete all the accelerator keys by repeatedly clicking the Delete button.

8. Insert the new accelerator Ctrl+D for the Date/Time command by clicking the New... button. App Studio displays the Accel Table: Accel Properties dialog box, which lets you specify the associated CM_*XXXX* identifier and accelerator key. Figure 5.3 shows a sample session as a new accelerator key is being added. The properties dialog box enables you to specify the accelerator key and choose among the Ctrl, Alt, or Shift keys. In addition, you can specify ASCII or virtual keys.

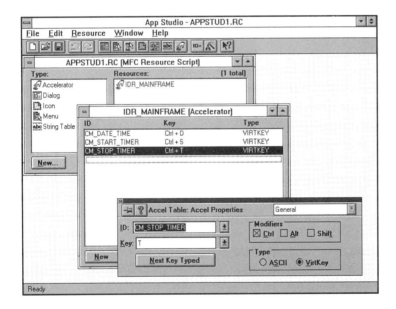

Figure 5.3
A new accelerator key being added.

9. Repeat step 9 to add the accelerator keys Ctrl+S and Ctrl+T for the menu options Start Timer and Stop Timer, respectively.

10. Save the edited menu resource by choosing the Save command from the File menu.

The third phase in crafting our application involves the ClassWizard utility. Use ClassWizard to add the following member functions in the view class:

- The member function OnLButtonDown responds to the Windows message WM_LBUTTONDOWN.

- The member function OnRButtonDown responds to the Windows message WM_RBUTTONDOWN.

- The member function OnChar responds to the Windows message WM_CHAR.

- The member function OnMouseMove responds to the Windows message WM_MOUSEMOVE.

- The member function CMGetDateTime responds to the Windows command message CM_DATETIME.

- The member function CMStartTimer responds to the Windows command message CM_START_TIMER.

- The member function CMStopTimer responds to the Windows command message CM_STOP_TIMER.

The fourth and final phase of creating the application is to tweak the code by manually inserting the statements in the member function definitions and inserting other declarations. I explain these manual code insertions shortly, when I present the relevant project listings. First, however, Listing 5.1 provides the source code for the header file RESOURCE.H, which displays the CM_*XXXX* commands.

Listing 5.1 Source Code for the Header File RESOURCE.H Showing the *CM_XXXX* Commands

```
//{{NO_DEPENDENCIES}}
// App Studio generated include file.
// Used by APPSTUD1.RC
//
#define IDR_MAINFRAME           2
#define IDD_ABOUTBOX            100
#define CM_DATE_TIME            32771
#define CM_START_TIMER          32772
#define CM_STOP_TIMER           32773

// Next default values for new objects
//
#ifdef APSTUDIO_INVOKED
#ifndef APSTUDIO_READONLY_SYMBOLS
```

```
#define _APS_NEXT_RESOURCE_VALUE        102
#define _APS_NEXT_COMMAND_VALUE         32774
#define _APS_NEXT_CONTROL_VALUE         1000
#define _APS_NEXT_SYMED_VALUE           101
#endif
#endif
```

Listing 5.1 contains the CM_*XXXX* constants for the three new menu options. The App Studio utility automatically assigns the values of these constants.

Listing 5.2 provides a partial listing for the resource file APPSTUD1.RC.

Listing 5.2 Partial Listing for the APPSTUD1.RC Resource File

```
//Microsoft App Studio generated resource script.
//
#include "resource.h"

#define APSTUDIO_READONLY_SYMBOLS
/////////////////////////////////////////////////////////////////////
//
// Generated from the TEXTINCLUDE 2 resource.
//
#include "afxres.h"


/////////////////////////////////////////////////////////////////////
  .
  .
  .
/////////////////////////////////////////////////////////////////////
//
// Menu
//

IDR_MAINFRAME MENU PRELOAD DISCARDABLE
BEGIN
    MENUITEM "E&xit",                      ID_APP_EXIT
    POPUP "&Time"
    BEGIN
        MENUITEM "&Date/Time",             CM_DATE_TIME
        MENUITEM SEPARATOR
        MENUITEM "&Start Timer",           CM_START_TIMER
        MENUITEM "S&top Timer",            CM_STOP_TIMER
    END
    POPUP "&Help"
    BEGIN
        MENUITEM "&About Appstud1...",     ID_APP_ABOUT
    END
END
```

(continues)

Listing 5.2 Continued

```
//////////////////////////////////////////////////////////////////
//
// Accelerator
//

IDR_MAINFRAME ACCELERATORS PRELOAD MOVEABLE PURE
BEGIN
    "D",            CM_DATE_TIME,           VIRTKEY,CONTROL, NOINVERT
    "S",            CM_START_TIMER,         VIRTKEY,CONTROL, NOINVERT
    "T",            CM_STOP_TIMER,          VIRTKEY,CONTROL, NOINVERT
END


//////////////////////////////////////////////////////////////////
//
// Dialog
//

IDD_ABOUTBOX DIALOG DISCARDABLE  34, 22, 217, 55
STYLE DS_MODALFRAME ¦ WS_POPUP ¦ WS_CAPTION ¦ WS_SYSMENU
CAPTION "About Appstud1"
FONT 8, "MS Sans Serif"
BEGIN
    ICON            IDR_MAINFRAME,IDC_STATIC,11,17,18,20
    LTEXT           "AppStudio1 Application Version 1.0",
                    IDC_STATIC,40,10, 119,8
    LTEXT           "Copyright \251 1993 Namir Shammas",
                    IDC_STATIC,40,25,119,8
    DEFPUSHBUTTON   "Close",IDOK,175,20,32,14,WS_GROUP
END


//////////////////////////////////////////////////////////////////
//
// String Table
//
.
.
.
//////////////////////////////////////////////////////////////////
#endif    // not APSTUDIO_INVOKED
```

Listing 5.2 contains a *partial* script of the APPSTUD1.RC resource file. This file shows the following relevant resources:

- The customized IDR_MMAINFRAME menu resource, including the Time pop-up menu selection and its nested options.

- The customized `IDR_MMAINFRAME` accelerators resource with its three items, Ctrl+D, Ctrl+S, and Ctrl+T.

- The dialog box resource `IDD_ABOUTBOX`. I manually edited the static text controls.

The source code for the customized header file STDAFX.H is provided in Listing 5.3.

Listing 5.3 Customized Source Code for the Header File STDAFX.H

```
// stdafx.h : include file for standard system include files,
//   or project specific include files that are used frequently, but
//      are changed infrequently
//

#include <afxwin.h>         // MFC core and standard components
#include <afxext.h>         // MFC extensions (including VB)


// define global project-wide constant
const MaxStringLen = 40;
```

The short, customized code shown in Listing 5.3 contains the project-wide global constant MaxStringLen, which I entered manually. I placed this constant in the file STDAFX.H because several project files use it, and those same files also include this header file.

Listing 5.4 displays the source code for the customized header file APPSTDOC.H.

Listing 5.4 Customized Source Code for the Header File APPSTDOC.H

```
// appstdoc.h : interface of the CAppstud1Doc class
//
/////////////////////////////////////////////////////////////////////

class CAppstud1Doc : public CDocument
{
protected: // create from serialization only
    CAppstud1Doc();
    DECLARE_DYNCREATE(CAppstud1Doc)

// Attributes
public:

  CTime tm;
```

(continues)

Introduction to Visual C++

Listing 5.4 Continued

```
    char szStr[MaxStringLen + 1];
    long nInitTickCount;
    int nCharIndex;
    BOOL bNew;
    BOOL bTimerOn;
```

```
// Operations
public:

// Implementation
public:
    virtual ~CAppstud1Doc();
    virtual void Serialize(CArchive& ar);   // overridden for
                                            // document i/o
#ifdef _DEBUG
    virtual void AssertValid() const;
    virtual void Dump(CDumpContext& dc) const;
#endif

protected:
    virtual BOOL OnNewDocument();

// Generated message map functions
protected:
    //{{AFX_MSG(CAppstud1Doc)
    // NOTE - the ClassWizard will add and remove member functions here.
    //    DO NOT EDIT what you see in these blocks of generated code !
    //}}AFX_MSG
    DECLARE_MESSAGE_MAP()
};


//////////////////////////////////////////////////////////////////////
```

The customized code shown in Listing 5.4 has the declaration for the application's document class CAppstdu1Doc. I manually inserted the declarations for the following data members:

■ The member tm, which is an instance of class CTime. This member provides the system date and time.

■ The member szStr, which stores the string of input characters.

■ The member nInitTickCount, which stores the tick count when you start the timer. The tick count is the number of milliseconds elapsed since Windows started running.

■ The member nCharIndex, which stores the index of the next character in member szStr (in which keyboard input is stored).

■ The Boolean member bNew, which stores TRUE if your keyboard input has not filled the first MaxStringLen characters in member szStr.

■ The Boolean member bTimerOn, which stores the timer-on mode.

The source code for the customized implementation file APPSTDOC.CPP is provided in Listing 5.5.

Listing 5.5 Customized Source Code for the Implementation File APPSTDOC.CPP

```
// appstdoc.cpp : implementation of the CAppstud1Doc class
//

#include "stdafx.h"
#include "appstud1.h"

#include "appstdoc.h"
#ifdef _DEBUG
#undef THIS_FILE
static char BASED_CODE THIS_FILE[] = __FILE__;
#endif

/////////////////////////////////////////////////////////////////
// CAppstud1Doc

IMPLEMENT_DYNCREATE(CAppstud1Doc, CDocument)

BEGIN_MESSAGE_MAP(CAppstud1Doc, CDocument)
    //{{AFX_MSG_MAP(CAppstud1Doc)
        // NOTE - the ClassWizard will add and remove mapping macros here.
        //    DO NOT EDIT what you see in these blocks of generated code!
    //}}AFX_MSG_MAP
END_MESSAGE_MAP()

/////////////////////////////////////////////////////////////////
// CAppstud1Doc construction/destruction
CAppstud1Doc::CAppstud1Doc()
{
    nCharIndex = 0;
    bNew = TRUE;
    bTimerOn = FALSE;
    szStr[0] = '\0';
}
```

(continues)

Listing 5.5 Continued

```
CAppstud1Doc::~CAppstud1Doc()
{
}

BOOL CAppstud1Doc::OnNewDocument()
{
    if (!CDocument::OnNewDocument())
        return FALSE;
    // TODO: add reinitialization code here
    // (SDI documents will reuse this document)

    return TRUE;
}

/////////////////////////////////////////////////////////////////////////
// CAppstud1Doc serialization

void CAppstud1Doc::Serialize(CArchive& ar)
{
    if (ar.IsStoring())
    {
        // TODO: add storing code here
    }
    else
    {
        // TODO: add loading code here
    }
}

/////////////////////////////////////////////////////////////////////////
// CAppstud1Doc diagnostics

#ifdef _DEBUG
void CAppstud1Doc::AssertValid() const
{
    CDocument::AssertValid();
}

void CAppstud1Doc::Dump(CDumpContext& dc) const
{
    CDocument::Dump(dc);
}
#endif //_DEBUG

/////////////////////////////////////////////////////////////////////////
// CAppstud1Doc commands
```

To the code shown in Listing 5.5, I added the statements inside the constructor to assign 0, TRUE, FALSE, and the null character to the members nCharIndex, bNew, bTimerOn, and szStr[0], respectively.

The source code for the customized header file APPSTVW.H is provided in
Listing 5.6.

Listing 5.6 Customized Source Code for the Header File APPSTVW.H

```
// appstvw.h : interface of the CAppstud1View class
//
/////////////////////////////////////////////////////////////////////

class CAppstud1View : public CView
{
protected: // create from serialization only
    CAppstud1View();
    DECLARE_DYNCREATE(CAppstud1View)

// Attributes
public:
    CAppstud1Doc* GetDocument();

// Operations
public:

// Implementation
public:
    virtual ~CAppstud1View();
    virtual void OnDraw(CDC* pDC);  // overridden to draw this view
#ifdef _DEBUG
    virtual void AssertValid() const;
    virtual void Dump(CDumpContext& dc) const;
#endif

protected:

// Generated message map functions
protected:
    //{{AFX_MSG(CAppstud1View)
    afx_msg void OnLButtonDown(UINT nFlags, CPoint point);
    afx_msg void OnChar(UINT nChar, UINT nRepCnt, UINT nFlags);
    afx_msg void OnRButtonDown(UINT nFlags, CPoint point);
    afx_msg void OnMouseMove(UINT nFlags, CPoint point);

    // next three members are manually inserted
    afx_msg void CMGetDateTime()
      { SendMessage(WM_RBUTTONDOWN); }
    afx_msg void CMStartTimer();
    afx_msg void CMStopTimer();
    //}}AFX_MSG
    DECLARE_MESSAGE_MAP()
};

#ifndef _DEBUG  // debug version in appstvw.cpp
inline CAppstud1Doc* CAppstud1View::GetDocument()
   { return (CAppstud1Doc*)m_pDocument; }
#endif

/////////////////////////////////////////////////////////////////////
```

ClassWizard customized the source code shown in Listing 5.6 by inserting the declaration of the member functions On*XXXX* and CM*XXXX* in the view class CAppstud1View. I manually inserted the statement defining the function CMGetDateTime.

The source code for the customized implementation file APPSTVW.CPP is provided in Listing 5.7.

Listing 5.7 Customized Source Code for the Implementation File APPSTVW.CPP

```
// appstvw.cpp : implementation of the CAppstud1View class
//

#include "stdafx.h"
#include "appstud1.h"

#include "appstdoc.h"
#include "appstvw.h"

// include additional header files needed to customize the program
#include <stdio.h>
#include <string.h>

#ifdef _DEBUG
#undef THIS_FILE
static char BASED_CODE THIS_FILE[] = __FILE__;
#endif

// define new constants
const X0 = 10;
const Y0 = 10;
const Y1 = 30;

/////////////////////////////////////////////////////////////////
// CAppstud1View

IMPLEMENT_DYNCREATE(CAppstud1View, CView)

BEGIN_MESSAGE_MAP(CAppstud1View, CView)
    //{{AFX_MSG_MAP(CAppstud1View)
    ON_WM_LBUTTONDOWN()
    ON_WM_CHAR()
    ON_WM_RBUTTONDOWN()
    ON_WM_MOUSEMOVE()

    ON_COMMAND(CM_DATE_TIME, CMGetDateTime)
    ON_COMMAND(CM_START_TIMER, CMStartTimer)
    ON_COMMAND(CM_STOP_TIMER, CMStopTimer)

    //}}AFX_MSG_MAP
END_MESSAGE_MAP()

/////////////////////////////////////////////////////////////////
// CAppstud1View construction/destruction
```

```
CAppstud1View::CAppstud1View()
{
    // TODO: add construction code here
}

CAppstud1View::~CAppstud1View()
{
}

/////////////////////////////////////////////////////////////////////
// CAppstud1View drawing
void CAppstud1View::OnDraw(CDC* pDC)
{
    CAppstud1Doc* pDoc = GetDocument();
    ASSERT_VALID(pDoc);
    // TODO: add draw code for native data here
}

/////////////////////////////////////////////////////////////////////
// CAppstud1View diagnostics

#ifdef _DEBUG
void CAppstud1View::AssertValid() const
{
    CView::AssertValid();
}

void CAppstud1View::Dump(CDumpContext& dc) const
{
    CView::Dump(dc);
}

CAppstud1Doc* CAppstud1View::GetDocument() // non-debug version is
                                           // inline
{
    ASSERT(m_pDocument->IsKindOf(RUNTIME_CLASS(CAppstud1Doc)));
    return (CAppstud1Doc*)m_pDocument;
}
#endif //_DEBUG

/////////////////////////////////////////////////////////////////////
// CAppstud1View message handlers
```

```
void CAppstud1View::OnLButtonDown(UINT nFlags, CPoint point)
{
  CAppstud1Doc* pDoc = GetDocument();
  char szStr[MaxStringLen+1];


  if (pDoc->bTimerOn) {
    pDoc->bTimerOn = FALSE;
    sprintf(szStr, "%3.3lf seconds elapsed",
            (GetTickCount() - pDoc->nInitTickCount) / 1000.0);
    MessageBox(szStr, "Timer Event",
               MB_OK | MB_ICONINFORMATION);
```

(continues)

Listing 5.7 Continued

```
  }
  else {
    pDoc->bTimerOn = TRUE;
    pDoc->nInitTickCount = GetTickCount();
    MessageBox("Timer is now On!", "Timer Event",
               MB_OK | MB_ICONEXCLAMATION);
  }
}

void CAppstud1View::OnChar(UINT nChar, UINT nRepCnt, UINT nFlags)
{
  CAppstud1Doc* pDoc = GetDocument();
  CClientDC dc(this);

  if (pDoc->nCharIndex < MaxStringLen) {
    pDoc->szStr[pDoc->nCharIndex++] = char(nChar);
    if (pDoc->bNew) // append null terminator when typing a new
string
      pDoc->szStr[pDoc->nCharIndex] = '\0';
  }
  else { // reached the end
    pDoc->nCharIndex = 0;
    pDoc->bNew = FALSE;
    pDoc->szStr[pDoc->nCharIndex++] = char(nChar);
  }
  dc.TextOut(X0, Y1, pDoc->szStr, strlen(pDoc->szStr));
}
void CAppstud1View::OnRButtonDown(UINT nFlags, CPoint point)
{
  CAppstud1Doc* pDoc = GetDocument();
  char szStr[MaxStringLen+1];
  pDoc->tm = CTime::GetCurrentTime();

  sprintf(szStr, "Date is %02d/%02d/%4d, Time is %02d:%02d:%02d",
             pDoc->tm.GetMonth(), pDoc->tm.GetDay(),
             pDoc->tm.GetYear(),  pDoc->tm.GetHour(),
             pDoc->tm.GetMinute(), pDoc->tm.GetSecond());
  MessageBox(szStr, "Current Date/Time",
             MB_OK | MB_ICONINFORMATION);
}

void CAppstud1View::OnMouseMove(UINT nFlags, CPoint point)
{
  char szStr[MaxStringLen+1];
  CClientDC dc(this);


  sprintf(szStr, "[%03d, %03d]", point.x, point.y);
  dc.TextOut(X0, Y0, szStr, strlen(szStr));
}
```

```
void CAppstud1View::CMStartTimer()
{
  CAppstud1Doc* pDoc = GetDocument();
  if (!pDoc->bTimerOn)
    SendMessage(WM_LBUTTONDOWN);
  else
    MessageBox("Timer is running!", "Information",
               MB_OK | MB_ICONINFORMATION);
}

void CAppstud1View::CMStopTimer()
{
  CAppstud1Doc* pDoc = GetDocument();
  if (pDoc->bTimerOn)
    SendMessage(WM_LBUTTONDOWN);
  else
    MessageBox("Timer is not running!", "Information",
               MB_OK | MB_ICONINFORMATION);
}
```

In the source code shown in Listing 5.7, ClassWizard inserted the following items:

■ The message map macros to handle the various WM_*XXXX* and CM_*XXXX* Windows messages.

■ The minimal definitions of the On*XXXX* and CM*XXXX* member functions.

I manually inserted the following items:

■ The #include directives to include the header files STDIO.H and STRING.H.

■ The definitions of the constants X0, Y0, and Y1.

■ The statements for the On*XXXX* and CM*XXXX* member functions.

The On*XXXX* and CM*XXXX* member functions include the following:

■ The member function OnLButtonDown, which performs the following tasks:

  • Obtains the address of the document and assigns it to the local pointer pDoc. The function uses this pointer to access the data member of the document.

- Determines if the timer is running by examining the document's data member bTimerOn (using the local pointer pDoc). If the timer is running, the function performs the following subtasks:

  Assigns FALSE to the document's data member bTimerOn.

  Builds a string image for the number of seconds since the timer started. This task uses the function sprintf and stores the string image in the local variable szStr.

  Displays the string image in a message dialog box.

  By contrast, if the timer is not running, the function performs the following subtasks:

  Assigns TRUE to the document's data member bTimerOn.

  Assigns the current tick count (obtained by invoking the Windows API function GetTickCount) to the document's data member nInitTickCount.

  Displays the text Timer is now On! in a message dialog box.

- The member function OnChar, which performs the following tasks:

  - Obtains the address of the document and assigns it to the local pointer pDoc. The function uses this pointer to access the data member of the document.

  - Declares the device context object dc as an instance of CClientDC.

  - Determines whether the value in the static variable i is less than that of the global constant MaxStringLen. If this condition is true, the function performs the following subtasks:

    Assigns the input character to the element nCharIndex (of the document's member szStr) and then increments the document's member nCharIndex.

    If the document's member bNew is nonzero, assigns the null terminator character to the element nCharIndex of the document's member szStr. This task stores a null terminator in the next character before the output starts to wrap.

The else clause of the if statement performs the following subtasks:

Assigns 0 to the document's member nCharIndex. This assignment helps the view window display further keyboard input at the beginning of the same line.

Assigns FALSE to the document's member bNew.

Assigns the input character to the element i of the document's member szStr and then increments the document's member nCharIndex.

Displays the contents of the variable szStr by sending the C++ message TextOut to the object dc. The arguments for this message specify the coordinates (X0, Y1), the document's member szStr, and the number of characters strlen(pDoc->szStr).

■ The member function OnRButtonDown. Displays the current system date and time in a message dialog box. The function performs the following tasks:

- Obtains the address of the document and assigns it to the local pointer pDoc. The function uses this pointer to access the data member of the document.

- Creates a formatted string image for the date and time. This task sends the C++ messages GetMonth(), GetDay(), GetYear(), GetHour(), GetMinute(), and GetSecond() to the document's data member tm. Each message obtains a component for the date or time.

- Displays the formatted string in a message dialog box.

■ The member function OnMouseMove. Displays the current mouse coordinates in the upper-left corner of the view window. The function performs the following tasks:

- Obtains the address of the document and assigns it to the local pointer pDoc. The function uses this pointer to access the data member of the document.

- Declares the device context object dc as an instance of CClientDC.

- Creates a formatted string image for the mouse location. This task involves accessing the members x and y from the CPoint parameter point.

- Displays the formatted string in a message dialog box.

■ The member function CMStartTimer. Starts the timer by sending the Windows message WM_LBUTTONDOWN to the view if the document's data member bTimerOn contains FALSE. Otherwise, the function displays an error note in a message dialog box. By sending the Windows message WM_LBUTTONDOWN, this function indirectly invokes the member function OnLButtonDown.

■ The member function CMStopTimer. Starts the timer by sending the Windows message WM_LBUTTONDOWN to the view if the document's data member bTimerOn contains TRUE. Otherwise, the function displays an error note in a message dialog box. By sending the Windows message WM_LBUTTONDOWN, this function indirectly invokes the member function OnLButtonDown.

Compile and run the program APPSTUD1.EXE. Use the Time menu commands to view the current date and time and to manipulate the simple timer. Figure 5.4 shows a sample session with the program APPSTUD1.EXE.

Figure 5.4

A sample session with the program APPSTUD1.EXE.

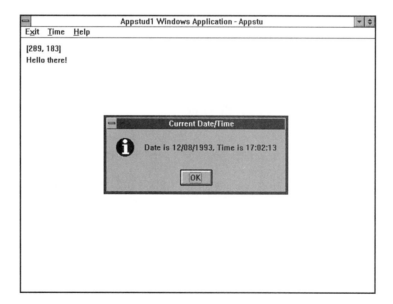

Adding a New Dialog Box Resource

You can modify the preceding project to use a custom message dialog box rather than the standard one. You can use this modification with App Studio to create a new dialog box resource. This dialog box also includes a custom exclamation icon (or any other custom icon you want to use) created using App Studio. As long as you are using the App Studio to create a new dialog box, you might as well customize the About dialog box resource (go ahead, be brave!). In addition, you can use the ClassWizard utility to create the class that supports the custom message dialog box.

The initial phases of building and customizing this application, APPSTUD2.EXE, include the same steps and tasks used with the APPSTUD1 project. You can build the new application from scratch using AppWizard, App Studio, and ClassWizard. The alternative to building the application from scratch is to create the APPSTUD1 subdirectory, copy the files from APPSTUD1, rename some of these files (the ones that include the project name), edit the source files (to change the names of those classes whose names depend on the project name), and then edit the project files to include the correct list of files. This multiple-step operation may seem more elaborate than starting from scratch, but it's really not. Therefore, the first phase of creating the application involves copying the files of the APPSTUD1 project and editing them.

After you make the files of the APPSTUD2 project equivalent to those of the APPSTUD1 project, you can move on to the second phase. The second phase invokes the App Studio to create the new icon and dialog box resources. Perform the following steps:

1. Select the icon resource type.

2. Select the IDR_MAINFRAME icon, which is the icon that appears in the About dialog box. App Studio responds by displaying the tools palette (which includes drawing tools and a color palette). Figure 5.5 shows a sample session with the tools palette as the IDR_MAINFRAME icon is being edited.

Figure 5.5

The tools palette
during editing of
IDR_MAINFRAME
icon.

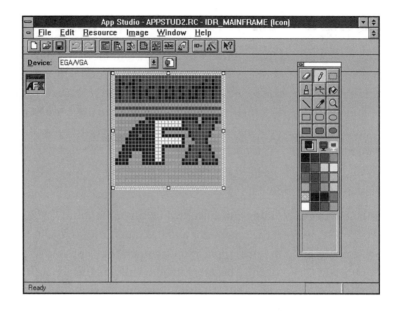

3. Alter the background colors for the IDR_MAINFRAME icon using colors of your choice. When you are finished coloring, save the icon and close its window.

4. Create a new icon by clicking the New... button, which is located at the bottom of the MFC Resource Script window.

5. Select the colors and tools to draw an exclamation icon. Figure 5.6 shows a sample session with the tools palette as the IDI_ICON1 icon is being created. When you are done drawing the icon, save it and close its window.

6. Select the dialog resource type in the MFC Resource Script window.

7. Choose the IDD_ABOUTBOX dialog resource.

8. Edit the caption of the OK button, changing it to *Close*. To edit the title of any dialog box control, double-click the item to bring up its properties dialog box. Make the changes in the dialog box and then press Enter to close it.

9. Edit the static text controls to modify the version and copyright information. Figure 5.7 shows the changes I made to my files (you can insert your own name in the copyright—you don't have to credit me for your work!). When you are finished with the About dialog box resource, save it, and then close it.

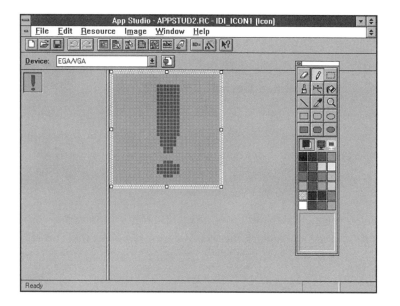

Figure 5.6
The tools palette as the IDI_ICON1 icon is being created.

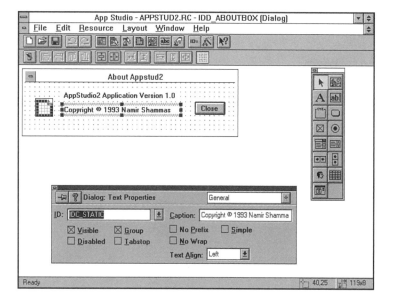

Figure 5.7
The customized IDD_ABOUTBOX dialog box resource.

10. Create a new dialog box resource by clicking the New... button located at the bottom of the MFC Resource Script window. App Studio displays a dialog box containing only the OK and Cancel buttons.

11. Delete the Cancel button by selecting it and then pressing the Delete key.

12. Double-click the OK button to bring up its properties dialog box. Type the caption **Close**. Move the control to the bottom of the dialog box.

13. Double-click the dialog box caption to bring up its properties dialog box. Type the caption **Message Box**.

14. Select the static text tool from the tools palette and draw the static text control above the Close button. In addition, make the text centered by selecting the Center option from the Text Align drop-down combo box in the properties dialog box. The static text control has the default text Static. There is no need to alter this text.

15. Select the picture control from the tools palette to draw the icon in the dialog box. Double-click the picture control to select the icon picture type and to specify the ID IDI_ICON1. Figure 5.8 shows the App Studio as the IDI_ICON1 dialog box resource is being created.

Figure 5.8

The App Studio as the IDI_ICON1 icon resource (in the IDD_DIALOG1 dialog box) is being created.

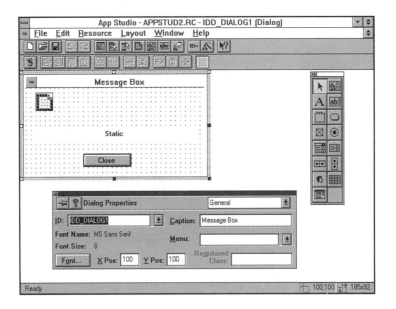

16. Save the new dialog box resource and close the App Studio.

The third phase of creating the APPSTUD2.EXE program involves the ClassWizard to create the new class CMsgDlg. Select the Class Info section in the MFC Class Wizard dialog box and create this new class as a descendant of class CDialog. After you create this class, you can use ClassWizard to add the message handler OnInitDialog to class CMsgDlg.

The fourth phase of creating the application includes manual customization of the code. I discuss this aspect when I present the relevant project files. First, I customized the file STDAFX.H to make it like Listing 5.1. The files APPSTUD1.H and APPSTVW.H in this project are just like their counterparts in project APPSTUD1. Listing 5.8 shows the source code for the header file RESOURCE.H.

Listing 5.8 Source Code for the Header File RESOURCE.H

```
//{{NO_DEPENDENCIES}}
// App Studio generated include file.
// Used by APPSTUD2.RC
//
#define IDR_MAINFRAME                   2
#define IDD_ABOUTBOX                    100
#define IDD_DIALOG1                     102
#define IDI_ICON1                       103
#define IDB_BITMAP1                     107
#define IDC_STATIC1                     1004
#define CM_DATE_TIME                    32771
#define CM_START_TIMER                  32772
#define CM_STOP_TIMER                   32773

// Next default values for new objects
//
#ifdef APSTUDIO_INVOKED
#ifndef APSTUDIO_READONLY_SYMBOLS

#define _APS_NEXT_RESOURCE_VALUE        112
#define _APS_NEXT_COMMAND_VALUE         32774
#define _APS_NEXT_CONTROL_VALUE         1005
#define _APS_NEXT_SYMED_VALUE           101
#endif
#endif
```

Listing 5.8 shows the declarations of the identifiers for the menu, menu options, dialog boxes, and icons. The App Studio utility inserted these declarations.

The partial script of the APPSTUD2.RC resource file is provided in Listing 5.9.

Listing 5.9 Partial Script of the APPSTUD2.RC Resource File

```
//Microsoft App Studio generated resource script.
//
#include "resource.h"
```

(continues)

Listing 5.9 Continued

```
#define APSTUDIO_READONLY_SYMBOLS
/////////////////////////////////////////////////////////
//
// Generated from the TEXTINCLUDE 2 resource.
//
#include "afxres.h"

/////////////////////////////////////////////////////////////////////
#undef APSTUDIO_READONLY_SYMBOLS

#ifdef APSTUDIO_INVOKED
/////////////////////////////////////////////////////////
//
// TEXTINCLUDE
//

1 TEXTINCLUDE DISCARDABLE
BEGIN
    "resource.h\0"
END

2 TEXTINCLUDE DISCARDABLE
BEGIN
    "#include ""afxres.h""\r\n"
    "\0"
END

3 TEXTINCLUDE DISCARDABLE
BEGIN
    "#include ""res\\appstud2.rc2""  // non-App Studio edited
                                    // resources\r\n"
    "\r\n"
    "#include ""afxres.rc""  \011// Standard components\r\n"
    "\0"
END

/////////////////////////////////////////////////////////
#endif    // APSTUDIO_INVOKED


/////////////////////////////////////////////////////////
//
// Icon
//

IDR_MAINFRAME           ICON    DISCARDABLE     "RES\\APPSTUD2.ICO"
IDI_ICON1               ICON    DISCARDABLE     "RES\\ICON1.ICO"

/////////////////////////////////////////////////////////
//
// Menu
//
```

```
IDR_MAINFRAME MENU PRELOAD DISCARDABLE
BEGIN
    MENUITEM "E&xit",                   ID_APP_EXIT
    POPUP "&Time"
    BEGIN
        MENUITEM "&Date/Time",          CM_DATE_TIME
        MENUITEM SEPARATOR
        MENUITEM "&Start Timer",        CM_START_TIMER
        MENUITEM "S&top Timer",         CM_STOP_TIMER
    END
    POPUP "&Help"
    BEGIN
        MENUITEM "&About Appstud2...",  ID_APP_ABOUT
    END
END


/////////////////////////////////////////////////////////
//
// Accelerator
//

IDR_MAINFRAME ACCELERATORS PRELOAD MOVEABLE PURE
BEGIN
    "D",            CM_DATE_TIME,       VIRTKEY,CONTROL, NOINVERT
    "S",            CM_START_TIMER,     VIRTKEY,CONTROL, NOINVERT
    "T",            CM_STOP_TIMER,      VIRTKEY,CONTROL, NOINVERT
END


/////////////////////////////////////////////////////////
//
// Dialog
//

IDD_ABOUTBOX DIALOG DISCARDABLE  34, 22, 217, 55
STYLE DS_MODALFRAME ¦ WS_POPUP ¦ WS_CAPTION ¦ WS_SYSMENU
CAPTION "About Appstud2"
FONT 8, "MS Sans Serif"
BEGIN
    ICON            IDR_MAINFRAME,IDC_STATIC,11,17,18,20
    LTEXT           "AppStudio2 Application Version 1.0",
                    IDC_STATIC,40,10,
                    119,8
    LTEXT           "Copyright \251 1993 Namir Shammas",
                    IDC_STATIC,40,25,119,
                    8
    DEFPUSHBUTTON   "Close",IDOK,175,20,32,14,WS_GROUP
END
```

(continues)

Listing 5.9 Continued

```
IDD_DIALOG1 DIALOG DISCARDABLE  100, 100, 185, 92
STYLE DS_MODALFRAME ¦ WS_POPUP ¦ WS_VISIBLE ¦ WS_CAPTION ¦ WS_SYSMENU
CAPTION "Message Box"
FONT 8, "MS Sans Serif"
BEGIN
    DEFPUSHBUTTON      "Close",IDOK,60,70,50,14
    ICON              IDI_ICON1,IDI_ICON1,10,5,18,20
    CTEXT             "Static",IDC_STATIC1,10,45,165,11
END


/////////////////////////////////////////////////////////
//
// String Table
//
.
.
.
/////////////////////////////////////////////////////////
#endif     // not APSTUDIO_INVOKED
```

The partial resource file script shown in Listing 5.9 displays the definitions of the main menu, the accelerators, the About dialog box, and the custom message dialog box. The AppWizard utility generated this file and App Studio customized it.

The source code for the header file MSGDLG.H is provided in Listing 5.10.

Listing 5.10 Source Code for the MSGDLG.H Header File

```
// msgdlg.h : header file
//

//#include "stdafx.h"
#include <string.h>

/////////////////////////////////////////////////////////////////////
// CMsgDlg dialog

class CMsgDlg : public CDialog
{
// Construction
public:
    CMsgDlg(LPCSTR lpszMsg,
            CWnd* pParent = NULL);  // standard constructor

// Dialog Data
    //{{AFX_DATA(CMsgDlg)
    enum { IDD = IDD_DIALOG1 };
    //}}AFX_DATA
```

```
// Implementation
protected:
    char szMsg[MaxStringLen+1];
    virtual void DoDataExchange(CDataExchange* pDX);    // DDX/DDV
                                                         // support

    // Generated message map functions
    //{{AFX_MSG(CMsgDlg)
    virtual BOOL OnInitDialog();
    //}}AFX_MSG
    DECLARE_MESSAGE_MAP()
};
```

The header file shown in Listing 5.10 contains the declaration for class CMsgDlg, which is a descendant of class CDialog and uses the resource ID IDD_DIALOG1 to create the custom message dialog box. The ClassWizard utility generated most of the source code in the header file MSGDLG.H, including the declarations for the constructor, untagged enumerated type, and the function DoDataExchange. The ClassWizard utility also added the declaration for the member function OnInitDialog. I manually inserted the following items:

- The constructor parameter lpszMsg, which passes the text for the message displayed by the custom dialog box.

- The declaration of the member szMsg to store the text of the message, which is supplied by the constructor's first parameter.

The source code for the implementation file MSGDLG.CPP is provided in Listing 5.11.

Listing 5.11 Source Code for the MSGDLG.CPP Implementation File

```
// msgdlg.cpp : implementation file
//

#include "stdafx.h"
#include "appstud2.h"
#include "msgdlg.h"

#ifdef _DEBUG
#undef THIS_FILE
static char BASED_CODE THIS_FILE[] = __FILE__;
#endif
```

(continues)

Listing 5.11 Continued

```
//////////////////////////////////////////////////////////////////////
// CMsgDlg dialog


CMsgDlg::CMsgDlg(LPCSTR lpszMsg,
                 CWnd* pParent /*=NULL*/
                 )
    : CDialog(CMsgDlg::IDD, pParent)
{
    _fstrcpy(szMsg, lpszMsg);
    //{{AFX_DATA_INIT(CMsgDlg)
    //}}AFX_DATA_INIT
}

void CMsgDlg::DoDataExchange(CDataExchange* pDX)
{
    CDialog::DoDataExchange(pDX);
    //{{AFX_DATA_MAP(CMsgDlg)
    //}}AFX_DATA_MAP
}

BEGIN_MESSAGE_MAP(CMsgDlg, CDialog)
    //{{AFX_MSG_MAP(CMsgDlg)
    //}}AFX_MSG_MAP
END_MESSAGE_MAP()


//////////////////////////////////////////////////////////////////////
// CMsgDlg message handlers

BOOL CMsgDlg::OnInitDialog()
{
    CDialog::OnInitDialog();

    // TODO: Add extra initialization here
    SetDlgItemText(IDC_STATIC1, szMsg);

    return TRUE;  // return TRUE  unless you set the focus to a
                  // control
}
```

Listing 5.11 shows the implementation file for the CMsgDlg class, which
contains definitions for the following members:

■ The constructor that invokes the constructor of the parent class and
then assigns the string of the parameter lpszMsg to the data member
szMsg. I inserted the statement to support this assignment; the
AppWizard generated the rest of the function definition.

■ The member function `DoDataExchange`, which simply invokes the function `DoDataExchange` of the parent class. The AppWizard generated this definition.

■ The member function `OnInitDialog`. The AppWizard generated the statements that invoke the function `OnInitDialog` of the parent class and return TRUE. I inserted the call to the inherited member function `SetDlgItemText`. This call has the arguments `IDC_STATIC1` and `szMsg`. The function `SetDlgItemText` assigns the string in the member `szStr` to the static text control in the dialog box.

Listing 5.12 provides the source code for the APPSTVW.CPP implementation file.

Listing 5.12 Customized Source Code for the Implementation File APPSTVW.CPP

```
// appstvw.cpp : implementation of the CAppstud2View class
//

#include "stdafx.h"
#include "appstud2.h"

#include "appstdoc.h"
#include "appstvw.h"
```

```
// include additional header files needed to customize the program
#include <stdio.h>
#include <string.h>
```

```
#include "msgdlg.h"
```

```
#ifdef _DEBUG
#undef THIS_FILE
static char BASED_CODE THIS_FILE[] = __FILE__;
#endif
```

```
// define new constants
const X0 = 10;
const Y0 = 10;
const Y1 = 30;
```

```
/////////////////////////////////////////////////////////////////
// CAppstud2View

IMPLEMENT_DYNCREATE(CAppstud2View, CView)
```

(continues)

Listing 5.12 Continued

```
BEGIN_MESSAGE_MAP(CAppstud2View, CView)
    //{{AFX_MSG_MAP(CAppstud2View)
    ON_WM_LBUTTONDOWN()
    ON_WM_CHAR()
    ON_WM_RBUTTONDOWN()
    ON_WM_MOUSEMOVE()

    ON_COMMAND(CM_DATE_TIME, CMGetDateTime)
    ON_COMMAND(CM_START_TIMER, CMStartTimer)
    ON_COMMAND(CM_STOP_TIMER, CMStopTimer)

    //}}AFX_MSG_MAP
END_MESSAGE_MAP()

/////////////////////////////////////////////////////////////////////
// CAppstud2View construction/destruction

CAppstud2View::CAppstud2View()
{
    // TODO: add construction code here
}

CAppstud2View::~CAppstud2View()
{
}

/////////////////////////////////////////////////////////////////////
// CAppstud2View drawing

void CAppstud2View::OnDraw(CDC* pDC)
{
    CAppstud2Doc* pDoc = GetDocument();
    ASSERT_VALID(pDoc);

    // TODO: add draw code for native data here
}

/////////////////////////////////////////////////////////////////////
// CAppstud2View diagnostics

#ifdef _DEBUG
void CAppstud2View::AssertValid() const
{
    CView::AssertValid();
}

void CAppstud2View::Dump(CDumpContext& dc) const
{
    CView::Dump(dc);
}

CAppstud2Doc* CAppstud2View::GetDocument() // non-debug version is
                                           // inline
{
    ASSERT(m_pDocument->IsKindOf(RUNTIME_CLASS(CAppstud2Doc)));
    return (CAppstud2Doc*)m_pDocument;
}
#endif //_DEBUG
```

```
///////////////////////////////////////////////////////////////
// CAppstud2View message handlers

void CAppstud2View::OnLButtonDown(UINT nFlags, CPoint point)
{
  CAppstud2Doc* pDoc = GetDocument();
  char szStr[MaxStringLen+1];

  if (pDoc->bTimerOn) {
    pDoc->bTimerOn = FALSE;
    sprintf(szStr, "%3.3lf seconds elapsed",
            (GetTickCount() - pDoc->nInitTickCount) / 1000.0);
    CMsgDlg MessageDlg(szStr);
    MessageDlg.DoModal();
  }
  else {
    pDoc->bTimerOn = TRUE;
    pDoc->nInitTickCount = GetTickCount();
    CMsgDlg MessageDlg("Timer is now On!");
    MessageDlg.DoModal();
  }
}

void CAppstud2View::OnChar(UINT nChar, UINT nRepCnt, UINT nFlags)
{
  CAppstud2Doc* pDoc = GetDocument();
  CClientDC dc(this);

  if (pDoc->nCharIndex < MaxStringLen) {
    pDoc->szStr[pDoc->nCharIndex++] = char(nChar);
    if (pDoc->bNew) // append null terminator when typing a new
                    // string
      pDoc->szStr[pDoc->nCharIndex] = '\0';
  }
  else { // reached the end
    pDoc->nCharIndex = 0;
    pDoc->bNew = FALSE;
    pDoc->szStr[pDoc->nCharIndex++] = char(nChar);
  }
  dc.TextOut(X0, Y1, pDoc->szStr, strlen(pDoc->szStr));
}

void CAppstud2View::OnRButtonDown(UINT nFlags, CPoint point)
{
  CAppstud2Doc* pDoc = GetDocument();
  char szStr[MaxStringLen+1];
  pDoc->tm = CTime::GetCurrentTime();

  sprintf(szStr, "Date is %02d/%02d/%4d, Time is %02d:%02d:%02d",
                 pDoc->tm.GetMonth(), pDoc->tm.GetDay(),
                 pDoc->tm.GetYear(),  pDoc->tm.GetHour(),
                 pDoc->tm.GetMinute(), pDoc->tm.GetSecond());
  CMsgDlg MessageDlg(szStr);
  MessageDlg.DoModal();
}
```

(continues)

Listing 5.12 Continued

```
void CAppstud2View::OnMouseMove(UINT nFlags, CPoint point)
{
  char szStr[MaxStringLen+1];
  CClientDC dc(this);

  sprintf(szStr, "[%03d, %03d]", point.x, point.y);
  dc.TextOut(X0, Y0, szStr, strlen(szStr));
}

void CAppstud2View::CMGetDateTime()
{
  SendMessage(WM_RBUTTONDOWN);
}

void CAppstud2View::CMStartTimer()
{
  CAppstud2Doc* pDoc = GetDocument();
  if (!pDoc->bTimerOn)
    SendMessage(WM_LBUTTONDOWN);
  else {
    CMsgDlg MessageDlg("Timer is running!");
    MessageDlg.DoModal();
  }
}

void CAppstud2View::CMStopTimer()
{
  CAppstud2Doc* pDoc = GetDocument();
  if (pDoc->bTimerOn)
    SendMessage(WM_LBUTTONDOWN);
  else {
    CMsgDlg MessageDlg("Timer is not running!");
    MessageDlg.DoModal();
  }
}
```

The customized source code shown in Listing 5.12 includes definitions for
the member functions OnLRButtonDown, OnRButtonDown, OnChar, CmInsertDate,
CmInsertTime, and CmInsertDateTime. The statements in these functions
greatly resemble those in the APPSTVW.CPP file of the APPSTUD1 project,
with one basic difference. The new version uses the class CMsgDlg to display
the custom message dialog box, which typically involves creating the instance of the class CMsgDlg and invoking it by sending it the C++ message
DoModal. The statement that creates the custom message dialog box also specifies the text of the message. This text comes from either a literal string or the
contents of a local string variable.

Compile and run the program APPSTUD2.EXE. Choose the commands from the Time menu (or click the left or right mouse button) to view the program's response, which involves displaying the custom dialog box. Figure 5.9 shows a sample session with the APPSTUD2.EXE program.

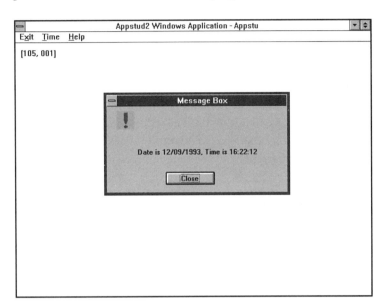

Figure 5.9
A sample session with the APPSTUD2.EXE program.

Creating a Form View

App Studio lets you create forms that are supported by the CFormView class. Forms, first implemented by Microsoft in Visual Basic, are very similar to dialog boxes. You can use the AppWizard utility to create an application using form views, and then use App Studio to draw the controls on the forms. Moreover, you can use ClassWizard to create any new classes and member functions to animate the form.

The following project, APPSTUD3, is a form view created with App Studio. APPSTUD3 is a variation of projects presented earlier in this chapter and uses an SDI-compliant application with a form view that contains the following controls:

- *A borderless read-only edit box*. Displays the current mouse coordinates.

- *A borderless read-only edit box*. Displays the elapsed time.

- *A borderless read-only edit box*. Displays the current system date and time.

- *Start pushbutton control.* Starts and stops the simple timer.

- *Date/Time pushbutton control.* Displays the current system date and time in the edit box just listed.

The APPSTUD3.EXE program has a very limited menu system that contains only the Exit and Help menus.

For the first phase of the project—creating the APPSTUD3.EXE application—you use AppWizard. Create the new project APPSTUD3 as an SDI-compliant application with no support for printing and no speed bar. Click the Classes... button in the AppWizard dialog box to make the view class a descendant of the class CFormView rather than a descendant of the default parent class CView. Give AppWizard the green light to generate the core source code for the application.

For the second phase of the project, you use App Studio. First, edit the menu resource IDR_MAINFRAME and delete most of the original menu commands. Create the command Exit and retain the command Help (with its nested option About...). When you have finished editing the menu resource, select the dialog resource type. App Studio displays the resources IDD_ABOUTBOX and IDD_APPSTUD3_FRM. Select IDD_APPSTUD3_FRM so that you can draw controls on the new, empty form. App Studio displays the empty form, which contains the default message TODO: Place form controls on this dialog. To customize the form, perform the following steps:

1. Select the initial static text control and then delete it by pressing the Delete key.

2. Draw the three read-only, borderless edit boxes. Select the control for each edit box from the Tools palette and then draw the control on the form.

3. Draw the two pushbutton controls. Select each pushbutton control from the Tools palette and then draw the control on the form. Figure 5.10 shows the pushbutton and edit box controls that have been drawn on the form.

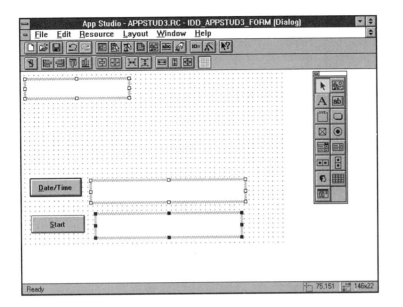

Figure 5.10
The pushbutton and edit box controls drawn on the form resource for the APPSTUD3 project.

4. Double-click the mouse-position edit box to display its properties dialog box. Type the control ID **IDC_MOUSEPOS_BOX**. Figure 5.11 shows the properties dialog box with this information displayed.

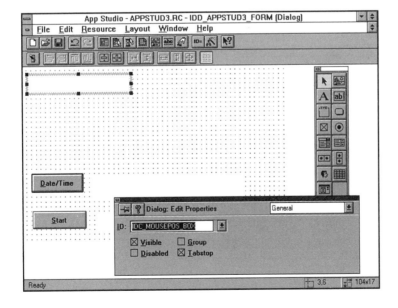

Figure 5.11
The properties dialog box for the IDC_MOUSEPOS_BOX edit box control.

5. Select the Styles item from the drop-down combo box in the properties dialog box. The properties dialog box reveals the check boxes and other controls that enable you to customize the style of the edit control. Check the Read-Only box and make sure that the other check boxes are clear (including the one labeled Border). Figure 5.12 shows the properties dialog box with this information displayed. When you are finished, close the dialog box.

Figure 5.12

The properties dialog box with the styles for the IDC_MOUSEPOS_BOX edit box control displayed.

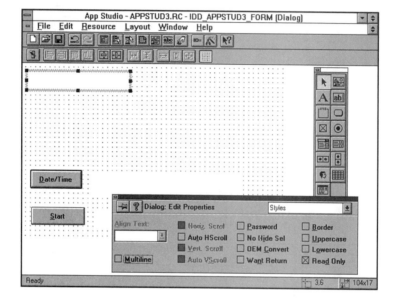

6. Repeat steps 4 and 5 for the other two edit boxes. Use the ID IDC_DATE_BOX for the date and time edit box and IDC_TIMER_BOX for the timer edit box.

7. Double-click the Date/Time button to display its properties dialog box. Type the caption string **&Date/Time** and the ID **IDC_DATE_BTN**. Close the properties dialog box.

8. Double-click the Start button to display its properties dialog box. Type the caption string **&Start** and the ID **IDC_TIMER_BTN**. Close the properties dialog box.

9. Save the updated resources.

For the third phase of the project, you use ClassWizard to add the message handling member functions and the special data members for the form view class. You invoke ClassWizard and then perform the following steps:

1. Select the Message Maps options.

2. Add the member function `OnMouseMove` that handles the Windows message `WM_MOUSEMOVE` for the `CAppstud3App` object.

3. Add to the Date/Time button (whose ID is `IDC_DATE_BTN`) the member function that handles the Windows notification message `BN_CLICKED`.

4. Add to the Start button (whose ID is `IDC_TIMER_BTN`) the member function that handles the Windows notification message `BN_CLICKED`.

5. Select the Member Variables options. The ClassWizard shows a list of the five controls in the form.

6. Select the control whose ID is `IDC_MOUSEPOS_BOX` and click the Add Variable... button. ClassWizard displays the Add Member Variable dialog box in which you can enter the name of the new variable and specify its kind and class. Type `m_MouseBoxBox` for the variable name. Select the `Value` property and the `CString` variable type.

7. Repeat step 6 for the other edit boxes. Enter the names `m_DateBox` and `m_TimerBox` for the date and timer edit controls, respectively. Also select the `Value` property and the `CString` variable type for both controls.

8. Select the control whose ID is `IDC_DATE_BTN` and click the Add Variable... button. ClassWizard displays the Add Member Variable dialog box in which you can enter the name of the new variable and specify its kind and class. Type `m_DateBtn` for the variable name. Select the `Control` property and the `CButton` variable type.

9. Select the control whose ID is `IDC_TIMER_BTN` and click the Add Variable... button. ClassWizard displays the Add Member Variable dialog box in which you can enter the name of the new variable and specify its kind and class. Type `m_TimerBtn` for the variable name. Select the `Control` property and the `CButton` variable type. Figure 5.13 shows the ClassWizard Member Variables dialog box with the list of variables for the APPSTUD3 project.

Figure 5.13

The ClassWizard Member Variables dialog box with the list of variables for the APPSTUD3 project.

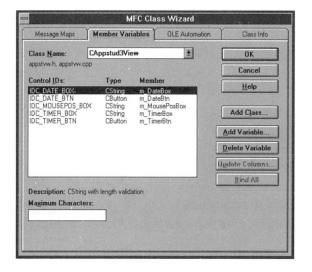

The fourth and final phase of the project involves manually customizing the source code. I discuss this customization as I present the relevant source code files. First, let's look at the source code for the RESOURCE.H header file in Listing 5.13.

Listing 5.13 Source Code for the RESOURCE.H Header File

```
//{{NO_DEPENDENCIES}}
// App Studio generated include file.
// Used by APPSTUD3.RC
//
#define IDR_MAINFRAME                   2
#define IDD_ABOUTBOX                    100
#define IDD_APPSTUD3_FORM               101
#define IDC_DATE_BTN                    1001
#define IDC_TIMER_BTN                   1002
#define IDC_MOUSEPOS_BOX                1006
#define IDC_DATE_BOX                    1007
#define IDC_TIMER_BOX                   1008

// Next default values for new objects
//
#ifdef APSTUDIO_INVOKED
#ifndef APSTUDIO_READONLY_SYMBOLS

#define _APS_NEXT_RESOURCE_VALUE        102
#define _APS_NEXT_COMMAND_VALUE         32772
#define _APS_NEXT_CONTROL_VALUE         1009
#define _APS_NEXT_SYMED_VALUE           101
#endif
#endif
```

Listing 5.13 was created by AppWizard and customized by App Studio to contain the definitions of the custom resource IDs. These IDs include those of the form and its controls.

Listing 15.14 provides the partial script of the APPSTUD3.RC resource file.

Listing 5.14 Partial Script of the APPSTUD3.RC Resource File

```
//Microsoft App Studio generated resource script.
//
#include "resource.h"

#define APSTUDIO_READONLY_SYMBOLS
/////////////////////////////////////////////////////////////
//
// Generated from the TEXTINCLUDE 2 resource.
//
#include "afxres.h"


/////////////////////////////////////////////////////////////
#undef APSTUDIO_READONLY_SYMBOLS

#ifdef APSTUDIO_INVOKED
/////////////////////////////////////////////////////////////
//
// TEXTINCLUDE
//

1 TEXTINCLUDE DISCARDABLE
BEGIN
    "resource.h\0"
END

2 TEXTINCLUDE DISCARDABLE
BEGIN
    "#include ""afxres.h""\r\n"
    "\0"
END

3 TEXTINCLUDE DISCARDABLE
BEGIN
    "#include ""res\\appstud3.rc2""  // non-App Studio edited
                                    // resources\r\n"
    "\r\n"
    "#include ""afxres.rc""  \011// Standard components\r\n"
    "\0"
END


/////////////////////////////////////////////////////////////
#endif    // APSTUDIO_INVOKED
```

(continues)

Listing 5.14 Continued

```
/////////////////////////////////////////////////////////
//
// Icon
//

IDR_MAINFRAME           ICON    DISCARDABLE     "RES\\APPSTUD3.ICO"

/////////////////////////////////////////////////////////
//
// Menu
//

IDR_MAINFRAME MENU PRELOAD DISCARDABLE
BEGIN
    MENUITEM "&Exit",                       ID_APP_EXIT
    POPUP "&Help"
    BEGIN
        MENUITEM "&About Appstud3...",      ID_APP_ABOUT
    END
END


/////////////////////////////////////////////////////////
//
// Accelerator
//

IDR_MAINFRAME ACCELERATORS PRELOAD MOVEABLE PURE
BEGIN
    "D",            IDC_DATE_BTN,           VIRTKEY,CONTROL, NOINVERT
    "S",            IDC_TIMER_BTN,          VIRTKEY,CONTROL, NOINVERT
END


/////////////////////////////////////////////////////////
//
// Dialog
//

IDD_ABOUTBOX DIALOG DISCARDABLE  34, 22, 217, 55
STYLE DS_MODALFRAME ¦ WS_POPUP ¦ WS_CAPTION ¦ WS_SYSMENU
CAPTION "About Appstud3"
FONT 8, "MS Sans Serif"
BEGIN
    ICON            IDR_MAINFRAME,IDC_STATIC,11,17,20,20
    LTEXT           "Appstud3 Application Version 1.0",
                    IDC_STATIC,40,10,119,
                    8
    LTEXT           "Copyright \251 1993",IDC_STATIC,40,25,119,8
    DEFPUSHBUTTON   "OK",IDOK,176,6,32,14,WS_GROUP
END
```

```
IDD_APPSTUD3_FORM DIALOG DISCARDABLE  0, 0, 267, 181
STYLE WS_CHILD
FONT 8, "MS Sans Serif"
BEGIN
    DEFPUSHBUTTON    "&Date/Time",IDC_DATE_BTN,5,110,54,20
    PUSHBUTTON       "&Start",IDC_TIMER_BTN,6,150,56,19
    EDITTEXT         IDC_MOUSEPOS_BOX,3,6,104,17,ES_READONLY ¦ NOT WS_BORDER
    EDITTEXT         IDC_DATE_BOX,70,115,155,20,ES_READONLY ¦ NOT WS_BORDER
    EDITTEXT         IDC_TIMER_BOX,75,151,146,22,ES_READONLY ¦ NOT WS_BORDER
END


/////////////////////////////////////////////////////////
//
// String Table
//
 .
 .
 .
/////////////////////////////////////////////////////////////////
#endif    // not APSTUDIO_INVOKED
```

The partial script of the APPSTUD3.RC resource file shown in Listing 5.14 defines various resources. Of special interest are the customized menu resource, the About dialog box resource, the form resource, and the accelerators resources used by the form's button controls. The form resource has the same syntax as that of an ordinary dialog box. The APPSTUD3.RC file originally was created by AppWizard and then modified by App Studio.

Listing 5.15 Source Code for the APPSTVW.H Header File

```
// appstvw.h : interface of the CAppstud3View class
//
/////////////////////////////////////////////////////////////////

const MaxStringLen = 40;

class CAppstud3View : public CFormView
{
protected: // create from serialization only
    CAppstud3View();
    DECLARE_DYNCREATE(CAppstud3View)

public:
    //{{AFX_DATA(CAppstud3View)
    enum { IDD = IDD_APPSTUD3_FORM };

    CButton m_TimerBtn;
    CButton m_DateBtn;
    CString m_MousePosBox;
    CString m_DateBox;
    CString m_TimerBox;
```

(continues)

Listing 5.15 Continued

```
        //}}AFX_DATA
        // additional members
        BOOL bTimerOn;
        long nInitTickCount;
        CTime tm;


    // Attributes
    public:
        CAppstud3Doc* GetDocument();

    // Operations
    public:

    // Implementation
    public:
        virtual ~CAppstud3View();
    #ifdef _DEBUG
        virtual void AssertValid() const;
        virtual void Dump(CDumpContext& dc) const;
    #endif

    protected:
        virtual void DoDataExchange(CDataExchange* pDX);    // DDX/DDV
                                                            // support

    // Generated message map functions
    protected:
        //{{AFX_MSG(CAppstud3View)
        afx_msg void OnDateBtn();
        afx_msg void OnTimerBtn();
        afx_msg void OnMouseMove(UINT nFlags, CPoint point);
        //}}AFX_MSG
        DECLARE_MESSAGE_MAP()
    };

    #ifndef _DEBUG  // debug version in appstvw.cpp
    inline CAppstud3Doc* CAppstud3View::GetDocument()
        { return (CAppstud3Doc*)m_pDocument; }
    #endif

    /////////////////////////////////////////////////////////////////////
```

The APPSTVW.H header file shown in Listing 5.15 contains the declaration
of the view class CAppstud3View. The listing declares this class as a descendant
of class CFormView. AppWizard created this file, and ClassWizard modified
it according to the steps that I described earlier. ClassWizard added the

declarations of the data members m_TimerBtn, m_DateBtn, m_MousePosBox, m_DateBox, and m_TimerBox. I added the data members bTimerOn, nInitTickCount, and tm. ClassWizard added the response handling member functions OnDateBtn, OnTimerBtn, and OnMouseMove. I also inserted at the beginning of the listing the declaration of the global constant MaxStringLen.

Listing 5.16 Source Code for the APPSTVW.CPP Implementation File

```
// appstvw.cpp : implementation of the CAppstud3View class
//

#include "stdafx.h"
#include "appstud3.h"

#include "appstdoc.h"
#include "appstvw.h"

#include <stdio.h>

#ifdef _DEBUG
#undef THIS_FILE
static char BASED_CODE THIS_FILE[] = __FILE__;
#endif

/////////////////////////////////////////////////////////////////////
// CAppstud3View

IMPLEMENT_DYNCREATE(CAppstud3View, CFormView)

BEGIN_MESSAGE_MAP(CAppstud3View, CFormView)
    //{{AFX_MSG_MAP(CAppstud3View)
    ON_BN_CLICKED(IDC_DATE_BTN, OnDateBtn)
    ON_BN_CLICKED(IDC_TIMER_BTN, OnTimerBtn)
    ON_WM_MOUSEMOVE()
    //}}AFX_MSG_MAP
END_MESSAGE_MAP()

/////////////////////////////////////////////////////////////////////
// CAppstud3View construction/destruction

CAppstud3View::CAppstud3View()
    : CFormView(CAppstud3View::IDD)
{
    //{{AFX_DATA_INIT(CAppstud3View)
    m_MousePosBox = "";
    m_DateBox = "";
    m_TimerBox = "";
    //}}AFX_DATA_INIT
    // TODO: add construction code here
    bTimerOn = FALSE;
}
```

(continues)

Listing 5.16 Continued

```
CAppstud3View::~CAppstud3View()
{
}

void CAppstud3View::DoDataExchange(CDataExchange* pDX)
{
    CFormView::DoDataExchange(pDX);
    //{{AFX_DATA_MAP(CAppstud3View)
    DDX_Control(pDX, IDC_TIMER_BTN, m_TimerBtn);
    DDX_Control(pDX, IDC_DATE_BTN, m_DateBtn);
    DDX_Text(pDX, IDC_MOUSEPOS_BOX, m_MousePosBox);
    DDX_Text(pDX, IDC_DATE_BOX, m_DateBox);
    DDX_Text(pDX, IDC_TIMER_BOX, m_TimerBox);
    //}}AFX_DATA_MAP
}

/////////////////////////////////////////////////////////////////
// CAppstud3View diagnostics

#ifdef _DEBUG
void CAppstud3View::AssertValid() const
{
    CFormView::AssertValid();
}

void CAppstud3View::Dump(CDumpContext& dc) const
{
    CFormView::Dump(dc);
}

CAppstud3Doc* CAppstud3View::GetDocument() // non-debug version is inline
{
    ASSERT(m_pDocument->IsKindOf(RUNTIME_CLASS(CAppstud3Doc)));
    return (CAppstud3Doc*)m_pDocument;
}
#endif //_DEBUG

/////////////////////////////////////////////////////////////////
// CAppstud3View message handlers
```

```
void CAppstud3View::OnDateBtn()
{

  char* pszStr = m_DateBox.GetBuffer(MaxStringLen);
  tm = CTime::GetCurrentTime();

  sprintf(pszStr,
          "Date is %02d/%02d/%4d, Time is %02d:%02d:%02d",
          tm.GetMonth(), tm.GetDay(), tm.GetYear(),
          tm.GetHour(), tm.GetMinute(), tm.GetSecond());
  m_DateBox.ReleaseBuffer(-1);
  SetDlgItemText(IDC_DATE_BOX, m_DateBox);
}
```

```
void CAppstud3View::OnTimerBtn()
{

  char* pszStr;

  if (bTimerOn) {
    bTimerOn = FALSE;
    pszStr = m_TimerBox.GetBuffer(MaxStringLen);
    SetDlgItemText(IDC_TIMER_BTN, "&Start");
    sprintf(pszStr, "%3.3lf seconds elapsed",
            (GetTickCount() - nInitTickCount) / 1000.0);
    m_TimerBox.ReleaseBuffer(-1);
    SetDlgItemText(IDC_TIMER_BOX, m_TimerBox);
  }
  else {
    bTimerOn = TRUE;
    SetDlgItemText(IDC_TIMER_BTN, "&Stop");
    nInitTickCount = GetTickCount();
  }
}

void CAppstud3View::OnMouseMove(UINT nFlags, CPoint point)
{
  char* pszStr = m_MousePosBox.GetBuffer(MaxStringLen);

  sprintf(pszStr, "[%03d, %03d]", point.x, point.y);
  m_MousePosBox.ReleaseBuffer(-1);
  SetDlgItemText(IDC_MOUSEPOS_BOX, m_MousePosBox);
}
```

The source code for the APPSTVW.CPP implementation file shown in Listing 5.16 was generated by AppWizard and then customized by ClassWizard. This customization incorporated the following elements:

- Inserting the message map macros for clicking the two pushbuttons in the form and for moving the mouse.

- Inserting the empty definitions of the On*XXXX* member functions.

- Initializing the data members m_MousePosBox, m_DateBox, and m_TimerBox by assigning empty strings to these CString instances. These initializations appear in the constructor of class CAppstud3View.

- Inserting the calls to DDX_Control and DDX_Text for the controls in the form.

I added the following statements:

- The #include directive to include the STDIO.H file.

■ The statements that define the member functions `OnDateBtn`, `OnTimerBtn`, and `OnMouseMove`. These statements are very similar to the ones that I presented earlier in the APPSTUD1 and APPSTUD2 projects. Notice that these functions use the inherited member function `SetDlgItemText` to alter the text in the edit boxes or to alter the caption of the Start pushbutton (the program toggles this caption between `Start` and `Stop`).

■ The statement that assigns FALSE to the data member `bTimerOn`. This statement is located in the view class constructor.

Compile and run the APPSTUD3.EXE program. Move the mouse and watch as the edit box in the upper-left corner displays the current mouse location. Click the Date/Time pushbutton to view the current system date and time in the adjacent edit box. Click the Start pushbutton and watch its caption change. Then click that button again and read the elapsed time in the adjacent edit box. To exit, click the Exit command. Figure 5.14 shows a sample session with the APPSTUD3.EXE program.

Figure 5.14
A sample session with the APPSTUD3.EXE program.

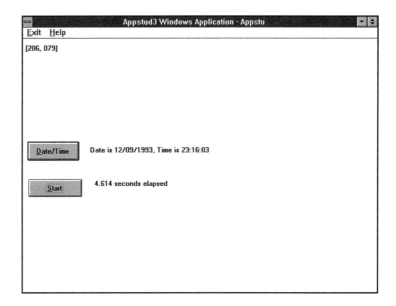

Summary

This chapter presented the versatile App Studio utility, which you can use to create and customize various resources. Here's what you learned:

- How to invoke App Studio from the Tools menu. The App Studio utility has its own menu system and client area. The menu system is not minimal and offers various commands to work with App Studio.

- How to use App Studio to modify a menu resource of an application generated by AppWizard. Through a sample project, you learned how to load an existing menu resource and then customize it by deleting and adding menu items.

- How to use App Studio to add a new dialog box resource to an application generated by AppWizard. Through a sample project, you learned how to create the dialog box resource, create an icon for the dialog box, and add the supporting dialog box class. The dialog box class supports the dialog box resource by initializing it and by responding to the proper messages.

- How to use App Studio to add new controls to a form view in an application generated by AppWizard. A sample project showed you how to create a form view class using AppWizard, how to use App Studio to draw its controls, and how to use ClassWizard to customize the code.

Introduction to Visual C++

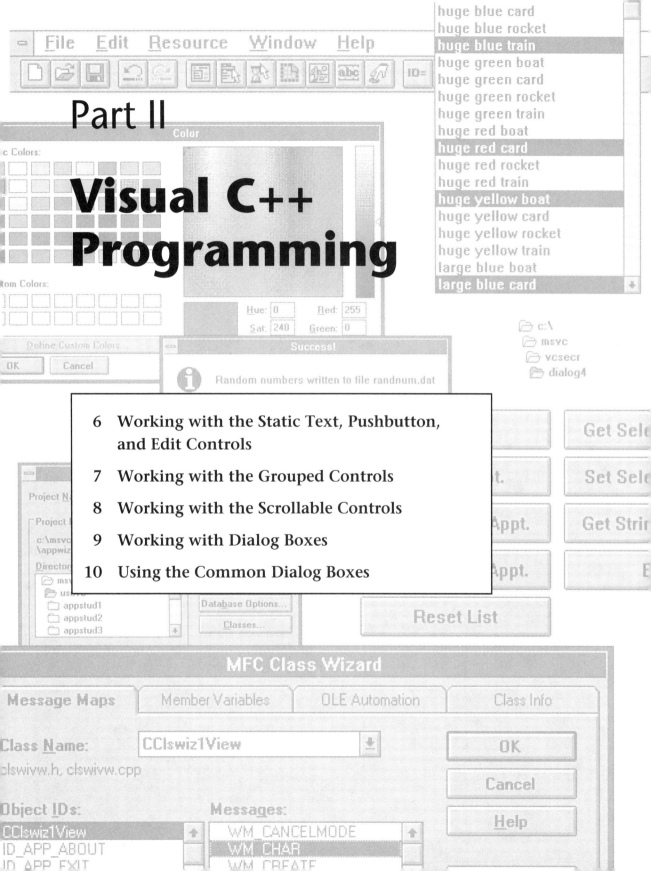

Part II

Visual C++ Programming

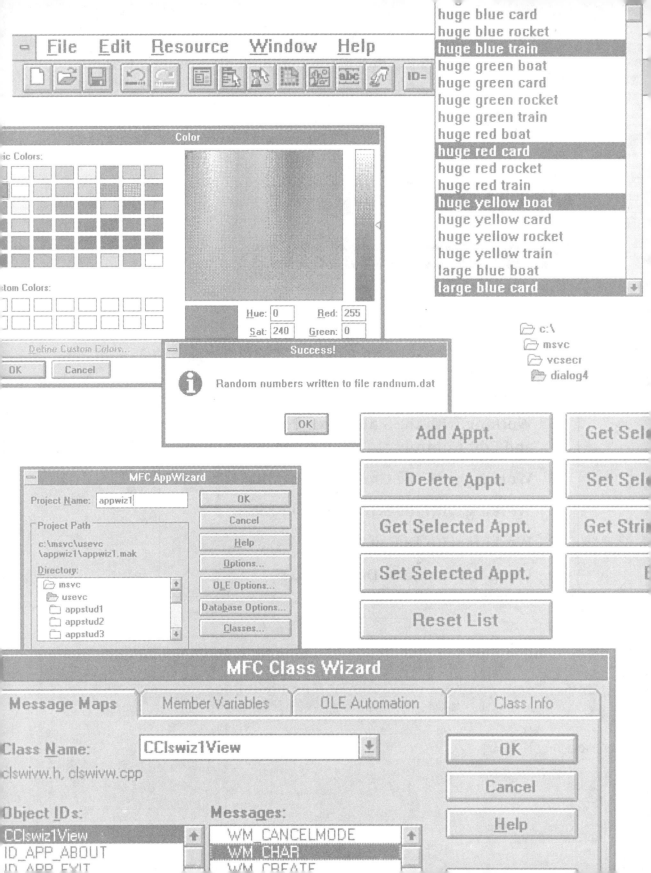

Chapter 6

Working with the Static Text, Pushbutton, and Edit Controls

Windows fosters a style of interaction between its applications and the users of those applications. This interaction takes place with menus, speed bars, and dialog boxes. As you learned in earlier chapters, dialog boxes are special windows that "pop up" following a particular event, such as when a certain menu command is invoked. Dialog boxes contain various controls that support communication and interaction between you and the application. Beginning with this chapter and continuing through Chapter 8, I present the various dialog box controls. Our safari into Windows Control Country begins with an examination of the three most basic controls:

- The static text control

- The edit control

- The pushbutton control

If you want to implement versatile applications, you must master the various controls and understand how they "behave"; this knowledge enables you to create highly interactive Windows applications. The material in this chapter and in Chapters 7 and 8 does not constitute a reference for the various controls. Instead, the main members of the classes that model these controls are presented.

The Static Text Control

The static text control supplies static text to a window or dialog box. Think of a static text control as text that the application user cannot change, but that the program can change at run time. Although you *can* alter the text associated with a static text control at run time, you have the option of establishing the text as permanent and unchangeable. Along with displaying text, static text controls can also display black, gray, and white rectangles and frames. The CStatic class implements the static text control. Now let's look at the class constructor and its members.

The *CStatic* Class

The CStatic class, a descendant of CWnd, models static text controls that possess a rectangular display area, visible text, and text attributes. You can only alter the visible text during run time. Here is the declaration of the Create member function:

```
BOOL Create(LPCSTR lpszText,      // control text
            DWORD dwStyle,         // control style
            const RECT& rect,      // control area
            CWnd* pParentWnd,      // parent window
            UINT nID = 0xffff);    // control ID
```

The parameter lpszText designates the pointer to the string that supplies the visible text for the static text control. The dwStyle parameter specifies the style of the control. Typically, the styles WS_CHILD and WS_VISIBLE are part of the arguments for the parameter dwStyle. Table 6.1 contains the set of SS_*XXXX* static text styles. The creation of a static text control includes one or more of these styles. The parameter rect specifies the rectangular area in which the static text control appears. The parameter pParentWnd is the pointer to the parent window. The parameter nID specifies the ID of the control; this ID may not be unique. The function Create assigns the default argument 0xffff, because a static text control typically does not send notification messages to its parent window. The Create function yields TRUE if it succeeds. Otherwise, it returns FALSE.

The parameter lpszText is the pointer which accesses the string that supplies the static text control with its text. This string can contain the ampersand character (&) to visually highlight a hot key character with an underline. Keep in mind that highlighting the character does not activate the hot key. (For the hot key to be activated, your application must load accelerator keys.) Place the ampersand character before the designated hot key character.

Should the argument of `lpszText` include more than one ampersand character, only the last occurrence of an ampersand is effective. The remaining occurrences are ignored and do not appear. In order to display the ampersand character, you must use `&&` or specify the `SS_NOPREFIX` style (to display `&` with a single ampersand character). Consequently, the `SS_NOPREFIX` style disables the capability to use the ampersand to designate other characters as hot keys.

The component of the static text control that you can change during run time is the text itself. If you specify the `SS_SIMPLE` style during the creation of a `CStatic` instance, however, you cannot alter its text. In this sense, the instance of `CStatic` is, indeed, etched in stone.

You can use the `CStatic` class to set, query, and clear the characters of the static text using the following functions inherited from class `CWnd`:

- The parameterless member function `GetWindowTextLength` yields the length of the text in a static text control. This function provides you with information related to the size of the buffer required to retrieve a copy of the control's text.

- The overloaded member function `GetWindowText` permits you to gain access to the characters of the control's text. The declarations of the overloaded `GetWindowText` functions are

    ```
    int GetWindowText(LPSTR lpszStringBuf, int nMaxCount) const;
    void GetWindowText(CString& rString) const;
    ```

    The parameter `lpszStringBuf` is a pointer to the ASCIIZ string buffer, which obtains a copy of the static text characters. The parameter `nMaxCount` specifies the maximum number of static text characters to copy. The result of the first overloaded function returns the actual number of characters copied to the buffer accessed by the pointer `lpszStringBuf`. The second overloaded function has a reference parameter that is a `CString` object. The function uses this string object to obtain a copy of the static text characters. The function has a `void` return type.

- The `SetWindowText` member function overwrites the current static text characters with those of a new string. The declaration of the `SetWindowText` function is

    ```
    void SetWindowText(LPCSTR lpszString);
    ```

II

Visual C++ Programming

The parameter lpszString is the pointer to the string that provides the control with new text. Use an empty string for the new text to clear the previous text in the targeted static text control.

Table 6.1 Static Text Style Values

Value	Meaning
SS_BLACKFRAME	Designates a box with a frame drawn that is the same color as the window frame. This color is black in the default Windows color scheme.
SS_BLACKRECT	Specifies a rectangle filled with the same color as the window frame. This color is black in the default Windows color scheme.
SS_CENTER	Centers the static text characters. The text is wrappable.
SS_GRAYFRAME	Specifies a box with a frame that is the same color as the screen background. This color is gray in the default Windows color scheme.
SS_GRAYRECT	Selects a rectangle filled with the same color as the screen background. This color is gray in the default Windows color scheme.
SS_LEFT	Indicates left-justified text. The text is wrappable.
SS_LEFTNOWORDWRAP	Indicates left-justified text that cannot be wrapped.
SS_NOPREFIX	Specifies that the ampersand character in the static text string should not be a hot key designator character. Instead, the & character appears as part of the static text character.
SS_RIGHT	Selects right-justified text that is wrappable.
SS_SIMPLE	Indicates that the static text characters cannot be altered at run time. In addition, the static text is displayed on a single line. Line breaks are ignored.
SS_WHITEFRAME	Specifies a box with a frame that is the same color as the window background. This color is white in the default Windows color scheme.
SS_WHITERECT	Selects a rectangle filled with the same color as the window background. This color is white in the default Windows color scheme.

Static Text Samplers

Let's look at a simple application that presents static text controls with different styles. The CTLSTAT1.EXE program gives you a feel for the various display attributes and how you can use them to show the following types of static text. The program uses the `#if`-`#elif`-`#else`-`#endif` compiler directive to compile into three different programs. These programs use a defined name to select which set of styles to illustrate. The first set illustrates the following styles:

- Simple static text

- Default single- and multi-line static text

- Left-justified single- and multi-line static text

- Long wrappable static text

The second set illustrates these styles:

- Right-justified single- and multi-line static text

- Centered single- and multi-line static text

- Long unwrappable static text

The third set demonstrates these styles:

- The black frame and rectangle

- The gray frame and rectangle

- The white frame and rectangle

- The black frame that contains text

- The gray frame that contains text

- The white frame that contains text

The CTLSTAT1.EXE program supports a special feature for the first two sets of static text controls: When you click the controls in the right column with the left mouse button, you convert the text of these controls to lowercase. By contrast, when you click these same controls with the right mouse button, you convert the text to uppercase.

Listing 6.1 displays the contents of the CTLSTAT1 definition file.

Listing 6.1 The CTLSTAT1 Definition File

```
NAME          CtlStat1
DESCRIPTION   'An MFC Windows Application'
EXETYPE       WINDOWS
STUB          'WINSTUB.EXE'
CODE          PRELOAD MOVEABLE DISCARDABLE
DATA          PRELOAD MOVEABLE MULTIPLE
HEAPSIZE      1024
```

Listing 6.2 shows the source code for the CTLSTAT1.H header file, which contains a single #define statement.

Listing 6.2 Source Code for the CTLSTAT1.H Header File

```
#define CM_EXIT (WM_USER + 200)
```

Listing 6.3 contains the script for the CTLSTAT1.RC resource file. The resource file defines the EXITMENU menu resource with a single item, Exit.

Listing 6.3 Script for the CTLSTAT1.RC Resource File

```
#include <windows.h>
#include <afxres.h>
#include "ctlstat1.h"
EXITMENU MENU LOADONCALL MOVEABLE PURE DISCARDABLE
BEGIN
    MENUITEM "E&xit", CM_EXIT
END
```

Listing 6.4 shows the source code for the CTLSTAT1.CPP program.

Listing 6.4 Source Code for the CTLSTAT1.CPP Program

```
/*

            Static Text Sampler version 1.0 11/3/93

    Program which demonstrates creating static text controls
    with different styles.  The program uses conditional compilation
    to display different sets of static text controls

*/

#include <stdlib.h>
#include <string.h>
#include <afxwin.h>
#include "ctlstat1.h"
```

```
// define selector for static text controls
// values range from 1 to 3
#define SET_SELECTOR 1

//----------- declare global "parameters"  -----------
// X coordinate for the upper-left corner of
// the left column of static text
const XLstat = 25;
const Ystat = 25;
const Hstat = 35;
const Wstat = 250;
// X coordinate for the upper-left corner of
// the right column of static text
const XRstat = XLstat + Wstat + 50;
// spacing between static text area
const Ydelta = 10;
// maximum size of a string in a static control
const MaxStringLen = 80;
// maximum number of static text controls
const MaxControls = 20;

// Define a window class derived from CFrameWnd
class CMainWnd : public CFrameWnd
{
public:

  CMainWnd();

  ~CMainWnd();

 protected:

  // declare array of pointers to static text controls
  CStatic* pEditText[MaxControls];

  // declare array of rectangles containing the static text
  // controls to manipulate
  CRect rectArr[MaxControls];

  int rectIdx[MaxControls];

  // the number of controls to manipulate
  int nControlsToManipulate;

  // handle creating the controls
  afx_msg int OnCreate(LPCREATESTRUCT lpCS);

  // handle clicking the left mouse button
  afx_msg void OnLButtonDown(UINT nFlags, CPoint point);

  // handle clicking the right mouse button
  afx_msg void OnRButtonDown(UINT nFlags, CPoint point);

  // handle closing the window
  afx_msg void OnClose();
```

(continues)

Listing 6.4 Continued

```cpp
    // handle exiting the application
    afx_msg void CMExit()
      { SendMessage(WM_CLOSE); }

    // declare message map macro
    DECLARE_MESSAGE_MAP();

};

// Define an application class derived from CWinApp
class CStaticTextApp : public CWinApp
{
public:

  virtual BOOL InitInstance();

};

CMainWnd::CMainWnd()
{
  UINT ClassStyle = CS_VREDRAW | CS_HREDRAW;
  HBRUSH hColor = (HBRUSH)(COLOR_HIGHLIGHTTEXT + 1);
  const char FAR* lpszClassName;

  // initialize the pointers to the static controls
  for (int i = 0; i < MaxControls; i++)
    pEditText[i] = NULL;

  // set the number of controls to manipulate to 7 or 0
  nControlsToManipulate =
      (SET_SELECTOR == 1 || SET_SELECTOR == 2) ? 7 : 0;

  // obtain the class registration name
  lpszClassName = AfxRegisterWndClass(ClassStyle, NULL,
                                      hColor, NULL);

    Create(lpszClassName, "A Static Text Control Sampler",
           WS_OVERLAPPEDWINDOW, rectDefault, NULL, "EXITMENU");

}

CMainWnd::~CMainWnd()
{
  for (int i = 0; i < MaxControls; i++)
    if (pEditText[i])
      delete pEditText[i];
}

int CMainWnd::OnCreate(LPCREATESTRUCT lpCS)
{
  int i = 0;
  int index = 0;
  char s[MaxStringLen+1];
  char longStr[161];
  char oneLine[] = "Single-line s&tatic text";
  char multiLine[] = "Multiline\nstatic t&ext";
```

```
    DWORD dwStaticStyle = WS_CHILD | WS_VISIBLE;
    DWORD dwLeftStaticStyle = dwStaticStyle | SS_LEFT;
    CRect r1(XLstat, Ydelta + Ystat,
            XLstat + Wstat, Ydelta + Ystat + Hstat);
    CRect r2(XRstat, Ydelta + Ystat,
            XRstat + Wstat, Ydelta + Ystat + Hstat);
    CPoint pt(0, Hstat + Ydelta);

#if SET_SELECTOR == 1

    // set the default single-line static text
    strcpy(s, "Default single-line static text");
    pEditText[i] = new CStatic();
    pEditText[i++]->Create(s, dwLeftStaticStyle, r1, this);
    pEditText[i] = new CStatic();
    pEditText[i]->Create(oneLine, dwLeftStaticStyle, r2, this);
    rectArr[index] = r2;
    rectIdx[index++] = i++;
    r1 += pt;
    r2 += pt;

    // set the default multiline static text
    strcpy(s, "Default multiline static text");
    pEditText[i] = new CStatic();
    pEditText[i++]->Create(s, dwLeftStaticStyle, r1, this);
    pEditText[i] = new CStatic();
    pEditText[i]->Create(multiLine, dwLeftStaticStyle, r2, this);
    rectArr[index] = r2;
    rectIdx[index++] = i++;
    r1 += pt;
    r2 += pt;

    // set the simple single-line static text
    strcpy(s, "Simple single-line static text");
    pEditText[i] = new CStatic();
    pEditText[i++]->Create(s, dwLeftStaticStyle, r1, this);
    pEditText[i] = new CStatic();
    pEditText[i]->Create(oneLine, dwLeftStaticStyle | SS_SIMPLE,
            r2, this);
    rectArr[index] = r2;
    rectIdx[index++] = i++;
    r1 += pt;
    r2 += pt;

    // set the simple multiline static text
    strcpy(s, "Simple multiline static text");
    pEditText[i] = new CStatic();
    pEditText[i++]->Create(s, dwLeftStaticStyle, r1, this);
    pEditText[i] = new CStatic();
    pEditText[i]->Create(multiLine, dwLeftStaticStyle | SS_SIMPLE,
            r2, this);
    rectArr[index] = r2;
    rectIdx[index++] = i++;
    r1 += pt;
    r2 += pt;
```

(continues)

Listing 6.4 Continued

```
      // set the left-justified single-line static text
      strcpy(s, "Left-justified single-line static text");
      pEditText[i] = new CStatic();
      pEditText[i++]->Create(s, dwLeftStaticStyle, r1, this);
      pEditText[i] = new CStatic();
      pEditText[i]->Create(oneLine, dwLeftStaticStyle, r2, this);
      rectArr[index] = r2;
      rectIdx[index++] = i++;
      r1 += pt;
      r2 += pt;

      // set the left-justified multiline static text
      strcpy(s, "Left-justified multiline static text");
      pEditText[i] = new CStatic();
      pEditText[i++]->Create(s, dwLeftStaticStyle, r1, this);
      pEditText[i] = new CStatic();
      pEditText[i]->Create(multiLine, dwLeftStaticStyle, r2, this);
      rectArr[index] = r2;
      rectIdx[index++] = i++;
      r1 += pt;
      r2 += pt;

      // set the left-justified long single-line static text
      strcpy(s, "Left-justified long single-line static text");
      pEditText[i] = new CStatic();
      pEditText[i++]->Create(s, dwLeftStaticStyle, r1, this);
      strcpy(longStr, "This string is longer than the other strings.");
      strcat(longStr, "  It illustrates text wrapping.");
      pEditText[i] = new CStatic();
      pEditText[i]->Create(longStr, dwLeftStaticStyle, r2, this);
      rectArr[index] = r2;
      rectIdx[index++] = i++;
      r1 += pt;
      r2 += pt;

#elif SET_SELECTOR == 2

      // set the left-justified long single-line static text
      strcpy(s, "Unwrappable long single-line static text");
      pEditText[i] = new CStatic();
      pEditText[i++]->Create(s, dwLeftStaticStyle, r1, this);
      strcpy(longStr, "This string is longer than the other strings.");
      strcat(longStr, "  It illustrates how to prevent text wrapping.");
      pEditText[i] = new CStatic();
      pEditText[i]->Create(longStr, dwLeftStaticStyle |
              SS_LEFTNOWORDWRAP, r2, this);
      rectArr[index] = r2;
      rectIdx[index++] = i++;
      r1 += pt;
      r2 += pt;

      // set the right-justified single-line static text
      strcpy(s, "Right-justified single-line static text");
      pEditText[i] = new CStatic();
```

```
pEditText[i++]->Create(s, dwLeftStaticStyle, r1, this);
pEditText[i] = new CStatic();
pEditText[i]->Create(oneLine, dwStaticStyle | SS_RIGHT, r2, this);
rectArr[index] = r2;
rectIdx[index++] = i++;
r1 += pt;
r2 += pt;

// set the right-justified multiline static text
strcpy(s, "Right-justified multiline static text");
pEditText[i] = new CStatic();
pEditText[i++]->Create(s, dwLeftStaticStyle, r1, this);
pEditText[i] = new CStatic();
pEditText[i]->Create(multiLine, dwStaticStyle | SS_RIGHT,
                     r2, this);
rectArr[index] = r2;
rectIdx[index++] = i++;
r1 += pt;
r2 += pt;

// set the centered single-line static text
strcpy(s, "Centered single-line static text");
pEditText[i] = new CStatic();
pEditText[i++]->Create(s, dwLeftStaticStyle, r1, this);
pEditText[i] = new CStatic();
pEditText[i]->Create(oneLine, dwStaticStyle | SS_CENTER, r2, this);
rectArr[index] = r2;
rectIdx[index++] = i++;
r1 += pt;
r2 += pt;

// set the centered multiline static text
strcpy(s, "Centered multiline static text");
pEditText[i] = new CStatic();
pEditText[i++]->Create(s, dwLeftStaticStyle, r1, this);
pEditText[i] = new CStatic();
pEditText[i]->Create(multiLine, dwStaticStyle | SS_CENTER,
                     r2, this);
rectArr[index] = r2;
rectIdx[index++] = i++;
r1 += pt;
r2 += pt;

// set the centered single-line static text with no prefix
strcpy(s, "Centered single-line static text with no prefix");
pEditText[i] = new CStatic();
pEditText[i++]->Create(s, dwLeftStaticStyle, r1, this);
pEditText[i] = new CStatic();
pEditText[i]->Create(oneLine, dwStaticStyle | SS_CENTER |
                     SS_NOPREFIX, r2, this);
rectArr[index] = r2;
rectIdx[index++] = i++;
r1 += pt;
r2 += pt;

#else
```

(continues)

Listing 6.4 Continued

```
// show a black frame
strcpy(s, "Black frame style");
pEditText[i] = new CStatic();
pEditText[i++]->Create(s, dwLeftStaticStyle, r1, this);
pEditText[i] = new CStatic();
pEditText[i++]->Create(oneLine, dwLeftStaticStyle | SS_BLACKFRAME,
        r2, this);
r1 += pt;
r2 += pt;

// show a black frame with text
strcpy(s, "Black frame with text");
pEditText[i] = new CStatic();
pEditText[i++]->Create(s, dwLeftStaticStyle, r1, this);
rectIdx[index++] = i++;
pEditText[i] = new CStatic();
pEditText[i++]->Create(oneLine, dwLeftStaticStyle, r2, this);
pEditText[i] = new CStatic();
pEditText[i++]->Create(oneLine, dwLeftStaticStyle | SS_BLACKFRAME,
        r2, this);
r1 += pt;
r2 += pt;

// show a black rectangle
strcpy(s, "Black rectangle style");
pEditText[i] = new CStatic();
pEditText[i++]->Create(s, dwLeftStaticStyle, r1, this);
pEditText[i] = new CStatic();
pEditText[i++]->Create(oneLine, dwLeftStaticStyle | SS_BLACKRECT,
        r2, this);
r1 += pt;
r2 += pt;

// show a gray frame
strcpy(s, "Gray frame style");
pEditText[i] = new CStatic();
pEditText[i++]->Create(s, dwLeftStaticStyle, r1, this);
pEditText[i] = new CStatic();
pEditText[i++]->Create(oneLine, dwLeftStaticStyle, r2, this);
pEditText[i] = new CStatic();
pEditText[i++]->Create(oneLine, dwLeftStaticStyle | SS_GRAYFRAME,
        r2, this);
r1 += pt;
r2 += pt;

// show a gray frame with text
strcpy(s, "Gray frame with text");
pEditText[i] = new CStatic();
pEditText[i++]->Create(s, dwLeftStaticStyle, r1, this);
pEditText[i] = new CStatic();
pEditText[i++]->Create(oneLine, dwLeftStaticStyle, r2, this);
pEditText[i] = new CStatic();
pEditText[i++]->Create(oneLine, dwLeftStaticStyle | SS_GRAYFRAME,
        r2, this);
```

```
    r1 += pt;
    r2 += pt;

    // show a gray rectangle
    strcpy(s, "Gray rectangle style");
    pEditText[i] = new CStatic();
    pEditText[i++]->Create(s, dwLeftStaticStyle, r1, this);
    pEditText[i] = new CStatic();
    pEditText[i++]->Create(oneLine, dwLeftStaticStyle, r2, this);
    pEditText[i] = new CStatic();
    pEditText[i++]->Create(oneLine, dwLeftStaticStyle | SS_GRAYRECT,
            r2, this);
    r1 += pt;
    r2 += pt;

    // show a white frame
    strcpy(s, "White frame style");
    pEditText[i] = new CStatic();
    pEditText[i++]->Create(s, dwLeftStaticStyle, r1, this);
    pEditText[i] = new CStatic();
    pEditText[i++]->Create(oneLine, dwLeftStaticStyle | SS_WHITEFRAME,
            r2, this);
    r1 += pt;
    r2 += pt;

    // show a white frame with text
    strcpy(s, "White frame with text");
    pEditText[i] = new CStatic();
    pEditText[i++]->Create(s, dwLeftStaticStyle, r1, this);
    pEditText[i] = new CStatic();
    pEditText[i++]->Create(oneLine, dwLeftStaticStyle, r2, this);
    pEditText[i] = new CStatic();
    pEditText[i++]->Create(oneLine, dwLeftStaticStyle | SS_WHITEFRAME,
            r2, this);
    r1 += pt;
    r2 += pt;

    // show a white rectangle
    strcpy(s, "White rectangle style");
    pEditText[i] = new CStatic();
    pEditText[i++]->Create(s, dwLeftStaticStyle, r1, this);
    pEditText[i] = new CStatic();
    pEditText[i++]->Create(oneLine, dwLeftStaticStyle | SS_WHITERECT,
            r2, this);
    r1 += pt;
    r2 += pt;

#endif

    return CFrameWnd::OnCreate(lpCS);
}


void CMainWnd::OnLButtonDown(UINT nFlags, CPoint point)
{
    int i = 0;
```

(continues)

Listing 6.4 Continued

```
      int j;
      BOOL notFound = TRUE;
      char s[MaxStringLen+1];
      CString w(' ', MaxStringLen);

      if (nControlsToManipulate) {
        while (i < nControlsToManipulate && notFound) {
          if (rectArr[i].PtInRect(point) == FALSE)
            i++;
          else
            notFound = FALSE;
        }

        // found a match?
        if (!notFound) {
          j = rectIdx[i];
          pEditText[j]->GetWindowText(s, MaxStringLen);
          strlwr(s);
          pEditText[j]->SetWindowText((const char*)w);
          pEditText[j]->SetWindowText(s);
        }
      }
    }

    void CMainWnd::OnRButtonDown(UINT nFlags, CPoint point)
    {
      int i = 0;
      int j;
      BOOL notFound = TRUE;
      char s[MaxStringLen+1];
      CString w(' ', MaxStringLen);


      if (nControlsToManipulate) {
        while (i < nControlsToManipulate && notFound) {
          if (rectArr[i].PtInRect(point) == FALSE)
            i++;
          else
            notFound = FALSE;
        }

        // found a match?
        if (!notFound) {
          j = rectIdx[i];
          pEditText[j]->GetWindowText(s, MaxStringLen);
          strupr(s);
          pEditText[j]->SetWindowText((const char*)w);
          pEditText[j]->SetWindowText(s);
        }
      }
    }

    void CMainWnd::OnClose()
    {
```

```
      if (MessageBox("Want to close this application",
            "Query", MB_YESNO | MB_ICONQUESTION) == IDYES)
      DestroyWindow();
}

BEGIN_MESSAGE_MAP(CMainWnd, CFrameWnd)
    ON_WM_CREATE()
    ON_WM_LBUTTONDOWN()
    ON_WM_RBUTTONDOWN()
    ON_WM_CLOSE()
    ON_COMMAND(CM_EXIT, CMExit)
END_MESSAGE_MAP()

// Construct the CStaticTextApp's m_pMainWnd data member
BOOL CStaticTextApp::InitInstance()
{
  m_pMainWnd = new CMainWnd();
  m_pMainWnd->ShowWindow(m_nCmdShow);
  m_pMainWnd->UpdateWindow();
  return TRUE;
}

// application's constructor initializes and runs the app
CStaticTextApp WindowApp;
```

I recommend that you compile and run the static text sampler application (CTLSTAT1.EXE) three times—each time altering the value that defines the symbol SET_SELECTOR. Click the controls in the right column with the left or right mouse buttons and watch the text of the controls change to lowercase or uppercase. Figures 6.1 through 6.3 show the three sets of static text controls generated by the CTLSTAT1.EXE application. The main window shows two columns of static text controls. The left column shows commenting text that explains the type of static text shown in the right column. On my system, the application window has a white background and the static text instances have a blue background. This contrast in color enables you to visually detect the area specified by the Create function when it creates the numerous static text instances.

After running the program CTLSTAT1.EXE to view the different sets of static text controls, you might notice these things:

■ Single- and multi-line default static text share the same appearance as the left-justified single- and multi-line static text, respectively.

■ The simple static text has a background color that extends only with the text characters.

II

Visual C++ Programming

■ Any attempt to display simple multi-line static text fails. In fact, the line break character appears with the rest of the text.

■ The normal left-justified long static text succeeds in wrapping to the next line in the rectangle defined by the constructor.

■ The left-justified long static text with the SS_LEFTNOWORDWRAP style does not wrap around and instead is truncated.

■ The multi-line right-justified static text has all lines right-justified, not just the first line.

■ The multi-line centered static text has all lines centered.

■ The characters of the static text with black, gray, and white rectangle styles are invisible.

■ The characters of the static text with black, gray, and white frame styles are essentially invisible. Using a simple programming trick that I present later, however, you can still display text inside these frames.

Figure 6.1

The first set of static text controls in a sample session with the CTLSTAT1.EXE application.

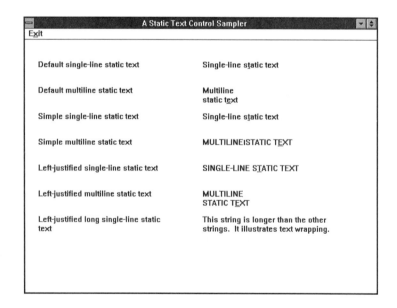

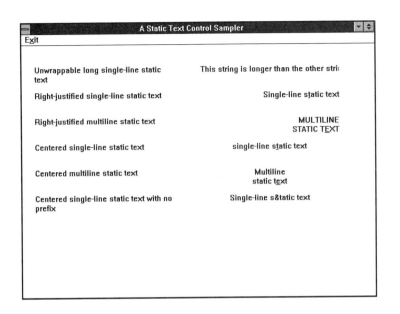

Figure 6.2

The second set of static text controls in CTLSTAT1.EXE.

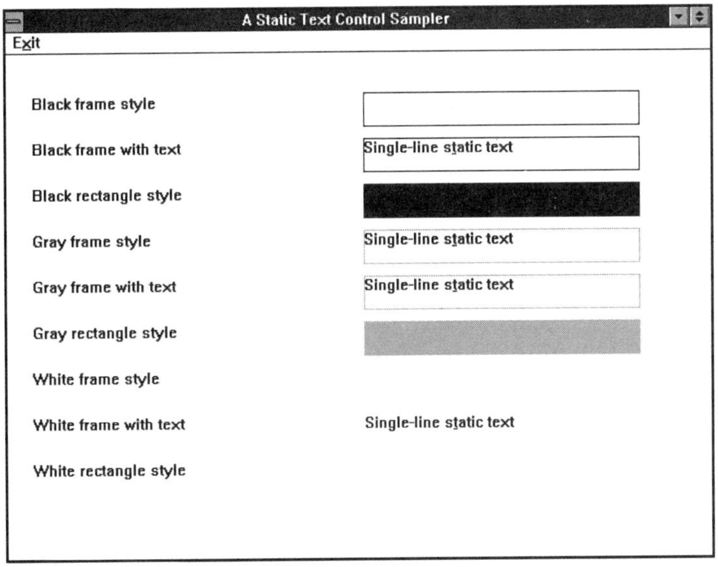

Figure 6.3

The third set of static text controls in CTLSTAT1.EXE.

Now let's focus on how the static text sampler works (refer to the source code shown in Listing 6.4). The program defines the global macro SET_SELECTOR, which is used to select the set of static text controls. The listing also declares a set of global constants (or program parameters, if you prefer) which specify the location, size, and spacing for the static text instances. The program declares the application class CStaticTextApp and the window class CMainWnd. The instance of CStaticTextApp owns the instance of CMainWnd, which in turn owns and manages the set of CStatic instances.

The CMainWnd class declares the array of CStatic* pointers, pEditText, to access the various instances of class CStatic. The data member pEditText has two roles. First, when the window generates the various CStatic instances, it uses members of the array pEditText to access these instances and to call the member function CStatic::Create. Second, the array of pointers is used in the ~CMainWnd destructor to destroy the various instances of class CStatic.

The CMainWnd class declares other data members:

- The data member rectArr is an array of rectangular areas occupied by the manipulated static text controls (that is, those whose text can be toggled between lowercase and uppercase characters).

- The data member rectIdx is an array of indices for the manipulated static text controls.

- The data member nControlsToManipulate stores the number of manipulated static text controls.

The CMainWnd class has a constructor, a destructor, and a set of protected member functions. The CMainWnd constructor declares a number of initialized local variables. These variables specify the Windows registration class name, attribute style, and background color. The constructor performs the following tasks:

- Assigns NULL to the members of the pEditText array.

- Obtains the class registration name by calling the global function AfxRegisterWndClass.

- Invokes the Create function to create the various controls. The call to Create also specifies the window title, attribute, rectangular area, and the menu resource EXITMENU.

The protected member function OnCreate creates the various controls owned by the main window. OnCreate declares a number of local variables. The variable i stores the row index of the static text. The other variables store various strings. The variable oneLine contains a sample single-line text, whereas the multiLine variable stores a string with a line break. The instance of CRect, r1, specifies the rectangular area for the *commenting text* located in the left column. The instance of CRect, r2, stores the rectangular areas for the various static text samples. The pt object stores the vertical spacing between the rows of static text samples.

The OnCreate function performs the following tasks for the first set of controls:

1. Constructs a default single-line static text sample. The sample static text is created by using the CStatic constructor and then the CStatic::Create member function. The Create function uses the oneLine string and the default style specified by the local variable dwLeftStaticStyle. The OnCreate function creates all other static text instances in a similar fashion.

2. Creates a default multi-line static text sample. Notice that the r1 and r2 objects are incremented by pt to adjust their coordinates for the next row of static text. This scheme of incrementing objects r1 and r2 is used systematically in this function. In addition, the local variable i is incremented in the same statement that invokes the Create function to build a static text sample.

3. Generates a simple single-line static text sample. Notice that the control style includes the SS_SIMPLE style.

4. *Attempts* to create a simple multi-line static text sample. The attempt fails, resulting in the display of a single-line simple static text.

5. Creates a left-justified, single-, and multi-line static text sample.

6. Generates a long, left-justified, single-line static text sample.

The OnCreate function performs the following tasks for the second set of controls:

1. Creates a long, left-justified, single-line static text sample that does not wrap around. The control style includes the SS_LEFTNOWORDWRAP style.

2. Generates a right-justified, single-, and multi-line static text sample. The control style includes the SS_RIGHT style.

3. Creates a centered, single-, and multi-line static text sample. The control style includes the SS_CENTER style.

II

Visual C++ Programming

4. Generates a centered, single-line static text sample with no prefix. The control style includes the SS_CENTER and SS_NOPREFIX styles.

The OnCreate function carries out the following tasks for the third set of controls:

1. Creates a black frame by specifying the SS_BLACKFRAME style. Notice in Figure 6.3 that the characters of the oneLine variable are not visible.

2. Generates a black frame that contains text. The programming trick here is to first create the visible text instance and then create the black frame. Using the reverse creation sequence causes the frame to block the text. Incidentally, the same trick does not work with the rectangle style.

3. Creates gray and white frames and rectangles. The frames are created both with text and without text inside, using the trick I just mentioned.

The member function OnLButtonDown responds to the left mouse click. The function converts to lowercase the characters of any right side static text control that you point to and click with the left mouse button. The function performs the following tasks if the value is positive in the data member nControlsToManipulate:

■ Searches for a matching static text control. This task uses a while loop to iterate over the nControlsToManipulate manipulated controls. Each loop iteration executes the nested if statement. This statement sends the C++ message PtInRect to the object rectArr[i] (an element of the data member rectArr). The argument of this message is the parameter point. The if statement compares the result of this message with FALSE. If the two Boolean values match (that is, if the rectangle rectArr[i] does not contain the point-type parameter point), the if statement increments the loop control variable i. Otherwise, the function executes the else clause, which assigns FALSE to the local Boolean variable notFound.

■ Determines whether the search in the preceding while loop found a match. If it did, the function performs the following subtasks:

• Assigns the index of the matching control (stored in the element rectIdx[i]) to the local variable j.

- Recalls the text in the matching static text control. This subtask sends the C++ message `GetWindowText` to the static text control that is accessed by the pointer `pEditText[j]`. The C++ message uses the local string s as the buffer to obtain the string in the matching static text control.

- Converts the characters of string s to lowercase.

- Assigns the uppercase characters to the matching static text control. This subtask involves sending the C++ message `SetWindowText` (with the argument s) to the object accessed by the pointer `pEditText[j]`.

The member function `OnRButtonDown` performs a set of tasks that is similar to that of the `OnLButtonDown` function. The difference is that the function `OnRButtonDown` converts the text of the matching static text control to uppercase.

The Edit Control

The MFC Library offers the `CEdit` class, which models an edit box control. The edit control permits you to type characters and edit the text. In this section, the operations of class `CEdit` are discussed in greater detail; you can enhance your applications by becoming familiar with the `CEdit` member functions.

The *CEdit* Class

The `CEdit` class, a child of class `CWnd`, implements a versatile edit control that supports single-line and multi-line text, as well as the capability to cut, paste, copy, delete, and clear text. The edit control also can undo the most recent text changes and exchange text with the Clipboard. The `CEdit` class has a constructor and a `Create` member function used in building the various class instances. Here is the declaration of the `Create` function:

```
BOOL Create(DWORD dwStyle,        // control style
            const RECT& rect,     // control area
            CWnd* pParentWnd,     // parent window
            UINT nID);            // control ID
```

The parameter `dwStyle` specifies the control style. The arguments for the `dwStyle` parameter typically include the `WS_CHILD` and `WS_VISIBLE` styles. Table 6.2 shows the collection of `ES_XXXX` edit control styles. Use a combination of these styles to create edit controls. The parameter rect specifies the rectangular area that contains the edit control. The parameter pParentWnd is the pointer to the parent window. The nID parameter represents the unique ID of the edit control. The Create function returns TRUE if it succeeds and yields FALSE if it fails.

Table 6.2 Values for the Edit Control Styles	
Value	**Meaning**
ES_AUTOHSCROLL	Lets the text scroll automatically 10 characters to the right when the user enters a character at the end of the line. When the user presses the Enter key, the text scrolls back all the way to the left.
ES_AUTOVSCROLL	Lets the text scroll up one page when the user presses the Enter key on the last visible line.
ES_CENTER	Centers the text in a multi-line edit control.
ES_LEFT	Left-justifies the text.
ES_LOWERCASE	Converts all letters that the user types into lowercase.
ES_MULTILINE	Specifies a multi-line edit control that recognizes line breaks (designated by the sequence of a carriage return and a line-feed character).
ES_NOHIDESEL	By default, the edit control hides the selected text when it loses focus and shows the selection when it gains focus again. Setting this style prevents the edit control from restoring the selected text.
ES_RIGHT	Right-justifies the text.
ES_UPPERCASE	Converts all letters that the user types into uppercase.

Typically, the edit control contains the styles WS_CHILD, WS_VISIBLE, WS_TABSTOP, ES_LEFT, ES_AUTOHSCROLL, and WS_BORDER. These styles generate an edit control with a frame and display left-justified text that can be scrolled horizontally if all the text does not fit in the frame. Multi-line edit controls require the inclusion of the following styles: ES_MULTILINE, ES_AUTOVSCROLL, WS_HSCROLL, and WS_VSCROLL. These additional styles provide for multiple text lines, support vertical text scrolling, and include both vertical and horizontal scroll bars.

The next sections examine a selection of member functions. Each section presents a set of member functions that support a certain category of operations.

Clipboard-Related Editing Functions

The CEdit class provides a set of member functions that manage editing operations involving the Windows Clipboard. These operations, with which you should be familiar, include Cut, Copy, Paste, Clear, Undo, and Delete. Table 6.3 shows the CEdit member functions and their purposes. These functions work with the Clipboard in the CF_TEXT format.

Table 6.3 CEdit Member Functions That Support the Clipboard- Related Editing Commands	
Member Function	**Purpose**
Cut	Deletes the current selection in the edit control and copies the text to the Clipboard.
Copy	Copies the current selection to the Clipboard.
Paste	Inserts the text from the Clipboard to the current cursor position in the edit control.
Clear	Deletes the current selection. Does not affect the Clipboard.
Undo	Undoes the last change made to the text of the edit control.

Query of Edit Controls

The class CEdit offers a set of member functions you can use to perform text queries. These functions enable you to obtain all or part of the text of the edit control or to query the control's text statistics (for example, the number of lines, the length of lines, and so on). The following list provides the relevant query member functions:

- The parameterless member function GetWindowTextLength yields the number of characters in the control's text. This member function is inherited from the parent class CWnd.

- The overloaded member function GetWindowText recalls characters in the edit control. This function also is inherited from the parent class. The declarations of the overloaded GetWindowText functions are

```
int GetWindowText(LPSTR lpszStringBuf, int nMaxCount) const;
void GetWindowText(CString& rString) const;
```

The parameter lpszStringBuf is a pointer to the string that receives a copy of the static text characters. The parameter nMaxCount specifies the maximum number of static text characters to copy to the buffer lpszStringBuf. The function returns the actual number of characters copied to the string accessed by the pointer lpszStringBuf. The second overloaded function has the reference parameter rString, which is an instance of class CString. The function passes the characters of the targeted edit control through this parameter. The function has a void return type.

■ The member function GetLineCount yields the number of lines in a multi-line edit control. The declaration of function GetLineCount is

```
int GetLineCount() const;
```

In the case of multiple-line edit controls, please take into account the characters involved in either the soft or hard line breaks. Hard line breaks use pairs of carriage return and line-feed characters at the end of each line. Soft line breaks use two carriage returns and a line feed as a line break. This information is relevant when you are counting the number of characters to process.

■ The member function LineFromChar yields the line number of a specified character index. The declaration of the function LineFromChar is

```
int LineFromChar(int nIndex = -1) const;
```

The function yields the line number for the nIndex character. The default argument for the parameter nIndex is –1. The function interprets this argument as a request to yield either of the following values:

• If the control has selected text, the function returns the line number where the first selected character is located.

• If the control has no selected text, the function returns the line number where character insertion occurs.

■ The member function LineIndex returns the character index of a specific line. The character index is also the number of characters in the edit control up to the specified line number. The declaration of the LineIndex function is

```
int LineIndex(int nLine = -1) const;
```

The parameter `nLine` represents the index of a line. This parameter has the default argument of –1, which selects the current line. The function returns the number of characters from the first line up to the specified line. The function returns –1 when the argument of `nLine` is greater than the actual number of lines.

- The member function `LineLength` returns the number of characters in a line for a specific character index. The declaration of function `LineLength` is

```
int LineLength(int nLine = -1) const;
```

The parameter `nLine` specifies the index of a character in the edit control. This parameter has the default argument of –1. This argument makes the function return the length of the current line. The `LineLength` function returns the total number of characters in a single-line edit control.

- The member function `GetSel` returns the starting and ending character positions of the selected text. The starting character position is the index of the first selected character. The ending position is the index of the first character *after* the selected text. The declaration of the `GetSel` function is

```
DWORD GetSel() const;
```

The function yields a 32-bit integer, which packs the starting position in the low word and the ending position in the high word. The predefined `HIWORD` and `LOWORD` macros help you extract the high and low words, respectively. If these two words are equal, there is no selected text—both words are the character indices to the current insertion point.

- The overloaded `GetLine` member function returns a line from a multi-line edit control. The declarations of the two versions of the `GetLine` function are

```
int GetLine(int nIndex, LPSTR lpszBuffer) const;
int GetLine(int nIndex, LPSTR lpszBuffer, int nMaxLength) const;
```

The parameter `nIndex` is the index of the line being retrieved. The parameter `lpszBuffer` is a buffer that stores the retrieved line. The first two bytes of `lpszBuffer` store the length of the line. The parameter `nMaxLength` indicates the maximum number of bytes to copy to the buffer `lpszBuffer`. The second version function `GetLine` copies the argument of the parameter `nMaxLength` to the first two bytes of the parameter `lpszBuffer`.

> **Note**
>
> It is very important to point out that the parameter lpszBuffer is not null termi-
> nated. The buffer simply contains an array of characters.

How to Alter the Edit Controls

Let's look at the member functions that change the text in the edit control.
These member functions perform operations such as writing new text to the
control, selecting text, and replacing the selected text. The member functions
you can use to change the edit control text are as follows:

- The member function SetWindowText (inherited from the parent class)
  supplies the edit control with new text. The declaration of the function
  SetWindowText is

  ```
  void SetWindowText(const char FAR* lpszString);
  ```

  The parameter lpszString is the pointer to the string that contains the
  new text for the edit control. If the argument for lpszString is an
  empty string, the function SetWindowText clears the text in the edit
  control.

- The overloaded member function SetSel delimits a block of characters
  as the new selected text. The declaration of function SetSel is

  ```
  void SetSel(DWORD dwSelection);
  void SetSel(int nStartChar, int nEndChar);
  ```

  The parameter dwSelection is a double-word containing the starting
  position in its low word and the ending position in its high word. The
  parameters nStartChar and nEndChar define the range of characters that
  specify the new selected text. You can select the entire text of the targeted edit control by setting the starting and ending positions at 0 and
  –1, respectively.

- The member function ReplaceSel substitutes the selected text with new
  characters. The declaration of the ReplaceSel function is

  ```
  void ReplaceSel(const char FAR* lpszNewText);
  ```

  The parameter lpszNewText is the pointer to the string containing the
  new selected text, which substitutes for the current selection. If there
  is no selected text, the function simply inserts at the current insertion

point the text accessed by the pointer `lpszNewText`. To delete text in an edit control, first select that text and then invoke the function `ReplaceSel` to replace the selected text with an empty string.

The Programmer's Calculator

In this section, I introduce you to an application that uses single-line and multi-line edit controls: the Programmer's Calculator (CTLEDIT1.EXE). Later in this chapter, and also in Chapter 7, I present additional calculator versions that use other controls to extend or modify the Programmer's Calculator. Figure 6.4 shows a sample session with the Programmer's Calculator program.

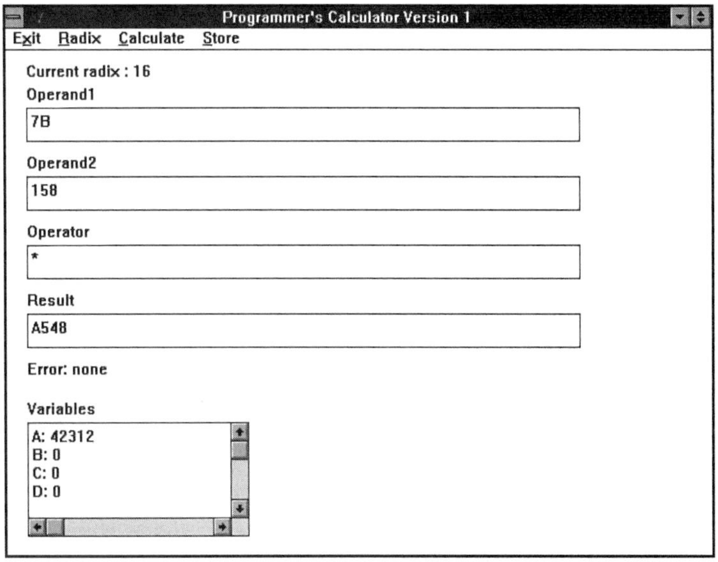

Figure 6.4
A sample session with the Programmer's Calculator application (CTLEDIT1.EXE).

The calculator consists of the following controls:

- *Menu bar.* Contains four menus: Exit, Radix, Calculate, and Store.

- *Exit menu.* Enables you to exit the application.

- *Radix menu.* Includes the Decimal, Hexadecimal, and Binary commands. These options let you select a different radix. The default radix is decimal numbers.

- *Calculate menu.* Enables you to perform a calculation using the numbers in the Operand edit controls and the operator in the Operator edit control.

- *Store menu.* Enables you to store the number found in the Result edit control. The storage target is the single-letter variable whose line contains the text insertion point.

- *Static text control.* Indicates the current radix.

- *First operand edit control, Operand1.* You can enter integers (which must conform to the currently selected radix) or the names of single-letter variables, A to Z. To distinguish between the name of a variable and a hexadecimal digit, you must insert the character @ before the name of a variable. Thus the string @A refers to the variable A, whereas A by itself refers to a hexadecimal integer.

- *Second operand edit control, Operand2.* You can enter integers (which must conform to the currently selected radix) or the names of single-letter variables, A to Z.

- *Operator edit control.* The current version of the calculator supports the four basic math operations as well as the bitwise operators ¦, &, ~, <<, and >>.

- *Result edit control.* Displays the result of the math operation.

- *Error message static text control.* Displays the current error status. If you move the mouse over this control and click the left mouse button, you reset the error message.

- *Variables multi-line edit control.* Enables you to copy a number from the Result edit control into one of 26 single-letter variables named A to Z. The multi-line edit control displays the current values stored in these variables as decimal integers (regardless of the current radix). You can view and edit the numbers in this control. You can also use the vertical scroll bar to inspect the values in the different variables.

- *Multiple static text controls.* Serve as labels for the various edit controls.

When you work with the calculator application, be sure to observe the following operational rules:

- Use the correct data type. The application uses the *long* data type to perform the math operations and data conversions.

- Make sure that your input is correct. You are responsible for entering integers that conform to the current radix. The decimal radix supports signed integers.

- Use the correct variable names. You are responsible for correctly entering the name of a variable.

- Remember that the application converts negative decimal integers into their equivalent unsigned hexadecimal and binary integers.

The calculator application demonstrates the following procedures:

- Utilizing single-line edit controls for simple input.

- Using a multi-line edit control to view and edit data.

- Accessing and editing text in a line.

- Manipulating the text in a static text control by clicking the mouse.

- Writing custom GetLine and GetLineLength member functions.

- Extending the CEdit class to accommodate the GetLine and GetLineLength member functions.

Before I discuss this nontrivial Windows program, I recommend that you first compile and run the calculator application. Experiment with these features:

- Enter unsigned integers (the program uses predefined type long in its math operations) in the operand edit boxes, enter one of the supported operators, and choose the Calculate menu.

- Select a hexadecimal or binary radix by choosing the appropriate command from the Radix menu. Watch the values in the two Operand edit boxes and in the Result edit box change to conform to the current radix. Also notice that the top static text control changes its text to indicate the current radix.

Using the single-letter variables is easy. These variables are all initialized with 0. Therefore, the first step in using single-letter variables is to store a nonzero value. Perform an operation and then click inside the Variables edit box. Select the first line that contains the variable A. Now click the Store menu (or press Alt+S) and watch the number in the Result edit box appear in the first line of the Variables edit box. The variable name, plus the colon and space characters that follow it, reappear with the new text line. Now replace the contents of the Operand1 edit box with the variable A (by entering @A); then choose the Calculate menu. The Result edit box displays the result of the latest operation. Also notice that the string @A is replaced with the value stored in variable A.

Listing 6.5 displays the contents of the CTLEDIT1.DEF definition file.

Listing 6.5 The CTLEDIT1.DEF Definition File

```
NAME          CtlEdit1
DESCRIPTION   'An MFC Windows Application'
CODE          PRELOAD MOVEABLE DISCARDABLE
DATA          PRELOAD MOVEABLE MULTIPLE
HEAPSIZE      1024
```

Listing 6.6 shows the source code for the CTLEDIT1.H header file. The header file declares the command constants for the Calculate and Store menus, as well as for the Decimal, Hexadecimal, and Binary menu commands.

Listing 6.6 Source Code for the CTLEDIT1.H Header File

```
#define CM_EXIT     (WM_USER + 200)
#define CM_DECIMAL  (WM_USER + 201)
#define CM_HEX      (WM_USER + 202)
#define CM_BINARY   (WM_USER + 203)
#define CM_CALC     (WM_USER + 204)
#define CM_STORE    (WM_USER + 205)
```

Listing 6.7 contains the script for the CTLEDIT1.RC resource file.

Listing 6.7 Script for the CTLEDIT1.RC Resource File

```
#include <windows.h>
#include <afxres.h>
#include "ctledit1.h"
COMMANDS MENU LOADONCALL MOVEABLE PURE DISCARDABLE
BEGIN
    MENUITEM "E&xit", CM_EXIT
    POPUP "&Radix"
    BEGIN
      MENUITEM "&Decimal", CM_DECIMAL
      MENUITEM "&Hexadecimal", CM_HEX
      MENUITEM "&Binary", CM_BINARY
    END
    MENUITEM "&Calculate", CM_CALC
    MENUITEM "&Store", CM_STORE
END
```

Listing 6.8 contains the source code for the CTLEDIT1.CPP program file.

Listing 6.8 Source Code for the CTLEDIT1.CPP Program File

```
/*
            Programmer's Calculator Version 1.0  11/3/93

  Program to test single-line and multi-line edit controls in
  implementing a programmer's calculator.
*/
#include <stdlib.h>
#include <ctype.h>
#include <stdio.h>
#include <string.h>
#include <afxwin.h>
#include "ctledit1.h"
// declare the constants that represent the sizes of the controls
const Wlbl = 100;
const Hlbl = 15;
const LblVertSpacing = 5;
const LblHorzSpacing = 40;
const Wbox = 500;
const Hbox = 30;
const BoxVertSpacing = 10;
const BoxHorzSpacing = 40;
const Wvarbox = 200;
const Hvarbox = 100;
const MaxStringLen = 80;
const MAX_MEMREG = 26;
// declare the ID_XXXX constants for the edit boxes
#define ID_OPERAND1_EDIT 101
#define ID_OPERATOR_EDIT 102
#define ID_OPERAND2_EDIT 103
#define ID_RESULT_EDIT    104
#define ID_ERRMSG_TXT     105
#define ID_VARIABLE_EDIT 106
#define ID_RADIX_TXT      107


class CxEdit : public CEdit
{
public:
  BOOL GetLine(LPSTR lpString, int nStrSize, int nLineNumber);
  int GetLineLength(int nLineNumber);

};
class CEditCtrlApp : public CWinApp
{
public:
    virtual BOOL InitInstance();
};
// expand the functionality of CFrameWnd by deriving class CMainWnd
class CMainWnd : public CFrameWnd
{
 public:
```

(continues)

Listing 6.8 Continued

```
CMainWnd();
~CMainWnd();
protected:
// declare the pointers to the various controls
// first, the edit box controls
CEdit* pOperand1Box;
CEdit* pOperatorBox;
CEdit* pOperand2Box;
CEdit* pResultBox;
CxEdit* pVariableBox;
// then the static text controls
CStatic* pRadixTxt;
CStatic* pOperand1Txt;
CStatic* pOperatorTxt;
CStatic* pOperand2Txt;
CStatic* pResultTxt;
CStatic* pErrMsgTxt;
CStatic* pVariableTxt;
// math mode
int nRadix;
// math error flag
BOOL bInError;
// coordinates for the error message static text area
CRect rectErrMsg;

// handle clicking the left mouse button
afx_msg void OnLButtonDown(UINT nFlags, CPoint point);
// handle selecting the decimal mode
afx_msg void CMDecimal();
// handle selecting the hexadecimal mode
afx_msg void CMHex();
// handle selecting the binary mode
afx_msg void CMBinary();
// handle the calculation
afx_msg void CMCalc();
// handle storing the result in a variable
afx_msg void CMStore();
// handle exiting the application
afx_msg void OnExit();
// handle creating the controls
afx_msg int OnCreate(LPCREATESTRUCT lpCS);
// handle closing the window
afx_msg void OnClose();

// return a reference to member r based on individual
// coordinates and dimensions
void makerect(int X, int Y, int W, int H, CRect& r)
 { r.SetRect(X, Y, X + W, Y + H); }
// obtain a number of a Variable edit box line
long getVar(int lineNum);
// store a number in the selected text of
// the Variable edit box line
void putVar(long x);
```

```
  // set contents of edit controls to integers in various bases
  void setDecimal(CEdit* pEdit);
  void setHexaDecimal(CEdit* pEdit);
  void setBinary(CEdit* pEdit);
  // declare message map macro
  DECLARE_MESSAGE_MAP();
};
BOOL CxEdit::GetLine(LPSTR lpString, int nStrSize, int nLineNumber)
{
  int nCopyCount;
  BOOL bResult;
  if (nStrSize <= 0)
    return FALSE;
  bResult = (nStrSize >= GetLineLength(nLineNumber) + 1) ?
              TRUE : FALSE;
  if (nStrSize == 1)
  {
    lpString[0] = '\0';
    return bResult;
  }
  ((WORD FAR *)lpString)[0] = nStrSize;

  nCopyCount = (WORD)(SendMessage(EM_GETLINE, nLineNumber,
                                  long(lpString)));
  if (nCopyCount)
  {
    // Windows returns non-null terminated string
    lpString[nCopyCount] = '\0';
    return bResult;
  }
  return FALSE;
}
int CxEdit::GetLineLength(int nLineNumber)
{
  int nStartPos = -1;
  if (nLineNumber > -1)
    nStartPos = LineIndex(nLineNumber);
  return (WORD) SendMessage(EM_LINELENGTH, nStartPos);
}
CMainWnd::CMainWnd()
{
  // load the main accelerator table to handle
  // keystroke input
  LoadAccelTable("MainAccelTable");
  // create the window
  Create(NULL,
    "Programmer's Calculator Version 1",
     WS_OVERLAPPEDWINDOW,
     rectDefault, NULL, "COMMANDS");
  // clear the bInError flag
  bInError = FALSE;
  // set the default math mode
  nRadix = 10;
}

int CMainWnd::OnCreate(LPCREATESTRUCT lpCS)
{
```

II

Visual C++ Programming

Listing 6.8 Continued

```
char s[81];
char bigStr[6 * MAX_MEMREG + 1];
char c;
int x0 = 20;
int y0 = 10;
int x = x0, y = y0;
CRect r;
DWORD dwStaticStyle = WS_CHILD | WS_VISIBLE | SS_LEFT;
DWORD dwBoxStyle = WS_CHILD | WS_VISIBLE | WS_BORDER |
                   ES_LEFT | ES_AUTOHSCROLL | ES_UPPERCASE;

// create the label for current radix (use Wbox width)
makerect(x, y, Wbox, Hlbl, r);
pRadixTxt = new CStatic();
pRadixTxt->Create("Current radix: 10", dwStaticStyle, r,
                  this, ID_RADIX_TXT);
// create the label for Operand1
y += Hlbl + LblVertSpacing;
makerect(x, y, Wlbl, Hlbl, r);
pOperand1Txt = new CStatic();
pOperand1Txt->Create("Operand1", dwStaticStyle, r, this, -1);
// create Operand1 edit box
y += Hlbl + LblVertSpacing;
makerect(x, y, Wbox, Hbox, r);
pOperand1Box = new CEdit();
pOperand1Box->Create(dwBoxStyle, r, this, ID_OPERAND1_EDIT);
pOperand1Box->LimitText(); // set no limit for text
// create the Operand2 label
y += Hbox + BoxVertSpacing;
makerect(x, y, Wlbl, Hlbl, r);
pOperand2Txt = new CStatic();
pOperand2Txt->Create("Operand2", dwStaticStyle, r, this, -1);

// create the Operand2 edit box
y += Hlbl + LblVertSpacing;
makerect(x, y, Wbox, Hbox, r);
pOperand2Box = new CEdit();
pOperand2Box->Create(dwBoxStyle, r, this, ID_OPERAND2_EDIT);
pOperand2Box->LimitText(); // set no limit for text

// create the Operator label
y += Hbox + BoxVertSpacing;
makerect(x, y, Wlbl, Hlbl, r);
pOperatorTxt = new CStatic();
pOperatorTxt->Create("Operator", dwStaticStyle, r, this, -1);

// create the Operator edit box
y += Hlbl + LblVertSpacing;
makerect(x, y, Wbox, Hbox, r);
pOperatorBox = new CEdit();
pOperatorBox->Create(dwBoxStyle, r, this, ID_OPERATOR_EDIT);
pOperatorBox->LimitText(); // set no limit for text
```

```
    // create the Result label
    y += Hbox + BoxVertSpacing;
    makerect(x, y, Wlbl, Hlbl, r);
    pResultTxt = new CStatic();
    pResultTxt->Create("Result", dwStaticStyle, r, this, -1);

    // create the Result edit box
    y += Hlbl + LblVertSpacing;
    makerect(x, y, Wbox, Hbox, r);
    pResultBox = new CEdit();
    pResultBox->Create(dwBoxStyle, r, this, ID_RESULT_EDIT);
    pResultBox->LimitText(); // set no limit for text

    // create the error message static text
    y += Hbox + BoxVertSpacing;
    // use the Wbox for the width of the error message static text
    makerect(x, y, Wbox, Hlbl, r);
    rectErrMsg = r; // store rectangular area for error message
    pErrMsgTxt = new CStatic();
    pErrMsgTxt->Create("Error: none", dwStaticStyle, r, this, -1);
    // create the Variables label
    y += 2 * Hlbl + LblVertSpacing;
    makerect(x, y, Wlbl, Hlbl, r);
    pVariableTxt = new CStatic();
    pVariableTxt->Create("Variables", dwStaticStyle, r, this, -1);

    // create the Variables edit box
    y += Hlbl + LblVertSpacing;
    bigStr[0] = '\0';
    // build the initial contents of the Variable edit box
    for (c = 'A'; c <= 'Z'; c++) {
      sprintf(s, "%c: 0\r\n", c);
      strcat(bigStr, s);
    }
    makerect(x, y, Wvarbox, Hvarbox, r);
    pVariableBox = new CxEdit();
    pVariableBox->Create(dwBoxStyle | ES_MULTILINE | WS_HSCROLL
                | WS_VSCROLL | ES_AUTOVSCROLL,
                        r, this, ID_VARIABLE_EDIT);
    pVariableBox->LimitText(); // set no limit for text
    pVariableBox->SetWindowText(bigStr);

    return CFrameWnd::OnCreate(lpCS);
}
CMainWnd::~CMainWnd()
{
    // delete the controls
    delete pOperand1Box;
    delete pOperatorBox;
    delete pOperand2Box;
    delete pResultBox;
    delete pVariableBox;
    delete pRadixTxt;
    delete pOperand1Txt;
    delete pOperatorTxt;
    delete pOperand2Txt;
    delete pResultTxt;
```

(continues)

Listing 6.8 Continued

```
    delete pErrMsgTxt;
    delete pVariableTxt;
}
void CMainWnd::OnLButtonDown(UINT nFlags, CPoint point)
{
  // did you click the mouse over the error message static text?
  if (rectErrMsg.PtInRect(point))
      pErrMsgTxt->SetWindowText("Error: none");
}
void CMainWnd::CMDecimal()
{
  setDecimal(pOperand1Box);
  setDecimal(pOperand2Box);
  setDecimal(pResultBox);
  nRadix = 10;
  pRadixTxt->SetWindowText("Current radix : 10");
}
void CMainWnd::CMHex()
{
  setHexaDecimal(pOperand1Box);
  setHexaDecimal(pOperand2Box);
  setHexaDecimal(pResultBox);
  nRadix = 16;
  pRadixTxt->SetWindowText("Current radix : 16");
}
void CMainWnd::CMBinary()
{
  setBinary(pOperand1Box);
  setBinary(pOperand2Box);
  setBinary(pResultBox);
  nRadix = 2;
  pRadixTxt->SetWindowText("Current radix : 2");
}
void CMainWnd::CMCalc()
{
  long x, y, z;
  char opStr[MaxStringLen+1];
  char s[MaxStringLen+1];
  char* ss;
  // obtain the string in the Operand1 edit box
  pOperand1Box->GetWindowText(s, MaxStringLen);
  // does the pOperand1Box contain the name
  // of a single-letter variable which begins with @?
  if (s[0] == '@') {
    // obtain value from the Variable edit control
    x = getVar(s[1] - 'A');
    // substitute variable name with its value
    _ltoa(x, s, nRadix);
    pOperand1Box->SetWindowText(s);
  }
  else
    // convert the string in the edit box
    x = strtol(s, &ss, nRadix);
  // obtain the string in the Operand2 edit box
```

```
pOperand2Box->GetWindowText(s, MaxStringLen);
// does the pOperand2Box contain the name
// of a single-letter variable which begins with @?
if (s[0] == '@') {
  // obtain value from the Variable edit control
  y = getVar(s[1] - 'A');
  // substitute variable name with its value
  _ltoa(y, s, nRadix);
  pOperand2Box->SetWindowText(s);
}
else
   // convert the string in the edit box
  y = strtol(s, &ss, nRadix);
// obtain the string in the Operator edit box
pOperatorBox->GetWindowText(opStr, MaxStringLen);
// clear the error message box
pErrMsgTxt->SetWindowText("Error: none");
bInError = FALSE;
// determine the requested operation
if (opStr[0] == '+')
  z = x + y;
else if (opStr[0] == '-')
  z = x - y;
else if (opStr[0] == '*') {
  if (x == 0 || y < (2147483647L / x))
    z = x * y;
  else {
    z = 0;
    bInError = TRUE;
    pErrMsgTxt->SetWindowText("Error: overflow error");
  }
}
else if (opStr[0] == '/') {
  if (y != 0)
    z = x / y;
  else {
    z = 0;
    bInError = TRUE;
    pErrMsgTxt->SetWindowText("Error: Division-by-zero error");
  }
}
else if (opStr[0] == '|')
  z = x | y;
else if (opStr[0] == '&')
  z = x & y;
else if (opStr[0] == '~')
  z = ~x;
else if (strcmp(opStr, "<<") == 0)
  z = x << y;
else if (strcmp(opStr, ">>") == 0)
  z = x >> y;
else {
  bInError = TRUE;
  pErrMsgTxt->SetWindowText("Error: Invalid operator");
}
// display the result if no error has occurred
```

II

Visual C++ Programming

(continues)

Listing 6.8 Continued

```
    if (!bInError) {
      _ltoa(z, s, nRadix);
      pResultBox->SetWindowText(s);
    }
}
void CMainWnd::CMStore()
{
  char s[MaxStringLen+1];
  char* ss;
  long z;
  // get the string in the Result edit box
  pResultBox->GetWindowText(s, MaxStringLen);
  // store the result in the selected text of
  // the Variable edit box
  z = strtol(s, &ss, nRadix);
  putVar(z);
}
long CMainWnd::getVar(int lineNum)
{
  int lineSize;
  char s[MaxStringLen+1];
  if (lineNum >= MAX_MEMREG) return 0;
  // get the size of the target line
  lineSize = pVariableBox->GetLineLength(lineNum);
  // get the line
  pVariableBox->GetLine(s, lineSize, lineNum);
  // delete the first three characters
  strcpy(s, (s+3));
  // return the number stored in the target line
  return atol(s);
}
void CMainWnd::putVar(long x)
{
  DWORD selPos;
  WORD startPos, endPos;
  int lineNum;
  int lineSize;
  char s[MaxStringLen+1];

  // locate the character position of the cursor
  selPos = pVariableBox->GetSel();
  startPos = LOWORD(selPos);
  endPos = HIWORD(selPos);
  // turn off the selected text
  if (startPos != endPos) {
    selPos = MAKELONG(startPos, startPos);
    pVariableBox->SetSel(selPos);
  }
  // get the line number where the cursor is located
  lineNum = pVariableBox->LineFromChar(-1);
  // get the line size of line lineNum
  lineSize = pVariableBox->GetLineLength(lineNum);
  // obtain the text of line lineNum
  pVariableBox->GetLine(s, lineSize, lineNum);
```

```
    // build the new text line
    sprintf(s, "%c: %ld", s[0], x);
    // get the character positions for the deleted line
    startPos = (WORD) (pVariableBox->LineIndex(-1));
    endPos = (WORD) (startPos + pVariableBox->LineLength(-1));
    // select the current line
    selPos = MAKELONG(startPos, endPos);
    pVariableBox->SetSel(selPos);
    // replace the current line with the new line
    pVariableBox->ReplaceSel(s);
}
void CMainWnd::OnExit()
{
    SendMessage(WM_CLOSE);
}
void CMainWnd::OnClose()
{
    if (MessageBox("Want to close this application",
                   "Query", MB_YESNO | MB_ICONQUESTION) == IDYES)
        DestroyWindow();
}

void CMainWnd::setDecimal(CEdit* pEdit)
{
    char s[MaxStringLen+1];
    char* ss;
    long n;
    pEdit->GetWindowText(s, MaxStringLen);
    n = strtol(s, &ss, nRadix);
    _ltoa(n, s, 10);
    pEdit->SetWindowText(s);
}
void CMainWnd::setHexaDecimal(CEdit* pEdit)
{
    char s[MaxStringLen+1];
    char *ss;
    long n;
    pEdit->GetWindowText(s, MaxStringLen);
    n = strtol(s, &ss, nRadix);
    _ltoa(n, s, 16);
    pEdit->SetWindowText(s);
}
void CMainWnd::setBinary(CEdit* pEdit)
{
    char s[MaxStringLen+1];
    char* ss;
    long n;
    pEdit->GetWindowText(s, MaxStringLen);
    n = strtol(s, &ss, nRadix);
    _ltoa(n, s, 2);
    pEdit->SetWindowText(s);
}
BEGIN_MESSAGE_MAP(CMainWnd, CFrameWnd)
    ON_WM_LBUTTONDOWN()
    ON_COMMAND(CM_DECIMAL, CMDecimal)
    ON_COMMAND(CM_HEX, CMHex)
```

II

Visual C++ Programming

(continues)

Listing 6.8 Continued

```
      ON_COMMAND(CM_BINARY, CMBinary)
      ON_COMMAND(CM_CALC, CMCalc)
      ON_COMMAND(CM_STORE, CMStore)
      ON_COMMAND(CM_EXIT, OnExit)
      ON_WM_CREATE()
      ON_WM_CLOSE()
END_MESSAGE_MAP()
// Construct the CEditCtrlApp's m_pMainWnd data member
BOOL CEditCtrlApp::InitInstance()
{
  m_pMainWnd = new CMainWnd();
  m_pMainWnd->ShowWindow(m_nCmdShow);
  m_pMainWnd->UpdateWindow();
  return TRUE;
}
// application's constructor initializes and runs the app
CEditCtrlApp WindowApp;
```

The program shown in Listing 6.8 contains two sets of constants. The first set declares the height, width, vertical spacing, and horizontal spacing used in dimensioning the different controls. The second set of constants declares the ID_XXXX values used in generating the various edit controls, the radix static text control, and the error message static text control.

The program also declares the application class CEditCtrlApp, the window class CMainWnd, and the extended edit box class CxEdit.

I declared the class CxEdit as a descendant of CEdit and incorporated the member functions GetLine and GetLineLength. GetLine works with ASCIIZ arguments, and the function is declared as follows:

```
      BOOL GetLine(LPSTR lpString, int nStrSize, int nLineNumber);
```

The parameter lpString is the pointer to an ASCIIZ string, the parameter nStrSize defines the maximum number of characters to copy, and the parameter nLineNumber specifies the target line number. The function returns TRUE if it succeeds and yields FALSE if it fails.

The member function GetLineLength yields the length of a specified line. The declaration of the function GetLineLength is

```
      int GetLineLength(int nLineNumber);
```

The parameter nLineNumber represents the index of the targeted line.

The class CMainWnd owns the static text and edit controls. The class also declares a group of data members and member functions. The class CMainWnd includes the following groups of data members:

- Pointers to the diverse instances of classes CStatic, CEdit, and CxEdit. Each pointer accesses one of the edit controls, as well as the radix and error message static text controls.

- The data member nRadix. Stores the radix; this member has the int type and stores the values 2, 10, and 16 to represent the binary, decimal, and hexadecimal radices, respectively.

- The Boolean data member bInError. Flags any error.

- The data member rectErrMsg. Stores the rectangular area occupied by the error message static text control. The mouse-click response member function OnLButtonDown examines whether the mouse is clicked inside that rectangle. If it is clicked inside, the member function resets the error message static text control.

The CMainWnd class has a constructor, a destructor, and a set of message response member functions that respond to the mouse click and to the menu options.

The window class constructor performs the following tasks:

- Builds the window instance by invoking the Create member function. The call to Create specifies the window title, the WS_OVERLAPPEDWINDOW style, and the COMMANDS menu resource.

- Assigns FALSE to the bInError data member.

- Assigns 10, the default radix, to the data member nRadix.

The member function makerect calculates the coordinates that define the rectangular area occupied by a control. The function has the following input parameters:

- The X and Y coordinates of the upper-left corner of the rectangular area.

- The parameter W, which represents the width of the rectangle.

- The parameter H, which defines the height of the rectangle.

The reference parameter r is an instance of class CRect, which passes the rectangle area object back to the function caller. The function makerect sends the C++ message SetRect to the object r so that the object r can define the sought rectangle. The arguments of the SetRect message are X, Y, X + W, and Y + H.

The OnCreate member function responds to the WM_CREATE message and builds the various controls attached to the window. The function carries out the following tasks:

■ Creates the radix static text control. This task involves the function makerect, which creates the required rectangle object r that defines the extent of the control. In addition, this task creates a new instance of class CStatic and assigns its address to the data member pRadixTxt. The function OnCreate also sends the C++ message Create to the newly created control and supplies it with the required arguments. These arguments set the initial control text, the control style (using the local variable dwStaticStyle), and specify the unique control ID ID_RADIX_TXT.

■ Creates the static text controls that label the Operand1, Operand1, Operator, and Result edit controls by invoking the CStatic constructor. This task also involves using the function makerect. The function OnCreate increases the local variable y by (Hlbl + LblVertSpacing) to calculate the Y coordinate for the next static text control. This approach enables you to systematically increment the Y coordinates for the control's area.

■ Creates the single-line edit boxes for the operands, operator, and the result. The data members pOperand1Box, pOperatorBox, pOperand2Box, and pResultBox access these edit box controls. The function OnCreate builds every CEdit instance with a unique ID_XXXX constant and an empty edit box. The single-line edit boxes have the same size. The style of the edit controls includes the ES_UPPERCASE style. This style results in automatically converting into uppercase the single-letter variable names that you type in these edit controls.

■ Creates the error message static text control.

■ Creates the static text control that labels the Variables box.

- Creates the Variables multi-line edit control. This task starts by putting together the contents of the Variables box using the local string variable bigStr. The function OnCreate creates the Variables edit control with the additional styles of ES_MULTILINE, WS_HSCROLL, WS_VSCROLL, and ES_AUTOVSCROLL. These styles generate an edit control with fully functioning vertical and horizontal scroll bars. The function OnCreate writes the contents of bigStr in the edit control by sending the C++ message SetWindowText to the edit box accessed by the member pVariableBox.

- Returns the expression CFrameWnd::OnCreate(lpCS).

To simplify calculating the coordinates of the various controls, the function OnCreate uses the local variables x and y, as well as the global constants that define the controls' dimensions. This technique makes it very easy to alter the application and avoid tedious manual recalculations.

The member function OnLButtonDown performs these tasks:

- Determines whether the mouse click location (supplied by the argument of the parameter point) is inside the rectangle that contains the error message static text. This task involves sending the C++ message PtInRect to the CRect object rectErrMsg. The argument for this message is point. If the message returns TRUE, the function performs the next task.

- Resets the error message static text by sending the C++ message SetWindowText to the static control accessed by the member pErrMsgTxt.

The CMDecimal function responds to the Decimal command and sets the decimal radix by carrying out the following tasks:

- Converts the contents of the Operand1, Operand2, and Result edit boxes to decimal integers. This task involves applying the setDecimal function for each of these edit controls.

- Assigns 10 to the data member nRadix.

- Updates the radix text control to reflect the new radix. This task involves sending the C++ message SetWindowText to the static text control accessed by the member pRadixTxt.

The CMHex function responds to the Hexadecimal command and sets the hexadecimal radix by carrying out the following tasks:

■ Converts the contents of the Operand1, Operand2, and Result edit boxes to hexadecimal integers. This task involves applying the setHexaDecimal function for each of these edit controls.

■ Assigns 16 to the data member nRadix.

■ Updates the radix text control to reflect the new radix. This task involves sending the C++ message SetWindowText to the static text control accessed by the member pRadixTxt.

The CMBinary function responds to the Binary command and sets the binary radix by carrying out the following tasks:

■ Converts the contents of the Operand1, Operand2, and Result edit boxes to binary integers. This task involves applying the setBinary function for each of these edit controls.

■ Assigns 2 to the data member nRadix.

■ Updates the radix text control to reflect the new radix. This task involves sending the C++ message SetWindowText to the static text control accessed by the member pRadixTxt.

The CMCalc member function responds to the Calculate command and carries out the calculation using the contents of the Operands and Operators edit box controls. The CMCalc function performs the following tasks:

■ Obtains the first operand from the Operand1 edit box. The control may contain the name of a single-letter variable (A to Z) or an integer. The function uses the function GetWindowText to copy the edit control text to the local variable s. The function then examines the first character in the variable s. If that character is the character @, the first operand is a single-letter variable. The function performs the following subtasks:

   • Calls the member function getVar to acquire the value associated with the single-letter variable. The name of the variable is located in the second character of the variable s. This task assigns the contents of the single-letter variable to the local variable x.

- Converts the integer in the variable x to a string image using the radix value in the member nRadix. This task calls the function ltoa.

- Updates the Operand1 edit box with the contents of the single-letter variable. This task involves sending the C++ message SetWindowText to the first operand edit box object.

If the first character in the variable s is not the character @, the function CMCalc uses the strtol function to convert the contents of the variable s into an integer. The function CMCalc assigns that integer to the variable x.

■ Obtains the second operand in a manner identical to the first one. The function stores the second operand in the variable y.

■ Copies the text in the Operator edit box to the local variable opStr.

■ Clears the error message text box and sets the bInError data member to FALSE.

■ Executes the requested operation by using a series of if and if-else statements. The operators supported are +, -, *, /, ¦, &, ~, <<, and >>. If the function detects an error, it sets the bInError data member to TRUE and displays a message in the error message static text control.

■ Displays the result of the operation in the Result box if the bInError data member is FALSE. The function first converts the result from an integer to a string. This step also uses the function _ltoa to create a string image of the integer using the current radix. Next, the function writes to the Result edit box by sending the C++ message SetWindowText to that control.

The CMStore member function stores the contents of the Result box in a single-letter variable by performing the following tasks:

■ Obtaining the string in the Result edit box by sending the C++ message GetWindowText to the Result edit box.

■ Converting the string in the variable s into an integer. This task involves calling the conversion function strtol. The function CMStore assigns the result of strtol to the local variable z.

- Invoking the member function putVar to store the contents of variable z at the current insertion point in the Variables edit box.

The member function getVar yields the number stored at line number lineNum of the Variables edit box. The function performs the following tasks:

- Exits and yields 0 if the lineNum is greater than or equal to the value of the constant MAX_MEMREG.

- Retrieves the size of the target line by sending the C++ message GetLineLength (with the argument lineNum) to the Variables edit box.

- Obtains the string at line number lineNum by sending the C++ message GetLine to the Variables edit box.

- Deletes the first three characters of the retrieved line. This step should leave the string with the number stored in the target line.

- Returns the double-typed number obtained by calling the function atof and supplying it with the argument s.

The member function putVar stores the contents of the Result edit box in the variable whose line contains the text insertion position. The function carries out the following tasks:

- Determines the character position of the cursor by sending the C++ message GetSel to the Variables edit box. The function stores the start and end character positions in the local DWORD-type variable selPos. The function putVar employs the predefined macros HIWORD and LOWORD to obtain the starting and ending positions. The function stores these positions in the local variables startPos and endPos.

- Turns off any selected text. The function compares the values in the variables startPos and endPos. If these values differ, the function obtains a new value for the variable selPos, such that both the low and high words are equal to the value of startPos. The function then sends the C++ message SetSel to the Variables edit box. The argument for this message is the selPos variable. This C++ message turns off any selected text.

- Obtains the line number where the cursor is located. This task involves sending the C++ message GetLineFromChar to the Variables edit box.

- Obtains the size of the target line by sending the C++ message `GetLineLength` to the Variables edit box.

- Retrieves the text in the target line by sending the C++ message `GetLine` to the Variables edit box.

- Builds the new text line.

- Recalls the starting and ending character positions for the line to be replaced.

- Selects the line to be replaced by sending the C++ message `SetSel` to the Variables edit box.

- Replaces the current line with a new line. This task involves sending the C++ message `ReplaceSel` to the Variables edit box. The argument for this message is the variable s.

The member function `setDecimal` sets the contents of an edit control (presumed to be a valid integer that is compliant with the current radix) into a decimal integer. The function performs the following tasks:

- Obtains the text in the edit control. This task involves sending the `GetWindowText` to the edit control accessed by the parameter `pEdit`.

- Converts the contents of the string s into an integer. This task uses the function `strtol` and assigns the result of the local integer variable n.

- Converts the value in the variable n to the equivalent decimal integer image. This task uses the function `_ltoa` and stores the resulting string in the variable s.

- Updates the text in the edit control. This task involves sending the message `SetWindowText` to the edit control accessed by the parameter `pEdit`. The argument for this message is the local variable s.

The member functions `setHexaDecimal` and `setBinary` perform similar tasks to convert the contents of edit boxes into hexadecimal and binary integers, respectively.

II

Visual C++ Programming

The Pushbutton Control

The Microsoft Foundation Classes library offers the class CButton to support pushbutton controls, group boxes, check boxes, and radio buttons. You specify different button styles to create these various controls. The examples presented in this book derive their own classes to distinctly model the button controls, group boxes, check boxes, and radio buttons.

For now, let's discuss the aspects of the CButton class that manage the pushbutton controls. The next chapter looks at the other aspects of CButton that are relevant to the group box, check box, and radio button controls.

Windows supports two basic types of pushbutton controls: default and nondefault buttons. Windows displays default buttons with slightly thicker edges than nondefault buttons. In addition, Windows supports the feature that makes pressing the Enter key equivalent to clicking the default button in a dialog box. You can choose a new default button by pressing the Tab key, but this feature works only when the buttons are in a dialog box. If a nondialog box window owns pushbutton control, it can visually display only a default button, so the capability of tabbing to other controls is not available.

The *CButton* Class

The CButton class, a descendant of CWnd, declares a relatively low number of member functions. The following CButton member functions are relevant to the pushbutton controls:

- The Create member function that works with the class constructor to create a pushbutton instance. Here is the declaration of the Create function:

```
BOOL Create(LPCSTR lpszCaption,          // button label
            DWORD dwStyle,               // style
            const RECT& rect,            // area
            CWnd* pParentWnd,            // parent window
            UINT nID);                   // control ID
```

The parameter lpszCaption designates the button's label or caption. The parameter dwStyle specifies the exact type of button. This parameter has a role that is more relevant in CButton::Create than in the Create function of any other class. The typical styles for pushbuttons are WS_CHILD, WS_VISIBLE, BS_PUSHBUTTON (or BS_DEFPUSHBUTTON), and WS_TABSTOP. WS_TABSTOP is typical only when the parent window is a dialog box.

The parameter rect defines the area and location of the control. The parameter pParent is the pointer to the owner window, which can be either a window or a dialog box. The parameter nID represents a unique control ID.

■ The member function GetButtonStyle enables you to query the style of a pushbutton. For example, you can use this function to determine whether a button is a default pushbutton. The declaration for the GetButtonStyle function is

```
UINT GetButtonStyle() const;
```

■ The member function SetButtonStyle permits you to set the style of a pushbutton. The declaration for the function SetButtonStyle is

```
void SetButtonStyle(UINT nStyle, BOOL bRedraw = TRUE);
```

The parameter nStyle defines the new style of the CButton instance. The Boolean parameter bRedraw signals whether or not to redraw the control. This parameter has a default argument of TRUE.

Button Messages

When you click a button, the control transmits the BN_CLICKED notification message to its parent window. The parent window responds to this message by invoking a message response member function based on the ID of the button. For example, if you have a button that was created with an ID of ID_STORE_BTN, the message handler function is as follows:

```
// other declarations
afx_msg void HandleStoreBtn();
// other declarations
BEGIN_MESSAGE_LOOP(_CMainWnd_, CFrameWnd)
// other possible message mapping macros
ON_BN_CLICKED(ID_STORE_BTN, HandleStoreBtn)
// other possible message mapping macros
END_MESSAGE_LOOP()
```

This example shows that the message map macro ON_BN_CLICKED is used to map the ID_STORE_BTN notification message with the member function HandleStoreBtn.

How to Manipulate Windows

My first programming language for Windows applications was Visual Basic. The Visual Basic implementation of BASIC enables you to draw the various controls on a form and then set the attributes of these controls. Among these attributes are the enabled and visible states. Thus, you can draw a button in Visual Basic and make it initially invisible or disabled.

II

Visual C++ Programming

When I moved to programming with the Microsoft C++ compiler, I noticed that the class CButton did not declare member functions to disable, enable, show, and hide pushbutton controls. My search led me to two member functions declared in class CWnd and inherited by the CButton class. These functions are CWnd::EnableWindow and CWnd::ShowWindow.

You can disable or enable a window (including a pushbutton control) by using the CWnd::EnableWindow function. Windows displays a disabled button with a faded gray caption and prevents it from responding to mouse clicks. The function accepts a single Boolean argument that indicates whether you want to enable the button (when the argument is TRUE) or disable the button (when the argument is FALSE). Here are sample calls to the function CWnd::EnableWindow:

```
pMyBtn->EnableWindow(FALSE); // disable button
pMyBtn->EnableWindow(TRUE);  // enable button
```

You can query the enabled state of a button by using the parameterless Boolean function CWnd::IsWindowEnabled. Here is a sample call to the IsWindowEnabled function:

```
// toggle the enabled state of a button
if (pMyBtn->IsWindowEnabled())
pMyBtn->EnableWindow(FALSE); // disable button
else
pMyBtn->EnableWindow(TRUE); // enable button
```

The function CWnd::ShowWindow permits you to hide and show a button. The function takes one argument—either the predefined constant SW_HIDE, used to hide the button, or the predefined constant SW_SHOW, used to show the button. The parameterless Boolean function CWnd::IsWindowVisible queries the visibility of a button. Here is a sample call to the functions CWnd::ShowWindow and CWnd::IsWindowVisible:

```
// toggle the visibility of a button
if (pMyBtn->IsWindowVisible())
pMyBtn->ShowWindow(SW_HIDE); // hide button
else
pMyBtn->ShowWindow(SW_SHOW); // show button
```

The Modified Programmer's Calculator

The first version of the Programmer's Calculator uses menus to execute calculations, store results, and exit the application. This modified version uses pushbuttons to perform these same tasks. For a quick look at the new user interface, refer to Figure 6.5. The two versions of the calculator have the same basic features. The differences are minor; they only affect the visual interface and how the applications operate. First, I changed the visual interface as follows:

- The menu system now contains only the Exit and Radix menus. The Radix menu still includes the Decimal, Hexadecimal, and Binary commands.

- Three pushbuttons have been added with the captions Calc, Store, and Exit. The first two buttons replace the Calculate and Store menus, found in the first version.

As for the operations supported by the new calculator version, the following new features have been added:

- The application disables the Store pushbutton if the application attempts to execute an invalid operator or perform an illegal operation. This feature shows you how to disable a pushbutton when a certain condition arises (in this case, a specific calculation error).

- The application enables the Store pushbutton when you click the mouse while the mouse is over the error message static text control. The application enables the Store button when it successfully executes a math operation.

- The application supports accelerator keys for the pushbuttons. This feature enables the program to maintain the same hot keys used by the menus in the previous version.

The listing for the second version of the calculator has notable additions and changes. Listing 6.9 displays the contents of the CTLBTN1.DEF definition file.

Listing 6.9 The CTLBTN1.DEF Definition File

```
NAME          CtlBtn1
DESCRIPTION   'An MFC Windows Application'
CODE          PRELOAD MOVEABLE DISCARDABLE
DATA          PRELOAD MOVEABLE MULTIPLE
HEAPSIZE      1024
```

II

Visual C++ Programming

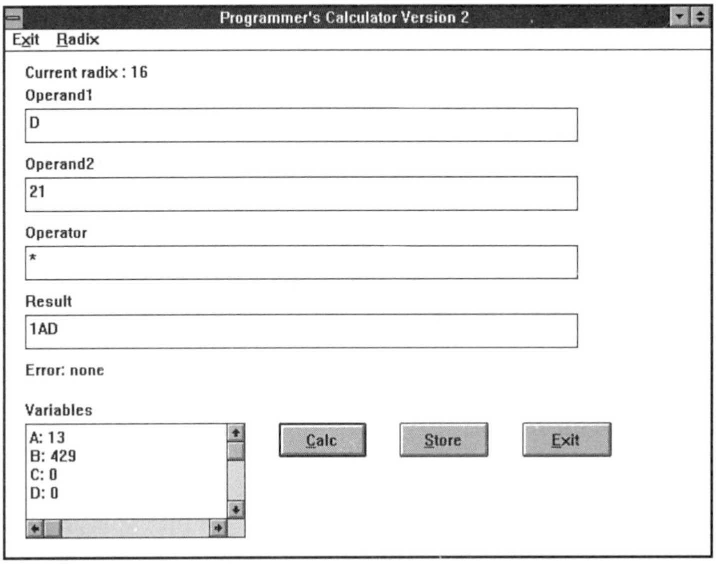

Figure 6.5

A sample session
with the second
version of the
Programmer's
Calculator.

Listing 6.10 shows the source code for the CTLBTN1.H header file.
This header file contains the ID_*XXXX* constants that define the various
pushbutton IDs.

Listing 6.10 Source Code for the CTLBTN1.H Header File

```
#define CM_EXIT    (WM_USER + 200)
#define CM_DECIMAL (WM_USER + 201)
#define CM_HEX     (WM_USER + 202)
#define CM_BINARY  (WM_USER + 203)
#define ID_CALC_BTN  100
#define ID_STORE_BTN 101
#define ID_EXIT_BTN  102
```

Listing 6.11 contains the script for the CTLBTN1.RC resource file. The resource file declares the COMMANDS menu resource. In addition, the resource file
also declares the BUTTONS accelerator keys resources. These accelerator keys
associate the Alt+C, Alt+S, and Alt+E keys with their respective button IDs.

Listing 6.11 Script for the CTLBTN1.RC Resource File

```
#include <windows.h>
#include <afxres.h>
#include "ctlbtn1.h"
BUTTONS ACCELERATORS
BEGIN
  "c", ID_CALC_BTN, ALT
  "s", ID_STORE_BTN, ALT
  "e", ID_EXIT_BTN, ALT
```

```
END
COMMANDS MENU LOADONCALL MOVEABLE PURE DISCARDABLE
BEGIN
    MENUITEM "E&xit", CM_EXIT
    POPUP "&Base"
    BEGIN
      MENUITEM "&Decimal", CM_DECIMAL
      MENUITEM "&Hexadecimal", CM_HEX
      MENUITEM "&Binary", CM_BINARY
    END
END
```

Listing 6.12 shows the source code for the CTLBTN1.CPP program file. Before
I explain what I added to or changed in the first version to create the second
version, let's examine the listing.

Listing 6.12 Source Code for the CTLBTN1.CPP Program File

```
#include <stdlib.h>
#include <ctype.h>
#include <stdio.h>
#include <string.h>
#include <afxwin.h>
#include "ctlbtn1.h"
// declare the constants that represent the sizes of the controls
const Wlbl = 100;
const Hlbl = 15;
const LblVertSpacing = 5;
const LblHorzSpacing = 40;
const Wbox = 500;
const Hbox = 30;
const BoxVertSpacing = 10;
const BoxHorzSpacing = 40;
const Wvarbox = 200;
const Hvarbox = 100;
const Hbtn = 30;
const Wbtn = 80;
const BtnHorzSpacing = 30;
const MaxStringLen = 80;
const MAX_MEMREG = 26;
// declare the ID_XXXX constants for the edit boxes
#define ID_OPERAND1_EDIT 101
#define ID_OPERATOR_EDIT 102
#define ID_OPERAND2_EDIT 103
#define ID_RESULT_EDIT   104
#define ID_ERRMSG_TXT    105
#define ID_VARIABLE_EDIT 106


class CxButton : public CButton
{
```

(continues)

Listing 6.12 Continued

```cpp
public:
    BOOL Create(const char FAR* lpCaption, const RECT& rect,
            CWnd* pParentWnd, UINT nID, BOOL bIsDefault);

};
class CxEdit : public CEdit
{
public:
  BOOL GetLine(LPSTR lpString, int nStrSize, int nLineNumber);
  int GetLineLength(int nLineNumber);

};
class CWindowApp : public CWinApp
{
public:
    virtual BOOL InitInstance();
};
// expand the functionality of CFrameWnd by deriving class CMainWnd
class CMainWnd : public CFrameWnd
{
 public:
  CMainWnd();
  ~CMainWnd();
 protected:
  // declare the pointers to the various controls
  // first, the edit box controls
  CEdit* pOperand1Box;
  CEdit* pOperatorBox;
  CEdit* pOperand2Box;
  CEdit* pResultBox;
  CxEdit* pVariableBox;
  // then the static text controls
  CStatic* pRadixTxt;
  CStatic* pOperand1Txt;
  CStatic* pOperatorTxt;
  CStatic* pOperand2Txt;
  CStatic* pResultTxt;
  CStatic* pErrMsgTxt;
  CStatic* pVariableTxt;
  // pushbuttons
  CxButton* pCalcBtn;
  CxButton* pStoreBtn;
  CxButton* pExitBtn;
  // math mode
  int nRadix;
  // math error flag
  BOOL bInError;
  // coordinates for the error message static text area
  CRect rectErrMsg;

  // handle clicking the left mouse button
  afx_msg void OnLButtonDown(UINT nFlags, CPoint point);
  // handle selecting the decimal mode
  afx_msg void CMDecimal();
```

```
  // handle selecting the hexadecimal mode
  afx_msg void CMHex();
  // handle selecting the binary mode
  afx_msg void CMBinary();
  // handle the calculation
  afx_msg void CMCalc();
  // handle storing the result in a variable
  afx_msg void CMStore();
  // handle exiting the application
  afx_msg void OnExit();
  // handle creating the controls
  afx_msg int OnCreate(LPCREATESTRUCT lpCS);
  // handle closing the window
  afx_msg void OnClose();

  // enable a pushbutton control
  virtual void EnableButton(CxButton* pBtn)
    { pBtn->EnableWindow( TRUE); }
  // disable a pushbutton control
  virtual void DisableButton(CxButton* pBtn)
    { pBtn->EnableWindow(FALSE); }

  // return a reference to member r based on individual
  // coordinates and dimensions
  void makerect(int X, int Y, int W, int H, CRect& r)
   { r.SetRect(X, Y, X + W, Y + H); }
  // obtain a number of a Variable edit box line
  long getVar(int lineNum);
  // store a number in the selected text of
  // the Variable edit box line
  void putVar(long x);

  // set contents of edit controls to integers in various bases
  void setDecimal(CEdit* pEdit);
  void setHexaDecimal(CEdit* pEdit);
  void setBinary(CEdit* pEdit);
  // declare message map macro
  DECLARE_MESSAGE_MAP();
};
BOOL CxButton::Create(const char FAR* lpCaption, const RECT& rect,
              CWnd* pParentWnd, UINT nID, BOOL bIsDefault)
{
  DWORD dwBtnStyle = (bIsDefault == TRUE) ?
             BS_DEFPUSHBUTTON : BS_PUSHBUTTON;
    return CButton::Create(lpCaption,
               WS_CHILD | WS_VISIBLE |
               WS_TABSTOP | dwBtnStyle,
               rect, pParentWnd, nID);
}
BOOL CxEdit::GetLine(LPSTR lpString, int nStrSize, int nLineNumber)
{
  int nCopyCount;
  BOOL bResult;
  if (nStrSize <= 0)
    return FALSE;
  bResult = (nStrSize >= GetLineLength(nLineNumber) + 1) ?
                TRUE : FALSE;
```

(continues)

II

Visual C++ Programming

Listing 6.12 Continued

```
      if (nStrSize == 1)
      {
        lpString[0] = '\0';
        return bResult;
      }
      ((WORD FAR *)lpString)[0] = nStrSize;

      nCopyCount = (WORD)(SendMessage(EM_GETLINE, nLineNumber,
                                      long(lpString)));
    if (nCopyCount)
    {
      // Windows returns non-null terminated string
      lpString[nCopyCount] = '\0';
      return bResult;
    }
    return FALSE;
}
int CxEdit::GetLineLength(int nLineNumber)
{
  int nStartPos = -1;
  if (nLineNumber > -1)
    nStartPos = LineIndex(nLineNumber);
  return (WORD) SendMessage(EM_LINELENGTH, nStartPos);
}
CMainWnd::CMainWnd()
{
  // load the main accelerator table to handle
  // keystroke input
  LoadAccelTable("BUTTONS");
  // create the window
  Create(NULL,
    "Programmer's Calculator Version 2",
    WS_OVERLAPPEDWINDOW,
    rectDefault, NULL, "COMMANDS");
  // clear the bInError flag
  bInError = FALSE;
  // set the default math mode
  nRadix = 10;
}

int CMainWnd::OnCreate(LPCREATESTRUCT lpCS)
{
  char s[81];
  char bigStr[6 * MAX_MEMREG + 1];
  char c;
  int x0 = 20;
  int y0 = 10;
  int x = x0, y = y0;
  CRect r;
  DWORD dwStaticStyle = WS_CHILD | WS_VISIBLE | SS_LEFT;
  DWORD dwBoxStyle = WS_CHILD | WS_VISIBLE | WS_BORDER |
                     ES_LEFT | ES_AUTOHSCROLL | ES_UPPERCASE;
```

```
// create the label for current radix (use Wbox width)
makerect(x, y, Wbox, Hlbl, r);
pRadixTxt = new CStatic();
pRadixTxt->Create("Current radix: 10", dwStaticStyle, r, this, -1);
// create the label for Operand1
y += Hlbl + LblVertSpacing;
makerect(x, y, Wlbl, Hlbl, r);
pOperand1Txt = new CStatic();
pOperand1Txt->Create("Operand1", dwStaticStyle, r, this, -1);
// create Operand1 edit box
y += Hlbl + LblVertSpacing;
makerect(x, y, Wbox, Hbox, r);
pOperand1Box = new CEdit();
pOperand1Box->Create(dwBoxStyle, r, this, ID_OPERAND1_EDIT);
pOperand1Box->LimitText(); // set no limit for text
// create the Operand2 label
y += Hbox + BoxVertSpacing;
makerect(x, y, Wlbl, Hlbl, r);
pOperand2Txt = new CStatic();
pOperand2Txt->Create("Operand2", dwStaticStyle, r, this, -1);

// create the Operand2 edit box
y += Hlbl + LblVertSpacing;
makerect(x, y, Wbox, Hbox, r);
pOperand2Box = new CEdit();
pOperand2Box->Create(dwBoxStyle, r, this, ID_OPERAND2_EDIT);
pOperand2Box->LimitText(); // set no limit for text

// create the Operator label
y += Hbox + BoxVertSpacing;
makerect(x, y, Wlbl, Hlbl, r);
pOperatorTxt = new CStatic();
pOperatorTxt->Create("Operator", dwStaticStyle, r, this, -1);

// create the Operator edit box
y += Hlbl + LblVertSpacing;
makerect(x, y, Wbox, Hbox, r);
pOperatorBox = new CEdit();
pOperatorBox->Create(dwBoxStyle, r, this, ID_OPERATOR_EDIT);
pOperatorBox->LimitText(); // set no limit for text

// create the Result label
y += Hbox + BoxVertSpacing;
makerect(x, y, Wlbl, Hlbl, r);
pResultTxt = new CStatic();
pResultTxt->Create("Result", dwStaticStyle, r, this, -1);

// create the Result edit box
y += Hlbl + LblVertSpacing;
makerect(x, y, Wbox, Hbox, r);
pResultBox = new CEdit();
pResultBox->Create(dwBoxStyle, r, this, ID_RESULT_EDIT);
pResultBox->LimitText(); // set no limit for text

// create the error message static text
y += Hbox + BoxVertSpacing;
```

(continues)

Listing 6.12 Continued

```cpp
// use the Wbox for the width of the error message static text
makerect(x, y, Wbox, Hlbl, r);
rectErrMsg = r; // store rectangular area for error message
pErrMsgTxt = new CStatic();
pErrMsgTxt->Create("Error: none", dwStaticStyle, r, this, -1);
// create the Variables label
y += 2 * Hlbl + LblVertSpacing;
makerect(x, y, Wlbl, Hlbl, r);
pVariableTxt = new CStatic();
pVariableTxt->Create("Variables", dwStaticStyle, r, this, -1);

// create the Variables edit box
y += Hlbl + LblVertSpacing;
bigStr[0] = '\0';
// build the initial contents of the Variable edit box
for (c = 'A'; c <= 'Z'; c++) {
  sprintf(s, "%c: 0\r\n", c);
  strcat(bigStr, s);
}
makerect(x, y, Wvarbox, Hvarbox, r);
pVariableBox = new CxEdit();
pVariableBox->Create(dwBoxStyle | ES_MULTILINE | WS_HSCROLL
            | WS_VSCROLL | ES_AUTOVSCROLL,
                r, this, ID_VARIABLE_EDIT);
pVariableBox->LimitText(); // set no limit for text
pVariableBox->SetWindowText(bigStr);

// create the Calc pushbutton
x += Wvarbox + BtnHorzSpacing;
makerect(x, y, Wbtn, Hbtn, r);
pCalcBtn = new CxButton();
pCalcBtn->Create("&Calc", r, this, ID_CALC_BTN, TRUE);
// create the Store Btn
x += Wbtn + BtnHorzSpacing;
makerect(x, y, Wbtn, Hbtn, r);
pStoreBtn = new CxButton();
pStoreBtn->Create("&Store", r, this, ID_STORE_BTN, FALSE);
// Create the Exit Btn
x += Wbtn + BtnHorzSpacing;
makerect(x, y, Wbtn, Hbtn, r);
pExitBtn = new CxButton();
pExitBtn->Create("&Exit", r, this, ID_EXIT_BTN, FALSE);

return CFrameWnd::OnCreate(lpCS);
}
CMainWnd::~CMainWnd()
{
  // delete the controls
  delete pOperand1Box;
  delete pOperatorBox;
  delete pOperand2Box;
  delete pResultBox;
  delete pVariableBox;
  delete pRadixTxt;
```

```
    delete pOperand1Txt;
    delete pOperatorTxt;
    delete pOperand2Txt;
    delete pResultTxt;
    delete pErrMsgTxt;
    delete pVariableTxt;
    delete pCalcBtn;
    delete pStoreBtn;
    delete pExitBtn;
}
void CMainWnd::OnLButtonDown(UINT nFlags, CPoint point)
{
    // did you click the mouse over the error message static text?
    if (rectErrMsg.PtInRect(point)) {
        pErrMsgTxt->SetWindowText("Error: none");
        EnableButton(pStoreBtn);
    }
}
void CMainWnd::CMDecimal()
{
    setDecimal(pOperand1Box);
    setDecimal(pOperand2Box);
    setDecimal(pResultBox);
    nRadix = 10;
    pRadixTxt->SetWindowText("Current radix : 10");
}
    // handle selecting the hexadecimal mode
void CMainWnd::CMHex()
{
    setHexaDecimal(pOperand1Box);
    setHexaDecimal(pOperand2Box);
    setHexaDecimal(pResultBox);
    nRadix = 16;
    pRadixTxt->SetWindowText("Current radix : 16");
}
    // handle selecting the binary mode
void CMainWnd::CMBinary()
{
    setBinary(pOperand1Box);
    setBinary(pOperand2Box);
    setBinary(pResultBox);
    nRadix = 2;
    pRadixTxt->SetWindowText("Current radix : 2");
}
void CMainWnd::CMCalc()
{
    long x, y, z;
    char opStr[MaxStringLen+1];
    char s[MaxStringLen+1];
    char* ss;
    // obtain the string in the Operand1 edit box
    pOperand1Box->GetWindowText(s, MaxStringLen);
    // does the pOperand1Box contain the name
    // of a single-letter variable which begins with @?
    if (s[0] == '@') {
        // obtain value from the Variable edit control
```

(continues)

Listing 6.12 Continued

```
  x = getVar(s[1] - 'A');
 // substitute variable name with its value
  _ltoa(x, s, nRadix);
  pOperand1Box->SetWindowText(s);
}
else
  // convert the string in the edit box
  x = strtol(s, &ss, nRadix);
// obtain the string in the Operand2 edit box
pOperand2Box->GetWindowText(s, MaxStringLen);
// does the pOperand2Box contain the name
// of a single-letter variable which begins with @?
if (s[0] == '@') {
  // obtain value from the Variable edit control
  y = getVar(s[1] - 'A');
 // substitute variable name with its value
  _ltoa(y, s, nRadix);
  pOperand2Box->SetWindowText(s);
}
else
    // convert the string in the edit box
  y = strtol(s, &ss, nRadix);
// obtain the string in the Operator edit box
pOperatorBox->GetWindowText(opStr, MaxStringLen);
// clear the error message box
pErrMsgTxt->SetWindowText("Error: none");
bInError = FALSE;
// determine the requested operation
if (opStr[0] == '+')
  z = x + y;
else if (opStr[0] == '-')
  z = x - y;
else if (opStr[0] == '*') {
  if (x == 0 || y < (2147483647L / x))
    z = x * y;
  else {
    z = 0;
    bInError = TRUE;
    pErrMsgTxt->SetWindowText("Error: overflow error");
  }
}
else if (opStr[0] == '/') {
  if (y != 0)
    z = x / y;
  else {
    z = 0;
    bInError = TRUE;
    pErrMsgTxt->SetWindowText("Error: Division-by-zero error");
  }
}
else if (opStr[0] == '|')
  z = x | y;
else if (opStr[0] == '&')
  z = x & y;
```

```
    else if (opStr[0] == '~')
      z = ~x;
    else if (strcmp(opStr, "<<") == 0)
      z = x << y;
    else if (strcmp(opStr, ">>") == 0)
      z = x >> y;
    else {
      bInError = TRUE;
      pErrMsgTxt->SetWindowText("Error: Invalid operator");
    }
    // display the result if no error has occurred
    if (!bInError) {
      _ltoa(z, s, nRadix);
      pResultBox->SetWindowText(s);
      EnableButton(pStoreBtn);
    }
    else
      DisableButton(pStoreBtn);
}
void CMainWnd::CMStore()
{
  char s[MaxStringLen+1];
  char* ss;
  long z;
  // get the string in the Result edit box
  pResultBox->GetWindowText(s, MaxStringLen);
  // store the result in the selected text of
  // the Variable edit box
  z = strtol(s, &ss, nRadix);
  putVar(z);
}
long CMainWnd::getVar(int lineNum)
{
  int lineSize;
  char s[MaxStringLen+1];
  if (lineNum >= MAX_MEMREG) return 0;
  // get the size of the target line
  lineSize = pVariableBox->GetLineLength(lineNum);
  // get the line
  pVariableBox->GetLine(s, lineSize, lineNum);
  // delete the first three characters
  strcpy(s, (s+3));
  // return the number stored in the target line
  return atol(s);
}
void CMainWnd::putVar(long x)
{
  DWORD selPos;
  WORD startPos, endPos;
  int lineNum;
  int lineSize;
  char s[MaxStringLen+1];

  // locate the character position of the cursor
  selPos = pVariableBox->GetSel();
  startPos = LOWORD(selPos);
```

(continues)

Listing 6.12 Continued

```
    endPos = HIWORD(selPos);
    // turn off the selected text
    if (startPos != endPos) {
      selPos = MAKELONG(startPos, startPos);
      pVariableBox->SetSel(selPos);
    }
    // get the line number where the cursor is located
    lineNum = pVariableBox->LineFromChar(-1);
    // get the line size of line lineNum
    lineSize = pVariableBox->GetLineLength(lineNum);
    // obtain the text of line lineNum
    pVariableBox->GetLine(s, lineSize, lineNum);
    // build the new text line
    sprintf(s, "%c: %ld", s[0], x);
    // get the character positions for the deleted line
    startPos = (WORD) (pVariableBox->LineIndex(-1));
    endPos = (WORD) (startPos + pVariableBox->LineLength(-1));
    // select the current line
    selPos = MAKELONG(startPos, endPos);
    pVariableBox->SetSel(selPos);
    // replace the current line with the new line
    pVariableBox->ReplaceSel(s);
}
void CMainWnd::OnExit()
{
    SendMessage(WM_CLOSE);
}
void CMainWnd::OnClose()
{
    if (MessageBox("Want to close this application",
                   "Query", MB_YESNO | MB_ICONQUESTION) == IDYES)
      DestroyWindow();
}

void CMainWnd::setDecimal(CEdit* pEdit)
{
    char s[MaxStringLen+1];
    char* ss;
    long n;
    pEdit->GetWindowText(s, MaxStringLen);
    n = strtol(s, &ss, nRadix);
    _ltoa(n, s, 10);
    pEdit->SetWindowText(s);
}
void CMainWnd::setHexaDecimal(CEdit* pEdit)
{
    char s[MaxStringLen+1];
    char *ss;
    long n;
    pEdit->GetWindowText(s, MaxStringLen);
    n = strtol(s, &ss, nRadix);
    _ltoa(n, s, 16);
    pEdit->SetWindowText(s);
}
```

```
void CMainWnd::setBinary(CEdit* pEdit)
{
  char s[MaxStringLen+1];
  char* ss;
  long n;
  pEdit->GetWindowText(s, MaxStringLen);
  n = strtol(s, &ss, nRadix);
  _ltoa(n, s, 2);
  pEdit->SetWindowText(s);
}
BEGIN_MESSAGE_MAP(CMainWnd, CFrameWnd)
    ON_WM_LBUTTONDOWN()
    ON_COMMAND(CM_DECIMAL, CMDecimal)
    ON_COMMAND(CM_HEX, CMHex)
    ON_COMMAND(CM_BINARY, CMBinary)
    ON_COMMAND(ID_CALC_BTN, CMCalc)
    ON_COMMAND(ID_STORE_BTN, CMStore)
    ON_COMMAND(ID_EXIT_BTN, OnExit)
    ON_COMMAND(CM_EXIT, OnExit)
    ON_WM_CREATE()
    ON_WM_CLOSE()
END_MESSAGE_MAP()
// Construct the CWindowApp's m_pMainWnd data member
BOOL CWindowApp::InitInstance()
{
  m_pMainWnd = new CMainWnd();
  m_pMainWnd->ShowWindow(m_nCmdShow);
  m_pMainWnd->UpdateWindow();
  return TRUE;
}
// application's constructor initializes and runs the app
CWindowApp WindowApp;
```

The program shown in Listing 6.12 declares additional constants for the sizes and dimensions of the pushbutton controls.

The program declares the class CxButton to model pushbutton controls. This class declares a more specialized version of the Create function. This version creates a normal or default pushbutton control by specifying the typical pushbutton styles. Thus, it becomes more straightforward for a client window or dialog box to create pushbutton controls using the class CxButton.

The window class CMainWnd adds new data members. These new members, pCalcBtn, pStoreBtn, and pExitBtn are pointers to the three pushbutton instances. As for the member functions, the new application version retains the OnLButtonDown, OnClose, OnExit, getVar, and putVar member functions from the previous version. All the other member functions are either new or have different names.

The CMainWnd constructor carries out these subsequent tasks:

- Loads the menu resource by invoking the LoadAccelTable function and specifying the BUTTONS accelerator resource.

- Creates the instances for the static text, edit box, and pushbuttons. This task involves calling the Create function.

- Assigns FALSE to the Boolean data member bInError.

- Assigns the default radix 10 to the data member nRadix.

The OnCreate member function creates the diverse controls. The function creates each instance of the class CxButton using a particular ID and caption. The caption string contains the ampersand (&) character to underline the hot key. The first pushbutton is created as the default control, by making TRUE the last argument of CxButton::Create. The function OnCreate creates the remaining pushbuttons as normal controls by specifying a FALSE argument to the last parameter of the function CxButton::Create. The Calc pushbutton, therefore, emerges as the default pushbutton. Just as appearances can be deceiving, however, the Calc button completely lacks the operations of a default button because its owner is a window and not a dialog box.

The OnLButtonDown member function in this version of the application adds a single statement to enable the Store button when you click the error message static text. This statement invokes the member function EnableButton and supplies it with the argument pStoreBtn (more about the function EnableButton later in this section).

The new version of member function CMCalc responds to the notification message sent by the Calc pushbutton. The function also responds to the Windows command messages transmitted by the Alt+C accelerator key. The corresponding message map macro uses the message ID of ID_CALC_BTN. The latter is the ID of the Calc button, used to create the Calc pushbutton. The statements in the function CMCalc are very similar to those in the first version. A few additional statements exist that enable or disable the Store button by calling the EnableButton and DisableButton member functions (more about these functions later in this section).

The new version of the member function CMStore works just like the function CMStore in the first version. The CMStore member function also intercepts the Alt+S accelerator key in the form of a command message with the ID number ID_STORE_BTN.

The CMExit member function responds to the notification message of the Exit button. The function sends the WM_CLOSE message to the parent window. The CMExit member function intercepts the Alt+E accelerator key in the form of a command message with the ID number ID_EXIT_BTN. The CMExit function also sends a WM_CLOSE message to the parent window.

The member functions EnableButton and DisableButton enable and disable a pushbutton, respectively. These functions send the C++ message CWnd::EnableWindow to the pointer-to-button parameter pBtn.

Summary

This chapter presented the basic controls: static text, edit box, and pushbutton. Typical Windows applications use these and other controls to animate the applications and to provide a more consistent user interface. You learned about the following topics:

- How to create static text controls and manipulate their text at run time.

- How to create single-line and multi-line edit box controls. These controls support versatile editing commands, such as cut, copy, paste, delete, and undo.

- How to create, use, and manipulate pushbutton controls. The control manipulation includes enabling, disabling, showing, and hiding the pushbutton controls at run time.

Chapter 7

Working with the Grouped Controls

In Chapter 6, I presented the first set of popular Windows controls. This chapter looks at another set of controls that includes the check box, radio button, and group box (also called the frame box). Check boxes and radio buttons behave as software switches. You probably have noticed these controls in typical search and replace dialog boxes, and you may have used these controls to direct particular aspects of a search or replacement operation, such as the direction, scope, and case-sensitivity of the operation. In this chapter, you learn about the following topics:

- The check box control

- The radio button control

- The group control, which groups the preceding controls in a logical manner

The Check Box Control

The check box control is a special button that toggles a check mark. The control includes a small square button, as well as a caption that appears, by default, to the right of the button. Clicking the square button toggles the check mark of the control. The check box is analogous to a binary digit that can be either set or cleared. You may place check boxes either inside or outside a group box. Check boxes (whether placed inside or outside a group box) are mutually nonexclusive. In other words, toggling any one check box does not affect the other check boxes. You might ask why you would want to place check boxes in a group box if this placement has no effect on the operation of the check boxes. The question has a two-part answer. First, the group box visually combines the check boxes so that the application user can more clearly see the purpose of the check boxes. Second, you can consolidate the notification messages sent by all the grouped check boxes to detect any change in the checked state of the check boxes.

A quick quiz! How many states does a check box have? If you answered two, you're in for a surprise! Actually, Windows supports three states: *checked*, *unchecked*, and *grayed* (also called the *indeterminate* state). You may interpret the third state in several ways. For example, you may consider the grayed state as a not-applicable (or "don't care") state. Table 7.1 shows the various check box control styles. The grayed state fills the controls rectangular button with a gray color.

Table 7.1 The Check Box Control Styles	
Style	**Meaning**
BS_CHECKBOX	Specifies a check box with the title to the right of the rectangular button.
BS_AUTOCHECKBOX	Same as BS_CHECKBOX, except that the button is automatically toggled when you click it.
BS_3STATE	Same as BS_CHECKBOX, except that the control has three states: checked, unchecked, and grayed.
BS_AUTO3STATE	Same as BS_3STATE, except that the button is automatically toggled when you click it.
BS_LEFTTEXT	Sets the control's title to the left of the button.

Examining the *CButton* Class and Check Boxes

In the last chapter, I presented the MFC class CButton and mentioned that this class models the check box control (among other controls). In this section, I focus on the aspects of the CButton class that relate to the check box control. As with the button control, you create a check box using both the class constructor and the member function CButton::Create. The check box styles shown in Table 7.1 imply that there are two basic modes for managing the check state of a check box control: automatic and nonautomatic. In the automatic mode (specified by the styles BS_AUTOCHECK or BS_AUTO3STATE), Windows toggles the check state when you click the control. By contrast, the manual mode (specified when you don't use the styles BS_AUTOCHECK or BS_AUTO3STATE) requires your application to be responsible for managing the check state of the check box.

The class CButton provides the following member functions to query and to set the state of the check box control:

- The parameterless member function GetCheck yields the state of the check box control. The declaration of the function GetCheck is

    ```
    int GetCheck() const;
    ```

    The function returns an int type value, which conveys the check state. The interpretation of this value is as follows:

    - A value of 0 means that the control is not checked.

    - A value of 1 indicates that the control is checked.

    - A value of 2 signals that the control is in a grayed state. This value is valid for check box controls set with the styles BS_3STATE or BS_AUTO3STATE.

    I suggest that your applications declare constants, such as BF_UNCHECKED, BF_CHECKED, and BF_GRAYED, to represent the preceding three states of the check box controls.

- The member function SetCheck lets you set the check state of a check box control. The declaration of the SetCheck function is

    ```
    void SetCheck(int nCheck);
    ```

    The parameter nCheck indicates the new state of the check box control. The arguments for the new state can be 0, 1, or 2.

Responding to Check Box Messages

Because check boxes are instances of CButton, with a BS_CHECKBOX or BS_AUTOCHECKBOX style, your MFC applications respond to the messages sent by check boxes in a manner similar to the way pushbuttons respond. The ON_BN_CLICKED macro maps the message sent by the check box control with the member function that responds to that message.

The Radio Button Control

To complement check boxes, Windows offers the mutually exclusive radio button controls. These controls enable you to choose one option from two or more options. Typically, a radio button includes a circular button and a title that appears, by default, to the right of the button. When you click a radio button, a tiny filled circle is displayed inside the circular button. You have to locate radio buttons in group boxes, which groups these buttons both logically and visually. Windows maintains only one selected radio button in each group box.

Examining the *CButton* Class and Radio Buttons

The MFC library enables the CButton class to model radio button controls by specifying the BS_RADIOBUTTON or BS_AUTORADIOBUTTON style. Table 7.2 provides the radio button styles. The constructor creates a radio button with the BS_AUTORADIOBUTTON style. As with the pushbutton and check box controls, creating the radio button controls involves using the class constructor and the member function Create. As with check box controls, you can use the member functions GetCheck and SetCheck to set and query the state of radio buttons. Unlike check box controls, however, radio buttons have only two states: checked and unchecked.

Table 7.2 Check Box Control Styles	
Style	**Meaning**
BS_RADIOBUTTON	Specifies a radio button with the title to the right of the circular button.
BS_AUTORADIOBUTTON	Same as BS_RADIOBUTTON, except that the button is automatically toggled when you click it.
BS_LEFTTEXT	Sets the control's title to the left of the button.

Responding to Radio Button Messages

The radio button controls transmit the same kind of notification messages to their parent windows as the check box controls do. Handling these messages for a radio button is identical to handling them for check boxes or pushbuttons.

The Group Control

The group box control is a special *container* control that includes radio buttons and/or check boxes. The group box serves these purposes:

- Logically combines multiple radio buttons so that when you select one radio button, the remaining buttons in the same group are automatically deselected.

- Visually combines radio buttons or check boxes. This grouping enables you to easily relate these controls to their tasks.

The MFC library supports the programming feature that enables the controls inside a group box to notify the parent of the group box that you have changed the state of its controls.

The class CButton, and its member function Create, build group boxes by specifying the style BS_GROUPBOX. This, however, is where the similarity ends between a group box and check box, radio button, and pushbutton controls. Group boxes have no state and do not send messages.

The Updated Calculator Application

At this point, I want to present a third version of the Programmer's Calculator. This version uses the controls discussed in this chapter to replace menu commands and to offer a new feature. This third version includes the following controls:

- *Single-line edit controls Operand1, Operand2, Operator, and Result.*

- *Error message static text control.*

- *Multi-line edit control labeled Variables.*

- *Static text controls.* Provide labels to the edit boxes.

- *Calc, Store, and Exit pushbuttons.*

- *Radix group box.* Contains the radio buttons Decimal, Hexadecimal, and Binary.

- *Substitute Vars check box.* Lets you enable or disable the substitution of values in place of names for the single-letter variables (that can appear in either of the Operand edit boxes). The replacement takes place after you click the Calc pushbutton.

■ *Exit menu.*

Figure 7.1 shows the controls contained in the new version of the calculator.

Figure 7.1.
A sample session with the third version of the Programmer's Calculator.

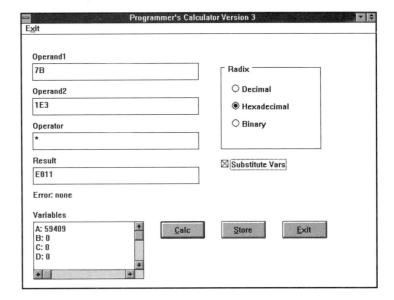

Compile and run the calculator application to get a good feel for the features supported by the radio buttons, check boxes, and the group box. When the application's window appears, maximize it to get a full view. Initially, the Decimal radio box is selected. Enter decimal integers in the Operand edit boxes and select a valid math operation, such as +. Click the Calc pushbutton to obtain the resulting value in the Result edit box. Now click the Hexadecimal radio box and watch the values in the Operands and Result edit boxes change from decimal to hexadecimal representation.

Store the current result in the single-letter variable A (click the mouse on the first line in the Variables edit box and then click the pushbutton Store). Enter the string @A in the Operand1 edit box and type a hexadecimal integer in the Operand2 edit box. Enter an appropriate operation in the Operator edit box and click the Calc pushbutton. What do you notice about the contents of the Operand1 edit box? It maintains the string @A because the Substitute Vars check box is unchecked. Click the Substitute Vars check box to mark it and then click again on the Calc pushbutton. This time, the application replaces the string @A with the contents of the single-letter variable A in the Variables edit box.

Listing 7.1 displays the contents of the CTLGRP1.DEF definition file.

Listing 7.1 CTLGRP1.DEF Definition File

```
NAME          CtlGrp1
DESCRIPTION   'An MFC Windows Application'
CODE          PRELOAD MOVEABLE DISCARDABLE
DATA          PRELOAD MOVEABLE MULTIPLE
HEAPSIZE      1024
```

Listing 7.2 shows the source code for the CTLGRP1.H header file.

Listing 7.2 Source Code for the CTLGRP1.H Header File

```
#define CM_EXIT      (WM_USER + 200)
#define ID_CALC_BTN  100
#define ID_STORE_BTN 101
#define ID_EXIT_BTN  102
```

Listing 7.3 contains the script for the CTLGRP1.RC resource file.

Listing 7.3 Script for the CTLGRP1.RC Resource File

```
#include <windows.h>
#include <afxres.h>
#include "ctlgrp1.h"
BUTTONS ACCELERATORS
BEGIN
  "c", ID_CALC_BTN, ALT
  "s", ID_STORE_BTN, ALT
  "e", ID_EXIT_BTN, ALT
END
EXITMENU MENU LOADONCALL MOVEABLE PURE DISCARDABLE
BEGIN
    MENUITEM "E&xit", CM_EXIT
END
```

Listing 7.4 contains the source code for the CTLGRP1.CPP program file.

Listing 7.4 Source Code for the CTLGRP1.CPP Program File

```
/*
                Programmer's Calculator version 3.0 11/3/93

  Program illustrates the group box, radio button, and
  check box controls.  These controls allow the application
  to select the radix and to enable/disable automatically
  substituting the name of a variable with its value.
*/
#include <stdlib.h>
#include <ctype.h>
#include <stdio.h>
#include <string.h>
#include <afxwin.h>
#include "ctlgrp1.h"
// declare the constants that represent the sizes of the controls
const Wlbl = 100;
const Hlbl = 15;
const LblVertSpacing = 5;
const LblHorzSpacing = 40;
const Wbox = 300;
const Hbox = 30;
const BoxVertSpacing = 10;
const BoxHorzSpacing = 40;
const Wvarbox = 200;
const Hvarbox = 100;
const Hbtn = 30;
const Wbtn = 80;
const BtnHorzSpacing = 30;
const Hgrp = 150;
const Wgrp = 180;
const GrpHorzSpacing = 30;
const GrpVertSpacing = 10;
const Hchk = 30;
const Wchk = 250;
const ChkHorzSpacing = 30;
const ChkVertSpacing = 10;
const Hrbt = 30;
const Wrbt = 120;
const RbtHorzSpacing = 30;
const RbtVertSpacing = 30;
const RbtLeftMargin = 20;
const MaxStringLen = 80;
const MAX_MEMREG = 26;
// declare the ID_XXXX constants for the edit boxes
#define ID_OPERAND1_EDIT 101
#define ID_OPERATOR_EDIT 102
#define ID_OPERAND2_EDIT 103
#define ID_RESULT_EDIT   104
#define ID_ERRMSG_TXT    105
#define ID_VARIABLE_EDIT 106
#define ID_AUTOSUBST_CHK 107
#define ID_RADIX_GRP     108
#define ID_DECIMAL_RBT   109
```

```
#define ID_HEX_RBT        110
#define ID_BINARY_RBT     111

// declare constants for the check box and radio button states
const BF_CHECKED = 1;
const BF_UNCHECKED = 0;
class CxButton : public CButton
{
public:
   BOOL Create(const char FAR* lpCaption, const RECT& rect,
          CWnd* pParentWnd, UINT nID, BOOL bIsDefault);

};
// declare check box class
class CCheckBox : public CButton
{
public:
   BOOL Create(const char FAR* lpCaption, const RECT& rect,
             CWnd* pParentWnd, UINT nID)
   {
       return CButton::Create(lpCaption,
                        WS_CHILD | WS_VISIBLE |
                        WS_TABSTOP | BS_AUTOCHECKBOX,
                        rect, pParentWnd, nID);
   }
   void Check()
     { SetCheck(BF_CHECKED); }

   void UnCheck()
     { SetCheck(BF_UNCHECKED); }
};
// declare radio button class
class CRadioButton : public CButton
{
public:
   BOOL Create(const char FAR* lpCaption, const RECT& rect,
             CWnd* pParentWnd, UINT nID)
   {
       return CButton::Create(lpCaption,
                        WS_CHILD | WS_VISIBLE |
                        WS_TABSTOP |
                        BS_AUTORADIOBUTTON,
                        rect, pParentWnd, nID);
   }

   void Check()
     { SetCheck(BF_CHECKED); }

   void UnCheck()
     { SetCheck(BF_UNCHECKED); }
};
// declare group box class
class CGroupBox : public CButton
{
public:
```

(continues)

II

Visual C++ Programming

Listing 7.4 Continued

```
        BOOL Create(const char FAR* lpCaption, const RECT& rect,
                    CWnd* pParentWnd, UINT nID)
        {
            return CButton::Create(lpCaption,
                                   WS_CHILD | WS_VISIBLE |
                                   WS_TABSTOP | BS_GROUPBOX,
                                   rect, pParentWnd, nID);
        }
};
class CxEdit : public CEdit
{
public:
  BOOL GetLine(LPSTR lpString, int nStrSize, int nLineNumber);
  int GetLineLength(int nLineNumber);

};
class CGroupedControlsApp : public CWinApp
{
public:
    virtual BOOL InitInstance();
};
// expand the functionality of CFrameWnd by deriving class CMainWnd
class CMainWnd : public CFrameWnd
{
 public:
  CMainWnd();
  ~CMainWnd();
 protected:
  // declare the pointers to the various controls
  // first, the edit box controls
  CEdit* pOperand1Box;
  CEdit* pOperatorBox;
  CEdit* pOperand2Box;
  CEdit* pResultBox;
  CxEdit* pVariableBox;
  // then the static text controls
  CStatic* pOperand1Txt;
  CStatic* pOperatorTxt;
  CStatic* pOperand2Txt;
  CStatic* pResultTxt;
  CStatic* pErrMsgTxt;
  CStatic* pVariableTxt;
  // pushbuttons
  CxButton* pCalcBtn;
  CxButton* pStoreBtn;
  CxButton* pExitBtn;
  // group box
  CGroupBox* pRadixGrp;
  // radio buttons
  CRadioButton* pDecimalRbt;
  CRadioButton* pHexRbt;
  CRadioButton* pBinaryRbt;
  // check box
  CCheckBox* pAutoSubstChk;
```

```
// math mode
int nRadix;
// math error flag
BOOL bInError;
// coordinates for the Error Message static text area
CRect rectErrMsg;

// handle clicking the left mouse button
afx_msg void OnLButtonDown(UINT nFlags, CPoint point);
// handle selecting the decimal mode
afx_msg void HandleDecimalRbt();
// handle selecting the hexadecimal mode
afx_msg void HandleHexRbt();
// handle selecting the binary mode
afx_msg void HandleBinaryRbt();
// handle the calculation
afx_msg void CMCalc();
// handle storing the result in a variable
afx_msg void CMStore();
// handle exiting the application
afx_msg void OnExit();
// handle creating the controls
afx_msg int OnCreate(LPCREATESTRUCT lpCS);
// handle closing the window
afx_msg void OnClose();

// enable a pushbutton control
virtual void EnableButton(CxButton* pBtn)
  { pBtn->EnableWindow( TRUE); }
// disable a pushbutton control
virtual void DisableButton(CxButton* pBtn)
  { pBtn->EnableWindow(FALSE); }

// return a reference to member r based on individual
// coordinates and dimensions
void makerect(int X, int Y, int W, int H, CRect& r)
 { r.SetRect(X, Y, X + W, Y + H); }
// obtain a number of a Variable edit box line
long getVar(int lineNum);
// store a number in the selected text of
// the Variable edit box line
void putVar(long x);

// set contents of edit controls to integers in various bases
void setDecimal(CEdit* pEdit);
void setHexaDecimal(CEdit* pEdit);
void setBinary(CEdit* pEdit);
// declare message map macro
DECLARE_MESSAGE_MAP();
};
BOOL CxButton::Create(const char FAR* lpCaption, const RECT& rect,
            CWnd* pParentWnd, UINT nID, BOOL bIsDefault)
{
  DWORD dwBtnStyle = (bIsDefault == TRUE) ?
            BS_DEFPUSHBUTTON : BS_PUSHBUTTON;
```

(continues)

II

Visual C++ Programming

Listing 7.4 Continued

```
      return CButton::Create(lpCaption,
                 WS_CHILD | WS_VISIBLE |
                 WS_TABSTOP | dwBtnStyle,
                 rect, pParentWnd, nID);
}
BOOL CxEdit::GetLine(LPSTR lpString, int nStrSize, int nLineNumber)
{
  int nCopyCount;
  BOOL bResult;
  if (nStrSize <= 0)
    return FALSE;
  bResult = (nStrSize >= GetLineLength(nLineNumber) + 1) ?
               TRUE : FALSE;
  if (nStrSize == 1)
  {
    lpString[0] = '\0';
    return bResult;
  }
  ((WORD FAR *)lpString)[0] = nStrSize;

  nCopyCount = (WORD)(SendMessage(EM_GETLINE, nLineNumber,
                                    long(lpString)));
  if (nCopyCount)
  {
    // Windows returns non-null terminated string
    lpString[nCopyCount] = '\0';
    return bResult;
  }
  return FALSE;
}
int CxEdit::GetLineLength(int nLineNumber)
{
  int nStartPos = -1;
  if (nLineNumber > -1)
    nStartPos = LineIndex(nLineNumber);
  return (WORD) SendMessage(EM_LINELENGTH, nStartPos);
}
CMainWnd::CMainWnd()
{
  // load the main accelerator table to handle
  // keystroke input
  LoadAccelTable("BUTTONS");
  // create the window
  Create(NULL,
    "Programmer's Calculator Version 3",
    WS_OVERLAPPEDWINDOW,
    rectDefault, NULL, "EXITMENU");
  // clear the bInError flag
  bInError = FALSE;
  // set the default math mode
  nRadix = 10;
}

int CMainWnd::OnCreate(LPCREATESTRUCT lpCS)
{
```

```
char s[81];
char bigStr[6 * MAX_MEMREG + 1];
char c;
int x0 = 20;
int y0 = 10;
int x = x0, y = y0;
int x1, y1;
CRect r;
DWORD dwStaticStyle = WS_CHILD | WS_VISIBLE | SS_LEFT;
DWORD dwBoxStyle = WS_CHILD | WS_VISIBLE | WS_BORDER |
                   ES_LEFT | ES_AUTOHSCROLL | ES_UPPERCASE;
// create the label for Operand1
y += Hlbl + LblVertSpacing;
makerect(x, y, Wlbl, Hlbl, r);
pOperand1Txt = new CStatic();
pOperand1Txt->Create("Operand1", dwStaticStyle, r, this, -1);
// create Operand1 edit box
y += Hlbl + LblVertSpacing;
makerect(x, y, Wbox, Hbox, r);
pOperand1Box = new CEdit();
pOperand1Box->Create(dwBoxStyle, r, this, ID_OPERAND1_EDIT);
pOperand1Box->LimitText(); // set no limit for text
x1 = x;
y1 = y;
// create the Operand2 label
y += Hbox + BoxVertSpacing;
makerect(x, y, Wlbl, Hlbl, r);
pOperand2Txt = new CStatic();
pOperand2Txt->Create("Operand2", dwStaticStyle, r, this, -1);

// create the Operand2 edit box
y += Hlbl + LblVertSpacing;
makerect(x, y, Wbox, Hbox, r);
pOperand2Box = new CEdit();
pOperand2Box->Create(dwBoxStyle, r, this, ID_OPERAND2_EDIT);
pOperand2Box->LimitText(); // set no limit for text

// create the Operator label
y += Hbox + BoxVertSpacing;
makerect(x, y, Wlbl, Hlbl, r);
pOperatorTxt = new CStatic();
pOperatorTxt->Create("Operator", dwStaticStyle, r, this, -1);

// create the Operator edit box
y += Hlbl + LblVertSpacing;
makerect(x, y, Wbox, Hbox, r);
pOperatorBox = new CEdit();
pOperatorBox->Create(dwBoxStyle, r, this, ID_OPERATOR_EDIT);
pOperatorBox->LimitText(); // set no limit for text

// create the Result label
y += Hbox + BoxVertSpacing;
makerect(x, y, Wlbl, Hlbl, r);
pResultTxt = new CStatic();
pResultTxt->Create("Result", dwStaticStyle, r, this, -1);
```

(continues)

II

Visual C++ Programming

Listing 7.4 Continued

```
// create the Result edit box
y += Hlbl + LblVertSpacing;
makerect(x, y, Wbox, Hbox, r);
pResultBox = new CEdit();
pResultBox->Create(dwBoxStyle, r, this, ID_RESULT_EDIT);
pResultBox->LimitText(); // set no limit for text

// create the error message static text
y += Hbox + BoxVertSpacing;
// use the Wbox for the width of the Error Message static text
makerect(x, y, Wbox, Hlbl, r);
rectErrMsg = r; // store rectangular area for error message
pErrMsgTxt = new CStatic();
pErrMsgTxt->Create("Error: none", dwStaticStyle, r, this, -1);
// create the Variables label
y += 2 * Hlbl + LblVertSpacing;
makerect(x, y, Wlbl, Hlbl, r);
pVariableTxt = new CStatic();
pVariableTxt->Create("Variables", dwStaticStyle, r, this, -1);

// create the Variables edit box
y += Hlbl + LblVertSpacing;
bigStr[0] = '\0';
// build the initial contents of the Variable edit box
for (c = 'A'; c <= 'Z'; c++) {
  sprintf(s, "%c: 0\r\n", c);
  strcat(bigStr, s);
}
makerect(x, y, Wvarbox, Hvarbox, r);
pVariableBox = new CxEdit();
pVariableBox->Create(dwBoxStyle ¦ ES_MULTILINE ¦ WS_HSCROLL
             ¦ WS_VSCROLL ¦ ES_AUTOVSCROLL,
                  r, this, ID_VARIABLE_EDIT);
pVariableBox->LimitText(); // set no limit for text
pVariableBox->SetWindowText(bigStr);

// create the Calc pushbutton
x += Wvarbox + BtnHorzSpacing;
makerect(x, y, Wbtn, Hbtn, r);
pCalcBtn = new CxButton();
pCalcBtn->Create("&Calc", r, this, ID_CALC_BTN, TRUE);
// create the Store Btn
x += Wbtn + BtnHorzSpacing;
makerect(x, y, Wbtn, Hbtn, r);
pStoreBtn = new CxButton();
pStoreBtn->Create("&Store", r, this, ID_STORE_BTN, FALSE);
// Create the Exit Btn
x += Wbtn + BtnHorzSpacing;
makerect(x, y, Wbtn, Hbtn, r);
pExitBtn = new CxButton();
pExitBtn->Create("&Exit", r, this, ID_EXIT_BTN, FALSE);

// create the group box
x = x1 + Wbox + BoxHorzSpacing;
y = y1;
```

```
    makerect(x, y, Wgrp, Hgrp, r);
    pRadixGrp = new CGroupBox();
    pRadixGrp->Create(" Radix ", r, this, ID_RADIX_GRP);

    // create the Decimal radio button
    y += RbtVertSpacing;
    makerect(RbtLeftMargin + x, y, Wrbt, Hrbt, r);
    pDecimalRbt = new CRadioButton();
    pDecimalRbt->Create("Decimal", r, this, ID_DECIMAL_RBT);

    // create the Hexadecimal radio button
    y += RbtVertSpacing;
    makerect(RbtLeftMargin + x, y, Wrbt, Hrbt, r);
    pHexRbt = new CRadioButton();
    pHexRbt->Create("Hexadecimal", r, this, ID_HEX_RBT);

    // create the Binary radio button
    y += RbtVertSpacing;
    makerect(RbtLeftMargin + x, y, Wrbt, Hrbt, r);
    pBinaryRbt = new CRadioButton();
    pBinaryRbt->Create("Binary", r, this, ID_BINARY_RBT);

    // check the decimal radix
    pDecimalRbt->SetCheck(BF_CHECKED);

    // create auto substitute check box
    y = y1 + Hgrp + BoxVertSpacing;
    makerect(x, y, Wrbt, Hrbt, r);
    pAutoSubstChk = new CCheckBox();
    pAutoSubstChk->Create("Substitute Vars", r,
                          this, ID_AUTOSUBST_CHK);
    return CFrameWnd::OnCreate(lpCS);
}
CMainWnd::~CMainWnd()
{
    // delete the controls
    delete pOperand1Box;
    delete pOperatorBox;
    delete pOperand2Box;
    delete pResultBox;
    delete pVariableBox;
    delete pOperand1Txt;
    delete pOperatorTxt;
    delete pOperand2Txt;
    delete pResultTxt;
    delete pErrMsgTxt;
    delete pVariableTxt;
    delete pCalcBtn;
    delete pStoreBtn;
    delete pExitBtn;
    delete pDecimalRbt;
    delete pHexRbt;
    delete pBinaryRbt;
    delete pRadixGrp;
    delete pAutoSubstChk;
}
```

II

Visual C++ Programming

(continues)

Listing 7.4 Continued

```
void CMainWnd::OnLButtonDown(UINT nFlags, CPoint point)
{
  // did you click the mouse over the Error Message static text?
  if (rectErrMsg.PtInRect(point)) {
      pErrMsgTxt->SetWindowText("Error: none");
      EnableButton(pStoreBtn);
  }
}
void CMainWnd::HandleDecimalRbt()
{
  setDecimal(pOperand1Box);
  setDecimal(pOperand2Box);
  setDecimal(pResultBox);
  nRadix = 10;
}
  // handle selecting the hexadecimal mode
void CMainWnd::HandleHexRbt()
{
  setHexaDecimal(pOperand1Box);
  setHexaDecimal(pOperand2Box);
  setHexaDecimal(pResultBox);
  nRadix = 16;
}
  // handle selecting the binary mode
void CMainWnd::HandleBinaryRbt()
{
  setBinary(pOperand1Box);
  setBinary(pOperand2Box);
  setBinary(pResultBox);
  nRadix = 2;
}
void CMainWnd::CMCalc()
{
  long x, y, z;
  char opStr[MaxStringLen+1];
  char s[MaxStringLen+1];
  char* ss;
  // obtain the string in the Operand1 edit box
  pOperand1Box->GetWindowText(s, MaxStringLen);
  // does the pOperand1Box contain the name
  // of a single-letter variable which begins with @?
  if (s[0] == '@') {
    // obtain value from the Variable edit control
    x = getVar(s[1] - 'A');
    if (pAutoSubstChk->GetCheck() == BF_CHECKED) {
      // substitute variable name with its value
      _ltoa(x, s, nRadix);
      pOperand1Box->SetWindowText(s);
    }
  }
  else
    // convert the string in the edit box
    x = strtol(s, &ss, nRadix);
  // obtain the string in the Operand2 edit box
  pOperand2Box->GetWindowText(s, MaxStringLen);
```

```
// does the pOperand2Box contain the name
// of a single-letter variable which begins with @?
if (s[0] == '@') {
  // obtain value from the Variable edit control
  y = getVar(s[1] - 'A');
  if (pAutoSubstChk->GetCheck() == BF_CHECKED) {
    // substitute variable name with its value
    _ltoa(y, s, nRadix);
    pOperand2Box->SetWindowText(s);
  }
}
else
    // convert the string in the edit box
  y = strtol(s, &ss, nRadix);
// obtain the string in the Operator edit box
pOperatorBox->GetWindowText(opStr, MaxStringLen);
// clear the error message box
pErrMsgTxt->SetWindowText("Error: none");
bInError = FALSE;
// determine the requested operation
if (opStr[0] == '+')
  z = x + y;
else if (opStr[0] == '-')
  z = x - y;
else if (opStr[0] == '*') {
  if (x == 0 || y < (2147483647L / x))
    z = x * y;
  else {
    z = 0;
    bInError = TRUE;
    pErrMsgTxt->SetWindowText("Error: overflow error");
  }
}
else if (opStr[0] == '/') {
  if (y != 0)
    z = x / y;
  else {
    z = 0;
    bInError = TRUE;
    pErrMsgTxt->SetWindowText("Error: Division-by-zero error");
  }
}
else if (opStr[0] == '|')
  z = x | y;
else if (opStr[0] == '&')
  z = x & y;
else if (opStr[0] == '~')
  z = ~x;
else if (strcmp(opStr, "<<") == 0)
  z = x << y;
else if (strcmp(opStr, ">>") == 0)
  z = x >> y;
else {
  bInError = TRUE;
  pErrMsgTxt->SetWindowText("Error: Invalid operator");
}
```

(continues)

Listing 7.4 Continued

```
    // display the result if no error has occurred
    if (!bInError) {
      _ltoa(z, s, nRadix);
      pResultBox->SetWindowText(s);
      EnableButton(pStoreBtn);
    }
    else
      DisableButton(pStoreBtn);
}
void CMainWnd::CMStore()
{
  char s[MaxStringLen+1];
  char* ss;
  long z;
  // get the string in the Result edit box
  pResultBox->GetWindowText(s, MaxStringLen);
  // store the result in the selected text of
  // the Variable edit box
  z = strtol(s, &ss, nRadix);
  putVar(z);
}
long CMainWnd::getVar(int lineNum)
{
  int lineSize;
  char s[MaxStringLen+1];
  if (lineNum >= MAX_MEMREG) return 0;
  // get the size of the target line
  lineSize = pVariableBox->GetLineLength(lineNum);
  // get the line
  pVariableBox->GetLine(s, lineSize, lineNum);
  // delete the first three characters
  strcpy(s, (s+3));
  // return the number stored in the target line
  return atol(s);
}
void CMainWnd::putVar(long x)
{
  DWORD selPos;
  WORD startPos, endPos;
  int lineNum;
  int lineSize;
  char s[MaxStringLen+1];

  // locate the character position of the cursor
  selPos = pVariableBox->GetSel();
  startPos = LOWORD(selPos);
  endPos = HIWORD(selPos);
  // turn off the selected text
  if (startPos != endPos) {
    selPos = MAKELONG(startPos, startPos);
    pVariableBox->SetSel(selPos);
  }
  // get the line number where the cursor is located
  lineNum = pVariableBox->LineFromChar(-1);
  // get the line size of line lineNum
```

```
    lineSize = pVariableBox->GetLineLength(lineNum);
    // obtain the text of line lineNum
    pVariableBox->GetLine(s, lineSize, lineNum);
    // build the new text line
    sprintf(s, "%c: %ld", s[0], x);
    // get the character positions for the deleted line
    startPos = (WORD) (pVariableBox->LineIndex(-1));
    endPos = (WORD) (startPos + pVariableBox->LineLength(-1));
    // select the current line
    selPos = MAKELONG(startPos, endPos);
    pVariableBox->SetSel(selPos);
    // replace the current line with the new line
    pVariableBox->ReplaceSel(s);
}
void CMainWnd::OnExit()
{
  SendMessage(WM_CLOSE);
}
void CMainWnd::OnClose()
{
  if (MessageBox("Want to close this application",
                 "Query", MB_YESNO ¦ MB_ICONQUESTION) == IDYES)
    DestroyWindow();
}

void CMainWnd::setDecimal(CEdit* pEdit)
{
  char s[MaxStringLen+1];
  char* ss;
  long n;
  pEdit->GetWindowText(s, MaxStringLen);
  n = strtol(s, &ss, nRadix);
  _ltoa(n, s, 10);
  pEdit->SetWindowText(s);
}
void CMainWnd::setHexaDecimal(CEdit* pEdit)
{
  char s[MaxStringLen+1];
  char *ss;
  long n;
  pEdit->GetWindowText(s, MaxStringLen);
  n = strtol(s, &ss, nRadix);
  _ltoa(n, s, 16);
  pEdit->SetWindowText(s);
}
void CMainWnd::setBinary(CEdit* pEdit)
{
  char s[MaxStringLen+1];
  char* ss;
  long n;
  pEdit->GetWindowText(s, MaxStringLen);
  n = strtol(s, &ss, nRadix);
  _ltoa(n, s, 2);
  pEdit->SetWindowText(s);
}
```

II

Visual C++ Programming

(continues)

Listing 7.4 Continued

```
BEGIN_MESSAGE_MAP(CMainWnd, CFrameWnd)
    ON_WM_LBUTTONDOWN()
    ON_COMMAND(ID_CALC_BTN, CMCalc)
    ON_COMMAND(ID_STORE_BTN, CMStore)
    ON_COMMAND(ID_EXIT_BTN, OnExit)
    ON_COMMAND(CM_EXIT, OnExit)
    ON_BN_CLICKED(ID_DECIMAL_RBT, HandleDecimalRbt)
    ON_BN_CLICKED(ID_HEX_RBT, HandleHexRbt)
    ON_BN_CLICKED(ID_BINARY_RBT, HandleBinaryRbt)
    ON_WM_CREATE()
    ON_WM_CLOSE()
END_MESSAGE_MAP()
// Construct the CGroupedControlsApp's m_pMainWnd data member
BOOL CGroupedControlsApp::InitInstance()
{
  m_pMainWnd = new CMainWnd();
  m_pMainWnd->ShowWindow(m_nCmdShow);
  m_pMainWnd->UpdateWindow();
  return TRUE;
}
// application's constructor initializes and runs the app
CGroupedControlsApp WindowApp;
```

The program just shown contains the source code for the CTLGRP1.CPP file and declares the following constants:

- Constants that specify the sizes of the various controls and the spacing between them.

- #define statements that define the IDs of the various controls.

- The constants BF_CHECKED and BF_UNCHECKED, which represent the checked and unchecked states of the check box and radio button controls.

The CTLGRP1.CPP program also declares the following classes:

- The class CxButton, a descendant of CButton, which supports pushbutton controls.

- The class CCheckBox, a descendant of CButton, which supports check box controls.

- The class CRadioButton, a descendant of CButton, which supports radio button controls.

- The class CGroupBox, a descendant of CButton, which supports group box controls.

- The class CxEdit, a descendant of CEdit, which supports an improved version of the edit controls.

- The window class CMainWnd.

- The application class CGroupedControlsApp.

The classes CCheckBox and CRadioButton declare the member functions Check and UnCheck to set and clear, respectively, the check state of these controls.

The CMainWnd window class includes a sizable collection of data members. Most of these members are pointers to the instances of the various controls used by the application. The remaining data members, nRadix, bInError, and rectErrMsg are the same as in the first two versions of the calculator program.

The CMainWnd class declares a constructor, a destructor, and a number of member functions to support the various operations. The constructor performs the following tasks:

- Loads the accelerator table resource BUTTONS.

- Creates the main window and attaches the menu resource EXITMENU to it.

- Assigns the Boolean value FALSE to the data member bInError.

- Assigns the initial radix value to the data member nRadix.

The member function OnCreate creates the various controls in a manner similar to the way they appeared in the earlier versions of the program. The relevant statements in the OnCreate function are the ones that create the check boxes, the group box, and the radio buttons. The function creates the CCheckBox instance using a unique control ID, a title, and a rectangular area. Notice that the function OnCreate does not use the style WS_GROUP to indicate that the check box is created outside a group box. The function OnCreate creates the group box control using a unique ID, a title, and a rectangular area. The function OnCreate creates each radio button control using a unique ID, a title, and a rectangular area.

Notice that these radio buttons have the main window, not the group box, as their parent, even though they are visually located inside the group box. Why? If you declare the group box as the parent window of these radio buttons, they will not appear in the main window! Consequently, you won't be able to use them.

The OnCreate function selects the Decimal radio button by sending the C++ message SetCheck to that control. The argument of this message is BF_CHECKED.

The member function CMCalc performs the calculations and replaces the name of single-letter variables if the Substitutes Vars check box is checked. The member function performs the following tasks:

■ Obtains the first operand from the Operand1 edit box. The control may contain the name of a single-letter variable (A to Z) or an integer. The CMCalc function uses the GetWindowText function to copy the edit control text to the local variable s. The function then examines the first character in the variable s. If that character is the character @, then the first operand is a single-letter variable, and the function performs the following subtasks:

  • Calls the member function getVar to acquire the value associated with the single-letter variable. The name of the variable is located in the second character of the variable s. This task assigns the contents of the single-letter variable to the local variable x.

  • Determines if the Substitute Vars check box is checked. This task involves sending the C++ message GetCheck to the check box control. The function compares the result of the message with the constant BF_CHECKED. If the two values match, the function converts the integer in variable x to a string image using the radix value in the member nRadix. This conversion involves the function _ltoa. The function then updates the Operand1 edit box with the contents of the single-letter variable. This task involves sending the C++ message SetWindowText to the first operand edit box object.

If the first character in the variable s is not the character @, the function CMCalc uses the function strtol to convert the contents of the variable s into an integer. The function CMCalc assigns that integer to the variable x.

- Obtains the second operand in a manner identical to the first one. The function stores the second operand in the variable y.

- Copies the text in the Operator edit box into the local variable opStr.

- Clears the error message text box and sets the bInError data member to FALSE.

- Executes the requested operation by using a series of if and if-else statements. The operators supported are +, -, *, /, ¦, &, ~, <<, and >>. If the function detects an error, its sets the bInError data member to TRUE and displays a message in the error message static text control.

- Displays the result of the operation in the Result box if the bInError data member is FALSE. The function first converts the result from an integer to a string. This step also uses the function _ltoa to create a string image of the integer using the current radix. Next, the function writes to the Result edit box by sending the C++ message SetWindowText to that control. The function enables the Store pushbutton if the member bInError contains TRUE, which involves the function EnableButton. Otherwise, the function disables the Store pushbutton, which involves the function DisableButton.

The member functions CMStore, CMExit, putVar, getVar, setDecimal, setHexaDecimal, and setBinary are the same as in the second version of the Programmer's Calculator.

The member functions HandleDecimalRbt, HandleHexRbt, and HandleBinaryRbt respond to the individual BN_CLICKED notification messages sent by the three radio buttons. These functions replace the member functions CMDecimal, CMHex, and CMBinary, which I presented in the first two versions of the Programmer's Calculator. The statements in the HandleXXXXRbt functions are identical to the CMXXXX functions they replace.

Summary

This chapter discussed the special switch controls: the group box, check box, and radio button controls. Here's what you learned:

- How to create check box, radio button, and group box controls.

- How to set and query the check state for check box and radio button controls.

- How to respond to notification messages sent by these controls to their parent window.

- How to initialize controls.

Chapter 8

Working with the Scrollable Controls

This chapter examines what I call *scrollable controls*—scroll bars, list boxes, and combo boxes—which all have the scroll bar in common. The scroll bar is a visual control that lets you quickly select from a wide range of integer values. The list box is an input tool that conveniently provides you with a list of items you can choose from, rather than forcing you to remember these items (and how they are spelled). It is far more convenient to provide you with a list of files from which you can pick one file, than for you to have to type the exact filename in an edit box. List controls have gradually become a typical way to retrieve information. In this chapter, I discuss the scroll bar, the list box, and the combo box. You learn about the following topics:

- The scroll bar control

- The single-selection list box control

- The multiple-selection list box control

- The combo box control in its various styles

The Scroll Bar Control

The scroll bar is, essentially, a control that enables you to scroll through integer values. Windows offers the scroll bar as a stand-alone control and also as a part of windows, lists, and combo boxes. The stand-alone scroll bar control appears and responds very much like the scroll bar of a window. The control contains a thumb box, which maintains the current value. Mouse clicks move the thumb box either by single lines (the smallest unit of movement) or by pages (a designated jump in value). The member functions OnVScroll and OnHScroll support vertical and horizontal scrolling, respectively. Moreover, the scroll bar responds to cursor control keys, such as Home, End, PgUp, and PgDown, and the member function OnKeyDown supports scrolling by these keys. The main role of the scroll bar control is to enable you to swiftly and efficiently choose an integer value in a predefined range of values.

The *CScrollBar* Class

The MFC library provides the CScrollBar class, a descendant of CWnd, which models the scroll bar controls. The makeup of the class CScrollBar includes a class constructor and a collection of member functions that set and query the current position and range of values for the scroll bar.

The class constructor, like many other MFC classes, is parameterless. The process of creating a scroll bar control involves the constructor and the member function Create. Here is the declaration of the Create function:

```
BOOL Create(DWORD dwStyle,      // control style
            const RECT& rect,    // location and dimensions
            CWnd* pParentWnd,    // pointer to parent window
            UINT nID);           // control ID
```

The parameter dwStyle indicates the style of the scroll bar control. Scroll bar styles include both the WS_*XXXX* window styles and the SBS_*XXXX* scroll bar styles. Table 8.1 illustrates the SBS_*XXXX* styles, which assist in fine-tuning the created CScrollBar instances. The parameter rect defines the location and the dimensions of the scroll bar control. The parameter pParentWnd is the pointer to the parent window. The parameter nID defines the unique ID of the scroll bar control.

Table 8.1 *SBS_XXXX* Styles for the Scroll Bar Control

Value	Description
SBS_BOTTOMALIGN	Used with the SBS_HORZ style to align the bottom of the scroll bar with the bottom edge of the rectangle specified in the Create function.
SBS_HORZ	Specifies a horizontal scroll bar. The scroll bar has the location, width, and height specified by the parameter rect in the Create function, if neither SBS_BOTTOMALIGN nor SBS_TOPALIGN styles are specified.

Value	Description
SBS_LEFTALIGN	Used with the SBS_VERT style to align the left edge of the scroll bar with the left edge of the rectangle specified in the Create function.
SBS_RIGHTALIGN	Used with the SBS_VERT style to align the right edge of the scroll bar with the right edge of the rectangle specified in the Create function.
SBS_SIZEBOX	Specifies a size box. The box has the location, width, and height specified by the parameter rect in the Create function, if neither the SBS_SIZEBOXBOTTOMRIGHTALIGN nor the SBS_SIZEBOXTOPLEFTALIGN styles is specified.
SBS_SIZEBOXBOTTOMRIGHTALIGN	Used with the SBS_SIZEBOX style to align the lower-right corner of the size box with the lower-right corner of the rectangle specified in the Create function.
SBS_SIZEBOXTOPLEFTALIGN	Used with the SBS_SIZEBOX style to align the top-left corner of the size box with the top-left corner of the rectangle specified in the Create function.
SBS_TOPALIGN	Used with the SBS_HORZ style to align the top of the scroll bar with the top edge of the rectangle specified in the Create function.
SBS_VERT	Specifies a vertical scroll bar. The location, width, and height of the scroll bar is specified by the rect parameter in the Create function, if neither the SBS_RIGHTALIGN nor the SBS_LEFTALIGN styles are specified.

The CScrollBar class declares a number of member functions. The relevant functions are as follows:

- The member function SetScrollRange, which permits you to set the range of values for the scroll bar. The declaration of the SetScrollRange function is

```
void SetScrollRange(int nMinPos, int nMaxPos,
                    BOOL bRedraw = TRUE);
```

The parameter nMinPos represents the minimum value that defines the range of scroll bar values. The parameter nMaxPos defines the maximum value that defines the range of scroll bar values. If you pass the argument 0 to both nMinPos and nMaxPos, you hide the standard scroll bar. The range defined by the parameters nMinPos and nMaxPos cannot exceed 32767. The Boolean parameter bRedraw indicates whether the scroll bar instance is to be redrawn using the new range.

■ The member function GetScrollRange queries the current range of values for the scroll bar. The declaration of the GetScrollRange function is

```
void GetScrollRange(LPINT lpMinPos, LPINT lpMaxPos) const;
```

The parameters lpMinPos and lpMaxPos are pointers to the minimum and maximum values, respectively. The minimum and maximum values define the current range for the scroll bar control.

■ The parameterless member function GetScrollPos yields the current position of the thumb box. (The *thumb box* is the small rectangle—within the scroll bar—that you can click and drag with your mouse to scroll the display.)

■ The member function SetScrollPos moves the thumb box to the specified position. The declaration of the SetScrollPos function is

```
void SetScrollPos(int nPos, BOOL bRedraw = TRUE);
```

The parameter nPos designates the new thumb box position. This position must be within the current scroll bar range. The Boolean parameter bRedraw indicates whether the scroll bar instance is to be redrawn using the new position.

How to Respond to Scroll Bar Notification Messages

The class CScrollBar instances require that your application override the inherited member functions CWnd::OnVScroll and CWnd::OnHScroll if thumb box scrolling is to be enabled. These functions require the ON_WM_VSCROLL and ON_WM_HSCROLL macros in the message map macro. The MFC library requires that you declare these scrolling functions as members of the parent window. The declaration of the functions OnVScroll and OnHScroll are as follows:

```
void OnVScroll(UINT nSBCode, UINT nPos,
               CScrollBar* pScrollBar);
void OnHScroll(UINT nSBCode, UINT nPos,
               CScrollBar* pScrollBar);
```

The parameter nSBCode specifies the scroll bar movement code. The parameter nPos represents the new thumb box position. The parameter pScrollBar is the pointer to the scroll bar control that is clicked by the user. The run-time message-handling system uses the member functions OnVScroll and OnHScroll of the parent window to handle the scroll bars in the window.

The small text program in the next section shows you how to manage multiple scroll bars using a single member function, `OnVScroll`.

The Random-Number Generator

Let's look at the random-number generating application CTLLST1.EXE—a small test program that uses the scroll bar controls. This program enables you to generate between 30 to 1000 random numbers and then write these numbers to a text file (one number per text file line). The program also enables you to define the range—between 0 and 32767—for the random numbers. Figure 8.1 shows a sample session with the program, which contains the following relevant controls:

- *Filename edit control.* Accepts the name of the output text file.

- *Count scroll bar control.* Enables you to specify the number of generated random numbers. The range for this control is 30 to 1000. The page increment value for this control is 100. The control has a set of associated static text controls that display the range of values and the current value.

- *Min scroll bar control.* Enables you to select the minimum value for the generated random numbers. The range for this control is 0 to 32767. The page increment value for this control is 1000. The control has a set of associated static text controls that display the range of values and the current value.

- *Max scroll bar control.* Enables you to select the maximum value for the generated random numbers. The range for this control is 0 to 32767. The page increment value for this control is 1000. The control has a set of associated static text controls that display the range of values and the current value.

- *Make pushbutton.* Generates the random numbers and writes them to the output text file. If that file is invalid, the program displays an error message dialog box. Otherwise, the program generates the random numbers, writes them to the output file, and then displays a dialog box with an affirming message.

- *Exit pushbutton.*

Figure 8.1

A sample
session with the
CTLLST1.EXE
application.

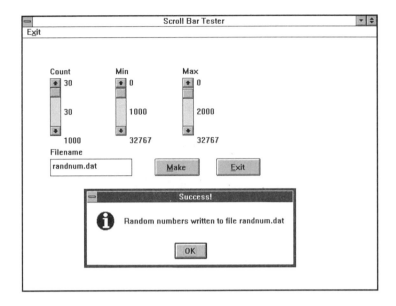

Compile and run the CTLLST1.EXE program. Enter a valid filename in the
Filename edit box, such as RANDNUM.DAT. In the Count scroll bar, select a
relatively low value, such as 50. Next, define the range of numbers, say 1000
to 2000, by clicking the Min and Max scroll bars. Click the Make pushbutton
(or press Alt+M) to generate the random numbers. The program displays a
message dialog box telling you that it successfully wrote the random numbers
to the designated output text file. You can minimize the application and
invoke your favorite text editor to view the contents of the output text file.
When you're done, restore the CTLLST1.EXE application; you can generate
more random numbers or exit by clicking the Exit pushbutton.

The CTLLST1.EXE application illustrates the following aspects of scroll bar
manipulation:

- Setting the scroll bar range of values.

- Moving and changing the scroll bar thumb box position. The program
  illustrates how these tasks are performed either internally or using the
  mouse.

- Employing the scroll bar controls to provide input.

Let's examine the code for the random-number generator application.
Listing 8.1 shows the contents of the CTLLST1.DEF definition file.

Listing 8.1 The CTLLST1.DEF Definition File

```
NAME          CtlLst1
DESCRIPTION   'An MFC Windows Application'
CODE          PRELOAD MOVEABLE DISCARDABLE
DATA          PRELOAD MOVEABLE MULTIPLE
HEAPSIZE      1024
```

Listing 8.2 shows the source code for the CTLLST1.H header file.

Listing 8.2 Source Code for the CTLLST1.H Header File

```
#define CM_EXIT       (WM_USER + 100)
#define ID_MAKE_BTN   (WM_USER + 101)
#define ID_EXIT_BTN   (WM_USER + 102)
#define ID_COUNT_SCR  (WM_USER + 103)
#define ID_MIN_SCR    (WM_USER + 103)
#define ID_MAX_SCR    (WM_USER + 103)
```

Listing 8.3 provides the script for the CTLLST1.RC resource file. The resource file contains the accelerator keys and menu resources. The program uses a menu with the single menu item Exit.

Listing 8.3 Script for the CTLLST1.RC Resource File

```
#include <windows.h>
#include <afxres.h>
#include "ctllst1.h"
BUTTONS ACCELERATORS
BEGIN
  "m", ID_MAKE_BTN, ALT
  "e", ID_EXIT_BTN, ALT
END
EXITMENU MENU LOADONCALL MOVEABLE PURE DISCARDABLE
BEGIN
    MENUITEM "E&xit", CM_EXIT
END
```

The source code for the CTLLST1.CPP program file is provided in Listing 8.4.

Listing 8.4 Source Code for the CTLLST1.CPP Program File

```
/*
                Program to test the scroll bar controls
        ----------------------------------------

        Program uses the scroll bar controls to generate random numbers
        which lie in a user-defined range.
```

(continues)

Listing 8.4 Continued

```
*/
#include <stdio.h>
#include <string.h>
#include <stdlib.h>
#include <fstream.h>
#include <afxwin.h>
#include "ctllst1.h"
const int MinIntVal = 0;
const int MaxIntVal = 32767;
const int MaxCount = 1000;
const int MinCount = 30;
const MaxStringLen = 80;
// set the dimensions of the various controls
const Hscr = 100;
const Wscr = 20;
const ScrVertSpacing = 20;
const ScrHorzSpacing = 100;
const ScrRightOffset = 5;
const Wlbl = 100;
const Wsmlbl = 40;
const Hlbl = 15;
const LblVertSpacing = 5;
const LblHorzSpacing = 40;
const Wbox = 150;
const Hbox = 30;
const BoxVertSpacing = 10;
const BoxHorzSpacing = 40;
const Hbtn = 30;
const Wbtn = 80;
const BtnHorzSpacing = 30;
const BtnVertSpacing = 30;
#define ID_COUNT_TXT      100
#define ID_MIN_TXT        101
#define ID_MAX_TXT        102
#define ID_LO_COUNT_TXT   103
#define ID_HI_COUNT_TXT   104
#define ID_LO_MIN_TXT     105
#define ID_HI_MIN_TXT     106
#define ID_LO_MAX_TXT     107
#define ID_HI_MAX_TXT     108
#define ID_FILENAME_BOX   109
#define ID_FILENAME_TXT   110
#define ID_COUNT_VAL_TXT 111
#define ID_MIN_VAL_TXT    112
#define ID_MAX_VAL_TXT    113
class CxButton : public CButton
{
public:
    BOOL Create(const char FAR* lpCaption, const RECT& rect,
             CWnd* pParentWnd, UINT nID)
    {
      return CButton::Create(lpCaption,
               WS_CHILD | WS_VISIBLE | BS_PUSHBUTTON,
                       rect, pParentWnd, nID);
    }
```

```
};
class CScrollBarApp : public CWinApp
{
public:
    virtual BOOL InitInstance();
};
// expand the functionality of CFrameWnd by deriving class CMainWnd
class CMainWnd : public CFrameWnd
{
 public:
  CMainWnd();
  ~CMainWnd();

 protected:
  // declare the pointers to the various controls
  CEdit* pFilenameBox;
  CxButton* pMakeBtn;
  CxButton* pExitBtn;
  CScrollBar* pCountScr;
  CScrollBar* pMinScr;
  CScrollBar* pMaxScr;
  CStatic* pCountTxt;
  CStatic* pMinTxt;
  CStatic* pMaxTxt;
  CStatic* pLoCountTxt;
  CStatic* pHiCountTxt;
  CStatic* pCountValTxt;
  CStatic* pLoMinTxt;
  CStatic* pHiMinTxt;
  CStatic* pMinValTxt;
  CStatic* pLoMaxTxt;
  CStatic* pHiMaxTxt;
  CStatic* pMaxValTxt;
  CStatic* pFilenameTxt;

  void makerect(int X, int Y, int W, int H, CRect& r)
  { r.SetRect(X, Y, X + W, Y + H); }
  // handle creating the controls
  afx_msg int OnCreate(LPCREATESTRUCT lpCS);
    // handle the vertical scrolling of the scroll bar
  afx_msg void OnVScroll(UINT nSBCode, UINT nPos,
                         CScrollBar* pScrollBar);
  // handle drawing the shape
  afx_msg void HandleMakeBtn();
  // handle starting the timer
  afx_msg void CMDrawBtn()
    { HandleMakeBtn(); }
  // handle exiting the program
  afx_msg void HandleExitBtn()
    { SendMessage(WM_CLOSE); }
  // handle exiting the program
  afx_msg void CMExitBtn()
    { SendMessage(WM_CLOSE); }
  // handle exiting the application
  afx_msg void OnExit()
    { SendMessage(WM_CLOSE); }
```

(continues)

Listing 8.4 Continued

```cpp
  // handle closing the window
  afx_msg void OnClose();

  // declare message map macro
  DECLARE_MESSAGE_MAP();
};

CMainWnd::CMainWnd()
{
  // load accelerator resources
  LoadAccelTable("BUTTONS");
  // create the window
  Create(NULL, "Scroll Bar Tester", WS_OVERLAPPEDWINDOW,
      rectDefault, NULL, "EXITMENU");
}

CMainWnd::~CMainWnd()
{
  delete pFilenameBox;
  delete pMakeBtn;
  delete pExitBtn;
  delete pCountScr;
  delete pMinScr;
  delete pMaxScr;
  delete pCountTxt;
  delete pMinTxt;
  delete pMaxTxt;
  delete pLoCountTxt;
  delete pHiCountTxt;
  delete pCountValTxt;
  delete pLoMinTxt;
  delete pHiMinTxt;
  delete pMinValTxt;
  delete pLoMaxTxt;
  delete pHiMaxTxt;
  delete pMaxValTxt;
  delete pFilenameTxt;
}

int CMainWnd::OnCreate(LPCREATESTRUCT lpCS)
{
  char s[81];
  int x0 = 50, y0 = 50;
  int x = x0, y = x0;
  DWORD dwStaticStyle = WS_CHILD | WS_VISIBLE | SS_LEFT;
  DWORD dwEditStyle = WS_CHILD | WS_VISIBLE | ES_LEFT | WS_BORDER;
  DWORD dwScrollStyle = WS_CHILD | WS_VISIBLE | SBS_VERT;
  CRect r;
  // create the labels for the scroll bars
  makerect(x, y, Wsmlbl, Hlbl, r);
  pCountTxt = new CStatic();
  pCountTxt->Create("Count", dwStaticStyle, r, this, ID_COUNT_TXT);
  x += Wscr + ScrHorzSpacing;
```

```
makerect(x, y, Wsmlbl, Hlbl, r);
pMinTxt = new CStatic();
pMinTxt->Create("Min", dwStaticStyle, r, this, ID_MIN_TXT);
x += Wscr + ScrHorzSpacing;
makerect(x, y, Wsmlbl, Hlbl, r);
pMaxTxt = new CStatic();
pMaxTxt->Create("Max", dwStaticStyle, r, this, ID_MAX_TXT);
x = x0;
y += Hlbl + LblVertSpacing;
// create Count scroll bar
makerect(x, y, Wscr, Hscr, r);
pCountScr = new CScrollBar();
pCountScr->Create(dwScrollStyle, r, this, ID_COUNT_SCR);
pCountScr->SetScrollRange(MinCount, MaxCount);
// create its minimum limit static text
makerect(x + Wscr + ScrRightOffset, y, Wsmlbl, Hlbl, r);
pLoCountTxt = new CStatic();
_itoa(MinCount, s, 10);
pLoCountTxt->Create(s, dwStaticStyle, r,
                       this, ID_LO_COUNT_TXT);
// create the current value static text
makerect(x + Wscr + ScrRightOffset, y + Hscr / 2, Wsmlbl, Hlbl, r);
pCountValTxt = new CStatic();
_itoa(MinCount, s, 10);
pCountValTxt->Create(s, dwStaticStyle, r,
                       this, ID_COUNT_VAL_TXT);
// create its maximum limit static text
makerect(x + Wscr + ScrRightOffset, y + Hscr, Wsmlbl, Hlbl, r);
pHiCountTxt = new CStatic();
_itoa(MaxCount, s, 10);
pHiCountTxt->Create(s, dwStaticStyle, r,
                       this, ID_HI_COUNT_TXT);
// create the Min scroll bar
x += Wscr + ScrHorzSpacing;
makerect(x, y, Wscr, Hscr, r);
pMinScr = new CScrollBar();
pMinScr->Create(dwScrollStyle, r, this, ID_MIN_SCR);
pMinScr->SetScrollRange(MinIntVal, MaxIntVal);
// create its minimum limit static text
makerect(x + Wscr + ScrRightOffset, y, Wsmlbl, Hlbl, r);
pLoMinTxt = new CStatic();
_itoa(MinIntVal, s, 10);
pLoMinTxt->Create(s, dwStaticStyle, r,
                     this, ID_LO_MIN_TXT);
// create the current value static text
makerect(x + Wscr + ScrRightOffset, y + Hscr / 2, Wsmlbl, Hlbl, r);
pMinValTxt = new CStatic();
pMinValTxt->Create(s, dwStaticStyle, r,
                       this, ID_MIN_VAL_TXT);
// create its maximum limit static text
makerect(x + Wscr + ScrRightOffset, y + Hscr, Wsmlbl, Hlbl, r);
pHiMinTxt = new CStatic();
_itoa(MaxIntVal, s, 10);
pHiMinTxt->Create(s, dwStaticStyle, r,
                       this, ID_HI_MIN_TXT);
```

(continues)

Listing 8.4 Continued

```
  // create the Max scroll bar
  x += Wscr + ScrHorzSpacing;
  makerect(x, y, Wscr, Hscr, r);
  pMaxScr = new CScrollBar();
  pMaxScr->Create(dwScrollStyle, r, this, ID_MAX_SCR);
  pMaxScr->SetScrollRange(MinIntVal, MaxIntVal);
  // create its minimum limit static text
  makerect(x + Wscr + ScrRightOffset, y, Wsmlbl, Hlbl, r);
  pLoMaxTxt = new CStatic();
  _itoa(MinIntVal, s, 10);
  pLoMaxTxt->Create(s, dwStaticStyle, r,
                    this, ID_LO_MAX_TXT);
  // create the current value static text
  makerect(x + Wscr + ScrRightOffset, y + Hscr / 2, Wsmlbl, Hlbl, r);
  pMaxValTxt = new CStatic();
  pMaxValTxt->Create(s, dwStaticStyle, r,
                     this, ID_MAX_VAL_TXT);
  // create its maximum limit static text
  makerect(x + Wscr + ScrRightOffset, y + Hscr, Wsmlbl, Hlbl, r);
  pHiMaxTxt = new CStatic();
  _itoa(MaxIntVal, s, 10);
  pHiMaxTxt->Create(s, dwStaticStyle, r,
                    this, ID_HI_MAX_TXT);

  x = x0;
  y += Hscr + ScrVertSpacing;
  // create the static text control which labels the filename
  // edit box control
  makerect(x, y, Wlbl, Hlbl, r);
  pFilenameTxt = new CStatic();
  pFilenameTxt->Create("Filename", dwStaticStyle, r, this,
                       ID_FILENAME_TXT);

  y += Hlbl + LblVertSpacing;
  makerect(x, y, Wbox, Hbox, r);
  pFilenameBox = new CEdit();
  pFilenameBox->Create(dwEditStyle, r, this, ID_FILENAME_BOX);
  pFilenameBox->LimitText(MaxStringLen);
  // create the Make button
  x += Wbox + BoxHorzSpacing;
  makerect(x, y, Wbtn, Hbtn, r);
  pMakeBtn = new CxButton();
  pMakeBtn->Create("&Make", r, this, ID_MAKE_BTN);
  // create the Exit button
  x += Wbtn + BtnHorzSpacing;
  makerect(x, y, Wbtn, Hbtn, r);
  pExitBtn  = new CxButton();
  pExitBtn->Create("&Exit", r, this, ID_EXIT_BTN);
  return CFrameWnd::OnCreate(lpCS);
}
void CMainWnd::HandleMakeBtn()
{
  char s[MaxStringLen+1];
  char filename[MaxStringLen+1];
```

```cpp
  fstream f;
  int minVal, maxVal, count, randNum;

  // get the filename in the edit box
  pFilenameBox->GetWindowText(filename, MaxStringLen);
  // open the file as an output text stream
  f.open(filename, ios::out);
  // stream opened successfully?
  if (f.good()) {
    // get the current values from the scroll bars
    minVal = pMinScr->GetScrollPos();
    maxVal = pMaxScr->GetScrollPos();
    count = pCountScr->GetScrollPos();
    // swap values of minVal and maxVal?
    if (minVal > maxVal) {
      int temp = minVal;
      minVal = maxVal;
      maxVal = temp;
    }
    // are minVal and maxVal equal?
    if (minVal == maxVal) {
      if(minVal < 32767)
        maxVal = minVal + 1;
      else
        minVal = maxVal - 1;
    }
    // reseed random number generator
    srand(13);
    // loop to generate random numbers and write them to the
    // output text stream
    while (count— > 0) {
      randNum = minVal + rand() % (maxVal - minVal);
      _itoa(randNum, s, 10);
      f << s << "\n";
    }
    f.close();
    strcpy(s, "Random numbers written to file ");
    strcat(s, filename);
    MessageBox(s, "Success!", MB_OK | MB_ICONINFORMATION);
  }
  else {
    // handle invalid filename
    strcpy(s, "Cannot open file ");
    strcat(s, filename);
    MessageBox(s, "Error!", MB_OK | MB_ICONEXCLAMATION);
  }
}
void CMainWnd::OnVScroll(UINT nSBCode, UINT nPos,
                         CScrollBar* pScrollBar)
{
  short nScrollInc;
  int nNewPos;
  int nVScrollMin, nVScrollMax;
  int nVScrollPos = pScrollBar->GetScrollPos();
  int nPageSize;
  int x;
  char s[MaxStringLen+1];
```

(continues)

II

Visual C++ Programming

Listing 8.4 Continued

```
// get the scroll bar range
pScrollBar->GetScrollRange(&nVScrollMin, &nVScrollMax);
nPageSize = (nVScrollMax > 1000) ? 1000 : 100;
switch (nSBCode) {
  case SB_TOP: // move to the top
      nScrollInc = -nVScrollPos;
      break;
  case SB_BOTTOM: // move to the bottom
      nScrollInc = nVScrollMax - nVScrollPos;
      break;
  case SB_LINEUP: // move one line up
      nScrollInc = -1;
      break;
  case SB_LINEDOWN: // move one line down
      nScrollInc = 1;
      break;
  case SB_PAGEUP: // move one page up
      nScrollInc = -nPageSize;
      break;
  case SB_PAGEDOWN: // move one page down
      nScrollInc = nPageSize;
      break;
  case SB_THUMBPOSITION: // track the thumb box
      nScrollInc = nPos - nVScrollPos;
      break;
  default:
      nScrollInc = 0;
}
// calculate new vertical thumb position so that:
//          0 <= nNewPos <= nVScrollMax
nNewPos = max(0, min(nVScrollPos + nScrollInc, nVScrollMax));
// adjust scroll increment
nScrollInc = nNewPos - nVScrollPos;
// is nScrollInc not zero?
if (nScrollInc) {
  // move the thumb box
  pScrollBar->SetScrollPos(nNewPos);
  // update the current values for the scroll bars
  if (pScrollBar == pCountScr) {
    // handle the Count scroll bar
    x = pCountScr->GetScrollPos();
    _itoa(x, s, 10);
    pCountValTxt->SetWindowText(s);
  }
  if (pScrollBar == pMinScr) {
    // handle the Min scroll bar
    x = pCountScr->GetScrollPos();
    _itoa(x, s, 10);
    pMinValTxt->SetWindowText(s);
  }
  if (pScrollBar == pMaxScr) {
    // handle the Max scroll bar
    x = pCountScr->GetScrollPos();
```

```
        _itoa(x, s, 10);
        pMaxValTxt->SetWindowText(s);
      }
    }
  }

  void CMainWnd::OnClose()
  {
    if (MessageBox("Want to close this application",
          "Query", MB_YESNO | MB_ICONQUESTION) == IDYES)
      DestroyWindow();
  }
  BEGIN_MESSAGE_MAP(CMainWnd, CFrameWnd)
    ON_WM_CREATE()
    ON_WM_VSCROLL()
    ON_BN_CLICKED(ID_MAKE_BTN, HandleMakeBtn)
    ON_COMMAND(ID_MAKE_BTN, HandleMakeBtn)
    ON_BN_CLICKED(ID_EXIT_BTN, HandleExitBtn)
    ON_COMMAND(ID_EXIT_BTN, CMExitBtn)
    ON_COMMAND(CM_EXIT, OnExit)
    ON_WM_CLOSE()
  END_MESSAGE_MAP()
  // Construct the CScrollBarApp's m_pMainWnd data member
  BOOL CScrollBarApp::InitInstance()
  {
    m_pMainWnd = new CMainWnd();
    m_pMainWnd->ShowWindow(m_nCmdShow);
    m_pMainWnd->UpdateWindow();
    return TRUE;
  }
  // application's constructor initializes and runs the app
  CScrollBarApp WindowApp;
```

The program just shown in Listing 8.4 contains declarations for the application class, CScrollBarApp, the window class, CMainWnd, and the button control class, CxButton. The window class CMainWnd declares a number of data members that are pointers to the application's controls. The class CMainWnd declares a constructor, a destructor, and a collection of member functions.

The CMainWnd class constructor creates the application window and performs the following tasks:

- Loads the BUTTONS accelerator keys resource.

- Creates the application window, specifying a title, a default size, a default location, and the EXITMENU menu resource.

The Create member function creates the various controls used by the application and performs the following tasks:

- Creates the three static text controls that label the three vertical scroll bars.

- Creates the Count scroll bar. The function CScrollBar::Create specifies a vertical scroll bar using the SBS_VERT style and supplies the argument ID_COUNT_SCR as the control's ID.

- Establishes the range of the Count scroll bar. This task involves sending the C++ message SetScrollRange to the newly created scroll bar. The arguments for this message are the global constants MinCount and MaxCount.

- Creates the static text controls that display the minimum, maximum, and current values for the Count scroll bar.

- Creates the Min scroll bar. The function CScrollBar::Create specifies a vertical scroll bar using the SBS_VERT style and supplies the argument ID_MIN_SCR as the control's ID.

- Establishes the range of the Min scroll bar. This task involves sending the C++ message SetScrollRange to the newly created scroll bar. The arguments for this message are the global constants MinIntVal and MaxIntVal.

- Creates the static text controls that display the minimum, maximum, and current values for the Min scroll bar.

- Creates the Max scroll bar. The function CScrollBar::Create specifies a vertical scroll bar using the SBS_VERT style and supplies the argument ID_MAX_SCR as the control's ID.

- Establishes the range of the Max scroll bar. This task involves sending the C++ message SetScrollRange to the newly created scroll bar. The arguments for this message are the global constants MinIntVal and MaxIntVal.

- Creates the static text controls that display the minimum, maximum, and current values for the Max scroll bar.

- Creates the static text control that provides a label for the Filename edit box.

- Creates the single-line Filename edit box control.

- Creates the pushbuttons Make and Exit.

The HandleMakeBtn member function triggers the creation of the random numbers and performs the following tasks:

- Retrieves the text in the Filename edit box and stores it in the local variable filename.

- Opens the output text stream object f. This task involves sending the C++ message open to the stream object f. The arguments for this message are the variable filename (which contains the name of the output text file) and the predefined value ios::out. This value requests opening the stream for text output.

- Verifies that the object f is properly opened for output. This task involves sending the C++ message good to the object f. If this message returns a 0 value, the program displays an error message using a message dialog box and then exits. Otherwise, the function performs the remaining tasks.

- Obtains the current value of the Min scroll bar. This task involves sending the C++ message GetScrollPos to the Min scroll control, which is accessed by the member pMinScr. The function stores the result of this message in the local variable minVal.

- Obtains the current value of the Max scroll bar. This task involves sending the C++ message GetScrollPos to the Max scroll control, which is accessed by the member pMaxScr. The function stores the result of this message in the local variable maxVal.

- Obtains the current value of the Count scroll bar. This task involves sending the C++ message GetScrollPos to the Count scroll control, which is accessed by the member pCountScr. The function stores the result of this message in the local variable count.

- Compares the values of minVal and maxVal. If the variable minVal contains an integer that is greater than that of the variable maxVal, the function swaps these values.

- Determines if the contents of the variables minVal and maxVal are equal. If they are equal, the function increases the value of the variable maxVal by 1 if minVal is less than 32767. If the two variables are not equal, the function decreases the value of minVal by 1.

- Reseeds the random-number generator by calling the function srand (declared in the file STDLIB.H) and supplying it with the argument 13.

- Generates the random numbers using a while loop. The first loop statement calculates the value of a random number using the function rand() and the variables minVal and maxVal. The statement stores the resulting number in the local variable randNum. The second loop statement converts the number in the variable randNum to a string and stores that string in the local variable s. The third loop statement writes the string in the variable s to the output stream object f.

- Closes the output stream object f by sending it the C++ message close.

- Displays a message box dialog box to confirm the success of the operation.

The CMMakeBtn member function traps the command message generated by the Alt+M keys. The function merely calls the HandleMakeBtn member function.

The HandleExitBtn and CMExitBtn member functions send a WM_CLOSE message to the application window.

The member function OnVScroll has the task of vertically scrolling the thumb box of the scroll bar control. The statements in the function use the pScrollBar parameter to query the current scroll bar range and to set the thumb box position. The OnVScroll function performs the following tasks:

- Obtains the current scroll bar range. This task involves sending the C++ message GetScrollRange to the object accessed by the pointer pScrollBar. The arguments for this message are the addresses of the local variables nVScrollMin and nVScrollMax.

- Sets the page size (stored in the variable nPageSize) to 1000 if the value in the variable nVScrollMax exceeds 1000. Otherwise, the OnVScroll function sets the page size to 100. The high page size value accommodates the Min and Max scroll bars, whereas the lower page size accommodates the Count scroll bar.

- Examines the value of the parameter nSBCode by using a switch statement. Each case value supports a specific scroll bar operation and affects the value in the local variable nScrollInc. This variable stores the amount of displacement in the thumb box.

■ Calculates the new vertical thumb box position and stores it in the variable nNewPos.

■ Recalculates the increment in the thumb box position and stores it in the variable nScrollInc.

■ Skips the remaining tasks if the value in the variable nScrollInc is 0.

■ Moves the thumb box by sending the C++ message SetScrollPos to the object accessed by the pointer pScrollBar. The argument for this message is nNewPos.

■ Compares the addresses of the pointer pScrollBar (which accesses the currently manipulated scroll bar) and the pointer pCountScr (the data member that accesses the Count scroll bar). If the two addresses match, the OnVScroll function updates the static text control which displays the current value of the Count scroll bar. This operation involves using the data member pCountValTxt to access the targeted static text control.

■ Compares the addresses of the pointers pScrollBar and pMinScr (the data member that accesses the Min scroll bar). If the two addresses match, the OnVScroll function updates the static text control, which displays the current value of the Min scroll bar. This operation involves using the data member pMinValTxt to access the targeted static text control.

■ Compares the addresses of the pointers pScrollBar and pMaxScr (the data member that accesses the Max scroll bar). If the two addresses match, the OnVScroll function updates the static text control, which displays the current value of the Max scroll bar. This operation involves using the data member pMaxValTxt to access the targeted static text control.

The List Box Controls

List boxes are input controls that enable the application user to choose from a list of items. Usually, list boxes are framed and include a vertical scroll bar. When you select an item by clicking it, the selection is highlighted. Microsoft suggests the following simple guidelines for making a selection:

- Use a single mouse click to select a new item or an additional item. A separate button control retrieves the selected item.

- Use a double-click as a shortcut to select and retrieve an item with a single action.

A list box control supports multiple selections only if you specify the multiple-selection style when you create the control. Making multiple selections is convenient when you want to process the selected items in a similar manner. For example, selecting multiple files for deletion speeds up the process and reduces your effort.

The *CListBox* Class

The MFC library offers the class CListBox, a descendant of CWnd, to implement list box controls. The CListBox class has a set of member functions that enable you to extensively set and query both the selected items and the other items in the list box. The class CListBox follows the typical MFC style in using a default constructor and the member function Create to create list box controls. The declaration of Create is as follows:

```
BOOL Create(DWORD dwStyle,       // control style
            const RECT& rect,     // location and dimensions
            CWnd* pParentWnd,     // pointer to parent window
            UINT nID);            // control ID
```

The dwStyle parameter defines the style of the list box control. The list box styles include the typical WS_*XXXX* window styles in addition to the special LBS_*XXXX* list box styles (shown in Table 8.2). The parameter rect specifies the location and dimensions of the list box control. The parameter pParentWnd is the pointer to the parent window. The parameter nID is the unique ID of the list box instance.

Table 8.2 List Box Control Styles	
Style	**Meaning**
LBS_EXTENDESEL	Enables the extension of multiple selections when the Shift key is used in the list box.
LBS_MULTICOLUMN	Designates a multi-column list box that scrolls horizontally. The number of columns is set by sending the message LB_SETCOLUMNWIDTH. Using this control style requires the use of the Windows API functions.
LBS_MULTIPLESEL	Supports multiple selections in a list box.

Style	Meaning
`LBS_NOINTEGRALHEIGHT`	Suppresses some parts of an item so that those parts are not shown.
`LBS_NOREDRAW`	Prevents the list box from being updated when the selection is changed. You can use the message `WM_SETREDRAW` to override this style when necessary.
`LBS_NOTIFY`	Notifies the parent window when you click or double-click in the list box.
`LBS_SORT`	Specifies that the items inserted in the list box be sorted automatically in ascending order.
`LBS_STANDARD`	Sets the `WS_BORDER`, `WS_VSCROLL`, `LBS_SORT`, and `LBS_NOTIFY` styles.
`LBS_WANTKEYBPARDINPUT`	Permits the list box owner to receive `WM_VKEYTOITEM` or `WM_CHARTOITEM` messages when you press a key while the list box has the focus. This style enables your application to manipulate the items in the list box.

It's worth pointing out that the `LBS_STANDARD` style is equivalent to the `WS_BORDER`, `WS_VSCROLL`, `LBS_SORT`, and `LBS_NOTIFY` styles. To maintain items in an unsorted and chronological fashion, you must eliminate the `LBS_SORT` style from the list box controls. Removing the `WS_VSCROLL` style gives you a list box without the vertical scroll bar. In this case, you need an external scroll bar to control scrolling the list box items. There are applications that resort to this method because they have to respond to the notification messages of the scroll bar control—something you cannot easily do with the scroll bar that is part of the list box control.

The `CListBox` class lets you refer to the items in a list box by index. The index of the first item is 0. The `CListBox` class offers the following member functions to set and query ordinary and selected list members:

■ The member function `AddString` adds a string to the list box and is declared as

```
int AddString(LPCSTR lpszItem);
```

The parameter `lpszItem` is the pointer to the string added in the list box. The `AddString` function yields the position of the string added in the control. In the case of any errors, the function returns the value `LB_ERR` or `LB_ERRSPACE` (out-of-memory error). If the `LBS_SORT` style is set, the string is inserted in such a way that the list order is maintained. If the LBS_SORT style is not set, the function inserts the new string at the end of the list.

■ The member function DeleteString removes a list member from a specified position and is declared as

```
int DeleteString(int nIndex);
```

The parameter nIndex specifies the position of the item to delete. The function yields the number of remaining list members. In case an error occurs, the function returns the value LB_ERR.

■ The parameterless member function ResetContent clears the list of strings in the list box control. This function serves to reset the contents of a list box before creating a new list of items.

■ The member function FindString performs a case-insensitive search for an item in the list box. The declaration of the function FindString is

```
int FindString(int nStartAfter, LPCSTR lpszItem) const;
```

The parameter nStartAfter specifies the index of the first list box member to be searched. The parameter lpszItem is the pointer to the search string. The function searches the entire list, starting at the nStartAfter position, and continues at the beginning of the list if necessary. The search ends when a list member matches the search string or the entire list has been searched. Supplying an argument of –1 to the parameter nStartAfter compels the function to start searching at the first item in the list. The FindString function yields the position of the matching list item, or the function returns the value LB_ERR if no match is found or when an error occurs.

> **Note**
>
> The function FindString implements a very interesting search algorithm, which enables you to accelerate the search by specifying a position located just before the most likely location of a match. The advantage of this method is that if you specify a position that is actually beyond that of the string you seek, you do not miss finding that string because the function resumes searching at the beginning of the list! Another benefit of FindString is its ability to find duplicate strings.

■ The parameterless member function GetCount returns the number of
items in the list box. The function returns the value LB_ERR if there is an
error.

■ The parameterless member function GetCurSel returns the location of
the selected item in a single-selection list box. The function returns a
negative value if there is no selected item. Keep in mind that this function is meant to work only with single-selection list boxes.

■ The member function GetSel returns the selection state of a list box
item, specified by index. The declaration of the function GetSel is

```
int GetSel(int nIndex) const;
```

The parameter nIndex represents the index of the queried list box item.
The function returns a positive number if the queried item is indeed
selected. Otherwise, the function yields 0. The function also returns the
value LB_ERR if an error occurs.

■ The parameterless member function GetSelCount returns the number of
selected items in the list box. For single-selection list boxes, the function returns the value LB_ERR.

■ The GetSelItems member function returns the number and positions of
the selected items in a multiple-selection list box. The declaration of
function GetSelItems is

```
int GetSelItems(int nMaxItems, LPINT rgIndex) const;
```

The parameter nMaxItems indicates the size of the array accessed by the
parameter rgIndex. This is the pointer to an array of integers that contains the positions of the selected items. The function returns the current number of selections. The function yields the value LB_ERR with
single-selection list boxes.

■ The overloaded member function GetText retrieves a copy of an item in
a list box by designating its index. The declarations for the function
GetText are

```
int GetText(int nIndex, LPSTR lpszBuffer) const;
void GetText(int nIndex, CString& rString) const;
```

II

Visual C++ Programming

The parameter `nIndex` specifies the index of the item retrieved from the list box. The first list box item has the index of 0. The parameter `lpszBuffer` points to a buffer that receives the retrieved item. You are responsible for guaranteeing that the buffer is large enough to hold the retrieved item. The reference parameter `rString` represents the `CString` object that obtains a copy of the targeted list box item. The first version of the overloaded function yields the size of the string retrieved from the list box.

■ The member function `GetTextLen` returns the size of a list box item specified by its index in the list. The declaration of the function `GetTextLen` is

```
int GetTextLen(int nIndex) const;
```

The `nIndex` parameter represents the index of the sought list item. The function yields the length of the targeted string item or returns the value `LB_ERR` if an error occurs.

■ The parameterless member function `GetTopIndex` yields the index of the first item that is visible in the list box control.

■ The member function `InsertString` inserts a string in a list box. The declaration of the function `InsertString` is

```
int InsertString(int nIndex, LPCSTR lpszItem);
```

The parameter `nIndex` represents the insertion position. The parameter `lpszItem` is the pointer to the inserted string. The function yields the actual insertion position or returns the value `LB_ERR` if an error occurs. If the argument for the parameter `nIndex` is –1, the function merely appends the inserted string to the end of the list.

Caution

Avoid using the `InsertString` member function with list boxes that have the `LBS_SORT` style set. Using the `InsertString` function in this way corrupts the ordered items in the list boxes.

■ The member function `SelectString` selects a list box item that matches a search string. The declaration of the function `SelectString` is

```
int SelectString(int nStartAfter, LPCSTR lpszItem);
```

The parameters and search mechanism of SelectString are similar to those of the function FindString. The difference is that the function SelectString finishes by selecting the list box item that matches the string accessed by the parameter lpszItem.

■ The member function SelItemRange is an additional function that selects a range of items in a single call. The declaration of the function SelItemRange is

```
int SelItemRange(BOOL bSelect, int nFirstItem, int nLastItem);
```

The parameter bSelect is a switch used to select or deselect the range of list box items bound by the arguments of the parameters nFirstItem and nLastItem.

■ The member function SetCurSel chooses a list item as the new selected item in a single-selection list box. The declaration of the function SetCurSel is

```
int SetCurSel(int nSelect);
```

The parameter nSelect designates the index of the new selected item. The argument of –1 clears a list box from any selection. The function returns the value LB_ERR if an error occurs.

■ The member function SetSel builds or removes a selection in a multiple-selection list box. The declaration of the function SetSel is

```
int SetSel(int nIndex, BOOL bSelect = TRUE);
```

The parameter nIndex represents the list box item when it is either selected (the argument of the parameter bSelect is TRUE) or deselected (the argument for the parameter bSelect is FALSE). The function yields the value LB_ERR if an error occurs and, thus, serves to flag selection/deselection errors. The function SetSel can toggle, one at a time, the selection of several items in a multiple-selection list box.

■ The member function SetTopIndex selects the list box item that becomes the first visible item in the list box control. The declaration for function SetTopIndex is

```
int SetTopIndex(int nIndex);
```

The parameter nIndex represents the index of the list box item that becomes the first visible item. This selection scrolls the list box, unless the item nIndex already is the first visible item. The function returns the value LB_ERR if an error occurs. Otherwise, the result is meaningless.

II

Visual C++ Programming

■ The member function Dir inserts in a list box filenames that match a specified wild card. The declaration of the function Dir is

```
int Dir(UINT attr, LPCSTR lpszWildCard);
```

The parameter attr specifies the combination of file attributes, shown in Table 8.3. This table also contains the equivalent file attribute constants that are declared in the DOS.H header file. The parameter lpszWildCard is the pointer to the filename wild card, such as *.H, C*.CPP, or B???.RC.

Table 8.3 Attributes for the *attr* Parameter in the *Dir* Member Function

Attribute Value	Equivalent Constant in DOS.H Header File	Meaning
0x0000	_A_NORMAL	File can be used for input and output.
0x0001	_A_RDONLY	File is read-only.
0x0002	_A_HIDDEN	File is hidden.
0x0004	_A_SYSTEM	System file.
0x0010	_A_SUBDIR	The name indicated by parameter lpszWildCard also supplies the directory.
0x0020	_A_ARCH	File has the archive bit set.
0x4000		Include all drives that match the filename supplied by lpszWildCard.
0x8000		Exclusive flag. Prevents normal files from being included with the specified files.

How to Respond to List Box Notification Messages

The list box control generates different kinds of messages, as shown in Table 8.4. The table also contains the message-mapping macros that are affiliated with the diverse command and notification messages. Each kind of command or notification message requires a distinct member function declared in the control's parent window class.

Table 8.4 List Box Notification Messages

Message	Macro	Meaning
WM_COMMAND	ON_COMMAND	A Windows command message.
LBN_CHANGE	ON_LBN_SELCHANGE	A list item is selected with a mouse click.
LBN_DBLCLK	ON_LBN_DBLCLK	A list item is selected with a double mouse click.
LBN_SETFOCUS	ON_LBN_SETFOCUS	The list box has gained focus.
LBN_KILLFOCUS	ON_LBN_KILLFOCUS	The list box has lost focus.
LBN_ERRSPACE	ON_LBNERRSPACE	The list box cannot allocate more dynamic memory to accommodate new list items.

A Simple List Manipulation Tester

In this section, I present a simple version of a program, CTLLST2.EXE, that manages appointments for a single day. This program demonstrates how to set and query normal and selected strings and how to set and query the current selection in a single-selection list box. Figure 8.2 shows the interface and a sample session with CTLLST2.EXE.

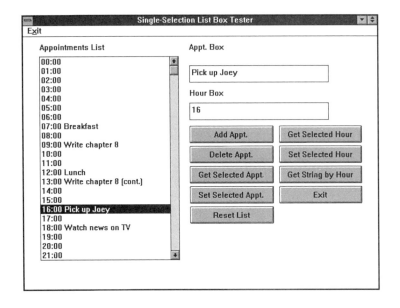

Figure 8.2
A sample session with the CTLLST2.EXE application.

The single-selection list tester program shows you how to use most of the CListBox member functions discussed earlier in this section. The program contains the following controls, which offer the test features indicated:

- *Appointments List list box control.* Initially, this list box control contains 24 empty appointments. The program limits the appointments to those on the hour. The program lets you add, delete, and change appointments.

- *Appt. Box edit control.* Lets you type and retrieve appointment text.

- *Hour Box edit control.* Enables you to type and retrieve the time of the appointment. Valid input includes integers in the range 0 to 23. By using on-the-hour appointments, the hour values become the indices for the list box items. If you enhance the program and include smaller time intervals, you must expand on the list box indexing scheme.

- *Add Appt. pushbutton.* Adds a new appointment to the list box using the contents of the Appt. Box and Hour Box edit controls. The program does not let you add duplicate appointments. If you attempt to add a duplicate appointment, the program displays a warning message. In addition, the program verifies the value you entered in the Hour Box edit control.

- *Delete Appt. pushbutton.* Deletes the currently selected appointment in the list box. The program automatically reinserts an empty time slot for the appointment you just deleted.

- *Get Selected Appt. pushbutton.* Retrieves the current list selection. In addition, the button displays the appointment text in the Appt. Box and the appointment time in the Hour Box edit control.

- *Set Selected Appt. pushbutton.* Overwrites the current list box selection with whatever text is currently displayed in the Appt. Box and with whatever time is displayed in the Hour Box.

- *Get Selected Hour pushbutton.* Writes the appointment hour of the current selection in the Hour Box edit control.

- *Set Selected Hour pushbutton.* Uses the value in the Hour Box edit control to choose a new list box selection.

■ *Get Appt. pushbutton.* Copies the appointment text of the time displayed in the Hour Box edit control to the Appt. Box edit control.

■ *Exit pushbutton.*

The preceding controls represent various aspects in the manipulation of a sorted list box and its members. The program is coded to retain a current selection and to prevent the insertion of duplicate names.

Compile and run the CTLLST2.EXE program. Enter appointment text and times in their respective edit controls. Use the various pushbutton controls to add, delete, and obtain appointment text and times. The program is straight-forward and easy to run.

Listing 8.5 shows the contents of the CTLLST2.DEF definition file.

Listing 8.5 The CTLLST2.DEF Definition File

```
NAME          CtlLst2
DESCRIPTION   'An MFC Windows Application'
CODE          PRELOAD MOVEABLE DISCARDABLE
DATA          PRELOAD MOVEABLE MULTIPLE
HEAPSIZE      1024
```

The source code for the CTLLST2.H header file is provided in Listing 8.6.

Listing 8.6 Source Code for the CTLLST2.H Header File

```
#define CM_EXIT (WM_USER + 100)
```

Listing 8.7 shows the script for the CTLLST2.RC resource file.

Listing 8.7 Script for the CTLLST2.RC Resource File

```
#include <windows.h>
#include <afxres.h>
#include "ctllst2.h"
EXITMENU MENU LOADONCALL MOVEABLE PURE DISCARDABLE
BEGIN
    MENUITEM "E&xit", CM_EXIT
END
```

The source code for the CTLLST2.CPP program file is provided in Listing 8.8.

Listing 8.8 Source Code for the CTLLST2.CPP Program File

```
/*
                    Single-Selection List Box Tester
                    --------------------------------

   Program tests single-selection list boxes by implementing a
   simple one-day appointment application.

*/
#include <stdio.h>
#include <stdlib.h>
#include <string.h>
#include <afxwin.h>
#include "ctllst2.h"
// declare constants for the size and spacing of controls
const Hlbl = 20;
const Wlbl = 150;
const LblVertSpacing = 5;
const LblHorzSpacing = 50;
const Hlst = 350;
const Wlst = 250;
const LstVertSpacing = 10;
const LstHorzSpacing = 20;
const Hbox = 30;
const Wbox = 250;
const BoxVertSpacing = 10;
const BoxHorzSpacing = 10;
const Hbtn = 30;
const Wbtn = 150;
const BtnVertSpacing = 5;
const BtnHorzSpacing = 10;
// declare miscellaneous constants
const MaxHours = 24;
const MaxStringLen = 40;
// declare the ID constants for the various controls
#define ID_APPT_LST        101
#define ID_APPT_EDIT       102
#define ID_HOUR_EDIT       103
#define ID_ADDAPPT_BTN     104
#define ID_DELAPPT_BTN     105
#define ID_GETSELAPPT_BTN 106
#define ID_SETSELAPPT_BTN 107
#define ID_GETSELHOUR_BTN 108
#define ID_SETSELHOUR_BTN 109
#define ID_EXIT_BTN        110
#define ID_GETAPPT_BTN     111
#define ID_CLEAR_BTN       112
class CxButton : public CButton
{
public:
   BOOL Create(const char FAR* lpCaption, const RECT& rect,
            CWnd* pParentWnd, UINT nID)
   {
     return CButton::Create(lpCaption,
              WS_CHILD | WS_VISIBLE | BS_PUSHBUTTON,
                    rect, pParentWnd, nID);
   }
```

```
};
class CListBoxApp : public CWinApp
{
public:
    virtual BOOL InitInstance();
};
// expand the functionality of CFrameWnd by deriving class CMainWnd
class CMainWnd : public CFrameWnd
{
 public:
  CMainWnd();
  ~CMainWnd();
 protected:
  // declare the pointers to the controls
  CStatic* pApptListTxt;
  CStatic* pApptBoxTxt;
  CStatic* pHourBoxTxt;
  CListBox* pApptLst;
  CEdit* pApptBox;
  CEdit* pHourBox;
  CxButton* pAddApptBtn;
  CxButton* pDelApptBtn;
  CxButton* pGetSelApptBtn;
  CxButton* pSetSelApptBtn;
  CxButton* pGetSelHourBtn;
  CxButton* pSetSelHourBtn;
  CxButton* pGetApptBtn;
  CxButton* pClearBtn;
  CxButton* pExitBtn;
  char apptStr[MaxStringLen+1];   // string for pApptBox
  char hourStr[MaxStringLen+1];   // string for pHourBox
  char formatApptStr[MaxStringLen+1]; // formatted appt. string
  // handle creating the controls
  afx_msg int OnCreate(LPCREATESTRUCT lpCS);

  // initialize the Appt list box
  void InitApptLst();

  // clear the list box
  void ClearList();

  // format the hour imag ein member hourStr
  void FormatHour(int hour);
  // handle adding an appointment to the list box
  afx_msg void HandleAddApptBtn();
  // handle deleting an appointment from the list box
  afx_msg void HandleDelApptBtn();
  // handle getting the selected text
  afx_msg void HandleGetSelApptBtn();
  // handle setting the selected text
  afx_msg void HandleSetSelApptBtn();
  // handle getting the hour of the selected text
  afx_msg void HandleGetSelHourBtn();
  // handle setting the hour of the selected text
  afx_msg void HandleSetSelHourBtn();
```

(continues)

Listing 8.8 Continued

```
      // handle getting an appointment from the list box
      afx_msg void HandleGetApptBtn();

      // handle clearning the list box
      afx_msg void HandleClearBtn()
        { ClearList(); }

      // handle double-clicking on the list box
      afx_msg void HandleListDblClk()
        { HandleGetApptBtn(); }
      // handle setting a string in the list box
      afx_msg void HandleExitBtn()
        { SendMessage(WM_CLOSE); }

      // handle exiting the application
      afx_msg void OnExit()
        { SendMessage(WM_CLOSE); }
      // handle closing the window
      afx_msg void OnClose();
      void makerect(int X, int Y, int W, int H, CRect& r)
        { r.SetRect(X, Y, X + W, Y + H); }
      // declare message map macro
      DECLARE_MESSAGE_MAP();
};
CMainWnd::CMainWnd()
{
    // create the window
    Create(NULL, "Single-Selection List Box Tester",
        WS_OVERLAPPEDWINDOW,
        rectDefault, NULL, "EXITMENU");

    // insert the initial list of names
    InitApptLst();
}
CMainWnd::~CMainWnd()
{
    delete pApptListTxt;
    delete pApptBoxTxt;
    delete pHourBoxTxt;
    delete pApptLst;
    delete pApptBox;
    delete pHourBox;
    delete pAddApptBtn;
    delete pDelApptBtn;
    delete pGetSelApptBtn;
    delete pSetSelApptBtn;
    delete pGetSelHourBtn;
    delete pSetSelHourBtn;
    delete pGetApptBtn;
    delete pExitBtn;
}
```

```
int CMainWnd::OnCreate(LPCREATESTRUCT lpCS)
{
  int x0 = 30;
  int x1 = x0 + Wlst + LstHorzSpacing;
  int x2 = x1 + Wbtn + BtnHorzSpacing;
  int y0 = 10;
  int x = x0;
  int y = y0;
  int y1;
  DWORD dwStaticStyle = WS_CHILD | WS_VISIBLE | SS_LEFT;
  DWORD dwEditStyle = WS_CHILD | WS_VISIBLE | ES_LEFT | WS_BORDER;
  DWORD dwScrollStyle = WS_CHILD | WS_VISIBLE | SBS_VERT;
  DWORD dwListBoxStyle = WS_CHILD | WS_VISIBLE | WS_VSCROLL |
                         LBS_STANDARD;
  CRect r;
  // create the list box and its label
  makerect(x, y, Wlbl, Hlbl, r);
  pApptListTxt = new CStatic();
  pApptListTxt->Create("Appointments List", dwStaticStyle, r, this);
  y += Hlbl + LblVertSpacing;
  makerect(x, y, Wlst, Hlst, r);
  pApptLst = new CListBox();
  pApptLst->Create(dwListBoxStyle, r, this, ID_APPT_LST);
  // create the edit boxes and their labels
  x = x1;
  y = y0;
  makerect(x, y, Wbox, Hbox, r);
  pApptBoxTxt = new CStatic();
  pApptBoxTxt->Create("Appt. Box", dwStaticStyle, r, this);
  y += Hbox + BoxVertSpacing;
  makerect(x, y, Wbox, Hbox, r);
  pApptBox = new CEdit();
  pApptBox->Create(dwEditStyle, r, this, ID_APPT_EDIT);
  y += Hbox + BoxVertSpacing;
  makerect(x, y, Wlbl, Hlbl, r);
  pHourBoxTxt = new CStatic();
  pHourBoxTxt->Create("Hour Box", dwStaticStyle, r, this);
  y += Hlbl + LblVertSpacing;
  makerect(x, y, Wbox, Hbox, r);
  pHourBox = new CEdit();
  pHourBox->Create(dwEditStyle, r, this, ID_HOUR_EDIT);
  // create the button controls
  y += Hbox + BoxVertSpacing;
  y1 = y;
  makerect(x, y, Wbtn, Hbtn, r);
  pAddApptBtn = new CxButton();
  pAddApptBtn->Create("Add Appt.", r, this, ID_ADDAPPT_BTN);
  y += Hbtn + BtnVertSpacing;
  makerect(x, y, Wbtn, Hbtn, r);
  pDelApptBtn = new CxButton();
  pDelApptBtn->Create("Delete Appt.", r, this, ID_DELAPPT_BTN);
  y += Hbtn + BtnVertSpacing;
  makerect(x, y, Wbtn, Hbtn, r);
  pGetSelApptBtn = new CxButton();
  pGetSelApptBtn->Create("Get Selected Appt.", r, this,
                         ID_GETSELAPPT_BTN);
```

II

Visual C++ Programming

(continues)

Listing 8.8 Continued

```
    y += Hbtn + BtnVertSpacing;
    makerect(x, y, Wbtn, Hbtn, r);
    pSetSelApptBtn = new CxButton();
    pSetSelApptBtn->Create("Set Selected Appt.", r, this,
                        ID_SETSELAPPT_BTN);
    y += Hbtn + BtnVertSpacing;
    makerect(x, y, Wbtn, Hbtn, r);
    pClearBtn = new CxButton();
    pClearBtn->Create("Reset List", r, this, ID_CLEAR_BTN);
    // create the second row of buttons
    y  = y1;
    x = x2;
    makerect(x, y, Wbtn, Hbtn, r);
    pGetSelHourBtn = new CxButton();
    pGetSelHourBtn->Create("Get Selected Hour", r, this,
                        ID_GETSELHOUR_BTN);

    y += Hbtn + BtnVertSpacing;
    makerect(x, y, Wbtn, Hbtn, r);
    pSetSelHourBtn = new CxButton();
    pSetSelHourBtn->Create("Set Selected Hour", r, this,
                        ID_SETSELHOUR_BTN);
    y += Hbtn + BtnVertSpacing;
    makerect(x, y, Wbtn, Hbtn, r);
    pGetApptBtn = new CxButton();
    pGetApptBtn->Create("Get String by Hour", r, this,
                    ID_GETAPPT_BTN);

    y += Hbtn + BtnVertSpacing;
    makerect(x, y, Wbtn, Hbtn, r);
    pExitBtn = new CxButton();
    pExitBtn->Create("Exit", r, this, ID_EXIT_BTN);
    return CFrameWnd::OnCreate(lpCS);
}
void CMainWnd::FormatHour(int hour)
{
    if (hour < 10)
        sprintf(hourStr, "0%d", hour);
    else
        sprintf(hourStr, "%2d", hour);
}
void CMainWnd::HandleAddApptBtn()
{
    int i;
    // get the string in the Appt. box
    pApptBox->GetWindowText(apptStr, MaxStringLen);
    // get the string in the Hor box
    pHourBox->GetWindowText(hourStr, MaxStringLen);
    i = atoi(hourStr);
    if (i < 0 || i >= 24) {
        MessageBox("Invalid hour value", "Error",
                    MB_OK | MB_ICONEXCLAMATION);
        return;
    }
```

```
  FormatHour(i);
  sprintf(formatApptStr, "%2s:00 %s", hourStr, apptStr);
  // add the string if it is not already in the list box
  if (pApptLst->FindString(-1, formatApptStr) < 0) {
    // delete empty time entry
    pApptLst->DeleteString(i);
    // add the string and store the position of the new string
    i = pApptLst->AddString(formatApptStr);
    // make the added string the new selection
    pApptLst->SetCurSel(i);
  }
  else
    // handle the duplicate appointment error
    MessageBox("Cannot add duplicate appointment", "Input Error",
            MB_OK | MB_ICONEXCLAMATION);
}
void CMainWnd::HandleDelApptBtn()
{
  // get the index of the currently selected list member
  int i = pApptLst->GetCurSel();
  // delete the currently selected list member
  pApptLst->DeleteString(i);
  // reinsert appointment time
  FormatHour(i);
  sprintf(formatApptStr, "%2s:00", hourStr);
  pApptLst->AddString(formatApptStr);
}
void CMainWnd::HandleGetSelApptBtn()
{
  // get the selected list item
  pApptLst->GetText(pApptLst->GetCurSel(), formatApptStr);
  // split formatted appointment
  if (strlen(formatApptStr) > 6)
    strcpy(apptStr, formatApptStr + 7);
  else
    strcpy(apptStr, "");
  strncpy(hourStr, formatApptStr, 2);
  // store it in the Appt. box
  pApptBox->SetWindowText(apptStr);
  pHourBox->SetWindowText(hourStr);
}
void CMainWnd::HandleSetSelApptBtn()
{
  // get the index of the currently selected list member
  int i = pApptLst->GetCurSel();
  FormatHour(i);
  // get the appointment to be replace the currently selected list item
  pApptBox->GetWindowText(apptStr, MaxStringLen);
  sprintf(formatApptStr, "%2s:00 %s", hourStr, apptStr);
  // is the candidate string not in the list?
  if (pApptLst->FindString(-1, formatApptStr) < 0) {
    // delete the current selection
    pApptLst->DeleteString(i);
    // insert the new selection
    i = pApptLst->AddString(formatApptStr);
```

(continues)

Listing 8.8 Continued

```
    // select the inserted string
    pApptLst->SetCurSel(i);
  }
  else
    MessageBox("Cannot add duplicate appointments", "Input Error!",
               MB_OK | MB_ICONEXCLAMATION);
}
void CMainWnd::HandleGetSelHourBtn()
{
  int n = pApptLst->GetCurSel();
  FormatHour(n);
  pHourBox->SetWindowText(hourStr);
}
void CMainWnd::HandleSetSelHourBtn()
{
  int i;
  pHourBox->GetWindowText(hourStr, MaxStringLen);
  i = atoi(hourStr);
  if (i >= 0 && i < 24)
    pApptLst->SetCurSel(i);
  else
    MessageBox("Invalid hour", "Error", MB_OK | MB_ICONEXCLAMATION);
}
void CMainWnd::HandleGetApptBtn()
{
  int i;
  // get the index from the Hour box
  pHourBox->GetWindowText(hourStr, MaxStringLen);
  i = atoi(hourStr);
  if (i >= 0 && i < 24) {
    // get the target string from the list box
    pApptLst->GetText(i, formatApptStr);
    if (strlen(formatApptStr) > 6)
      strcpy(apptStr, formatApptStr + 7);
    else
      strcpy(apptStr, "");
    // write the list member in the Appt. box
    pApptBox->SetWindowText(apptStr);
  }
  else
    MessageBox("Invalid hour", "Error", MB_OK | MB_ICONEXCLAMATION);
}
void CMainWnd::OnClose()
{
  if (MessageBox("Want to close this application",
         "Query", MB_YESNO | MB_ICONQUESTION) == IDYES)
    DestroyWindow();
}
void CMainWnd::InitApptLst()
{
  ClearList();
  // select the second item
  pApptLst->SetCurSel(8);
```

```
    // assign data to the Appt. and Hour boxes
    pApptBox->SetWindowText("Lunch");
    pHourBox->SetWindowText("12");
}
void CMainWnd::ClearList()
{
    pApptLst->ResetContent();
    // add data in the list box
    for (int hour = 0; hour < MaxHours; hour++) {
        FormatHour(hour);
        strcat(hourStr, ":00");
        pApptLst->AddString(hourStr);
    }
}
BEGIN_MESSAGE_MAP(CMainWnd, CFrameWnd)
    ON_WM_CREATE()
    ON_BN_CLICKED(ID_ADDAPPT_BTN, HandleAddApptBtn)
    ON_BN_CLICKED(ID_DELAPPT_BTN, HandleDelApptBtn)
    ON_BN_CLICKED(ID_GETSELAPPT_BTN, HandleGetSelApptBtn)
    ON_BN_CLICKED(ID_SETSELAPPT_BTN, HandleSetSelApptBtn)
    ON_BN_CLICKED(ID_GETSELHOUR_BTN, HandleGetSelHourBtn)
    ON_BN_CLICKED(ID_SETSELHOUR_BTN, HandleSetSelHourBtn)
    ON_BN_CLICKED(ID_GETAPPT_BTN, HandleGetApptBtn)
    ON_BN_CLICKED(ID_CLEAR_BTN, HandleClearBtn)
    ON_LBN_DBLCLK(ID_APPT_LST, HandleListDblClk)
    ON_BN_CLICKED(ID_EXIT_BTN, HandleExitBtn)
    ON_COMMAND(CM_EXIT, OnExit)
    ON_WM_CLOSE()
END_MESSAGE_MAP()
// Construct the CListBoxApp's m_pMainWnd data member
BOOL CListBoxApp::InitInstance()
{
    m_pMainWnd = new CMainWnd();
    m_pMainWnd->ShowWindow(m_nCmdShow);
    m_pMainWnd->UpdateWindow();
    return TRUE;
}
// application's constructor initializes and runs the app
CListBoxApp WindowApp;
```

The source code shown in Listing 8.8 declares three sets of constants. The
first set contains the constants that dimension the sizes and spacings of the
various controls; the second set defines miscellaneous constants; and the
third set specifies the ID for the various controls.

The program listing declares the application class, CListBoxApp, the window
class, CMainWnd, and the button class, CxButton. The class CMainWnd declares a
number of data members that are pointers to the controls owned by the main
window. The class also declares three strings to handle the contents of the
Appt. Box and Hour Box edit controls, and the contents of the selected list

box item. The CMainWnd class also declares a constructor, a destructor, and a number of member functions that respond to the notification messages sent by the various pushbutton controls.

The CMainWnd constructor performs two tasks: invokes the member function Create to build the application window, and calls the InitApptLst member function to initialize the list box with empty appointments.

The OnCreate member function creates the controls using the appropriate styles. For example, the list box control appears with a vertical scroll bar and automatically maintains a sorted list of strings.

The member function FormatHour converts the argument of the int-type parameter hour into a string image. The function stores that image in the data member hourStr. If the argument for the parameter hour is less than 10, the function appends a 0 to the string image of the parameter hour.

The HandleAddApptBtn member function adds the appointment in the list box control. The function performs the following tasks:

- Obtains the string in the Appt. Box edit control and stores it in the data member apptStr.

- Obtains the string in the Hour Box edit control and stores it in the data member hourStr.

- Converts the contents of the member hourStr into an integer value using the function atoi. This task assigns the result of the function atoi to the local variable i.

- Determines if the variable i contains either a negative value or an integer that exceeds 23. If this condition is true, the function displays an error message dialog box and then exits.

- Formats the value in the variable i by calling the member function FormatHour. The formatted string image of the variable i is now in the member hourStr.

- Creates a formatted image of an appointment by using the function sprintf. This function converts members hourStr and apptStr into the formatted string image stored in the member formatApptStr.

- Verifies that the added appointment does not already exist in the list box. The function uses the FindString function to detect an attempt to add duplicate strings. If the `FindString` function returns a negative number, the function `HandleAddApptBtn` resumes the subsequent tasks. Otherwise, the function displays a message informing you that you cannot add duplicate strings in the list box.

■ Deletes the appointment at hour `i`. This task involves sending the C++ message `DeleteString` to the list box. The argument for this message is the local variable `i`.

■ Adds the string of the member `formatApptStr` to the list box and assigns the position of the string to the local variable `i`. The function performs this task by sending the C++ message `AddString` to the list box.

■ Makes the added appointment the current selection by sending the C++ message `SetCurSel` to the list box. The argument for this message is the local variable `i`, which contains the index of the inserted string.

The `HandleDelApptBtn` member function deletes the current selection. Here are the tasks that the `HandleDelApptBtn` function performs:

■ Obtains the position of the current selection by sending the C++ message `GetCurSel` to the list box. The function stores the result of this message (that is, the index of the selected item) in the local variable `i`.

■ Deletes the selection by sending the C++ message `DeleteString` and supplying the message with the argument `i`.

■ Inserts an empty appointment entry. This task involves using the function `FormatHour` to obtain and store the string image of the variable `i` in the member `hourStr`. Then, the function creates a formatted image of an empty appointment and stores it in the member `formatApptStr`. Finally, the function sends the C++ message `AddString` to the list box and supplies the message with the argument `formatApptStr`.

The `HandleGetSelApptBtn` member function recalls the current appointment and writes its text and hour to the Appt. Box and Hour Box edit controls, respectively. The function performs the following tasks:

■ Copies the current selection to the member `formatApptStr` by sending the C++ message `GetText` to the list box. The first argument of this message is the C++ message `GetCurSel`, which is also sent to the list box. The second argument of the message `GetText` is the data member `formatApptStr`.

- Copies the appointment text from the member `formatApptStr` to the member `apptStr`.

- Copies the appointment time from the member `formatApptStr` to the member `hourStr`.

- Writes the string of the member `apptStr` to the Appt. Box edit control.

- Writes the string of the member `hourStr` to the Hour Box edit control.

The `HandleSetSelApptBtn` member function overwrites the current selection with the string in the Appt. Box edit control. The function performs the following tasks:

- Obtains the position of the current selection by sending the C++ message `GetCurSel` to the list box. The function assigns the result of the message to the local variable `i`.

- Obtains a formatted image of the variable `i` and stores it in the member `hourStr`. This task involves the member function `FormatHour`.

- Copies the text in the Appt. Box to the member `apptStr`.

- Creates a formatted image of the appointment using the members `apptStr` and `hourStr`. This task uses the function `sprintf` and stores the resulting string in the member `formatApptStr`.

- Verifies that the string in the member `formatApptStr` does not already exist in the list box. This task involves sending the C++ message `FindString` to the list box. If the string in `formatApptStr` is new to the list, the function deletes the current selection (by sending the C++ message `DeleteString` to the list box), adds the string of `formatApptStr` (by sending the C++ message `AddString` to the list box), and then selects the added string (by sending the C++ message `SetCurSel` to the list box). By contrast, if the string in `formatApptStr` has a matching list item, the function displays a message informing you that you cannot add duplicate strings in the list box. This warning also appears if you attempt to overwrite the current selection with the same string!

The member function `HandleGetSelHourBtn` writes the time (which is also the index) of the current selection in the Hour Box edit control. The function sends the C++ message `GetCurSel` to the list box in order to obtain the sought time.

The member function `HandleSetSelHourBtn` reads the value in the Hour Box edit control and uses that value (after validating it) to set the new current selection. The function sends the C++ message `SetCurSel` to the list box to make the new selection.

The member function `HandleGetApptBtn` enables you to retrieve the appointment whose time (also index) appears in the Hour Box edit control. The function performs the following tasks:

- Copies the string of the Hour Box edit control to the data member `hourStr`.

- Converts the string in `hourStr` to the int-typed local variable `i`. This task uses the function `atoi`.

- Performs the remaining tasks if the value in variable `i` is in the range 0 to 23. Otherwise, the function displays an error message dialog box.

- Copies the string of the list item at position `i` to the member `formatApptStr`.

- Extracts the appointment text from the member `formatApptStr` and stores it in the member `apptStr`.

- Writes the string of the member `apptStr` in the Appt. Box edit control.

Multiple-Selection Lists

Let's shift the focus from single-selection list boxes to multiple-selection list boxes. In this section, I present the CTLLST3.EXE program. This program demonstrates the use of multiple-selection lists and focuses on selecting and retrieving the selection strings and their indices. It is worthwhile to point out that there are two modes for making multiple selections in a list box. These modes depend on whether you set the style `LBS_EXTENDEDSEL` when you create a `CListBox` instance. If you set this style, you can quickly extend the range of selected items by simply holding down the Shift key and clicking the mouse.

However, using the `LBS_EXTENDEDSEL` multiple-selection feature has a limitation: You are restricted to manually (that is, using the mouse or cursor keys) selecting blocks of contiguous items in the list box. The member functions `SetSel` and `SetItemRange` enable your application to select noncontiguous items; however, using either of these functions requires the user to do additional work, and a few extra controls are required to support this type of selection. By contrast, if you avoid the style LBS_EXTENDEDSEL, you can easily make dispersed selections by clicking the mouse button on the individual items you want to select. The disadvantage to this selection method is that you must click each item to select it, including neighboring items. Choose the selection method you feel best fulfills the user-interface needs of your MFC applications.

The Multiple-Selection List Tester

Now let's look at the program that illustrates how to set and query multiple selections in a list box. Figure 8.3 shows a sample session with the CTLLST3.EXE application and shows the controls available in the application.

Figure 8.3

A sample session with the CTLLST3.EXE application.

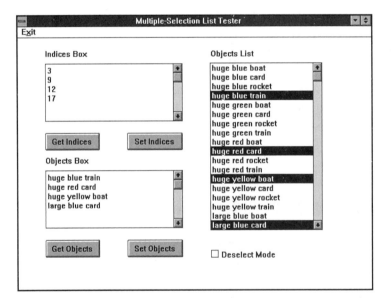

Here is a list of the controls used by the CTLLST3.EXE program, along with the operations they support:

■ *Indices Box multi-line edit box control.* Contains the indices of the selected strings. Each index appears on a separate line. Every time you click the Get Indices button, you lose the previous contents of this edit control.

■ *Get Indices pushbutton.* Copies the indices of the list box selections to the Indices Box edit control.

- *Set Indices pushbutton.* Selects (or deselects) the list box items using the values in the Indices Box edit control.

- *Objects Box multi-line edit box control.* Contains the names of the selected objects. Each selection appears on a separate line in the edit box. Every time you click the Get Objects button, you lose the previous contents of this edit control.

- *Get Objects pushbutton.* Copies the selections from the list box selections to the Objects Box edit control.

- *Set Objects pushbutton.* Selects (or deselects) the list box items that match those in the Objects Box edit control. The match does not have to be exact—the strings in the Objects Box edit control only have to match the leading characters of the list items.

- *Objects List multiple-selection list.* Created by the style LBS_MULTIPLESEL, this list box contains a list of physical objects (various kinds of cars, boats, trains, and rockets), sorted in ascending order.

- *Deselect Mode check box control.* Determines whether the pushbuttons Set Objects and Set Indices select or deselect list items.

- *Static text controls.* Provide labels for the list and edit boxes.

Compile and run the program. The application initializes the list box with the names of 64 objects. Select a few list items and click the pushbuttons Get Objects and Get Indices. The selected strings and indices become visible in the Objects Box and Indices Box edit controls. Now edit the lines in the Objects Box edit control by deleting one or two trailing characters from each line to create partial names. Click the Set Objects pushbutton. Notice that the selections are the same because the strings in the Objects Box edit control still match the same list box selection. Now type a new set of indices in the Indices Box edit control and click the Set Indices pushbutton. The program now shows a new set of selected items in the list box. You also can make a new selection by deleting the text in the Objects Box edit control and then typing names found in the list box. Now click the Set Objects button and view the new list box selections. When you are done experimenting with the program, click Exit or press Alt+X.

Listing 8.9 shows the contents of the CTLLST3.DEF definition file.

Listing 8.9 The CTLLST3.DEF Definition File

```
NAME         CtlLst3
DESCRIPTION  'An MFC Windows Application'
CODE         PRELOAD MOVEABLE DISCARDABLE
DATA         PRELOAD MOVEABLE MULTIPLE
HEAPSIZE     1024
```

The source code for the CTLLST3.H header file is provided in Listing 8.10.

Listing 8.10 Source Code for the CTLLST3.H Header File

```
#define CM_EXIT (WM_USER + 100)
```

Listing 8.11 provides the script for the CTLLST3.RC resource file.

Listing 8.11 Script for the CTLLST3.RC Resource File

```
#include <windows.h>
#include <afxres.h>
#include "ctllst3.h"
EXITMENU MENU LOADONCALL MOVEABLE PURE DISCARDABLE
BEGIN
    MENUITEM "E&xit", CM_EXIT
END
```

Listing 8.12 shows the source code for the CTLLST3.CPP program file.

Listing 8.12 Source Code for the CTLLST3.CPP Program File

```
/*
                Multi-Selection List Box Tester
             -------------------------------
   Program tests multi-selection list boxes to select and deselect
   items from a list of objects.
*/
#include <stdio.h>
#include <string.h>
#include <afxwin.h>
#include "ctllst3.h"
// declare the constants for the dimensions and spacing
// of the various controls
const Wtxt = 100;
const Htxt = 20;
const TxtVertSpacing = 5;
const Wlst = 200;
const Hlst = 300;
```

```
const LstHorzSpacing = 50;
const LstVertSpacing = 20;
const Wbox = 250;
const Hbox = 100;
const BoxVertSpacing = 20;
const BoxHorzSpacing = 50;
const Wbtn = 100;
const Hbtn = 30;
const BtnHorzSpacing = 50;
const BtnVertSpacing = 10;
const Wchk = 200;
const Hchk = 20;
const MaxStringLen = 80;
const MaxSelections = 64; // maximum number of selections

// declare the ID constants for the various controls
#define ID_OBJECTS_LST      101
#define ID_OBJECTS_EDIT     102
#define ID_INDICES_EDIT   103
#define ID_GETOBJECTS_BTN   104
#define ID_SETOBJECTS_BTN   105
#define ID_GETINDICES_BTN 106
#define ID_SETINDICES_BTN 107
#define ID_SELECT_CHK      108
// declare constants for the check box and radio button states
const BF_CHECKED = 1;
const BF_UNCHECKED = 0;
class CxEdit : public CEdit
{
public:
  BOOL GetLine(LPSTR lpString, int nStrSize, int nLineNumber);
  int GetLineLength(int nLineNumber);
  int GetNumOfLines();

};
// declare the extended button class
class CxButton : public CButton
{
public:
   BOOL Create(const char FAR* lpCaption, const RECT& rect,
            CWnd* pParentWnd, UINT nID)
   {
       return CButton::Create(lpCaption,
                           WS_CHILD | WS_VISIBLE |
                           WS_TABSTOP | BS_PUSHBUTTON,
                           rect, pParentWnd, nID);
   }
};
// declare the check box class
class CCheckBox : public CButton
{
public:
   BOOL Create(const char FAR* lpCaption, const RECT& rect,
            CWnd* pParentWnd, UINT nID)
```

(continues)

Listing 8.12 Continued

```
    {
        return CButton::Create(lpCaption,
                               WS_CHILD | WS_VISIBLE |
                               WS_TABSTOP | BS_AUTOCHECKBOX,
                               rect, pParentWnd, nID);
    }
};

// expand the functionality of CFrameWnd by deriving class CMainWnd
class CMainWnd : public CFrameWnd
{
 public:
  CMainWnd();
  ~CMainWnd();
 protected:
  // declare pointers to controls
  CStatic* pObjectsListTxt;
  CStatic* pObjectsBoxTxt;
  CStatic* pIndicesBoxTxt;
  CListBox* pObjectsLst;
  CxEdit* pObjectsBox;
  CxEdit* pIndicesBox;
  CxButton* pGetObjectsBtn;
  CxButton* pSetObjectsBtn;
  CxButton* pGetIndicesBtn;
  CxButton* pSetIndicesBtn;
  CCheckBox* pSelectChk;
  // declare edit control insertion buffer
  CString insertBuffer;

  // array of string pointers
  LPSTR objects[MaxSelections];

  // array of integers to store the selection indices
  int indices[MaxSelections];
  // handle creating the controls
  afx_msg int OnCreate(LPCREATESTRUCT lpCS);
  // initialize the list box
  void InitObjectsLst();
  // handle getting the selections
  afx_msg void HandleGetObjectsBtn();
  // handle setting the selections
  afx_msg void HandleSetObjectsBtn();
  // handle getting the selection indices
  afx_msg void HandleGetIndicesBtn();
  // handle setting the selection indices
  afx_msg void HandleSetIndicesBtn();
  // handle exiting the application
  afx_msg void OnExit()
    { SendMessage(WM_CLOSE); }
  // handle closing the window
  virtual void OnClose();
  // reset the selections
  void resetSelections();
```

```
    void makerect(int X, int Y, int W, int H, CRect& r)
      { r.SetRect(X, Y, X + W, Y + H); } }
    // declare message map macro
    DECLARE_MESSAGE_MAP();

};
class CListBoxApp : public CWinApp
{
public:
    virtual BOOL InitInstance();
};
BOOL CxEdit::GetLine(LPSTR lpString, int nStrSize, int nLineNumber)
{
  int nCopyCount;
  BOOL bResult;
  if (nStrSize <= 0)
    return FALSE;
  bResult = (nStrSize >= GetLineLength(nLineNumber) + 1) ? TRUE : FALSE;
  if (nStrSize == 1)
  {
    lpString[0] = '\0';
    return bResult;
  }
  ((WORD FAR *)lpString)[0] = nStrSize;

  nCopyCount = (WORD)(SendMessage(EM_GETLINE, nLineNumber,
                                  long(lpString)));
  if (nCopyCount)
  {
    // Windows returns non-null terminated string
    lpString[nCopyCount] = '\0';
    return bResult;
  }
  return FALSE;
}
int CxEdit::GetLineLength(int nLineNumber)
{
  int nStartPos = -1;
  if (nLineNumber > -1)
    nStartPos = LineIndex(nLineNumber);
  return (WORD) SendMessage(EM_LINELENGTH, nStartPos);
}
int CxEdit::GetNumOfLines()
{
  // get the size of the text in the edit control
  int size = GetWindowTextLength();
  // initialize the function's result
  int count = (size == 0) ? 0 : 1;
  // return 0 if the edit box is empty
  if (size == 0)
    return 0;
  // create a string object of the same size
  CString s(' ', size);
  // copy the text in the edit control to the string object
```

(continues)

Visual C++ Programming

Listing 8.12 Continued

```
    GetWindowText(s.GetBuffer(size), size);
    s.ReleaseBuffer(); // release any extra space
    // loop to count the number of lines by counting the number
    // of '\n' characters (assuming they only occur at a line
    // break)
    for (int i = 0; i < (s.GetLength() - 1);)
      if (s[i++] == '\r' && s[i] == '\n') {
        count++;
        i++;
      }

    return count;
}
CMainWnd::CMainWnd()
{
  // create the window
  Create(NULL, "Multiple-Selection List Tester",
    WS_OVERLAPPEDWINDOW,
    rectDefault, NULL, "EXITMENU");

  // insert the initial Objects list
  InitObjectsLst();
}
CMainWnd::~CMainWnd()
{
  delete pObjectsListTxt;
  delete pObjectsBoxTxt;
  delete pIndicesBoxTxt;
  delete pObjectsLst;
  delete pObjectsBox;
  delete pIndicesBox;
  delete pGetObjectsBtn;
  delete pSetObjectsBtn;
  delete pGetIndicesBtn;
  delete pSetIndicesBtn;
  delete pSelectChk;

  // deallocate the dynamic string space
  for (int i = 0; i < MaxSelections; i++)
    delete objects[i];
}
int CMainWnd::OnCreate(LPCREATESTRUCT lpCS)
{
  int x0 = 50;
  int y0 = 20;
  int x = x0;
  int y = y0;
  DWORD dwStaticStyle = WS_CHILD | WS_VISIBLE | SS_LEFT;
  DWORD dwEditStyle = WS_CHILD | WS_VISIBLE | WS_TABSTOP |
              WS_BORDER | WS_VSCROLL | ES_LEFT |
              ES_AUTOHSCROLL | ES_AUTOVSCROLL | ES_MULTILINE;
  DWORD dwListBoxStyle = WS_CHILD | WS_VISIBLE | LBS_STANDARD |
                    LBS_MULTIPLESEL;

  CRect r;
```

```
// create the multi=line Indices Box edit control and its label
makerect(x, y, Wtxt, Htxt, r);
pIndicesBoxTxt = new CStatic();
pIndicesBoxTxt->Create("Indices Box", dwStaticStyle, r, this);
y += Htxt + TxtVertSpacing;
makerect(x, y, Wbox, Hbox, r);
pIndicesBox = new CxEdit();
pIndicesBox->Create(dwEditStyle, r, this, ID_INDICES_EDIT);
// create the GetIndices button
y += Hbox + BoxVertSpacing;
makerect(x, y, Wbtn, Hbtn, r);
pGetIndicesBtn = new CxButton();
pGetIndicesBtn->Create("Get Indices", r, this, ID_GETINDICES_BTN);
// create the Set Indices button
x += Wbtn + BtnHorzSpacing;
makerect(x, y, Wbtn, Hbtn, r);
pSetIndicesBtn = new CxButton();
pSetIndicesBtn->Create("Set Indices", r, this, ID_SETINDICES_BTN);
x = x0;
y += Hbtn + BtnVertSpacing;
// creates the multiline Objects Box edit control and its label
makerect(x, y, Wtxt, Htxt, r);
pObjectsBoxTxt = new CStatic();
pObjectsBoxTxt->Create("Objects Box", dwStaticStyle, r, this);
y += Htxt + TxtVertSpacing;
makerect(x, y, Wbox, Hbox, r);
pObjectsBox = new CxEdit();
pObjectsBox->Create(dwEditStyle, r, this, ID_OBJECTS_EDIT);
// create the Get Objects button
y += Hbox + BoxVertSpacing;
makerect(x, y, Wbtn, Hbtn, r);
pGetObjectsBtn = new CxButton();
pGetObjectsBtn->Create("Get Objects", r, this, ID_GETOBJECTS_BTN);
// create the Set Objects button
x += Wbtn + BtnHorzSpacing;
makerect(x, y, Wbtn, Hbtn, r);
pSetObjectsBtn = new CxButton();
pSetObjectsBtn->Create("Set Objects", r, this, ID_SETOBJECTS_BTN);
// allocate the dynamic space for the array of strings accessed
// by the array of pointers objects
for (int i = 0; i < MaxSelections; i++)
  objects[i] = new char[MaxStringLen + 1];
// create the name list box and its label
x0 += Wbox + BoxHorzSpacing;
x = x0;
y = y0;
makerect(x, y, Wtxt, Htxt, r);
pObjectsListTxt = new CStatic();
pObjectsListTxt->Create("Objects List", dwStaticStyle, r, this);
y += Htxt + TxtVertSpacing;
makerect(x, y, Wlst, Hlst, r);
pObjectsLst = new CListBox();
pObjectsLst->Create(dwListBoxStyle, r, this, ID_OBJECTS_LST);
// create the Deselect Mode check box
y += Hlst + LstVertSpacing;
```

II

Visual C++ Programming

(continues)

Listing 8.12 Continued

```
  makerect(x, y, Wchk, Hchk, r);
  pSelectChk = new CCheckBox();
  pSelectChk->Create("Deselect Mode", r, this, ID_SELECT_CHK);
  return CFrameWnd::OnCreate(lpCS);
}
void CMainWnd::InitObjectsLst()
{
  char* ps1[4] = { "small", "medium", "large" ,"huge" };
  char* ps2[4] = { " red", " blue", " yellow", " green" };
  char* ps3[4] = { " card", " boat", " train", " rocket" };
  char s[MaxStringLen+1];

  // add objects in the Objects list box
  for (int i = 0; i < 4; i++)
    for (int j = 0; j < 4; j++)
      for (int k = 0; k < 4; k++) {
        strcpy(s, ps1[i]);
        strcat(s, ps2[j]);
        strcat(s, ps3[k]);
        pObjectsLst->AddString(s);
      }
}
void CMainWnd::HandleGetObjectsBtn()
{
  char s[MaxStringLen+1];
  // get the indices of the selected strings
  int n = pObjectsLst->GetSelItems(MaxSelections, indices);

  // exit if n is not positive
  if (n <= 0) return;
  // clear the insertion buffer
  insertBuffer = "";
  // concatenate the selected strings in the insertion buffer
  for (int i = 0; i < n; i++) {
    pObjectsLst->GetText(indices[i], objects[i]);
    sprintf(s, "%s\r\n", objects[i]);
    insertBuffer += s;
  }
  // copy the insertion buffer to the Objects Box edit control
  pObjectsBox->SetWindowText((const char*) insertBuffer);
}
void CMainWnd::HandleSetObjectsBtn()
{
  char s[MaxStringLen+1];
  int j;
  // get the number of lines in the Objects Box edit control
  int n = pObjectsBox->GetNumOfLines();
  // get the select status from the Deselect Mode check box
  BOOL shouldSet =
    (pSelectChk->GetCheck() == BF_UNCHECKED) ? TRUE : FALSE;
  resetSelections();
  // read the lines from the Objects Box control
  for (int i = 0; i < n; i++) {
    // get the i'th name from the Objects Box edit control
    pObjectsBox->GetLine(s, MaxStringLen, i);
```

```
      // find its match in the list box
      j = pObjectsLst->FindString(-1, s);
      // select the matching element
      if (j >= 0)
        pObjectsLst->SetSel(j, shouldSet);
  }
}
void CMainWnd::HandleGetIndicesBtn()
{
  char s[MaxStringLen+1];
  // get the selected indices
  int n = pObjectsLst->GetSelItems(MaxSelections, indices);

  // exit if n is not positive
  if (n <= 0) return;
  // initialize the insertion buffer
  insertBuffer = "";
  // concatenate the selected indices in the insertion buffer
  for (int i = 0; i < n; i++) {
    sprintf(s, "%d\r\n", indices[i]);
    insertBuffer += s;
  }
  // copy the insertion buffer to the Objects edit control
  pIndicesBox->SetWindowText((const char*) insertBuffer);
}
void CMainWnd::HandleSetIndicesBtn()
{
  char s[MaxStringLen + 1];
  int j;
  resetSelections();
  // get the number of lines in the Indices Box edit control
  int n = pIndicesBox->GetNumOfLines();
  // get the select status from the Deselect Mode check box
  BOOL shouldSet =
    (pSelectChk->GetCheck() == BF_UNCHECKED) ? TRUE : FALSE;

  // read the lines from the Indices Box control and set the
  // corresponding objects in the list box
  for (int i = 0; i < n; i++) {
    pIndicesBox->GetLine(s, MaxStringLen, i);
    j = atoi(s);
    pObjectsLst->SetSel(j, shouldSet);
  }
}
void CMainWnd::OnClose()
{
  if (MessageBox("Want to close this application",
        "Query", MB_YESNO | MB_ICONQUESTION) == IDYES)
    DestroyWindow();
}
void CMainWnd::resetSelections()
{
  int n = pObjectsLst->GetSelItems(MaxSelections, indices);
  for (int i = 0; i < n; i++)
      pObjectsLst->SetSel(indices[i], FALSE);
}
```

(continues)

Listing 8.12 Continued

```
BEGIN_MESSAGE_MAP(CMainWnd, CFrameWnd)
  ON_WM_CREATE()
  ON_BN_CLICKED(ID_GETOBJECTS_BTN, HandleGetObjectsBtn)
  ON_BN_CLICKED(ID_SETOBJECTS_BTN, HandleSetObjectsBtn)
  ON_BN_CLICKED(ID_GETINDICES_BTN, HandleGetIndicesBtn)
  ON_BN_CLICKED(ID_SETINDICES_BTN, HandleSetIndicesBtn)
  ON_COMMAND(CM_EXIT, OnExit)
  ON_WM_CLOSE()
END_MESSAGE_MAP()
// Construct the CListBoxApp's m_pMainWnd data member
BOOL CListBoxApp::InitInstance()
{
  m_pMainWnd = new CMainWnd();
  m_pMainWnd->ShowWindow(m_nCmdShow);
  m_pMainWnd->UpdateWindow();
  return TRUE;
}
// application's constructor initializes and runs the app
CListBoxApp WindowApp;
```

Essentially, the program shown in Listing 8.12 tests the use of the member functions GetSelIndexes, GetSelStrings, SetSelIndexes, and SetSelStrings of the class CListBox. The program listing declares the following sets of constants:

■ The set that designates the dimensions and spacing for the various application controls.

■ The set that specifies the maximum string size and the maximum number of selections.

■ The set that defines the ID numbers for the various controls.

■ The set that declares the check box state constants, BF_CHECKED and BF_UNCHECKED.

The program CTTLST3.EXE declares the following classes:

■ The application class, CListBoxApp.

■ The window class, CMainWnd.

■ The edit control class, CxEdit.

■ The button class, CxButton.

■ The check box class, CCheckBox.

The last three classes extend the CEdit and CButton classes in a manner similar to that shown in previous programs. The current implementation of the class CxEdit introduces an additional member function, GetNumOfLines. This function counts the number of lines in an edit control. The program must have this result to read individual lines in a multiple-line edit control.

The CMainWnd class declares two sets of data members. The first set represents pointers to the diverse controls employed in the application. The second set includes the array of string pointers, objects, and the array of integers, indices. Both arrays have MaxSelections members.

The CMainWnd class declares a class constructor, a destructor, and a collection of member functions. The class destructor removes the dynamic control instances and the dynamic strings. The CMainWnd constructor invokes the Create function and calls the InitApptLst function to initialize the appointments list box.

The member function OnCreate creates the various controls and creates the array of dynamic strings. The function sets the style for the CListBox instance to include the LBS_MULTIPLESEL style. If you want to make the application extend the list box selections with the Shift key, just add ¦ **LBS_EXTENDEDSEL** to the expression that initializes the local variable dwListBoxStyle.

The member function HandleGetObjectsBtn responds to the notification message sent by clicking the Get Objects pushbutton. The function performs the following tasks:

- Sends the C++ message GetSelItems to the list box to obtain the current selections. The message copies the indices of the selections to the member indices, which is an array of integers. The message also specifies that up to MaxSelections indices can be copied. The function assigns the result of the message GetSelItems to the local variable n.

- Exits the function if the variable n stores zero or a negative value.

- Initializes the insertion buffer insertBuffer.

- Uses a loop to append the strings accessed by the array objects to the insertion buffer insertBuffer.

- Writes the contents of the insertion buffer to the Objects Box edit control.

The member function HandleSetObjectsBtn responds to the notification message of the Set Objects pushbutton control. The function carries out the following tasks:

- Retrieves the number of lines in the Objects Box edit control. This task involves sending the C++ message GetNumOfLines to the edit control, accessed by the member pObjectsBox.

- Obtains the check state of the Deselect Mode check box. This task involves sending the C++ message GetCheck to the check box, which is accessed by the member pSelectChk. The function compares the result of the GetCheck message with the constant BF_UNCHECKED and then assigns a Boolean value, equivalent to the check state, to the local variable shouldSet.

- Invokes the member function resetSelections to deselect the current selections.

- Copies the lines of the Objects Box edit control to the array objects. This task employs a loop to read each line from the Objects Box edit control and then select that line. The selection involves sending the C++ message FindString to the list box in order to locate the index of the matching list box item. The function also sends the C++ message SetSel to the list box in order to select or deselect the matching element. The argument for this message includes the local variable shouldSet, whose value determines whether the items are selected or deselected.

The member function HandleGetIndicesBtn responds to the notification message sent by the Get Indices pushbutton control. The function performs the following tasks:

- Sends the C++ message GetSelItems to the list box in order to obtain the list box selections. The GetSellItems message copies the selections to the integer array indices. The message argument also specifies that up to MaxSelections indices can be copied to the array indices. The function assigns the result of the message to the local variable n.

- Exits the function if the variable n stores zero or a negative value.

- Assigns an empty string to the insertion buffer insertBuffer.

- Uses a `for` loop to convert the selected indices to their string images and to concatenate these strings with the insertion buffer. The conversion involves the function `sprintf`, which appends a pair of line-feed and carriage return characters to each string image.

- Copies the string of the insertion buffer to the Indices Box edit control.

The member function `HandleSetIndicesBtn` responds to the notification message of the Set Indices pushbutton control. The function carries out the following tasks:

- Invokes the member function `resetSelections` to reset the current selections.

- Retrieves the number of lines in the Indices Box control. This task involves sending the C++ message `GetNumOfLines` to the Indices Box edit control.

- Obtains the check state of the Deselect Mode check box. This task involves sending the C++ message `GetCheck` to the check box accessed by the member `pSelectChk`. The function compares the result of the `GetCheck` message with the constant `BF_UNCHECKED` and then assigns a Boolean value, equivalent to the check state, to the local variable `shouldSet`.

- Uses a `for` loop to read each line from the Indices Box control, converts that line into an index, and then uses that index to select (or deselect, depending on the value of the local variable `shouldSet`) a list box item. Reading the lines involves sending the C++ message `GetLine` to the targeted edit box. Selecting (or deleting) a list box item involves sending the C++ message `SetSel` to the list box. The local variable `shouldSet`, which determines the selection mode, is one of the arguments of the `SetSel` message.

The member function `resetSelections` deselects the list box items. The function performs the following tasks:

- Obtains the current number of selections by sending the C++ message `GetSelItems` to the list box. The arguments for this message are `MaxSelections` and the array `indices`. The first argument specifies the maximum number of selections. The array indices obtains the indices of the selected items. The function assigns the result of this message to the local variable n.

■ Uses a for loop to repeat the list box selections and to deselect each one. This task involves sending the C++ message SetSel to the list box. The arguments for this message are indices[i] (the index of the deselected item) and FALSE, which requests that the indexed item be deselected.

The Combo Box Control

The combo box control combines an edit box with a list box, which enables you to select an item in the list box component or to type your own input. Thus, the list box part of the combo box includes convenient or frequently chosen selections. However, unlike a list box, a combo box does not limit your selection to items in the list box. As you learned in Chapter 2, there are three kinds of combo boxes: simple, drop-down, and drop-down list. As you may recall from Chapter 2, the simple combo box contains the edit box and the list box that is always displayed. The drop-down combo box varies from the simple type by the fact that the list box is visible only when you click the down arrow. The drop-down list combo box also provides a drop-down list only when you click the down arrow, but the drop-down list combo box contains no edit box.

The *CComboBox* Class

The MFC library provides the class CComboBox, a descendant of the class CWnd, to model the combo box controls. The class CComboBox declares a constructor and an ample set of member functions to maintain both the list box and the edit control components. The member function Create helps the class constructor in creating class instances. The declaration of the function Create is as follows:

```
BOOL Create(DWORD dwStyle,        // control style
            const RECT& rect,     // location and dimensions
            CWnd* pParentWnd,     // pointer to parent window
            UINT nID);            // control ID
```

The parameter dwStyle specifies the style of the list box control. The combo box styles include the usual WS_*XXXX* window styles as well as the special CBS_*XXXX* combo box styles (shown in Table 8.5). The parameter rect defines the location and dimensions of the control. The parameter pParentWnd is the pointer to the parent window. The parameter nID specifies the unique ID of the combo box instance.

Table 8.5 Combo Box Control Styles	
Style	**Meaning**
CBS_AUTOHSCROLL	Automatically scrolls the text in the edit control to the left when you enter a character at the end of the line. Removing this style limits the text to the characters that fit inside the rectangular boundary of the edit control.
CBS_DROPDOWN	Specifies a drop-down combo box.
CBS_DROPDOWNLIST	Designates a drop-down list combo box.
CBS_SIMPLE	Specifies a simple combo box.
CBS_SORT	Automatically sorts the items in the list box.

The dwStyle parameter may contain the following arguments: CBS_SIMPLE for a simple combo box, CBS_DROPDOWN for a drop-down combo box, or CBS_DROPDOWNLIST for a drop-down list combo box. Typical instances of CComboBox are generated with the styles WS_CHILD, WS_VISIBLE, WS_GROUP, WS_TABSTOP, CBS_SORT, CBS_AUTOHSCROLL, and WS_VSCROLL.

The class CComboBox declares member functions to oversee the list box and the edit control components. Most of these functions are similar to the members of the classes CEdit and CListBox. The MFC library redeclares these member functions for the class CComboBox because CComboBox is not a descendant of the classes CListBox and CEdit.

Among the functions that handle the list box component are the following:

- The parameterless member function GetCount yields the number of items in the list box component.

- The parameterless member function GetCurSel returns the index of the current selection in the list box component. If there is no current selection, the function returns the value CB_ERR.

- The member function SetCurSel selects a new item in the list box component. The declaration of the function SetCurSel is

```
int SetCurSel(int nSelect);
```

The parameter nSelect specifies the index of the new selection in the list box component. The function yields the index of the selected item, or returns the value CB_ERR if an error occurs.

■ The overloaded member function GetLBText resembles the function CListBox::GetText. The overloaded functions yield the selected item of the list box component and have the following declarations:

```
int GetLBText(int nIndex, LPSTR lpszItem) const;
void GetLBText(int nIndex, CString& rString) const;
```

The parameter nIndex specifies the index of the retrieved list box item. The parameter lpszItem is the pointer to the buffer that obtains the list box item. The buffer must be large enough to hold the retrieved items. The reference parameter rString is a CString object that obtains a copy of the list box item. The first version of the function yields the length of the retrieved list box item or returns the value CB_ERR if an error occurs.

■ The member function GetLBTextLen yields the length of a list box item specified by an index. The declaration of the function GetLBTextLen is

```
int GetLBTextLen(int nIndex) const;
```

The parameter nIndex specifies the list box item. The function yields the length of the targeted list box item or returns the value CB_ERR if the argument for the parameter nIndex is invalid.

■ The member function ShowDropDown displays or hides the list box components of a combo box control. The declaration of the function ShowDropDown is

```
void ShowDropDown(BOOL bShowIt = TRUE);
```

The Boolean parameter bShowIt is a flag that is used to show (when its argument is TRUE) or hide (when its argument is FALSE) the drop-down list box. The function helps in toggling the visibility of the drop-down list box in an application.

■ The member function AddString adds a string to the list box component of a combo box control. The declaration of the function AddString is

```
int AddString(LPCSTR lpszString);
```

The parameter lpszString is the pointer to the added string. The function yields the index of the successfully added string. Otherwise, the function returns the value CB_ERR. If the combo box is created with

the style CBS_SORT, the function inserts the added string in the appropriate location to maintain a sorted list. Otherwise, the function merely
adds the new string at the end of the list.

■ The member function DeleteString deletes an item from the list box
component. The declaration of the function DeleteString is

```
int DeleteString(int nIndex);
```

The parameter nIndex specifies the index of the removed list box item.
The function yields the number of remaining strings if the deletion is
successful. Otherwise, the function returns the value CB_ERR.

■ The member function InsertString inserts a string at a designated
index in the list box component. The declaration of the function
InsertString is

```
int InsertString(int nIndex, LPCSTR lpszString);
```

The parameter nIndex specifies the index for inserting the new string.
The parameter lpszString is the pointer to the inserted string. Avoid
using InsertString with combo boxes created with the style CBS_SORT,
unless you are inserting an item in such a way that the order of the list
box component is not corrupted. The function returns the index of the
inserted string or yields the value CB_ERR if an error occurs. When the
list box component runs out of memory space to store a new string, the
function produces the value CB_ERRSPACE.

■ The parameterless member function ResetContent clears the list box
component of a combo box control.

■ The member function Dir inserts filenames in the list box component.
The declaration of the function Dir is

```
int Dir(UINT attr, LPCSTR lpszWildCard);
```

The parameter attr specifies the combination of attributes. The file
attributes are identical to the ones for the CListBox::Dir function,
shown in Table 8.3. The parameter lpszWildCard is the pointer to the
filename wild card, such as *.*, A*.CPP, or B???.H.

■ The member function FindString carries out a case-insensitive search
for an item in the list box component. The declaration of the function
FindString is

```
int FindString(int nStartAfter, LPCSTR lpszItem) const;
```

The parameter nStartAfter specifies the index of the first list box member to be searched. The parameter lpszItem is the pointer to the search string. The function searches the entire list, starting at the index nStartAfter and resuming at the beginning of the list, if necessary. The search ends when either a list member matches the search string or the entire list has been searched. Supplying the parameter nStartAfter with an argument of –1 makes the function start searching at the first list item. The FindString function yields the index of the matching list item, or the function produces the value LB_ERR if no match is found or when an error occurs.

■ The member function SelectString chooses a list box item that matches a search string. The declaration of the function SelectString is

```
int SelectString(int nStartAfter, LPCSTR lpszItem);
```

The parameters and the search mechanism of SelectString are identical to those of FindString. The difference is that SelectString selects the list box item that matches the string accessed by the parameter lpszItem.

Following are some of the the functions declared by the class CComboBox to manage the edit control component:

■ The member function GetEditSel yields the starting and ending character positions for the selected text. The declaration for the function GetEditSel is

```
DWORD GetEditSel() const;
```

The function returns a double word result. The lower word holds the starting character position (that is, the index of the first selected character). The higher word holds the ending character position (that is, the index of the first character that is not in the selected text).

■ The member function LimitText limits the number of characters that you can type in the edit box component of a combo box control. The declaration of the function LimitText is

```
BOOL LimitText(int nMaxChars);
```

The nMaxChars parameter specifies the limit of the text in the edit box. The function yields TRUE when successful and returns FALSE otherwise.

- The parameterless member function `Clear` clears the selected text.

- The parameterless member function `Copy` copies the selected text to the Clipboard.

- The member function `Cut` deletes the selected text and copies it to the Clipboard.

- The member function `Paste` copies the contents of the Clipboard to the current insertion point of the edit box.

How to Respond to Combo Box Notification Messages

The combo box control generates different types of messages, shown in Table 8.6. The table also shows the message-mapping macros that are associated with the different command and notification messages. Each type of command or notification message requires a separate member function that is declared in the control's parent window class.

II

Visual C++ Programming

Table 8.6 Combo Box Notification Messages

Message	Macro	Meaning
WM_COMMAND	ON_COMMAND	A Windows command message.
CBN_SELCHANGE	ON_CBN_SELCHANGE	A combo item is selected with a mouse click.
CBN_DBLCLK	ON_CBN_DBLCLK	A combo item is selected with a double mouse click.
CBN_SETFOCUS	ON_CBN_SETFOCUS	The combo box has gained focus.
CBN_KILLFOCUS	ON_CBN_KILLFOCUS	The combo box has lost focus.
CBN_ERRSPACE	ON_CBN_ERRSPACE	The combo box cannot allocate more dynamic memory to accommodate new list items.
CBN_EDITCHANGE	ON_CBN_EDITCHANGE	The contents of the edit box are changed.
CB__EDITUPDATE	ON_CBN_EDITUPDATE	The contents of the edit box are updated.

(continues)

Table 8.6 Continued

Message	Macro	Meaning
CBN_DROPDOWN	ON_CBN_DROPDOWN	The list box is about to be dropped down on a CBS_DROPDOWN or CBS_DROPDOWN list combo box.
CBN_CLOSEUP	ON_CBN_CLOSEUP	The list box of a combo box has closed. This message is sent with the style CBS_SIMPLE to the combo box.
CBN_SELENDCANCEL	ON_CBN_SELENDCANCEL	Notification message which indicates that the user's selection should be canceled.
CBN_SELENDOK	ON_CBN_SELENDOK	Notification message which indicates that the user has selected and then pressed Enter or clicked the down arrow.

Combo Boxes as History List Boxes

Often it makes sense to store in the list box component what you type in the edit box component (of a combo box control). In other words, your input expands the list of items. This mode of operation turns a combo box into what is commonly called a *history list.* History list boxes store the user's input in chronological order. Typically, history list boxes observe the following operations:

- History boxes usually limit the number of items in the list box component to prevent running out of memory. This memory conservation method requires that the oldest list item be purged when the number of list items attains a maximum limit.

- The combo list box is created without the style CBS_SORT to chronologically insert the items in the list box component. Newly inserted items are placed at position 0, pushing the older items further down the list. The oldest item in the list box is the one at the bottom of the list box component.

- If the edit control component has a string that doesn't have an exact match in the accompanying list box component, the edit control string is inserted in the list box at position 0.

■ If the edit control component has a string that finds an exact match in the accompanying list box component, the matching list member is moved up to position 0. This relocation involves first deleting the matching list member from its current position and then reinserting it at position 0.

The Programmer's Calculator Version 4

Now, let's examine yet another version of the Programmer's Calculator program. Figure 8.4 shows a sample session with the CTLLST4.EXE application.

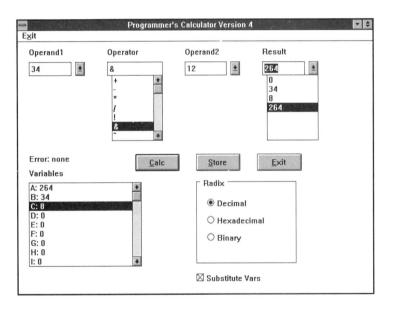

Figure 8.4
A sample session with the CTLLST4.EXE application.

The following controls are used in the fourth version of the calculator application:

■ *Operand1 drop-down combo box.* Behaves like a history list box.

■ *Operator simple combo box.* Contains the list of supported operators: +, -, /, *, !, |, &, ~, <<, and >>.

■ *Operand2 drop-down combo box.* Behaves like a history list box.

■ *Result drop-down combo box.* Behaves like a history list box.

- *Error message static text control.*

- *Variables list box.* Supports a new variable-name substitution feature. If you enter the # character in the Operand edit boxes and double-click a Variables list item, the number stored in that item replaces the # character in the Operand edit boxes.

- *Calc pushbutton control.*

- *Store pushbutton control.* Stores the current result (the number in the edit control component of the Result combo box) in the currently selected item of the Variables list box.

- *Exit pushbutton control.*

- *Radix group box.* Contains the Decimal, Hexadecimal, and Binary radio buttons. These controls select the current radix. When you select a new radix, the program updates only the edit box components of the Operand1, Operand2, and Result combo boxes. The list box components are not updated. (Therefore, avoid recalling integers with incompatible radices, from the list box components.)

- *Substitute Vars check box.*

Compile and run the CTLLST4.EXE program. Experiment with entering and executing numbers and operators. Notice that entries in the Operand and Result combo boxes are inserted into the list boxes in chronological order. The Operand combo boxes "remember" the last 35 different operands you entered. The Result combo box "remembers" the last 35 different results calculated. In a way, the Result combo box acts as a temporary transient memory. You can even select older results and then store them in the Variables list box. Type the # character in the edit box component of either Operand combo box and then double-click an item in the Variables list box. This action immediately replaces the # character with the item you double-clicked in the list box.

Listing 8.13 shows the contents of the CTLLST4.DEF definition file.

Listing 8.13 The CTLLST4.DEF Definition File

```
NAME          CtlLst4
DESCRIPTION   'An MFC Windows Application'
CODE          PRELOAD MOVEABLE DISCARDABLE
DATA          PRELOAD MOVEABLE MULTIPLE
HEAPSIZE      1024
```

Listing 8.14 shows the source code for the CTLLST4.H header file.

Listing 8.14 Source Code for the CTLLST4.H Header File

```
#define CM_EXIT    (WM_USER + 200)
#define ID_CALC_BTN  100
#define ID_STORE_BTN 101
#define ID_EXIT_BTN  102
```

Listing 8.15 shows the script for the CTLLST4.RC resource file.

Listing 8.15 Script for the CTLLST4.RC Resource File

```
#include <windows.h>
#include <afxres.h>
#include "ctllst4.h"
BUTTONS ACCELERATORS
BEGIN
  "c", ID_CALC_BTN, ALT
  "s", ID_STORE_BTN, ALT
  "e", ID_EXIT_BTN, ALT
END
EXITMENU MENU LOADONCALL MOVEABLE PURE DISCARDABLE
BEGIN
    MENUITEM "E&xit", CM_EXIT
END
```

The source code for the CTLLST4.CPP program file is provided in Listing 8.16.

Listing 8.16 Source Code for the CTLLST4.CPP Program File

```
/*
                 Programmer's Calculator version 4.0 11/8/93
                 -------------------------------------------

     Program illustrates the combo box and list box.
     These controls support history list and pick lists.
     The program uses a list box to store and recall the
     single-letter variables.
*/
#include <stdlib.h>
#include <ctype.h>
#include <stdio.h>
#include <string.h>
#include <afxwin.h>
#include "ctllst4.h"
// declare the constants that represent the sizes of the controls
const WErrMsglbl = 150;
const Wlbl = 100;
const Hlbl = 20;
const LblVertSpacing = 5;
```

(continues)

Listing 8.16 Continued

```
const LblHorzSpacing = 40;
const Wlst = 200;
const Hlst = 150;
const LstVertSpacing = 10;
const LstHorzSpacing = 40;
const Hbtn = 30;
const Wbtn = 80;
const BtnHorzSpacing = 30;
const BtnVertSpacing = 10;
const Wcmb = 100;
const Hcmb = 150;
const CmbVertSpacing = 10;
const CmbHorzSpacing = 40;
const Hgrp = 150;
const Wgrp = 180;
const GrpHorzSpacing = 30;
const GrpVertSpacing = 10;
const Hchk = 30;
const Wchk = 250;
const ChkHorzSpacing = 30;
const ChkVertSpacing = 10;
const Hrbt = 30;
const Wrbt = 120;
const RbtHorzSpacing = 30;
const RbtVertSpacing = 30;
const RbtLeftMargin = 20;
const MaxStringLen = 80;
const MAX_MEMREG = 26;
// maximum number of items in a combo box that doubles up as
// history list box
const MaxHistory = 25;
// declare the ID_XXXX constants for the edit boxes
#define ID_OPERAND1_CMB   101
#define ID_OPERATOR_CMB   102
#define ID_OPERAND2_CMB   103
#define ID_RESULT_CMB     104
#define ID_ERRMSG_TXT     105
#define ID_VARIABLE_LST   106
#define ID_AUTOSUBST_CHK 107
#define ID_RADIX_GRP      108
#define ID_DECIMAL_RBT    109
#define ID_HEX_RBT        110
#define ID_BINARY_RBT     111

// declare constants for the check box and radio button states
const BF_CHECKED = 1;
const BF_UNCHECKED = 0;
class CxButton : public CButton
{
public:
   BOOL Create(const char FAR* lpCaption, const RECT& rect,
           CWnd* pParentWnd, UINT nID, BOOL bIsDefault);

};
```

```
// declare check box class
class CCheckBox : public CButton
{
public:
   BOOL Create(const char FAR* lpCaption, const RECT& rect,
               CWnd* pParentWnd, UINT nID)
   {
       return CButton::Create(lpCaption,
                              WS_CHILD ¦ WS_VISIBLE ¦
                              WS_TABSTOP ¦ BS_AUTOCHECKBOX,
                              rect, pParentWnd, nID);
   }
   void Check()
     { SetCheck(BF_CHECKED); }

   void UnCheck()
     { SetCheck(BF_UNCHECKED); }
};
// declare radio button class
class CRadioButton : public CButton
{
public:
   BOOL Create(const char FAR* lpCaption, const RECT& rect,
               CWnd* pParentWnd, UINT nID)
   {
       return CButton::Create(lpCaption,
                              WS_CHILD ¦ WS_VISIBLE ¦
                              WS_TABSTOP ¦
                              BS_AUTORADIOBUTTON,
                              rect, pParentWnd, nID);
   }

   void Check()
     { SetCheck(BF_CHECKED); }

   void UnCheck()
     { SetCheck(BF_UNCHECKED); }
};
// declare group box class
class CGroupBox : public CButton
{
public:
   BOOL Create(const char FAR* lpCaption, const RECT& rect,
               CWnd* pParentWnd, UINT nID)
   {
       return CButton::Create(lpCaption,
                              WS_CHILD ¦ WS_VISIBLE ¦
                              WS_TABSTOP ¦ BS_GROUPBOX,
                              rect, pParentWnd, nID);
   }
};
class CComboListApp : public CWinApp
{
public:
    virtual BOOL InitInstance();
};
```

(continues)

Listing 8.16 Continued

```
// expand the functionality of CFrameWnd by deriving class CMainWnd
class CMainWnd : public CFrameWnd
{
 public:
  CMainWnd();
  ~CMainWnd();
 protected:
  // declare the pointers to the various controls
  // first, the combo box controls
  CComboBox* pOperand1Cmb;
  CComboBox* pOperatorCmb;
  CComboBox* pOperand2Cmb;
  CComboBox* pResultCmb;
  // then the list box control
  CListBox* pVariableLst;
  // then the static text controls
  CStatic* pOperand1Txt;
  CStatic* pOperatorTxt;
  CStatic* pOperand2Txt;
  CStatic* pResultTxt;
  CStatic* pErrMsgTxt;
  CStatic* pVariableTxt;
  // pushbuttons
  CxButton* pCalcBtn;
  CxButton* pStoreBtn;
  CxButton* pExitBtn;
  // group box
  CGroupBox* pRadixGrp;
  // radio buttons
  CRadioButton* pDecimalRbt;
  CRadioButton* pHexRbt;
  CRadioButton* pBinaryRbt;
  // check box
  CCheckBox* pAutoSubstChk;

  // math mode
  int nRadix;
  // math error flag
  BOOL bInError;
  // coordinates for the Error Message static text area
  CRect rectErrMsg;

  // handle the notification messages from the Operator combo box
  afx_msg void HandleOperatorCmb();
  // handle the Variables list box when it gets the focus
  afx_msg void HandleVariableLst();
  // initialize the instances of CAppWindow
  void InitAppWindow();
  // update the combo box with the text in the
  // accompanying edit box, assuming that the text
  // is not already in the box
  void updateComboBox(CComboBox* pComboBox);
```

```
  // handle clicking the left mouse button
  afx_msg void OnLButtonDown(UINT nFlags, CPoint point);
  // handle selecting the decimal mode
  afx_msg void HandleDecimalRbt();
  // handle selecting the hexadecimal mode
  afx_msg void HandleHexRbt();
  // handle selecting the binary mode
  afx_msg void HandleBinaryRbt();
  // handle the calculation
  afx_msg void CMCalc();
  // handle storing the result in a variable
  afx_msg void CMStore();
  // handle exiting the application
  afx_msg void OnExit();
  // handle creating the controls
  afx_msg int OnCreate(LPCREATESTRUCT lpCS);
  // handle closing the window
  afx_msg void OnClose();

  // enable a pushbutton control
  virtual void EnableButton(CxButton* pBtn)
    { pBtn->EnableWindow( TRUE); }
  // disable a pushbutton control
  virtual void DisableButton(CxButton* pBtn)
    { pBtn->EnableWindow(FALSE); }

  // return a reference to member r based on individual
  // coordinates and dimensions
  void makerect(int X, int Y, int W, int H, CRect& r)
   { r.SetRect(X, Y, X + W, Y + H); }
  // obtain a number of a Variable edit box line
  long getVar(int lineNum);
  // store a number in the selected text of
  // the Variable edit box line
  void putVar(long x);

  // set contents of edit controls to integers in various bases
  void setDecimal(CComboBox* pEdit);
  void setHexaDecimal(CComboBox* pEdit);
  void setBinary(CComboBox* pEdit);
  // declare message map macro
  DECLARE_MESSAGE_MAP();
};
BOOL CxButton::Create(const char FAR* lpCaption, const RECT& rect,
           CWnd* pParentWnd, UINT nID, BOOL bIsDefault)
{
  DWORD dwBtnStyle = (bIsDefault == TRUE) ?
            BS_DEFPUSHBUTTON : BS_PUSHBUTTON;
    return CButton::Create(lpCaption,
            WS_CHILD ¦ WS_VISIBLE ¦
            WS_TABSTOP ¦ dwBtnStyle,
            rect, pParentWnd, nID);
}
CMainWnd::CMainWnd()
{
  // load the main accelerator table to handle
```

Listing 8.16 Continued

```
  // keystroke input
  LoadAccelTable("BUTTONS");
  // create the window
  Create(NULL,
    "Programmer's Calculator Version 4",
    WS_OVERLAPPEDWINDOW,
    rectDefault, NULL, "EXITMENU");

  // initialize application
  InitAppWindow();
}

int CMainWnd::OnCreate(LPCREATESTRUCT lpCS)
{
  int x0 = 20;
  int y0 = 10;
  int x = x0, y = y0;
  int x1, y1;                       •
  DWORD dwStaticStyle = WS_CHILD | WS_VISIBLE | SS_LEFT;
  DWORD dwEditStyle = WS_CHILD | WS_VISIBLE | WS_BORDER |
               ES_LEFT | ES_AUTOHSCROLL | ES_UPPERCASE;
  DWORD dwComboStyle = WS_CHILD | WS_VISIBLE | WS_VSCROLL;
  DWORD dwListStyle = WS_CHILD | WS_VISIBLE | WS_VSCROLL |
                      WS_HSCROLL | LBS_STANDARD;
  CRect r;
  // create the first set of labels for the edit boxes
  makerect(x, y, Wlbl, Hlbl, r);
  pOperand1Txt = new CStatic();
  pOperand1Txt->Create("Operand1", dwStaticStyle, r, this);
  x += Wlbl + LblHorzSpacing;
  makerect(x, y, Wlbl, Hlbl, r);
  pOperatorTxt = new CStatic();
  pOperatorTxt->Create("Operator", dwStaticStyle, r, this);
  x += Wlbl + LblHorzSpacing;
  makerect(x, y, Wlbl, Hlbl, r);
  pOperand2Txt = new CStatic();
  pOperand2Txt->Create("Operand2", dwStaticStyle, r, this);
  x += Wlbl + LblHorzSpacing;
  makerect(x, y, Wlbl, Hlbl, r);
  pResultTxt = new CStatic();
  pResultTxt->Create("Result", dwStaticStyle, r, this);
  // create the Operand1, Operator, Operand2, and Result
  // combo list boxes
  x = x0;
  y += Hlbl + LblVertSpacing;
  makerect(x, y, Wcmb, Hcmb, r);
  pOperand1Cmb = new CComboBox();
  pOperand1Cmb->Create(dwComboStyle | CBS_DROPDOWN, r,
                       this, ID_OPERAND1_CMB);
  // create the Operator combo box
  x += Wcmb + CmbHorzSpacing;
  makerect(x, y, Wcmb, Hcmb, r);
  pOperatorCmb = new CComboBox();
  pOperatorCmb->Create(dwComboStyle | CBS_SIMPLE, r,
                       this, ID_OPERATOR_CMB);
```

```
x += Wcmb + CmbHorzSpacing;
makerect(x, y, Wcmb, Hcmb, r);
pOperand2Cmb = new CComboBox();
pOperand2Cmb->Create(dwComboStyle | CBS_DROPDOWN, r,
                     this, ID_OPERAND2_CMB);
x += Wcmb + CmbHorzSpacing;
makerect(x, y, Wcmb, Hcmb, r);
pResultCmb = new CComboBox();
pResultCmb->Create(dwComboStyle | CBS_DROPDOWN, r,
                   this, ID_RESULT_CMB);
// create the static text and edit box for the error message
x = x0;
y += Hcmb + CmbVertSpacing;
// store coordinates for the button controls
x1 = x + WErrMsglbl + LblHorzSpacing;
y1 = y;
makerect(x, y, WErrMsglbl, Hlbl, r);
pErrMsgTxt = new CStatic();
pErrMsgTxt->Create("Error: none", dwStaticStyle, r, this);
// create the static text and list box for the single-letter
// variable selection
y += Hlbl + LblVertSpacing;
makerect(x, y, Wlbl, Hlbl, r);
pVariableTxt = new CStatic();
pVariableTxt->Create("Variables", dwStaticStyle, r, this);
y += Hlbl + LblVertSpacing;
makerect(x, y, Wlst, Hlst, r);
pVariableLst = new CListBox();
pVariableLst->Create(dwListStyle, r, this, ID_VARIABLE_LST);
// create the Calc pushbutton
x = x1;
y = y1;
makerect(x, y, Wbtn, Hbtn, r);
pCalcBtn = new CxButton();
pCalcBtn->Create("&Calc", r, this, ID_CALC_BTN, TRUE);
// create the Store Btn
x += Wbtn + BtnHorzSpacing;
makerect(x, y, Wbtn, Hbtn, r);
pStoreBtn = new CxButton();
pStoreBtn->Create("&Store", r, this, ID_STORE_BTN, FALSE);
// Create the Exit Btn
x += Wbtn + BtnHorzSpacing;
makerect(x, y, Wbtn, Hbtn, r);
pExitBtn = new CxButton();
pExitBtn->Create("&Exit", r, this, ID_EXIT_BTN, FALSE);
// create the group box
x = x1 + Wbtn + BtnHorzSpacing;
y = y1 + Hbtn + BtnVertSpacing;
makerect(x, y, Wgrp, Hgrp, r);
pRadixGrp = new CGroupBox();
pRadixGrp->Create(" Radix ", r, this, ID_RADIX_GRP);
y1 = y;
x1 = x;

// create the Decimal radio button
y += RbtVertSpacing;
```

(continues)

Listing 8.16 Continued

```
    makerect(RbtLeftMargin + x, y, Wrbt, Hrbt, r);
    pDecimalRbt = new CRadioButton();
    pDecimalRbt->Create("Decimal", r, this, ID_DECIMAL_RBT);

    // create the Hexadecimal radio button
    y += RbtVertSpacing;
    makerect(RbtLeftMargin + x, y, Wrbt, Hrbt, r);
    pHexRbt = new CRadioButton();
    pHexRbt->Create("Hexadecimal", r, this, ID_HEX_RBT);

    // create the Binary radio button
    y += RbtVertSpacing;
    makerect(RbtLeftMargin + x, y, Wrbt, Hrbt, r);
    pBinaryRbt = new CRadioButton();
    pBinaryRbt->Create("Binary", r, this, ID_BINARY_RBT);
    // create auto substitute check box
    x = x1;
    y = y1 + Hgrp + GrpVertSpacing;
    makerect(x, y, Wrbt, Hrbt, r);
    pAutoSubstChk = new CCheckBox();
    pAutoSubstChk->Create("Substitute Vars", r,
                          this, ID_AUTOSUBST_CHK);
    // check the decimal radix
    pDecimalRbt->SetCheck(BF_CHECKED);
    return CFrameWnd::OnCreate(lpCS);
}
CMainWnd::~CMainWnd()
{
    // delete the controls
    delete pOperand1Cmb;
    delete pOperatorCmb;
    delete pOperand2Cmb;
    delete pResultCmb;
    delete pVariableLst;
    delete pOperand1Txt;
    delete pOperatorTxt;
    delete pOperand2Txt;
    delete pResultTxt;
    delete pErrMsgTxt;
    delete pVariableTxt;
    delete pCalcBtn;
    delete pStoreBtn;
    delete pExitBtn;
    delete pDecimalRbt;
    delete pHexRbt;
    delete pBinaryRbt;
    delete pRadixGrp;
    delete pAutoSubstChk;
}
void CMainWnd::InitAppWindow()
{
    char s[MaxStringLen];
    // disable the Store button
    DisableButton(pStoreBtn);
```

```
  // build the initial contents of the Variable list box
  for (char c = 'Z'; c >= 'A'; c--) {
    sprintf(s, "%c: 0", c);
    pVariableLst->AddString(s);
  }
  // select the first item
  pVariableLst->SetCurSel(0);
  // add the operators in the Operator combo box
  pOperatorCmb->AddString("+");
  pOperatorCmb->AddString("-");
  pOperatorCmb->AddString("*");
  pOperatorCmb->AddString("/");
  pOperatorCmb->AddString("!");
  pOperatorCmb->AddString("&");
  pOperatorCmb->AddString("~");
  pOperatorCmb->AddString("<<");
  pOperatorCmb->AddString(">>");

  // clear the bInError flag
  bInError = FALSE;
  // set the default math mode
  nRadix = 10;
}
void CMainWnd::HandleOperatorCmb()
{
  char s[MaxStringLen+1];
  // get the text in the Operator combo box edit area
  pOperatorCmb->GetWindowText(s, MaxStringLen);
  // use it to search for a matching list item
  pOperatorCmb->SelectString(-1, s);
}

void CMainWnd::OnLButtonDown(UINT nFlags, CPoint point)
{
  // did you click the mouse over the Error Message static text?
  if (rectErrMsg.PtInRect(point)) {
      pErrMsgTxt->SetWindowText("Error: none");
      EnableButton(pStoreBtn);
  }
}
void CMainWnd::HandleDecimalRbt()
{
  setDecimal(pOperand1Cmb);
  setDecimal(pOperand2Cmb);
  setDecimal(pResultCmb);
  nRadix = 10;
}
  // handle selecting the hexadecimal mode
void CMainWnd::HandleHexRbt()
{
  setHexaDecimal(pOperand1Cmb);
  setHexaDecimal(pOperand2Cmb);
  setHexaDecimal(pResultCmb);
  nRadix = 16;
}
```

II

Visual C++ Programming

(continues)

Listing 8.16 Continued

```
    // handle selecting the binary mode
void CMainWnd::HandleBinaryRbt()
{
  setBinary(pOperand1Cmb);
  setBinary(pOperand2Cmb);
  setBinary(pResultCmb);
  nRadix = 2;
}
void CMainWnd::CMCalc()
{
  long x, y, z;
  char opStr[MaxStringLen+1];
  char s[MaxStringLen+1];
  char* ss;
  // obtain the string in the Operand1 edit box
  pOperand1Cmb->GetWindowText(s, MaxStringLen);
  // does the pOperand1Cmb contain the name
  // of a single-letter variable which begins with @?
  if (s[0] == '@') {
    // obtain value from the Variable edit control
    x = getVar(s[1] - 'A');
    if (pAutoSubstChk->GetCheck() == BF_CHECKED) {
      // substitute variable name with its value
      _ltoa(x, s, nRadix);
      pOperand1Cmb->SetWindowText(s);
    }
  }
  else
    // convert the string in the edit box
    x = strtol(s, &ss, nRadix);
  // obtain the string in the Operand2 edit box
  pOperand2Cmb->GetWindowText(s, MaxStringLen);
  // does the pOperand2Cmb contain the name
  // of a single-letter variable which begins with @?
  if (s[0] == '@') {
    // obtain value from the Variable edit control
    y = getVar(s[1] - 'A');
    if (pAutoSubstChk->GetCheck() == BF_CHECKED) {
      // substitute variable name with its value
      _ltoa(y, s, nRadix);
      pOperand2Cmb->SetWindowText(s);
    }
  }
  else
    // convert the string in the edit box
    y = strtol(s, &ss, nRadix);
  // obtain the string in the Operator edit box
  pOperatorCmb->GetWindowText(opStr, MaxStringLen);
  // clear the error message box
  pErrMsgTxt->SetWindowText("Error: none");
  bInError = FALSE;
  // determine the requested operation
  if (opStr[0] == '+')
    z = x + y;
```

```
    else if (opStr[0] == '-')
      z = x - y;
    else if (opStr[0] == '*') {
      if (x == 0 || y < (2147483647L / x))
        z = x * y;
      else {
        z = 0;
        bInError = TRUE;
        pErrMsgTxt->SetWindowText("Error: overflow error");
      }
    }
    else if (opStr[0] == '/') {
      if (y != 0)
        z = x / y;
      else {
        z = 0;
        bInError = TRUE;
        pErrMsgTxt->SetWindowText("Error: Division-by-zero error");
      }
    }
    else if (opStr[0] == '|')
      z = x | y;
    else if (opStr[0] == '&')
      z = x & y;
    else if (opStr[0] == '~')
      z = ~x;
    else if (strcmp(opStr, "<<") == 0)
      z = x << y;
    else if (strcmp(opStr, ">>") == 0)
      z = x >> y;
    else {
      bInError = TRUE;
      pErrMsgTxt->SetWindowText("Error: Invalid operator");
    }
    // display the result if no error has occurred
    if (!bInError) {
      _ltoa(z, s, nRadix);
      pResultCmb->SetWindowText(s);
      // update the Result comb box
      updateComboBox(pResultCmb);
      EnableButton(pStoreBtn);
    }
    else
      DisableButton(pStoreBtn);
    // update the operand combo boxes
    updateComboBox(pOperand1Cmb);
    updateComboBox(pOperand2Cmb);
}
void CMainWnd::CMStore()
{
  char s[MaxStringLen+1];
  char* ss;
  long z;
  // get the string in the Result edit box
  pResultCmb->GetWindowText(s, MaxStringLen);
  // store the result in the selected text of
```

Listing 8.16 Continued

```
      // the Variable edit box
      z = strtol(s, &ss, nRadix);
      putVar(z);
    }
    void CMainWnd::HandleVariableLst()
    {
      char s[MaxStringLen+1];
      char operandText[MaxStringLen];
      pVariableLst->GetText(pVariableLst->GetCurSel(), s);
      strcpy(s, (s+3));
      // get the text in the Operand1 combo box
      pOperand1Cmb->GetWindowText(operandText, MaxStringLen);
      // is the first character in the Operand1 combo box a #?
      if (operandText[0] == '#')
        pOperand1Cmb->SetWindowText(s);
      // get the text in the Operand2 edit box
      pOperand2Cmb->GetWindowText(operandText, MaxStringLen);
      // is the first character in the Operand2 combo box a #?
      if (operandText[0] == '#')
        pOperand2Cmb->SetWindowText(s);
    }
    long CMainWnd::getVar(int lineNum)
    {
      char s[MaxStringLen+1];
      if (lineNum >= pVariableLst->GetCount())
        return 0;
      pVariableLst->GetText(lineNum, s);
      strcpy(s, (s+3));
      // return the number stored in the target line
      return atol(s);
    }
    void CMainWnd::putVar(long x)
    {
      char s[MaxStringLen+1];
      char c;
      int selectIndex = pVariableLst->GetCurSel();
      pVariableLst->DeleteString(selectIndex);
      strcpy(s, "A:");
      c = selectIndex + 'A';
      // locate the character position of the cursor
      sprintf(s, "%c: %ld", c, x);
      // insert it
      pVariableLst->InsertString(selectIndex, s);
      pVariableLst->SetCurSel(selectIndex);
    }
    void CMainWnd::updateComboBox(CComboBox* pComboBox)
    {
      char s[MaxStringLen+1];
      int i;
      pComboBox->GetWindowText(s, MaxStringLen);
      // is string s in the combo list
      i = pComboBox->FindString(-1, s);
      if (i == 0) return;
      else if (i < 0) {
        pComboBox->InsertString(0, s);
```

```
    // delete extra history list members?
    while (pComboBox->GetCount() >= MaxHistory)
      pComboBox->DeleteString(pComboBox->GetCount()-1);
  }
  else {
    // delete the current selection
    pComboBox->DeleteString(i);
    // insert the string s at the first position
    pComboBox->InsertString(0, s);
    // select the first combo box item
    pComboBox->SetCurSel(0);
  }
}
void CMainWnd::OnExit()
{
  SendMessage(WM_CLOSE);
}
void CMainWnd::OnClose()
{
  if (MessageBox("Want to close this application",
                 "Query", MB_YESNO | MB_ICONQUESTION) == IDYES)
    DestroyWindow();
}

void CMainWnd::setDecimal(CComboBox* pEdit)
{
  char s[MaxStringLen+1];
  char* ss;
  long n;
  pEdit->GetWindowText(s, MaxStringLen);
  n = strtol(s, &ss, nRadix);
  _ltoa(n, s, 10);
  pEdit->SetWindowText(s);
}
void CMainWnd::setHexaDecimal(CComboBox* pEdit)
{
  char s[MaxStringLen+1];
  char *ss;
  long n;
  pEdit->GetWindowText(s, MaxStringLen);
  n = strtol(s, &ss, nRadix);
  _ltoa(n, s, 16);
  pEdit->SetWindowText(s);
}
void CMainWnd::setBinary(CComboBox* pEdit)
{
  char s[MaxStringLen+1];
  char* ss;
  long n;
  pEdit->GetWindowText(s, MaxStringLen);
  n = strtol(s, &ss, nRadix);
  _ltoa(n, s, 2);
  pEdit->SetWindowText(s);
}
BEGIN_MESSAGE_MAP(CMainWnd, CFrameWnd)
    ON_CBN_EDITUPDATE(ID_OPERATOR_CMB, HandleOperatorCmb)
```

II

Visual C++ Programming

(continues)

Listing 8.16 Continued

```
      ON_LBN_DBLCLK(ID_VARIABLE_LST, HandleVariableLst)
      ON_WM_LBUTTONDOWN()
      ON_COMMAND(ID_CALC_BTN, CMCalc)
      ON_COMMAND(ID_STORE_BTN, CMStore)
      ON_COMMAND(ID_EXIT_BTN, OnExit)
      ON_COMMAND(CM_EXIT, OnExit)
      ON_BN_CLICKED(ID_DECIMAL_RBT, HandleDecimalRbt)
      ON_BN_CLICKED(ID_HEX_RBT, HandleHexRbt)
      ON_BN_CLICKED(ID_BINARY_RBT, HandleBinaryRbt)
      ON_WM_CREATE()
      ON_WM_CLOSE()
END_MESSAGE_MAP()
// Construct the CComboListApp's m_pMainWnd data member
BOOL CComboListApp::InitInstance()
{
  m_pMainWnd = new CMainWnd();
  m_pMainWnd->ShowWindow(m_nCmdShow);
  m_pMainWnd->UpdateWindow();
  return TRUE;
}
// application's constructor initializes and runs the app
CComboListApp WindowApp;
```

The Code for the COCA Application

The source code for the CTLLST4.CPP program, just shown in Listing 8.16, declares three sets of constants. The first set specifies the dimensions and spacing for the various application controls. The second set of constants declares the maximum string size, maximum number of single-letter variables, and maximum number of items to maintain in the list box components of the combo box. The third set of constants establishes the ID numbers for the various controls.

The calculator program declares the application class, CComboListApp, the window class, CMainWnd, and the button class, CxButton. The CMainWnd class declares two sets of data members. The first set represents pointers to the various controls used in the application, and the second set contains the bInError and nRadix data members.

The CMainWnd class declares a constructor, a destructor, and a collection of member functions to handle the various messages. The CMainWnd constructor performs the following tasks:

■ Loads the BUTTONS accelerator keys resource.

■ Invokes the `Create` function to create the application window. The window uses the `EXITMENU` resource menu.

■ Calls the `InitAppWindow` function to initialize the application.

The member function `OnCreate` creates the instances for the various controls. The Operand and Result combo boxes are created with the `CBS_DROPDOWN` style. These same combo boxes avoid including the `CBS_SORT` style to enable them to work as history list boxes. The Operator combo box is created with the `CBS_SIMPLE` style and maintains the ordered items in the accompanying list box. The Variables list box is created using the default styles.

The member function `InitAppWindow` initializes the window instance by performing the following tasks:

■ Disabling the Store pushbutton control.

■ Building the Variables list box. This task involves a `for` loop that inserts the single-letter variables in the list box. This insertion involves sending the C++ message `AddString` to the Variables list box.

■ Selecting the first item in the Variables list box. This task involves sending the C++ message `SetCurSel` to the Variables list box.

■ Adding the supported operators in the list box component of the Operator combo box. This task involves sending the C++ message `AddString` to the Operator combo box.

■ Assigning FALSE to the member `bInError`.

■ Assigning the initial radix value, 10, to the member `nRadix`.

The `HandleOperatorCmb` member function responds to the `CBN_EDITUPDATE` notification message sent by the Operator combo box. The function carries out the following tasks:

■ Obtains the text from the edit box component by sending the C++ message `GetText` to the Operator combo box.

■ Sends the C++ message `SelectString` to the combo box in order to search for a list box member that matches the retrieved string. If the message `SelectString` finds a match, the matching item appears as selected text in the edit control area of the combo box.

The member function HandleCalcBtn responds to the notification message of the Calc button and performs the requested calculation. The function performs these tasks:

- Obtains the first operand from the edit box component of the Operand1 combo box. The control may contain the name of a single-letter variable (A to Z) or an integer. The function uses the function GetWindowText to copy the edit control text to the local variable s. The function then examines the first character in the variable s. If that character is the character @, the first operand is a single-letter variable. The function performs the following subtasks:

  - Calls the member function getVar to acquire the value associated with the single-letter variable. The name of the variable is located in the second character of the variable s. This task assigns the contents of the single-letter variable to the local variable x.

  - Determines if the Substitute Vars check box is checked. This task involves sending the C++ message GetCheck to the check box control. The function compares the result of the message with the constant BF_CHECKED. If the two values match, the function converts the integer in the variable x to a string image using the radix value in the member nRadix. This conversion involves the function _ltoa. The function then updates the edit box component of the Operand1 combo box with the contents of the single-letter variable. This task involves sending the C++ message SetWindowText to the edit box component of Operand1.

- If the first character in the variable s is not the character @, the function uses the function strtol to convert the contents of the variable s into an integer. The function CMCalc assigns that integer to the variable x.

- Obtains the second operand in a manner identical to the first one. The function stores the second operand in the variable y.

- Copies the text in the edit box component of the Operator combo box into the local variable opStr.

- Clears the error message text box and sets the bInError data member to FALSE.

- Executes the requested operation by using a series of `if` and `if-else` statements. The operators supported are +, -, *, /, |, &, ~, <<, and >>. If the function detects an error, it sets the `bInError` data member to TRUE and displays a message in the error message static text control.

- Displays the result of the operation in the edit box of the Result combo box if the `bInError` data member is FALSE. The function first converts the result from an integer to a string. This step also uses the function `_ltoa` to create a string image of the integer using the current radix. Next, the function writes to the edit control component of the Result combo box by sending the C++ message `SetWindowText` to that control. If the member `bInError` contains TRUE, the `HandleCalcBtn` function causes the Store pushbutton to be enabled, which in turn requires the `EnableButton` function. Otherwise, the function disables the Store pushbutton, which involves the function `DisableButton`.

The member function `CMStore` responds to the notification message sent by the Store pushbutton. The function stores the number found in the edit box of the Result combo box in the currently selected Variables list box item. The function performs the following tasks:

- Retrieves the string in the edit box of the Result combo box by sending the C++ message `GetWindowText`. The message copies the obtained string to the local variable `result`.

- Stores the obtained string in the Variables list box by calling the member function `putVar` with an argument of `atof(result)`.

The member function `HandleVariablesLst` responds to the `LBN_DBLCLK` notification messages sent by the Variables list box when you double-click a list item. The purpose of double-clicking is to replace the character in either Operand edit box with the number in the double-clicked item. The function carries out the following tasks:

- Copies the characters of the new selection (chosen by the double-click action) to the local string variable s. This task involves sending the C++ messages `GetText` and `GetCurSel` to the Variables list box.

- Deletes the first three characters of the variable s.

- Retrieves a copy of the text in the edit control of the Operand1 combo box and stores it in the local variable `operandText`.

- If the first character in the string `operandText` is the # character, the function sets the edit control of the Operand1 combo box to the string variable `s`. This task involves sending the C++ message `SetWindowText` to the Operand1 combo box.

- Repeats the last two tasks with the Operand2 combo box.

The member function `getVar` obtains the value from the Variables list box by specifying the item number. The function performs the following tasks:

- Returns a 0 value if the index of the item exceeds the position of the last item in the Variables list box. This task involves sending the C++ message `GetCount` to the Variables list box. The `GetCount` message returns the number of items in the list box.

- Obtains the list item at the specified item position by sending the C++ message `GetText` to the Variables list box.

- Deletes the first three characters of the list item obtained in the preceding step.

- Returns the expression `atol(s)` that represented the long integer stored in the selected list box item.

The member function `putVar` stores the value of the Result edit box in the selected Variables list item. The function carries out the following tasks:

- Retrieves the index of the current selection by sending the C++ message `GetCurSel` to the Variables list box. The function stores the retrieved index in the local variable `selectIndex`.

- Deletes the current selection by sending the C++ message `DeleteString` to the Variables list box. The argument for this message is the local variable `selectIndex`.

- Creates the string image of the new list item using the `sprintf` function.

- Inserts the new list item at the `selectIndex` position. This particular fashion of inserting an item in a sorted list box with the function `InsertString` does not corrupt the order of the item.

- Selects the newly inserted item. The net effect is that the same item remains selected but now has a different value associated with it.

The member function updateComboBox enables the operands and result combo boxes to work as history list boxes. The function performs the following tasks:

■ Obtains the text in the edit box component of the manipulated combo box (accessed using the parameter pComboBox). This task involves sending the C++ message GetWindowText to the manipulated combo box. The message stores the obtained string in the local string variable s.

■ Searches for the string s in the list box component of the manipulated combo box. This task involves sending the C++ message FindString to the manipulated combo box. The arguments for this message are –1 and the variable s. These arguments force the search to start at index 0. The function assigns the result of the message to the local variable i.

■ Exits if the variable contains 0; the edit box already contains the most recent item in the list box component.

■ If variable i contains a negative number, the function adds the string s to the list box component. This task involves sending the C++ message InsertString to the manipulated combo box. The arguments for this message are 0 and the variable s. Following the insertion, the function deletes any extra history list members if the number of items in the list box component exceeds the allowed limit. This trimming step involves a while loop. The statement in this loop sends the C++ message DeleteString to the manipulated combo box.

■ If the variable i contains a positive value, the function changes the visual location of the matching item, moving it to the top of the list box component. The function performs the following subtasks:

• Deletes the matching item in the list box component of the manipulated combo box. This subtask involves sending the C++ message DeleteString to the manipulated combo box. The argument for this message is the variable i.

• Inserts the variable s in the list box component. This subtask involves sending the C++ message InsertString to the list box component. The arguments for this message are 0 and the variable s. This message insets the string in the variable s at the top of the list.

- Selects the newly inserted string. This subtack involves sending the C++ message `SetCurSel` to the manipulated combo box.

The remaining member functions are similar to those included in the earlier versions of the program.

Summary

This chapter presented the scroll bar, list box, and combo box controls. These controls share the common factor of being input objects. You learned about the following topics:

- How you can use the scroll bar control to quickly select from a wide range of integers.

- How the list box control provides you with a list of items from which you can select.

- How you can use the multiple-selection list box to select multiple items for collective processing.

- How to use the various combo box control types: simple, drop-down, and drop-down list. In addition, you learned how to make a history list box from a drop-down combo box.

Chapter 9

Working with Dialog Boxes

Dialog boxes play a vital role in Windows applications because you can use them to obtain and supply information. In this chapter, I present the modal and modeless dialog boxes, which were briefly discussed in Chapter 2. Modal dialog boxes usually exchange critical information and therefore require that you close them before you can continue with the application. To support this exclusivity feature, modal dialog boxes disable their parent windows while they have the focus. By comparison, modeless dialog boxes do not dictate that you first close them before you continue with the application.

This chapter discusses the following topics:

- Creating instances of the class CDialog

- Executing a modal dialog box

- Creating a dialog box as a window

- Transferring control data both with and without the function DoDataExchange

Constructing Dialog Boxes

The MFC library offers the class CDialog, a descendant of class CWnd, to represent both modal and modeless dialog boxes. The CDialog class contains overloaded constructors (for both modal and modeless dialog boxes) and a set of member functions. The MFC library declares as a protected member the `CDialog` constructor for modeless dialog boxes. This kind of declaration dictates that you derive your own modeless dialog box classes from `CDialog`. Your custom dialog classes may declare one or both of the following kinds of constructors:

- A public constructor with an adequate set of parameters. This kind of constructor uses its parameters to call the inherited member function `CDialog::Create`.

- A public constructor and a `Create` member function. This approach builds dialog boxes in two steps: the first step calls the class constructor, and the second step calls the member function `Create`.

The class `CDialog` declares the following overloaded constructors:

```
CDialog();
CDialog(LPCSTR lpszTemplateName, CWnd* pParentWnd = NULL);
CDialog(UINT nIDTemplate, CWnd* pParentWnd = NULL);
```

The parameters `lpszTemplateName` and `nIDTemplate` are the dialog box resource template name and ID, respectively. The parameter `pParentWnd` is the pointer to the parent window. You can use the NULL default argument when the dialog box instance is also the main application window.

The class also declares the following overloaded versions of the member function `Create`:

```
BOOL Create(LPCSTR lpszTemplateName, CWnd* pParentWnd = NULL);
BOOL Create(UINT nIDTemplate, CWnd* pParentWnd = NULL);
```

The parameters of these overloaded functions are the same as the second and third overloaded `CDialog` constructors.

> **Note**
>
> The declarations of the `CDialog` contructors and the function `Create` indicate that dialog boxes rely extensively on dialog box resources. You may ask "Why this dependence?" The answer lies in the fact that defining dialog boxes and their controls using resources has the advantage of defining the location, dimensions, style, and caption of the various controls beyond the application's source code. This scheme empowers you to modify the resource file, recompile it, and then bind it in the .EXE application file without recompiling the source file itself. This advantage translates into your ability to create varying resource versions with different colors, styles, and even languages without resorting to multiple copies of the application code.

Executing Modal Dialog Boxes

Executing modal dialog boxes involves the following steps:

1. Create a dialog box using your custom dialog box class constructor.

2. Send the C++ message `DoModal` (which is a member function declared in the class `CDialog`) to the dialog box object to display the dialog box. Every dialog box contains the OK and Cancel pushbuttons—the OK button is the default button. Windows assigns the predefined IDs of `IDOK` and `IDCANCEL` to the OK and Cancel buttons, respectively.

   In addition, Windows permits you to assign different captions for the OK and Cancel pushbutton controls. For example, you can replace the captions *OK* and *Cancel* with *Yes* and *No*. In all cases, the ID of these buttons must still be `IDOK` and `IDCANCEL`. A reason to obey this rule is that you can take advantage of the automatic response to `IDOK` and `IDCANCEL` offered by the member functions `OnOK` and `OnCancel` defined in your dialog box class. Clicking the OK pushbutton (which is equivalent to pressing the Enter key when it is the default button) usually signals your acceptance of the current data in the dialog box. In contrast, clicking the Cancel button indicates that you are dissatisfied with the current data (either in its default state or after the changes you made). The declaration of the function `DoModal` is

   ```
   int DoModal();
   ```

   The function yields an integer that reflects the outcome of clicking the OK or Cancel pushbutton. As such, the function returns the value `IDOK` or `IDCANCEL`.

3. Compare the result of the function `DoModal` with the value `IDOK` (or even the value `IDCANCEL`). This comparison determines the next statements to execute. Typically, when the function `DoModal` returns `IDOK`, the program executes statements that access the dialog box data.

The class `CDialog` offers the member functions `OnInitDialog`, `OnOK`, and `OnCancel` to support the execution of the modal dialog boxes. The class `CDialog` declares these parameterless functions as virtual so that you override them with functions that are void of any parameters.

The *OnInitDialog* Function

The member function `OnInitDialog` initializes the dialog box and its controls. The declaration of the function `OnInitDialog` is

```
virtual BOOL OnInitDialog();
```

The function yields a Boolean result to indicate whether or not the dialog box was successfully initialized. Typically, the function `OnInitDialog` has the role of initializing the controls of the dialog box. This initialization usually involves copying data from buffers or data members to the dialog box controls.

The *OnOk* Function

The member function `OnOK` responds to clicking the OK pushbutton. The declaration of the function `OnOK` is

```
virtual void OnOK();
```

The function `OnOK` copies data from the dialog box controls to data members or buffers. The function `OnOk` employs the member function `EndDialog` to supply the function `DoModal` with its return value. Typically, the last statement in the member function `OnOK` is the statement `EndDialog(IDOK)`. The statement `EndDialog(IDOK)` makes the function `DoModal` return the value `IDOK`.

The *OnCancel* Function

The member function `OnCancel` responds to clicking the Cancel pushbutton. The declaration of the function `OnCancel` is

```
virtual void OnCancel();
```

The function `OnCancel` cleans up before the dialog box is closed. This cleanup operation might include closing data files or de-allocating special dynamic data. Typically, the last statement in the member function `OnCancel` is `EndDialog(IDCANCEL)`. The statement makes the function `DoModal` return the value `IDCANCEL`.

Using Simple Modal Dialog Boxes

In this section, the MFC DIALOG1.EXE program is presented, which provides a pair of simple dialog boxes defined in a resource file. These dialog boxes represent an alternate form that usually is found in separate resource files. The first dialog box uses ordinary, formal wording to request that you confirm that you are closing the application. The second dialog box uses more informal wording to accomplish the same purpose. This simple application consists of an empty window with two menu items: Exit and Time. When you click the Exit menu (or press Alt+X) a dialog box appears that asks whether you want to exit the application. The dialog box has a title, a message, and two buttons (I deliberately made it look like the dialog boxes created with the CWnd::MessageBox function).

The program switches between the two versions of the dialog box. When you first click the Exit menu, you see the formal version—with OK and Cancel pushbuttons—shown in Figure 9.1.

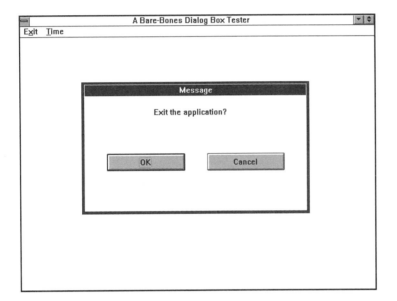

Figure 9.1
The DIALOG1.EXE application showing pushbuttons with formal wording.

If you click the Cancel button and then click the Exit menu again, the informal version of the dialog box appears—with Cool! and Bummer! pushbuttons—shown in Figure 9.2. Each time you choose the Cancel or Bummer! button and then click the Exit menu, you switch between the two versions of the dialog box. To exit the application, click the OK or Cool! pushbutton, depending on the current version of the dialog box. If you click the Time menu, the program displays a message dialog box that shows the current date and time.

Figure 9.2

The DIALOG1.EXE application showing pushbuttons with informal wording.

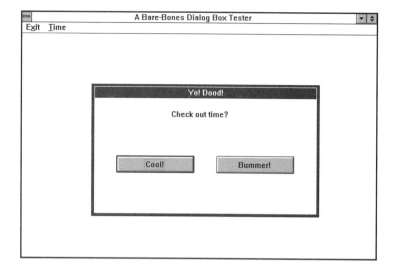

Listing 9.1 shows the contents of the DIALOG1.DEF definition file.

Listing 9.1 The DIALOG1.DEF Definition File

```
NAME            Dialog1
DESCRIPTION     'An MFC Windows Application'
CODE            PRELOAD MOVEABLE DISCARDABLE
DATA            PRELOAD MOVEABLE MULTIPLE
HEAPSIZE        1024
```

Listing 9.2 contains the source code for the DIALOG1.H header file.

Listing 9.2 Source Code for the DIALOG1.H Header File

```
#define CM_EXIT (WM_USER + 100)
#define CM_TIME (WM_USER + 101)
```

The script for the DIALOG1.RC resource file is provided in Listing 9.3.

Listing 9.3 Script for the DIALOG1.RC Resource File

```
#include <windows.h>
#include <afxres.h>
#include "dialog1.h"
EXITMENU MENU LOADONCALL MOVEABLE PURE DISCARDABLE
BEGIN
    MENUITEM "E&xit", CM_EXIT
    MENUITEM "&Time", CM_TIME
END
FORMAL DIALOG DISCARDABLE LOADONCALL PURE MOVEABLE 30, 50, 200, 100
STYLE WS_POPUP ¦ DS_MODALFRAME
```

```
CAPTION "Message"
BEGIN
  CTEXT "Exit the application?", 1, 10, 10, 170, 15
  CONTROL "OK", IDOK, "BUTTON", WS_CHILD | WS_VISIBLE |
    WS_TABSTOP | BS_DEFPUSHBUTTON, 20, 50, 70, 15
  CONTROL "Cancel", IDCANCEL, "BUTTON", WS_CHILD | WS_VISIBLE |
    WS_TABSTOP | BS_PUSHBUTTON, 110, 50, 70, 15
END
INFORMAL DIALOG DISCARDABLE LOADONCALL PURE MOVEABLE 30, 50, 200, 100
STYLE WS_POPUP | DS_MODALFRAME
CAPTION "A Message From Our Sponsor"
BEGIN
  CTEXT "Time for your disappearing act?", 1, 10, 10, 170, 15
  CONTROL "For sure!", IDOK, "BUTTON", WS_CHILD | WS_VISIBLE |
    WS_TABSTOP | BS_DEFPUSHBUTTON, 20, 50, 70, 15
  CONTROL "No way!", IDCANCEL, "BUTTON", WS_CHILD | WS_VISIBLE |
    WS_TABSTOP | BS_PUSHBUTTON, 110, 50, 70, 15
END
```

The DIALOG1.RC resource file shown in Listing 9.3 defines the BUTTONS accelerator resource, the EXITMENU menu resource, and two dialog box resources. These dialog box resources are named FORMAL and INFORMAL. Each dialog box has a title, a message, and pushbuttons with the IDs IDOK and IDCANCEL. Each version has different captions for these pushbuttons.

The resource definition of dialog boxes and controls may be new to you. Appendix B discusses the resource files for dialog boxes and their controls in more detail. The CTEXT keyword specifies centered text; the CONTROL keyword enables you to define any control and requires the caption, ID, control class, control style, location, and dimensions of the control.

Listing 9.4 contains the source code for the DIALOG1.CPP program file.

Listing 9.4 Source Code for the DIALOG1.CPP Program File

```cpp
#include <afxwin.h>
#include <stdio.h>
#include <string.h>
#include "dialog1.h"
class CDialogBoxApp : public CWinApp
{
public:
    virtual BOOL InitInstance();
};
// expand the functionality of CFrameWnd by deriving class CMainWnd
class CMainWnd : public CFrameWnd
{
 public:
  CMainWnd();
```

(continues)

Listing 9.4 Continued

```
  protected:
   // handle the current time
   afx_msg void CMTime();
   // handle exiting the application
   afx_msg void OnExit()
     { SendMessage(WM_CLOSE); }
   // Handle closing the window
   afx_msg void OnClose();
   // format date and time components
   void formatInt(char* s, int n);
   DECLARE_MESSAGE_MAP();
};
CMainWnd::CMainWnd()
{
  // create the window
  Create(NULL, "A Bare-Bones Dialog Box Tester",
         WS_OVERLAPPEDWINDOW, rectDefault, NULL, "EXITMENU");
}
void CMainWnd::formatInt(char* s, int n)
{
  if (n < 10)
    sprintf(s, "0%1d", n);
  else
    sprintf(s, "%2d", n);
}
void CMainWnd::CMTime()
{
  char s[41];
  char dateStr[81] = "Date: ";
  CTime tm = CTime::GetCurrentTime();
  formatInt(s, tm.GetMonth());
  strcat(dateStr, s);
  formatInt(s, tm.GetDay());
  strcat(dateStr, "/");
  strcat(dateStr, s);
  sprintf(s, "%d", tm.GetYear());
  strcat(dateStr, "/");
  strcat(dateStr, s);
  strcat(dateStr, "\r\n");
  strcat(dateStr, "Time: ");
  formatInt(s, tm.GetHour());
  strcat(dateStr, s);
  formatInt(s, tm.GetMinute());
  strcat(dateStr, ":");
  strcat(dateStr, s);
  formatInt(s, tm.GetSecond());
  strcat(dateStr, ":");
  strcat(dateStr, s);
  MessageBox(dateStr, "Current Date and Time",
             MB_OK | MB_ICONINFORMATION);
}
void CMainWnd::OnClose()
{
  static BOOL bFlag = FALSE;
  CDialog* pDialogBox;
```

```
    BOOL bCloseIt;
    // toggle flag that selects alternate dialog box resources
    bFlag = (bFlag == TRUE) ? FALSE : TRUE;
    if (bFlag) {
      pDialogBox = new CDialog("FORMAL", this);
      // use FORMAL dialog box
      bCloseIt = (pDialogBox->DoModal() == IDOK) ? TRUE : FALSE;
    }
    else {
      pDialogBox = new CDialog("INFORMAL", this);
      // use INFORMAL dialog box
      bCloseIt = (pDialogBox->DoModal() == IDOK) ? TRUE : FALSE;
    }
    if (bCloseIt)
        DestroyWindow();
}
BEGIN_MESSAGE_MAP(CMainWnd, CFrameWnd)
  ON_COMMAND(CM_TIME, CMTime)
  ON_COMMAND(CM_EXIT, OnExit)
  ON_WM_CLOSE()
END_MESSAGE_MAP()
// Construct the CDialogBoxApp's m_pMainWnd data member
BOOL CDialogBoxApp::InitInstance()
{
  m_pMainWnd = new CMainWnd();
  m_pMainWnd->ShowWindow(m_nCmdShow);
  m_pMainWnd->UpdateWindow();
  return TRUE;
}
// application's constructor initializes and runs the app
CDialogBoxApp WindowApp;
```

The source code for the DIALOG1.CPP program file shown in Listing 9.4
declares two classes: the application class, CDialogBoxApp, and the window
class, CMainWnd. The application employs the class CDialog to create simple
modal dialog boxes because it requires no additional dialog box operations.

The member function CMainWnd::OnClose is most relevant. It responds to the
command message WM_CLOSE sent by the Exit menu. The function utilizes the
local static Boolean variable flag to switch between the two dialog box resources FORMAL and INFORMAL. The function invokes the formal dialog box
using the following statement:

```
    pDialogBox = new CDialog("FORMAL", this);
```

The dialog box, which is executed using the function DoModal, disables
the parent window until you click either pushbutton control. The function
OnClose compares the value returned by the function DoModal with the
constant IDOK. This comparison assigns either TRUE or FALSE to the local

Boolean variable bCloseIt. The function OnClose inspects the value in the variable bCloseIt to decide whether to close the application window.

The program creates the informal dialog box using the following statement:

```
pDialogBox = new CDialog("INFORMAL", this);
```

The member function CDialog::OnOK responds to the IDOK command by closing the dialog boxes and returning the IDOK result.

The member function CMTime responds to the Time menu. The function declares the CTime object tm to obtain the current date and time by using the member function CTime::GetCurrentTime. The function CMTime sends the messages GetMonth, GetDay, GetYear, GetHour, GetMinute, and GetSecond to the object tm to obtain the month, day, year, hour, minute, and second, respectively. The function converts these date and time components to their string images and stores these images in the local variable dateStr. After the function completes these tasks, it invokes the message dialog box to display the properly formatted current date and time.

Using Dialog Boxes as Windows

Windows permits dialog boxes to appear as independent windows, and many simple applications use dialog boxes as stand-alone windows. In fact, if your application requires multiple controls and has little use for a typical parent window, you can create a dialog box instance as a direct child of the application class instance. This approach correctly bypasses the classic parent window when that window has nothing to offer the application. In addition, the stand-alone dialog box provides a fixed-size window that cannot be resized.

A good example of a stand-alone dialog box is a calculator application. A calculator usually is loaded with controls, which makes it suitable for a dialog box. Unless you are collecting the results from the various calculator instances in a parent window (or doing some other meaningful management task) a parent window is not necessary. It is more suitable for you to use a dialog box as the application window.

In previous chapters, I presented several versions of the Programmer's Calculator that had its controls attached to a window. In this section, I present the floating-point math calculator program, DIALOG2.EXE, which uses a dialog box. This version is somewhat similar to the first version of the Programmer's Calculator and contains the following controls:

■ *Operand1 edit box*. Accepts floating-point numbers or the name of a single-letter variable. In this program, you do not have to begin the name of a single-letter variable with the character @.

■ *Operator edit box*. Accepts the operations +, -, /, *, or ^ (raising to power).

■ *Operand2 edit box*. Accepts floating-point numbers or the name of a single-letter variable.

■ *Result edit box*. Displays the result of an operation.

■ *Error Message edit box*. Displays any error messages.

■ *Variables multi-line edit box*. Displays the contents of the single-letter variables. These variables store floating-point numbers.

■ *Calc pushbutton*. Executes the operation that appears in the Operator edit box using the operands in the Operand1 and Operand2 edit boxes.

■ *Store pushbutton*. Stores the value of the Result edit box in the current line of the Variables edit box.

■ *Exit pushbutton*. Exits the application.

Figure 9.3 shows a sample session with the DIALOG2.EXE program.

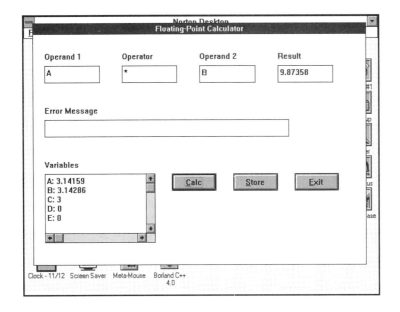

Figure 9.3

DIALOG2.EXE application—the floating-point calculator.

II

Visual C++ Programming

> **Note**
>
> Because the DIALOG2.EXE program uses a dialog box, you can use the Tab key to move between the various controls (if the control includes the WS_TABSTOP style in its related resource file). In addition, the dialog box also supports a default push-button that is invoked when you press the Enter key. All these features are supported by the dialog boxes with a few resource file declarations and no extra coding in DIALOG2.CPP.

Listing 9.5 shows the contents of the floating-point math calculator program definition file, DIALOG2.DEF.

Listing 9.5 The DIALOG2.DEF Definition File

```
NAME          Dialog2
DESCRIPTION   'An MFC Windows Application'
CODE          PRELOAD MOVEABLE DISCARDABLE
DATA          PRELOAD MOVEABLE MULTIPLE
HEAPSIZE      1024
```

Listing 9.6 contains the source code for the DIALOG2.H header file.

Listing 9.6 Source Code for the DIALOG2.H Header File

```
/* declare the ID_XXXX #define constants for the edit boxes */
#define ID_OPERAND1_EDIT 101
#define ID_OPERATOR_EDIT 102
#define ID_OPERAND2_EDIT 103
#define ID_RESULT_EDIT   104
#define ID_ERRMSG_EDIT   105
#define ID_VARIABLE_EDIT 106
#define ID_CALC_BTN      107
#define ID_STORE_BTN     108
#define ID_EXIT_BTN      109
```

The script for the DIALOG2.RC resource file is shown in Listing 9.7.

Listing 9.7 Script for the DIALOG2.RC Resource File

```
#include <windows.h>
#include <afxres.h>
#include "dialog2.h"
/* declare the constants that represent the sizes of the controls
*/
#define Wtxt 50
#define Htxt 10
#define TxtVertSpacing 2
#define TxtHorzSpacing 20
```

```
#define Wbox 50
#define Hbox 15
#define BoxVertSpacing 20
#define BoxHorzSpacing 20
#define WLongbox (Wbox + Wbox + Wbox + Wbox + BoxHorzSpacing)
#define Wvarbox (Wbox + Wbox)
#define Hvarbox (Hbox + Hbox + Hbox + Hbox)
#define Hbtn 15
#define Wbtn 40
#define BtnHorzSpacing 15
#define X0 10
#define Y0 15
#define X1 (X0 + Wtxt + TxtHorzSpacing)
#define X2 (X1 + Wtxt + TxtHorzSpacing)
#define X3 (X2 + Wtxt + TxtHorzSpacing)
#define Y1 (Y0 + Htxt + TxtVertSpacing)
#define Y2 (Y1 + Hbox + BoxVertSpacing)
#define Y3 (Y2 + Htxt + TxtVertSpacing)
#define Y4 (Y3 + Hbox + BoxVertSpacing)
#define Y5 (Y4 + Htxt + TxtVertSpacing)
#define X4 (X0 + Wvarbox + BtnHorzSpacing)
#define X5 (X4 + Wbtn + BtnHorzSpacing)
#define X6 (X5 + Wbtn + BtnHorzSpacing)
BUTTONS ACCELERATORS
BEGIN
  "c", ID_CALC_BTN, ALT
  "s", ID_STORE_BTN, ALT
  "e", ID_EXIT_BTN, ALT
END
CALC DIALOG DISCARDABLE LOADONCALL PURE MOVEABLE 10, 10, 300, 200
STYLE WS_VISIBLE | WS_POPUP | WS_DLGFRAME
CAPTION "Floating-Point Calculator"
BEGIN
  CONTROL "Operand 1", 0xffff, "STATIC",
          WS_CHILD | WS_VISIBLE | ES_LEFT, X0, Y0, Wtxt, Htxt
  CONTROL "", ID_OPERAND1_EDIT, "EDIT",
          WS_CHILD | WS_VISIBLE | WS_TABSTOP | WS_BORDER |
          ES_AUTOHSCROLL, X0, Y1, Wbox, Hbox
  CONTROL "Operator", 0xffff, "STATIC",
          WS_CHILD | WS_VISIBLE | ES_LEFT, X1, Y0, Wtxt, Htxt
  CONTROL "", ID_OPERATOR_EDIT, "EDIT",
          WS_CHILD | WS_VISIBLE | WS_TABSTOP | WS_BORDER |
          ES_AUTOHSCROLL, X1, Y1, Wbox, Hbox
  CONTROL "Operand 2", 0xffff, "STATIC",
          WS_CHILD | WS_VISIBLE | ES_LEFT, X2, Y0, Wtxt, Htxt
  CONTROL "", ID_OPERAND2_EDIT, "EDIT",
          WS_CHILD | WS_VISIBLE | WS_TABSTOP | WS_BORDER |
          ES_AUTOHSCROLL, X2, Y1, Wbox, Hbox
  CONTROL "Result", 0xffff, "STATIC",
          WS_CHILD | WS_VISIBLE | ES_LEFT, X3, Y0, Wtxt, Htxt
  CONTROL "", ID_RESULT_EDIT, "EDIT",
          WS_CHILD | WS_VISIBLE | WS_TABSTOP | WS_BORDER |
          ES_AUTOHSCROLL, X3, Y1, Wbox, Hbox
  CONTROL "Error Message", 0xffff, "STATIC",
          WS_CHILD | WS_VISIBLE | ES_LEFT, X0, Y2, Wtxt, Htxt
```

(continues)

Listing 9.7 Continued

```
CONTROL "", ID_ERRMSG_EDIT, "EDIT",
        WS_CHILD ¦ WS_VISIBLE ¦ WS_TABSTOP ¦ WS_BORDER ¦
        ES_AUTOHSCROLL, X0, Y3, WLongbox, Hbox
CONTROL "Variables", 0xffff, "STATIC",
        WS_CHILD ¦ WS_VISIBLE ¦ ES_LEFT, X0, Y4, Wtxt, Htxt
CONTROL "", ID_VARIABLE_EDIT, "EDIT",
        WS_CHILD ¦ WS_VISIBLE ¦ WS_BORDER ¦
        WS_VSCROLL ¦ WS_HSCROLL ¦ ES_MULTILINE ¦
        ES_AUTOVSCROLL ¦ ES_AUTOHSCROLL,
        X0, Y5, Wvarbox, Hvarbox
CONTROL "&Calc", ID_CALC_BTN, "BUTTON",
        WS_CHILD ¦ WS_VISIBLE ¦ WS_TABSTOP ¦ WS_BORDER ¦
        BS_DEFPUSHBUTTON, X4, Y5, Wbtn, Hbtn
CONTROL "&Store", ID_STORE_BTN, "BUTTON",
        WS_CHILD ¦ WS_VISIBLE ¦ WS_TABSTOP ¦ WS_BORDER ¦
        BS_PUSHBUTTON, X5, Y5, Wbtn, Hbtn
CONTROL "&Exit", ID_EXIT_BTN, "BUTTON",
        WS_CHILD ¦ WS_VISIBLE ¦ WS_TABSTOP ¦ WS_BORDER ¦
        BS_PUSHBUTTON, X6, Y5, Wbtn, Hbtn
END
```

The resource file shown in Listing 9.7 provides the definition of the CALC dialog box resource. I coded this dialog box using macros for the sizes and locations of the various controls. These macros let you adjust the sizes and locations of the various controls with minimum effort.

The source code for the DIALOG2.CPP program file is provided in Listing 9.8.

Listing 9.8 Source Code for the DIALOG2.CPP Program File

```
#include <stdlib.h>
#include <ctype.h>
#include <stdio.h>
#include <math.h>
#include <string.h>
#include <afxwin.h>
#include "dialog2.h"
// declare global constants
const MaxStringLen = 30;
const MAX_MEMREG = 26;
class CModalDialogApp : public CWinApp
{
public:
    virtual BOOL InitInstance();
};
class CxEdit : public CEdit
{
public:
  // get an ASCIIZ string from a line
  BOOL GetLine(LPSTR lpString, int nStrSize, int nLineNumber);
```

```
  // get the line length given a line number
  int GetLineLength(int nLineNumber);

};
// expand the functionality of CDialog by deriving class CMainWnd
class CMainWnd : public CDialog
{
 public:
  CMainWnd();
 protected:
  // math error flag
  BOOL bInError;
  // handle the accelerator key for the Calculate button
  afx_msg void HandleCalcBtn();
  // handle the accelerator key for the Calculate button
  afx_msg void CMCalcBtn()
    { HandleCalcBtn(); }
  // handle storing the result in a variable
  afx_msg void HandleStoreBtn();
  // handle the accelerator key for the Store button
  afx_msg void CMStoreBtn()
    { HandleStoreBtn(); }
  // handle exiting the application
  afx_msg void HandleExitBtn()
    { SendMessage(WM_CLOSE); }
  // handle the accelerator key for the Exit button
  afx_msg void CMExitBtn()
    { SendMessage(WM_CLOSE); }

  // enable a pushbutton-control
  void EnableButton(CButton* pBtn)
    { pBtn->EnableWindow(TRUE); }
  // disable a pushbutton control
  void DisableButton(CButton* pBtn)
    { pBtn->EnableWindow(FALSE); }

  // handle closing the window
  afx_msg void OnClose();
  // obtain a number of a Variable edit box line
  double getVar(int lineNum);
  // store a number in the selected text of
  // the Variable edit box line
  void putVar(double x);
  // declare message map macro
  DECLARE_MESSAGE_MAP();
};
BOOL CxEdit::GetLine(LPSTR lpString, int nStrSize, int nLineNumber)
{
  int nCopyCount;
  BOOL bResult;
  if (nStrSize <= 0)
    return FALSE;
  bResult = (nStrSize >= GetLineLength(nLineNumber) + 1) ? TRUE :
FALSE;
```

                                                                (continues)

Listing 9.8 Continued

```
    if (nStrSize == 1)
    {
      lpString[0] = '\0';
      return bResult;
    }
    ((WORD FAR *)lpString)[0] = nStrSize;

    nCopyCount = (WORD)(SendMessage(EM_GETLINE, nLineNumber,
                                    long(lpString)));
    if (nCopyCount)
    {
      // Windows returns non-null-terminated string
      lpString[nCopyCount] = '\0';
      return bResult;
    }
    return FALSE;
}
int CxEdit::GetLineLength(int nLineNumber)
{
  int nStartPos = -1;
  if (nLineNumber > -1)
    nStartPos = LineIndex(nLineNumber);
  return (WORD) SendMessage(EM_LINELENGTH, nStartPos);
}
CMainWnd::CMainWnd()
{
  CString bigStr;
  char s[10];
  char c;

  Create("CALC", NULL);

  bigStr = "";
  for (c = 'A'; c <= 'Z'; c++) {
    sprintf(s, "%c: 0\r\n", c);
    bigStr += s;
  }
  SetDlgItemText(ID_VARIABLE_EDIT, (const char*) bigStr);
  // clear the bInError flag
  bInError = FALSE;
}
void CMainWnd::HandleCalcBtn()
{
  double x, y, z;
  char opStr[MaxStringLen+1];
  char s[MaxStringLen+1];
  // obtain the string in the Operand1 edit box
  GetDlgItemText(ID_OPERAND1_EDIT, s, MaxStringLen);
  // does the Operand1Box contain the name
  // of a single-letter variable?
  if (isalpha(s[0]))
    // obtain value from the Variable edit control
    x = getVar(s[0] - 'A');
  else
```

```
    // convert the string in the edit box
    x = atof(s);
// obtain the string in the Operand2 edit box
GetDlgItemText(ID_OPERAND2_EDIT, s, MaxStringLen);
// does the Operand2 Box contain the name
// of a single-letter variable?
if (isalpha(s[0]))
    // obtain value from the Variable edit control
    y =getVar(s[0] - 'A');
else
    // convert the string in the edit box
    y = atof(s);
// obtain the string in the Operator edit box
GetDlgItemText(ID_OPERATOR_EDIT, opStr, MaxStringLen);
// clear the error message box
SetDlgItemText(ID_ERRMSG_EDIT, "");
bInError = FALSE;
// determine the requested operation
if (opStr[0] == '+')
    z = x + y;
else if (opStr[0] == '-')
    z = x - y;
else if (opStr[0] == '*')
    z = x * y;
else if (opStr[0] == '/') {
    if (y != 0)
        z = x / y;
    else {
        z = 0;
        bInError = TRUE;
        SetDlgItemText(ID_ERRMSG_EDIT, "Division-by-zero error");
    }
}
else if (opStr[0] == '^') {
    if (x > 0)
        z = exp(y * log(x));
    else {
        bInError = TRUE;
        SetDlgItemText(ID_ERRMSG_EDIT,
            "Cannot raise the power of a negative number");
    }
}
else {
    bInError = TRUE;
    SetDlgItemText(ID_ERRMSG_EDIT, "Invalid operator");
}
CButton* StoreBtn = (CButton*) (GetDlgItem(ID_STORE_BTN));
// display the result if no error has occurred
    if (!bInError) {
    sprintf(s, "%g", z);
    SetDlgItemText(ID_RESULT_EDIT, s);
    // enable the Store button
    CButton* StoreBtn = (CButton*) (GetDlgItem(ID_STORE_BTN));
    EnableButton(StoreBtn);
}
else
```

II

Visual C++ Programming

(continues)

Listing 9.8 Continued

```
      // disable the Store button
      DisableButton(StoreBtn);
}
void CMainWnd::HandleStoreBtn()
{
  char result[MaxStringLen+1];
  // get the string in the Result edit box
  GetDlgItemText(ID_RESULT_EDIT, result, MaxStringLen);
  // store the result in the selected text of
  // the Variable edit box
  putVar(atof(result));
}
double CMainWnd::getVar(int lineNum)
{
  int lineSize;
  char s[MaxStringLen+1];
  CxEdit* VariableBox = (CxEdit*) (GetDlgItem(ID_VARIABLE_EDIT));
  if (lineNum >= MAX_MEMREG) return 0;
  // get the size of the target line
  lineSize = VariableBox->GetLineLength(lineNum);
  // get the line
  VariableBox->GetLine(s, lineSize, lineNum);
  // delete the first three characters
  strcpy(s, (s+3));
  // return the number stored in the target line
  return atof(s);
}

void CMainWnd::putVar(double x)
{
  DWORD selPos;
  WORD startPos, endPos;
  int lineNum;
  int lineSize;
  char s[MaxStringLen+1];
  CxEdit* VariableBox = (CxEdit*) (GetDlgItem(ID_VARIABLE_EDIT));

  // locate the character position of the cursor
  selPos = VariableBox->GetSel();
  startPos = LOWORD(selPos);
  endPos = HIWORD(selPos);
  // turn off the selected text
  if (startPos != endPos) {
    selPos = MAKELONG(startPos, startPos);
    VariableBox->SetSel(selPos);
  }
  // get the line number where the cursor is located
  lineNum = VariableBox->LineFromChar(-1);
  // get the line size of line lineNum
  lineSize = VariableBox->GetLineLength(lineNum);
  // obtain the text of line lineNum
  VariableBox->GetLine(s, lineSize, lineNum);
  // build the new text line
  sprintf(s, "%c: %g", s[0], x);
```

```
  // get the character positions for the deleted line
  startPos = (WORD) (VariableBox->LineIndex(-1));
  endPos = (WORD) (startPos + VariableBox->LineLength(-1));
  // select the current line
  selPos = MAKELONG(startPos, endPos);
  VariableBox->SetSel(selPos);
  // replace the current line with the new line
  VariableBox->ReplaceSel(s);
}
void CMainWnd::OnClose()
{
  if (MessageBox("Want to close this application",
                 "Query", MB_YESNO | MB_ICONQUESTION) == IDYES)
    DestroyWindow();
}
BEGIN_MESSAGE_MAP(CMainWnd, CDialog)
  ON_COMMAND(ID_CALC_BTN, CMCalcBtn)
  ON_BN_CLICKED(ID_CALC_BTN, HandleCalcBtn)
  ON_COMMAND(ID_STORE_BTN, CMStoreBtn)
  ON_BN_CLICKED(ID_STORE_BTN, HandleStoreBtn)
  ON_COMMAND(ID_EXIT_BTN, CMExitBtn)
  ON_BN_CLICKED(ID_EXIT_BTN, HandleExitBtn)
  ON_WM_CLOSE()
END_MESSAGE_MAP()
// Construct the CModalDialogApp's m_pMainWnd data member
BOOL CModalDialogApp::InitInstance()
{
  m_pMainWnd = new CMainWnd();
  m_pMainWnd->ShowWindow(m_nCmdShow);
  m_pMainWnd->UpdateWindow();
  return TRUE;
}
// application's constructor initializes and runs the app
CModalDialogApp WindowApp;
```

The source code for the DIALOG2.CPP program, just shown in Listing 9.8, is similar to the source code of the file CTLBTN1.CPP (the second version of the Programmer's Calculator) provided in Listing 6.12. The two listings have the following differences:

■ The program declares CMainWnd as a descendant of the class CDialog.

■ The application creates an instance of CMainWnd, the custom dialog box class. Notice that the creation of the dialog box is very similar to that of a typical window.

■ The dialog box class does not have the member function OnCreate. The constructor creates the dialog box and its controls, in one swoop, using the statement

```
    Create("CALC", NULL)
```

II

Visual C++ Programming

- The modeless calculator dialog box closes in response to WM_CLOSE messages transmitted by the Exit pushbutton control.

- The program accesses the text in the single-line edit controls by sending the C++ messages GetDlgItemText and SetDlgItemText to these controls. These messages use member functions inherited from the class CWnd. The arguments of these messages include the ID of the targeted control.

- The program accesses the multiple-line edit control and the other pushbuttons by using local pointers that are initialized by the inherited function CWnd::GetDlgItem and the ID of the target control. The program typecasts the result of the function GetDlgItem to obtain the pointer of the sought object. This method also works smoothly with classes that are descendants of MFC classes, such as CxEdit.

- The program performs its operations using the type double instead of the type long. Likewise, the program uses conversion functions, such as atof to convert from string to floating-point.

Transferring Control Data

The MFC library provides the class CDataExchange to assist in the *automatic* and *command-induced* transfer of data between the dialog box controls and the special data members of the related dialog box class. Moreover, the class CDataExchange provides data validation services. The data transfer and validation mechanisms work with edit controls, check boxes, radio buttons, list boxes, and combo boxes.

The Basics

You implement the basic data transfer mechanism by overriding the inherited member function CDialog::DoDataExchange. The general syntax for overriding this member function is as follows:

```
void CAppDialog::DoDataExchange(CDataExchange* pDX)
{
  // call base class
  CDialog::DoDataExchange(pDX);
  //{{AFX_DATA_MAP(CAppDialog)
    data_exchange_function_call_1
    [data_validation_function_call_1]
    data_exchange_function_call_2
    [data_validation_function_call_2]
    ...
    data_exchange_function_call_n
```

```
      [data_validation_function_call_n]
    //}}AFX_DATA_MAP
  }
```

The `DoDataExchange` has one parameter that is a pointer to the class
`CDataExchange` instance. The special comments that begin and end with `//{{`
and `//}}` are placed and utilized by the ClassWizard to manage the sequence
of calls to data exchange and validation functions. If you manually code the
member function `DoDataExchange`, you can leave out these comments.

The general syntax for calling a data exchange function is

```
DDX_control(pDX, controlID, associatedDataMember);
```

Here are the declarations for exchanging various kinds of data types with an
edit control in a dialog box:

```
void AFXAPI DDX_Text(CDataExchange* pDX, int nIDC, int& value);
void AFXAPI DDX_Text(CDataExchange* pDX, int nIDC, UINT& value);
void AFXAPI DDX_Text(CDataExchange* pDX, int nIDC, long& value);
void AFXAPI DDX_Text(CDataExchange* pDX, int nIDC, DWORD& value);
void AFXAPI DDX_Text(CDataExchange* pDX, int nIDC, CString& value);
void AFXAPI DDX_Text(CDataExchange* pDX, int nIDC, float& value);
void AFXAPI DDX_Text(CDataExchange* pDX, int nIDC, double& value);
```

The header file AFXDD_.H includes the declarations of the data exchange and
validation functions. The header file AFXEXT.H contains similar functions for
VBX controls. The following example employs a selection from the preceding
DDX functions. The example shows how to exchange data with three text
boxes—one that contains ordinary text and the other two which accept
integers:

```
#define ID_FILENAME_BOX = 100;
#define ID_FIRSTLINE_VAL_BOX = 101;
#define ID_LASTLINE_VAL_BOX = 102;
class CMyDialog : public CDialog
{
 public:
  CString FilenameBuff;
  int nFirstLineValBuff;
  int nLastLineValBuff;
  // other data members ...
  // other member functions ...

  virtual void DoDataExchange(CDataExchange* pDX);
  // other member functions ...
 protected:
  // other data members ...
  // other member functions ...
};
void CMyDialog::DoDataExchange(CDataExchange* pDX)
```

```
{
  CDialog::DoDataExchange(pDX);
  DDX_Text(pDX, ID_FIND_BOX, FilenameBuff); // swaps CString
  DDX_Text(pDX, ID_FIRST_VAL_BOX, nFirstLineValBuff); // swaps int
  DDX_Text(pDX, ID_LAST_VAL_BOX, nLastLineValBuff); // swaps int
}
```

In addition, the MFC library provides the following functions to swap data with check boxes, radio controls, the current selection of a list box, and the current selection of a combo box:

```
// special control types
void AFXAPI DDX_Check(CDataExchange* pDX, int nIDC, int& value);
void AFXAPI DDX_Radio(CDataExchange* pDX, int nIDC, int& value);
void AFXAPI DDX_LBString(CDataExchange* pDX, int nIDC,
                         CString& value);
void AFXAPI DDX_CBString(CDataExchange* pDX, int nIDC,
                         CString& value);
void AFXAPI DDX_LBIndex(CDataExchange* pDX, int nIDC, int& index);
void AFXAPI DDX_CBIndex(CDataExchange* pDX, int nIDC, int& index);
// for Windows 3.1 and greater
void AFXAPI DDX_LBStringExact(CDataExchange* pDX, int nIDC,
                              CString& value);
void AFXAPI DDX_CBStringExact(CDataExchange* pDX, int nIDC,
                              CString& value);
```

Here is a snippet of code that uses a selection from the preceding DDX functions. The example illustrates how to swap data with a list box, two radio buttons, and two check boxes:

```
#define ID_GLOBAL_RADIO         100
#define ID_SELECTED_TEXT_RADIO  101
#define ID_CASE_SENSITIVE_CHECK 102
#define ID_WHOLE_WORD_CHECK     103
#define ID_LIST_BOX             104
class CMyDialog : public CDialog
{
 public:
  CString SelectionBuff;
  int nSelectionIndexBuff;
  int nGlobalRadioBuff;
  int nSelectedTextRadioBuff;
  int nCaseSensitiveCheckBuff;
  int nWholeWordCheckBuff;
  // other data members ...
  // other member functions ...

  virtual void DoDataExchange(CDataExchange* pDX);
  // other member functions ...
 protected:
  // other data members ...
  // other member functions ...
};
void CMyDialog::DoDataExchange(CDataExchange* pDX)
```

```
{
    CDialog::DoDataExchange(pDX);
    DDX_LBString(pDX, ID_LIST_BOX, SelectionBuff);
    DDX_LBIndex(pDX, ID_LIST_BOX, nSelectionIndexBuff);
    DDX_Radio(pDX, ID_GLOBAL_RADIO, nGlobalRadioBuff);
    DDX_Radio(pDX, ID_SELECTED_TEXT_RADIO, nSelectedTextRadioBuff);
    DDX_Check(pDX, ID_CASE_SENSITIVE_CHECK, nCaseSensitiveCheckBuff);
    DDX_Check(pDX, ID_WHOLE_WORD_CHECK, nWholeWordCheckBuff);
}
```

You can use the following DDX function to access a dialog box control:

```
void AFXAPI DDX_Control(CDataExchange* pDX, int nIDC, CWnd& rControl);
```

The MFC library also offers the following data validation functions:

```
// range - value must be >= minVal and <= maxVal
// NOTE: you will require casts for 'minVal' and 'maxVal' to use the
//    UINT, DWORD or float types
void AFXAPI DDV_MinMaxInt(CDataExchange* pDX, int value,
                          int minVal, int maxVal);
void AFXAPI DDV_MinMaxLong(CDataExchange* pDX, long value,
                           long minVal, long maxVal);
void AFXAPI DDV_MinMaxUInt(CDataExchange* pDX, UINT value,
                           UINT minVal, UINT maxVal);
void AFXAPI DDV_MinMaxDWord(CDataExchange* pDX, DWORD value,
                            DWORD minVal, DWORD maxVal);
void AFXAPI DDV_MinMaxFloat(CDataExchange* pDX, float const& value,
                            float minVal, float maxVal);
void AFXAPI DDV_MinMaxDouble(CDataExchange* pDX, double const& value,
                             double minVal, double maxVal);
// number of characters
void AFXAPI DDV_MaxChars(CDataExchange* pDX, CString const& value,
                         int nChars);
```

The data-validating functions just shown monitor the values in their respective controls. After you close the dialog box, the data validation functions check the value in the various controls (that have a DDV function assigned to them) and display a warning in a message box if the input values do not adhere to the appropriate ranges of values or to the string lengths.

> **Note**
>
> You must declare every DDV function immediately after its corresponding DDX function.

Here is an example that uses data validation:

```
#define ID_FILENAME_BOX = 100;
#define ID_FIRSTLINE_VAL_BOX = 101;
#define ID_LASTLINE_VAL_BOX = 102;
```

```
const int MaxChars = 30;
const int MinValue = 1;
const int MaxValue = 7;
class CMyDialog : public CDialog
{
 public:
  CString FilenameBuff;
  int nFirstLineValBuff;
  int nLastLineValBuff;
  // other data members ...
  // other member functions ...

  virtual void DoDataExchange(CDataExchange* pDX);
  // other member functions ...
 protected:
  // other data members ...
  // other member functions ...
};
void CMyDialog::DoDataExchange(CDataExchange* pDX)
{
  CDialog::DoDataExchange(pDX);
  DDX_Text(pDX, ID_FILENAME_BOX, FilenameBuff);
  DDV_MaxChars(pDX, ID_FILENAME_BOX, MaxChars);
  DDX_Text(pDX, ID_FIRSTLINE_VAL_BOX, nFirstLineValBuff);
  DDV_MinMaxInt(pDX, nFirstLineValBuff, MinValue, MaxValue);
  DDX_Text(pDX, ID_LASTLINE_VAL_BOX, nLastLineValBuff);
  DDV_MinMaxInt(pDX, nLastLineValBuff, MinValue, MaxValue);
}
```

Data Transfer Mechanisms

The DDX functions transfer data between dialog box controls and their related data members in the dialog box class. The transfer mechanism utilizes the function CWnd::UpdateData to transfer data to and from the dialog box controls. The function requires a single argument, a BOOL value that determines the direction of data flow. The C++ message UpdateData(TRUE) moves the data from the dialog box controls to their associated data members. By contrast, the C++ message UpdateData(FALSE) moves the data from the data members to their associated dialog box controls.

To use the DDX and DDV functions with your custom dialog box class, you can choose from the following options:

■ Use the constructor of your custom dialog box class to initialize the data members that are mapped onto the dialog box controls. This initialization method applies when the dialog box presents the same values every time it pops up. This scheme absolves you from declaring the overriding member functions OnInitDialog and OnOK. This method works because the inherited member function CDialog::OnOK sends the C++ message UpdateData(TRUE). Likewise, the inherited member function `CDialog::OnInitDialog` sends the C++ message `UpdateData(FALSE)`. How and where do you access the data in the dialog box control? The answer lies in the member function of the window class, which invokes the dialog box. This function should have statements that obtain the data in the public data members of the dialog box (when the function `DoModal` yields the value `IDOK`).

■ Use a modified version of the preceding method to implement a two-way data transfer for simple controls (that is, edit controls, check boxes, and radio buttons). This scheme requires initialization statements in a window's member function (which brings up the dialog box). These statements appear before the ones that send the C++ message `DoModal` to the dialog box. They initialize the public data members of the dialog box class. Therefore, this method permits the dialog box to show the states or values of its controls since the last time you clicked the OK button.

■ Use the member function `OnInitDialog` to initialize the items in a list box or combo box.

■ Use the member function `OnOK` to update the data in a combo box. This scheme enables you to use a combo box as a history list box.

The *CDataExchange* Class

The `CDataExchange` class is not a very complicated one. Here is the declaration of this class in the AFXWIN.H header file:

```
class AFX_STACK_DATA CDataExchange
{
// Attributes
public:
 BOOL m_bSaveAndValidate;    // TRUE => save and validate data
 CWnd* m_pDlgWnd;             // container usually a dialog
// Operations (for implementors of DDX and DDV procs)
 HWND PrepareCtrl(int nIDC);     // return HWND of control
 HWND PrepareEditCtrl(int nIDC); // return HWND of control
 CVBControl* PrepareVBCtrl(int nIDC);   // return VB control
 void Fail();                    // will throw exception
// Implementation
 CDataExchange(CWnd* pDlgWnd, BOOL bSaveAndValidate);
 HWND m_hWndLastControl;     // last control used (for validation)
 BOOL m_bEditLastControl;    // last control was an edit item
};
```

The public data member `m_bSaveAndValidate` specifies the action taken. When this member is TRUE, the data flows from the dialog box data members to the related controls. By contrast, when the member is FALSE, the data flows from the controls to the related data members. The public member `m_pDlgWnd` is the pointer to the dialog box that contains the controls.

The member functions `PrepareCtrl` and `PrepareEditCtrl` prepare a dialog box for data exchange. These functions store the handle of the control in order to reselect these controls if data validation fails. The function `PrepareCtrl` works with non-edit controls; whereas the function `PrepareEditCtrl` works with edit controls.

The member function `Fail` is invoked after data validation fails. The function presents a message box to alert the user to an error in the input. This function restores the focus to the offending control.

In the following sections, I present examples of data being transferred between dialog boxes and their buffers. These examples show how to transfer data with modal and modeless dialog boxes. In the case of the modeless dialog box, I show you another method for transferring data—one which does not rely on the function `DoDataExchange`.

Transferring Data with a Simple Modal Dialog Box

Let's look at a simple example of transferring data between the controls of a modal dialog box and a buffer. I present a simple application which creates a dialog box that might be used to number the lines of a text file (I say *might* because the program does not actually perform the line numbering). Figure 9.4 shows the dialog box in question during a sample session with the DIALOG3.EXE application.

The dialog box contains the following controls:

- *Input File edit box.* Accepts the name of the input file.

- *Output File edit box.* Accepts the name of the output file.

- *Keywords group box.* Contains the Uppercase and Lowercase radio button controls. These radio buttons offer the options of making the keywords in the output file either uppercase or lowercase.

- *Bold keywords check box.* Makes the keywords in the output file appear in bold letters.

- *Add colon check box.* Adds a colon after the line number.

- *OK and Cancel pushbutton controls.*

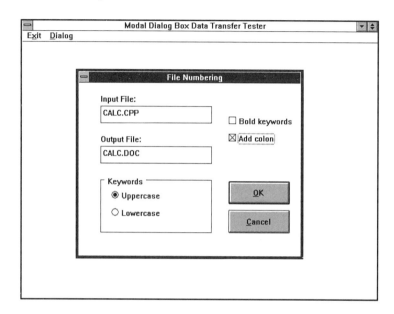

Figure 9.4
A sample
session with the
DIALOG3.EXE
application.

The application has a menu bar that includes Exit and Dialog menus. To
access the dialog box, click the Dialog menu or press Alt+D. When you invoke the dialog box for the first time, the controls have the following initial
values and states:

- The Input File edit box contains the string CALC.CPP.

- The Output File edit box contains the string CALC.DOC.

- The Uppercase radio button is checked.

- The Add colon check box is checked.

- The Bold keywords check box is checked.

Try entering other filenames in the edit boxes and changing the check states
of the radio buttons and check boxes. Now, click the OK button (or press
Alt+O) to close the dialog box. The program displays a message dialog box
that states the values and states of the dialog box controls. Invoke the Dialog
menu again to open the dialog box. Notice that the dialog controls have the
same values and states as when you last closed the dialog box.

Listing 9.9 shows the contents of the DIALOG3.DEF definition file.

Listing 9.9 The DIALOG3.DEF Definition File

```
NAME         Dialog3
DESCRIPTION  'An MFC Windows Application'
EXETYPE      WINDOWS
CODE         PRELOAD MOVEABLE DISCARDABLE
DATA         PRELOAD MOVEABLE MULTIPLE
HEAPSIZE     1024
```

Listing 9.10 contains the source code for the DIALOG3.H header file.

Listing 9.10 Source Code for the DIALOG3.H Header File

```
#define CM_EXIT    (WM_USER + 100)
#define CM_DIALOG (WM_USER + 101)
#define ID_INPUTFILE_TXT    101
#define ID_INPUTFILE_EDIT   102
#define ID_OUTPUTFILE_TXT   103
#define ID_OUTPUTFILE_EDIT  104
#define ID_KEYWORDS_GRP     105
#define ID_UPPERCASE_RBT    106
#define ID_LOWERCASE_RBT    107
#define ID_ADDCOLON_CHK     108
#define ID_BOLDKEYWORD_CHK  109
#define IDD_FILENUM_DLG     200
```

Listing 9.11 shows the script for the DIALOG3.RC resource file.

Listing 9.11 Script for the DIALOG3.RC Resource File

```
#include <windows.h>
#include <afxres.h>
#include "dialog3.h"
BUTTONS ACCELERATORS MOVEABLE PURE
BEGIN
    "o", IDOK, ALT
    "c", IDCANCEL, ALT
END
MAINMENU MENU LOADONCALL MOVEABLE PURE DISCARDABLE
BEGIN
    MENUITEM "E&xit", CM_EXIT
    MENUITEM "&Dialog", CM_DIALOG
END
IDD_FILENUM_DLG DIALOG DISCARDABLE  10, 10, 200, 150
STYLE DS_MODALFRAME ¦ WS_POPUP ¦ WS_CLIPSIBLINGS ¦ WS_CAPTION ¦ WS_SYSMENU
CAPTION "File Numbering"
FONT 8, "System"
BEGIN
    LTEXT            "Input File:",ID_INPUTFILE_TXT,
                     20,10,100,8,NOT WS_GROUP
```

```
        EDITTEXT        ID_INPUTFILE_EDIT,20,20,100,15
        LTEXT           "Output File:",ID_OUTPUTFILE_TXT,
                        20,45,100,8, NOT WS_GROUP
        EDITTEXT        ID_OUTPUTFILE_EDIT,20,55,100,15
        GROUPBOX        " Keywords ",ID_KEYWORDS_GRP,
                        20,80,100,50,WS_GROUP
        CONTROL         "Uppercase",ID_UPPERCASE_RBT,"Button",
                        BS_AUTORADIOBUTTON | WS_GROUP | WS_TABSTOP,
                        30,90,50,15
        CONTROL         "Lowercase",ID_LOWERCASE_RBT,"Button",
                        BS_AUTORADIOBUTTON | WS_TABSTOP,30,105,60,15
        CONTROL         "Add colon",ID_ADDCOLON_CHK,"Button",
                        BS_AUTOCHECKBOX | WS_TABSTOP,135,40,60,15
        CONTROL         "Bold keywords",ID_BOLDKEYWORD_CHK,"Button",
                        BS_AUTOCHECKBOX | WS_TABSTOP,135,25,60,15
        DEFPUSHBUTTON   "&OK",IDOK,135,85,55,20,WS_GROUP
        PUSHBUTTON      "&Cancel",IDCANCEL,135,110,55,20,WS_GROUP
    END
```

The script for the DIALOG3.RC resource file shown in Listing 9.11 defines the resources for the accelerator keys, the menu, and the dialog box, including its controls. Looking at the dialog box resource definitions, notice that the OK and Cancel pushbuttons have the predefined IDOK and IDCANCEL IDs, respectively. Also notice that the OK button is defined as a DEFPUSHBUTTON control to indicate that it is the default pushbutton. The Cancel button, however, is defined as a PUSHBUTTON control. In addition, notice that the group box, radio buttons, and check boxes have the BUTTON class name. The styles associated with these controls determine their final form. Appendix B provides more details about declaring the resources for controls that are owned by dialog boxes.

The source code for the DIALOG3.CPP program file is provided in Listing 9.12.

Listing 9.12 Source Code for the DIALOG3.CPP Program File

```cpp
#include <string.h>
#include <afxwin.h>
#include "dialog3.h"
// declare constants
const int MAX_CHARS = 30;
const int BF_CHECKED = 1;
const int BF_UNCHECKED = 0;
class CModalDialogApp : public CWinApp
{
public:
    virtual BOOL InitInstance();
};
```

(continues)

Listing 9.12 Continued

```cpp
// expand the functionality of CDialog by
// deriving class CAppDialog
class CAppDialog : public CDialog
{
 public:
  CAppDialog(CWnd* pParentWnd = NULL)
    : CDialog(CAppDialog::IDD, pParentWnd) {}
  // data exchange buffer
  enum { IDD = IDD_FILENUM_DLG };
  CString InputFileBoxBuff;
  CString OutputFileBoxBuff;
  int nUpperCaseRbtBuff;
  int nLowerCaseRbtBuff;
  int nAddColonChkBuff;
  int nBoldKeywordChkBuff;
 protected:
  virtual void DoDataExchange(CDataExchange* pDX);
};
// expand the functionality of CFrameWnd by deriving class CMainWnd
class CMainWnd : public CFrameWnd
{
 public:
  CMainWnd();
 protected:
  CString InputFileBoxBuff;
  CString OutputFileBoxBuff;
  int nUpperCaseRbtBuff;
  int nLowerCaseRbtBuff;
  int nAddColonChkBuff;
  int nBoldKeywordChkBuff;
  // handle the dialog command
  afx_msg void CMDialog();
  // handle exiting the application
  afx_msg void OnExit()
    { SendMessage(WM_CLOSE); }
  // handle closing the window
  afx_msg void OnClose();
  // declare message map macro
  DECLARE_MESSAGE_MAP()
};
void CAppDialog::DoDataExchange(CDataExchange* pDX)
{
  CDialog::DoDataExchange(pDX); // call base class
  // update the Input File edit box
  DDX_Text(pDX, ID_INPUTFILE_EDIT, InputFileBoxBuff);
  DDV_MaxChars(pDX, InputFileBoxBuff, MAX_CHARS);
  // update the Output File edit box
  DDX_Text(pDX, ID_OUTPUTFILE_EDIT, OutputFileBoxBuff);
  DDV_MaxChars(pDX, OutputFileBoxBuff, MAX_CHARS);
  // update the Uppercase radio button
  DDX_Radio(pDX, ID_UPPERCASE_RBT, nUpperCaseRbtBuff);
  // update the Lowercase radio button
  DDX_Radio(pDX, ID_LOWERCASE_RBT, nLowerCaseRbtBuff);
  // update the Add colon check box
```

```
    DDX_Check(pDX, ID_ADDCOLON_CHK, nAddColonChkBuff);
    // update the Bold keyword check box
    DDX_Check(pDX, ID_BOLDKEYWORD_CHK, nBoldKeywordChkBuff);
}
CMainWnd::CMainWnd()
{
    // load the accelerator keys resource
    LoadAccelTable("BUTTONS");
    // create the window
    Create(NULL, "Modal Dialog Box Data Transfer Tester",
           WS_OVERLAPPEDWINDOW, rectDefault, NULL, "MAINMENU");
    // assign the initial values for the dialog controls
    InputFileBoxBuff = "CALC.CPP";
    OutputFileBoxBuff = "CALC.DOC";
    nUpperCaseRbtBuff = BF_CHECKED;
    nLowerCaseRbtBuff = BF_UNCHECKED;
    nAddColonChkBuff = BF_CHECKED;
    nBoldKeywordChkBuff = BF_CHECKED;

};
void CMainWnd::CMDialog()
{
    CString msgStr;
    CAppDialog Dlg(this);

    // copy the current values from the window's members to
    // the dialog box members
    Dlg.InputFileBoxBuff = InputFileBoxBuff;
    Dlg.OutputFileBoxBuff = OutputFileBoxBuff;
    Dlg.nUpperCaseRbtBuff = nUpperCaseRbtBuff;
    Dlg.nLowerCaseRbtBuff = nLowerCaseRbtBuff;
    Dlg.nAddColonChkBuff = nAddColonChkBuff;
    Dlg.nBoldKeywordChkBuff = nBoldKeywordChkBuff;
    if (Dlg.DoModal() == IDOK) {
      // build string which reflects the current dialog box data
      msgStr = "Input File: ";
      msgStr += Dlg.InputFileBoxBuff;
      msgStr += "\nOutput File: ";
      msgStr += Dlg.OutputFileBoxBuff;
      msgStr += "\nUppercase: ";
      msgStr += (Dlg.nUpperCaseRbtBuff == BF_CHECKED) ?
                                          "TRUE" : "FALSE";
      msgStr += "\nLowercase: ";
      msgStr += (Dlg.nLowerCaseRbtBuff == BF_CHECKED) ?
                                          "TRUE" : "FALSE";
      msgStr += "\nAdd colon: ";
      msgStr += (Dlg.nAddColonChkBuff == BF_CHECKED) ?
                                          "TRUE" : "FALSE";
      msgStr += "\nBold keyword: ";
      msgStr += (Dlg.nBoldKeywordChkBuff == BF_CHECKED) ?
                                          "TRUE" : "FALSE";
      // display the contents of msgStr
      MessageBox((const char*) msgStr, "Dialog Box Data",
               MB_OK | MB_ICONINFORMATION);
      // update copy of window for the next dialog box invocation
      InputFileBoxBuff = Dlg.InputFileBoxBuff;
      OutputFileBoxBuff = Dlg.OutputFileBoxBuff;
```

II

Visual C++ Programming

(continues)

Listing 9.12 Continued

```
      nUpperCaseRbtBuff = Dlg.nUpperCaseRbtBuff;
      nLowerCaseRbtBuff = Dlg.nLowerCaseRbtBuff;
      nAddColonChkBuff = Dlg.nAddColonChkBuff;
      nBoldKeywordChkBuff = Dlg.nBoldKeywordChkBuff;
    }
  }
  void CMainWnd::OnClose()
  {
    if (MessageBox("Want to close this application",
                   "Query", MB_YESNO | MB_ICONQUESTION) == IDYES)
      DestroyWindow();
  }
  BEGIN_MESSAGE_MAP(CMainWnd, CFrameWnd)
    ON_COMMAND(CM_DIALOG, CMDialog)
    ON_COMMAND(CM_EXIT, OnExit)
    ON_WM_CLOSE()
  END_MESSAGE_MAP()
  // Construct the CModalDialogApp's m_pMainWnd data member
  BOOL CModalDialogApp::InitInstance()
  {
    m_pMainWnd = new CMainWnd();
    m_pMainWnd->ShowWindow(m_nCmdShow);
    m_pMainWnd->UpdateWindow();
    return TRUE;
  }
  // application's constructor initializes and runs the app
  CModalDialogApp WindowApp;
```

The source code for the DIALOG3.CPP program file (just shown in Listing 9.12) declares three classes: an application class, a window class, and a modal dialog box class.

The dialog box class CAppDialog declares a class constructor, the set of public data members, and the member function DoDataExchange. These data members map the controls of the dialog box whose data is exchanged. Notice that the declaration of these data members starts with the declaration of an untagged enumerated type which defines a single value, IDD. The CAppDialog constructor uses the enumerated value IDD in invoking the CDialog constructor. The class CAppDialog only declares the member function DoDataExchange because the operations of the inherited member functions OnInitDialog and OnOK are adequate. This example shows how the two-way data transfer for simple controls requires only the DoDataExchange. In fact, notice that the dialog box constructor just calls the parent class constructor. This is another programming aspect that is involved in this kind of two-way data transfer.

The member function DoDataExchange uses a set of DDX and DDV functions to associate the data members of the class with the dialog box controls. The function uses the DDV_MaxChars to validate the size of the strings entered in the Input File and Output File edit controls. Moreover, the function uses DDX to move the data of the radio button and check box controls.

The application window class, CMainWnd, declares a constructor, a set of data members, and three member functions. The data members parallel those in the class CAppDialog—in fact they have the same names. The window class uses these data members to store the dialog box data between invocations of the dialog box.

The CMainWnd constructor creates the window (which also loads the menu resource) and then initializes the control data buffers. The constructor assigns the "CALC.CPP" and "CALC.DOC" strings to the buffers of the Input File and Output File edit boxes, respectively. The constructor also assigns the following values:

- The constant BF_CHECKED to the members nUpperCaseRbtBuff, nAddColorCaseChkBuff, and nBoldKeywordChkBuf.

- The constant BF_UNCHECKED to the member nLowerCaseRbtBuff.

The CMainWnd class declares the CMDialog member function to handle the command message transmitted by the Dialog menu. The CMDialog function performs the following tasks:

- Creates the instance Dlg of the class CAppDialog.

- Copies the values in the data members of the window object to the corresponding members of the dialog box object. This task both initializes and updates the controls of the dialog box before invoking the dialog box.

- Invokes the dialog box by sending the C++ message DoModal to the Dlg object. If the message yields the value IDOK, the function performs the remaining tasks.

- Builds the display string (stored in the local CString instance, msgStr). This task involves accessing the various public dialog box data members.

- Displays a message box that shows the strings you typed in the edit controls, as well as the state of the radio buttons and check boxes. Figure 9.5 shows a sample session with the DIALOG3.EXE program showing this message dialog box.

- Copies the values in the data members of the dialog box object to the corresponding members of the window object. This task updates the window's data member with the latest dialog box data after invoking the dialog box.

Figure 9.5

The DIALOG3.EXE program showing the message dialog box.

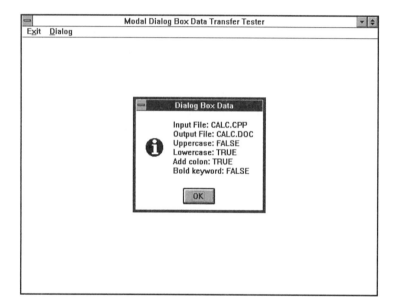

Transferring Data with a Complex Modal Dialog Box

Let's look at a more advanced example of using the class CDataExchange in a dialog box with combo boxes. These combo boxes work like history boxes. The next program, DIALOG4.EXE, is an advanced version of the program DIALOG3.EXE. Figure 9.6 shows a sample session with the new version of the dialog box. The Input File and Output File combo boxes permit you to enter text in their edit control areas. If you close the dialog box by clicking the OK button, the program inserts into the list box component of the combo box any text you typed in the corresponding edit box. The next time you invoke the dialog box, the list box (and edit box) components of the combo box contain the previous input. As you type a new string in either combo box and then exit the dialog box, the corresponding list box component builds a list of your previous input. The latest input is always inserted at the top of the list box. As with the DIALOG3.EXE program, clicking the OK button causes a message dialog box to be displayed that shows the values and states of the various dialog box controls.

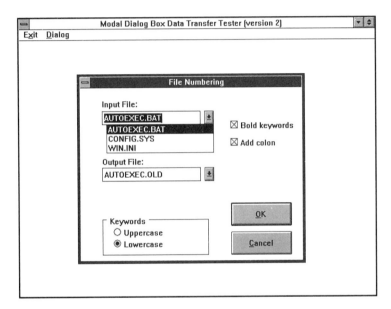

Figure 9.6

A sample session with the DIALOG4.EXE program.

II

Visual C++ Programming

Listing 9.13 contains the contents of the DIALOG4.DEF definition file.

Listing 9.13 The DIALOG4.DEF Definition File

```
NAME          Dialog4
DESCRIPTION   'An MFC Windows Application'
EXETYPE       WINDOWS
CODE          PRELOAD MOVEABLE DISCARDABLE
DATA          PRELOAD MOVEABLE MULTIPLE
HEAPSIZE      1024
```

Listing 9.14 shows the source code for the DIALOG4.H header file.

Listing 9.14 Source Code for the DIALOG4.H Header File

```
#define CM_EXIT    (WM_USER + 100)
#define CM_DIALOG  (WM_USER + 101)
#define ID_INPUTFILE_TXT    101
#define ID_INPUTFILE_CMB    102
```

(continues)

Listing 9.14 Continued

```
#define ID_OUTPUTFILE_TXT    103
#define ID_OUTPUTFILE_CMB    104
#define ID_KEYWORDS_GRP      105
#define ID_UPPERCASE_RBT     106
#define ID_LOWERCASE_RBT     107
#define ID_ADDCOLON_CHK      108
#define ID_BOLDKEYWORD_CHK   109
#define IDD_FILENUM_DLG      200
```

Listing 9.15 shows the script for the DIALOG4.RC resource file.

Listing 9.15 Script for the DIALOG4.RC Resource File

```
#include <windows.h>
#include <afxres.h>
#include "dialog4.h"
BUTTONS ACCELERATORS MOVEABLE PURE
BEGIN
    "o", IDOK, ALT
    "c", IDCANCEL, ALT
END
MAINMENU MENU DISCARDABLE
BEGIN
    MENUITEM "E&xit", CM_EXIT
    MENUITEM "&Dialog", CM_DIALOG
END
IDD_FILENUM_DLG DIALOG DISCARDABLE  10, 10, 200, 150
STYLE DS_MODALFRAME | WS_POPUP | WS_CLIPSIBLINGS |
                    WS_CAPTION | WS_SYSMENU
CAPTION "File Numbering"
FONT 8, "System"
BEGIN
    LTEXT           "Input File:",ID_INPUTFILE_TXT,20,10,100,8,
                    NOT WS_GROUP
    COMBOBOX        ID_INPUTFILE_CMB,20,20,100,36,
                    CBS_DROPDOWN | WS_BORDER | WS_TABSTOP
    LTEXT           "Output File:",ID_OUTPUTFILE_TXT,20,60,100,8,
                    NOT WS_GROUP
    COMBOBOX        ID_OUTPUTFILE_CMB,20,69,100,36,
                    CBS_DROPDOWN | WS_BORDER | WS_TABSTOP
    GROUPBOX        " Keywords ",ID_KEYWORDS_GRP,20,110,95,35,WS_GROUP
    CONTROL         "Uppercase",ID_UPPERCASE_RBT,"Button",
                    BS_AUTORADIOBUTTON | WS_TABSTOP,30,120,50,10
    CONTROL         "Lowercase",ID_LOWERCASE_RBT,"Button",
                    BS_AUTORADIOBUTTON | WS_TABSTOP,30,130,60,10
    CONTROL         "Add colon",ID_ADDCOLON_CHK,"Button",
                    BS_AUTOCHECKBOX | WS_TABSTOP,135,40,60,15
    CONTROL         "Bold keywords",ID_BOLDKEYWORD_CHK,"Button",
                    BS_AUTOCHECKBOX | WS_TABSTOP,135,25,60,15
    DEFPUSHBUTTON   "&OK",IDOK,135,100,55,20,WS_GROUP
    PUSHBUTTON      "&Cancel",IDCANCEL,135,125,55,20,WS_GROUP
END
```

Listing 9.16 contains the source code for the DIALOG4.CPP program file.

Listing 9.16 Source Code for the DIALOG4.CPP Program File

```
#include <string.h>
#include <afxwin.h>
#include <afxcoll.h>
#include "dialog4.h"
// declare constants
const int MaxStringLen = 40;
const int BF_CHECKED = 1;
const int BF_UNCHECKED = 0;
class CComboBoxData
{
public:
  CString Selection;
  CStringArray DataList;

  CComboBoxData() {}
  // set the combo box data
  void GetComboBoxData(CComboBox* pCombo);
  // get the data from the combo box
  void SetComboBoxData(CComboBox* pCombo);
};
class CModalDialogApp : public CWinApp
{
 public:
    virtual BOOL InitInstance();
};
// expand the functionality of CDialog by
// deriving class CAppDialog
class CAppDialog : public CDialog
{
 public:
  CAppDialog(CWnd* pParentWnd = NULL)
    : CDialog(CAppDialog::IDD, pParentWnd) {}

  // data exchange buffer
  enum { IDD = IDD_FILENUM_DLG };
  int nUpperCaseRbtBuff;
  int nLowerCaseRbtBuff;
  int nAddColonChkBuff;
  int nBoldKeywordChkBuff;

 protected:

  // handle initializing the dialog box
  virtual BOOL OnInitDialog();
  // handle pressing the OK button
  virtual void OnOK();
  // handle data transfer
  virtual void DoDataExchange(CDataExchange* pDX);
};
```

(continues)

Listing 9.16 Continued

```cpp
// expand the functionality of CFrameWnd by deriving
// class CMainWnd
class CMainWnd : public CFrameWnd
{

  friend CAppDialog;

public:

  CMainWnd();
protected:
  CComboBoxData InputFileList;
  CComboBoxData OutputFileList;
  int nUpperCaseRbtBuff;
  int nLowerCaseRbtBuff;
  int nAddColonChkBuff;
  int nBoldKeywordChkBuff;
  // handle the dialog command
  afx_msg void CMDialog();
  // handle exiting the application
  afx_msg void OnExit()
    { SendMessage(WM_CLOSE); }
  // handle closing the window
  afx_msg void OnClose();
  // declare message map macro
  DECLARE_MESSAGE_MAP()
};
void CComboBoxData::GetComboBoxData(CComboBox* pCombo)
{
  char szStr[MaxStringLen+1];

  if (pCombo) {
    // get the selection text
    pCombo->GetWindowText(Selection.GetBuffer(MaxStringLen),
                          MaxStringLen);
    Selection.ReleaseBuffer();
    // get the number of items in the combo list
    int n = pCombo->GetCount();
    // remove all of the previous array members
    DataList.RemoveAll();
    // update the array with current data
    for (int i = 0; i < n; i++) {
      pCombo->GetLBText(i, szStr);
      DataList.Add(szStr);
    }
    DataList.SetSize(n);
  }
}

void CComboBoxData::SetComboBoxData(CComboBox* pCombo)
{
  if (pCombo) {
    int n = DataList.GetSize();
    // get the selection text
    pCombo->SetWindowText((const char*)Selection);
```

```
    // get the number of items in the combo list
    for (int i = 0; i < n; i++)
      pCombo->InsertString(i, (const char*) DataList[i]);
  }
}
BOOL CAppDialog::OnInitDialog()
{
  CMainWnd* pW = (CMainWnd*)(GetParent());
  // copy data from the buffer to the dialog box controls
  CComboBox* pCombo = (CComboBox*)(GetDlgItem(ID_INPUTFILE_CMB));
  pW->InputFileList.SetComboBoxData(pCombo);
  pCombo = (CComboBox*)(GetDlgItem(ID_OUTPUTFILE_CMB));
  pW->OutputFileList.SetComboBoxData(pCombo);
  UpdateData(FALSE);
  return TRUE;
}
void CAppDialog::OnOK()
{
  CMainWnd* pW = (CMainWnd*)(GetParent());
  char szStr[MaxStringLen+1];
  int i;

  // copy data from the dialog box controls to the buffer
  CComboBox* pCombo = (CComboBox*)(GetDlgItem(ID_INPUTFILE_CMB));
  if (!pCombo)
    MessageBox("pCombo is NULL", "Error!");
  // get the string from the edit control
  pCombo->GetWindowText(szStr, MaxStringLen);
  // is string not empty?
  if (szStr[0] != '\0') {
    i = pCombo->FindString(-1, szStr);
    if (i >= 0) {
      // delete the matching list item
      pCombo->DeleteString(i);
      // write s back to the edit area (MFC bug fix??)
      pCombo->SetWindowText(szStr);
    }
    // insert string at the head of the list
    pCombo->InsertString(0, szStr);
  }
  pW->InputFileList.GetComboBoxData(pCombo);
  pCombo = (CComboBox*)(GetDlgItem(ID_OUTPUTFILE_CMB));
  // get the string from the edit control
  pCombo->GetWindowText(szStr, MaxStringLen);
  // is string not empty?
  if (szStr[0] != '\0') {
    i = pCombo->FindString(-1, szStr);
    if (i >= 0) {
      // delete the matching list item
      pCombo->DeleteString(i);
      // write s back to the edit area (MFC bug fix??)
      pCombo->SetWindowText(szStr);
    }
    // insert string at the head of the list
    pCombo->InsertString(0, szStr);
  }
```

(continues)

Listing 9.16 Continued

```
    pW->OutputFileList.GetComboBoxData(pCombo);
    UpdateData(TRUE);
    // return dialog box value
    EndDialog(IDOK);
}

void CAppDialog::DoDataExchange(CDataExchange* pDX)
{
    CDialog::DoDataExchange(pDX); // call base class
    // update the Global radio button
    DDX_Radio(pDX, ID_UPPERCASE_RBT, nUpperCaseRbtBuff);
    // update the Selected Text radio button
    DDX_Radio(pDX, ID_LOWERCASE_RBT, nLowerCaseRbtBuff);
    // update the Case Sensitive check box
    DDX_Check(pDX, ID_ADDCOLON_CHK, nAddColonChkBuff);
    // update the Whole Word check box
    DDX_Check(pDX, ID_BOLDKEYWORD_CHK, nBoldKeywordChkBuff);
}
CMainWnd::CMainWnd()
{
    // load the accelerator keys resource
    LoadAccelTable("BUTTONS");
    // create the window
    Create(NULL, "Modal Dialog Box Data Transfer Tester (version 2)",
           WS_OVERLAPPEDWINDOW, rectDefault, NULL, "MAINMENU");

    nUpperCaseRbtBuff = BF_CHECKED;
    nLowerCaseRbtBuff = BF_UNCHECKED;
    nAddColonChkBuff = BF_CHECKED;
    nBoldKeywordChkBuff = BF_CHECKED;
};
void CMainWnd::CMDialog()
{
    CString msgStr;
    CAppDialog Dlg(this);
    Dlg.nUpperCaseRbtBuff = nUpperCaseRbtBuff;
    Dlg.nLowerCaseRbtBuff = nLowerCaseRbtBuff;
    Dlg.nAddColonChkBuff = nAddColonChkBuff;
    Dlg.nBoldKeywordChkBuff = nBoldKeywordChkBuff;
    if (Dlg.DoModal() == IDOK) {
        nUpperCaseRbtBuff = Dlg.nUpperCaseRbtBuff;
        nLowerCaseRbtBuff = Dlg.nLowerCaseRbtBuff;
        nAddColonChkBuff = Dlg.nAddColonChkBuff;
        nBoldKeywordChkBuff = Dlg.nBoldKeywordChkBuff;
        msgStr = "Input File: " +
                 InputFileList.Selection +
                 "\nOutput File: " +
                 OutputFileList.Selection +
                 "\nUppercase: ";
        msgStr += (Dlg.nUpperCaseRbtBuff == BF_CHECKED) ?
                                            "TRUE" : "FALSE";
        msgStr += "\nLowercase: ";
        msgStr += (Dlg.nLowerCaseRbtBuff == BF_CHECKED) ?
                                            "TRUE" : "FALSE";
```

```
      msgStr += "\nAdd colon: ";
      msgStr += (Dlg.nAddColonChkBuff == BF_CHECKED) ?
                                       "TRUE" : "FALSE";
      msgStr += "\nBold keyword: ";
      msgStr += (Dlg.nBoldKeywordChkBuff == BF_CHECKED) ?
                                       "TRUE" : "FALSE";
      // display the contents of msgStr
      MessageBox((const char*) msgStr, "Dialog Box Data",
              MB_OK | MB_ICONINFORMATION);
    }
  }
}
void CMainWnd::OnClose()
{
  if (MessageBox("Want to close this application",
                 "Query", MB_YESNO | MB_ICONQUESTION) == IDYES)
    DestroyWindow();
}
BEGIN_MESSAGE_MAP(CMainWnd, CFrameWnd)
  ON_COMMAND(CM_DIALOG, CMDialog)
  ON_COMMAND(CM_EXIT, OnExit)
  ON_WM_CLOSE()
END_MESSAGE_MAP()
// Construct the CModalDialogApp's m_pMainWnd data member
BOOL CModalDialogApp::InitInstance()
{
  m_pMainWnd = new CMainWnd();
  m_pMainWnd->ShowWindow(m_nCmdShow);
  m_pMainWnd->UpdateWindow();
  return TRUE;
}
// application's constructor initializes and runs the app
CModalDialogApp WindowApp;
```

The source code for the DIALOG4.CPP program file, just shown in Listing 9.16, declares the class CComboBoxData, the dialog box class, the window class, and the application class. The class CComboBoxData supports the data transfer between the combo box controls and the data buffer. The class defines the member functions GetComboBoxData and SetComboBoxdata.

The member function CComboBoxData::GetComboBoxData copies the contents of a combo box control to the data buffer. The function performs the following tasks:

■ Verifies that the parameter pCombo is not a NULL pointer. If this condition is true, the function performs the remaining tasks.

■ Copies the contents of the edit control to the object Selection.

■ Obtains the number of items in the combo box accessed by the pointer pCombo and stores it in the local variable n.

■ Deletes all the current members of the string array DataList. This task involves sending the C++ message RemoveAll to the object DataList.

■ Uses a loop to obtain the list items from the combo box and adds them to the string array DataList.

■ Sets the size of the string array to the number of items contained in the list box portion of the combo box control. This task involves sending the C++ message SetSize to the object DataList. The argument of the message SetSize is the local variable n.

The member function CComboBoxData::SetComboBoxData copies data from the buffer to the combo box control that is accessed by the pointer pCombo. The function performs the following tasks:

■ Verifies that the parameter pCombo is not a NULL pointer. If this condition is true, the function performs the remaining tasks.

■ Obtains the number of elements in the string array DataList and assigns the result to the local variable n. This task involves sending the C++ message GetSize to the object DataList.

■ Assigns the string in the data member Selection to the edit control portion of the combo box control.

■ Uses a for loop to insert elements of the string array DataList into the list box of the target combo box control.

The CAppDialog class declares the member functions OnInitDialog, OnOK, and DoDataExchange. In addition, the class declares the public data members to exchange data with the check box and radio button controls. Notice that the class does not declare members as buffers for the combo list boxes. Why? The answer lies in the fact that the DDX functions do not support the kind of data transfer implemented in this program. The class CComboBoxData supports the transfer of combo box data.

The member function OnInitDialog initializes the dialog box by performing the following tasks:

■ Obtaining a pointer to the parent window, which is the main window. This task invokes the inherited function GetParent. The function assigns the pointer to the parent window to the local pointer pW.

- Obtaining the pointer to the Input File combo box. This task involves the function GetDlgItem, which has the argument ID_INPUTFILE_CMD (the ID of the targeted control). This task assigns the address of the Input File combo box to the local pointer pCombo.

- Copying the data from the buffer to the Input File combo box. This task involves sending the C++ message SetComboBoxData to the InputFileList member of the main window class.

- Repeating the preceding two tasks to similarly transfer data from the buffer to the Output File combo box.

- Invoking the function UpdateData to transfer the data to the radio buttons and the check boxes.

- Returning the value TRUE.

The member function OnOK copies the data from the controls of the dialog box to the buffer. The function uses the local pointer pCombo to access the data in the combo boxes. The OnOK function treats the combo boxes as history boxes. The string in the edit control component, therefore, is inserted as the first item in the list box. If that string already exists in the list box, the matching list box item is deleted. This sequence of statements is applied to each combo box. The OnOK function uses the function GetComboBoxData to retrieve the data from the combo boxes after updating the list box component.

> **Note**
>
> This program example shows how to use the member functions OnInitDialog and OnOK to implement a data transfer that is beyond the capabilities of the DDX functions. In this case, the data transfer concerns the entire list of items in the combo box controls.

The member function DoDataExchange uses the DDX functions to link the radio buttons and check boxes with their respective data members.

The window class declares a constructor, a set of data members, and a group of member functions. The data members include two instances of the class CComboBoxData, which are used to store combo box data between the invocations of the dialog box. In addition, the class declares data members that correspond to the public data members of the class CAppDialog.

II

Visual C++ Programming

The window constructor creates the main window and assigns the BF_CHECKED and BF_UNCHECKED values to the initialized dialog box controls.

The member function CMDialog responds to the CM_DIALOG Windows command message by performing the following tasks:

- Creating the instance Dlg of the class CAppDialog.

- Copying the values in the data members of the window object to the corresponding members of the dialog box object. This task both initializes and updates the controls of the dialog box before invoking the dialog box.

- Invoking the dialog box by sending the C++ message DoModal to the object Dlg. If the message yields the value IDOK, the function performs the remaining tasks.

- Copying the values in the data members of the dialog box object to the corresponding members of the window object. This task updates the window's data member with the latest dialog box data after invoking the dialog box.

- Building the display string (stored in the local CString instance, msgStr). This task involves accessing the public dialog box data members InputFileBoxBuff and OutputFileBoxBuff.

- Displaying a message box that shows the strings you typed in the Input File and Output File edit controls, as well as the states of the radio buttons and check boxes.

Transferring Dialog Box Data without Using *DoDataExchange*

You can transfer data between the dialog box controls and their buffers without using the function DoDataExchange. This method has its advantages and disadvantages compared to the MFC method. The advantages include better control over the transfer of scroll bars, list boxes, and combo boxes. The disadvantages include difficulty in implementing data validation.

The transfer method just mentioned also uses a buffer to store the values and states of the dialog box controls. This buffer usually is a data member of the parent window. The first step in supporting data transfer, therefore, is to define a transfer buffer type. The buffer declares the data fields to hold the information of the controls transferring their data. These controls usually include static text, edit boxes, list boxes, combo boxes, scroll bars, check boxes, and radio buttons. The group box and pushbutton controls have no data to transfer and therefore do not have to be included in the declaration of the data transfer buffer type. The following is a sample data buffer type that includes a single instance of each allowable control:

```
struct TAppTransferBuffer {
    char szStaticText[MaxStaticTextLen+1];
    char szEditBox[MaxEditBoxLen+1];
    CListBoxData ListBoxData;     // user-defined class
    CComboBoxData ComboBoxData;   // user-defined class
    CScrollBarData ScrollBarData; // user-defined class
    int nCheckBox;
    int nRadioButton;
};
```

The buffer structure only has to include the controls that participate in the data transfer. You don't have to declare the fields of the buffer structure in any particular order. The preceding sample buffer type includes three special user-defined classes that transfer data between dialog boxes and list boxes, combo boxes, and scroll bars.

Let's look at the various members of the data transfer buffer type:

■ The member szStaticText assists in moving data between a static text control and the data buffer. The data member defines a character array that should be equal to or greater than the number of characters in the static text control.

■ The member szEditBox helps in transferring data between the edit box control and the data buffer. The data member defines a character array that should be equal to or greater than the number of characters in the edit box control.

■ The member ListBoxData helps in transferring data between a list box control and the data buffer. The ListBoxData is an instance of the class that you declare to manage the data transfer between a dialog box and a list box. Why use a special data transfer class? The answer lies in the fact that this kind of class successfully encapsulates the data and operations related to the transferred data. A typical declaration for the CListBoxData class is shown in the following:

```
class CListBox
{
public:
     // array of CString to store the list box items
     CStringArray DataList;
     CListBoxData();
     // transfer data to the buffer
     void GetListBoxData(CListBox* pListBox);
     // transfer data to the list box
     void SetListBoxData(CListBox* pListBox);
};
```

The member DataList is a dynamic array of CString objects that store the list box items. The MFC library declares the class CStringArray and provides adequate operations to manipulate the array of strings. The absence of a data member to keep track of the number of list box items is justified by the fact that the CStringArray class offers the GetSize member function to provide the number of string objects in a CStringArray instance.

The GetListBoxData and SetListBoxData member functions provide the two-way data transfer between a list box control and the data buffer.

■ The member ComboBoxData helps to transfer data between a combo box control and the data buffer. The ComboBoxData is an instance of the CComboBoxData class that you declare. Here is a typical declaration for the class CComboBoxData:

```
class CComboBox
{
public:
     // the combo box selection
     CString Selection;
     // array of CString to store the list box items
     CStringArray DataList;
     CComboBoxData();
     // transfer data to the buffer
     void GetComboBoxData(CListBox* pComboBox);
     // transfer data to the combo box
     void SetComboBoxData(CListBox* pComboBox);
};
```

The suggested declaration of the class CComboBoxData is similar to that of the class CListBoxData. The class ComboBoxData has an additional data member, Selection, to store the combo box selection located in its edit control.

■ The member ScrollBarData assists in transferring data between a scroll bar control and the data buffer. This member has the suggested CScollBarData class, which is defined as follows:

```
class CScrollBarData
{
public:
    int nMinVal;
    int nMaxVal;
    int nCurVal;
    CScrollBarData();
    // move data to the buffer
    void GetScrollBarData(CScrollBar* pScrollBar);
    // move data to the scroll bar
    void SetScrollBarData(CScrollBar* pScrollBar);
};
```

The members nMinVal, nMaxVal, and nCurVal store the scroll bar range and the current thumb position.

■ The member nCheckBox stores the current check state of a check box in an int data type.

■ The member nRadioButton stores the current check state of a radio button in an int data type.

Transferring Data Using a Simple Modeless Dialog Box

An earlier section dealt with the transfer of data from the controls of a modal dialog box. In this section, I discuss the transfer of data for a modeless dialog box. The DIALOG5.EXE program also shows how to transfer data without using DoDataExchange and, at your discretion, using a special pushbutton control. This next application is a variation on the first version of the File Numbering dialog box. This new version, DIALOG5.EXE, is very similar to DIALOG3.EXE, which was presented earlier in this chapter. The two differ in the following aspects:

■ The dialog box is modeless.

■ The dialog box has an additional Send pushbutton.

When you click the Send button (see Figure 9.7), the dialog box copies the text in its Input File and Output File edit boxes to the edit boxes in the parent window that likewise are labeled Input File and Output File.

Visual C++ Programming

II

Figure 9.7

A sample
session with the
DIALOG5.EXE
program.

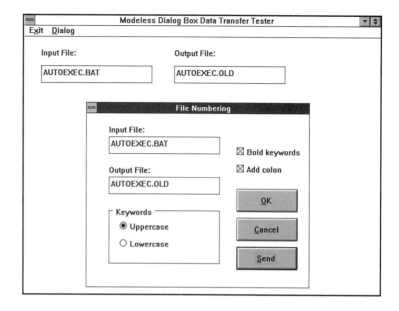

When you click the Dialog menu item in the program, the application causes
a modeless dialog box to pop up. The dialog box contains the filenames
AUTOEXEC.BAT and AUTOEXEC.OLD in the Input File and Output File edit
boxes, respectively. The program initially checks the Uppercase radio button,
Add colon check box, and the Bold keywords check box. Type new filenames
in either or both of the edit boxes and click the OK pushbutton. This action
causes the following to occur:

- The File Numbering dialog box closes.

- A message dialog box is displayed that contains the strings in the edit
  box controls and the states of the radio buttons and check boxes.

- The text of the dialog box is echoed in the edit boxes of the window.

Invoke the dialog box again, and type new filenames in both edit boxes.
Now click the Send button and watch how the new filenames appear in the
window's edit boxes.

Listing 9.17 contains the contents of the DIALOG5.DEF definition file.

Listing 9.17 The DIALOG5.DEF Definition File

```
NAME           Dialog5
DESCRIPTION    'An MFC Windows Application'
EXETYPE        WINDOWS
```

```
CODE          PRELOAD MOVEABLE DISCARDABLE
DATA          PRELOAD MOVEABLE MULTIPLE
HEAPSIZE      1024
```

Listing 9.18 shows the source code for the DIALOG5.H header file.

Listing 9.18 Source Code for the DIALOG5.H Header File

```
#define CM_EXIT   (WM_USER + 100)
#define CM_DIALOG (WM_USER + 101)
#define ID_INPUTFILE_TXT      101
#define ID_INPUTFILE_EDIT     102
#define ID_OUTPUTFILE_TXT     103
#define ID_OUTPUTFILE_EDIT    104
#define ID_KEYWORDS_GRP       105
#define ID_UPPERCASE_RBT      106
#define ID_LOWERCASE_RBT      107
#define ID_ADDCOLON_CHK       108
#define ID_BOLDKEYWORD_CHK    109
#define ID_INPUTFILE_BOX      110
#define ID_OUTPUTFILE_BOX     112
#define ID_SEND_BTN           113
```

Listing 9.19 shows the script for the DIALOG5.RC resource file.

Listing 9.19 Script for the DIALOG5.RC Resource File

```
#include <windows.h>
#include <afxres.h>
#include "dialog5.h"
BUTTONS ACCELERATORS
BEGIN
  "o", IDOK, ALT
  "c", IDCANCEL, ALT
  "s", ID_SEND_BTN, ALT
END
MAINMENU MENU LOADONCALL MOVEABLE PURE DISCARDABLE
BEGIN
    MENUITEM "E&xit", CM_EXIT
    MENUITEM "&Dialog", CM_DIALOG
END

FILENUM DIALOG DISCARDABLE LOADONCALL PURE MOVEABLE 10, 10,
                                               200, 150
STYLE WS_POPUP ¦ WS_CLIPSIBLINGS ¦ WS_CAPTION ¦ WS_SYSMENU ¦
      WS_DLGFRAME ¦ WS_VISIBLE
CAPTION "File Numbering"
FONT 8, "System"
BEGIN
    LTEXT           "Input File:",ID_INPUTFILE_TXT,
                    20,10,100,8,NOT WS_GROUP
```

(continues)

Listing 9.19 Continued

```
        EDITTEXT        ID_INPUTFILE_EDIT,20,20,100,15
        LTEXT           "Output File:",ID_OUTPUTFILE_TXT,
                        20,45,100,8, NOT WS_GROUP
        EDITTEXT        ID_OUTPUTFILE_EDIT,20,55,100,15
        GROUPBOX        " Keywords ",ID_KEYWORDS_GRP,
                        20,80,100,50,WS_GROUP
        CONTROL         "Uppercase",ID_UPPERCASE_RBT,"Button",
                         BS_AUTORADIOBUTTON | WS_TABSTOP,30,90,50,15
        CONTROL         "Lowercase",ID_LOWERCASE_RBT,"Button",
                        BS_AUTORADIOBUTTON | WS_TABSTOP,30,105,60,15
        CONTROL         "Add colon",ID_ADDCOLON_CHK,"Button",
                        BS_AUTOCHECKBOX | WS_TABSTOP,135,40,60,15
        CONTROL         "Bold keywords",ID_BOLDKEYWORD_CHK,"Button",
                        BS_AUTOCHECKBOX | WS_TABSTOP,135,25,60,15
        DEFPUSHBUTTON   "&OK",IDOK,135,65,55,20,WS_GROUP
        PUSHBUTTON      "&Cancel",IDCANCEL,135,90,55,20,WS_GROUP
        PUSHBUTTON      "&Send",ID_SEND_BTN,135,115,55,20,WS_GROUP
END
```

The source code for the DIALOG5.CPP program file is provided in Listing 9.20.

Listing 9.20 Source Code for the DIALOG5.CPP Program File

```cpp
#include <string.h>
#include <afxwin.h>
#include "dialog5.h"
// declare constants for sizing and dimensioning the
// application window's controls
const Wtxt = 200;
const Htxt = 20;
const TxtVertSpacing = 10;
const Wbox = 200;
const Hbox = 30;
const BoxHorzSpacing = 40;
// declare other constants
const MaxStringLen = 30;
const BF_CHECKED = 1;
const BF_UNCHECKED = 0;
// declare the application buffer
struct TAppTransferBuf {
  char szInputFileBoxBuff[MaxStringLen+1];
  char szOutputFileBoxBuff[MaxStringLen+1];
  int nUpperCaseRbtBuff;
  int nLowerCaseRbtBuff;
  int nAddColonChkBuff;
  int nBoldKeywordChkBuff;
};
class CModelessDialogApp : public CWinApp
```

```
{
 public:
    virtual BOOL InitInstance();
};
// expand the functionality of CDialog by
// deriving class CModelessDialog
class CModelessDialog : public CDialog
{
 public:
  CModelessDialog(LPCSTR lpszTemplateName, CWnd* pParentWnd);
  // handle pressing the OK button
  afx_msg void OnOK();
  afx_msg void CMOK()
    { OnOK(); }
  // handle pressing the Cancel button
  afx_msg void OnCancel();
  afx_msg void CMCancel()
    { OnCancel(); }
  // handle sending data without closing the modal dialog box
  afx_msg void HandleSendBtn();
  afx_msg void CMSendBtn()
    { HandleSendBtn(); }
 protected:
  // pointer to data buffer in parent window
  TAppTransferBuf* pAppBuffer;

  // handle initializing the dialog box
  virtual BOOL OnInitDialog();

  // transfer data from the controls to the buffer
  void TransferData();

  // declare message map macro
  DECLARE_MESSAGE_MAP();
};
// expand the functionality of CFrameWnd by deriving
// class CMainWnd
class CMainWnd : public CFrameWnd
{
 public:
  // declare data transfer buffer
  TAppTransferBuf AppBuffer;
  CMainWnd();
  ~CMainWnd();
  // handle the dialog command
  afx_msg void CMDialog();
  // handle a message sent by the Send button of
  // the dialog box
  afx_msg void HandleSendBtn();
  // handle exiting the application
  afx_msg void OnExit()
    { SendMessage(WM_CLOSE); }

  BOOL IsDialogActive() { return bDialogActive; }
  void DialogIsActive() { bDialogActive = TRUE; }
  void DialogIsNotActive() { bDialogActive = FALSE; }
```

II

Visual C++ Programming

(continues)

Listing 9.20 Continued

```
protected:
  // declare the pointers to the window's controls
  // and the modeless dialog box
  CStatic* pInputFileTxt;
  CEdit* pInputFileBox;
  CStatic* pOutputFileTxt;
  CEdit* pOutputFileBox;
  CModelessDialog* pDlg;
  // flag to indicate whether or not the
  // modeless dialog box is active
  BOOL bDialogActive;

  // handle creating the controls
  afx_msg int OnCreate(LPCREATESTRUCT lpCS);
  // handle closing the window
  afx_msg void OnClose();
  // return a reference to member r based on individual
  // coordinates and dimenions
  void makerect(int X, int Y, int W, int H, CRect& r)
    { r.SetRect(X, Y, X + W, Y + H); }
  // declare message map macro
  DECLARE_MESSAGE_MAP();
};
CModelessDialog::CModelessDialog(LPCSTR lpszTemplateName,
                                 CWnd* pParentWnd)
{
  Create(lpszTemplateName, pParentWnd);
}
BOOL CModelessDialog::OnInitDialog()
{
  CMainWnd* pW = (CMainWnd*)(GetParent());
  pAppBuffer = &pW->AppBuffer;
  // copy data from the buffer to the dialog box controls
  SetDlgItemText(ID_INPUTFILE_EDIT, pAppBuffer->szInputFileBoxBuff);
  SetDlgItemText(ID_OUTPUTFILE_EDIT,
                 pAppBuffer->szOutputFileBoxBuff);
  CButton* pBtn = (CButton*)(GetDlgItem(ID_UPPERCASE_RBT));
  pBtn->SetCheck(pAppBuffer->nUpperCaseRbtBuff);
  pBtn = (CButton*)(GetDlgItem(ID_LOWERCASE_RBT));
  pBtn->SetCheck(pAppBuffer->nLowerCaseRbtBuff);
  pBtn = (CButton*)(GetDlgItem(ID_ADDCOLON_CHK));
  pBtn->SetCheck(pAppBuffer->nAddColonChkBuff);
  pBtn = (CButton*)(GetDlgItem(ID_BOLDKEYWORD_CHK));
  pBtn->SetCheck(pAppBuffer->nBoldKeywordChkBuff);
  return TRUE;
}
void CModelessDialog::OnOK()
{
  CString msgStr;
  CMainWnd* pParent = (CMainWnd*)(GetParent());
  // transfer data to the buffer
  TransferData();
  // notify parent of transfer
  pParent->SendMessage(WM_COMMAND, ID_SEND_BTN);
```

```
    // clear active dialog flag
    pParent->DialogIsNotActive();
    // close the modeless dialog box
    DestroyWindow();

    msgStr = "Input File: ";
    msgStr += pAppBuffer->szInputFileBoxBuff;
    msgStr += "\nOutput File: ";
    msgStr += pAppBuffer->szOutputFileBoxBuff;
    msgStr += "\nUppercase: ";
    msgStr += (pAppBuffer->nUpperCaseRbtBuff == BF_CHECKED) ?
                                     "TRUE" : "FALSE";
    msgStr += "\nLowercase: ";
    msgStr += (pAppBuffer->nLowerCaseRbtBuff == BF_CHECKED) ?
                                     "TRUE" : "FALSE";
    msgStr += "\nAdd colon: ";
    msgStr += (pAppBuffer->nAddColonChkBuff == BF_CHECKED) ?
                                     "TRUE" : "FALSE";
    msgStr += "\nBold keyword: ";
    msgStr += (pAppBuffer->nBoldKeywordChkBuff == BF_CHECKED) ?
                                     "TRUE" : "FALSE";
    // display the contents of msgStr
    MessageBox((const char*) msgStr, "Dialog Box Data",
            MB_OK | MB_ICONINFORMATION);
}
void CModelessDialog::OnCancel()
{
    CMainWnd* pParent = (CMainWnd*)(GetParent());
    // clear active dialog flag
    pParent->DialogIsNotActive();
    // close the modeless dialog box
    DestroyWindow();
}
void CModelessDialog::HandleSendBtn()
{
    CMainWnd* pParent = (CMainWnd*)(GetParent());

    // transfer data to the buffer
    TransferData();
    // notify parent of transfer
    pParent->SendMessage(WM_COMMAND, ID_SEND_BTN);
}

void CModelessDialog::TransferData()
{
    // copy data from the dialog box controls to the buffer
    GetDlgItemText(ID_INPUTFILE_EDIT, pAppBuffer->szInputFileBoxBuff,
                   MaxStringLen);
    GetDlgItemText(ID_OUTPUTFILE_EDIT,
                   pAppBuffer->szOutputFileBoxBuff,
                   MaxStringLen);
    CButton* pBtn = (CButton*)(GetDlgItem(ID_UPPERCASE_RBT));
    pAppBuffer->nUpperCaseRbtBuff = pBtn->GetCheck();
    pBtn = (CButton*)(GetDlgItem(ID_LOWERCASE_RBT));
    pAppBuffer->nLowerCaseRbtBuff = pBtn->GetCheck();
```

II

Visual C++ Programming

(continues)

Listing 9.20 Continued

```
      pBtn = (CButton*)(GetDlgItem(ID_ADDCOLON_CHK));
      pAppBuffer->nAddColonChkBuff = pBtn->GetCheck();
      pBtn = (CButton*)(GetDlgItem(ID_BOLDKEYWORD_CHK));
      pAppBuffer->nBoldKeywordChkBuff = pBtn->GetCheck();
    }
    CMainWnd::CMainWnd()
    {
      // load the accelerator keys resource
      LoadAccelTable("BUTTONS");
      // create the window
      Create(NULL, "Modeless Dialog Box Data Transfer Tester",
             WS_OVERLAPPEDWINDOW, rectDefault, NULL, "MAINMENU");
      // fill buffer with 0's
      memset(&AppBuffer, 0x0, sizeof(AppBuffer));
      strcpy(AppBuffer.szInputFileBoxBuff, "AUTOEXEC.BAT");
      strcpy(AppBuffer.szOutputFileBoxBuff, "AUTOEXEC.OLD");
      AppBuffer.nUpperCaseRbtBuff = BF_CHECKED;
      AppBuffer.nAddColonChkBuff = BF_CHECKED;
      AppBuffer.nBoldKeywordChkBuff = BF_CHECKED;
      // clear the active dialog flag
      DialogIsNotActive();
    };
    CMainWnd::~CMainWnd()
    {
      delete pInputFileTxt;
      delete pInputFileBox;
      delete pOutputFileTxt;
      delete pOutputFileBox;
    }
    int CMainWnd::OnCreate(LPCREATESTRUCT lpCS)
    {
      int nX0 = 30;
      int nY0 = 20;
      int nX = nX0;
      int nY = nY0;
      CRect r;
      DWORD dwStaticStyle = WS_CHILD | WS_VISIBLE | SS_LEFT;
      DWORD dwEditStyle = WS_CHILD | WS_VISIBLE | WS_BORDER |
                  ES_LEFT | ES_AUTOHSCROLL;
      // create InputFile static text
      makerect(nX, nY, Wtxt, Htxt, r);
      pInputFileTxt = new CStatic();
      pInputFileTxt->Create("Input File:", dwStaticStyle, r, this);
      // create InputFile edit control
      nY += Htxt + TxtVertSpacing;
      makerect(nX, nY, Wbox, Hbox, r);
      pInputFileBox = new CEdit();
      pInputFileBox->Create(dwEditStyle, r, this, ID_INPUTFILE_BOX);
      // create OutputFile static text
      nX += Wbox + BoxHorzSpacing;
      nY = nY0;
      makerect(nX, nY, Wtxt, Htxt, r);
      pOutputFileTxt = new CStatic();
      pOutputFileTxt->Create("Output File:", dwStaticStyle, r, this);
```

```
        // create OutputFile edit control
        nY += Htxt + TxtVertSpacing;
        makerect(nX, nY, Wbox, Hbox, r);
        pOutputFileBox = new CEdit();
        pOutputFileBox->Create(dwEditStyle, r, this, ID_OUTPUTFILE_BOX);
        return CFrameWnd::OnCreate(lpCS);
    }
    void CMainWnd::CMDialog()
    {
        if (IsDialogActive()) return;
        pDlg = new CModelessDialog("FILENUM", this);
        DialogIsActive();
        pDlg->SendMessage(WM_INITDIALOG);
    }
    void CMainWnd::HandleSendBtn()
    {
        pInputFileBox->SetWindowText(AppBuffer.szInputFileBoxBuff);
        pOutputFileBox->SetWindowText(AppBuffer.szOutputFileBoxBuff);
    }
    void CMainWnd::OnClose()
    {
        if (MessageBox("Want to close this application",
                        "Query", MB_YESNO | MB_ICONQUESTION) == IDYES)
            DestroyWindow();
    }
    BEGIN_MESSAGE_MAP(CModelessDialog, CDialog)
      ON_BN_CLICKED(IDOK, OnOK)
      ON_COMMAND(IDOK, CMOK)
      ON_BN_CLICKED(IDCANCEL, OnCancel)
      ON_COMMAND(IDCANCEL, CMCancel)
      ON_BN_CLICKED(ID_SEND_BTN, HandleSendBtn)
      ON_COMMAND(ID_SEND_BTN, CMSendBtn)
    END_MESSAGE_MAP()
    BEGIN_MESSAGE_MAP(CMainWnd, CFrameWnd)
      ON_COMMAND(CM_DIALOG, CMDialog)
      ON_COMMAND(ID_SEND_BTN, HandleSendBtn)
      ON_COMMAND(CM_EXIT, OnExit)
      ON_WM_CREATE()
      ON_WM_CLOSE()
    END_MESSAGE_MAP()
    // Construct the CModelessDialogApp's pMainWnd data member
    BOOL CModelessDialogApp::InitInstance()
    {
        m_pMainWnd = new CMainWnd();
        m_pMainWnd->ShowWindow(m_nCmdShow);
        m_pMainWnd->UpdateWindow();
        return TRUE;
    }
    // application's constructor initializes and runs the app
    CModelessDialogApp WindowApp;
```

II

Visual C++ Programming

The source code for the DIALOG5.CPP program file, just shown in Listing 9.20, declares a group of constants for sizing and spacing the controls in the window application. The listing also contains the declaration of the data transfer buffer type, `TAppTransferBuf`, in the manner that I described in the last section. The buffer type has the following members:

- The string `szInputFileBoxBuff`, which is a buffer for the Input File edit box.

- The string `szOutputFileBoxBuff`, which is a buffer for the Output File edit box.

- The int-type member `nUpperCaseRbtBuff`, which is the buffer for the UpperCase radio button.

- The int-type member `nLowerCaseRbtBuff`, which is the buffer for the LowerCase radio button.

- The int-type member `nAddColonChkBuff`, which is the buffer for the Add colon check box.

- The int-type member `nBoldKeywordChkBuff`, which is the buffer for the Bold keywords check box.

The DIALOG5.EXE application declares three classes: the application class, the window class, and the dialog box class.

The dialog box class `CModelessDialog` declares a constructor; the public member functions `OnOK`, `CMOK`, `OnCancel`, `CMCancel`, `HandleSendBtn`, and `CMSendBtn`; the protected member `pAppBuffer` (a pointer to the transfer buffer type); and the protected member functions `OnInitDialog` and `TransferData`.

The dialog box class constructor simply invokes the inherited function `Create` to build a dialog box. The `CAppDialog` class declares member functions to handle each pushbutton. The dialog class declares the `TransferData` member function to transfer data from the dialog box controls to the buffer. This function is called by the `OnOK` and `HandleSendBtn` member functions.

The virtual member function `OnInitDialog` initializes the dialog box by copying the data from the buffer to the dialog box controls. The function performs the following tasks:

- Obtains the pointer to the parent window. This task uses the inherited member function `GetParent` and assigns the address of the parent window to the local pointer `pW`.

■ Obtains the address of the parent window's data buffer. This task accesses that buffer using the pointer pW and assigns the address of the buffer to the member pAppBuffer.

■ Copies the string from the parent window's szInputFileBoxBuff member to the Input File edit box. This task uses the function SetDlgItemText and specifies the ID of the targeted edit control in the dialog box.

■ Copies the string from the parent window's szOutputFileBoxBuff member to the Output File edit box. This task uses the function SetDlgItemText and specifies the ID of the targeted edit control in the dialog box.

■ Obtains the address of the UpperCase radio button and assigns it to the local pointer pBtn. This task uses the function GetDlgItem and specifies the ID of the targeted radio button.

■ Assigns the value in the buffer member nUpperCaseRbtBuff to the radio button accessed by the pointer pBtn. This task involves sending the C++ message SetCheck to the targeted control. The argument for this message is the expression

        pAppBuffer->nUpperCaseRbtBuff

■ Obtains the address of the LowerCase radio button and assigns it to the local pointer pBtn. This task uses the function GetDlgItem and specifies the ID of the targeted radio button.

■ Assigns the value in the buffer member nLowerCaseRbtBuff to the radio button accessed by the pointer pBtn. This task involves sending the C++ message SetCheck to the targeted control. The argument for this message is the expression

        pAppBuffer->nLowerCaseRbtBuff

■ Obtains the address of the Add colon check box and assigns it to the local pointer pBtn. This task uses the function GetDlgItem and specifies the ID of the targeted check box.

■ Assigns the value in the buffer member nAddColonChkBuff to the check box accessed by the pointer pBtn. This task involves sending the C++ message SetCheck to the targeted control. The argument for this message is the expression

        pAppBuffer->nAddColonChkBuff

- Obtains the address of the Bold keywords check box and assigns it to the local pointer pBtn. This task uses the function GetDlgItem and specifies the ID of the targeted check box.

- Assigns the value in the buffer member nBoldKeywordChkBuff to the check box accessed by the pointer pBtn. This task involves sending the C++ message SetCheck to the targeted control. The argument for this message is the expression

  ```
  pAppBuffer->nBoldKeywordChkBuff
  ```

- Returns TRUE.

The virtual OnOK member function responds to the IDOK notification message transmitted by the OK button. The function performs the following tasks:

- Transfers the data from the controls to the buffer by sending the C++ message TransferData.

- Sends an ID_SEND_BTN Windows message to the parent window using the SendMessage function.

- Sets the parent window data member, bDialogActive, to FALSE by sending that window the C++ message DialogIsNotActive.

- Closes the dialog box by invoking the DestroyWindow function.

- Builds the local CString object msgStr to contain the strings in the edit boxes and the states of both the radio buttons and the check boxes.

- Displays the contents of the object msgStr in a message dialog box.

The member function OnCancel handles the IDCANCEL notification message sent by the Cancel pushbutton. The function performs the following tasks:

- Obtains the address of the parent window and assigns that address to the local pointer pParent.

- Sets the parent window data member bDialogActive to FALSE by sending that window the C++ message DialogIsNotActive.

- Closes the dialog box by invoking the function DestroyWindow.

The HandleSendBtn member function handles the ID_SEND_BTN notification message transmitted by the Send button. The function carries out the following tasks:

- Transfers the data from the controls to the buffer by sending the C++ message `TransferData` member.

- Sends the message `ID_SEND_BTN` to the parent window using the `SendMessage` function.

The `CMSendBtn` member function handles the `ID_SEND_BTN` command message generated by the accelerator key Alt+S. The function simply calls the `HandleSendBtn` member function.

The member function `TransferData` copies the data from the dialog box controls to the buffer. The function performs tasks that are similar to those of the function `OnInitDialog`, except that the transfer is in the reverse direction. The function `TransferData` uses the inherited functions `GetDlgItemText`, `GetDlgItem`, and `GetCheck` to move the data to the buffer.

The window class `CMainWnd` declares one public data member, six protected data members, a constructor, a destructor, and six member functions. The data member `AppBuffer` is the data transfer buffer. The window class declares five protected pointers. The pointers, `pInputFileBox` and `pOutputFileBox`, access the edit box instance pointers s. The member `pDlg` is the pointer to the dialog box instance. The Boolean data member `bDialogActive` indicates whether or not the dialog box instance exists. Using this flag ensures one instance of the modeless dialog box. The member functions `IsDialogActive`, `DialogIsActive`, and `DialogIsNotActive` query and set the Boolean state of the member `bDialogActive`.

The `CMainWnd` constructor performs the following tasks:

- Loads the `BUTTONS` accelerator resource.

- Creates the application window by calling the `Create` function.

- Initializes the buffer by filling it with zeros.

- Assigns the strings AUTOEXEC.BAT and AUTOEXEC.OLD to the edit box buffers; assigns the constant `BF_CHECKED` to the check box buffers and the Add colon radio button buffer.

- Sets the data member `bDialogActive` to FALSE. This task involves using the member function `DialogIsNotActive`.

The OnCreate member function actually creates the controls that are attached to the application window. The function carries out the following tasks:

- Creates the static text instance that labels the Input File edit box.

- Creates the Input File edit box.

- Creates the static text instance that labels the Output File edit box.

- Creates the Output File edit box.

- Returns the function value.

The application window class declares the CMDialog member function to create a modeless dialog box. The function carries out these subsequent tasks:

- Exits if the sending message IsDialogActive yields TRUE.

- Creates a CModelessDialog instance that is accessed by the pDlg pointer.

- Sets the bDialogActive data member to TRUE by using the member function DialogIsActive.

- Brings the modeless dialog box on-screen by sending it a WM_INITDIALOG message. This task involves using the pDlg pointer to make the dialog box receive the intended message.

The HandleSendBtn member function responds to the message sent by the Send button in the dialog box by copying the InputFileBoxBuff and OutputFileBoxBuff buffer members to the Input File and Output File edit boxes in the window.

Summary

This chapter presented you with powerful dialog boxes that serve as input tools. You learned about:

- Constructing the modal and modeless dialog boxes using the class CDialog.

- Executing a modal dialog box using the DoModal member function.

- Creating a floating-point calculator program using a dialog box as a stand-alone window. In this case, the dialog box is the child of the application class.

■ Two methods for transferring the data of dialog box controls to and from the buffer. The first method uses the MFC member function `DoDataExchange`, whereas the second method employs user-defined classes to model a data transfer buffer type.

In addition, this chapter provided examples on transferring data for dialog boxes. These examples showed you how to transfer data for a simple modal dialog box, a complex modal dialog box, and a simple modeless dialog box.

II

Visual C++ Programming

Chapter 10

Using the Common Dialog Boxes

Windows supports five common dialog boxes that enable you to select a file, print, select a color, select a font, and search and replace text. In this chapter, I present the MFC classes and supporting structures that model these common dialog boxes. You learn about the following topics:

- Software requirements for using the common dialog boxes

- The color selection dialog box class CColorDialog

- The font selection dialog box class CFontDialog

- The printer setup dialog box class CPrintDialog

- The file selection dialog box class CFileDialog, which creates dialog boxes that support either opening or saving a file

- The text find/replace dialog box class CFindReplaceDialog, which creates dialog boxes that support either finding or replacing text

The common dialog boxes are supported by a family of Windows API functions, structures, and constants. As with other MFC library classes, Microsoft provides C++ classes to encapsulate the data and API functions to support the common dialog boxes. As I present each common dialog box class, I also show you the supporting data structures and constants.

The common dialog boxes merely present the visual user interface for their respective tasks. The client programs that invoke the common dialog boxes are responsible for providing the related operations based on the information supplied or selected through the common dialog boxes. The examples in this chapter focus on creating, invoking, and obtaining the data from the common dialog boxes.

Software Requirements

Compiling a program that uses the common dialog boxes requires the Windows 3.1 COMMDLG functions. Common dialog boxes, however, do not require Windows 3.1 to run, provided that COMMDLG.DLL is included with the programs targeted for Windows 3.0. When you are incorporating the common dialog boxes in your Windows applications, consider the following:

- Include the header file AFXDLGS.H in the client source files.

- Link with the COMMDLG.LIB library.

- Ensure that the dynamic library file COMMDLG.DLL is present in the Windows system directory (the default name of this directory is \WINDOWS\SYSTEM).

The *CColorDialog* Class

The class CColorDialog models the color selection common dialog box. Figure 10.1 shows a session with the COMMDLG1.EXE program (presented later in this chapter), which brings up the Color dialog box. The dialog box includes diverse controls to choose a color, define custom colors, and add to custom colors. And, as in most dialog boxes, the Color dialog box also includes OK and Cancel pushbuttons.

Supporting Classes and Structures

The class CColorDialog encapsulates the structure CHOOSECOLOR and the Windows API function ChooseColor. The declaration of the structure CHOOSECOLOR is as follows:

```
typedef struct tagCHOOSECOLOR
{
    DWORD   lStructSize;
    HWND    hwndOwner;
```

```
    HWND     hInstance;
    COLORREF rgbResult;
    COLORREF FAR* lpCustColors;
    DWORD    Flags;
    LPARAM   lCustData;
    UINT     (CALLBACK* lpfnHook)(HWND, UINT, WPARAM, LPARAM);
    LPCSTR   lpTemplateName;
} CHOOSECOLOR;
```

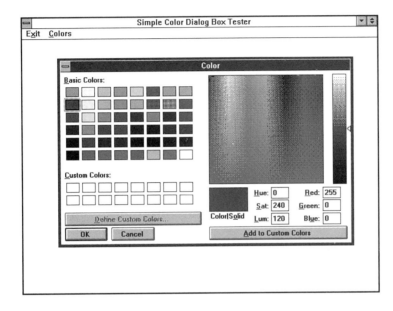

Figure 10.1

The program
COMMDLG1.EXE
showing the Color
dialog box.

The structure CHOOSECOLOR employs the following CC_*xxxx* constants:

```
#define CC_RGBINIT              0x00000001
#define CC_FULLOPEN             0x00000002
#define CC_PREVENTFULLOPEN      0x00000004
#define CC_SHOWHELP             0x00000008
#define CC_ENABLEHOOK           0x00000010
#define CC_ENABLETEMPLATE       0x00000020
#define CC_ENABLETEMPLATEHANDLE 0x00000040
```

The class CColorDialog, which is a descendant of the class CDialog, is declared
as follows:

```
class CColorDialog : public CDialog
{
  DECLARE_DYNAMIC(CColorDialog)
 public:
 // Attributes
  // color chooser parameter block
  CHOOSECOLOR m_cc;
```

```
                  // Constructors
                  CColorDialog(COLORREF clrInit = 0, DWORD dwFlags = 0,
                               CWnd* pParentWnd = NULL);
              // Operations
                  virtual int DoModal();
                  // Set the current color while dialog is displayed
                  void SetCurrentColor(COLORREF clr);
                  // Helpers for parsing information after successful return
                  COLORREF GetColor() const;
                  // Custom colors are held here and saved between calls
                  static COLORREF AFXAPI_DATA clrSavedCustom[16];
              // Overridable callbacks
              protected:
                  friend UINT CALLBACK AFX_EXPORT _AfxCommDlgProc(HWND, UINT,
                                                                  WPARAM, LPARAM);

                  virtual BOOL OnColorOK();        // validate color
              // Implementation
#ifdef _DEBUG
              public:
                  virtual void Dump(CDumpContext& dc) const;
#endif
              protected:
                  virtual void OnOK();
                  virtual void OnCancel();
                  //{{AFX_MSG(CColorDialog)
                  afx_msg HBRUSH OnCtlColor(CDC* pDC, CWnd* pWnd, UINT nCtlColor);
                  //}}AFX_MSG
                  DECLARE_MESSAGE_MAP()
              };
```

The class constructor has three parameters that fine-tune the Color dialog
boxes. The COLORREF-type parameter clrInit defines the initial color selection.
The default argument for this parameter is 0, which is also equal to the result
of the function call RGB(0, 0, 0). The RGB function yields the numeric color
code based in the values for the red, green, and blue components. The parameter dwFlags contains the set of flags that customizes the Color dialog box.
The default argument for this parameter is 0. The parameter pParentWnd is a
pointer to the parent window.

The class CColorDialog declares the data member m_cc, which has the
CHOOSECOLOR structure type. This data member enables the class instances to
exchange data with the supporting API functions.

Invoking the Color Dialog Box

After the program creates the CColorDialog instance using the constructor,
it can invoke the dialog box using the virtual member function DoModal.
To accept the dialog box selection, click the OK button, which makes the

DoModal function return the IDOK result. To close the dialog box without accepting the current selection, click the Cancel button or select the Close command from the system menu. Either action causes the DoModal function to return IDCANCEL.

Note

The IDCANCEL result doubles as a flag for rejecting the current selection and for signaling an error. If your application must detect any error, call the Windows API function CommDlgExtendedError. This function returns 0 if there is no error and a nonzero value if there is an error.

Using the *CColorDialog* Helper Functions

The class CColorDialog provides the function GetColor, which yields a COLORREF-type result to indicate the selected color. In addition, the class offers the member function SetCurrentColor to set the color while the dialog box is active.

Testing the Class *CColorDialog*

Let's look at a simple program that opens the Color dialog box and then displays the numeric value for the selected color.

Listing 10.1 shows the contents of the COMMDLG1.DEF definition file.

Listing 10.1 The COMMDLG1.DEF Definition File

```
NAME         CommDlg1
DESCRIPTION  'An MFC Windows Application'
EXETYPE      WINDOWS
CODE         PRELOAD MOVEABLE DISCARDABLE
DATA         PRELOAD MOVEABLE MULTIPLE
HEAPSIZE     1024
```

Listing 10.2 shows the COMMDLG1.H header file.

Listing 10.2 Source Code for the COMMDLG1.H Header File

```
#define CM_EXIT         (WM_USER + 100)
#define CM_COLORCHANGE  (WM_USER + 101)
```

Listing 10.3 contains the script for the COMMDLG1.RC resource file.

Listing 10.3 Script for the COMMDLG1.RC Resource File

```
#include <windows.h>
#include <afxres.h>
#include "commdlg1.h"
MAINMENU MENU LOADONCALL MOVEABLE PURE DISCARDABLE
BEGIN
    MENUITEM "E&xit", CM_EXIT
    MENUITEM "&Colors", CM_COLORCHANGE
END
```

The source code for the COMMDLG1.CPP program file is provided in
Listing 10.4.

Listing 10.4 Source Code for the COMMDLG1.CPP Program File

```
/*
  Program tests the class CColorDialog which creates the
  color selection dialog box
*/
#include <stdio.h>
#include <string.h>
#include <afxwin.h>
#include <afxdlgs.h>
#include "commdlg1.h"
const MaxStringLen = 41;
// declare the custom application class as
class CColorDialogApp : public CWinApp
{
public:
    virtual BOOL InitInstance();
};
// expand the functionality of CFrameWnd by deriving class CMainWnd
class CMainWnd : public CFrameWnd
{
 public:
  CMainWnd();
 protected:
  // handle the Colors menu item
  afx_msg void CMColorChange();
  // handle exiting the application
  afx_msg void OnExit()
    { SendMessage(WM_CLOSE); }
  // handle closing the window
  afx_msg void OnClose();
  // declare message map macro
  DECLARE_MESSAGE_MAP()
};
```

```
CMainWnd::CMainWnd()
{
  // create the window
  Create(NULL, "Simple Color Dialog Box Tester",
         WS_OVERLAPPEDWINDOW, rectDefault, NULL, "MAINMENU");
}
void CMainWnd::CMColorChange()
{
  char s[MaxStringLen+1];
  CColorDialog aColorDialogBox(0, 0, this);

  if (aColorDialogBox.DoModal() == IDOK) {
    sprintf(s, "Selected Color Value = %lu",
            aColorDialogBox.GetColor());
    MessageBox(s, "Color Selection", MB_OK | MB_ICONINFORMATION);
  }
}
void CMainWnd::OnClose()
{
  if (MessageBox("Want to close this application",
                 "Query", MB_YESNO | MB_ICONQUESTION) == IDYES)
    DestroyWindow();
}
BEGIN_MESSAGE_MAP(CMainWnd, CFrameWnd)
  ON_COMMAND(CM_COLORCHANGE, CMColorChange)
  ON_COMMAND(CM_EXIT, OnExit)
  ON_WM_CLOSE()
END_MESSAGE_MAP()
// Construct the CColorDialogApp's m_pMainWnd data member
BOOL CColorDialogApp::InitInstance()
{
  m_pMainWnd = new CMainWnd();
  m_pMainWnd->ShowWindow(m_nCmdShow);
  m_pMainWnd->UpdateWindow();
  return TRUE;
}
// application's constructor initializes and runs the app
CColorDialogApp WindowApp;
```

Let's look at the source code shown in Listing 10.4. The window class
CMainWnd declares a constructor and a number of member functions. The relevant member function is CMColorChange, which declares a local string variable and an instance of CColorDialog—ColorDialogBox. The function invokes
the Color dialog box using the function DoModal in an if statement. The if
statement compares the value returned by the function DoModal with the
predefined constant IDOK. If the two values are equal, the function
CMColorChange converts the numeric result of the helper function GetColor
into its string image, and then displays that string in a message dialog box.

II

Visual C++ Programming

Compile and run the COMMDLG1.EXE program. Click the Colors menu item to invoke the Color dialog box. Experiment with selecting different colors. Click the OK button to close the dialog box. The program then displays a message dialog box that contains the integer code for the currently selected color. Figure 10.2 shows a sample session with COMMDGL1.EXE in which the message dialog box appears after the Color dialog box has been closed.

Figure 10.2

The program COMMDGL1.EXE showing the message dialog box that appears after the Color dialog box is closed.

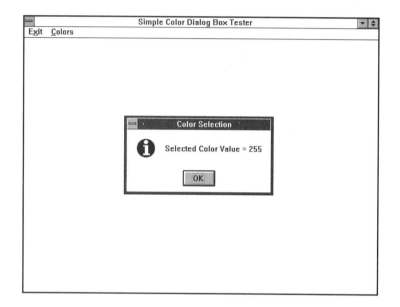

The *CFontDialog* Class

The CFontDialog class supports the Font dialog box, which enables you to select different fonts. Figure 10.3 shows the Font dialog box, which contains the following controls:

- *Font selection combo box.*

- *Font Style combo box.*

- *Size combo box.*

- *Effects group box.* Contains the Strikeout and Underline check boxes.

- *Color selection combo box.*

- *Sample group box.* Displays a sample of the currently selected font.

- *OK and Cancel pushbuttons.*

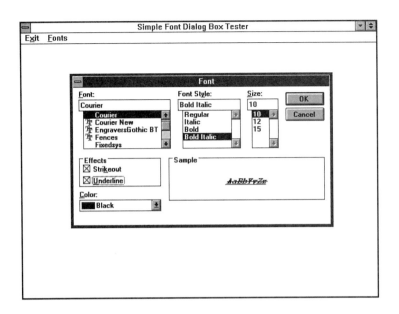

Figure 10.3
A session with
the program
COMMDLG2.EXE
showing the Font
dialog box.

Supporting Classes and Structures

The class CFontDialog encapsulates the structure CHOOSEFONT and the Windows
API function ChooseFont. Here's the declaration of the structure CHOOSEFONT:

```
typedef struct tagCHOOSEFONT
{
    DWORD lStructSize;
    HWND hwndOwner;  /* caller's window handle */
    HDC hDC; /* printer DC/IC or NULL */
    LOGFONT FAR* lpLogFont;  /* ptr. to a LOGFONT struct */
    int iPointSize; /* 10 * size in points of selected font */
    DWORD Flags; /* enum. type flags */
    COLORREF rgbColors; /* returned text color */
    LPARAM lCustData; /* data passed to hook fn. */
    UINT (CALLBACK* lpfnHook)(HWND, UINT, WPARAM, LPARAM);
                            /* ptr. to hook function */
    LPCSTR lpTemplateName; /* custom template name */
    HINSTANCE hInstance; /* instance handle of.EXE that
                            contains cust. dlg. template */
    LPSTR lpszStyle; /* return the style field here
                        must be LF_FACESIZE or bigger */
    UINT nFontType; /* same value reported to the EnumFonts
                        call back with the extra FONTTYPE_
                        bits added */
    int nSizeMin; /* minimum pt size allowed & */
    int nSizeMax; /* max pt size allowed if
                    CF_LIMITSIZE is used */
} CHOOSEFONT;
```

The structure CHOOSEFONT and the API function ChooseFont use the following CF_*XXXX* constants:

```
#define CF_SCREENFONTS          0x00000001
#define CF_PRINTERFONTS         0x00000002
#define CF_BOTH                 (CF_SCREENFONTS |
                                 CF_PRINTERFONTS)
#define CF_SHOWHELP             0x00000004L
#define CF_ENABLEHOOK           0x00000008L
#define CF_ENABLETEMPLATE       0x00000010L
#define CF_ENABLETEMPLATEHANDLE 0x00000020L
#define CF_INITTOLOGFONTSTRUCT  0x00000040L
#define CF_USESTYLE             0x00000080L
#define CF_EFFECTS              0x00000100L
#define CF_APPLY                0x00000200L
#define CF_ANSIONLY             0x00000400L
#define CF_NOVECTORFONTS        0x00000800L
#define CF_NOOEMFONTS           CF_NOVECTORFONTS
#define CF_NOSIMULATIONS        0x00001000L
#define CF_LIMITSIZE            0x00002000L
#define CF_FIXEDPITCHONLY       0x00004000L
#define CF_WYSIWYG              0x00008000L /* must also have
                                              CF_SCREENFONTS &
                                              CF_PRINTERFONTS */

#define CF_FORCEFONTEXIST       0x00010000L
#define CF_SCALABLEONLY         0x00020000L
#define CF_TTONLY               0x00040000L
#define CF_NOFACESEL            0x00080000L
#define CF_NOSTYLESEL           0x00100000L
#define CF_NOSIZESEL            0x00200000L

/* these are extra nFontType bits that are added to what is
   returned to the EnumFonts callback routine */

#define SIMULATED_FONTTYPE      0x8000
#define PRINTER_FONTTYPE        0x4000
#define SCREEN_FONTTYPE         0x2000
#define BOLD_FONTTYPE           0x0100
#define ITALIC_FONTTYPE         0x0200
#define REGULAR_FONTTYPE        0x0400
```

The class CFontDialog, with a descendant of CDialog, is declared as follows:

```
class CFontDialog : public CDialog
{
  DECLARE_DYNAMIC(CFontDialog)
 public:
 // Attributes
 // font choosing parameter block
  CHOOSEFONT m_cf;
 // Constructors
```

```
    CFontDialog(LPLOGFONT lplfInitial = NULL,
                DWORD dwFlags = CF_EFFECTS | CF_SCREENFONTS,
                CDC* pdcPrinter = NULL,
                CWnd* pParentWnd = NULL);
// Operations
  virtual int DoModal();
  // Retrieve the currently selected font while dialog is displayed
  void GetCurrentFont(LPLOGFONT lplf);
  // Helpers for parsing information after successful return
  CString GetFaceName() const;  // return the face name of the font
  CString GetStyleName() const; // return the style name of the font
  int GetSize() const;          // return the pt size of the font
  COLORREF GetColor() const;    // return the color of the font
  int GetWeight() const;        // return the chosen font weight
  BOOL IsStrikeOut() const;     // return TRUE if strikeout
  BOOL IsUnderline() const;     // return TRUE if underline
  BOOL IsBold() const;          // return TRUE if bold font
  BOOL IsItalic() const;        // return TRUE if italic font
// Implementation
  LOGFONT m_lf; // default LOGFONT to store the info
#ifdef _DEBUG
 public:
  virtual void Dump(CDumpContext& dc) const;
#endif
 protected:
  virtual void OnOK();
  virtual void OnCancel();
  char m_szStyleName[64]; // contains style name after return
};
```

The class `CFontDialog` declares a constructor with four parameters that fine-tune the creation of the Font dialog box instance. The parameter `lplfInitial` is a pointer to the initial settings of the dialog box. The default argument for this parameter is NULL. The parameter `dwFlags` provides the flags that fine-tune the dialog box. The default argument for this parameter is the expression (`CF_EFFECTS | CF_SCREENFONTS`). The parameter `pdcPrinter` is a pointer to a `CDC` object for the printer, for which the fonts are chosen. The parameter `pParentWnd` is the pointer to the parent window.

The class declares the data member `m_cf`, which is the `CHOOSEFONT` structure. This data member permits the instances of the class `CFontDialog` to transfer information to and from the supporting Windows API functions.

Invoking a Font dialog box is very similar to invoking the Color dialog box. The OK button, Cancel button, and the Close command from the system menu play the same role in influencing the result returned by the `DoModal` member function. The Windows API function `CommDlgExtendedError` also can be used to detect errors when the `DoModal` function returns `IDCANCEL`.

Using the *CFontDialog* Helper Functions

The class CFontDialog offers the following helper member functions to recall the data from the dialog box:

- The function GetFaceName yields a CString object that has the name of the selected font.

- The function GetStyleName returns a CString object that provides the name of the selected font style.

- The function GetSize returns the point size (multiplied by ten) of the selected font.

- The function GetColor yields the numeric color code of the selected font.

- The function GetWeight returns the weight of the selected font.

- The function IsStrikeOut yields TRUE if the strikeout effect is selected; otherwise, it returns FALSE.

- The function IsUnderline yields TRUE if the underline effect is selected; otherwise it returns FALSE.

- The function IsBold returns TRUE if the bold style is selected; otherwise, it yields FALSE.

- The function IsItalic returns TRUE if the italic style is selected; otherwise, it yields FALSE.

Testing the *CFontDialog* Class

Let's look at a simple program that opens the Font dialog box and then displays the results returned by the various CFontDialog helper functions. The program focuses on creating, using, and accessing the data in a Font dialog box.

Listing 10.5 shows the contents of the COMMDLG2.DEF definition file.

Listing 10.5 The COMMDLG2.DEF Definition File

```
NAME           CommDlg2
DESCRIPTION    'An MFC Windows Application'
EXETYPE        WINDOWS
CODE           PRELOAD MOVEABLE DISCARDABLE
DATA           PRELOAD MOVEABLE MULTIPLE
HEAPSIZE       1024
```

Listing 10.6 shows the COMMDLG2.H header file.

Listing 10.6 Source Code for the COMMDLG2.H Header File

```
#define CM_EXIT      (WM_USER + 100)
#define CM_FONTCHANGE (WM_USER + 101)
```

Listing 10.7 contains the script for the COMMDLG2.RC resource file.

Listing 10.7 Script for the COMMDLG2.RC Resource File

```
#include <windows.h>
#include <afxres.h>
#include "commdlg2.h"
MAINMENU MENU LOADONCALL MOVEABLE PURE DISCARDABLE
BEGIN
    MENUITEM "E&xit", CM_EXIT
    MENUITEM "&Fonts", CM_FONTCHANGE
END
```

The source code for the COMMDLG2.CPP program file is provided in Listing 10.8.

Listing 10.8 Source Code for the COMMDLG2.CPP Program File

```
/*
  Program tests the class CFontDialog which creates a font
  selection dialog box
*/
#include <stdio.h>
#include <string.h>
#include <afxwin.h>
#include <afxdlgs.h>
#include "commdlg2.h"
const MaxStringLen = 20;
CString BoolString(BOOL bBoolVal)
{
  return (bBoolVal) ? CString(": Yes") : CString(": No");
}
// declare the custom application class as
class CFontDialogApp : public CWinApp
{
public:
    virtual BOOL InitInstance();
};
// expand the functionality of CFrameWnd by deriving
// class CMainWnd
class CMainWnd : public CFrameWnd
```

(continues)

Listing 10.8 Continued

```
{
 public:
  CMainWnd();
 protected:
  // handle the Fonts menu item
  afx_msg void CMFontChange();
  // handle exiting the application
  afx_msg void OnExit()
    { SendMessage(WM_CLOSE); }
  // handle closing the window
  afx_msg void OnClose();
  // declare message map macro
  DECLARE_MESSAGE_MAP()
};
CMainWnd::CMainWnd()
{
  // create the window
  Create(NULL, "Simple Font Dialog Box Tester",
         WS_OVERLAPPEDWINDOW, rectDefault, NULL, "MAINMENU");
}
void CMainWnd::CMFontChange()
{
  CString msgStr;
  char szSizeStr[MaxStringLen+1];
  char szWeightStr[MaxStringLen+1];
  char szColorStr[MaxStringLen+1];
  CFontDialog FontDialogBox(NULL, CF_EFFECTS | CF_SCREENFONTS,
                            NULL, this);
  if (FontDialogBox.DoModal() == IDOK) {
    // convert numeric results to their string images
    sprintf(szSizeStr, "%d", FontDialogBox.GetSize());
    sprintf(szWeightStr, "%d", FontDialogBox.GetWeight());
    sprintf(szColorStr, "%lu", FontDialogBox.GetColor());
    // build message box string
    msgStr = "Font Name: " + FontDialogBox.GetFaceName();
    msgStr += "\nFont Style: " + FontDialogBox.GetStyleName();
    msgStr += CString("\nFont Size: ") + szSizeStr;
    msgStr += CString("\nColor Code: ") + szColorStr;
    msgStr += CString("\nFont Weight: ") + szWeightStr;
    msgStr += "\nIs Bold" +
              BoolString(FontDialogBox.IsBold());
    msgStr += "\nIs Italic" +
              BoolString(FontDialogBox.IsItalic());
    msgStr += "\nIs Underline" +
              BoolString(FontDialogBox.IsUnderline());
    msgStr += "\nIs StrikeOut" +
              BoolString(FontDialogBox.IsStrikeOut());
    // display font information
    MessageBox((const char*) msgStr, "Selected Font Information",
               MB_OK | MB_ICONINFORMATION);
  }
}
void CMainWnd::OnClose()
```

```
  {
    if (MessageBox("Want to close this application",
                   "Query", MB_YESNO | MB_ICONQUESTION) == IDYES)
      DestroyWindow();
  }
  BEGIN_MESSAGE_MAP(CMainWnd, CFrameWnd)
    ON_COMMAND(CM_FONTCHANGE, CMFontChange)
    ON_COMMAND(CM_EXIT, OnExit)
    ON_WM_CLOSE()
  END_MESSAGE_MAP()
  // Construct the CFontDialogApp's m_pMainWnd data member
  BOOL CFontDialogApp::InitInstance()
  {
    m_pMainWnd = new CMainWnd();
    m_pMainWnd->ShowWindow(m_nCmdShow);
    m_pMainWnd->UpdateWindow();
    return TRUE;
  }
  // application's constructor initializes and runs the app
  CFontDialogApp WindowApp;
```

Let's examine the source code just shown in Listing 10.8. The program declares the general function BoolString, which converts a BOOL value into a
": Yes" or ": No" CString object. The window class CMainWnd declares a constructor and a set of member functions. The relevant member function is the
function CMFontChange. The member function CMFontChange declares three
ASCIIZ strings (szSizeStr, szWeightStr, and szColorStr) and an instance of
CFontDialog—FontDialogBox. The function invokes the Font dialog box using
the DoModal function in an if statement. The if statement compares the
value returned by the function DoModal with the predefined constant IDOK. If
the two values are equal, the function CMFontChange performs the following
tasks:

- Obtains the data from the various helper functions. The function converts numerical data into strings images using the function sprintf. The
  function also translates BOOL data into strings using the general function
  BoolString.

- Tags and concatenates the individual results, inserting line breaks
  between the various individual results.

- Displays the results string a message dialog box.

Compile and run the COMMDLG2.EXE program. Click the Fonts menu item
to invoke the Font dialog box. Experiment with choosing different fonts,
font sizes, font styles, font colors, and font effects. Click the OK button to

close the dialog box. The program then displays a message dialog box that shows you the results retrieved from the helper functions. Figure 10.4 shows a sample session with COMMDLG4.EXE in which the message dialog box appears after the Font dialog box has been closed.

Figure 10.4

The program COMMDLG4.EXE showing the message dialog box that appears after the Font dialog box is closed.

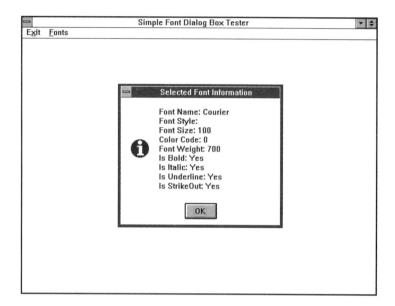

The *CPrintDialog* Class

The class CPrintDialog supports common dialog boxes for printing files and setting up the printer. Figure 10.5 shows the Print dialog box that assists in printing files. The Print dialog box contains the following controls:

- *Static text control.* Enables you to specify the current printer.

- *Print Range group box.* Contains a set of controls including the radio buttons All, Selection, and Pages, and the edit controls From and To.

- *Print Quality combo box.* Lets you choose between draft and final quality printing.

- *Copies edit control.* Lets you choose the number of printed copies.

- *Collate Copies check box.* Enables you to choose whether to collate the pages of your print job.

- *Print to File check box.* Enables you to print to a file.

- *Setup pushbutton.* Lets you open the Print Setup dialog box.

- *OK and Cancel pushbuttons.*

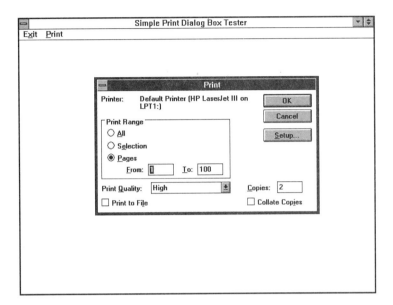

Figure 10.5
The program
COMMDLG3.EXE
showing the Print
dialog box.

The Print Setup dialog box is shown in Figure 10.6 and contains the following controls:

- *Printer group box.* Contains the radio buttons Default Printer and Specific Printer. When you choose Specific Printer, you can use the printer selection combo box located inside the group box.

- *Orientation group box.* Contains the radio buttons Portrait and Landscape, which enable you to print in portrait mode (across the page) or landscape mode (lengthwise on the page).

- *Paper group box.* Contains the Size and Source combo boxes. The Size combo box enables you to specify the paper size on which you want to print. The Source combo box enables you to indicate where that paper is located, such as in a particular printer tray.

- *Options... pushbutton.* Invokes the Options dialog box, which offers advanced options, such as choices for the output bin, gray scale, printing TrueType graphics, and so on.

- *OK and Cancel pushbuttons.*

Figure 10.6

The program
COMMDLG3.EXE
showing the Print
Setup dialog box.

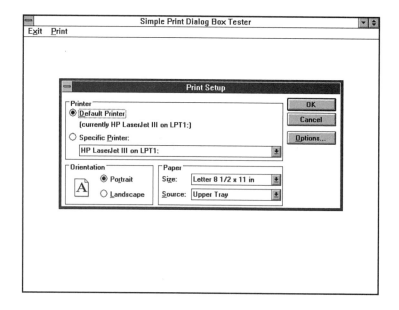

The Supporting Structures and Classes

The class CPrintDialog encapsulates the structure PRINTDLG and the supporting Windows API functions. The declaration of the structure PRINTDLG is as
follows:

```
typedef struct tagPD
{
DWORD    lStructSize;
HWND     hwndOwner;
HGLOBAL  hDevMode;
HGLOBAL  hDevNames;
HDC      hDC;
DWORD    Flags;
UINT     nFromPage;
UINT     nToPage;
UINT     nMinPage;
UINT     nMaxPage;
UINT     nCopies;
HINSTANCE hInstance;
LPARAM   lCustData;
UINT     (CALLBACK* lpfnPrintHook)(HWND, UINT,
                                    WPARAM,LPARAM);
UINT     (CALLBACK* lpfnSetupHook)(HWND, UINT,
                                    WPARAM, LPARAM);
LPCSTR   lpPrintTemplateName;
LPCSTR   lpSetupTemplateName;
HGLOBAL  hPrintTemplate;
HGLOBAL  hSetupTemplate;
} PRINTDLG;
```

The structure `PRINTDLG` and the associated Windows API functions use the following PD_*XXXX* constants:

```
#define PD_ALLPAGES                      0x00000000
#define PD_SELECTION                     0x00000001
#define PD_PAGENUMS                      0x00000002
#define PD_NOSELECTION                   0x00000004
#define PD_NOPAGENUMS                    0x00000008
#define PD_COLLATE                       0x00000010
#define PD_PRINTTOFILE                   0x00000020
#define PD_PRINTSETUP                    0x00000040
#define PD_NOWARNING                     0x00000080
#define PD_RETURNDC                      0x00000100
#define PD_RETURNIC                      0x00000200
#define PD_RETURNDEFAULT                 0x00000400
#define PD_SHOWHELP                      0x00000800
#define PD_ENABLEPRINTHOOK               0x00001000
#define PD_ENABLESETUPHOOK               0x00002000
#define PD_ENABLEPRINTTEMPLATE           0x00004000
#define PD_ENABLESETUPTEMPLATE           0x00008000
#define PD_ENABLEPRINTTEMPLATEHANDLE     0x00010000
#define PD_ENABLESETUPTEMPLATEHANDLE     0x00020000
#define PD_USEDEVMODECOPIES              0x00040000
#define PD_DISABLEPRINTTOFILE            0x00080000
#define PD_HIDEPRINTTOFILE               0x00100000
```

The class `CPrintDialog`, which is a descendant of `CDialog`, has the following declaration:

```
class CPrintDialog : public CDialog
{
  DECLARE_DYNAMIC(CPrintDialog)
 public:
 // Attributes
   // print dialog parameter block (note this is a reference)
#ifdef AFX_CLASS_MODEL
   PRINTDLG FAR& m_pd;
#else
   PRINTDLG& m_pd;
#endif
   // Constructors
   CPrintDialog(BOOL bPrintSetupOnly, // TRUE for Print Setup,
                                      // FALSE for Print Dialog
              DWORD dwFlags = PD_ALLPAGES | PD_USEDEVMODECOPIES |
                              PD_NOPAGENUMS | PD_HIDEPRINTTOFILE |
                              PD_NOSELECTION,
              CWnd* pParentWnd = NULL);
 // Operations
   virtual int DoModal();
   // GetDefaults will not display a dialog but will get
   // device defaults
   BOOL GetDefaults();
   // Helpers for parsing information after successful return
   int GetCopies() const;            // num. copies requested
   BOOL PrintCollate() const;        // TRUE if collate checked
```

```
          BOOL PrintSelection() const;      // TRUE if printing selection
          BOOL PrintAll() const;            // TRUE if printing all pages
          BOOL PrintRange() const;          // TRUE if printing page range
          int GetFromPage() const;          // starting page if valid
          int GetToPage() const;            // starting page if valid
          LPDEVMODE GetDevMode() const;     // return DEVMODE
          CString GetDriverName() const;    // return driver name
          CString GetDeviceName() const;    // return device name
          CString GetPortName() const;      // return output port name
          HDC GetPrinterDC() const;         // return HDC (caller must delete)
          // This helper creates a DC based on the DEVNAMES and DEVMODE
          // structures. This DC is returned, but also stored in m_pd.hDC
          // as though it had been returned by CommDlg. It is assumed
          // that any previously obtained DC has been/will be deleted by
          // the user. This may be used without ever invoking the
          // print/print setup dialogs.
          HDC CreatePrinterDC();
        // Implementation
#ifdef _DEBUG
 public:
          virtual void Dump(CDumpContext& dc) const;
#endif
 private:
          PRINTDLG m_pdActual; // the Print/Print Setup need to share this
 protected:
          virtual void OnOK();
          virtual void OnCancel();
// The following handle the case of print setup... from the print
// dialog
#ifdef AFX_CLASS_MODEL
          CPrintDialog(PRINTDLG FAR& pdInit);
#else
          CPrintDialog(PRINTDLG& pdInit);
#endif
          virtual CPrintDialog* AttachOnSetup();
          //{{AFX_MSG(CPrintDialog)
            afx_msg void OnPrintSetup();
          //}}AFX_MSG
          DECLARE_MESSAGE_MAP()
        }
```

The class constructor has three parameters. The logical parameter
bPrintSetUpOnly indicates whether to invoke the Print Setup dialog box
(when its argument is TRUE) or the Print dialog box (when its argument is
FALSE). The parameter dwFlags contains the flags that fine tune the printer
dialog box. The default argument for this parameter is the expression

```
PD_ALLPAGES ¦ PD_USEDEVMODECOPIES ¦ PD_NOPAGENUMS ¦
    PD_HIDEPRINTTOFILE ¦ PD_NOSELECTION
```

The default parameter value is for all pages to be printed without showing the
range of pages in the From and To edit boxes. The default flags also hide the
Print to File check box. The parameter pParentWnd is the pointer to the parent
window.

The class CPrintDialog declares the data member m_pd, which is a PRINTDLG structure. This member permits the class instances to transfer information with the supporting Windows API functions.

Using the *CPrintDialog* Helper Functions

The CPrintDialog class offers the following helper member functions so that you can query the various print parameters:

- The function GetCopies yields the number of requested copies.

- The function PrintCollate returns TRUE if the check box Collate Copies is checked.

- The function PrintSelection yields TRUE if the radio button Selection is selected.

- The function PrintAll returns TRUE if the radio button All is selected.

- The function PrintRange yields TRUE if the radio button Pages is selected.

- The function GetFromPage returns the number in the edit control From (assuming this control has a valid integer.)

- The function GetToPage yields the number in the edit control To (assuming this control has a valid integer.)

- The function GetDevMode returns a pointer to the device mode.

- The function GetDriverName yields a CString object that contains the printer driver name.

- The function GetDeviceName returns a CString object that contains the device name.

- The function GetPortName returns a CString object that contains the printer port name.

- The function GetPrinterDC returns an HDC result for the selected printer.

Invoking the Print and Setup Dialog Boxes

Invoking the Print and Setup dialog boxes is very similar to invoking the Color dialog box. The OK button, Cancel button, and the Close command from the system menu play the same role in influencing the result returned by the DoModal member function. The Windows API function CommDlgExtendedError can also be used to detect errors when the DoModal function returns IDCANCEL.

Testing the *CPrintDialog* Class

This section presents a simple program that uses the Print and Print Setup common dialog boxes. Listing 10.9 shows the contents of the COMMDLG3.DEF definition file.

Listing 10.9 The COMMDLG3.DEF Definition File

```
NAME         CommDlg3
DESCRIPTION  'An MFC Windows Application'
EXETYPE      WINDOWS
CODE         PRELOAD MOVEABLE DISCARDABLE
DATA         PRELOAD MOVEABLE MULTIPLE
HEAPSIZE     1024
```

Listing 10.10 shows the COMMDLG3.H header file.

Listing 10.10 Source Code for the COMMDLG3.H Header File

```
#define CM_EXIT     (WM_USER + 100)
#define CM_PRINTDLG (WM_USER + 101)
#define CM_SETUPDLG (WM_USER + 102)
```

Listing 10.11 contains the script for the COMMDLG3.RC resource file.

Listing 10.11 Script for the COMMDLG3.RC Resource File

```
#include <windows.h>
#include <afxres.h>
#include "commdlg3.h"
MAINMENU MENU LOADONCALL MOVEABLE PURE DISCARDABLE
BEGIN
    MENUITEM "E&xit", CM_EXIT
    POPUP "&Print"
    BEGIN
      MENUITEM "&SetUp...", CM_SETUPDLG
      MENUITEM "&Print...", CM_PRINTDLG
    END
END
```

The source code for the COMMDLG3.CPP program file is provided in
Listing 10.12.

Listing 10.12 Source Code for the COMMDLG3.CPP Program File

```
/*
  Program tests the class CPrintDialog to create the Print and
  Print Setup dialog boxes
*/
#include <stdio.h>
#include <string.h>
#include <afxwin.h>
#include <afxdlgs.h>
#include "commdlg3.h"
const MaxStringLen = 40;
CString BoolString(BOOL bBOOL)
{
  return (bBOOL) ? CString(" : Yes") : CString(" : No");
}
// declare the custom application class as
class CPrintDialogApp : public CWinApp
{
public:
    virtual BOOL InitInstance();
};
// expand the functionality of CFrameWnd by deriving class CMainWnd
class CMainWnd : public CFrameWnd
{
 public:
  CMainWnd();
 protected:
  // handle the Print menu item
  afx_msg void CMPrintDialogBox();

  // handle the SetUp menu item
  afx_msg void CMSetupDialogBox();

  // handle exiting the application
  afx_msg void OnExit()
    { SendMessage(WM_CLOSE); }
  // handle closing the window
  afx_msg void OnClose();
  // display the parameters of the Print dialog box
  void displayDialogBoxData(CPrintDialog& PrintDlgBox);
  // declare message map macro
  DECLARE_MESSAGE_MAP();
};
CMainWnd::CMainWnd()
{
  // create the window
  Create(NULL, "Simple Print Dialog Box Tester",
         WS_OVERLAPPEDWINDOW, rectDefault, NULL, "MAINMENU");
}
```

(continues)

Listing 10.12 Continued

```
void CMainWnd::CMPrintDialogBox()
{
  CPrintDialog PrintDialogBox(FALSE, PD_USEDEVMODECOPIES , this);

  // assign value sto some of the members of member m_pd
  PrintDialogBox.m_pd.nMinPage = 1;
  PrintDialogBox.m_pd.nMaxPage = 100;
  PrintDialogBox.m_pd.nFromPage = 1;
  PrintDialogBox.m_pd.nToPage = 100;
  PrintDialogBox.m_pd.nCopies = 2;

  if (PrintDialogBox.DoModal() == IDOK)
    displayDialogBoxData(PrintDialogBox);
}
void CMainWnd::CMSetupDialogBox()
{
  CPrintDialog PrintDialogBox(TRUE, PD_USEDEVMODECOPIES , this);

  // assign value sto some of the members of member m_pd
  PrintDialogBox.m_pd.nMinPage = 1;
  PrintDialogBox.m_pd.nMaxPage = 200;
  PrintDialogBox.m_pd.nFromPage = 1;
  PrintDialogBox.m_pd.nToPage = 200;
  PrintDialogBox.m_pd.nCopies = 3;

  if (PrintDialogBox.DoModal() == IDOK)
    displayDialogBoxData(PrintDialogBox);
}
void CMainWnd::displayDialogBoxData(CPrintDialog& PrintDlgBox)
{
  CString msgStr;
  char szCopiesStr[MaxStringLen];
  char szFromPageStr[MaxStringLen];
  char szToPageStr[MaxStringLen];

  // convert numeric results into their string images
  sprintf(szCopiesStr, "%d", PrintDlgBox.GetCopies());
  sprintf(szFromPageStr, "%d", PrintDlgBox.GetFromPage());
  sprintf(szToPageStr, "%d", PrintDlgBox.GetToPage());
  // build the results message
  msgStr = "Driver Name: " + PrintDlgBox.GetDriverName();
  msgStr += "\nDevice Name: " + PrintDlgBox.GetDeviceName();
  msgStr += "\nPort Name: " + PrintDlgBox.GetPortName();
  msgStr += "\nNumber of Copies: " + CString(szCopiesStr);
  msgStr += "\nCollate" +
            BoolString(PrintDlgBox.PrintCollate());
  msgStr += "\nSelection" +
            BoolString(PrintDlgBox.PrintSelection());
  msgStr += "\nPrint All" + BoolString(PrintDlgBox.PrintAll());
  msgStr += "\nPrint Range" +
            BoolString(PrintDlgBox.PrintRange());
```

```
      msgStr += "\nFrom Page " + CString(szFromPageStr);
      msgStr += "\nTo Page " + CString(szToPageStr);
      // display the results message
      MessageBox(msgStr, "Print Dialog Box Parameters",
                 MB_OK | MB_ICONINFORMATION);
}
void CMainWnd::OnClose()
{
   if (MessageBox("Want to close this application",
                  "Query", MB_YESNO | MB_ICONQUESTION) == IDYES)
     DestroyWindow();
}
BEGIN_MESSAGE_MAP(CMainWnd, CFrameWnd)
   ON_COMMAND(CM_PRINTDLG, CMPrintDialogBox)
   ON_COMMAND(CM_SETUPDLG, CMSetupDialogBox)
   ON_COMMAND(CM_EXIT, OnExit)
   ON_WM_CLOSE()
END_MESSAGE_MAP()
// Construct the CPrintDialogApp'msgStr m_pMainWnd data member
BOOL CPrintDialogApp::InitInstance()
{
   m_pMainWnd = new CMainWnd();
   m_pMainWnd->ShowWindow(m_nCmdShow);
   m_pMainWnd->UpdateWindow();
   return TRUE;
}
// application'msgStr constructor initializes and runs the app
CPrintDialogApp WindowApp;
```

Now let's examine the source code in Listing 10.12. The program declares the general function BoolString, which is identical to the one in Listing 10.8. The window class CMainWnd declares a constructor and a set of member functions. The member functions CMPrintDialog, CMSetupDialog, and displayDialogBoxData are relevant to the program.

The member functions CMPrintDialog and CMSetupDialog respond to the menu commands Print and SetUp, respectively. The CMPrint function creates the object PrintDialogBox, an instance of CPrintDialog, which specifies the Print dialog box. The constructor call uses flags that enable the dialog box to support printing all pages, the current selection, and a range of pages. The function CMPrint performs the following tasks:

■ Assigns values to the following members of data member m_pd: nMinPage, nMaxPage, nFromPage, nToPage, and nCopies. These values assign a page range used by the dialog box API functions to validate the requested page range.

■ Sends the C++ message DoModal to the PrintDialogBox object in an if statement. This if statement compares the result of DoModal with the predefined constant IDOK. If the two values are equal, the function invokes the member function displayDialogBoxData. The argument for the displayDialogBoxData function is the object PrintDialogBox, which is passed by reference.

The statements of the member function CMSetUp greatly resemble those of the function CMPrint. The only difference is in the first CPrintDialog constructor argument—CMSetupDialog passes the argument TRUE to invoke the Print Setup dialog box.

The member function displayDialogBoxData has the task of displaying the printer status by invoking the various helper functions. The function has a single reference parameter that passes the address of the CPrintDialog object. The function declares a CString object and three ASCIIZ strings (szCopiesStr, szFromPageStr, and szToPageStr). The displayDialogBoxData function performs the following tasks:

■ Converts the numeric results of the helper functions GetCopies, GetFromPage, and GetToPage into their string images. These strings are stored in the local variables szCopiesStr, szFromPageStr, and szToPageStr.

■ Builds the results string (using the local variable msgStr). This task involves several statements that concatenate the string images mentioned in the preceding item with the results of the BoolString function calls. These calls convert the results of the Boolean helper functions into the string ": Yes" or ": No".

■ Displays the results string in a message dialog box.

Compile and run the test COMMDLG3.EXE program. The program contains the Exit and Print menus, and the Print menu includes the Print and SetUp commands. The Print command opens the Print dialog box, and the SetUp command opens the Print Setup dialog box. Choose either command and make your selections in the corresponding dialog box. When you click the OK button, the program removes the dialog box and displays the current printer parameter in a message dialog box. The program displays the same type of message box for either common dialog box. Figure 10.7 shows a sample session with the program COMMDLG3.EXE, which shows the message dialog box after the Print dialog box has been closed.

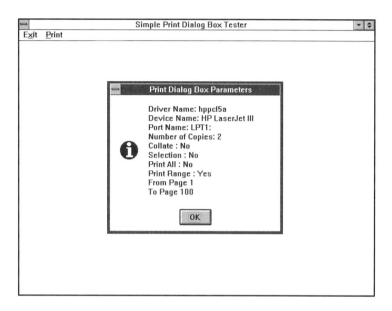

Figure 10.7
The program COMMDLG3.EXE showing the message box that appears after the Print dialog box has been closed.

Figure 10.8 shows a sample session with the program COMMDLG3.EXE, which shows the message dialog box after closing the Print Setup dialog box.

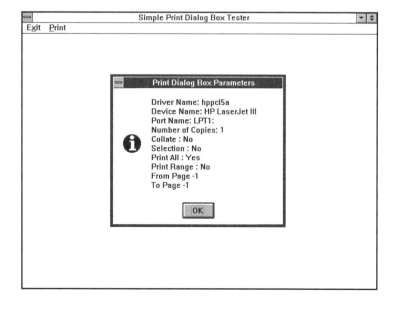

Figure 10.8
The program COMMDLG3.EXE showing the message box that appears after the Print Setup dialog box has been closed.

II

Visual C++ Programming

The *CFileDialog* Class

The CFileDialog class implements the modal common dialog boxes that support opening and saving a file. Figure 10.9 shows a standard file dialog box in the open file mode.

Figure 10.9

A session with COMMDLG4.EXE showing the Open dialog box.

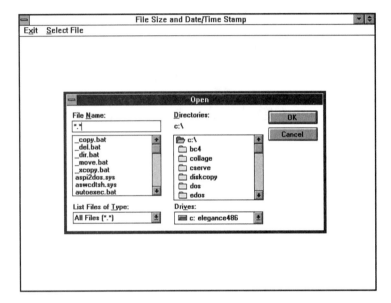

The Open and Save As dialog boxes have the following controls:

■ *File Name combo box.*

■ *File filter combo box.*

■ *Current directory static text control.*

■ *Directories list box.* Shows the current directory, its sibling directories, and its parent directory.

■ *Drives combo box.*

■ *OK and Cancel pushbuttons.*

■ *Help pushbutton.*

■ *Read-only check box.* Enables you to select read-only files.

The Supporting Classes and Structures

The class `CFileDialog` encapsulates the structure `OPENFILENAME` and the Windows API functions `GetOpenFileName` and `GetSaveFileName`. The structure `OPENFILENAME` is declared as follows:

```
typedef struct tagOFN
{
    DWORD     lStructSize;
    HWND      hwndOwner;
    HINSTANCE hInstance;
    LPCSTR    lpstrFilter;
    LPSTR     lpstrCustomFilter;
    DWORD     nMaxCustFilter;
    DWORD     nFilterIndex;
    LPSTR     lpstrFile;
    DWORD     nMaxFile;
    LPSTR     lpstrFileTitle;
    DWORD     nMaxFileTitle;
    LPCSTR    lpstrInitialDir;
    LPCSTR    lpstrTitle;
    DWORD     Flags;
    UINT      nFileOffset;
    UINT      nFileExtension;
    LPCSTR    lpstrDefExt;
    LPARAM    lCustData;
    UINT      (CALLBACK *lpfnHook)(HWND, UINT, WPARAM, LPARAM);
    LPCSTR    lpTemplateName;
}   OPENFILENAME;
```

The structure `OPENFILENAME` and its related Windows API functions use the following `OFN_XXXX` constants:

```
#define OFN_READONLY                0x00000001
#define OFN_OVERWRITEPROMPT         0x00000002
#define OFN_HIDEREADONLY            0x00000004
#define OFN_NOCHANGEDIR             0x00000008
#define OFN_SHOWHELP                0x00000010
#define OFN_ENABLEHOOK              0x00000020
#define OFN_ENABLETEMPLATE          0x00000040
#define OFN_ENABLETEMPLATEHANDLE    0x00000080
#define OFN_NOVALIDATE              0x00000100
#define OFN_ALLOWMULTISELECT        0x00000200
#define OFN_EXTENSIONDIFFERENT      0x00000400
#define OFN_PATHMUSTEXIST           0x00000800
#define OFN_FILEMUSTEXIST           0x00001000
#define OFN_CREATEPROMPT            0x00002000
#define OFN_SHAREAWARE              0x00004000
#define OFN_NOREADONLYRETURN        0x00008000
#define OFN_NOTESTFILECREATE        0x00010000
```

II

Visual C++ Programming

The declaration of the class CFileDialog, which is a descendant of CDialog, is as follows:

```
class CFileDialog : public CDialog
{
  DECLARE_DYNAMIC(CFileDialog)
 public:
  // Attributes
  // open file parameter block
  OPENFILENAME m_ofn;
  // Constructors
  CFileDialog(BOOL bOpenFileDialog, // TRUE for FileOpen,
                                    // FALSE for FileSaveAs
              LPCSTR lpszDefExt = NULL,
              LPCSTR lpszFileName = NULL,
              DWORD dwFlags = OFN_HIDEREADONLY |
                              OFN_OVERWRITEPROMPT,
              LPCSTR lpszFilter = NULL,
              CWnd* pParentWnd = NULL);
  // Operations
  virtual int DoModal();
  // Helpers for parsing filename after successful return
  CString GetPathName() const;  // return full path name
  CString GetFileName() const;  // return only filename
  CString GetFileExt() const;   // return only ext
  CString GetFileTitle() const; // return file title
  BOOL GetReadOnlyPref() const; // return TRUE if readonly checked
  // Overridable callbacks
 protected:
  friend UINT CALLBACK AFX_EXPORT _AfxCommDlgProc(HWND, UINT,
                                                  WPARAM, LPARAM);
  virtual UINT OnShareViolation(LPCSTR lpszPathName);
  virtual BOOL OnFileNameOK();
  virtual void OnLBSelChangedNotify(UINT nIDBox, UINT iCurSel,
                                    UINT nCode);
  // Implementation
#ifdef _DEBUG
 public:
  virtual void Dump(CDumpContext& dc) const;
#endif
 protected:
  virtual void OnOK();
  virtual void OnCancel();
  BOOL m_bOpenFileDialog; // TRUE for file open, FALSE for file save
  CString m_strFilter; // filter string separate fields with '|',
                       // terminate with '||\0'
  char m_szFileTitle[64];        // contains file title after return
  char m_szFileName[_MAX_PATH];  // contains full path name
                                 // after return
};
```

The class CFileDialog constructor creates a modal dialog box defined by the various parameters. The parameter bOpenFileDialog selects either the Open or the Save As file dialog box. Passing the argument TRUE for this parameter brings up the Open dialog box, and passing the argument FALSE for the parameter brings up the Save As dialog box. The parameter `lpszDefExt` designates the default file extension name, which is appended automatically to the file if you do not type one. The default argument for this parameter is NULL. The parameter `lpszFileName` specifies the initial filename. The default argument for this parameter is NULL. The parameter `dwFlags` sets the flags that fine-tune the file dialog box. The default argument for this parameter is the expression

```
OFN_HIDEREADONLY | OFN_OVERWRITEPROMPT
```

The parameter `lpszFilter` is a pointer to a string that is made up of pairs of substrings that are involved in filtering the selected file. (More about the filter strings in the next paragraph.) The parameter `pParentWnd` is the pointer to the parent window that owns the file dialog box.

As I just mentioned, the argument for the parameter `lpszFilter` is a string with a particular format: it is made up of substring pairs. The first pair member contains the wording of the filter, for example, `string resource file (*.RC)`. This wording is selected by the dialog box user and does not have to include any filename wild cards. The second pair member contains the actual wild card used in filtering the selected files, for example, `*.RC`. The formatting rules to observe are as follows:

- Use the bar character, ¦, to separate the substrings.

- Use pairs of strings, one for wording and one for the corresponding filename wild card. The dialog box actually uses this wild card to filter the file selection.

- The string must end with an empty substring. That is, the last two string characters must be a pair of bar characters, ¦¦.

An example of the argument for the `lpszFilter` parameter is the following string:

```
char szFilter[] =
"All files (*.*)¦*.*¦"
"Header files (*.h)¦*.h¦"
"Resource script (*.rc)¦*.rc¦"
"C++ files¦*.cpp¦¦";
```

The preceding string displays four file selections. The first permits you to select from all files, the second lets you choose a *.CPP file, the third one permits you to select an .RC file, and the last one lets you pick a header file.

The class `CFileDialog` declares the data member `m_ofn` as an `OPENFILENAME` structure. This member enables the class `CFileDialog` to transfer information to and from the `OPENFILENAME` structure used by the supporting Windows API functions.

Invoking the File Dialog Box

Invoking the Open and Save As dialog boxes is very similar to invoking the Color dialog box. The OK button, Cancel button, and the Close command from the system menu play the same roles (in both the Open and Save As dialog boxes) in influencing the result returned by the `DoModal` member function. The Windows API function `CommDlgExtendedError` also can be used to detect errors when the `DoModal` function returns `IDCANCEL`.

Using the *CFileDialog* Helper Functions

The class `CFileDialog` provides the following helper member functions to query the members of the data member `m_ofn` after the dialog box is successfully created and invoked (with a call to `DoModal`):

■ The function `GetPathName` returns a `CString` object that contains the full path name.

■ The function `GetFileName` yields a `CString` object that holds only the main filename (without the extension.)

■ The function `GetFileExt` returns a `CString` object that holds the extension name.

■ The function `GetFileTitle` yields a `CString` object that contains the file title which should be utilized as the caption of the frame window.

■ The function `GetReadOnlyPref` returns TRUE if the dialog box user has the read-only check box checked.

Testing the Class *CFileDialog*

In this section, the COMMDLG4.EXE program is presented, which uses the class `CFileDialog`. The COMMDLG4.EXE program also lets you query the statistics of a file: the file size and the date/time stamp.

Listing 10.13 contains the COMMDLG4.DEF definition file.

Listing 10.13 The COMMDLG4.DEF Definition File

```
NAME          CommDlg4
DESCRIPTION   'An MFC Windows Application'
EXETYPE       WINDOWS
CODE          PRELOAD MOVEABLE DISCARDABLE
DATA          PRELOAD MOVEABLE MULTIPLE
HEAPSIZE      1024
```

Listing 10.14 shows the COMMDLG4.H header file.

Listing 10.14 Source Code for the COMMDLG4.H Header File

```
#define CM_EXIT       (WM_USER + 100)
#define CM_SELECTFILE (WM_USER + 101)
```

Listing 10.15 shows the script for the COMMDLG4.RC resource file.

II

Visual C++ Programming

Listing 10.15 Script for the COMMDLG4.RC Resource File

```
#include <windows.h>
#include <afxres.h>
#include "commdlg4.h"
MAINMENU MENU LOADONCALL MOVEABLE PURE DISCARDABLE
BEGIN
    MENUITEM "E&xit", CM_EXIT
    MENUITEM "&File Stats", CM_SELECTFILE
END
```

The source code for the COMMDLG4.CPP program file is provided in Listing 10.16.

Listing 10.16 Source Code for the COMMDLG4.CPP Program File

```
/*
  Program tests the class CFileDialog to create the
  Open dialog box
*/
#include <stdlib.h>
#include <stdio.h>
#include <string.h>
#include <dos.h>
#include <afxwin.h>
#include <afxdlgs.h>
#include "commdlg4.h"
const MaxStringLen = 255;
// declare the custom application class as
class CFileDialogApp : public CWinApp
{
```

(continues)

Listing 10.16 Continued

```cpp
public:
    virtual BOOL InitInstance();
};
// expand the functionality of CFrameWnd by deriving
// class CMainWnd
class CMainWnd : public CFrameWnd
{
 public:
  CMainWnd();
 protected:
  // handle the Files menu item
  afx_msg void CMSelectFile();
  // handle exiting the application
  afx_msg void OnExit()
    { SendMessage(WM_CLOSE); }
  // handle closing the window
  afx_msg void OnClose();
  // declare message map macro
  DECLARE_MESSAGE_MAP()
};
CMainWnd::CMainWnd()
{
  // create the window
  Create(NULL, "File Size and Date/Time Stamp",
         WS_OVERLAPPEDWINDOW, rectDefault, NULL, "MAINMENU");
}
void CMainWnd::CMSelectFile()
{
  CString selectedFile;
  char szFileFilter[] =
          "All Files (*.*)|*.*|"
          "Header files (*.h)|*.h|"
          "Resource files (*.rc)|*.rc|"
          "C++ Programs (*.cpp)"
          "||";
  char szMsgStr[MaxStringLen+1];
  char szFormat[MaxStringLen+1];
  _find_t selFileInfo;
  unsigned uDate, uTime;
  unsigned uHour, uMinute, uSecond;
  unsigned uDay, uMonth, uYear;
  unsigned attrib = _A_ARCH | _A_NORMAL;
  CFileDialog FileDialogBox(
      TRUE,  // use file open dialog
      NULL, // ".* is the default extension"
      "*.*",
      OFN_HIDEREADONLY | OFN_OVERWRITEPROMPT,
      szFileFilter,
      this);
    if (FileDialogBox.DoModal() == IDOK) {
    // get the file information
    selectedFile = FileDialogBox.GetPathName();
    // obtain attributes from the DOS function _dos_findfirst
    _dos_findfirst((const char*) selectedFile, attrib, &selFileInfo);
```

```
    // build the szFormat string
    strcpy(szFormat, "Filename: %s\n");
    strcat(szFormat, "Time Stamp: %02u:%02u:%02u\n");
    strcat(szFormat, "Date Stamp: %02u/%02u/%u\n");
    strcat(szFormat, "Size: %ld\n");
    // get the time stamp
    uTime = selFileInfo.wr_time;
    // extract the seconds
    uSecond = 2 * (uTime & 0x1f);
    // extract the minutes
    uMinute = (uTime >> 5) & 0x3f;
    // extract the hours
    uHour = (uTime >> 11) & 0x1f;
    // obtain the date stamp
    uDate = selFileInfo.wr_date;
    // extract the uDay
    uDay  =  uDate & 0x1f;
    // extract the month
    uMonth = (uDate >> 5) & 0xf;
    // extract the year
    uYear = (uDate >> 9) & 0x7f;

    sprintf(szMsgStr, szFormat,
            selFileInfo.name,          // filename
            uHour, uMinute, uSecond,   // time stamp
            uMonth, uDay, uYear + 1980U, // date stamp
            selFileInfo.size);         // filesize
    MessageBox(szMsgStr, "File Information",
               MB_OK | MB_ICONINFORMATION);
  }
}
void CMainWnd::OnClose()
{
  if (MessageBox("Want to close this application",
                 "Query", MB_YESNO | MB_ICONQUESTION) == IDYES)
    DestroyWindow();
}
BEGIN_MESSAGE_MAP(CMainWnd, CFrameWnd)
  ON_COMMAND(CM_SELECTFILE, CMSelectFile)
  ON_COMMAND(CM_EXIT, OnExit)
  ON_WM_CLOSE()
END_MESSAGE_MAP()
// Construct the CFileDialogApp's m_pMainWnd data member
BOOL CFileDialogApp::InitInstance()
{
  m_pMainWnd = new CMainWnd();
  m_pMainWnd->ShowWindow(m_nCmdShow);
  m_pMainWnd->UpdateWindow();
  return TRUE;
}
// application's constructor initializes and runs the app
CFileDialogApp WindowApp;
```

II

Visual C++ Programming

Let's take a closer look at the COMMDLG4.CPP program code shown in Listing 10.16. The window class `CMainWnd` declares a constructor and three member functions: `OnExit`, `OnClose`, and `CMSelectFile`. The most relevant component of the class is the member function `CMSelectFile`. The function declares a number of local variables, among them the string `szFileFilter`, which stores the four sets of file filters. The function also declares the `_find_t`-type variable `selFileInfo`. This variable contains the structure for the DOS file data, including the file size and date/time stamp. In addition, the function `CMSelectFile` declares the `FileDialogBox` object as an instance of `CFileDialog`. The arguments for creating the object `FileDialogBox` create an Open dialog box with no default filename, with a *.* initial filename, with default flags, and with the filter string `szFileFilter`.

The function `CMSelectFile`, using an `if` statement, sends the C++ message `DoModal` to the `FileDialogBox` object. This `if` statement compares the result of the `DoModal` message with the predefined constant `IDOK`. If the two values are equal, the function performs the following tasks:

- Retrieves the full name of the selected file by sending the C++ message `GetPathName` to the `FileDialogBox` object. The function assigns the result of this message to the `CString` object `selectedFile`.

- Invokes the function `_dos_findfirst` to obtain the information for the selected file and stores it in the local variable `selFileInfo`. The arguments for the function `_dos_findfirst` are the string object `selectedFile`, the local variable `attrib` (which stores the file attributes), and the address of the local structured variable `selFileInfo`.

- Builds the string `szFormat`, which contains the format for the output.

- Obtains the time stamp from the member `wr_time` of the variable `selFileInfo`. This task stores the time stamp in the local variable `uTime`.

- Extracts the seconds, minutes, and hours from the variable `uTime` and stores them in the variables `uSecond`, `uMinute`, and `uHour`, respectively.

- Obtains the date stamp from the member `wr_date` of the variable `selFileInfo`. This task stores the date stamp in the local variable `uDate`.

- Extracts the day, month, and year from the variable `uDate`, and stores them in the variables `uDay`, `uMonth`, and `uYear`, respectively.

- Generates the results string using the function `sprintf`. This function uses the format specified by the variable `szFormat` to obtain the information from the various local variables and from the members `name` and `size` of the variable `selFileInfo`.

- Displays the results string in a message dialog box.

Compile and run the COMMDLG4.EXE program. Click the Stats command from the File menu to invoke the Open dialog box. The file filter combo box has four items: all files, header files, resource files, and .CPP files. You can pick a file from the current directory, or you can move to another directory. After you have selected a file, click the OK button. The program removes the Open dialog box and displays a message dialog box. This message box shows you the name of the file you selected, its size, and the date/time stamp. Figure 10.10 shows a sample session with the COMMDLG4.EXE program, which shows the message dialog box that appears after the Open dialog box has been closed.

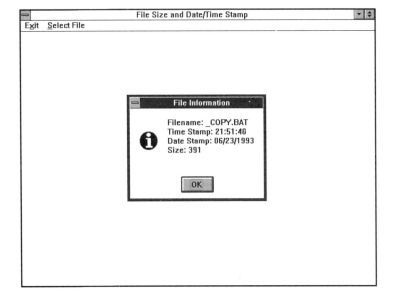

Figure 10.10
The program COMMDLG4.EXE showing the message dialog box that appears after the Open dialog box has been closed.

The *CFindReplaceDialog* Class

The class `CFindReplaceDialog` models the modeless Find and Replace dialog boxes. Figure 10.11 shows the Find dialog box.

Figure 10.11

The program
COMMDLG5.EXE
showing the Find
dialog box.

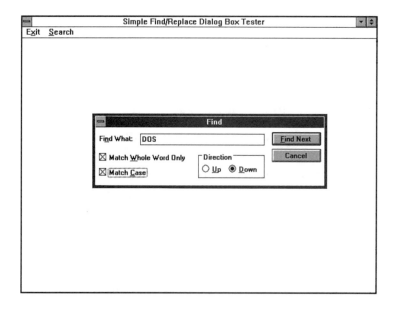

The Find dialog box contains the following controls:

- *Find What edit control.* Contains the search text.

- *Match Whole Word Only check box.* Forces the Find dialog box to match complete words only.

- *Match Case check box.* Forces the Find dialog box to match the case of the search string with the text.

- *Direction group box.* Contains the radio buttons Up and Down.

- *Find Next pushbutton.* Parallels the OK button of a typical modal dialog box.

- *Cancel pushbutton.*

- *Help pushbutton.*

Figure 10.12 shows a sample Replace dialog box, which contains the following controls:

- *Find What edit control.* Contains the search text.

- *Replace With edit control.* Contains the replacement text.

- *Match Whole Word Only check box.* Forces the Find dialog box to match complete words only.

- *Match Case check box.* Forces the Find dialog box to match the case of the search string with the text.

- *Find Next pushbutton.* Parallels the OK button of a typical modal dialog box.

- *Replace pushbutton.* Replaces the next matching string only.

- *Replace All pushbutton.* Replaces all the matching strings in the direction specified.

- *Cancel pushbutton.*

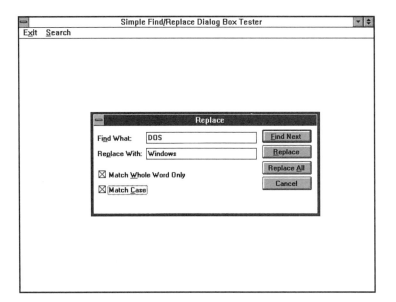

Figure 10.12
The program
COMMDLG5.EXE
showing the
Replace dialog
box.

Supporting Classes and Structures

The class `CFindReplaceDialog` encapsulates the structure `FINDREPLACE` and the Windows API functions `FindText` and `ReplaceText`. The declaration of the structure `FINDREPLACE` is as follows:

```
typedef struct tagFINDREPLACE
{
    DWORD lStructSize; /* size of this struct 0x20 */
    HWND hwndOwner; /* handle to owner's window    */
    HINSTANCE hInstance; /* instance handle of.EXE that
                            contains  cust. dlg. template */
```

```
            DWORD Flags; /* one or more of the FR_?? */
            LPSTR lpstrFindWhat; /* ptr. to search string */
            LPSTR lpstrReplaceWith; /* ptr. to replace string */
            UINT wFindWhatLen; /* size of find buffer */
            UINT wReplaceWithLen;  /* size of replace buffer */
            LPARAM lCustData; /* data passed to hook fn. */
            UINT (CALLBACK* lpfnHook)(HWND, UINT, WPARAM, LPARAM);
                 /* ptr. to hook fn. or NULL    */
            LPCSTR lpTemplateName; /* custom template name */
        } FINDREPLACE;
```

The structure FINDREPLACE and the related Windows API functions use the
following FR_*XXXX* constants:

```
#define FR_DOWN                    0x00000001
#define FR_WHOLEWORD               0x00000002
#define FR_MATCHCASE               0x00000004
#define FR_FINDNEXT                0x00000008
#define FR_REPLACE                 0x00000010
#define FR_REPLACEALL              0x00000020
#define FR_DIALOGTERM              0x00000040
#define FR_SHOWHELP                0x00000080
#define FR_ENABLEHOOK              0x00000100
#define FR_ENABLETEMPLATE          0x00000200
#define FR_NOUPDOWN                0x00000400
#define FR_NOMATCHCASE             0x00000800
#define FR_NOWHOLEWORD             0x00001000
#define FR_ENABLETEMPLATEHANDLE    0x00002000
#define FR_HIDEUPDOWN              0x00004000
#define FR_HIDEMATCHCASE           0x00008000
#define FR_HIDEWHOLEWORD           0x00010000
```

The class CFindReplaceDialog, which is a descendant of CDialog, supports the
typical Find and Replace modeless dialog boxes that you use to find and replace text. The instances of class CFindReplaceDialog work better as modeless
dialog boxes because they stay visible during the text search operations. As
such, the Find and Replace dialog boxes enable programs to shift the focus to
the related window that contains the edited text. Therefore, you can reselect
these dialog boxes at any time and perform a further text search. This approach keeps the dialog boxes on stand by and prevents you from having to
repeatedly reinvoke the dialog boxes. This flexibility does have its price—a
slightly more elaborate coding requirement. Here's the declaration of the
class CFindReplaceDialog:

```
class CFindReplaceDialog : public CDialog
{
  DECLARE_DYNAMIC(CFindReplaceDialog)
 public:
// Attributes
  FINDREPLACE m_fr;
// Constructors
```

```
CFindReplaceDialog();
// NOTE: you must allocate these on the heap.
// If you do not, you must derive and override PostNcDestroy()
BOOL Create(BOOL bFindDialogOnly, // TRUE for Find,
                                  // FALSE for FindReplace
            LPCSTR lpszFindWhat,
            LPCSTR lpszReplaceWith = NULL,
            DWORD dwFlags = FR_DOWN,
            CWnd* pParentWnd = NULL);
// find/replace parameter block
static CFindReplaceDialog* PASCAL GetNotifier(LPARAM lParam);
// Operations
// Helpers for parsing information after successful return
CString GetReplaceString() const;// get replacement string
CString GetFindString() const;   // get find string
BOOL SearchDown() const;         // TRUE if search down,
                                 // FALSE is up
BOOL FindNext() const;           // TRUE if command is find next
BOOL MatchCase() const;          // TRUE if matching case
BOOL MatchWholeWord() const;     // TRUE if matching whole words
                                 // only
BOOL ReplaceCurrent() const;     // TRUE if replacing current string
BOOL ReplaceAll() const;         // TRUE if replacing all
                                 // occurrences
BOOL IsTerminating() const;      // TRUE if terminating dialog
// Implementation
protected:
  virtual void OnOK();
  virtual void OnCancel();
  virtual void PostNcDestroy();
#ifdef _DEBUG
public:
  virtual void Dump(CDumpContext& dc) const;
#endif
protected:
  char m_szFindWhat[128];
  char m_szReplaceWith[128];
};
```

> **Note**
>
> The instances of class `CFindReplaceDialog` generate modeless dialog boxes, so they should be dynamically created on the heap using the operator new. To allocate the instances of `CFindReplaceDialog` on the stack, you must derive a descendant and override the default behavior of the `PostNcDestroy` member function.

The class `CFindReplaceDialog` constructor requires no arguments. Creating the instances of this class requires invoking the constructor and then sending the C++ message `Create` to the newly created dialog box object. The member function `Create` has five parameters. The logical parameter `bFindDialogOnly` selects the Find dialog box (when its argument is TRUE) or the Replace dialog box (when its argument is FALSE.) The parameter `lpszFindWhat` is the pointer to the searched string. The parameter `lpszReplaceWith` is the pointer to the replacement string. The default argument for this parameter is NULL, and NULL is appropriate for invoking the Find dialog box and for deleting text using a Replace dialog box. The parameter `dwFlags` sets the flags that fine-tune the dialog box. The default argument for this parameter is `FR_DOWN` (search down.) Arguments for the parameter `dwFlags` may combine the constants `FR_XXXX`. The parameter `pParentWnd` is the pointer to the parent window.

Notifying the Parent Window

The instances of class `CFindReplaceDialog` notify their parent windows using a special protected data member that assists the notification mechanism. This mechanism involves the following members:

- A static pointer to the `CFindReplaceDialog` instance.

- A static UINT-type data member that stores a message number.

- A message response member function.

Here is a code fragment that illustrates, in general, how to code and initialize the members just listed:

```
class CMainWnd : public CFrameWnd
{
public:
    // member declarations
protected:
    static CFindReplaceDialog* pDialog;
    static UINT nMsgNumber;
    afx_msg LONG CMdFindHelper(UINT wParam, LONG lParam);
    // other delacrations
    DECLARE_MESSAGE_MAP();
};
BEGIN_MESSAGE_MAP(CMainWnd, CFrameWnd)
    // other message maps
    ON_REGISTERED_MESSAGE(nMsgNumber, CMFindReplaceHelper)
    // other message maps
END_MESSAGE_MAP()
UINT CMainWnd::nMsgNumber = ::RegisterMessage(FINDMSGSTRING);
CFindReplaceDialog* CMainWnd::pDialog = NULL
```

Notice that this code fragment contains the declarations of special data members: two static members and the message response member function. Such a member function uses the special message map macro `ON_REGISTERED_MESSAGE`, which takes two arguments. The first argument of the macro is the static member `nMsgNumber`. The second argument is the name of the message response member function, `CMFindReplaceHelper`. The code fragment also initializes the static members that follow the message mapping macros. The code initializes the member `nMsgNumber` using the Windows API function call `::RegisterMessage(FINDMSGSTRING)`. This function yields a message number that is unique to the application instance. The code fragment initializes the static pointer member `pDialog` with NULL.

Using the *CFindReplaceDialog* Helper Functions

The class `CFindReplaceDialog` offers the following helper member functions:

- The function `GetReplaceString` returns a `CString` object that contains the replacement string.

- The function `GetFindString` yields a `CString` object that contains the search string.

- The function `SearchDown` returns TRUE if the search direction is down. Otherwise, the function yields FALSE.

- The function `FindNext` yields TRUE if the button Find Next is clicked.

- The function `MatchCase` returns TRUE if the check box Match Case is checked.

- The function `MatchWholeWord` yields TRUE if the check box Match Whole Word is checked.

- The function `ReplaceCurrent` returns true if the Replace button (in a Replace dialog box) is clicked.

- The function `ReplaceAll` yields TRUE if the button Replace All (in a Replace dialog box) is clicked.

- The function `IsTerminating` returns TRUE if the dialog box is terminating.

> **Note**
>
> The special helper member function uses the results of the functions `FindNext`, `ReplaceCurrent`, `ReplaceAll`, and `IsTerminating` to determine the action to take, based on the button clicked by the user.

Testing the Class *CFindReplaceDialog*

Now let's look at a program that invokes the Find and Replace dialog boxes: the simple program COMMDLG5.EXE.

Listing 10.17 shows the contents of the COMMDLG5.DEF definition file.

Listing 10.17 The COMMDLG5.DEF Definition File

```
NAME          CommDlg5
DESCRIPTION   'An MFC Windows Application'
EXETYPE       WINDOWS
CODE          PRELOAD MOVEABLE DISCARDABLE
DATA          PRELOAD MOVEABLE MULTIPLE
```

Listing 10.18 shows the COMMDLG5.H header file.

Listing 10.18 Source Code for the COMMDLG5.H Header File

```
#define CM_EXIT    (WM_USER + 100)
#define CM_FIND    (WM_USER + 101)
#define CM_REPLACE (WM_USER + 102)
```

Listing 10.19 contains the script for the COMMDLG5.RC resource file.

Listing 10.19 Script for the COMMDLG5.RC Resource File

```
#include <windows.h>
#include <afxres.h>
#include "commdlg5.h"
MAINMENU MENU LOADONCALL MOVEABLE PURE DISCARDABLE
BEGIN
    MENUITEM "E&xit", CM_EXIT
    POPUP "&Search"
    BEGIN
      MENUITEM "&Find...", CM_FIND
      MENUITEM "&Replace...", CM_REPLACE
    END
END
```

The source code for the COMMDLG5.CPP program file is provided in Listing 10.20.

**Listing 10.20 Source Code for the COMMDLG5.CPP
Program File**

```
/*
  Program tests the class CFindReplaceDialog to create the
  Find and Replace dialog boxes.
*/
#include <stdio.h>
#include <string.h>
#include <afxwin.h>
#include <afxdlgs.h>
#include "commdlg5.h"
CString BoolString(BOOL bBool)
{
  return (bBool) ? CString(": Yes") : CString(": No");
}

// declare the custom application class as
class CFindReplaceApp : public CWinApp
{
public:
    virtual BOOL InitInstance();
};
// expand the functionality of CFrameWnd by deriving class CMainWnd
class CMainWnd : public CFrameWnd
{
public:
  CMainWnd();
 protected:
  // declare static members
  static UINT nFindMsg;
  static CFindReplaceDialog* pFindReplaceDialog;
  static bIsReplaceDialog;
  // handle the Find menu item
  afx_msg void CMFind();

  // handle the Replace menu item
  afx_msg void CMReplace();

  // handle exiting the application
  afx_msg void OnExit()
    { SendMessage(WM_CLOSE); }

  // define the helper function
  afx_msg LONG CMFindReplaceHelper(UINT wParam, LONG lParam);

  // handle closing the window
  afx_msg void OnClose();
  // declare message map macro
  DECLARE_MESSAGE_MAP()
};
UINT CMainWnd::nFindMsg = ::RegisterWindowMessage(FINDMSGSTRING);
CFindReplaceDialog* CMainWnd::pFindReplaceDialog = NULL;
```

(continues)

Listing 10.20 Continued

```
BOOL CMainWnd::bIsReplaceDialog = FALSE;
LONG CMainWnd::CMFindReplaceHelper(UINT wParam, LONG lParam)
{
  CString msgStr;
  CFindReplaceDialog* pDialogBox =
        CFindReplaceDialog::GetNotifier(lParam);
  if (pDialogBox->FindNext()        ||
      pDialogBox->ReplaceCurrent()  ||
      pDialogBox->ReplaceAll()) {
    msgStr = "Find: " + pDialogBox->GetFindString();
    if (bIsReplaceDialog)
      msgStr += "\nReplace: " + pDialogBox->GetReplaceString();
    msgStr += "\nSearch Down" +
          BoolString(pDialogBox->SearchDown());
    msgStr += "\nMatch Case" +
          BoolString(pDialogBox->MatchCase());
    msgStr += "\nMatch Whole Word" +
          BoolString(pDialogBox->MatchWholeWord());
    msgStr += "\nFind Next" +
          BoolString(pDialogBox->FindNext());
    if (bIsReplaceDialog) {
      msgStr += "\nReplace Current" +
            BoolString(pDialogBox->ReplaceCurrent());
      msgStr += "\nReplace All" +
            BoolString(pDialogBox->ReplaceAll());
    }
    if (bIsReplaceDialog)
      MessageBox(msgStr, "Replace Dialog Box Settings",
              MB_OK | MB_ICONINFORMATION);
    else
      MessageBox(msgStr, "Find Dialog Box Settings",
              MB_OK | MB_ICONINFORMATION);
  }
  // is dialog box closing?
  else if (pDialogBox->IsTerminating()) {
    // remove dialog box instance
    delete pFindReplaceDialog;
    pFindReplaceDialog = NULL;
  }
  return 0;
}
CMainWnd::CMainWnd()
{
  // create the window
  Create(NULL, "Simple Find/Replace Dialog Box Tester",
        WS_OVERLAPPEDWINDOW, rectDefault, NULL, "MAINMENU");
}
void CMainWnd::CMFind()
{
  if (pFindReplaceDialog)
    return;
  pFindReplaceDialog = new CFindReplaceDialog();
  bIsReplaceDialog = FALSE;
```

```
    pFindReplaceDialog->Create(TRUE, "DOS", NULL,
                              FR_DOWN, this);
    pFindReplaceDialog->SendMessage(WM_INITDIALOG);
}

void CMainWnd::CMReplace()
{

    if (pFindReplaceDialog) return;
    pFindReplaceDialog = new CFindReplaceDialog();
    bIsReplaceDialog = TRUE;
    pFindReplaceDialog->Create(FALSE, "DOS", "Windows",
                              FR_DOWN, this);
    pFindReplaceDialog->SendMessage(WM_INITDIALOG);
}
void CMainWnd::OnClose()
{
    if (MessageBox("Want to close this application",
                   "Query", MB_YESNO | MB_ICONQUESTION) == IDYES)
      DestroyWindow();
}
BEGIN_MESSAGE_MAP(CMainWnd, CFrameWnd)
  ON_COMMAND(CM_FIND, CMFind)
  ON_COMMAND(CM_REPLACE, CMReplace)
  ON_REGISTERED_MESSAGE(nFindMsg, CMFindReplaceHelper)
  ON_COMMAND(CM_EXIT, OnExit)
  ON_WM_CLOSE()
END_MESSAGE_MAP()

// Construct the CFindReplaceApp'msgStr m_pMainWnd data member
BOOL CFindReplaceApp::InitInstance()
{
  m_pMainWnd = new CMainWnd();
  m_pMainWnd->ShowWindow(m_nCmdShow);
  m_pMainWnd->UpdateWindow();
  return TRUE;
}
// application'msgStr constructor initializes and runs the app
CFindReplaceApp WindowApp;
```

Let's take a closer look at the source code shown in Listing 10.20. The window class CMainWnd declares a constructor and a set of member functions. These members include the special static members nFindMsg, pFindReplaceDialog, and bIsReplaceDialog. The member bIsReplaceDialog stores TRUE when you invoke the Replace dialog box and stores FALSE when you invoke the Find dialog box. The class also declares the member function CMFindReplaceHelper to handle notification messages sent by the instance of class CFindReplaceDialog.

The member function CMFind brings up the Find dialog box and performs the following tasks:

■ Exits if the static member pFindReplaceDialog is not NULL. This task ensures that there is only a single instance of the Find dialog box.

■ Invokes the constructor CFindReplaceDialog with the member pFindReplaceDialog.

■ Creates a dialog box by sending the C++ message Create to the newly created CFindReplaceDialog instance. This message specifies the Find dialog box by passing TRUE as the first argument. In addition, the message selects the string "DOS" as the initial search text. The argument for the replacement string is NULL. The constant FR_DOWN is the setting flag.

■ Sends the Windows message WM_INITDIALOG to the dialog box instance to visually bring up the Find dialog box.

The CMReplace member function is similar to the CMFind function. The differences are in the arguments of the C++ message Create. The CMReplace function passes FALSE as the first argument and "Windows" as the replacement string.

The member function CMFindReplaceHelper is the special helper function. This function handles the notification messages generated by the pushbutton controls of the Find and Replace dialog boxes. The function declares the CString object msgStr and the dialog box pointer pDialogBox. The function initializes the latter pointer with the result of the member function GetNotifier. The GetNotifier function yields to the local pointer pDialogBox the address of the member m_pFindReplace (which is from the notifying dialog box). This assignment gives the pointer pDialogBox access to the data of the structure FINDREPLACE. The function responds to clicking the Find Next, Replace, or Replace All pushbuttons by testing the expression that logically ORs the results of the C++ messages FindNext, ReplaceCurrent, and ReplaceAll, which are sent to the dialog box object. If the tested expression is TRUE, the function CMFindReplaceHelper retrieves the values returned by the various helper functions and accumulates them in the results string object msgStr. The function then displays the results string in a message box. Notice that the function uses the static member bIsReplaceDialog to determine whether to include certain information that is relevant to the Replace dialog box. In addition, the function uses the `bIsReplaceDialog` static member to display a message box with the appropriate caption.

If the first Boolean expression is FALSE, the `CMFindReplaceHelper` function determines whether the function `IsTerminating` yields TRUE. When this condition is true, the function deletes the dynamically allocated dialog box and assigns NULL to the static pointer `pDialogBox`. This assignment ensures that you can create a Find or a Replace dialog box when you select the Find or Replace menu options.

Compile and run the COMMDLG5.EXE test program. The program contains a menu bar with two menus: Exit and Search. The Search menu contains the Find and Replace commands. Choosing the Find command opens the Find dialog box; choosing Replace invokes the Replace dialog box. Choose either command and experiment with making new selections and typing new text in the corresponding dialog box. Click the Find Next button (available in both the Find and Replace dialog boxes) and watch the program display a message box containing information about the dialog box you invoked. When you finish experimenting with one dialog box, select the other one. When you are finished testing the program, click the Cancel button of the current dialog box to exit. Figure 10.13 shows the message box after the Find Next pushbutton has been clicked.

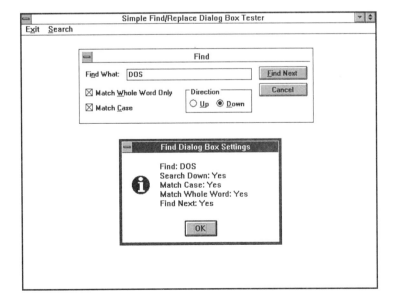

Figure 10.13

The message dialog box after the Find Next pushbutton in the Find dialog box has been clicked.

Figure 10.14 shows the message dialog box after the Replace pushbutton in the Replace dialog box has been clicked.

Figure 10.14

The message dialog box after the Replace pushbutton in the Replace dialog box has been clicked.

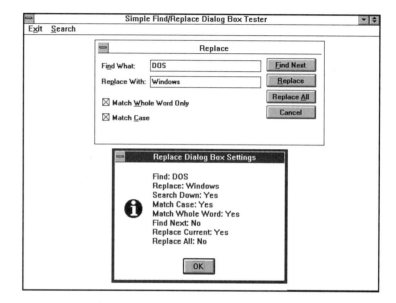

Summary

This chapter presented the common dialog boxes supported by Windows. You learned about the following topics:

- Software requirements for using the common dialog boxes. This included using the AFXDLGS.H header file, linking with the COMMDLG.LIB library, and making sure that the COMMDLG.DLL file is in the Windows system directory.

- The color selection dialog box class CColorDialog.

- The font selection dialog box class CFontDialog.

- The printer setup dialog box class CPrintDialog.

- The file selection dialog box class CFileDialog. This class creates dialog boxes that support either opening or saving a file.

- The text find/replace dialog box class CFindReplaceDialog. This class creates dialog boxes that support either finding or replacing text.

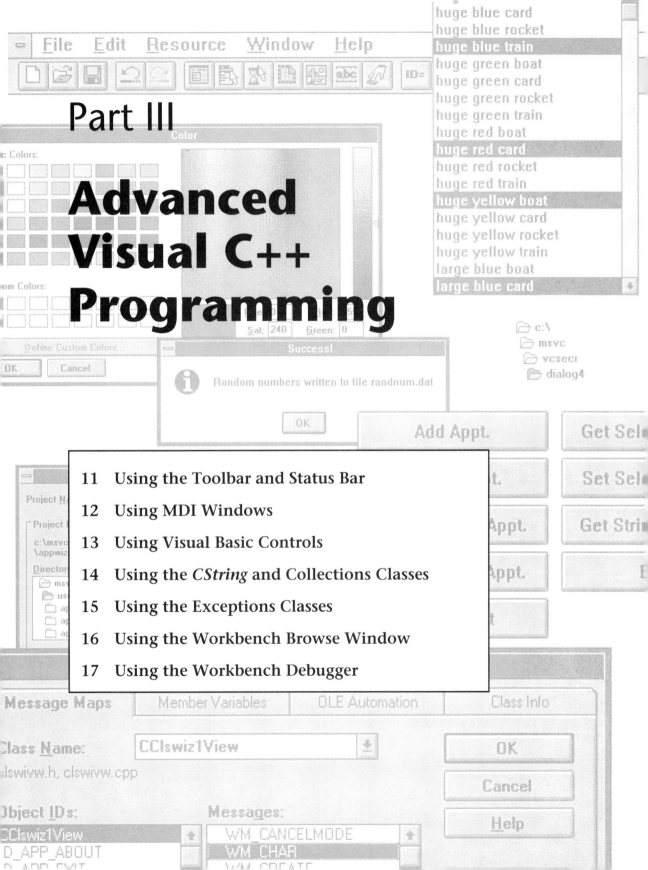

Part III

Advanced
Visual C++
Programming

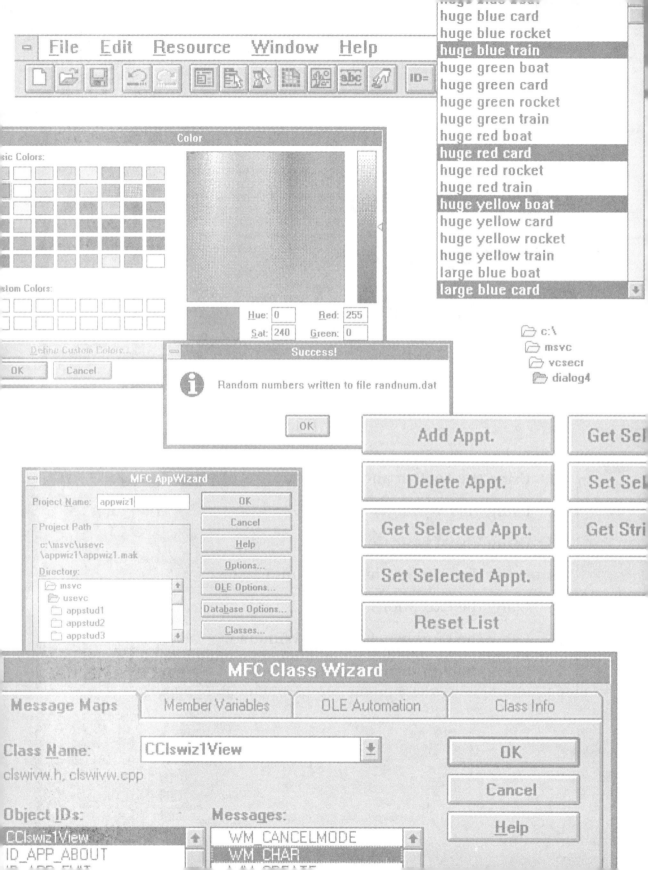

Chapter 11

Using the Toolbar and Status Bar

The toolbar and the status bar are special windows that have become increasingly popular with the proliferation of Windows applications. The toolbar contains bitmapped buttons that offer shortcut commands; they have become so popular in major applications (such as Word for Windows and WordPerfect for Windows) that their implementations are proliferating. Currently, for example, you can choose between fixed and customizable toolbars, as well as small and large toolbars. The status bar also is becoming popular in major applications, such as word processors. Word for Windows 6.0, for example, uses the status bar to display such information as the page number, the total number of pages, the location of the insertion cursor, and the current time. In this chapter, I introduce the classes that support the toolbar and the status bar, and you learn about the following topics:

- The CToolBar class

- Guidelines for programming a toolbar in an application

- A sample program that uses a toolbar

- The CStatusBar class

- Guidelines for programming a status bar in an application

- A sample program that uses a status bar

The *CToolBar* Class

The MFC library declares the class CToolBar as a descendant of class CControlBar. The class CToolBar supports the toolbar window and is declared as follows:

```
class CToolBar : public CControlBar
{
  DECLARE_DYNAMIC(CToolBar)
// Construction
public:
  CToolBar();
  BOOL Create(CWnd* pParentWnd,
              DWORD dwStyle = WS_CHILD | WS_VISIBLE | CBRS_TOP,
              UINT nID = AFX_IDW_TOOLBAR);

  void SetSizes(SIZE sizeButton, SIZE sizeImage);
  // button size should be bigger than image
  void SetHeight(int cyHeight);
  // call after SetSizes, height overrides bitmap size
  BOOL LoadBitmap(LPCSTR lpszResourceName);
  BOOL LoadBitmap(UINT nIDResource);
  BOOL SetButtons(const UINT FAR* lpIDArray, int nIDCount);
                    // lpIDArray can be NULL to allocate empty
                    // buttons

// Attributes
public: // standard control bar things
  int CommandToIndex(UINT nIDFind) const;
  UINT GetItemID(int nIndex) const;
  virtual void GetItemRect(int nIndex, LPRECT lpRect) const;

public:
  // for changing button info
  void GetButtonInfo(int nIndex, UINT& nID, UINT& nStyle,
                     int& iImage) const;
  void SetButtonInfo(int nIndex, UINT nID, UINT nStyle,
                     int iImage);

// Implementation
public:
  virtual ~CToolBar();
  inline UINT _GetButtonStyle(int nIndex) const;
  void _SetButtonStyle(int nIndex, UINT nStyle);

#ifdef _DEBUG
  virtual void AssertValid() const;
  virtual void Dump(CDumpContext& dc) const;
#endif

protected:
  inline AFX_TBBUTTON* _GetButtonPtr(int nIndex) const;
  void InvalidateButton(int nIndex);
  void CreateMask(int iImage, CPoint offset,
                  BOOL bHilite, BOOL bHiliteShadow);
```

```
      // for custom drawing
      struct DrawState
      {
        HBITMAP hbmMono;
        HBITMAP hbmMonoOld;
        HBITMAP hbmOldGlyphs;
      };
      BOOL PrepareDrawButton(DrawState& ds);
      BOOL DrawButton(HDC hdC, int x, int y, int iImage, UINT nStyle);
      void EndDrawButton(DrawState& ds);

  protected:
      CSize m_sizeButton;        // size of button
      CSize m_sizeImage;         // size of glyph
      HBITMAP m_hbmImageWell;       // glyphs only
      int m_iButtonCapture;   // index of button with capture
                              // (-1 => none)
      HRSRC m_hRsrcImageWell; // handle to loaded resource for image
                              // well
      HINSTANCE m_hInstImageWell; // instance handle to load image
                                  // well from

      virtual void DoPaint(CDC* pDC);
      virtual void OnUpdateCmdUI(CFrameWnd* pTarget,
                                 BOOL bDisableIfNoHndler);
      virtual int HitTest(CPoint point);

  //{{AFX_MSG(CToolBar)
      afx_msg void OnLButtonDown(UINT nFlags, CPoint point);
      afx_msg void OnMouseMove(UINT nFlags, CPoint point);
      afx_msg void OnLButtonUp(UINT nFlags, CPoint point);
      afx_msg void OnCancelMode();
      afx_msg LRESULT OnHelpHitTest(WPARAM wParam, LPARAM lParam);
      afx_msg void OnSysColorChange();
  //}}AFX_MSG
      DECLARE_MESSAGE_MAP()
  };
```

The class `CToolBar` declares the default constructor, which creates an invisible empty toolbar object. The member function `Create` builds the visible toolbar control by specifying its style, ID, and parent window. The member function `Create` has default arguments for the style parameter, `dwStyle`, and the ID parameter, `nID`. The default argument for the parameter `dwStyle` is the expression

```
    WS_CHILD ¦ WS_VISIBLE ¦ CBRS_TOP
```

The default argument for the parameter `nID` is the identifier `AFX_IDW_TOOLBAR`. The class also offers the member function `LoadBitmap` to load the bitmaps for the toolbar from a bitmap resource. The member function `SetButtons` assigns the IDs for the bitmapped buttons in the toolbar. The sequence for creating a toolbar, therefore, involves the constructor, the function `Create`, the function `LoadBitmap`, and the function `SetButtons`.

III

Advanced Programming

A toolbar is made up of a set of bitmapped buttons and may include separators to visually group certain buttons. Each button must have a unique ID. The separators also have IDs, although they all share the same identifier: ID_SEPARATOR.

The class CToolBar provides the following member functions that help you manage the bitmapped buttons of the toolbar:

■ The member function CommandToIndex yields the index of the first toolbar button that matches the argument for the parameter nIDFind (the indices of the toolbar buttons are 0-based).

■ The member function GetItemID returns the ID of the button or separator selected by its positional index nIndex. If the argument for the parameter nIndex refers to a separator, the function yields the identifier ID_SEPARATOR.

■ The member function SetButtonInfo enables you to assign a new ID, style, and bitmap to a toolbar button. The parameter nIndex specifies the manipulated toolbar button; the parameter nID specifies the command ID of the button (which can be new); the parameter nStyle indicates the new style of the button; and the parameter iImage is the index for the button's new image, which is selected from the bitmap.

■ The member function GetButtonInfo obtains the ID, style, and image index for a toolbar button.

The header file AFXEXT.H, which declares the class CToolBar, also contains the declarations for the toolbar button styles, as shown here:

```
// Styles for toolbar buttons
#define TBBS_BUTTON     0x00    // this entry is button
#define TBBS_SEPARATOR  0x01    // this entry is a separator
#define TBBS_CHECKBOX   0x02    // this is an auto check/radio
                                // button

// styles for display states
#define TBBS_CHECKED        0x0100  // button is checked/down
#define TBBS_INDETERMINATE  0x0200  // third state
#define TBBS_DISABLED       0x0400  // element is disabled
#define TBBS_PRESSED        0x0800  // button is being pressed -
                                    // mouse down
```

Toolbar Programming Guidelines

A toolbar requires two primary components: a bitmap resource and support for command messages. The bitmap resource contains the contiguous set of bitmaps that represents each toolbar button. Each toolbar bitmap is 15 pixels high and 16 pixels wide. You don't have to draw the borders or separators—the application framework handles these visual components. The AppWizard stores the toolbar bitmap in the file TOOLBAR.BMP. Figure 11.1 shows a sample toolbar bitmap and the actual toolbar it produces. Notice that the bitmap has no edges or separators, but the actual toolbar does.

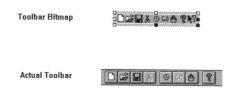

Toolbar Bitmap

Actual Toolbar

Figure 11.1
A sample toolbar bitmap and the actual toolbar it produces.

The second aspect of creating a working toolbar is supporting the commands it generates. Typically, the generated commands duplicate menu commands. Consequently, when assigning IDs to toolbar buttons, the program must assign IDs that match the corresponding menu commands. The program then responds to any command message that is generated (regardless of whether the message is issued by a menu command or its associated toolbar button) by invoking the appropriate member function (as specified by the message macros).

Having menu commands and toolbar pushbuttons send the same command messages brings up the following question. What is the easiest way to handle enabling and disabling a menu command and its associated toolbar button? The answer lies in responding to the UPDATE_COMMAND_UI command message that is associated with the ID of the menu command and the toolbar button. The ClassWizard helps in declaring the member functions for the UPDATE_COMMAND_UI message. The general syntax for the member function that responds to an UPDATE_COMMAND_UI message type is

```
void CViewClass::OnUpdateMenuOption(CCmdUI* pCmdUI)
{
  // other statements below
  .
  .
  .
  pCmdUI->Enable(BooleanExpression);
}
```

The member function OnUpdate*MenuOption* sends the C++ message Enable to the object accessed by the parameter pCmdUI. The argument for this message is a Boolean expression that, when true, enables the command *MenuOption*; otherwise, the command is disabled.

A Sample Toolbar Program

In this section, I use the AppWizard, App Studio, and ClassWizard utilities to create a simple application, TOOLBAR1.EXE, that displays the current system date and time and manipulates a simple timer. The program includes a menu command that displays the current date and time in a message dialog box. Other menu commands start and stop the simple timer. When you start the timer, the program displays a message dialog box which tells you that the timer is on. When you stop the timer, the program resets the timer and displays the elapsed number of seconds in a message dialog box. Each of these menu commands has an associated toolbar button.

This application supports the feature that disables the menu command (and its associated toolbar button) that stops the timer when the timer is not running. Likewise, the program disables the menu command (and its associated toolbar button) that starts the timer when the timer is running.

Creating the program TOOLBAR1.EXE requires several stages that involve the AppWizard utility, the App Studio utility, the ClassWizard utility, and some manual coding. Here are the required stages:

1. Use the AppWizard utility to create source code files for an SDI-compliant program that has initial toolbars (but no print-related feature). The project name is TOOLBAR1, and the files reside in the directories \MSVC\USEVC\TOOLBAR1 and \MSVC\USEVC\TOOLBAR1\RES.

2. Use the App Studio application to edit the IDR_MAINFRAME menu resource generated by the AppWizard. Make the following changes:

   ■ Change the File pop-up menu resource into the nonpop-up Exit menu. This change deletes automatically the original menu commands of the File menu. Assign the ID ID_APP_EXIT to the Exit menu and type the one line of help text that appears in the status bar when the Exit menu is chosen.

   ■ Change the caption of the Edit menu to *Time*.

- Remove the original commands from the Edit menu.

- Insert the menu commands Date/Time, Start Timer, and Stop Timer. Use the IDs ID_DATE_TIME, ID_START_TIMER, and ID_STOP_TIMER, respectively, for these commands.

- Save the menu resource and return to the main window of the App Studio.

Listing 11.1 shows the source code for the RESOURCE.H header file, which contains the new menu command IDs you defined in step 2 using App Studio.

Listing 11.1 Source Code for the RESOURCE.H Header File

```
//{{NO_DEPENDENCIES}}
// App Studio generated include file.
// Used by TOOLBAR1.RC
//
#define IDR_MAINFRAME                   2
#define IDD_ABOUTBOX                    100
#define ID_DATE_TIME                    32772
#define ID_START_TIMER                  32773
#define ID_STOP_TIMER                   32775

// Next default values for new objects
//
#ifdef APSTUDIO_INVOKED
#ifndef APSTUDIO_READONLY_SYMBOLS

#define _APS_NEXT_RESOURCE_VALUE        102
#define _APS_NEXT_COMMAND_VALUE         32776
#define _APS_NEXT_CONTROL_VALUE         1000
#define _APS_NEXT_SYMED_VALUE           101
#endif
#endif
```

Listing 11.2 shows the partial script of the TOOLBAR1.RC resource file, which contains the menu resource you modified previously in step 2.

Listing 11.2 Partial Script of the TOOLBAR1.RC Resource File

```
//Microsoft App Studio generated resource script.
//
#include "resource.h"
```

(continues)

III

Advanced Programming

Listing 11.2 Continued

```
#define APSTUDIO_READONLY_SYMBOLS
/////////////////////////////////////////////////////////////
//
// Generated from the TEXTINCLUDE 2 resource.
//
#include "afxres.h"
  .
  .
  .
/////////////////////////////////////////////////////////////
//
// Bitmap
//

IDR_MAINFRAME            BITMAP  MOVEABLE PURE    "RES\\TOOLBAR.BMP"

/////////////////////////////////////////////////////////////
//
// Menu
//

IDR_MAINFRAME MENU PRELOAD DISCARDABLE
BEGIN
    MENUITEM "&Exit",                    ID_APP_EXIT
    POPUP "&Time"
    BEGIN
        MENUITEM "&Date/Time    ",       ID_DATE_TIME
        MENUITEM SEPARATOR
        MENUITEM "&Start Timer",         ID_START_TIMER
        MENUITEM "S&top Timer",          ID_STOP_TIMER
    END
    POPUP "&View"
    BEGIN
        MENUITEM "&Toolbar",             ID_VIEW_TOOLBAR
        MENUITEM "&Status Bar",          ID_VIEW_STATUS_BAR
    END
    POPUP "&Help"
    BEGIN
        MENUITEM "&About Toolbar1...",   ID_APP_ABOUT
    END
END
  .
  .
  .
/////////////////////////////////////////////////////////////
#endif    // not APSTUDIO_INVOKED
```

3. Select the `IDR_MAINFRAME` bitmap resource and edit the bitmaps for the original copy, paste, and print toolbar buttons. Replace these bitmaps as follows so that your toolbar includes the bitmaps shown in Figure 11.1:

- Replace the copy bitmap with a clock bitmap. This bitmap will be associated with the Date/Time menu command.

- Substitute the paste bitmap with the GO bitmap. This bitmap will be associated with the Start Timer menu command.

- Replace the print bitmap with the hand bitmap. This bitmap will be associated with the Stop Timer menu command.

After you have replaced the preceding bitmaps, save the bitmap resource and exit App Studio.

4. Load the file MAINFRM.CPP into an edit window and edit the static array called `buttons`. Replace the IDs for the Copy, Paste, and Print commands with these IDs: `ID_DATE_TIME`, `ID_START_TIMER`, and `ID_STOP_TIMER`, respectively. Make sure that these identifiers have an `ID_SEPARATOR` before and after them.

Listing 11.3 shows the source code for the MAINFRM.CPP implementation file with the ID changes you just made.

Listing 11.3 Source Code for the MAINFRM.CPP
Implementation File

```
// mainfrm.cpp : implementation of the CMainFrame class
//

#include "stdafx.h"
#include "toolbar1.h"

#include "mainfrm.h"

#ifdef _DEBUG
#undef THIS_FILE
static char BASED_CODE THIS_FILE[] = __FILE__;
#endif

///////////////////////////////////////////////////////////////
// CMainFrame

IMPLEMENT_DYNCREATE(CMainFrame, CFrameWnd)
```

(continues)

Listing 11.3 Continued

```
BEGIN_MESSAGE_MAP(CMainFrame, CFrameWnd)
    //{{AFX_MSG_MAP(CMainFrame)
  // NOTE - the ClassWizard will add and remove mapping macros
here.
  //    DO NOT EDIT what you see in these blocks of generated code !
    ON_WM_CREATE()
    //}}AFX_MSG_MAP
END_MESSAGE_MAP()

/////////////////////////////////////////////////////////////
// arrays of IDs used to initialize control bars

// toolbar buttons - IDs are command buttons
static UINT BASED_CODE buttons[] =
{
    // same order as in the bitmap 'toolbar.bmp'
    ID_FILE_NEW,
    ID_FILE_OPEN,
    ID_FILE_SAVE,
    ID_EDIT_CUT,
        ID_SEPARATOR,
    ID_DATE_TIME,
    ID_START_TIMER,
    ID_STOP_TIMER,
        ID_SEPARATOR,
    ID_APP_ABOUT,
};

static UINT BASED_CODE indicators[] =
{
    ID_SEPARATOR,           // status line indicator
    ID_INDICATOR_CAPS,
    ID_INDICATOR_NUM,
    ID_INDICATOR_SCRL,
};

/////////////////////////////////////////////////////////////
// CMainFrame construction/destruction

CMainFrame::CMainFrame()
{
    // TODO: add member initialization code here
}

CMainFrame::~CMainFrame()
{
}

int CMainFrame::OnCreate(LPCREATESTRUCT lpCreateStruct)
{
    if (CFrameWnd::OnCreate(lpCreateStruct) == -1)
        return -1;
```

```
    if (!m_wndToolBar.Create(this) ¦¦
        !m_wndToolBar.LoadBitmap(IDR_MAINFRAME) ¦¦
        !m_wndToolBar.SetButtons(buttons,
          sizeof(buttons)/sizeof(UINT)))
    {
        TRACE("Failed to create toolbar\n");
        return -1;       // fail to create
    }

    if (!m_wndStatusBar.Create(this) ¦¦
        !m_wndStatusBar.SetIndicators(indicators,
          sizeof(indicators)/sizeof(UINT)))
    {
        TRACE("Failed to create status bar\n");
        return -1;       // fail to create
    }

    return 0;
}

/////////////////////////////////////////////////////////////
// CMainFrame diagnostics

#ifdef _DEBUG
void CMainFrame::AssertValid() const
{
    CFrameWnd::AssertValid();
}

void CMainFrame::Dump(CDumpContext& dc) const
{
    CFrameWnd::Dump(dc);
}

#endif //_DEBUG

/////////////////////////////////////////////////////////////
// CMainFrame message handlers
```

5. Load the ClassWizard utility, select the view class, and then perform the following tasks to add the message-handling member functions:

   ■ Select the CToolbar1View object and add the handler for the message WM_MOUSEMOVE. The ClassWizard utility adds the member function OnMouseMove to the list of member functions.

   ■ Select the ID_DATE_TIME object and add the handler for the COMMAND message. The ClassWizard utility adds the member function OnDateTime to the list of member functions.

III

Advanced Programming

- Select the ID_START_TIMER object and add handlers for the COMMAND and UPDATE_COMMAND_UI messages. The ClassWizard utility adds the member functions OnStartTimer and OnUpdateStartTimer to the list of member functions.

- Select the ID_STOP_TIMER object and add handlers for the COMMAND and UPDATE_COMMAND_UI messages. ClassWizard adds the member functions OnStopTimer and OnUpdateStopTimer to the list of member functions.

Listing 11.4 shows the source code for the TOOLBVW.H header file, which contains the declarations of the new member functions that ClassWizard just added.

Listing 11.4 Source Code for the TOOLBVW.H Header File

```
// toolbvw.h : interface of the CToolbar1View class
//
/////////////////////////////////////////////////////////////

class CToolbar1View : public CView
{
protected: // create from serialization only
    CToolbar1View();
    DECLARE_DYNCREATE(CToolbar1View)

// Attributes
public:
    CToolbar1Doc* GetDocument();

// Operations
public:

// Implementation
public:
    virtual ~CToolbar1View();
    virtual void OnDraw(CDC* pDC);  // overridden to draw
                                    // this view
#ifdef _DEBUG
    virtual void AssertValid() const;
    virtual void Dump(CDumpContext& dc) const;
#endif

protected:

// Generated message map functions
protected:
    //{{AFX_MSG(CToolbar1View)
    afx_msg void OnDateTime();
    afx_msg void OnStartTimer();
```

```
    afx_msg void OnUpdateStartTimer(CCmdUI* pCmdUI);
    afx_msg void OnUpdateStopTimer(CCmdUI* pCmdUI);
    afx_msg void OnStopTimer();
    afx_msg void OnMouseMove(UINT nFlags, CPoint point);
    //}}AFX_MSG
    DECLARE_MESSAGE_MAP()
};

#ifndef _DEBUG  // debug version in toolbvw.cpp
inline CToolbar1Doc* CToolbar1View::GetDocument()
   { return (CToolbar1Doc*)m_pDocument; }
#endif

/////////////////////////////////////////////////////////////////
```

6. To the TOOLBDOC.H header file, manually add the declarations of the following data members to class `CToolbar1Doc`:

- The Boolean data member `bTimerOn`, which stores the on/off mode of the simple timer.

- The long-type member `lInitTickCount`, which stores the tick counts (the number of milliseconds since Windows started running).

- The data member `tm`, which is an instance of class `CTime`. The program uses this instance to obtain the current system date and time.

Listing 11.5 shows the source code for the TOOLBDOC.H header file with the preceding data members inserted.

Listing 11.5 Source Code for the TOOLBDOC.H Header File

```
// toolbdoc.h : interface of the CToolbar1Doc class
//
/////////////////////////////////////////////////////////////////

class CToolbar1Doc : public CDocument
{
protected: // create from serialization only
    CToolbar1Doc();
    DECLARE_DYNCREATE(CToolbar1Doc)

// Attributes
public:
  BOOL bTimerOn;
```

III

Advanced Programming

(continues)

Listing 11.5 Continued

```
    long lInitTickCount;
    CTime tm;

// Operations
public:

// Implementation
public:
    virtual ~CToolbar1Doc();
    virtual void Serialize(CArchive& ar); // overridden for
                                          // document i/o
#ifdef _DEBUG
    virtual void AssertValid() const;
    virtual void Dump(CDumpContext& dc) const;
#endif

protected:
    virtual BOOL OnNewDocument();

// Generated message map functions
protected:
    //{{AFX_MSG(CToolbar1Doc)
    // NOTE - the ClassWizard will add and remove member
    // functions here.
    //    DO NOT EDIT what you see in these blocks of
    // generated code !
    //}}AFX_MSG
    DECLARE_MESSAGE_MAP()
};

/////////////////////////////////////////////////////////////
```

---

7. Manually insert into the TOOLBDOC.CPP file the constructor statement that assigns FALSE to the document's data member bTimerOn. Listing 11.6 shows the source code for the TOOLBDOC.CPP implementation file after the constructor statement has been inserted.

Listing 11.6 Source Code for the TOOLBDOC.CPP Implementation File

```
// toolbdoc.cpp : implementation of the CToolbar1Doc class
//

#include "stdafx.h"
#include "toolbar1.h"

#include "toolbdoc.h"
```

```
#ifdef _DEBUG
#undef THIS_FILE
static char BASED_CODE THIS_FILE[] = __FILE__;
#endif


/////////////////////////////////////////////////////////
// CToolbar1Doc

IMPLEMENT_DYNCREATE(CToolbar1Doc, CDocument)

BEGIN_MESSAGE_MAP(CToolbar1Doc, CDocument)
    //{{AFX_MSG_MAP(CToolbar1Doc)
        // NOTE - the ClassWizard will add and remove mapping macros here.
        //    DO NOT EDIT what you see in these blocks of generated code!
    //}}AFX_MSG_MAP
END_MESSAGE_MAP()

/////////////////////////////////////////////////////////
// CToolbar1Doc construction/destruction

CToolbar1Doc::CToolbar1Doc()
{
  bTimerOn = FALSE;
}

CToolbar1Doc::~CToolbar1Doc()
{
}

BOOL CToolbar1Doc::OnNewDocument()
{
    if (!CDocument::OnNewDocument())
        return FALSE;

    // TODO: add reinitialization code here
    // (SDI documents will reuse this document)

    return TRUE;
}

/////////////////////////////////////////////////////////
// CToolbar1Doc serialization

void CToolbar1Doc::Serialize(CArchive& ar)
{
    if (ar.IsStoring())
    {
        // TODO: add storing code here
    }
    else
    {
        // TODO: add loading code here
    }
}
```

III

Advanced Programming

(continues)

Listing 11.6 Continued

```
//////////////////////////////////////////////////////////////
// CToolbar1Doc diagnostics

#ifdef _DEBUG
void CToolbar1Doc::AssertValid() const
{
    CDocument::AssertValid();
}

void CToolbar1Doc::Dump(CDumpContext& dc) const
{
    CDocument::Dump(dc);
}
#endif //_DEBUG


//////////////////////////////////////////////////////////////
// CToolbar1Doc commands
```

8. Manually insert statements for the following items into the
    TOOLBVW.CPP file:

    ■ The definitions of the member functions `OnDateTime`, `OnMouseMove`,
      `OnStartTimer`, `OnStopTimer`, `OnUpdateStartTimer`, and
      `OnUpdateStopTimer`.

    ■ The inclusion of header files STDIO.H and STRING.H.

    ■ The declarations of the constants `MaxStringLen`, `X0`, `Y0`, and `Y1`.

    Listing 11.7 shows the source code for the TOOLBVW.CPP implementa-
    tion file with the preceding statements inserted.

**Listing 11.7 Source Code for the TOOLBVW.CPP
Implementation File**

```
// toolbvw.cpp : implementation of the CToolbar1View class
//

#include "stdafx.h"
#include "toolbar1.h"

#include "toolbdoc.h"
#include "toolbvw.h"

// include additional header files needed to customize the program
#include <stdio.h>
#include <string.h>
```

```
#ifdef _DEBUG
#undef THIS_FILE
static char BASED_CODE THIS_FILE[] = __FILE__;
#endif

// define a new constant
const MaxStringLen = 40;
const X0 = 10;
const Y0 = 10;

/////////////////////////////////////////////////////////////
// CToolbar1View

IMPLEMENT_DYNCREATE(CToolbar1View, CView)

BEGIN_MESSAGE_MAP(CToolbar1View, CView)
    //{{AFX_MSG_MAP(CToolbar1View)
    ON_COMMAND(ID_DATE_TIME, OnDateTime)
    ON_COMMAND(ID_START_TIMER, OnStartTimer)
    ON_UPDATE_COMMAND_UI(ID_START_TIMER, OnUpdateStartTimer)
    ON_UPDATE_COMMAND_UI(ID_STOP_TIMER, OnUpdateStopTimer)
    ON_COMMAND(ID_STOP_TIMER, OnStopTimer)
    ON_WM_MOUSEMOVE()
    //}}AFX_MSG_MAP
END_MESSAGE_MAP()

/////////////////////////////////////////////////////////////
// CToolbar1View construction/destruction

CToolbar1View::CToolbar1View()
{
    // TODO: add construction code here
}

CToolbar1View::~CToolbar1View()
{
}

/////////////////////////////////////////////////////////////
// CToolbar1View drawing

void CToolbar1View::OnDraw(CDC* pDC)
{
    CToolbar1Doc* pDoc = GetDocument();
    ASSERT_VALID(pDoc);

    // TODO: add draw code for native data here
}

/////////////////////////////////////////////////////////////
// CToolbar1View diagnostics

#ifdef _DEBUG
void CToolbar1View::AssertValid() const
```

(continues)

Advanced Programming

Listing 11.7 Continued

```
    {
        CView::AssertValid();
    }

    void CToolbar1View::Dump(CDumpContext& dc) const
    {
        CView::Dump(dc);
    }

    CToolbar1Doc* CToolbar1View::GetDocument() // non-debug version
                                               // is inline
    {
        ASSERT(m_pDocument->IsKindOf(RUNTIME_CLASS(CToolbar1Doc)));
        return (CToolbar1Doc*)m_pDocument;
    }
    #endif //_DEBUG

    ///////////////////////////////////////////////////////////
    // CToolbar1View message handlers

    void CToolbar1View::OnDateTime()
    {
      CToolbar1Doc* pDoc = GetDocument();
      char szStr[MaxStringLen+1];
      pDoc->tm = CTime::GetCurrentTime();

      sprintf(szStr, "Date is %02d/%02d/%4d, Time is %02d:%02d:%02d",
                     pDoc->tm.GetMonth(), pDoc->tm.GetDay(),
                     pDoc->tm.GetYear(), pDoc->tm.GetHour(),
                     pDoc->tm.GetMinute(), pDoc->tm.GetSecond());
      MessageBox(szStr, "Current Date/Time",
                 MB_OK | MB_ICONINFORMATION);
    }

    void CToolbar1View::OnStartTimer()
    {
      CToolbar1Doc* pDoc = GetDocument();

      pDoc->bTimerOn = TRUE;
      pDoc->lInitTickCount = GetTickCount();
      MessageBox("Timer is now On!", "Timer Event",
                 MB_OK | MB_ICONEXCLAMATION);
    }

    void CToolbar1View::OnUpdateStartTimer(CCmdUI* pCmdUI)
    {
      CToolbar1Doc* pDoc = GetDocument();
      pCmdUI->Enable(!pDoc->bTimerOn);
    }

    void CToolbar1View::OnUpdateStopTimer(CCmdUI* pCmdUI)
    {
      CToolbar1Doc* pDoc = GetDocument();
      pCmdUI->Enable(pDoc->bTimerOn);
    }
```

```
void CToolbar1View::OnStopTimer()
{
  CToolbar1Doc* pDoc = GetDocument();
  char szStr[MaxStringLen+1];

  pDoc->bTimerOn = FALSE;
  sprintf(szStr, "%3.3lf seconds elapsed",
          (GetTickCount() - pDoc->lInitTickCount) / 1000.0);
  MessageBox(szStr, "Timer Event",
             MB_OK | MB_ICONINFORMATION);
}

void CToolbar1View::OnMouseMove(UINT nFlags, CPoint point)
{
  char szStr[MaxStringLen+1];
  CClientDC dc(this);

  sprintf(szStr, "[%03d, %03d]", point.x, point.y);
  dc.TextOut(X0, Y0, szStr, strlen(szStr));
}
```

The AppWizard utility generated this file. The ClassWizard utility added the entries in the message map and also inserted the minimal definitions of the member functions OnDateTime, OnMouseMove, OnStartTimer, OnStopTimer, OnUpdateStartTimer, and OnUpdateStopTimer. Let's examine these functions in their final form:

■ The member function OnDateTime responds to the Windows command message ID_DATE_TIME by displaying the current system date and time. The function performs the following tasks:

- Stores the address of the document in the local pointer pDoc.

- Obtains the current system date and time by assigning the result of the static member function CTime::GetCurrentTime to the document's member tm.

- Creates the string image for the date and time. This task uses the function sprintf and sends the C++ messages GetMonth, GetYear, GetDay, GetHour, GetMinute, and GetSecond to the document's data member tm.

- Displays the string image of the date and time in a message dialog box.

III

Advanced Programming

- The member function `OnStartTimer` responds to the Windows command message `ID_START_TIMER` by starting the simple timer. The function carries out the following tasks:

  - Assigns the address of the document to the local pointer `pDoc`.

  - Assigns TRUE to the document's data member `bTimerOn`.

  - Assigns the result of the API function `GetTickCount` to the document's data member `lInitTickCount`.

  - Displays a message, in a message dialog box, telling you that the timer is now on.

> **Note**
>
> Notice that the function `OnStartTimer` does not examine the document's data member `bTimerOn` to determine the state of the timer. Such an examination is not necessary; once the timer is running, the program disables both the menu command and the toolbar button that starts the timer. The champions of this feature are the member functions `OnUpdateStartTimer` and `OnUpdateStopTimer`.

- The member function `OnStopTimer` responds to the Windows command message `ID_STOP_TIMER` by stopping the simple timer. The function carries out the following tasks:

  - Assigns the address of the document to the local pointer `pDoc`.

  - Assigns FALSE to the document's data member `bTimerOn`.

  - Calculates the number of elapsed seconds and creates a string image for that result.

  - Displays the string image of the elapsed time in a message dialog box.

- The member function `OnUpdateStartTimer` responds to the `UPDATE_COMMAND_UI` command and performs the following tasks:

  - Assigns the address of the document to the local pointer `pDoc`.

- Sends the C++ message Enable to the parameter pCmdUI. The argument for this message is the expression !pDoc->bTimerOn. When the member bTimerOn is FALSE, the Enable message enables the Start Timer menu command and its associated toolbar button. Otherwise, the function disables the Start Timer menu command and toolbar button.

■ The member function OnUpdateStopTimer responds to the UPDATE_COMMAND_UI command and performs the following tasks:

- Assigns the address of the document to the local pointer pDoc.

- Sends the C++ message Enable to the parameter pCmdUI. The argument for this message is the expression pDoc->bTimerOn. When the member bTimerOn is TRUE, the Enable message enables the Stop Timer menu command and its associated toolbar button. Otherwise, the function disables the Stop Timer menu command and toolbar buttons.

■ The member function OnMouseMove responds to the Windows message WM_MOUSEMOVE by displaying the current mouse location in the upper-left corner of the view. The function performs the following tasks:

- Creates the device context object dc.

- Creates a string image for the current mouse coordinates. The members x and y of the parameter point provide the current mouse coordinates. This task involves the function sprintf and stores the string image in the local variable szStr.

- Displays the contents of the string szStr by sending the C++ message TextOut to the object dc. The arguments for this message are X0, Y0, szStr, and strlen(szStr).

III

Advanced Programming

9. Compile and run the TOOLBAR1.EXE program. Notice that initially the program has disabled the Stop Timer menu command and the hand toolbar button. Click the clock toolbar button to display the current date and time in a message dialog box. Then click the GO toolbar button to start the simple timer. Notice that after you close the message dialog box, the program disables the GO toolbar button and enables the hand toolbar button. Move the mouse around the view for a while and then click the hand toolbar button. The program responds by displaying a message dialog box containing the elapsed number of seconds (see Figure 11.2). When you are finished experimenting with the program, click the Exit menu.

Figure 11.2
The program
TOOLBAR1.EXE
showing the
message box with
the timer's elapsed
time.

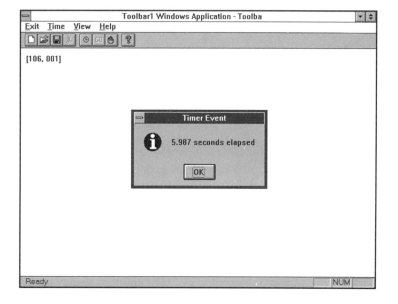

The *CStatusBar* Class

The MFC library offers class CStatusBar to support the status bar in Windows applications. The class CStatusBar, a descendant of class CControlBar, is declared as follows:

```
class CStatusBar : public CControlBar
{
  DECLARE_DYNAMIC(CStatusBar)
// Construction
public:
  CStatusBar();
```

```
   BOOL Create(CWnd* pParentWnd,
               DWORD dwStyle = WS_CHILD ¦ WS_VISIBLE ¦ CBRS_BOTTOM,
               UINT nID = AFX_IDW_STATUS_BAR);
   BOOL SetIndicators(const UINT FAR* lpIDArray, int nIDCount);

// Attributes
public: // standard control bar things
   int CommandToIndex(UINT nIDFind) const;
   UINT GetItemID(int nIndex) const;
   void GetItemRect(int nIndex, LPRECT lpRect) const;
public:
   void GetPaneText(int nIndex, CString& s) const;
   BOOL SetPaneText(int nIndex, LPCSTR lpszNewText,
                    BOOL bUpdate = TRUE);
   void GetPaneInfo(int nIndex, UINT& nID, UINT& nStyle,
                    int& cxWidth) const;
   void SetPaneInfo(int nIndex, UINT nID, UINT nStyle, int cxWidth);

// Implementation
public:
   virtual ~CStatusBar();
   inline UINT _GetPaneStyle(int nIndex) const;
   void _SetPaneStyle(int nIndex, UINT nStyle);

#ifdef _DEBUG
   virtual void AssertValid() const;
   virtual void Dump(CDumpContext& dc) const;
#endif

protected:
   HFONT m_hFont;
   int m_cxRightBorder;      // right borders (panes get clipped)

   inline AFX_STATUSPANE* _GetPanePtr(int nIndex) const;
   static void PASCAL DrawStatusText(HDC hDC, CRect const& rect,
                                     LPCSTR lpszText, UINT nStyle);
   virtual void DoPaint(CDC* pDC);
   virtual void OnUpdateCmdUI(CFrameWnd* pTarget,
                              BOOL bDisableIfNoHndler);
   //{{AFX_MSG(CStatusBar)
   afx_msg void OnSize(UINT nType, int cx, int cy);
   afx_msg LRESULT OnSetFont(WPARAM wParam, LPARAM lParam);
   afx_msg LRESULT OnGetFont(WPARAM wParam, LPARAM lParam);
   afx_msg LRESULT OnSetText(WPARAM wParam, LPARAM lParam);
   afx_msg LRESULT OnGetText(WPARAM wParam, LPARAM lParam);
   afx_msg LRESULT OnGetTextLength(WPARAM wParam, LPARAM lParam);
   //}}AFX_MSG
   DECLARE_MESSAGE_MAP()
};
```

The class CStatusBar declares a default constructor and also declares the
member function Create, which enables you to specify the parent window,
the status bar style, and the ID. The style parameter dwStyle and the ID

III

Advanced Programming

parameter nID have default arguments. The default argument for the parameter dwStyle is the expression

```
WS_CHILD ¦ WS_VISIBLE ¦ CBRS_BOTTOM
```

This default value causes the status bar to appear at the bottom of the frame window. The default argument for the parameter nID is AFX_IDW_STATUS_BAR. To create a status bar, you employ the constructor, the member function Create, and the member function SetIndicators. The SetIndicators function assigns the IDs to the indicators that appear in the status bar. The CStatusBar regards these indicators as arrays with 0-based indices.

The class CStatusBar has other member functions that can help you manage the indicators of the status bar:

- The member function CommandToIndex yields the index of the first indicator that matches the argument for the parameter nIDFind.

- The member function GetItemID returns the ID of the indicator selected by its positional index nIndex.

- The member function SetPaneInfo enables you to assign a new ID, style, and width to a status bar pane. The parameter nIndex specifies the manipulated pane. The parameter nID specifies the command ID of the pane. The parameter nStyle indicates the new style of the pane. The parameter cxWidth sets the width of the pane.

- The member function GetPaneInfo obtains the ID, style, and width of a pane in the status bar.

- The member function SetPaneText assigns a string to appear in a status bar pane. The parameter nIndex specifies the index of the targeted pane. The parameter lpszNextText is the pointer to the string supplying the text to the targeted pane.

Status Bar Programming Guidelines

The status bar contains panes that are message lines and status indicators. The left panes are message lines, whereas the rest are status indicators. The AppWizard creates a status bar with a single message line and three status indicators. These indicators tell you when the Num Lock, Caps Lock, and Scroll Lock keys are on or off. The message line typically displays one line of help, which comments on the operation of the currently selected menu item.

The following components are involved in programming the status bar:

■ Assigning the IDs that define both the panes of the status bar and the custom status bar

■ Creating a custom status bar

■ Accessing the message lines

■ Updating the status indicators

The status bar requires that you list its IDs in the static UINT-typed array indicators. The MAINFRM.CPP contains the declaration for the array indicators. If the IDs used to initialize this array are new, you must define them in a string table resource using App Studio. As for the ID of the status bar, AppWizard uses the ID AFX_IDW_STATUS_BAR. You have to define your own ID for the custom status bar. Use this ID when you create the status bar.

After you define the ID of the status bar and its panes, your program can proceed and create the status bar—a process that involves the member functions Create and LoadIndicators. The arguments of the function Create let you specify where the status bar appears (bottom, left, or right). The invocation of the function LoadIndicators specifies the IDs of the panes.

Now let's focus on accessing the panes of the status bar. To access the message lines, you first have to obtain a pointer to the status bar. Because the status bar is a sibling to the client window, you have to obtain a pointer to the application using the function AfxGetApp. This pointer gives you access to the application's data member m_pMainWnd. In turn, the pointer m_pMainWnd gives you access to the address of the status bar by using the function GetDescendantWindow. The argument for the latter function is the ID of your custom status bar. Here is sample code that clarifies this method of accessing the status bar:

```
CStatusBar* pSB =
  (CStatusBar*)AfxGetApp()->m_pMainWnd >GetDescendantWindow(ID_SB);
```

After you obtain the pointer to the status bar, you can write to any message line by using the member function SetPaneText. The arguments for this function specify the index of the message line and the new message line text. Here is a sample statement:

```
int nIndex = 1;
char szStr[81] = "Hello There!";
pSB->SetPane(nIndex, szStr);
```

Updating the indicators involves using an OnUpdateXXXX member function that responds to the ON_UPDATE_COMMAND_UI type of message with a specific indicator ID. As with toolbar buttons, the OnUpdateXXXX function sends the C++ message Enable to the function's parameter pCmdUI. The argument for this function is the expression

```
GetKeyState(VK_key) < 0
```

The identifier VK_key represents the virtual key you want to test.

A Sample Status Bar Program

Let's modify the toolbar program I presented earlier in this chapter to use the status bar. The new version displays the current mouse location in a message line and the date and timer information in another message line. The new program supports the date, timer, and mouse location features using the same kind of menu used in the program TOOLBAR1.EXE. To simplify the example, the new program does not have the toolbar used in TOOLBAR1.EXE. Instead, this new program uses the default toolbar created by AppWizard.

The new program demonstrates using the indicators of the status bar by displaying the strings Shift, Ctrl, and Alt when you press the Shift, Ctrl, and Alt keys, respectively.

The creation of the status bar program STATBAR1.EXE requires the following stages:

1. Use the AppWizard utility to create the source code files for an SDI-compliant program that has initial toolbars (but no print-related feature). The project name is STATBAR1, and the files reside in the directories \MSVC\USEVC\STATBAR1 and \MSVC\USEVC\STATBAR1\RES.

2. Use the App Studio application to edit the menu resource generated by the AppWizard. Make the following changes:

    ■ Change the File pop-up menu resource into the nonpop-up Exit menu. This change automatically deletes the original menu commands from the File menu. Assign the ID ID_APP_EXIT to the Exit menu and type the one line of help text that appears in the status bar when the Exit menu is chosen.

- Change the caption of the Edit menu to *Time*.

- Remove the original commands from the Edit menu.

- Insert the menu commands Date/Time, Start Timer, and Stop Timer. Use the IDs `ID_DATE_TIME`, `ID_START_TIMER`, and `ID_STOP_TIMER`, respectively, for these commands.

- Save the menu resource and return to the main window of App Studio.

3. Use the App Studio to add the following string resources:

- The string `Shift` with the ID `ID_KEY_SHIFT`.

- The string `Ctrl` with the ID `ID_KEY_CTRL`.

- The string `Alt` with the ID `ID_KEY_ALT`.

When you are done adding these string resources, save them.

4. Use the App Studio to add the ID for the custom status bar. Choose the Symbols menu command from the Edit menu (or press Ctrl+I); the Symbol Browser dialog box appears. Click the New... button and then enter the new symbol `ID_THE_STATUS_BAR`. Close the dialog boxes and save the resources.

Listing 11.8 shows the source code for the RESOURCE.H header file. This header file contains the new IDs for the new menu commands, the indicators, and the custom status bar.

Listing 11.8 Source Code for the RESOURCE.H Header File

```
//{{NO_DEPENDENCIES}}
// App Studio generated include file.
// Used by STATBAR1.RC
//
#define IDR_MAINFRAME                  2
#define IDD_ABOUTBOX                   100
#define ID_THE_STATUS_BAR              101
#define ID_DATE_TIME                   32771
#define ID_START_TIMER                 32772
#define ID_STOP_TIMER                  32773
#define ID_KEY_SHIFT                   61204
#define ID_KEY_CTRL                    61205
#define ID_KEY_ALT                     61206
```

(continues)

III

Advanced Programming

Listing 11.8 Continued

```
// Next default values for new objects
//
#ifdef APSTUDIO_INVOKED
#ifndef APSTUDIO_READONLY_SYMBOLS

#define _APS_NEXT_RESOURCE_VALUE        102
#define _APS_NEXT_COMMAND_VALUE         32774
#define _APS_NEXT_CONTROL_VALUE         1000
#define _APS_NEXT_SYMED_VALUE           102
#endif
#endif
```

5. In the MAINFRM.H header file, manually insert the declarations of
the member functions that update the new indicators to the class
CMainFrame. Listing 11.9 shows the source code for the MAINFRM.H
header file after the declarations have been added for the member
functions OnUpdateKeyAlt, OnUpdateKeyCtrl, and OnUpdateKeyAlt.

Listing 11.9 Source Code for the MAINFRM.H Header File

```
// mainfrm.h : interface of the CMainFrame class
//
/////////////////////////////////////////////////////////////

class CMainFrame : public CFrameWnd
{
protected: // create from serialization only
    CMainFrame();
    DECLARE_DYNCREATE(CMainFrame)

// Attributes
public:

// Operations
public:

// Implementation
public:
    virtual ~CMainFrame();
#ifdef _DEBUG
    virtual void AssertValid() const;
    virtual void Dump(CDumpContext& dc) const;
#endif

protected:  // control bar embedded members
    CStatusBar  m_wndStatusBar;
    CToolBar    m_wndToolBar;
```

```
// Generated message map functions
protected:
    //{{AFX_MSG(CMainFrame)
    afx_msg int OnCreate(LPCREATESTRUCT lpCreateStruct);
    afx_msg void OnViewStatusBar();
    afx_msg void OnUpdateViewStatusBar(CCmdUI* pCmdUI);
    // next three members were manually added
    afx_msg void OnUpdateKeyShift(CCmdUI* pCmdUI);
    afx_msg void OnUpdateKeyCtrl(CCmdUI* pCmdUI);
    afx_msg void OnUpdateKeyAlt(CCmdUI* pCmdUI);
    //}}AFX_MSG
    DECLARE_MESSAGE_MAP()
};

/////////////////////////////////////////////////////////////
```

6. Edit the file MAINFRM.CPP to modify the declaration of the static array indicators. The new declaration should be as follows:

```
static UINT BASED_CODE indicators[] =
{
    ID_SEPARATOR,          // mouse coordinates message
    ID_SEPARATOR,          // date/time and timer messages
    ID_KEY_SHIFT,
    ID_KEY_CTRL,
    ID_KEY_ALT,
};
```

7. Modify the code of the member function CMainFrame::OnCreate (also in the file MAINFRM.CPP) by changing the following if statement:

```
if (!m_wndStatusBar.Create(this) ¦¦
    !m_wndStatusBar.SetIndicators(indicators,
       sizeof(indicators)/sizeof(UINT)))
```

The new code is as follows:

```
if (!m_wndStatusBar.Create(this,
    WS_CHILD ¦ WS_VISIBLE ¦ CBRS_BOTTOM,
    ID_THE_STATUS_BAR) ¦¦
    !m_wndStatusBar.SetIndicators(indicators,
       sizeof(indicators)/sizeof(UINT)))
```

The new code specifies the ID of the custom status bar.

III

Advanced Programming

8. Manually insert the following message map macros to handle messages for the `OnUpdateKeyXXXX` member functions:

```
ON_UPDATE_COMMAND_UI(ID_KEY_SHIFT, OnUpdateKeyShift)
ON_UPDATE_COMMAND_UI(ID_KEY_CTRL, OnUpdateKeyCtrl)
ON_UPDATE_COMMAND_UI(ID_KEY_ALT, OnUpdateKeyAlt)
```

These message macros connect the `ID_KEY_XXXX` Windows command messages with their respective `OnUpdateKeyXXXX` member functions. This connection enables the status bar to properly display the indicators for the Shift, Ctrl, and Alt keys.

9. Manually insert the following definitions of the `OnUpdateKeyXXXX` member functions:

```
void CMainFrame::OnUpdateKeyShift(CCmdUI* pCmdUI)
{
  pCmdUI->Enable(::GetKeyState(VK_SHIFT) & 0x80);
}

void CMainFrame::OnUpdateKeyCtrl(CCmdUI* pCmdUI)
{
  pCmdUI->Enable(::GetKeyState(VK_CONTROL) & 0x80);
}

void CMainFrame::OnUpdateKeyAlt(CCmdUI* pCmdUI)
{
  pCmdUI->Enable(::GetKeyState(VK_MENU) & 0x80);
}
```

The preceding code shows that the identifiers `VK_SHIFT`, `VK_CONTROL`, and `VK_MENU` represent the Shift, Ctrl, and Alt keys, respectively. Each `OnUpdateKeyXXXX` function sends the C++ message `Enable` to the parameter `pCmdUI` with an argument involving the function `GetKeyState`.

10. Manually insert into the MAINFRM.CPP file the following statements to define the member function `CMainFrame::OnViewStatusBar`:

```
void CMainFrame::OnViewStatusBar()
{
  CWnd* pStatusBar = GetDescendantWindow(ID_THE_STATUS_BAR);

  if (pStatusBar) {
    pStatusBar->ShowWindow((pStatusBar->GetStyle() &
                            WS_VISIBLE) == 0);
    RecalcLayout();
  }
}
```

11. Manually insert into the MAINFRM.CPP file the following statements to define the member function CMainFrame::OnUpdateViewStatusBar:

```
void CMainFrame::OnUpdateViewStatusBar(CCmdUI* pCmdUI)
{
  CWnd* pStatusBar = GetDescendantWindow(ID_THE_STATUS_BAR);

  if (pStatusBar)
    pCmdUI->SetCheck((pStatusBar->GetStyle() & WS_VISIBLE) != 0);
}
```

Listing 11.10 shows the source code for the MAINFRM.CPP implementation file after the preceding modifications and manual code insertions have been completed.

Listing 11.10 Source Code for the MAINFRM.CPP Implementation File

```
// mainfrm.cpp : implementation of the CMainFrame class
//

#include "stdafx.h"
#include "statbar1.h"

#include "mainfrm.h"

#ifdef _DEBUG
#undef THIS_FILE
static char BASED_CODE THIS_FILE[] = __FILE__;
#endif

/////////////////////////////////////////////////////////////
// CMainFrame

IMPLEMENT_DYNCREATE(CMainFrame, CFrameWnd)

BEGIN_MESSAGE_MAP(CMainFrame, CFrameWnd)
    //{{AFX_MSG_MAP(CMainFrame)
    ON_WM_CREATE()
    ON_COMMAND(ID_VIEW_STATUS_BAR, OnViewStatusBar)
    ON_UPDATE_COMMAND_UI(ID_VIEW_STATUS_BAR, OnUpdateViewStatusBar)
    // manually added macros
    ON_UPDATE_COMMAND_UI(ID_KEY_SHIFT, OnUpdateKeyShift)
    ON_UPDATE_COMMAND_UI(ID_KEY_CTRL, OnUpdateKeyCtrl)
    ON_UPDATE_COMMAND_UI(ID_KEY_ALT, OnUpdateKeyAlt)
    //}}AFX_MSG_MAP
END_MESSAGE_MAP()

/////////////////////////////////////////////////////////////
// arrays of IDs used to initialize control bars
```

(continues)

III

Advanced Programming

Listing 11.10 Continued

```cpp
// toolbar buttons - IDs are command buttons
static UINT BASED_CODE buttons[] =
{
    // same order as in the bitmap 'toolbar.bmp'
    ID_FILE_NEW,
    ID_FILE_OPEN,
    ID_FILE_SAVE,
        ID_SEPARATOR,
    ID_EDIT_CUT,
    ID_EDIT_COPY,
    ID_EDIT_PASTE,
        ID_SEPARATOR,
    ID_FILE_PRINT,
    ID_APP_ABOUT,
};

static UINT BASED_CODE indicators[] =
{
    ID_SEPARATOR,           // mouse coordinates message
    ID_SEPARATOR,           // date/time and timer messages
    ID_KEY_SHIFT,
    ID_KEY_CTRL,
    ID_KEY_ALT,
};

/////////////////////////////////////////////////////////////
// CMainFrame construction/destruction

CMainFrame::CMainFrame()
{
    // TODO: add member initialization code here
}

CMainFrame::~CMainFrame()
{
}

int CMainFrame::OnCreate(LPCREATESTRUCT lpCreateStruct)
{
    if (CFrameWnd::OnCreate(lpCreateStruct) == -1)
        return -1;

    if (!m_wndToolBar.Create(this) ||
        !m_wndToolBar.LoadBitmap(IDR_MAINFRAME) ||
        !m_wndToolBar.SetButtons(buttons,
          sizeof(buttons)/sizeof(UINT)))
    {
        TRACE("Failed to create toolbar\n");
        return -1;      // fail to create
    }
/*
    if (!m_wndStatusBar.Create(this) ||
        !m_wndStatusBar.SetIndicators(indicators,
          sizeof(indicators)/sizeof(UINT)))
```

```
*/
// edited code is
    if (!m_wndStatusBar.Create(this,
        WS_CHILD ¦ WS_VISIBLE ¦ CBRS_BOTTOM,
        ID_THE_STATUS_BAR) ¦¦
        !m_wndStatusBar.SetIndicators(indicators,
          sizeof(indicators)/sizeof(UINT)))

    {
        TRACE("Failed to create status bar\n");
        return -1;      // fail to create
    }

    return 0;
}


/////////////////////////////////////////////////////////////
// CMainFrame diagnostics

#ifdef _DEBUG
void CMainFrame::AssertValid() const
{
    CFrameWnd::AssertValid();
}

void CMainFrame::Dump(CDumpContext& dc) const
{
    CFrameWnd::Dump(dc);
}

#endif //_DEBUG

/////////////////////////////////////////////////////////////
// CMainFrame message handlers

void CMainFrame::OnViewStatusBar()
{
  CWnd* pStatusBar = GetDescendantWindow(ID_THE_STATUS_BAR);

  if (pStatusBar) {
    pStatusBar->ShowWindow((pStatusBar->GetStyle() &
                           WS_VISIBLE) == 0);
    RecalcLayout();
  }
}

void CMainFrame::OnUpdateViewStatusBar(CCmdUI* pCmdUI)
{
  CWnd* pStatusBar = GetDescendantWindow(ID_THE_STATUS_BAR);

  if (pStatusBar)
    pCmdUI->SetCheck((pStatusBar->GetStyle() & WS_VISIBLE) != 0);
}
```

(continues)

III

Advanced Programming

Listing 11.10 Continued

```
void CMainFrame::OnUpdateKeyShift(CCmdUI* pCmdUI)
{
  pCmdUI->Enable(::GetKeyState(VK_SHIFT) & 0x80);
}

void CMainFrame::OnUpdateKeyCtrl(CCmdUI* pCmdUI)
{
  pCmdUI->Enable(::GetKeyState(VK_CONTROL) & 0x80);
}

void CMainFrame::OnUpdateKeyAlt(CCmdUI* pCmdUI)
{
  pCmdUI->Enable(::GetKeyState(VK_MENU) & 0x80);
}
```

12. Manually insert into the STATBDOC.H file the data members bTimeOn, lInitTickCount, and tm in the class CStatbar1Doc. These data members are identical to the ones used in the TOOLBAR1.EXE program.

13. Manually insert into the STATBDOC.CPP file the statement that assigns FALSE to the member bTimerOn in the constructor of class CStatbar1Doc.

14. Invoke the ClassWizard utility and add a member function to handle the Windows message WM_MOUSEMOVE. Then perform the following tasks to add message-handling member functions:

- Select the CStatbar1View object and add the handler for the message WM_MOUSEMOVE. ClassWizard adds the member function OnMouseMove to the list of member functions.

- Select the ID_DATE_TIME object and add the handler for the COMMAND message. ClassWizard adds the member function OnDateTime to the list of functions.

- Select the ID_START_TIMER object and add handlers for the COMMAND and UPDATE_COMMAND_UI messages. ClassWizard adds the member functions OnStartTimer and OnUpdateStartTimer to the list of functions.

- Select the ID_STOP_TIMER object and add handlers for the COMMAND and UPDATE_COMMAND_UI messages. ClassWizard adds the member functions OnStopTimer and OnUpdateStopTimer to the list of functions.

Listing 11.11 shows the source code for the STATBVW.H header file, which contains the declarations of the member functions you just added.

Listing 11.11 Source Code for the STATBVW.H Header File

```
// statbvw.h : interface of the CStatbar1View class
//
/////////////////////////////////////////////////////////////////

class CStatbar1View : public CView
{
protected: // create from serialization only
    CStatbar1View();
    DECLARE_DYNCREATE(CStatbar1View)

// Attributes
public:
    CStatbar1Doc* GetDocument();

// Operations
public:

// Implementation
public:
    virtual ~CStatbar1View();
    virtual void OnDraw(CDC* pDC);   // overridden to draw this view
#ifdef _DEBUG
    virtual void AssertValid() const;
    virtual void Dump(CDumpContext& dc) const;
#endif

protected:

// Generated message map functions
protected:
    //{{AFX_MSG(CStatbar1View)
    afx_msg void OnStartTimer();
    afx_msg void OnUpdateStartTimer(CCmdUI* pCmdUI);
    afx_msg void OnUpdateStopTimer(CCmdUI* pCmdUI);
    afx_msg void OnStopTimer();
    afx_msg void OnMouseMove(UINT nFlags, CPoint point);
    afx_msg void OnDateTime();
    //}}AFX_MSG
    DECLARE_MESSAGE_MAP()
};

#ifndef _DEBUG  // debug version in statbvw.cpp
inline CStatbar1Doc* CStatbar1View::GetDocument()
   { return (CStatbar1Doc*)m_pDocument; }
#endif

/////////////////////////////////////////////////////////////////
```

III

Advanced Programming

15. Manually insert the following statements into the STATBVW.CPP file:

- The definitions the member functions `OnDateTime`, `OnMouseMove`, `OnStartTimer`, `OnStopTimer`, `OnUpdateStartTimer`, and `OnUpdateStopTimer`.

- The inclusion of header files STDIO.H and STRING.H.

- The declaration of the constant `MaxStringLen`.

Listing 11.12 shows the source code for the STATBVW.CPP implementation file with the preceding statements inserted.

Listing 11.12 Source Code for the STATBVW.CPP Implementation File

```cpp
// statbvw.cpp : implementation of the CStatbar1View class
//

#include "stdafx.h"
#include "statbar1.h"

#include "statbdoc.h"
#include "statbvw.h"

// include additional header files needed to customize the program
#include <stdio.h>
#include <string.h>

#ifdef _DEBUG
#undef THIS_FILE
static char BASED_CODE THIS_FILE[] = __FILE__;
#endif

// define a new constant
const MaxStringLen = 40;


/////////////////////////////////////////////////////////////////
// CStatbar1View

IMPLEMENT_DYNCREATE(CStatbar1View, CView)

BEGIN_MESSAGE_MAP(CStatbar1View, CView)
    //{{AFX_MSG_MAP(CStatbar1View)
    ON_COMMAND(ID_START_TIMER, OnStartTimer)
    ON_UPDATE_COMMAND_UI(ID_START_TIMER, OnUpdateStartTimer)
    ON_UPDATE_COMMAND_UI(ID_STOP_TIMER, OnUpdateStopTimer)
    ON_COMMAND(ID_STOP_TIMER, OnStopTimer)
    ON_WM_MOUSEMOVE()
    ON_COMMAND(ID_DATE_TIME, OnDateTime)
    //}}AFX_MSG_MAP
END_MESSAGE_MAP()
```

```
/////////////////////////////////////////////////////////////
// CStatbar1View construction/destruction

CStatbar1View::CStatbar1View()
{
    // TODO: add construction code here
}

CStatbar1View::~CStatbar1View()
{
}

/////////////////////////////////////////////////////////////
// CStatbar1View drawing

void CStatbar1View::OnDraw(CDC* pDC)
{
    CStatbar1Doc* pDoc = GetDocument();
    ASSERT_VALID(pDoc);

    // TODO: add draw code for native data here
}

/////////////////////////////////////////////////////////////
// CStatbar1View diagnostics

#ifdef _DEBUG
void CStatbar1View::AssertValid() const
{
    CView::AssertValid();
}

void CStatbar1View::Dump(CDumpContext& dc) const
{
    CView::Dump(dc);
}

CStatbar1Doc* CStatbar1View::GetDocument() // non-debug version
                                           // is inline
{
    ASSERT(m_pDocument->IsKindOf(RUNTIME_CLASS(CStatbar1Doc)));
    return (CStatbar1Doc*)m_pDocument;
}
#endif //_DEBUG

/////////////////////////////////////////////////////////////
// CStatbar1View message handlers

void CStatbar1View::OnStartTimer()
{
  CStatbar1Doc* pDoc = GetDocument();
  CStatusBar* pStatusBar =
    (CStatusBar*)AfxGetApp()->m_pMainWnd->GetDescendantWindow(
                                        ID_THE_STATUS_BAR);
```

(continues)

Listing 11.12 Continued

```
    pDoc->bTimerOn = TRUE;
    pDoc->lInitTickCount = GetTickCount();
    pStatusBar->SetPaneText(0, "Timer is on!");

}

void CStatbar1View::OnUpdateStartTimer(CCmdUI* pCmdUI)
{
  CStatbar1Doc* pDoc = GetDocument();
  pCmdUI->Enable(!pDoc->bTimerOn);
}

void CStatbar1View::OnUpdateStopTimer(CCmdUI* pCmdUI)
{
  CStatbar1Doc* pDoc = GetDocument();
  pCmdUI->Enable(pDoc->bTimerOn);
}

void CStatbar1View::OnStopTimer()
{
  CStatbar1Doc* pDoc = GetDocument();
  char szStr[MaxStringLen+1];
  CStatusBar* pStatusBar =
    (CStatusBar*)AfxGetApp()->m_pMainWnd->GetDescendantWindow(
                                      ID_THE_STATUS_BAR);

  pDoc->bTimerOn = FALSE;
  sprintf(szStr, "%3.3lf seconds elapsed",
          (GetTickCount() - pDoc->lInitTickCount) / 1000.0);
  pStatusBar->SetPaneText(0, szStr);
}

void CStatbar1View::OnMouseMove(UINT nFlags, CPoint point)
{
  char szStr[MaxStringLen+1];
  CStatusBar* pStatusBar =
    (CStatusBar*)AfxGetApp()->m_pMainWnd->GetDescendantWindow(
                                      ID_THE_STATUS_BAR);

  sprintf(szStr, "[%03d, %03d]", point.x, point.y);
  pStatusBar->SetPaneText(1, szStr);

}

void CStatbar1View::OnDateTime()
{
  CStatbar1Doc* pDoc = GetDocument();
  char szStr[MaxStringLen+1];
  pDoc->tm = CTime::GetCurrentTime();
  CStatusBar* pStatusBar =
    (CStatusBar*)AfxGetApp()->m_pMainWnd->GetDescendantWindow(
                                      ID_THE_STATUS_BAR);
```

```
    sprintf(szStr, "Date is %02d/%02d/%4d, Time is %02d:%02d:%02d",
                    pDoc->tm.GetMonth(), pDoc->tm.GetDay(),
                    pDoc->tm.GetYear(), pDoc->tm.GetHour(),
                    pDoc->tm.GetMinute(), pDoc->tm.GetSecond());
    pStatusBar->SetPaneText(0, szStr);
}
```

Let's look at the definitions of the relevant member functions in the view class:

■ The member function OnDateTime responds to the Windows command message ID_DATE_TIME by displaying the current system date and time. The function performs the following tasks:

- Stores the address of the document in the local pointer pDoc.

- Obtains the current system date and time by assigning the result of the static member function CTime::GetCurrentTime to the document's member tm.

- Stores the address of the status bar in the local pointer pStatusBar.

- Creates the string image for the date and time. This task uses the function sprintf and sends the C++ messages GetMonth, GetYear, GetDay, GetHour, GetMinute, and GetSecond to the document's data member tm.

- Displays the string image of the date and time in the first message line (which has the pane index 0). This task involves sending the C++ message SetPaneText to the status bar. The arguments for this message are 0 and szStr.

■ The member function OnStartTimer responds to the Windows command message ID_START_TIMER by starting the simple timer. The function carries out the following tasks:

- Assigns the address of the document to the local pointer pDoc.

III

Advanced Programming

- Assigns the address of the status bar to the local pointer `pStatusBar`.

- Assigns TRUE to the document's data member `bTimerOn`.

- Assigns the result of the API function `GetTickCount` to the document's data member `lInitTickCount`.

- Displays a message in the status line telling you that the timer is now on. The message appears in the first message line (which has the pane index 0). This task involves sending the C++ message `SetPaneText` to the status bar. The arguments for this message are 0 and `"Timer is on!"`.

■ The member function `OnStopTimer` responds to the Windows command message `ID_STOP_TIMER` by stopping the simple timer. The function carries out the following tasks:

- Assigns the address of the document to the local pointer `pDoc`.

- Assigns the address of the status bar to the local pointer `pStatusBar`.

- Assigns FALSE to the document's data member `bTimerOn`.

- Calculates the number of elapsed seconds and creates a string image for that result.

- Displays the string image of the elapsed time in the first message line (which has the pane index 0). This task involves sending the C++ message `SetPaneText` to the status bar. The arguments for this message are 0 and `szStr`.

■ The member function `OnUpdateStartTimer` responds to the `UPDATE_COMMAND_UI` command. The function performs the following tasks:

- Assigns the address of the document to the local pointer `pDoc`.

- Sends the C++ message `Enable` to the parameter
  `pCmdUI`. The argument for this message is the expression
  `!pDoc->bTimerOn`. When the member `bTimerOn` is FALSE,
  this message enables the Start Timer menu command.
  Otherwise, the function disables the Start Timer
  command.

■ The member function `OnUpdateStopTimer` responds to the
`UPDATE_COMMAND_UI` command. The function performs the
following tasks:

- Assigns the address of the document to the local pointer
  `pDoc`.

- Sends the C++ message `Enable` to the parameter `pCmdUI`. The
  argument for this message is the expression `pDoc->bTimerOn`.
  When the member `bTimerOn` is TRUE, this message enables
  the Stop Timer menu command. Otherwise, the function
  disables the Stop Timer command.

■ The member function `OnMouseMove` responds to the Windows
message `WM_MOUSEMOVE` by displaying the current mouse location
in the upper-left corner of the view. The function performs the
following tasks:

- Creates the device context object `dc`.

- Assigns the address of the status bar to the local pointer
  `pStatusBar`.

- Creates a string image for the current mouse coordinates.
  The members `x` and `y` of the parameter `point` provide the
  current mouse coordinates. This task involves the function
  `sprintf` and stores the string image in the local variable
  `szStr`.

- Displays the contents of the string `szStr` in the second
  message line (which has the pane index 1). This task involves sending the C++ message `SetPaneText` to the status
  bar. The arguments for this message are 1 and `szStr`.

16. Compile and run the STATBAR1.EXE program. Notice that initially the program has disabled the Stop Timer menu command. Invoke the Date/Time menu command to display the current date and time in the leftmost message line in the status bar (see Figure 11.3). Move the mouse around and notice that the second message line displays the current mouse coordinates. Invoke the Start Timer menu command to start the simple timer. The program displays a message, in the first message line, telling you that the timer is on. Invoke the Stop Timer menu command. The program responds by displaying the elapsed number of seconds in the leftmost message line. When you are finished experimenting with the program, click the Exit menu.

Figure 11.3

The program STATBAR1.EXE showing the current date and time in the status bar.

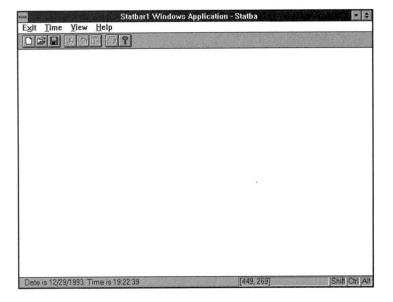

Summary

This chapter presented the MFC classes that support the toolbar and status bar. Here's what you learned:

- The CToolBar class supports the toolbar window and manages mapping the toolbar bitmap onto the visible toolbar buttons.

- Guidelines for programming a toolbar in an application. The basic ingredients for using the toolbar are defining the resources and the member functions that handle the toolbar button commands.

- The CStatusBar class supports the status bar window and manages the panes that provide the message lines and status indicators.

- Guidelines for programming a status bar in an application. The basic components for programming a status bar are the IDs for the status bar, the IDs for the panes, accessing message lines, and updating the status indicators.

In addition, this chapter presented a sample program that used a toolbar to display the current system date and time and to start and stop a simple timer. The program showed how to disable and enable toolbar buttons, as well as their associated menu commands.

This chapter also offered a sample program that used a status bar to display the current system date and time, display the elapsed seconds of a simple timer, and to show the indicators for the Shift, Ctrl, and Alt keys.

III

Advanced Programming

Chapter 12

Using MDI Windows

Many Windows applications, such as the Windows Program Manager, Windows File Manager, and most word processors, use a standard Windows interface. This interface is the *Multiple Document Interface* (MDI). The MDI standard also is part of the *Common User Access* (CUA) standard set by IBM. The MDI-compliant applications support the opening of multiple child windows of different documents within a single application for jobs such as creating a spreadsheet, editing a document, drawing graphics, and managing a database. This chapter discusses the following topics about managing MDI windows and objects:

- Understanding the basic characteristics and makeup of MDI-compliant applications.

- Examining the basics of constructing MDI-compliant applications.

- Declaring the class CMDIFrameWnd.

- Constructing MDI frame windows.

- Declaring the class CMDIChildWnd.

- Constructing MDI child windows.

- Handling messages in MDI-compliant applications.

Understanding MDI-Compliant Applications: Features and Components

An MDI-compliant application consists of the following objects:

- The visible *MDI frame window*, which holds the remaining MDI objects. The MDI frame window is an instance of class CMDIFrameWnd or its descendants. Each MDI application has a single MDI frame window.

- The invisible *MDI client window*, which supports the underlying management of the MDI child windows that are created and removed dynamically. Each MDI application has a single MDI client window.

- The visible *MDI child window*. An MDI application dynamically creates and removes multiple instances of MDI child windows. An MDI child window is an instance of CMDIChildWnd or its descendants. MDI-compliant applications support locating, resizing, moving, minimizing, and maximizing MDI child windows inside the area defined by the MDI frame window. As with non-MDI windows, only one MDI child window is active at any given time.

The maximized MDI child window occupies the area defined by the MDI client. The minimized MDI child window appears as an icon, located at the bottom area of the MDI frame window.

> **Note**
>
> The MDI frame window contains a menu that manipulates the MDI child windows and their contents. The MDI child windows cannot have menus but may contain controls. The MFC library supports the ability to change the menu attached to the MDI frame window when you select a different MDI child window. This feature supports MDI child windows that have different uses and data.

Before I discuss the details of creating the diverse components of an MDI application, let me quickly state the strategy involved. The CMDIFrameWnd class supports the following tasks:

- Creating and handling the MDI client windows.

- Creating and handling the MDI child windows.

- Managing menus.

Declaring the *CMDIFrameWnd* Class

The class CMDIFrameWnd, which is a descendant of CFrameWnd, supports the MDI
frame window of an MDI application. Following is the declaration of class
CMDIFrameWnd:

```
class CMDIFrameWnd : public CFrameWnd
{
    DECLARE_DYNCREATE(CMDIFrameWnd)
public:
// Constructors
    CMDIFrameWnd();
// Operations
    void MDIActivate(CWnd* pWndActivate);
    CMDIChildWnd* MDIGetActive(BOOL* pbMaximized = NULL) const;
    void MDIIconArrange();
    void MDIMaximize(CWnd* pWnd);
    void MDINext();
    void MDIRestore(CWnd* pWnd);
    CMenu* MDISetMenu(CMenu* pFrameMenu, CMenu* pWindowMenu);
    void MDITile();
    void MDICascade();
#if (WINVER >= 0x030a)
    void MDITile(int nType);
    void MDICascade(int nType);
#endif
// Overridables
    // MFC V1 backward-compatible CreateClient hook (called by
    // OnCreateClient)
    virtual BOOL CreateClient(LPCREATESTRUCT lpCreateStruct,
                    CMenu* pWindowMenu);
    // customize if using a 'Window' menu with non-standard IDs
    virtual HMENU GetWindowMenuPopup(HMENU hMenuBar);
// Implementation
public:
    HWND m_hWndMDIClient;        // MDI Client window handle
    HMENU m_hMenuDefault;        // menu when no active child
                                 // (owned)
#ifdef _DEBUG
    virtual void AssertValid() const;
    virtual void Dump(CDumpContext& dc) const;
#endif
    virtual BOOL PreCreateWindow(CREATESTRUCT& cs);
    virtual BOOL LoadFrame(UINT nIDResource,
                DWORD dwDefaultStyle = WS_OVERLAPPEDWINDOW |
                                      FWS_ADDTOTITLE,
                CWnd* pParentWnd = NULL,
                CCreateContext* pContext = NULL);
    virtual BOOL OnCreateClient(LPCREATESTRUCT lpcs,
                        CCreateContext* pContext);
    virtual BOOL PreTranslateMessage(MSG* pMsg);
    virtual void OnUpdateFrameTitle(BOOL bAddToTitle);
    virtual BOOL OnCmdMsg(UINT nID, int nCode, void* pExtra,
        AFX_CMDHANDLERINFO* pHandlerInfo);
```

```
protected:
    virtual LRESULT DefWindowProc(UINT nMsg, WPARAM wParam,
                                  LPARAM lParam);
    virtual BOOL OnCommand(WPARAM wParam, LPARAM lParam);
    //{{AFX_MSG(CMDIFrameWnd)
    afx_msg void OnDestroy();
    afx_msg void OnSize(UINT nType, int cx, int cy);
    afx_msg void OnActivate(UINT nState, CWnd* pWndOther,
                            BOOL bMinimized);
    afx_msg void OnUpdateMDIWindowCmd(CCmdUI* pCmdUI);
    afx_msg BOOL OnMDIWindowCmd(UINT nID);
    afx_msg void OnWindowNew();
    afx_msg LRESULT OnCommandHelp(WPARAM wParam, LPARAM lParam);
    //}}AFX_MSG
    DECLARE_MESSAGE_MAP()
};
```

The class `CMDIFrameWnd` and its descendants use both the constructor and the inherited `Create` function to generate the MDI frame windows. A number of the `Create` function's parameters specify the `Windows` class (a `WNDCLASS` structure), the MDI window title, the window style, the window location and position (specified using the `CRect` parameter), the pointer to the parent window, and the name of the associated menu resource. When the MDI frame window is the top-level window, the argument for the parent pointer is NULL.

The member function `CreateClient` creates the invisible MDI client window. The function has an `LPCREATESTRUCT` parameter and a `CMenu*` menu pointer parameter.

The member functions of `CMDIFrameWnd` support operations such as the following:

- Activating an MDI child window with the `MDIActive` member function.

- Cascading and tiling MDI child windows using the member functions `MDICascade` and `MDITile`, respectively.

- Obtaining the pointer to the currently active MDI child window using the member function `MDIGetActive`.

- Selecting the next MDI child window. This window is directly behind the currently active MDI child window.

- Maximizing and restoring an MDI child window using the member functions `MDIMaximize` and `MDIRestore`, respectively.

Creating MDI Frame Windows

Typically, an MFC application starts to generate the application's object by first creating the application instance followed by the main window. In the case of an MDI-compliant application, the application's main window is a descendant of class CMDIFrameWnd. The application's member function InitInstance creates this MDI window. The constructor of the MDI frame window class, along with the function Create, produces both the MDI frame and MDI client windows. The MDI frame window, however, need not be void of MDI child windows. It is possible to load one or more initial MDI child windows.

Declaring the *CMDIChildWnd* Class

The class CMDIChildWnd, which is a descendant CFrameWnd, supports the MDI child windows. Following is the declaration of class CMDIChildWnd:

```
class CMDIChildWnd : public CFrameWnd
{
    DECLARE_DYNCREATE(CMDIChildWnd)
// Constructors
public:
    CMDIChildWnd();
    BOOL Create(LPCSTR lpszClassName,
                LPCSTR lpszWindowName,
                DWORD dwStyle = WS_CHILD | WS_VISIBLE |
                                WS_OVERLAPPEDWINDOW,
                const RECT& rect = rectDefault,
                CMDIFrameWnd* pParentWnd = NULL,
                CCreateContext* pContext = NULL);
// Attributes
    CMDIFrameWnd* GetMDIFrame();
// Operations
    void MDIDestroy();
    void MDIActivate();
    void MDIMaximize();
    void MDIRestore();
// Implementation
protected:
    HMENU m_hMenuShared;        // menu when we are active
public:
#ifdef _DEBUG
    virtual void AssertValid() const;
    virtual void Dump(CDumpContext& dc) const;
#endif
    virtual BOOL PreCreateWindow(CREATESTRUCT& cs);
    virtual BOOL LoadFrame(UINT nIDResource, DWORD dwDefaultStyle,
                CWnd* pParentWnd,
                CCreateContext* pContext = NULL);
```

```
                    // 'pParentWnd' parameter is required for MDI Child
                    virtual BOOL DestroyWindow();
                    virtual BOOL PreTranslateMessage(MSG* pMsg);
                    virtual void ActivateFrame(int nCmdShow = -1);
              protected:
                    virtual CWnd* GetMessageBar();
                    virtual void OnUpdateFrameTitle(BOOL bAddToTitle);
                    virtual LRESULT DefWindowProc(UINT nMsg, WPARAM wParam,
                                             LPARAM lParam);
                    //{{AFX_MSG(CMDIChildWnd)
                    afx_msg void OnMDIActivate(BOOL bActivate, CWnd*, CWnd*);
                    afx_msg int OnCreate(LPCREATESTRUCT lpCreateStruct);
                    afx_msg void OnSize(UINT nType, int cx, int cy);
                    //}}AFX_MSG
                    DECLARE_MESSAGE_MAP()
              };
```

The class declares a constructor, a Create function, a set of member functions, and a data member. The member functions enable you to destroy, activate, maximize, restore, and obtain the pointer to the parent window.

Creating MDI Child Windows

Creating MDI child windows is akin to creating application windows in the programs that I presented earlier. The differences are as follows:

■ The MDI child window is an instance of CMDIChildWnd or its descendants.

■ The MDI child window lacks its own menu. The menu of the MDI frame window manages the currently active MDI child window or all of the MDI children.

■ An MDI child window can have controls.

Managing MDI Messages

The message loop directs the flow of command messages first to the currently active MDI child window. If this MDI window does not handle the incoming message, the message loop redirects that message to the parent MDI frame window. In addition, the currently active MDI child window handles the notification messages sent by its own controls. This response is akin to that of windows and dialog boxes.

Using the System File Viewer

Now look at a simple MDI-compliant application. I present the MDIWIN1.EXE program, which enables you to view the AUTOEXEC.BAT, CONFIG.SYS, WIN.INI, and SYSTEM.INI files. The program assumes that the .INI files are located in the directory \WINDOWS. If your files are not located in this directory in your system, edit the filenames assigned the global constant FILES in the program to reflect your actual Windows directory.

The program's menu system offers Exit, File, and MDI Children. The File menu contains a list of commands made up of the AUTOEXEC.BAT, CONFIG.SYS, WIN.INI, and SYSTEM.INI filenames. The MDI Children menu contains commands to cascade, tile, arrange icons, close all, and count MDI child windows. These menu commands are typical of MDI-compliant applications.

Compile and run the program. Open a file using one of the File menu commands. The program displays in a list box the file that you select. Use the list's vertical scroll bar (if visible) to inspect the file. You can open the four files, maximize, minimize, arrange the icons, and query the number of MDI child windows. If you close an individual MDI window, the program requests that you confirm closing that window. When you finish viewing the files, click the Exit menu. Figure 12.1 shows a sample session with the MDIWIN1.EXE program.

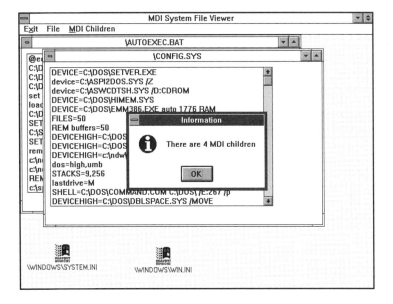

Figure 12.1

A sample session with the MDIWIN1.EXE program.

III

Advanced Programming

MDIWIN1.EXE illustrates creating and managing somewhat specialized MDI child windows. The program can open up to four special MDI child windows. Typical MDI-compliant programs do not have such limitations on the number of MDI child windows. In fact, the second program in this chapter illustrates this aspect.

Listing 12.1 shows the contents of the MDIWIN1.DEF definition file.

Listing 12.1 The MDIWIN1.DEF Definition File

```
NAME         MDIWin1
DESCRIPTION  'An MFC Windows Application'
EXETYPE      WINDOWS
CODE         PRELOAD MOVEABLE DISCARDABLE
DATA         PRELOAD MOVEABLE MULTIPLE
HEAPSIZE     1024
```

Listing 12.2 shows the source code for the MDIWIN1.H header file.

Listing 12.2 Source Code for the MDIWIN1.H Header File

```
#define CM_EXIT              (WM_USER + 100)
#define CM_COUNTCHILDREN     (WM_USER + 101)
#define CM_LOAD_AUTOEXEC     (WM_USER + 102)
#define CM_LOAD_CONFIG       (WM_USER + 103)
#define CM_LOAD_WIN          (WM_USER + 104)
#define CM_LOAD_SYSTEM       (WM_USER + 105)
#define CM_CASCADECHILDREN   (WM_USER + 106)
#define CM_TILECHILDREN      (WM_USER + 107)
#define CM_ARRANGEICONS      (WM_USER + 108)
#define CM_CLOSECHILDREN     (WM_USER + 109)
#define WM_CHILDDESTROY      (WM_USER + 110)
#define ID_TEXT_LST     100
```

Listing 12.3 contains the script for the MDIWIN1.RC resource file.

Listing 12.3 Script for the MDIWIN1.RC Resource File

```
#include <windows.h>
#include <afxres.h>
#include "mdiwin1.h"
FILEMENU MENU LOADONCALL MOVEABLE PURE DISCARDABLE
BEGIN
  MENUITEM "E&xit", CM_EXIT
  POPUP "&File"
  BEGIN
    MENUITEM  "&AUTOEXEC.BAT", CM_LOAD_AUTOEXEC
    MENUITEM  "&CONFIG.SYS", CM_LOAD_CONFIG
    MENUITEM  "&WIN.INI", CM_LOAD_WIN
    MENUITEM  "&SYSTEM.INI", CM_LOAD_SYSTEM
```

```
      END
      POPUP "&MDI Children"
      BEGIN
        MENUITEM  "&Cascade", CM_CASCADECHILDREN
        MENUITEM  "&Tile", CM_TILECHILDREN
        MENUITEM  "Arrange &Icons", CM_ARRANGEICONS
        MENUITEM  "C&lose All", CM_CLOSECHILDREN
        MENUITEM  "C&ount Children", CM_COUNTCHILDREN
      END
    END
```

Listing 12.4 shows the source code for the MDIWIN1.CPP program.

Listing 12.4 Source Code for the MDIWIN1.CPP Program File

```
/*
    Program which views the AUTOEXEC.BAT, CONFIG.SYS,
    WIN.INI, and SYSTEM.INI files in four MDI child windows

*/
#include <stdlib.h>
#include <stdio.h>
#include <fstream.h>
#include <string.h>
#include <afxwin.h>
#include "mdiwin1.h"
const MaxStringLen = 80;
const char* MenuName = "FILEMENU";
const Hctl = 250;
const Wctl = 400;
const MAX_FILES = 4;
char* FILES[MAX_FILES] = { "\\AUTOEXEC.BAT",
                           "\\CONFIG.SYS",
                           "\\WINDOWS\\WIN.INI",
                           "\\WINDOWS\\SYSTEM.INI" };
// function used by MDI classes
void makerect(int X, int Y, int W, int H, CRect& r)
{
  r.SetRect(X, Y, X + W, Y + H);
}
// Define an application class derived from CWinApp
class CMDIDemoApp : public CWinApp
{
 public:
  virtual BOOL InitInstance();
};
class CAppMDIChild : public CMDIChildWnd
{
 public:
  int nChildNum;
  // pointer to the list box control
```

(continues)

III

Advanced Programming

Listing 12.4 Continued

```
      CListBox* pTextLst;
      CAppMDIChild();
      ~CAppMDIChild();
      BOOL Create(LPSTR szFilename, int nChildNum);

   protected:
      // handle closing the MDI child window
      afx_msg void OnClose();
      // handle destroying an MDI child window
      afx_msg void OnDestroy();
      afx_msg int OnCreate(LPCREATESTRUCT lpCS);
      BOOL OpenFile(const char* szFilename);

      // declare message map macro
      DECLARE_MESSAGE_MAP()
   };
   class CMDIMainWnd : public CMDIFrameWnd
   {
    public:
      // flag to quickly close all MDI children windows
      BOOL bExpressClose;
      BOOL bLoadedFile[MAX_FILES];
      char szFilename[MaxStringLen+1];
      CMDIMainWnd();
      ~CMDIMainWnd() { delete pMenu; }

    protected:
      CMenu* pMenu;
      int nNumMDIChildren;
      // create a new client window area
      afx_msg int OnCreate(LPCREATESTRUCT lpCS);
      // create MDI child windows
      afx_msg void CMLoadAutoexec();
      afx_msg void CMLoadConfig();
      afx_msg void CMLoadWin();
      afx_msg void CMLoadSystem();
      // helper function which creates the actual MDI child windows
      void CreateChild(int nChildIndex);

      // cascade MDI children
      afx_msg void CMCascadeChildren()
        { MDICascade(); }
      // tile MDI children
      afx_msg void CMTileChildren()
        { MDITile(); }
      // arrange MDI children icons
      afx_msg void CMArrangeIcons()
        { MDIIconArrange(); }
      // close all MDI children
      afx_msg void CMCloseChildren();
      // get the number of MDI children
      int GetChildCount()
        { return nNumMDIChildren; }
      // handle the command for counting the MDI children
      afx_msg void CMCountChildren();
```

```
  // handle the child destroy message
  afx_msg LONG OnChildDestroy(UINT wParam, LONG lParam);
  // handle exiting the application
  afx_msg void OnExit()
    { SendMessage(WM_CLOSE); }
  // handle closing the MDI frame window
  virtual void OnClose();

  // declare message map macro
  DECLARE_MESSAGE_MAP();
};
CAppMDIChild::CAppMDIChild()
{
  pTextLst = NULL;
}
CAppMDIChild::~CAppMDIChild()
{
  if (pTextLst)
    delete pTextLst;
}
BOOL CAppMDIChild::Create(LPSTR szFilename, int nChildNumber)
{
  nChildNum = nChildNumber;
  return CMDIChildWnd::Create(NULL, szFilename);
}
int CAppMDIChild::OnCreate(LPCREATESTRUCT lpCS)
{
  CMDIMainWnd* pParent = (CMDIMainWnd*)(GetParentFrame());
  CRect r;
  char msgStr[MaxStringLen+1];
  DWORD dwListBoxStyle = WS_CHILD | WS_VISIBLE | WS_VSCROLL |
                         LBS_STANDARD;
  // disable sorting of items in the list box
  dwListBoxStyle &= ~LBS_SORT;

  // create the output list box
  makerect(10, 10, Wctl, Hctl, r);
  pTextLst = new CListBox();
  pTextLst->Create(dwListBoxStyle, r, this, ID_TEXT_LST);
  if (!OpenFile(pParent->szFilename)) {
    strcpy(msgStr, "Cannot open file ");
    strcat(msgStr, pParent->szFilename);
    MessageBox(msgStr, "File Input Error",
               MB_OK | MB_ICONINFORMATION);
  }
  return 0;
}
void CAppMDIChild::OnClose()
{
  CMDIMainWnd* pParent = (CMDIMainWnd*)(GetParentFrame());

  // is the express-close flag of the parent window set?
  if (pParent->bExpressClose == TRUE)
    pParent->bLoadedFile[nChildNum] = FALSE;
```

(continues)

Advanced Programming

III

Listing 12.4 Continued

```cpp
    else
      // prompt the user and return the prompt result
      if (MessageBox("Close this MDI window?",
            "Query", MB_YESNO | MB_ICONQUESTION) == IDYES) {
        MDIDestroy();
        pParent->bLoadedFile[nChildNum] = FALSE;
      }
  }
}
void CAppMDIChild::OnDestroy()
{
  CMDIMainWnd* pParent = (CMDIMainWnd*)(GetParentFrame());
  pParent->SendMessage(WM_CHILDDESTROY, (UINT)m_hWnd, 0);
}

BOOL CAppMDIChild::OpenFile(const char* szFilename)
{
  fstream f(szFilename, ios::in);
  char szStr[MaxStringLen+1];

  if (f.good()) {
   while (!f.eof()) {
     f.getline(szStr, MaxStringLen);
     pTextLst->AddString(szStr);
   }
   f.close();
   return TRUE;
  }
  else
   return FALSE;
}

CMDIMainWnd::CMDIMainWnd()
{
    Create(NULL, "MDI System File Viewer",
           WS_OVERLAPPEDWINDOW, rectDefault,
        NULL, MenuName);
    // clear the express-close flag
    bExpressClose = FALSE;
    // initialize the number of MDI child windows
    nNumMDIChildren = 0;
    // initialize the file flags
    for (int i = 0; i < MAX_FILES; i++)
      bLoadedFile[i] = FALSE;
}
int CMDIMainWnd::OnCreate(LPCREATESTRUCT lpCS)
{
  pMenu = new CMenu();
  pMenu->LoadMenu(MenuName);
  CreateClient(lpCS, pMenu->GetSubMenu(0));
  return 0;
}
void CMDIMainWnd::CMLoadAutoexec()
{
```

```
  if (!bLoadedFile[0])
    CreateChild(0);
}
void CMDIMainWnd::CMLoadConfig()
{
  if (!bLoadedFile[1])
    CreateChild(1);
}
void CMDIMainWnd::CMLoadWin()
{
  if (!bLoadedFile[2])
    CreateChild(2);
}
void CMDIMainWnd::CMLoadSystem()
{
  if (!bLoadedFile[3])
    CreateChild(3);
}
void CMDIMainWnd::CreateChild(int nChildIndex)
{
  CRect r;
  CAppMDIChild* pChild = new CAppMDIChild();
  makerect(10 * nChildIndex, 10 * nChildIndex,
           Wctl + 10, Hctl + 10, r);
  strcpy(szFilename, FILES[nChildIndex]);
  if (!pChild->Create(szFilename, nChildIndex)) {
    delete pChild;
    return;
  }
  bLoadedFile[nChildIndex] = TRUE;
  nNumMDIChildren++;
  // show the new MDI child window
  pChild->ShowWindow(SW_SHOW);
}
void CMDIMainWnd::CMCloseChildren()
{
  CAppMDIChild* pChild = (CAppMDIChild*) MDIGetActive();

  // set the bExpressClose flag
  bExpressClose = TRUE;
  while (pChild) {
    // close the active MDI child
    pChild->MDIDestroy();
    MDINext; // get the next MDI child
    pChild = (CAppMDIChild*) MDIGetActive();
  }
  // clear the bExpressClose flag
  bExpressClose = FALSE;
  // clear file flags
  for (int i = 0; i < MAX_FILES; i++)
    bLoadedFile[i] = FALSE;
}
//  display a message box which shows the number of children
void CMDIMainWnd::CMCountChildren()
{
```

(continues)

III

Advanced Programming

Listing 12.4 Continued

```
    char msgStr[MaxStringLen+1];
    sprintf(msgStr, "There are %d MDI children", nNumMDIChildren);
    MessageBox(msgStr, "Information", MB_OK | MB_ICONINFORMATION);
}
LONG CMDIMainWnd::OnChildDestroy(UINT wParam, LONG lParam)
{
    nNumMDIChildren--;
    return 0;
}
void CMDIMainWnd::OnClose()
{
    if (MessageBox("Want to close this application",
                   "Query", MB_YESNO | MB_ICONQUESTION) == IDYES)
        DestroyWindow();
}
BEGIN_MESSAGE_MAP(CAppMDIChild, CMDIChildWnd)
    ON_WM_CREATE()
    ON_WM_CLOSE()
    ON_WM_DESTROY()
END_MESSAGE_MAP()
BEGIN_MESSAGE_MAP(CMDIMainWnd, CMDIFrameWnd)
    ON_WM_CREATE()
    ON_COMMAND(CM_LOAD_AUTOEXEC, CMLoadAutoexec)
    ON_COMMAND(CM_LOAD_CONFIG, CMLoadConfig)
    ON_COMMAND(CM_LOAD_WIN, CMLoadWin)
    ON_COMMAND(CM_LOAD_SYSTEM, CMLoadSystem)
    ON_COMMAND(CM_CASCADECHILDREN, CMCascadeChildren)
    ON_COMMAND(CM_TILECHILDREN, CMTileChildren)
    ON_COMMAND(CM_ARRANGEICONS, CMArrangeIcons)
    ON_COMMAND(CM_CLOSECHILDREN, CMCloseChildren)
    ON_COMMAND(CM_COUNTCHILDREN, CMCountChildren)
    ON_MESSAGE(WM_CHILDDESTROY, OnChildDestroy)
    ON_COMMAND(CM_EXIT, OnExit)
    ON_WM_CLOSE()
END_MESSAGE_MAP()
// Construct the CMDIDemoApp's m_pMainWnd data member
BOOL CMDIDemoApp::InitInstance()
{
    m_pMainWnd = new CMDIMainWnd();
    m_pMainWnd->ShowWindow(m_nCmdShow);
    m_pMainWnd->UpdateWindow();
    return TRUE;
}
// application's constructor initializes and runs the app
CMDIDemoApp WindowApp;
```

The source code for the MDIWIN1.CPP program file shown in Listing 12.4 declares the following sets of constants (some of these sets are made up of individual constants):

- The constant MaxStringLen, which defines the size of data members that are strings, and strings that are local to member functions.

- The constant MenuName, which defines the name of the menu resource passed as an argument to the functions Create and CreateClient.

- The constants Hctl and Wctl, which define the size of the list box controls that are attached to the MDI child windows.

- The constant MAX_FILES, which specifies the number of viewed files (which also is the maximum number of MDI child windows).

The global array of strings FILES contains the names of the viewed system files. The general function makerect calculates the rectangular area. The MDI classes use this general function.

The program listing declares three classes: the application class, CMDIDemoApp; the MDI frame class, CMDIMainWnd; and the MDI child window class, CAppMDIChild.

The Application Class

The code for the application class CMDIDemoApp closely resembles the ones in the programs that I've presented, with one exception. The member function InitInstance generates an instance of the MDI frame class CMDIMainWnd instead of an instance of the main window class.

The MDI Frame Class

The class CMDIMainWnd, which is a descendant of class CMDIFrameWnd, declares five data members, a constructor, a destructor, and a set of member functions. The class contains three public and two protected data members, as follows:

- The public data member bExpressClose is a Boolean flag that helps in quickly closing all the windows. This process bypasses the confirmation normally requested when you close an individual MDI child window.

- The public data member bLoadedFile is an array of flags that track the state of loading the four system files. The array bLoadedFile has MAX_FILES elements.

- The public data member szFilename stores the name of the file to be loaded in an MDI child window.

- The protected data member pMenu is the pointer to the menu attached to the MDI frame window.

- The protected data member nNumMDIChildren stores the current number of MDI child windows.

The class constructor creates an MDI frame window by performing the following tasks:

- Invoking the Create member function to specify the window title, over-lapped style, and the MAINMENU menu resource (using the global constant MenuName).

- Initializing the data member bExpressClose by assigning it FALSE.

- Initializing the data member nNumMDIChildren by assigning it zero.

- Assigning FALSE to the elements of the member bLoadedFile.

The class destructor deletes the dynamic menu accessed by the pMenu pointer.

The member function OnCreate creates the MDI frame window by performing the following tasks:

- Creating a new instance of CMenu, the menu class, and linking that instance with the pMenu data member.

- Attaching the resource menu MAINMENU to the MDI frame window by sending the C++ message LoadMenu to the menu object accessed by the pointer pMenu.

- Creating the invisible MDI client window by calling the member function CreateClient. The first argument of the CreateClient function is the parameter of the OnCreate function itself. The second argument of the CreateClient function is the pointer to the first menu item, accessed by the expression pMenu->GetSubMenu(0).

- Returning zero as the function result.

The member functions CMLoadAutoexec, CMLoadConfig, CMLoadWin, and CMLoadSystem load the AUTOEXEC.BAT, CONFIG.SYS, WIN.INI, and SYSTEM.INI files, respectively. These functions have a similar if statement, which invokes the member function CreateChild only if the corresponding element of the member bLoadedFile is false.

The member function CreateChild creates an MDI child window by performing the following tasks:

- Creating a new instance of class CAppMDIChild and accessing that instance with the local pointer pChild.

■ Calculating the size and location of the MDI child window by calling the general function `makerect`.

■ Assigning the string `FILES[nChildIndex]` to the member `szFilename`.

■ Creating the MDI child window by sending the C++ message `Create` to the MDI child window object accessed by the pointer `pChild`. The arguments for this message include the filename and the child number. If the message yields FALSE, the function `CreateChild` deletes the dynamic instance of `CAppMDIChild` and then exits.

■ Assigning TRUE to the element number `nChildIndex` of the member `bLoadedFile`.

■ Incrementing the value in the member `nNumMDIChildren`.

■ Displaying the new MDI child window by sending the C++ message `ShowWindow` to that window.

The member function `CMCloseChildren` closes all the MDI child windows. This function performs the following tasks:

■ Retrieves the address of the currently active MDI child window by invoking the member function `MDIGetActive`. This task assigns the retrieved address to the local pointer `pChild`.

■ Assigns TRUE to the data member `bExpressClose`.

■ Employs a `while` loop statement to close each MDI child window, starting with the currently active window. The first loop statement sends the C++ message `MDIDestroy` to the currently active MDI child window (accessed by the local pointer `pChild`). The second loop statement selects the next MDI child by invoking the function `MDINext`. The third loop statement invokes the function `MDIGetActive` to store the address of the new active child in the pointer `pChild`. When the loop closes all MDI child windows, the `MDIGetActive` function assigns a NULL to the `pChild` pointer. This NULL value terminates the loop iteration.

■ Assigns FALSE to the `bExpressClose` data member.

■ Assigns FALSE to each element of the member `bLoadedFile`.

III

Advanced Programming

The member function CMCountChildren displays the current number of MDI child windows in a message dialog box. The function first translates the value stored in the member nNumMDIChildren into a formatted string. Then the function displays that string in a message dialog box.

The member function OnChildDestroy responds to the messages sent by an MDI child window when it is destroyed. The function decrements the value stored in the member nNumMDIChildren and returns 0.

The member functions CMCascadeChildren, CMTileChildren, and CMArrangeIcons simply invoke the inherited member functions MDICascade, MDITile, and MDIIconArrange, respectively.

The MDI Child Window Class

The class CAppMDIChild declares the public members nChildNum and pTextLst. The member pTextLst is the pointer to the list box control that displays the contents of a system file. The data member nChildNum stores the child number of an MDI child window for self-identification. The class also declares a constructor, a destructor, a Create function, and a number of member functions.

The class constructor simply assigns NULL to the member pTextLst. The class destructor deletes the dynamic instance of the list box control accessed by the member pTextLst.

The member function Create is a short version of the inherited Create function, and it has two parameters: szFilename and nChildNumber. The function assigns the argument of nChildNumber to the member nChildNum and then invokes the Create member function of the parent class.

The member function OnCreate creates the MDI child window by carrying out the following tasks:

- Obtaining the address of the parent window and assigning that address to the local pointer pParent.

- Calculating the size and location of the list box control to be created.

- Creating a list box control and assigning its address to the member pTextLst.

- Opening the file specified by member szFilename of the parent window. This task invokes the member function OpenFile. If this function yields FALSE, the program displays an error message in a message dialog box.

- Returning zero.

The member function `OnClose` closes an MDI child window with or without user confirmation. The function declares the local pointer `pParent` and assigns it the address of the parent MDI frame window. This pointer enables the function to then obtain the Boolean value of `bExpressClose` and, depending on that value, determine whether to prompt the user before closing the window.

The member function `OnDestroy` sends the parent MDI frame window the Windows message `WM_CHILDDESTROY` when an MDI child window is removed. This message enables the parent MDI frame window to take appropriate action, which in this case is decrementing the `nNumMDIChildren` member.

The member function `OpenFile` loads a system file in an MDI child window. The function uses the C++ input text stream object `f` and initializes this object (an instance of class `fstream`) using the member `szFilename` and with the I/O mode `ios::in`. The function then sends the C++ message `good` to the stream object to determine whether the stream is opened successfully. If this message yields a nonzero value, the function `OpenFile` uses a `while` loop to read the lines from the input text stream. The first loop statement sends the C++ message `getline` to the object `f` to read the next line. The second loop statement then sends the C++ message `AddString` to the list box to insert the line just read. The loop iterates while the C++ message `eof`, which is sent to object `f`, returns a nonzero value. After the loop iterates, the function sends the C++ message close to the object `f` to close the stream. The function then returns TRUE. By contrast, if the stream was not opened, the function `OpenFile` returns FALSE.

Using the Timer MDI Program

Now look at another example for an MDI-compliant application. The new program, MDIWIN2.EXE, produces MDI child windows that display the current date and time and also support an electronic stopwatch. Each MDI child window has the following controls:

- *Start pushbutton control.* Starts the electronic stopwatch; when you click this control, the program alters the control's caption to *Stop*. This scheme enables the control's caption to indicate the status of the stopwatch.

- *Time pushbutton control.* Displays the current system date and time.

- *Can Close check box.* Replaces the confirmation dialog box. Use this box when you want to close the MDI child window; it enables you to predetermine whether you can close the MDI child window.

The program's menu system manages the MDI child windows. On the Time menu are the commands that start and stop the stopwatch and obtain the current date and time. These commands affect the currently active MDI child windows.

MDIWIN2.EXE illustrates three main aspects of an MDI-compliant application:

- The MDI child windows are similar.

- The application can generate as many MDI child windows as the Windows resources allow.

- The MDI child windows contain controls.

Now you're ready to compile and run the MDIWIN2.EXE application. Create a few MDI children and use their pushbutton controls to display the current date and time, and start and stop the stopwatch. Try to close the MDI children with the Can Close check box marked and unmarked. Only the MDI children that have the Can Close control checked will close individually. Use the MDI Children menu's Close All command and watch all the MDI children close, regardless of the check state of the Can Close control. Figure 12.2 shows a sample session with the MDIWIN2.EXE program.

Listing 12.5 shows the contents of the MDIWIN2.DEF definition file.

Listing 12.5 The MDIWIN2.DEF Definition File

```
NAME         MDIWin2
DESCRIPTION  'An MFC Windows Application'
EXETYPE      WINDOWS
CODE         PRELOAD MOVEABLE DISCARDABLE
DATA         PRELOAD MOVEABLE MULTIPLE
HEAPSIZE     1024
```

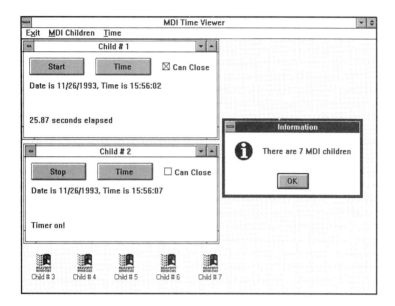

Figure 12.2

A sample
session with the
MDIWIN2.EXE
program.

Listing 12.6 shows the source code for the MDIWIN2.H header file.

Listing 12.6 Source Code for the MDIWIN2.H Header File

```
#define CM_EXIT            (WM_USER + 100)
#define CM_COUNTCHILDREN   (WM_USER + 101)
#define CM_CREATECHILD     (WM_USER + 102)
#define CM_CASCADECHILDREN (WM_USER + 103)
#define CM_TILECHILDREN    (WM_USER + 104)
#define CM_ARRANGEICONS    (WM_USER + 105)
#define CM_CLOSECHILDREN   (WM_USER + 106)
#define CM_LAPSE           (WM_USER + 107)
#define CM_NOW             (WM_USER + 108)
#define WM_CHILDDESTROY    (WM_USER + 109)
#define ID_TIME_TXT     100
#define ID_LAPSE_TXT    101
#define ID_LAPSE_BTN    102
#define ID_NOW_BTN      103
#define ID_CLOSE_CHK    104
```

Listing 12.7 contains the script for the MDIWIN2.RC resource file.

Listing 12.7 Script for the MDIWIN2.RC Resource File

```
#include <windows.h>
#include <afxres.h>
#include "mdiwin2.h"
MAINMENU MENU LOADONCALL MOVEABLE PURE DISCARDABLE
```

(continues)

III

Advanced Programming

Listing 12.7 Continued

```
BEGIN
  MENUITEM "E&xit", CM_EXIT
  POPUP "&MDI Children"
  BEGIN
    MENUITEM   "C&reate", CM_CREATECHILD
    MENUITEM   "&Cascade", CM_CASCADECHILDREN
    MENUITEM   "&Tile", CM_TILECHILDREN
    MENUITEM   "Arrange &Icons", CM_ARRANGEICONS
    MENUITEM   "C&lose All", CM_CLOSECHILDREN
    MENUITEM   "C&ount Children", CM_COUNTCHILDREN
  END
  POPUP "&Time"
  BEGIN
    MENUITEM "&Start/Stop Timer", CM_LAPSE
    MENUITEM "&Time", CM_NOW
  END
END
```

Listing 12.8 shows the source code for the MDIWIN2.CPP program.

**Listing 12.8 Source Code for the MDIWIN2.CPP
Program File**

```
/*
    Program which displays time and invokes a timer in each
    MDI child window.  All MDI child windows are similar.
    Program is limited by the amount of memory resources in
    creating MDI child windows.

*/
#include <stdlib.h>
#include <stdio.h>
#include <string.h>
#include <afxwin.h>
#include "mdiwin2.h"
const char* MenuName = "MAINMENU";
const Hlbl = 50;
const Wlbl = 400;
const Wbtn = 100;
const Hbtn = 30;
const Wchk = 100;
const Hchk = 30;
const VertSpacing = 10;
const HorzSpacing = 20;
const BUFFER_SIZE = 80;
// declare constants for the check box states
const BF_CHECKED = 1;
const BF_UNCHECKED = 0;

// declare global function to calculate the location
// and size of a control
```

```
void makeRect(int X, int Y, int W, int H, CRect& r)
{
  r.SetRect(X, Y, X + W, Y + H);
}
// declare extended button class
class CxButton : public CButton
{
public:
   BOOL Create(const char FAR* lpCaption, const RECT& rect,
               CWnd* pParentWnd, UINT nID)
   {
       return CButton::Create(lpCaption,
                              WS_CHILD | WS_VISIBLE | BS_PUSHBUTTON,
                              rect, pParentWnd, nID);
   }
};
// declare check box class
class CCheckBox : public CButton
{
public:
   BOOL Create(const char FAR* lpCaption, const RECT& rect,
               CWnd* pParentWnd, UINT nID)
   {
       return CButton::Create(lpCaption,
                              WS_CHILD | WS_VISIBLE | BS_AUTOCHECKBOX,
                              rect, pParentWnd, nID);
   }
   void Check()
     { SetCheck(BF_CHECKED); }

   void UnCheck()
     { SetCheck(BF_UNCHECKED); }
};
// Define an application class derived from CWinApp
class CMDIDemoApp : public CWinApp
{
public:
  virtual BOOL InitInstance();
};
class CAppMDIChild : public CMDIChildWnd
{
  friend class CMDIMainWnd;
 public:
  // pointer to the controls
  CStatic* pTimeTxt;
  CStatic* pLapseTxt;
  CxButton* pLapseBtn;
  CxButton* pTimeNowBtn;
  CCheckBox* pCanCloseChk;
  CAppMDIChild();

  ~CAppMDIChild();
```

III

Advanced Programming

(continues)

Listing 12.8 Continued

```
protected:
 int nChildNum;
 long nInitTickCount;
 BOOL bTimerOn;
 BOOL Create(LPSTR szTitle, int ChildNumber);

 afx_msg int OnCreate(LPCREATESTRUCT lpCS);

 // handle the Lapse pushbutton
 afx_msg void HandleLapseBtn();
 afx_msg void CMLapseBtn()
   { HandleLapseBtn(); }
 // handle the Time Now pushbutton
 afx_msg void HandleTimeNowBtn();
 afx_msg void CMTimeNowBtn()
   { HandleTimeNowBtn(); }
 // handle closing the MDI child window
 afx_msg void OnClose();
 // handle destroying an MDI child window
 afx_msg void OnDestroy();
 // get the current time
 void getTime(CString& StrObj);
 // declare message map macro
 DECLARE_MESSAGE_MAP();
};
class CMDIMainWnd : public CMDIFrameWnd
{
 public:
  // flag to quickly close all MDI chidren windows
  BOOL ExpressClose;
  CMDIMainWnd();
  ~CMDIMainWnd()
    { delete pMenu; }
 protected:
  CMenu* pMenu;
  int nNumMDIChildren;
  int nLastMDIChild;
  // create a new client window area
  afx_msg int OnCreate(LPCREATESTRUCT lpCS);
  // create an MDI child window
  afx_msg void CMCreateChild();
  // cascade MDI children
  afx_msg void CMCascadeChildren()
    { MDICascade(); }

  // tile MDI children
  afx_msg void CMTileChildren()
    { MDITile(); }

  // arrange MDI children icons
  afx_msg void CMArrangeIcons()
    { MDIIconArrange(); }
  // close all MDI children
  afx_msg void CMCloseChildren();
```

```
  // get the number of MDI children
  int GetChildCount()
    { return nNumMDIChildren; }
  // handle the command for counting the MDI children
  afx_msg void CMCountChildren();
  // handle the Lapse menu item
  afx_msg void CMLapse()
    { SendMessage(WM_COMMAND, ID_LAPSE_BTN); }

  // handle the Time menu item
  afx_msg void CMNow()
    { SendMessage(WM_COMMAND, ID_NOW_BTN); }
  // handle the child destroy message
  afx_msg LONG OnChildDestroy(UINT wParam, LONG lParam);
  // handle exiting the application
  afx_msg void OnExit()
    { SendMessage(WM_CLOSE); }
  // handle closing the MDI frame window
  virtual void OnClose();

  // declare message map macro
  DECLARE_MESSAGE_MAP();
};
CAppMDIChild::CAppMDIChild()
{
  pTimeTxt = NULL;
  pLapseTxt = NULL;
  bTimerOn = FALSE;
}
CAppMDIChild::~CAppMDIChild()
{
  delete pTimeTxt;
  delete pLapseTxt;
  delete pLapseBtn;
  delete pTimeNowBtn;
  delete pCanCloseChk;
}
BOOL CAppMDIChild::Create(LPSTR szTitle, int ChildNumber)
{
  nChildNum = ChildNumber;
  return CMDIChildWnd::Create(NULL, szTitle);
}
CAppMDIChild::OnCreate(LPCREATESTRUCT lpCS)
{
  int x0 = 10;
  int y0 = 10;
  int x = x0, y = y0;
  CString s;
  CRect r;
  DWORD dwStaticStyle = WS_CHILD | WS_VISIBLE | SS_LEFT;

  // create the pushbuttons
  makeRect(x, y, Wbtn, Hbtn, r);
  pLapseBtn = new CxButton();
  pLapseBtn->Create("Start", r, this, ID_LAPSE_BTN);
```

III

Advanced Programming

(continues)

Listing 12.8 Continued

```
      x+= Wbtn + HorzSpacing;
      makeRect(x, y, Wbtn, Hbtn, r);
      pTimeNowBtn = new CxButton();
      pTimeNowBtn->Create("Time", r, this, ID_NOW_BTN);

      x+= Wbtn + HorzSpacing;
      makeRect(x, y, Wchk, Hchk, r);
      pCanCloseChk = new CCheckBox();
      pCanCloseChk->Create("Can Close", r, this, ID_CLOSE_CHK);
      x = x0;
      y += Hbtn + VertSpacing;
      // get the current time
      getTime(s);

      // create the time static text
      makeRect(x, y, Wlbl, Hlbl, r);
      pTimeTxt = new CStatic();
      pTimeTxt->Create(s, dwStaticStyle, r, this, ID_TIME_TXT);
      // create the lapse static text
      y += Hlbl + VertSpacing;
      makeRect(x, y, Wlbl, Hlbl, r);
      pLapseTxt = new CStatic();
      pLapseTxt->Create("0 second elapsed", dwStaticStyle,
                        r, this, ID_LAPSE_TXT);
      return 0;
    }
    void CAppMDIChild::HandleLapseBtn()
    {
      char szStr[BUFFER_SIZE];

      if (bTimerOn) {
        bTimerOn = FALSE;
        sprintf(szStr, "%g seconds elapsed",
                double((GetTickCount() - nInitTickCount) / 1000.0));
        // alter the lapse static text
        pLapseTxt->SetWindowText(szStr);
        // alter the Start/Stop button
        pLapseBtn->SetWindowText("Start");

      }
      else {
        bTimerOn = TRUE;
        // store current tick count
        nInitTickCount = GetTickCount();
        // alter the lapse static text
        pLapseTxt->SetWindowText("Timer on!");
        // alter the Start/Stop button
        pLapseBtn->SetWindowText("Stop");
      }
    }

    void CAppMDIChild::HandleTimeNowBtn()
    {
      CString s;
```

```
  // build new text
  getTime(s);

  // insert text in the edit control
  pTimeTxt->SetWindowText((const char*) s);
}
void CAppMDIChild::OnClose()
{
   CMDIMainWnd* pParent = (CMDIMainWnd*)(GetParentFrame());
  if (pParent->ExpressClose == TRUE ||
      pCanCloseChk->GetCheck() == BF_CHECKED)
    MDIDestroy();
}
void CAppMDIChild::OnDestroy()
{
  CMDIMainWnd* pParent = (CMDIMainWnd*)(GetParentFrame());
  pParent->SendMessage(WM_CHILDDESTROY, (UINT)m_hWnd, 0);
}
void CAppMDIChild::getTime(CString& StrObj)
{
  char* pszStr = StrObj.GetBuffer(BUFFER_SIZE);
  CTime tm = CTime::GetCurrentTime();
  sprintf(pszStr, "Date is %02d/%02d/%4d, Time is %02d:%02d:%02d",
                  tm.GetMonth(), tm.GetDay(), tm.GetYear(),
                  tm.GetHour(), tm.GetMinute(), tm.GetSecond());
  StrObj.ReleaseBuffer(-1);
}
CMDIMainWnd::CMDIMainWnd()
{

   Create(NULL, "MDI Time Viewer",
          WS_OVERLAPPEDWINDOW, rectDefault,
      NULL, MenuName);
   // clear the express-close flag
   ExpressClose = FALSE;
   // initialize the number of MDI children
   nLastMDIChild = 0;
   nNumMDIChildren = 0;
}
int CMDIMainWnd::OnCreate(LPCREATESTRUCT lpCS)
{
  pMenu = new CMenu();
  pMenu->LoadMenu(MenuName);
  CreateClient(lpCS, pMenu->GetSubMenu(0));
  return 0;
}
void CMDIMainWnd::CMCreateChild()
{
  char s[81];
  CAppMDIChild* pChild = new CAppMDIChild();
  nLastMDIChild++;
  sprintf(s, "Child # %d", nLastMDIChild);
  if (!pChild->Create(s, nLastMDIChild)) {
    delete pChild;
    nLastMDIChild--; // decrement highest child index
    return;
  }
```

III

Advanced Programming

(continues)

Listing 12.8 Continued

```
  nNumMDIChildren++;
  // show the new MDI child window
  pChild->ShowWindow(SW_SHOW);

}
void CMDIMainWnd::CMCloseChildren()
{
  CAppMDIChild* pChild = (CAppMDIChild*) MDIGetActive();

  // set the ExpressClose flag
  ExpressClose = TRUE;

  while (pChild) {
    // close the active MDI child
    pChild->MDIDestroy();
    MDINext; // get the next MDI child
    pChild = (CAppMDIChild*) MDIGetActive();
  }
  // clear the ExpressClose flag
  ExpressClose = FALSE;
}
//  display a message box which shows the number of children
void CMDIMainWnd::CMCountChildren()
{
  char msgStr[81];
  sprintf(msgStr, "There are %d MDI children", nNumMDIChildren);
  MessageBox(msgStr, "Information", MB_OK ¦ MB_ICONINFORMATION);
}
LONG CMDIMainWnd::OnChildDestroy(UINT wParam, LONG lParam)
{
  nNumMDIChildren--;
  // reset nLastMDIChild to 0, if there are no MDI children
  nLastMDIChild = (nNumMDIChildren == 0) ? 0 : nLastMDIChild;
  return 0;
}
void CMDIMainWnd::OnClose()
{
  if (MessageBox("Want to close this application",
                 "Query", MB_YESNO ¦ MB_ICONQUESTION) == IDYES)
    DestroyWindow();
}
BEGIN_MESSAGE_MAP(CAppMDIChild, CMDIChildWnd)
  ON_WM_CREATE()
  ON_BN_CLICKED(ID_LAPSE_BTN, HandleLapseBtn)
  ON_COMMAND(ID_LAPSE_BTN, CMLapseBtn)
  ON_BN_CLICKED(ID_NOW_BTN, HandleTimeNowBtn)
  ON_COMMAND(ID_NOW_BTN, CMTimeNowBtn)
  ON_WM_CLOSE()
  ON_WM_DESTROY()
END_MESSAGE_MAP()
BEGIN_MESSAGE_MAP(CMDIMainWnd, CMDIFrameWnd)
  ON_WM_CREATE()
  ON_COMMAND(CM_CREATECHILD, CMCreateChild)
  ON_COMMAND(CM_CASCADECHILDREN, CMCascadeChildren)
```

```
    ON_COMMAND(CM_TILECHILDREN, CMTileChildren)
    ON_COMMAND(CM_ARRANGEICONS, CMArragenIcons)
    ON_COMMAND(CM_CLOSECHILDREN, CMCloseChildren)
    ON_COMMAND(CM_COUNTCHILDREN, CMCountChildren)
    ON_COMMAND(CM_LAPSE, CMLapse)
    ON_COMMAND(CM_NOW, CMNow)
    ON_MESSAGE(WM_CHILDDESTROY, OnChildDestroy)
    ON_COMMAND(CM_EXIT, OnExit)
    ON_WM_CLOSE()
END_MESSAGE_MAP()
// Construct the CMDIDemoApp's m_pMainWnd data member
BOOL CMDIDemoApp::InitInstance()
{
    m_pMainWnd = new CMDIMainWnd();
    m_pMainWnd->ShowWindow(m_nCmdShow);
    m_pMainWnd->UpdateWindow();
    return TRUE;
}
// application's constructor initializes and runs the app
CMDIDemoApp WindowApp;
```

The source code for the MDIWIN2.CPP program file shown in Listing 12.8 declares the following constants:

- The constant MenuName, which stores the menu resource name.

- The set of constants that size and space the controls of each MDI child window.

- The constant BUFFER_SIZE, which defines the string sizes.

- The constants BF_CHECKED and BF_UNCHECKED, which represent the state of a check box control.

In addition, the program listing declares the general function makerect.

The new application declares five classes: the CxButton button class, the CCheckBox check box class, the CAppMDIChild MDI child window class, the CMDIMainWnd MDI frame class, and the CMDIDemoApp application class. The CxButton and CCheckBox classes are similar to the ones used in programs I presented earlier.

The MDI Child Class

The MDI child class declares the following data members:

- The public member pTimeTxt, which is a pointer to the static text control that displays the current system date and time when you click the Time button or invoke the Time menu command.

III

Advanced Programming

■ The public member `pLapseTxt`, which is a pointer to the static text control that displays the stopwatch time when you click the Start button or invoke the Start/Stop Timer menu command.

■ The public member `pLapseBtn`, which is the pointer to the Start button.

■ The public member `pTimeNowBtn`, which is the pointer to the Time button.

■ The public member `pCanCloseChk`, which is the pointer to the Can Close check box.

■ The protected member `nChildNum`, which stores the MDI child window number.

■ The protected member `nInitTickCount`, which stores the initial tick count (that is, the number of milliseconds Windows has been running).

■ The protected Boolean member `bTimerOn`, which flags whether the stopwatch is running.

The `CAppMDIChild` constructor assigns NULLs to the members `pTimeTxt` and `pLapseTxt` and assigns FALSE to the member `bTimerOn`. The class destructor deletes the instances of the various controls in an MDI child window.

The member function `OnCreate` builds the contents of an MDI child window by performing the following tasks:

■ Creating the Start pushbutton.

■ Creating the Time pushbutton.

■ Creating the Can Close check box control.

■ Creating the static text that displays the current date and time.

■ Creating the static text that displays the stopwatch time. Initially, this control displays the string `Time elapsed: 0 seconds`.

The member function `HandleLapseBtn` responds to the command message sent by the Start pushbutton. The function then uses the member `bTimerOn` to determine whether to start or stop the stopwatch. When the member `bTimerOn` contains TRUE, the function performs the following tasks:

■ Assigns FALSE to member `bTimerOn` to toggle its value.

- Calculates the elapsed time and converts the result into a string image. This task uses the function sprintf to store the string image in the local variable szStr. The number of milliseconds is calculated by taking the difference between the result of API function GetTickCount and the member nInitTickCount.

- Displays the elapsed time in the stopwatch static text.

- Alters the caption of the stopwatch button to *Start*.

By contrast, when the member bTimerOn contains FALSE, the function performs the following tasks:

- Assigns TRUE to member bTimerOn to toggle its value.

- Assigns the starting tick count to the member nInitTickCount.

- Displays the string Timer on! in the stopwatch static text.

- Alters the caption of the stopwatch button to *Stop*.

The member function HandleTimeNowBtn responds to the command message sent by the Time pushbutton. The function invokes the member function getTime to obtain the string image of the current date and time. The function then writes that string image to the current time static text.

The MDI child window class also declares the CMLapseBtn and CMTimeNowBtn member functions. These functions respond to commands sent by the parent MDI frame window and simply invoke the corresponding Handle*XXXX* member functions.

The CanClose member function responds to the WM_CLOSE message sent by the Close command in the system menu available in each MDI child window. If the MDI frame window's bExpressClose variable is TRUE or the Can Close check box is marked, the function destroys the MDI child window.

The member function getTime obtains the current date and time using the local instance of class CTime, which is tm. The function uses the member function CTime::GetCurrentTime to obtain the current date and time. The function getTime also uses the function sprintf along with the CTime helper functions GetMonth, GetDay, GetYear, GetHour, GetMinute, and GetSecond to create a formatted string image of the current date and time. The function returns the formatted string using the function's reference parameter StrObj.

III

Advanced Programming

The MDI Frame Window Class

The class CMDIMainWnd, which is a descendant of class CMDIFrameWnd, declares four data members, a constructor, a destructor, and a set of member functions. The class contains one public and three protected data members, as follows:

- The public data member bExpressClose is a Boolean flag that helps in quickly closing all the windows. This data member works just like the one in the source code MDIWIN1.CPP.

- The protected data member pMenu is the pointer to the menu attached to the MDI frame window.

- The protected data member nNumMDIChildren stores the current number of MDI child windows.

- The protected data member nLastMDIChild stores the number of the last MDI child window. The program uses the member along with member nNumMDIChildren to control the number of the MDI child windows.

The class constructor creates an MDI frame window by performing the following tasks:

- Invoking the Create member function to specify the window title, the overlapped style, and the MAINMENU menu resource (using the global constant MenuName).

- Initializing the data member bExpressClose by assigning it FALSE.

- Initializing the data member nLastMDIChild by assigning it zero.

- Initializing the data member nNumMDIChildren by assigning it zero.

The class destructor deletes the dynamic menu accessed by the pMenu pointer.

The member function OnCreate creates the MDI frame window by performing the following tasks:

- Creating a new instance of CMenu, the menu class, and linking that instance with the pMenu data member.

- Attaching the resource menu MAINMENU to the MDI frame window by sending the C++ message LoadMenu to the menu object accessed by the pointer pMenu.

- Creating the invisible MDI client window by calling the member function CreateClient. The first argument of the CreateClient function is the parameter of the OnCreate function itself. The second argument of the CreateClient function is the pointer to the first menu item, accessed by the expression pMenu->GetSubMenu(0).

- Returning zero as the function result.

The member function CMCreateChild creates an MDI child window by performing the following tasks:

- Creating a new instance of class CAppMDIChild and accessing that instance with the local pointer pChild.

- Incrementing the member nLastMDIChild.

- Storing a string image of the member nLastMDIChild in the local string variable s.

- Creating the MDI child window by sending the C++ message Create to the MDI child window object accessed by the pointer pChild. The arguments for this message include the filename and the child number. If the message yields FALSE, the function CreateChild deletes the dynamic instance of CAppMDIChild, decrements the member nLastMDIChild, and then exits.

- Incrementing the value in the member nNumMDIChildren.

- Displaying the new MDI child window by sending the C++ message ShowWindow to that window.

The member function CMCloseChildren closes all the MDI child windows. The function performs the following tasks:

- Retrieves the address of the currently active MDI child window by invoking the member function MDIGetActive. This task assigns the retrieved address to the local pointer pChild.

- Assigns TRUE to the data member bExpressClose.

- Employs a while loop statement to close each MDI child window, starting with the currently active window. The first loop statement sends the C++ message MDIDestroy to the currently active MDI child window (accessed by the local pointer pChild). The second loop statement selects the next MDI child by invoking the function MDINext. The third loop statement invokes the function MDIGetActive to store the address of the new active child in the pointer pChild. When the loop closes all MDI child windows, the MDIGetActive function assigns NULL to the pChild pointer. This NULL value terminates the loop iteration.

■ Assigns FALSE to the bExpressClose data member.

The member function CMCountChildren displays the current number of MDI child windows in a message dialog box. The function first translates the value stored in the member nNumMDIChildren into a formatted string. Then the function displays that string in a message dialog box.

The member function OnChildDestroy responds to the messages sent by an MDI child window when it is destroyed. The function decrements the value stored in member nNumMDIChildren and returns 0.

The member functions CMCascadeChildren, CMTileChildren, and CMArrangeIcons simply invoke the inherited member functions MDICascade, MDITile, and MDIIconArrange, respectively.

Summary

This chapter presented the Multiple Document Interface (MDI), which is an interface standard in Windows. You learned about the following topics:

■ The fundamental features and components of an MDI-compliant application. These components include the MDI frame window, the invisible MDI client window, and the dynamically created MDI child window.

■ The basics of building an MDI application.

■ The CMDIFrameWnd class, which manages the MDI client window, the MDI child window, and the execution of the menu commands.

■ Building MDI frame windows as objects that are owned by the application and that own the MDI children.

■ The CMDIChildWnd class, which is used in building MDI child windows. This class handles operations such as activating, maximizing, restoring, and destroying MDI child windows.

Chapter 13

Using the Visual Basic Controls

Microsoft scored two hits with Visual Basic. First, the product was well received by the industry. Second, Microsoft made the Visual Basic (VBX) controls available to programming languages other than Visual Basic. Today, products such as Visual C++ and Borland C++ support VBX controls. Many software developers, including Borland, sell VBX controls. This chapter introduces you to programming VBX controls using the MFC library. You learn about the following topics:

- Using VBX control properties, methods, and events

- Declaring the CVbControl class

- Using AppWizard and ClassWizard support for VBX controls

- Installing VBX controls in App Studio

- Creating a simple spreadsheet application that uses the VBX grid control

Understanding VBX Control Properties, Methods, and Events

Visual Basic has succeeded in making Windows programming available for the masses. Although it is more limited than Visual C++, Visual Basic supports many common controls and operations. Programming in Visual Basic is centered around drawing controls on forms—similar to the view forms in Visual Basic. Using a toolbar (much like the one in App Studio), you draw the

III

Advanced Programming

controls on a form. These controls have predefined properties—similar to data members. These properties enable you to fine-tune the appearance and behavior of the Visual Basic controls. Initially, these controls perform practically nothing—they're just pretty little gizmos! Visual Basic, however, offers for each kind of control a set of events (that is, Windows messages) that the control can handle. Typically, you select one or two events to handle for each control. After you make your choice, Visual Basic creates empty procedures whose names are derived from the names of the control and the handled event. If you have a pushbutton whose control name is `QuitBtn`, for example, and you decide to handle the Click command, then the handler routine is `SUB QuitBtn_Click`.

To manipulate the Visual Basic controls, you use predefined functions, called *methods*, to perform this task. The list box control, for example, offers methods to add, delete, and search for items.

Declaring the *CVbControl* Class

The MFC library offers the class `CVbControl`, a descendant of class `CWnd`, to support VBX controls. Following is the declaration of the class `CVbControl`:

```
class CVbControl : public CWnd
{
  DECLARE_DYNAMIC(CVbControl)
// Constructors
public:
  CVbControl();

  BOOL Create(LPCSTR lpszWindowName, DWORD dwStyle,
    const RECT& rect, CWnd* pParentWnd, UINT nID,
    CFile* pFile = NULL, BOOL bAutoDelete = FALSE);


// Attributes
  // Property Access Routines
  BOOL SetNumProperty(int nPropIndex, LONG lValue, int index = 0);
  BOOL SetNumProperty(LPCSTR lpszPropName, LONG lValue,
                      int index = 0);

  BOOL SetFloatProperty(int nPropIndex, float value, int index = 0);
  BOOL SetFloatProperty(LPCSTR lpszPropName, float value,
                        int index = 0);

  BOOL SetStrProperty(int nPropIndex, LPCSTR lpszValue,
                      int index = 0);
```

```
    BOOL SetStrProperty(LPCSTR lpszPropName, LPCSTR lpszValue,
                        int index = 0);

    BOOL SetPictureProperty(int nPropIndex, HPIC hPic, int index = 0);
    BOOL SetPictureProperty(LPCSTR lpszPropName, HPIC hPic,
                            int index = 0);

    LONG GetNumProperty(int nPropIndex, int index = 0);
    LONG GetNumProperty(LPCSTR lpszPropName, int index = 0);

    float GetFloatProperty(int nPropIndex, int index = 0);
    float GetFloatProperty(LPCSTR lpszPropName, int index = 0);

    CString GetStrProperty(int nPropIndex, int index = 0);
    CString GetStrProperty(LPCSTR lpszPropName, int index = 0);

    HPIC GetPictureProperty(int nPropIndex, int index = 0);
    HPIC GetPictureProperty(LPCSTR lpszPropName, int index = 0);

    // Get the index of a property
    int GetPropIndex(LPCSTR lpszPropName) const;
    LPCSTR GetPropName(int nIndex) const;

    // Get the index of an Event
    int GetEventIndex(LPCSTR lpszEventName) const;
    LPCSTR GetEventName(int nIndex) const;

    // Class name of control
    LPCSTR GetVBXClass() const;

    // Class information
    int GetNumProps() const;
    int GetNumEvents() const;
    BOOL IsPropArray(int nIndex) const;

    UINT GetPropType(int nIndex) const;
    DWORD GetPropFlags(int nIndex) const;

    // Error reporting variable
    // Contains the VB error code returned by a control
    int m_nError;

// Operations
    // BASIC file number (channel) to CFile association

    static void PASCAL OpenChannel(CFile* pFile, WORD wChannel);
    static BOOL PASCAL CloseChannel(WORD wChannel);
    static CFile* PASCAL GetChannel(WORD wChannel);
    static void BeginNewVBHeap();

    void AddItem(LPCSTR lpszItem, LONG lIndex);
    void RemoveItem(LONG lIndex);
    void Refresh();
    void Move(RECT& rect);
```

```
// Implementation
public:
  virtual ~CVBControl();
#ifdef _DEBUG
  virtual void AssertValid() const;
  virtual void Dump(CDumpContext& dc) const;
#endif

  DWORD GetModelFlags();
  DWORD GetModelStyles();
  void ReferenceFile(BOOL bReference);
  static void EnableVBXFloat();

  static BOOL ParseWindowText(LPCSTR lpszWindowName,
                             CString& strFileName,
                             CString& strClassName,
                             CString& strCaption);

  HCTL GetHCTL();

  // Control Defined Structure -- Dangerous to use directly
  BYTE FAR* GetUserSpace();

  struct CRecreateStruct  // Implementation structure
  {
    char* pText;
    DWORD dwStyle;
    CRect rect;
    HWND hWndParent;
    UINT nControlID;
  };

  enum
  {
    TYPE_FROMVBX,          // Coming from VBX, assume proper type
    TYPE_INTEGER,          // int or LONG
    TYPE_REAL,             // float
    TYPE_STRING,
    TYPE_PICTURE
  };

  virtual LRESULT DefControlProc(UINT message, WPARAM wParam,
                                 LPARAM lParam);
  void Recreate(CRecreateStruct& rs);
  CVBControlModel* GetModel();

public:
  int GetStdPropIndex(int nStdID) const;
  BOOL SetPropertyWithType(int nPropIndex, WORD wType,
              LONG lValue, int index);
  LONG GetNumPropertyWithType(int nPropIndex, UINT nType, int index);
  HSZ GetStrProperty(int nPropIndex, int index, BOOL& bTemp);
  CString m_ctlName;            // Read only at run-time
```

```
    // Trace routine to allow one library version
    static void CDECL Trace(BOOL bFatal, UINT nFormatIndex, ...);
    void VBXAssertValid() const;     // non-virtual helper

    static BOOL EnableMemoryTracking(BOOL bTracking);

protected:

    static CVBControl* NEW();
    void DELETE();

    virtual BOOL OnChildNotify(UINT, WPARAM, LPARAM, LRESULT*);
    LRESULT CallControlProc(UINT message, WPARAM wParam, LPARAM lParam);

    BOOL CommonInit();
    void SetDefaultValue(int nPropIndex, BOOL bPreHwnd);

    BOOL SetStdProp(WORD wPropId, WORD wType, LONG lValue);
    LONG GetStdNumProp(WORD wPropId);
    CString GetStdStrProp(WORD wPropId);

    BOOL SetFontProperty(WORD wPropId, LONG lData);
    void BuildCurFont(HDC hDC, HFONT hCurFont, LOGFONT& logFont);
    LONG GetNumFontProperty(WORD wPropId);
    WORD GetCharSet(HDC hDC, LPCSTR lpFaceName);

    virtual LRESULT DefWindowProc(UINT message, WPARAM wParam,
                                  LPARAM lParam);
    virtual void PostNcDestroy();

    void FireMouseEvent(WORD event, WORD wButton, WPARAM wParam,
                        LPARAM lParam);
    BOOL CreateAndSetFont(LPLOGFONT lplf);

    BOOL LoadProperties(CFile* pFile, BOOL bPreHwnd);
    BOOL LoadProp(int nPropIndex, CFile* pFile);
    BOOL LoadPropData(int nPropIndex, CFile* pFile);

    BOOL IsPropDefault(int nPropIndex);

    CVBControlModel* LoadControl(LPCSTR lpszFileName,
                                 LPCSTR lpszControlName);
    afx_msg void OnVBXLoaded();

    void AllocateHCTL(size_t nSize);
    void DeallocateHCTL();

    static int ConvertFontSizeToTwips(LONG lFontSize);
    // This actually returns a float masquerading as a long
    static LONG ConvertTwipsToFontSize(int nTwips);

protected:
  CVBControlModel* m_pModel;
```

III

Advanced Programming

```
        BOOL m_bRecreating;          // Do not destroy on this NCDestroy
        BOOL m_bAutoDelete;          // TRUE if automatically created
        BOOL m_bInPostNcDestroy;     // TRUE if deleting from Destroy
        BOOL m_bLoading;             // TRUE if loading properties from
                                     // formfile
        int m_nCursorID;

        // variables for stack overrun protection
        UINT m_nInitialStack;        // SP when control recieved first message
        UINT m_nRecursionLevel;      // Level of control proc recursion
        BOOL m_bStackFault;          // TRUE if stack fault hit
        UINT m_nFaultRecurse;        // level at which stack faulted

        HBRUSH m_hbrBkgnd;           // brush used in WM_CTLCOLOR
        HFONT m_hFontCreated;        // Font created by control
        HCURSOR m_hcurMouse;
        HCTL m_hCtl;                 // Control handle
        COLORREF m_clrBkgnd;
        COLORREF m_clrFore;
        CRect m_rectCreate;          // Created Size
        CString m_strTag;

        // friends required for VB API access
        friend LRESULT CALLBACK AFX_EXPORT _AfxVBWndProc(HWND hWnd,
                UINT msg, WPARAM wParam, LPARAM lParam);
        friend LRESULT CALLBACK AFX_EXPORT _AfxVBProxyProc(HWND hWnd,
                UINT msg, WPARAM wParam, LPARAM lParam);
        friend WORD CALLBACK AFX_EXPORT _AfxVBFireEvent(HCTL hControl,
                WORD idEvent, LPVOID lpParams);
        friend WORD CALLBACK AFX_EXPORT _AfxVBRecreateControlHwnd(
                HCTL hControl);

        DECLARE_MESSAGE_MAP()

        /////////////////////
        // Implementation
        // These APIs cannot be referenced by applications
public:
    DWORD Save(CFile* pFile);
    BOOL Load(CFile* pData);

protected:
    BOOL m_bCreatedInDesignMode;
    BOOL m_bVisible;

    friend class CVBPopupWnd;

    BOOL SaveProperties(CFile* pFile, BOOL bPreHwnd);
    BOOL SaveProp(int nPropIndex, CFile* pFile);
    BOOL SavePropData(int nPropIndex, CFile* pFile);
    LONG InitPropPopup(WPARAM wParam, LPARAM lParam);
    void DoPictureDlg(int m_nPropId);
    void DoColorDlg(int m_nPropId);
    void DoFontDlg(int m_nPropId);
    void FillList(CListBox* pLB, LPCSTR lpszEnumList);
};
```

The declaration of class CVbControl indicates that this versatile class is capable of handling VBX controls that have not yet been written. The various member functions permit the class to handle properties that are integers, floating-point, strings, and bitmaps. The public member functions serve to create VBX controls, access control properties, manipulate attributes, apply special methods to the VBX controls, and perform special file I/O with the VBX controls. The example in this chapter focuses on the following member functions, which access the various properties of a VBX control:

- The overloaded member function GetFloatProperty obtains the floating-point value of the property specified by index or by name. The parameter index (common to both overloaded versions of the function) enables you to specify the index for a control array (Visual Basic enables you to declare an array of control, whose members are accessed using indices).

- The overloaded member function GetNumProperty obtains the long integer value of the property specified by index or by name. The parameter index (common to both overloaded versions of the function) enables you to specify the index for a control array.

- The overloaded member function GetPictureProperty obtains the picture handle of the property specified by index or by name. The parameter index (common to both overloaded versions of the function) enables you to specify the index for a control array.

- The overloaded member function GetStrProperty obtains the string value of the property specified by index or by name. The parameter index (common to both overloaded versions of the function) enables you to specify the index for a control array.

- The overloaded member function SetFloatProperty assigns the floating-point value to the property specified by index or by name. The parameter index (common to both overloaded versions of the function) enables you to specify the index for a control array.

- The overloaded member function SetNumProperty assigns the long integer value to the property specified by index or by name. The parameter index (common to both overloaded versions of the function) enables you to specify the index for a control array.

- The overloaded member function `SetPictureProperty` assigns the picture handle to the property specified by index or by name. The parameter index (common to both overloaded versions of the function) enables you to specify the index for a control array.

- The overloaded member function `SetStrProperty` assigns the string value to the property specified by index or by name. The parameter index (common to both overloaded versions of the function) enables you to specify the index for a control array.

Using AppWizard and ClassWizard Support for VBX Controls

Programming VBX controls requires some extra effort compared to programming standard controls. This effort includes using special VBX support libraries, using specific functions to set up the message mapping for the VBX control, and so on. The good news is that the AppWizard and ClassWizard utilities perform a good part of the systematic preparation for using VBX controls. This preparation enables you to focus on creating the resources that use the VBX controls and on inserting the code to animate these controls.

> **Note**
>
> When you use AppWizard to create a program that uses one or more VBX controls, make sure that you check the Custom VBX Controls box in the Options dialog box. Checking the control signals the AppWizard utility to insert the code that prepares for using VBX controls.

Installing VBX Controls in App Studio

App Studio complements the AppWizard and ClassWizard utilities in the area of VBX control just as it complements them in Visual C++ as a whole. The App Studio offers the Install Controls menu command (in the File menu) to install and remove VBX controls. This command displays the Install Controls dialog box, as shown in Figure 13.1. This dialog box is essentially a superset of the com-mon Open File dialog box; it contains the following controls:

- *Control Filename edit box.* Displays either the wild card for the files to select or the name of the currently selected .VBX file (hence, the name VBX controls).

- *Unlabeled list box.* Lists the matching .VBX files.

- *Drives drop-down combo box.* Enables you to select other drives.

- *Directories list box.* Shows the current directory along with its parent and child directories.

- *Static text control.* States the current directory.

- *Installed Files list box.* Lists the currently installed VBX controls.

- *Install pushbutton.* Enables you to install the VBX control from the currently selected .VBX file.

- *Remove pushbutton.* Enables you to delete the currently selected VBX control.

- *OK, Cancel, and Help pushbuttons.* Perform their typical operations.

Figure 13.1 shows that the list of installed VBX controls contains the GRID control, which I use in a sample program in the next section. If the VBX grid control is not yet installed in your system, install it now. The file GRID.VBX usually is located in the directory \WINDOWS\SYSTEM.

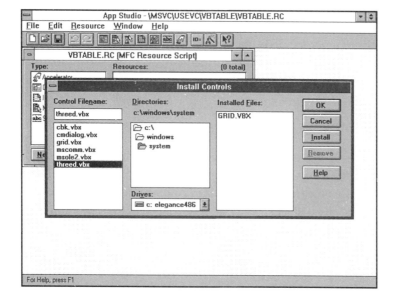

Figure 13.1

The Install Controls dialog box.

III

Advanced Programming

Using the Grid VBX Control

The program VBTABLE.EXE, presented in this section, uses the VBX grid control to emulate a numerical spreadsheet—each cell contains the image of a number. This control supports a form of spreadsheet that stores text. Figure 13.2 shows a sample session with the VBTABLE.EXE program.

Figure 13.2

A session with the VBTABLE.EXE spreadsheet program.

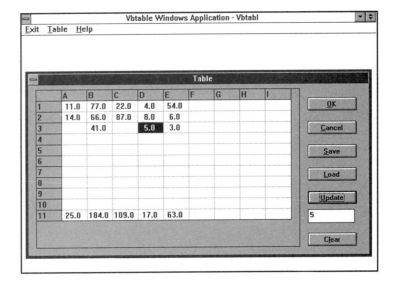

About the VBTABLE.EXE Program

The VBTABLE.EXE program offers a menu system with Exit, Table, and Help menus. The Table menu has three commands: Table1, Table2, and Table3. Thus, the program supports not one, but three spreadsheets (which I also call tables). Each command in the Table menu invokes the modal Table dialog box with a different set of data. Initially, each TableX command invokes an empty Table dialog box.

The Table dialog box contains the following controls:

- *VBX grid control.* Contains 10 columns (9 of which are labeled A through I) and 12 rows (11 of which are labeled 1 through 11). The VBX grid control has a single fixed column and a single fixed row that are used to label the other rows and columns. The bottom row shows the summations of the rows above it.

- *Edit box.* Enables you to enter a new value for the currently selected cell in the VBX grid control.

- *Update pushbutton.* Updates the currently selected cell with the value in the edit box.

- *Clear pushbutton.* Clears the contents of the VBX grid control.

- *Save pushbutton.* Stores the numbers whose string images appear in the VBX grid control. The program stores the data in files TABLE1.DAT, TABLE2.DAT, and TABLE3.DAT when you select the menu commands Table1, Table2, and Table3, respectively.

- *Load pushbutton.* Loads the numbers used to fill the VBX grid control. The program recalls the data from files TABLE1.DAT, TABLE2.DAT, and TABLE3.DAT when you select the menu commands Table1, Table2, and Table3, respectively. The program ignores a request to load a nonexistent TABLEx.DAT file.

- *OK and Cancel pushbuttons.*

The Save and Load pushbuttons override the effect of the Cancel pushbutton. After you commit to saving or loading data from the VBX grid control, you also commit to accepting the contents of the grid.

I coded the application to avoid displaying 0 in the cells of the VBX grid control. This design enables you to locate nonzero values quickly in various cells.

The Relevant Grid Properties and Methods

The VBX grid control has many properties. Table 13.1 shows the properties that are relevant to the VBTABLE.EXE program. The properties Row and Col specify the currently selected grid cell and can be altered at run time. By contrast, the properties Rows and Cols are fixed by App Studio during the creation of the VBX grid control. The Text property enables you to access the text in the selected cell (determined by the current values of the Row and Col properties). The CellSelected property is a Boolean flag, which tells you whether a grid cell is selected.

The relevant event (that is, Visual Basic control message) is SelChange, which is sent by the grid when you select a new cell. This event notifies the host dialog box to update the summation of the column that contains the previously selected cell.

Table 13.1 Relevant Properties for the VBX Grid Control

Property	Type	Comments
Col	Numeric	Current column
Cols	Numeric	Total number of columns
Row	Numeric	Current row
Rows	Numeric	Total number of rows
Text	String	Text of the selected VBX grid cell
CellSelected	Numeric	−1 if a cell is selected; otherwise, 0

Note

The properties Rows and Cols can be set only in App Studio.

How to Build the VBTABLE.EXE Program

Building the VBTABLE.EXE program involves adding manual code to supplement using the AppWizard, App Studio, and ClassWizard utilities. This section presents the source code files that are directly mentioned in the stages of building and customizing the application. The next section presents the relevant source code files that are generated by AppWizard but require no editing.

To build VBTABLE.EXE, follow these steps:

1. Invoke the AppWizard utility to create the source code files for project VBTABLE. The directory for this project is a child of the directory \MSVC\USEVC.

2. Invoke the Options dialog box and clear the check boxes for the MDI, toolbar, and print-related features. Check the Custom VBX Support box and then close the Options dialog box.

3. Invoke the Classes dialog box and edit the names of the classes that contain the word *table*. Change the lowercase *t* in the word *table* into an uppercase *T*. Then close the Classes dialog box.

4. Click the OK pushbutton in the MFC AppWizard dialog box. The AppWizard utility displays the New Application Information dialog box, as shown in Figure 13.3.

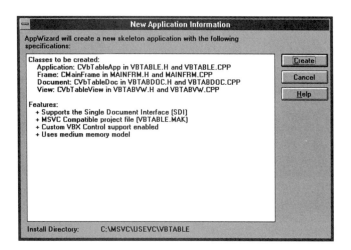

Figure 13.3
The New Application Information dialog box for the VBTABLE.EXE program.

5. Invoke the App Studio utility from the Visual Workbench. If you missed installing the GRID control, do so now (see "Installing VBX Controls in App Studio" earlier in this chapter).

6. Edit the menu system to make it look like the one shown in Figure 13.4.

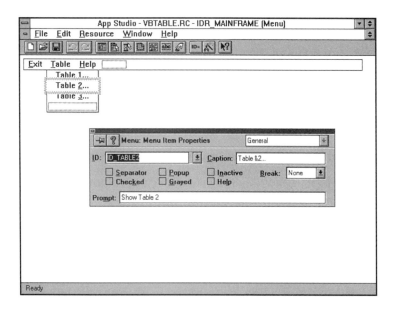

Figure 13.4
The menu resource for the VBTABLE project.

III

Advanced Programming

Perform the following edits:

■ Replace the pop-up File menu with the nonpop-up Exit menu. Assign the ID ID_APP_EXIT to this selection.

- Change the caption of the Edit menu to *Table*.

- Delete the original commands from the Edit menu.

- Insert the menu commands Table1, Table2, and Table3 into the Table menu. Use the IDs ID_TABLE1, ID_TABLE2, and ID_TABLE3, respectively, for these commands.

- Save the menu resource and exit back to the main resource list.

7. Select the dialog resources and create the new dialog resource with the caption *Table* and with the ID IDD_TABLE_DLG. Figure 13.5 shows the App Studio utility after the various controls on the dialog box were pasted. Perform the following edits:

   - Enlarge the size of the dialog box.

   - Insert the VBX grid control. Its Toolbox icon appears as a tiny grid. Set the Cols and Rows properties to 10 and 12, respectively. Figure 13.5 shows the Properties dialog box for the VBX grid control; the figure shows the columns that list the various properties of the VBX grid control. Assign the ID IDC_TABLE to the grid control.

   - Insert four pushbuttons and label them Update, Clear, Save, and Load. The IDs for these controls are IDC_UPDATE_BTN, IDC_CLEAR_BTN, IDC_SAVE_BTN, and IDC_LOAD_BTN, respectively. Check the default pushbutton box (in the Properties dialog box) for the Update pushbutton.

   - Insert an edit box and assign it the ID IDC_UPDATE_BOX.

   - Save the dialog box resource and exit App Studio.

Listing 13.1 shows the source code for the RESOURCE.H header file. The listing also shows the definitions of the identifiers used in the menu system and in the Table dialog box.

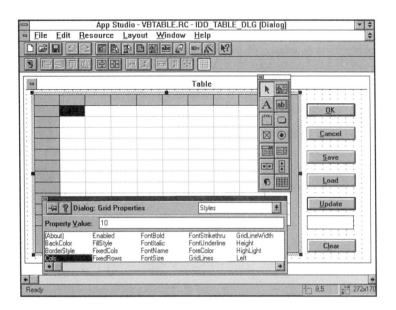

Figure 13.5
The App Studio
utility with the
various controls
on the dialog box.

Listing 13.1 Source Code for the RESOURCE.H Header File

```
//{{NO_DEPENDENCIES}}
// App Studio generated include file.
// Used by VBTABLE.RC
//
#define IDR_MAINFRAME                   2
#define IDC_UPDATE_BTN                  3
#define IDC_LOAD_BTN                    4
#define IDC_SAVE_BTN                    5
#define IDC_CLEAR_BTN                   6
#define IDD_ABOUTBOX                    100
#define IDD_TABLE_DLG                   102
#define IDC_UPDATE_BOX                  1000
#define IDC_TABLE                       1001
#define ID_TABLE1                       32775
#define ID_TABLE2                       32776
#define ID_TABLE3                       32777

// Next default values for new objects
//
#ifdef APSTUDIO_INVOKED
#ifndef APSTUDIO_READONLY_SYMBOLS

#define _APS_NEXT_RESOURCE_VALUE        104
#define _APS_NEXT_COMMAND_VALUE         32778
#define _APS_NEXT_CONTROL_VALUE         1003
#define _APS_NEXT_SYMED_VALUE           101
#endif
#endif
```

Listing 13.2 shows the partial script of the VBTABLE.RC resource file.

Listing 13.2 Partial Script of the VBTABLE.RC Resource File

```
//Microsoft App Studio generated resource script.
//
#include "resource.h"

#define APSTUDIO_READONLY_SYMBOLS
.
.
.
/////////////////////////////////////////////////////////////////
//
// Menu
//

IDR_MAINFRAME MENU PRELOAD DISCARDABLE
BEGIN
    MENUITEM "&Exit",                       ID_APP_EXIT
    POPUP "&Table"
    BEGIN
        MENUITEM "Table &1...",             ID_TABLE1
        MENUITEM "Table &2...",             ID_TABLE2
        MENUITEM "Table &3...",             ID_TABLE3
    END
    POPUP "&Help"
    BEGIN
        MENUITEM "&About VbTable...",       ID_APP_ABOUT
    END
END
.
.
.
/////////////////////////////////////////////////////////////////
//
// Dialog
//

IDD_ABOUTBOX DIALOG DISCARDABLE  34, 22, 217, 55
STYLE DS_MODALFRAME ¦ WS_POPUP ¦ WS_CAPTION ¦ WS_SYSMENU
CAPTION "About VbTable"
FONT 8, "MS Sans Serif"
BEGIN
    ICON            IDR_MAINFRAME,IDC_STATIC,11,17,18,20
    LTEXT           "VbTable Application Version 1.0",
                    IDC_STATIC,40,10,119,8
    LTEXT           "Copyright \251 1994",IDC_STATIC,40,25,119,8
    DEFPUSHBUTTON   "OK",IDOK,176,6,32,14,WS_GROUP
END

IDD_TABLE_DLG DIALOG DISCARDABLE  0, 0, 351, 183
STYLE DS_MODALFRAME ¦ WS_POPUP ¦ WS_VISIBLE ¦ WS_CAPTION ¦ WS_SYSMENU
CAPTION "Table"
FONT 8, "MS Sans Serif"
```

```
BEGIN
    DEFPUSHBUTTON   "&OK",IDOK,288,15,50,14
    PUSHBUTTON      "&Cancel",IDCANCEL,288,40,50,14
    DEFPUSHBUTTON   "&Update",IDC_UPDATE_BTN,288,115,50,14
    EDITTEXT        IDC_UPDATE_BOX,288,135,48,15,ES_AUTOHSCROLL
    CONTROL         "GRID.VBX;Grid;Grid1",IDC_TABLE,"VBControl",
                    WS_CLIPSIBLINGS | WS_BORDER | WS_TABSTOP,8,5,272,170
    PUSHBUTTON      "&Load",IDC_LOAD_BTN,288,90,50,14
    PUSHBUTTON      "&Save",IDC_SAVE_BTN,288,65,50,14
    PUSHBUTTON      "C&lear",IDC_CLEAR_BTN,288,160,50,14
END
.
.
.
#endif    // not APSTUDIO_INVOKED
```

Listing 13.2 shows the resources for the menu system and the
IDD_TABLE_DLG dialog resource. Notice that the VBX grid control has the
following resource statement:

```
CONTROL         "GRID.VBX;Grid;Grid1",IDC_TABLE,"VBControl",
                WS_CLIPSIBLINGS | WS_BORDER | WS_TABSTOP,8,5,272,170
```

The first literal string in the preceding statement specifies the VBX control filename, type, and default name. The second literal string indicates
that the control is a VBX control.

8. Invoke the ClassWizard utility to create a class for the dialog box containing the VBX grid control. Specify the name **CVbTblDlg** for the
   new dialog box.

9. Use the ClassWizard utility to add the member functions OnTable1,
   OnTable2, and OnTable3 to the view class CVbTableView. These member
   functions handle the Windows command messages ID_TABLE1,
   ID_TABLE2, and ID_TABLE3, respectively.

10. Manually insert the following code in the VBTABVW.H header file:

    ■ Insert the #include directive to include the header file
      VBTABDOC.H.

    ■ The #ifndef _VBTABVW_H_ and #define _VBTABVW_H_ directives,
      which protect the header file declarations from being processed
      twice by the compiler. Also add the #endif directive at the end of
      the file.

III

Advanced Programming

■ Insert the declarations of the constants MAX_TABLES, MAX_ROWS, and MAX_COLS. You must update the values assigned to these constants if you increase the number of the menu commands in the Table menu or expand the size of the VBX grid control.

■ The data member m_dData, which is a three-dimensional array of floating-point numbers. This member stores the data for the three versions of the Table dialog box (it's really the same dialog box invoked by three different menu commands, each with its own data).

Listing 13.3 shows the source code for the VBTABVW.H header file after the preceding changes have been made. The file also reflects the member functions OnTableX, which were inserted in step 9 by ClassWizard.

Listing 13.3 Source Code for the VBTABVW.H Header File

```
// vbtabvw.h : interface of the CVbTableView class
//
/////////////////////////////////////////////////////////////////

#ifndef _VBTABVW_H_
#define _VBTABVW_H_

#include "vbtabdoc.h"

// these constants must conform to the number of tables, rows,
// and columns in each table
const MAX_TABLES = 3;
const MAX_ROWS = 12;
const MAX_COLS = 10;

class CVbTableView : public CView
{
protected: // create from serialization only
    CVbTableView();
    DECLARE_DYNCREATE(CVbTableView)

// Attributes
public:
    CVbTableDoc* GetDocument();
    double m_dData[MAX_TABLES][MAX_ROWS][MAX_COLS];
// Operations
public:

// Implementation
public:
    virtual ~CVbTableView();
    virtual void OnDraw(CDC* pDC);  // overridden to draw this view
```

```
#ifdef _DEBUG
    virtual void AssertValid() const;
    virtual void Dump(CDumpContext& dc) const;
#endif

protected:

// Generated message map functions
protected:
    //{{AFX_MSG(CVbTableView)
    afx_msg void OnTable1();
    afx_msg void OnTable2();
    afx_msg void OnTable3();
    //}}AFX_MSG
    DECLARE_MESSAGE_MAP()
};

#ifndef _DEBUG  // debug version in vbtabvw.cpp
inline CVbTableDoc* CVbTableView::GetDocument()
    { return (CVbTableDoc*)m_pDocument; }
#endif

/////////////////////////////////////////////////////////////////////

#endif
```

11. Use the ClassWizard to add the message handling member functions for class CVbTblDlg, as shown in Table 13.2.

Table 13.2 Message-Handling Member Functions for the CVbTblDlg Class		
Object ID	**Message Handled**	**Member Function**
CVbTblDlg	WM_INITDIALOG	OnInitDialog
IDC_TABLE	VBN_SELCHANGE	OnSelChangeTable
IDC_UPDATE_BTN	BN_CLICKED	OnUpdateBtn
IDC_CLEAR_BTN	BN_CLICKED	OnClearBtn
IDC_SAVE_BTN	BN_CLICKED	OnSaveBtn
IDC_LOAD_BTN	BN_CLICKED	OnLoadBtn
IDCANCEL	BN_CLICKED	OnCancel
IDOK	BN_CLICKED	OnOK

III

Advanced Programming

12. Use the ClassWizard utility to add two new data members to the dialog box class CVbTblDlg. Table 13.3 shows these new data members.

Table 13.3	New Data Members of the Dialog Box Class *CVbTblDlg*		
Control ID	**Member Name**	**Property**	**Member Type**
IDC_UPDATE_BOX	m_cellCopy	Value	CString
IDC_TABLE	m_pVbTable	Control	CVBControl

13. Manually insert into (or modify in) the header file VBTBLDLG.H the following members in the declaration of class CVbTblDlg:

- The parameter int nIndex, which is inserted before the pParent parameter in the constructor.

- The data member m_pView, which is the pointer to the view that owns the dialog box. This pointer allows the dialog box to access the view's data member m_dData to store and recall the grid's data.

- The data member m_nIndex, which stores the index of the dialog box version. The dialog box instances use this member to access the matrix in the view's member m_dData.

- The member function CalcSums, which sums up the numbers in the grid column specified by parameter lCellIndex. This member function performs a smart update of the sums by limiting itself to updating only one column—the one that contains the previously selected cell.

In addition, insert the #include directive to include the header file VBTABDVW.H. Listing 13.4 shows the source code for the VBTBLDLG.H header file after the members listed in step 13 are inserted. The listing also shows the member functions OnInitDialog, OnSelChange, OnUpdateBtn, OnCancel, OnOK, OnClearBtn, OnLoadBtn, and OnSaveBtn, which are inserted by ClassWizard.

Listing 13.4 Source Code for the VBTBLDLG.H Header File

```
// vbtbldlg.h : header file
//

//////////////////////////////////////////////////////////////////
// CVbTblDlg dialog

#include "vbtabvw.h"

class CVbTblDlg : public CDialog
{
// Construction
public:
    CVbTblDlg(int nIndex, CWnd* pParent = NULL);

// Dialog Data
    CVbTableView* m_pView;
    int m_nIndex;
    //{{AFX_DATA(CVbTblDlg)
    enum { IDD = IDD_TABLE_DLG };
    CVBControl* m_pVbTable;
    CString m_cellCopy;
    //}}AFX_DATA

// Implementation
protected:
    virtual void DoDataExchange(CDataExchange* pDX);//DDX/DDV support
    // the following member was manually added
    void CalcSums(long lCellIndex);
    // Generated message map functions
    //{{AFX_MSG(CVbTblDlg)
    virtual BOOL OnInitDialog();
    afx_msg void OnSelchangeTable(UINT, int, CWnd*, LPVOID);
    afx_msg void OnUpdateBtn();
    virtual void OnCancel();
    virtual void OnOK();
     afx_msg void OnClearBtn();
     afx_msg void OnLoadBtn();
     afx_msg void OnSaveBtn();
     //}}AFX_MSG
    DECLARE_MESSAGE_MAP()
};
```

14. Manually insert #include directives to include the header files FSTREAM.H, STDIO.H, STDLIB.H, and STRING.H. In addition, insert the code for the member functions CVbTblDlg, OnInitDialog, OnSelChange, OnUpdateBtn, OnCancel, OnOK, OnClearBtn, OnLoadBtn, and OnSaveBtn.

I added the declarations for the constants MaxStringLen, FIRST_COL, FIRST_ROW, and FILES. The constant FILES accesses the names of the data file for each command in the Table menu.

III

Advanced Programming

Listing 13.5 shows the code for the member functions and other statements that I added manually.

Listing 13.5 Source Code for the VBTBLDLG.CPP Implementation File

```
// vbtbldlg.cpp : implementation file
//

#include "stdafx.h"
#include "vbtable.h"
#include "vbtbldlg.h"

#include <fstream.h>
#include <stdio.h>
#include <stdlib.h>
#include <string.h>

#ifdef _DEBUG
#undef THIS_FILE
static char BASED_CODE THIS_FILE[] = __FILE__;
#endif

const MaxStringLen = 40;
const long FIRST_COL = 1;
const long FIRST_ROW = 1;
const char* FILES[3] = { "table1.dat", "table2.dat", "table3.dat" };

/////////////////////////////////////////////////////////////////////
// CVbTblDlg dialog


CVbTblDlg::CVbTblDlg(int nIndex, CWnd* pParent /*=NULL*/)
    : CDialog(CVbTblDlg::IDD, pParent)
{
    m_pView = (CVbTableView*)pParent;
    m_nIndex = nIndex;
    //{{AFX_DATA_INIT(CVbTblDlg)
    m_pVbTable = NULL;
    m_cellCopy = "";
    //}}AFX_DATA_INIT
}

void CVbTblDlg::DoDataExchange(CDataExchange* pDX)
{
    CDialog::DoDataExchange(pDX);
    //{{AFX_DATA_MAP(CVbTblDlg)
    DDX_VBControl(pDX, IDC_TABLE, m_pVbTable);
    DDX_Text(pDX, IDC_UPDATE_BOX, m_cellCopy);
    //}}AFX_DATA_MAP
}

BEGIN_MESSAGE_MAP(CVbTblDlg, CDialog)
    //{{AFX_MSG_MAP(CVbTblDlg)
    ON_VBXEVENT(VBN_SELCHANGE, IDC_TABLE, OnSelchangeTable)
```

```
    ON_BN_CLICKED(IDC_UPDATE_BTN, OnUpdateBtn)
    ON_BN_CLICKED(IDC_CLEAR_BTN, OnClearBtn)
    ON_BN_CLICKED(IDC_LOAD_BTN, OnLoadBtn)
    ON_BN_CLICKED(IDC_SAVE_BTN, OnSaveBtn)
    //}}AFX_MSG_MAP
END_MESSAGE_MAP()


/////////////////////////////////////////////////////////////////
// CVbTblDlg message handlers

BOOL CVbTblDlg::OnInitDialog()
{
  CDialog::OnInitDialog();
  // manually added code starts here
  char szLabel[10];
  long MaxRows = m_pVbTable->GetNumProperty("Rows");
  long MaxCols = m_pVbTable->GetNumProperty("Cols");
  char szStr[MaxStringLen+1];

  // select column 0
  m_pVbTable->SetNumProperty("Col", 0L);
  // label rows 1 through MaxRows-1 of column 0
  for (long row = FIRST_ROW; row < MaxRows; row++) {
    m_pVbTable->SetNumProperty("Row", row);
    sprintf(szLabel, "%ld", row);
    m_pVbTable->SetStrProperty("Text", szLabel);
  }

  // reset labeling string
  strcpy(szLabel, "A");
  // select row 0
  m_pVbTable->SetNumProperty("Row", 0L);
  // label columns 1 through MaxCols-1 of row 0
  for (long col = FIRST_COL; col < MaxCols; col++) {
    m_pVbTable->SetNumProperty("Col", col);
    m_pVbTable->SetStrProperty("Text", LPSTR(szLabel));
    szLabel[0]++;
  }

  // restore table values
  for (col = FIRST_COL; col < MaxCols; col++) {
    m_pVbTable->SetNumProperty("Col", col);
    for (row = FIRST_ROW; row < MaxRows; row++) {
      m_pVbTable->SetNumProperty("Row", row);
      if (m_pView->m_dData[m_nIndex][row][col] != 0.0) {
        sprintf(szStr, "%5.1lf",
                m_pView->m_dData[m_nIndex][row][col]);
        m_pVbTable->SetStrProperty("Text", szStr);
      }
    }
  }

      // select the first unfixed cell
      m_pVbTable->SetNumProperty("Row", FIRST_ROW);
```

III

Advanced Programming

(continues)

Listing 13.5 Continued

```
    m_pVbTable->SetNumProperty("Col", FIRST_COL);
    // get a copy of the selected cell
    m_cellCopy = m_pVbTable->GetStrProperty("Text");
    // place the copy of the selected cell in the edit box
    UpdateData(FALSE);
    // manually added code ends here
    return TRUE;   // return TRUE  unless you set the focus
                   // to a control
}

void CVbTblDlg::OnSelchangeTable(UINT, int, CWnd*, LPVOID)
{
    if (m_pVbTable) {
        m_cellCopy = m_pVbTable->GetStrProperty("Text");
        UpdateData(FALSE); // update edit box
        // select the edit box
        GotoDlgCtrl(GetDlgItem(IDC_UPDATE_BOX));
    }
}

void CVbTblDlg::OnUpdateBtn()
{
    double x;
    long row, col;
    char szStr[MaxStringLen+1];

    if (m_pVbTable->GetNumProperty("CellSelected") == 0)
        return;

    UpdateData(TRUE);
    x = atof(m_cellCopy);
    sprintf(szStr, "%5.1lf", x);

    // store selected cell
    col = m_pVbTable->GetNumProperty("Col");
    row = m_pVbTable->GetNumProperty("Row");

    // store new value in selected cell
    m_pVbTable->SetStrProperty("Text", szStr);
    CalcSums(col); // update sums

    // reselect the last cell
    m_pVbTable->SetNumProperty("Col", col);
    m_pVbTable->SetNumProperty("Row", row);
}

void CVbTblDlg::OnCancel()
{
```

```
      CDialog::OnCancel();
}

void CVbTblDlg::OnOK()
{
  long MaxRows = m_pVbTable->GetNumProperty("Rows");
  long MaxCols = m_pVbTable->GetNumProperty("Cols");

  // store the values of the table's cell in the
  // array m_pView->m_dData
  for (long col = FIRST_COL; col < MaxCols; col++) {
    m_pVbTable->SetNumProperty("Col", col);
    for (long row = FIRST_ROW; row < MaxRows; row++) {
      m_pVbTable->SetNumProperty("Row", row);
      m_pView->m_dData[m_nIndex][row][col] =
        atof(m_pVbTable->GetStrProperty("Text"));
    }
  }
  CDialog::OnOK();
}

void CVbTblDlg::CalcSums(long lColIndex)
{
  long MaxRows = m_pVbTable->GetNumProperty("Rows");
  long WorkRows = MaxRows - 1;
  double sumCol;
  char szStr[MaxStringLen+1];

  m_pVbTable->SetNumProperty("Col", lColIndex);
  sumCol = 0.0;
  for (long row = FIRST_ROW; row < WorkRows; row++) {
    m_pVbTable->SetNumProperty("Row", row);
    sumCol += atof(m_pVbTable->GetStrProperty("Text"));
  }
  sprintf(szStr, "%5.1lf", sumCol);
  m_pVbTable->SetNumProperty("Row", WorkRows);
  m_pVbTable->SetStrProperty("Text", szStr);
}
void CVbTblDlg::OnClearBtn()
{
  long MaxRows = m_pVbTable->GetNumProperty("Rows");
  long MaxCols = m_pVbTable->GetNumProperty("Cols");

  for (long col = 1; col < MaxCols; col++) {
    m_pVbTable->SetNumProperty("Col", col);
    for (long row = 1; row < MaxRows; row++) {
      m_pVbTable->SetNumProperty("Row", row);
      m_pVbTable->SetStrProperty("Text", "");
    }
  }
```

Listing 13.5 Continued

```cpp
    // select the first unfixed cell
    m_pVbTable->SetNumProperty("Row", FIRST_ROW);
    m_pVbTable->SetNumProperty("Col", FIRST_COL);
    // get a copy of the selected cell
    m_cellCopy = m_pVbTable->GetStrProperty("Text");
    // place the copy of the selected cell in the edit box
    UpdateData(FALSE);
}

void CVbTblDlg::OnLoadBtn()
{
  fstream f;
  long MaxRows = m_pVbTable->GetNumProperty("Rows");
  long MaxCols = m_pVbTable->GetNumProperty("Cols");
  char szStr[MaxStringLen+1];

  f.open(FILES[m_nIndex], ios::in | ios::binary);

  if (f.good) {
    // read array from input stream
    f.read((unsigned char*)&m_pView->m_dData[m_nIndex],
           sizeof(m_pView->m_dData) / MAX_TABLES);
    f.close();

    // restore table values
    for (long col = FIRST_COL; col < MaxCols; col++) {
      m_pVbTable->SetNumProperty("Col", col);
      for (long row = FIRST_ROW; row < MaxRows; row++) {
        m_pVbTable->SetNumProperty("Row", row);
        if (m_pView->m_dData[m_nIndex][row][col] != 0.0) {
          sprintf(szStr, "%5.1lf",
                  m_pView->m_dData[m_nIndex][row][col]);
          m_pVbTable->SetStrProperty("Text", szStr);
        }
      }
    }
  }
  else
    MessageBox("Cannot load table", "File I/O Error",
               MB_OK | MB_ICONEXCLAMATION);
}

void CVbTblDlg::OnSaveBtn()
{
  fstream f;
  long MaxRows = m_pVbTable->GetNumProperty("Rows");
  long MaxCols = m_pVbTable->GetNumProperty("Cols");

  f.open(FILES[m_nIndex], ios::out | ios::binary);

  if (f.good) {
    // store the values of the table's cell in the
    // array m_pView->m_dData
```

```
    for (long col = FIRST_COL; col < MaxCols; col++) {
      m_pVbTable->SetNumProperty("Col", col);
      for (long row = FIRST_ROW; row < MaxRows; row++) {
        m_pVbTable->SetNumProperty("Row", row);
        m_pView->m_dData[m_nIndex][row][col] =
          atof(m_pVbTable->GetStrProperty("Text"));
      }
    }

    // write array to output stream
    f.write((const unsigned char*)&m_pView->m_dData[m_nIndex],
            sizeof(m_pView->m_dData) / MAX_TABLES);
    f.close();
  }
  else
    MessageBox("Cannot save table", "File I/O Error",
               MB_OK | MB_ICONEXCLAMATION);
}
```

Notice that the listing contains the message map, which links the various messages with member functions. Of particular interest is the macro ON_VBXEVENT, which has three arguments: the special VBN_SELCHANGE notification message, the ID of the VBX grid, and the handler member function OnSelChangeTable.

Listing 13.5 contains the statements that define the following members:

■ The constructor, which performs the following tasks:

  • Assigns the parameter pParent to the member m_pView. This assignment uses a typecast to allow member m_pView access to the view's member m_dData.

  • Assigns the value of the parameter nIndex to the data member m_nIndex.

  • Assigns NULL to the member m_pVbTable. The ClassWizard inserted this statement.

  • Assigns an empty string to the member m_cellCopy. The ClassWizard also inserted this statement.

■ The member function DoDataExchange, which was inserted by ClassWizard. It swaps data between the Table dialog box controls and the data members m_pVbTable and m_cellCopy. Notice that the function uses the DDX_VBControl function to swap data with a VBX control.

- The member function `OnInitDialog`, which initializes the dialog box mainly by preparing the VBX grid control. The function performs the following tasks:

  - Sets the single-letter labels for column 0.

  - Sets the numeric labels for row 0.

  - Restores the table by using the data of the matrix `m_dData[m_nIndex]` (the view's member `m_dData` is a three-dimensional array, which also can be regarded as an array of matrices).

  - Selects the first unfixed cell.

  - Updates the edit control.

Table 13.4 shows the `CVbControl` functions used to access the various properties of the VBX grid control. Notice that the function declares and initializes the local variables `MaxRows` and `MaxCols`. These variables store the maximum number of rows and columns, respectively, in the VBX grid control. The function obtains these values by sending the C++ message `GetNumProperty` to the VBX grid control. Thus, if you go back to the App Studio utility and alter the number of columns and rows, the initialization of `MaxRows` and `MaxCols` still provides the correct information.

Table 13.4 *CVbControl* Functions Used to Access Various Properties of the VBX Grid Control

Function Call	Comment
`GetNumProperty("Rows")`	Obtains the integer-type property `Rows`
`GetNumProperty("Cols")`	Obtains the integer-type property `Cols`
`GetNumProperty("Row")`	Obtains the integer-type property `Row`
`GetNumProperty("Col")`	Obtains the integer-type property `Col`
`GetStrProperty("Text")`	Obtains the string-type property `Text`

Function Call	Comment
SetNumProperty("Row", *row*)	Assigns the value of *row* to the integer-type property Row
SetNumProperty("Col", *col*)	Assigns the value of *col* to the integer-type property Col
SetStrProperty("Text", *str*)	Assigns the string *str* to the string-type property Text

The remaining member functions, which follow, also use the CVbControl member functions in Table 13.4 to access the various VBX grid properties.

■ The member function OnSelChange, which handles changing the selected cell. The function updates the edit box control to display the value of the new selected cell and then selects the edit control. This selection makes it very convenient to edit the copy of the currently selected cell.

■ The member function OnUpdateBtn, which responds to clicking the Update pushbutton. The function performs the following tasks:

• Exits if no cell is selected. The function tests the CellSelected property of the VBX grid to determine whether a cell is selected.

• Updates the VBX grid control.

• Converts the string in the edit box into a number and then back into a string (this process filters out invalid numbers), which then is inserted in the selected cell. This task involves obtaining the Row and Col properties of the VBX grid and assigning the latter string to the Text property of the grid.

• Updates the sum of the current column. This task involves calling the member function CalcSums and supplying it the argument col.

• Reselects the last cell.

■ The member function OnOK, which handles pressing the OK pushbutton. The function basically stores the *values* of the VBX grid in the matrix m_dData[m_nIndex].

III

Advanced Programming

■ The member function CalcSums, which calculates the sum for rows in the column specified by parameter lColIndex. The function performs the following tasks:

- Selects the targeted column.

- Initializes the summation variable sumCol.

- Obtains the sum of rows for column lColIndex. This task uses a for loop, which selects each row and adds the value of that row to variable sumCol.

- Displays the calculated sum in the bottom row of the column lColIndex.

■ The member function OnClearBtn, which clears the strings in the VBX grid control and then selects the first unfixed cell.

■ The member function OnLoadBtn, which reads the data for the VBX grid from a binary data file. The function performs the following tasks:

- Opens the input stream in binary input mode. This task opens the file FILES[m_nIndex].

- Performs the remaining tasks if the input stream was opened successfully. Otherwise, the function displays an error message dialog box and then exits.

- Reads the targeted data matrix (using the view's member m_dData).

- Closes the input stream.

- Restores the contents of the VBX grid control using the matrix m_dData[m_nIndex].

■ The member function OnSaveBtn, which writes the data of the VBX grid to a binary data file. The function performs the following tasks:

- Opens the input stream in binary output mode. This task opens the file FILES[m_nIndex].

- Performs the remaining tasks if the input stream was opened successfully.

- Stores the *values* of the VBX grid into the targeted data matrix (using the view's member `m_dData`).

- Writes the matrix `m_pView->m_dData[m_nIndex]` to the output stream.

- Closes the output stream.

- Restores the contents of the VBX grid control using the matrix `m_dData[m_nIndex]`.

15. Manually insert into the VBTABVW.CPP implementation file the code to define the `OnTableX` member function in the view class `CVbTableView`.

Listing 13.6 shows the source code for the VBTABVW.CPP implementation file after various statements were inserted manually. The listing shows the `#include` statement, which includes the header file VBTBLDLG.H. The definitions of the member functions `OnTableX` require this header file to declare instances of class `CVbTblDlg` locally. Listing 13.6 also contains the statements that define the member functions `OnTable1`, `OnTable2`, and `OnTable3`. These definitions are similar. Each `OnTableX` member function creates an instance of class `CVbTblDlg` and then invokes it as a modal dialog box. This invocation involves sending the C++ message `DoModal` to the dialog box instance.

Listing 13.6 Source Code for the VBTABVW.CPP Implementation File

```
// vbtabvw.cpp : implementation of the CVbTableView class
//

#include "stdafx.h"
#include "vbtable.h"

#include "vbtabdoc.h"
#include "vbtabvw.h"

// include the declaration of the VbTable dialog class
#include "vbtbldlg.h"

#ifdef _DEBUG
#undef THIS_FILE
static char BASED_CODE THIS_FILE[] = __FILE__;
#endif

/////////////////////////////////////////////////////////////////
// CVbTableView
```

(continues)

Advanced Programming

III

Listing 13.6 Continued

```cpp
IMPLEMENT_DYNCREATE(CVbTableView, CView)

BEGIN_MESSAGE_MAP(CVbTableView, CView)
    //{{AFX_MSG_MAP(CVbTableView)
    ON_COMMAND(ID_TABLE1, OnTable1)
    ON_COMMAND(ID_TABLE2, OnTable2)
    ON_COMMAND(ID_TABLE3, OnTable3)
    //}}AFX_MSG_MAP
END_MESSAGE_MAP()

/////////////////////////////////////////////////////////////////////////
// CVbTableView construction/destruction

CVbTableView::CVbTableView()
{
  // initialize the table of data
  for (long i = 0; i < MAX_TABLES; i++)
    for (long row = 0; row < MAX_ROWS; row++)
      for (long col = 0; col < MAX_COLS; col++)
        m_dData[i][row][col] = 0.0;
}

CVbTableView::~CVbTableView()
{
}

/////////////////////////////////////////////////////////////////////////
// CVbTableView drawing

void CVbTableView::OnDraw(CDC* pDC)
{
    CVbTableDoc* pDoc = GetDocument();
    ASSERT_VALID(pDoc);

    // TODO: add draw code for native data here
}

/////////////////////////////////////////////////////////////////////////
// CVbTableView diagnostics

#ifdef _DEBUG
void CVbTableView::AssertValid() const
{
    CView::AssertValid();
}

void CVbTableView::Dump(CDumpContext& dc) const
```

```
{
    CView::Dump(dc);
}

CVbTableDoc* CVbTableView::GetDocument() // non-debug version is inline
{
    ASSERT(m_pDocument->IsKindOf(RUNTIME_CLASS(CVbTableDoc)));
    return (CVbTableDoc*)m_pDocument;
}
#endif //_DEBUG

/////////////////////////////////////////////////////////////////////////
// CVbTableView message handlers

void CVbTableView::OnTable1()
{
  CVbTblDlg TableDlg(0, this);
  TableDlg.DoModal();
}

void CVbTableView::OnTable2()
{
  CVbTblDlg TableDlg(1, this);
  TableDlg.DoModal();
}

void CVbTableView::OnTable3()
{
  CVbTblDlg TableDlg(2, this);
  TableDlg.DoModal();
}
```

The source code shown in Listing 13.6 contains three nested `for` loops in the view class constructor. These loops assign zeros to the elements of the three-dimensional array `m_dData`.

16. Manually insert the leading directives `#ifndef` and `#define`, and insert the last `#endif` directive in the VBTABDOC.H header file. These directives ensure that the compiler processes only after the declarations are in the header file; otherwise, you get redefinition errors from the compiler. Listing 13.7 shows the source code for the VBTABDOC.H header file.

Listing 13.7 Source Code for the VBTABDOC.H Header File

```
// vbtabdoc.h : interface of the CVbTableDoc class
//
/////////////////////////////////////////////////////////////////

#ifndef _VBTABDOC_H_
#define _VBTABDOC_H_

class CVbTableDoc : public CDocument
{
protected: // create from serialization only
    CVbTableDoc();
    DECLARE_DYNCREATE(CVbTableDoc)

// Attributes
public:
// Operations
public:

// Implementation
public:
    virtual ~CVbTableDoc();
    virtual void Serialize(CArchive& ar);   // overridden for
                                            // document i/o
#ifdef _DEBUG
    virtual void AssertValid() const;
    virtual void Dump(CDumpContext& dc) const;
#endif

protected:
    virtual BOOL OnNewDocument();

// Generated message map functions
protected:
    //{{AFX_MSG(CVbTableDoc)
        // NOTE - the ClassWizard will add and remove member
        // functions here.
        //    DO NOT EDIT what you see in these blocks of
        //    generated code !
    //}}AFX_MSG
    DECLARE_MESSAGE_MAP()
};

/////////////////////////////////////////////////////////////////

#endif
```

The Unedited Files of the VBTABLE Project

The files VBTABLE.H and VBTABLE.CPP contain a few VBX-related statements that were generated by AppWizard. Listing 13.8 shows the source code
for the VBTABLE.H header file.

Listing 13.8 Source Code for the VBTABLE.H Header File

```
// vbtable.h : main header file for the VBTABLE application
//

#ifndef __AFXWIN_H__
    #error include 'stdafx.h' before including this file for PCH
#endif

#include "resource.h"        // main symbols

/////////////////////////////////////////////////////////////////////////
// CVbTableApp:
// See vbtable.cpp for the implementation of this class
//

class CVbTableApp : public CWinApp
{
public:
    CVbTableApp();

// Overrides
    virtual BOOL InitInstance();

// Implementation

    //{{AFX_MSG(CVbTableApp)
    afx_msg void OnAppAbout();
  // NOTE - the ClassWizard will add and remove member functions here.
  //    DO NOT EDIT what you see in these blocks of generated code !
    //}}AFX_MSG
    DECLARE_MESSAGE_MAP()
};

/////////////////////////////////////////////////////////////////////////
// VB-Event extern declarations

//{{AFX_VBX_REGISTER()
    extern UINT NEAR VBN_SELCHANGE;
//}}AFX_VBX_REGISTER

/////////////////////////////////////////////////////////////////////////
```

III

Advanced Programming

The VBTABLE.H header file makes an external declaration for the VBN_SELCHANGE message. Listing 13.9, which contains the source code for the VBTABLE.CPP implementation file, invokes the global function AfxRegisterVBEvent to register the VBN_SELCHANGE message. The member function InitInstance (in Listing 13.9) contains the statement EnableVBX(), which prepares the application for VBX support.

Listing 13.9 Source Code for the VBTABLE.CPP Implementation File

```cpp
// vbtable.cpp : Defines the class behaviors for the application.
//

#include "stdafx.h"
#include "vbtable.h"

#include "mainfrm.h"
#include "vbtabdoc.h"
#include "vbtabvw.h"

#ifdef _DEBUG
#undef THIS_FILE
static char BASED_CODE THIS_FILE[] = __FILE__;
#endif

/////////////////////////////////////////////////////////////////////
// CVbTableApp

BEGIN_MESSAGE_MAP(CVbTableApp, CWinApp)
    //{{AFX_MSG_MAP(CVbTableApp)
    ON_COMMAND(ID_APP_ABOUT, OnAppAbout)
    // NOTE - the ClassWizard will add and remove mapping macros here.
    //    DO NOT EDIT what you see in these blocks of generated code!
    //}}AFX_MSG_MAP
    // Standard file-based document commands
    ON_COMMAND(ID_FILE_NEW, CWinApp::OnFileNew)
    ON_COMMAND(ID_FILE_OPEN, CWinApp::OnFileOpen)
END_MESSAGE_MAP()

/////////////////////////////////////////////////////////////////////
// CVbTableApp construction

CVbTableApp::CVbTableApp()
{
    // TODO: add construction code here,
    // Place all significant initialization in InitInstance
}

/////////////////////////////////////////////////////////////////////
```

```
// The one and only CVbTableApp object

CVbTableApp NEAR theApp;

/////////////////////////////////////////////////////////////////////
// CVbTableApp initialization

BOOL CVbTableApp::InitInstance()
{
    // Standard initialization
    // If you are not using these features and wish to reduce the size
    //  of your final executable, you should remove from the following
    //  the specific initialization routines you do not need.

    SetDialogBkColor();          // Set dialog background color to gray
    LoadStdProfileSettings();    // Load standard INI file options
                                 // (including MRU)
    EnableVBX();                 // Initialize VBX support

    // Register the application's document templates.
     // Document templates serve as the connection between
     // documents, frame windows, and views.

    CSingleDocTemplate* pDocTemplate;
    pDocTemplate = new CSingleDocTemplate(
        IDR_MAINFRAME,
        RUNTIME_CLASS(CVbTableDoc),
        RUNTIME_CLASS(CMainFrame),      // main SDI frame window
        RUNTIME_CLASS(CVbTableView));
    AddDocTemplate(pDocTemplate);

    // create a new (empty) document
    OnFileNew();

    if (m_lpCmdLine[0] != '\0')
    {
        // TODO: add command line processing here
    }


    return TRUE;
}

/////////////////////////////////////////////////////////////////////
// CAboutDlg dialog used for App About

    .
    .
    .
/////////////////////////////////////////////////////////////////////
// VB-Event registration
```

(continues)

III

Advanced Programming

Listing 13.9 Continued

```
// (calls to AfxRegisterVBEvent will be placed here by ClassWizard)

//{{AFX_VBX_REGISTER_MAP()
    UINT NEAR VBN_SELCHANGE = AfxRegisterVBEvent("SELCHANGE");
//}}AFX_VBX_REGISTER_MAP

//////////////////////////////////////////////////////////////////
// CVbTableApp commands
```

Summary

This chapter introduced you to programming VBX controls, which enables you to tap into a wealth of third-party controls. You learned about the following:

- The VBX control properties, methods, and events are similar to data members, member functions, and messages, respectively, in Visual C++. This chapter briefly described the basic concepts for programming in Visual Basic.

- The MFC library offers the CVbControl class, which supports VBX controls. The class contains member functions to access the various properties, attributes, and methods of VBX controls.

- The AppWizard utility supports VBX controls by generating code that typically initializes the applications to use VBX controls. The ClassWizard enables you to add classes, data members, and member functions to animate the VBX controls.

- VBX controls can be installed using the App Studio utility. This feature allows the App Studio to extend the Toolbox palette and include buttons for VBX controls. In addition, the App Studio supports pasting VBX controls on dialog box and form views.

In addition, a simple spreadsheet application using the VBX grid control was created in this chapter. The VBTABLE.EXE program simulated the support for three distinct spreadsheets—each with the capability to save and load its information in a data file. The text explained the steps involved in building the project and showed you how to involve the AppWizard, ClassWizard, and App Studio utilities. The discussion also pointed out the steps for manually inserting the code and presented the listings relevant to using the VBX grid control.

Chapter 14

Using the *CString* and Collections Classes

A sophisticated library like the Microsoft Foundation Classes (MFC) requires and incorporates the services of supporting classes for strings, arrays, lists, and hash-table-based maps. These classes provide auxiliary support for the various MFC classes and for Windows applications. This chapter introduces you to the various collection classes:

- The CString class

- The array classes

- The list classes

- The map classes

The *CString* Class

The MFC library contains the class CString to model string objects in a manner that closely resembles strings in the various Microsoft Basic implementations. In fact, some of the member functions of class CString are fashioned after built-in Microsoft Basic string functions. The header file AFX.H contains the declaration of class CString shown in Listing 14.1. The listing also shows the helper-friend functions that implement relational operators.

Listing 14.1 Declaration of the *CString* Class in the File AFX.H

```
class CString
{
public:
// Constructors
```

(continues)

Listing 14.1 Continued

```
            CString();
            CString(const CString& stringSrc);
            CString(char ch, int nRepeat = 1);
            CString(const char* psz);
            CString(const char* pch, int nLength);
    #ifdef _NEARDATA
        // Additional versions for far string data
        CString(LPCSTR lpsz);
        CString(LPCSTR lpch, int nLength);
    #endif
        ~CString();
    // Attributes & Operations
        // as an array of characters
        int GetLength() const;
        BOOL IsEmpty() const;
        void Empty();                       // free up the data
        char GetAt(int nIndex) const;       // 0 based
        char operator[](int nIndex) const;  // same as GetAt
        void SetAt(int nIndex, char ch);
        operator const char*() const;       // as a C string
        // overloaded assignment
        const CString& operator=(const CString& stringSrc);
        const CString& operator=(char ch);
        const CString& operator=(const char* psz);
        // string concatenation
        const CString& operator+=(const CString& string);
        const CString& operator+=(char ch);
        const CString& operator+=(const char* psz);
        friend CString AFXAPI operator+(const CString& string1,
                const CString& string2);
        friend CString AFXAPI operator+(const CString& string, char ch);
        friend CString AFXAPI operator+(char ch, const CString& string);
           friend CString AFXAPI operator+(const CString& string,
                                           const char* psz);
           friend CString AFXAPI operator+(const char* psz,
                                           const CString& string);
        // string comparison
        int Compare(const char* psz) const;        // straight character
        int CompareNoCase(const char* psz) const;  // ignore case
        int Collate(const char* psz) const;        // NLS aware
        // simple sub-string extraction
        CString Mid(int nFirst, int nCount) const;
        CString Mid(int nFirst) const;
        CString Left(int nCount) const;
        CString Right(int nCount) const;
        CString SpanIncluding(const char* pszCharSet) const;
        CString SpanExcluding(const char* pszCharSet) const;
        // upper/lower/reverse conversion
        void MakeUpper();
        void MakeLower();
        void MakeReverse();
        // searching (return starting index, or -1 if not found)
        // look for a single character match
        int Find(char ch) const;                   // like "C" strchr
        int ReverseFind(char ch) const;
        int FindOneOf(const char* pszCharSet) const;
```

```
      // look for a specific sub-string
      int Find(const char* pszSub) const;         // like "C" strstr
      // input and output
#ifdef _DEBUG
      friend CDumpContext& AFXAPI operator<<(CDumpContext& dc,
                    const CString& string);
#endif
         friend CArchive& AFXAPI operator<<(CArchive& ar,
                                       const CString& string);
      friend CArchive& AFXAPI operator>>(CArchive& ar, CString& string);
      // Windows support
#ifdef _WINDOWS
      BOOL LoadString(UINT nID);          // load from string resource
                                          // 255 chars max
      // ANSI<->OEM support (convert string in place)
      void AnsiToOem();
      void OemToAnsi();
      // OLE 2.0 BSTR support (use for OLE automation)
      BSTR AllocSysString();
      BSTR SetSysString(BSTR FAR* pbstr);
#endif //_WINDOWS
      // Access to string implementation buffer as "C" character array
      char* GetBuffer(int nMinBufLength);
      void ReleaseBuffer(int nNewLength = -1);
      char* GetBufferSetLength(int nNewLength);
// Implementation
public:
      int GetAllocLength() const;
protected:
      // lengths/sizes in characters
      //  (note: an extra character is always allocated)
      char* m_pchData;              // actual string (zero terminated)
      int m_nDataLength;            // does not include terminating 0
      int m_nAllocLength;           // does not include terminating 0
      // implementation helpers
      void Init();
         void AllocCopy(CString& dest, int nCopyLen, int nCopyIndex,
                        int nExtraLen) const;
      void AllocBuffer(int nLen);
      void AssignCopy(int nSrcLen, const char* pszSrcData);
         void ConcatCopy(int nSrc1Len, const char* pszSrc1Data,
                         int nSrc2Len, const char* pszSrc2Data);
      void ConcatInPlace(int nSrcLen, const char* pszSrcData);
      static void SafeDelete(char* pch);
      static int SafeStrlen(const char* psz);
};

// Compare helpers
BOOL AFXAPI operator==(const CString& s1, const CString& s2);
BOOL AFXAPI operator==(const CString& s1, const char* s2);
BOOL AFXAPI operator==(const char* s1, const CString& s2);
BOOL AFXAPI operator!=(const CString& s1, const CString& s2);
BOOL AFXAPI operator!=(const CString& s1, const char* s2);
BOOL AFXAPI operator!=(const char* s1, const CString& s2);
BOOL AFXAPI operator<(const CString& s1, const CString& s2);
BOOL AFXAPI operator<(const CString& s1, const char* s2);
```

(continues)

Listing 14.1 Continued

```
BOOL AFXAPI operator<(const char* s1, const CString& s2);
BOOL AFXAPI operator>(const CString& s1, const CString& s2);
BOOL AFXAPI operator>(const CString& s1, const char* s2);
BOOL AFXAPI operator>(const char* s1, const CString& s2);
BOOL AFXAPI operator<=(const CString& s1, const CString& s2);
BOOL AFXAPI operator<=(const CString& s1, const char* s2);
BOOL AFXAPI operator<=(const char* s1, const CString& s2);
BOOL AFXAPI operator>=(const CString& s1, const CString& s2);
BOOL AFXAPI operator>=(const CString& s1, const char* s2);
BOOL AFXAPI operator>=(const char* s1, const CString& s2);
```

The declaration of class CString includes a set of constructors, a destructor, and a medley of member functions. The following sections look at the majority of the members and friend functions by groups.

Constructors

The class CString declares seven constructors, including the default and copy constructors. Two of these constructors work with far-string data. Other class constructors build CString objects by replicating a character for a specified number of times or by using an ASCIIZ string. Following are some examples for creating instances of CString:

```
CString str1;                  // string object is empty
CString str2('+', 5);          // contains "+++++"
CString str3("Blue Thunder");  // contains "Blue Thunder"
CString str4('X');             // contains "X"
CString str4(str3);            // also contains "Blue Thunder"
```

Access Functions

The class CString contains the following member functions that store and recall the particular characters or string in a CString object. The indexing of characters in the CString class is zero based. The access functions are as follows:

- The member function GetAt and operator [ ] recall the character specified by the index parameter, nIndex.

- The member function SetAt and operator [ ] store a character at a specified index.

- The parameterless operator const char* accesses the ASCIIZ string stored in the targeted CString object.

   Following are examples of how to use the preceding functions and operators:

```
CString CStringObj("Visual C++");
char szString[81] = "VISUAL C++";
cout << "Strings '" << szString << "' and '"
```

```
         << (const char*)CStringObj << "' are "
         << (strcmp(szString, (const char*)CStringObj) != 0) ?
                "not equal" : "equal";
// replace each character with a +
for (int i = 0; i < CStringObj.GetLength(); i++)
  CStringObj.SetAt(i, '+');
cout << "CStringObj is '" << (const char*)CStringObj << "'\n";
// replace each character with a *
cout << "CStringObj is '";
for (i = 0; i < CStringObj.GetLength(); i++) {
  CStringObj[i] = '*';
  cout << CStringObj[i];
}
cout << "'\n";
```

■ The member functions GetBuffer, ReleaseBuffer, and
GetBufferSetLength store characters in a CString object. These functions
help you use a CString object as an argument for char* parameters.

The function GetBuffer returns a char* pointer to the string in a CString
object. Your program can use the function's result directly or assign it to
a char* pointer to assign a new group of characters. After your program
carries out this task, it must send a C++ message ReleaseBuffer to the
CString object before sending that object any other messages.

The function GetBuffer uses the single parameter nMinBufLength.
This parameter designates the minimum size of the CString character
buffer (that can exclude the null terminator). The member function
ReleaseBuffer has the single parameter nNewLength, which has a default
argument of -1. This parameter specifies the new length of the string,
excluding the null terminator. The default argument sets the size of
the CString object to the current string length. The member function
GetBufferSetLength yields the pointer to the string in a CString object
and sets the size of the string to the value indicated by the parameter
nNewLength. The function can increase or reduce the size of the buffer
to conform with the argument of the parameter nNewLength.

Following is an example of how to use the functions GetBuffer and
ReleaseBuffer to obtain an input string using a pointer-to-character:

```
const STRING_LEN = 80;
CString CStringObj;
char *pszStr = CStringObj.GetBuffer(STRING_LEN+1);
cout << "Type in a string: ";
cin.getline(pszStr, STRING_LEN);
CStringObj.ReleaseBuffer(-1);
cout << "\nYou entered '<< (const char*)CStringObj < "'\n";
```

III

Advanced Programming

Assignment Operators

The class CString declares a set of operators to assign and concatenate strings and characters. There are three = operators that assign CString instances, ASCIIZ strings, and characters to instances of CString. Similar += operators concatenate the same three types of items to CString instances.

Attributes Functions

The class CString has the following member functions that yield the general attributes of a CString object:

- The member function GetLength yields the number of characters stored in the targeted CString object.

- The Boolean member function IsEmpty returns TRUE if the targeted CString object contains no characters; otherwise, the function returns FALSE.

- The member function Empty removes the allocated memory for the characters of a CString object.

Following are examples of how to use these three member functions:

```
CString langStr("Visual C++");
cout << "String has " << lanStr.GetLength() << "characters\n";
langStr.Empty();
cout << (langStr.IsEmpty()) ?
   "String object langStr is now empty\n" :
   "Looks like function Empty is out to lunch!\n";
```

The preceding code fragment displays the following output:

```
String has 10 characters
String object langStr is now empty
```

Concatenation Operators

The class CString declares five versions of the friend + operators that concatenate CString objects with other CString objects, ASCIIZ strings, and even characters. These functions are coded to follow the C++ programming rules that dictate that one of the two arguments of a + operator must have the type of the befriended class.

The following code gives an example of how to use the operators =, +=, and +:

```
CString StrObj1 = "I program ";
CString StrObj2 = "with ";
CString StrObj3 = "Visual C++";
CString StrObj4;
StrObj4 = StrObj1 + "a lot " + StrObj2 + "Microsoft " + StrObj3 + '!';
// next statement displays the following string
```

```
// "I program a lot with Microsoft Visual C++!"
cout << (const char*)StrObj4 << "\n";
StrObj4 = StrObj1;
StrObj4 += "a lot ";
StrObj4 += StrObj2 + "Visual";
StrObj4 += ' ';
StrObj4 += "C++";
StrObj4 += '!';
// next statement displays the following string
// "I program a lot with Microsoft Visual C++!"
cout << (const char*)StrObj4 << "\n";
```

String-Comparison Functions

The CString class declares the following member functions to compare strings:

- The member function Compare performs a case-sensitive comparison between an ASCIIZ string with the targeted CString object. The function yields the following values:

    0 if the strings are equal

    +1 if the CString object is greater than the ASCIIZ string

    –1 if the CString object is less than the ASCIIZ string

- The member function CompareNoCase is a case-insensitive version of the Compare member function.

- The member function Collate carries out a locale-specific comparison between the targeted CString object and an ASCIIZ string. The function returns 0 if the strings are equal, +1 if the CString is greater than the ASCIIZ string, and –1 if otherwise.

The CString class has a number of helper relational operators <, <=, >, >=, ==, and != that contrast CString objects with other CString objects or with ASCIIZ strings. These helper functions empower you to write more readable source code. The following chart describes each of these operators:

Following is an example that uses the functions Compare and CompareNoCase:

```
CString StrObj = "Visual Basic";
char szStr[] = "Visual BASIC;
int result;
cout << "*** Case-sensitive comparison ***\n";
result = StrObj.Compare(szStr);
// subsequent if-else statement displays:
// String 'Visual Basic' > 'Visual BASIC'
if (result > 0)
  cout << "String '" << (const char*)StrObj << "' > '"
       << szStr << "'\n";
else if (result < 0)
```

```
        cout << "String '" << (const char*)StrObj << "' < '"
             << szStr << "'\n";
      else
        cout << "String '" << (const char*)StrObj << "' == '"
             << szStr << "'\n";
      cout << "*** Case-insensitive comparison ***\n";
      result = StrObj.CompareNoCase(szStr);
      // subsequent if-else statement displays:
      // String 'Visual Basic' == 'Visual BASIC'
      if (result > 0)
        cout << "String '" << (const char*)StrObj << "' > '"
             << szStr << "'\n";
      else if (result < 0)
        cout << "String '" << (const char*)StrObj << "' < '"
             << szStr << "'\n";
      else
        cout << "String '" << (const char*)StrObj << "' == '"
             << szStr << "'\n";
```

String-Extraction Functions

The class `CString` declares the following member functions to pull out, or extract, portions of a `CString` object:

- The member function `Left`, which is fashioned after the BASIC function LEFT$, extracts the first characters of a `CString` object. The function returns a `CString` object.

- The member function `Right`, which is fashioned after the BASIC function RIGHT$, extracts the trailing characters of a `CString` object. The function returns a `CString` object.

- The overloaded member function `Mid`, which is fashioned after the BASIC function MID$, extracts the middle portion of a `CString` object and returns a `CString` object. In one version, `Mid` extracts from a specified character index to the end of the string. In the other version, `Mid` extracts a specified number of characters starting with a certain character.

- The member function `SpanExcluding` extracts the largest substring chunk that excludes the characters specified in the parameter `pszCharSet`. The function ends the extraction process at the first character found in the argument of parameter `pszCharSet`.

- The member function `SpanIncluding` extracts the largest substring chunk that includes the characters specified in the parameter `pszCharSet`. The function ends the extraction process at the first character *not* in the argument of the parameter `pszCharSet`.

Following is an example that uses these five member functions:

```
CString StrObj = "Visual Basic";
CString CharsObj = "aioue";
CString ResultObj;
ResultObj = StrObj.Left(6);
cout << (const char*)ResultObj << "\n"; // displays Visual
ResultObj = StrObj.Right(5);
cout << (const char*)ResultObj << "\n"; // displays Basic
ResultObj = StrObj.Mid(6);
cout << (const char*)ResultObj << "\n"; // displays Basic
ResultObj = StrObj.Mid(6, 2);
cout << (const char*)ResultObj << "\n"; // displays Ba
ResultObj = StrObj.SpanExcluding((const char*)CharsObj);
cout << (const char*)ResultObj << "\n"; // displays Vis
CharsObj = "lausiV";
ResultObj = StrObj.SpanIncluding((const char*)CharsObj);
cout << (const char*)ResultObj << "\n"; // displays Visual
```

Character-Conversion Functions

The class CString provides the following member functions to manage the characters of a CString object:

- The member function MakeUpper converts the characters of a CString object to uppercase.

- The member function MakeLower converts the characters of a CString object to lowercase.

- The member function MakeReverse reverses the order of the characters of a CString object.

Following are examples of how to use the character-conversion functions:

```
CString StrObj("Visual Basic");
cout << (const char*)StrObj << "\n";     // displays "Visual Basic"
StrObj.MakeLower();
cout << (const char*)StrObj << "\n";     // displays "visual basic"
StrObj.MakeUpper();
cout << (const char*)StrObj << "\n";     // displays "VISUAL BASIC"
StrObj.MakeReverse();
cout << (const char*)StrObj << "\n";     // displays "CISAB LAUSIV"
```

Search Functions

The CString class offers the following member functions to search for characters and strings in CString objects:

- The overloaded member function Find looks for a character or an ASCIIZ string in a CString object. The character-searching version of the Find function has a char-type parameter that defines the search character. The function produces the index of the first matching character, or returns –1 if no match is found. The string-searching version of the Find function has a const char*-type parameter that specifies the search string. The function returns the index of the first matching character or –1 if no match is found.

■ The member function ReverseFind finds the last occurrence of a character in a CString object. The function returns the index of the last matching character, or produces –1 if no match is found.

■ The member function FindOneOf looks for the first character that matches any character in a search string. The function returns –1 if no matching character is found.

Following is an example that shows how to use these three functions:

```
CString StrObj = "QWERTYUIOP";
CString SearchStr = "ERTY";
CString CharSet = "OIUYTR";
char chFind = 'R';
int i;
int j;
i = StrObj.Find(chFind);
if (i >= 0)
  cout << "Character " << chFind << " has a match at index "
      << i << "\n";
else
  cout << "No match for character " << chFind << "\n";
i = StrObj.ReverseFind(chFind);
if (i >= 0)
  cout << "Character " << chFind << " has a match at index "
      << i << "\n";
else
  cout << "No match for character " << chFind << "\n";
i = StrObj.Find((const char*)SearchStr);
if (i >= 0)
  cout << "String " << (const char*) SearchStr
      << " has a match at index " << i << "\n";
else
  cout << "No match for string " << (const char*) SearchStr << "\n";
i = StrObj.FindOneOf((const char*)SearchStr);
if (i >= 0)
  cout << "A character in " << (const char*)SearchStr
      << " has a match in " << (const char*)StrObj << "\n";
```

Test of the *CString* Class

This section presents a simple Windows program that tests some of the member functions in class CString. The program STRING1.EXE is menu driven and contains the following controls:

■ *Static text control.* Displays the last operation.

■ *Main String edit box.*

- *String Argument edit box.*

- *Result edit box.*

- *Static text controls.* Label the three edit boxes.

Figure 14.1 shows a session with the STRING1.EXE program.

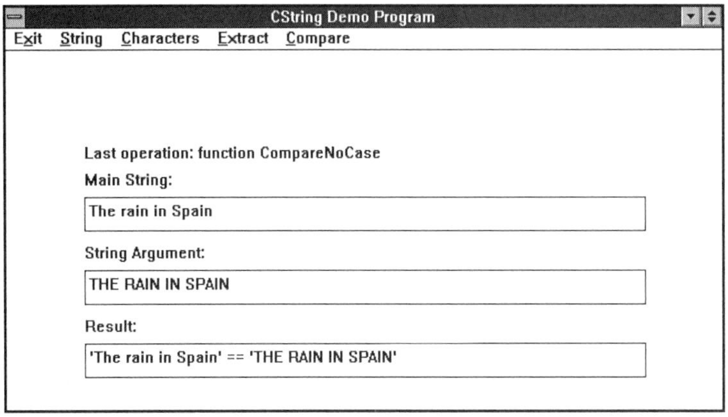

Figure 14.1
A sample
session
with the
STRING1.EXE
program.

The STRING1.EXE program has the following menus:

- The Exit menu enables you to exit the test program.

- The String menu contains the commands Is, Length, and Append. The Is command copies the main string to the result string. The Length command displays the length of the CString object in the Result edit box. The Append command displays, in the Result edit box, the result of appending the strings in the edit boxes Main String and String Argument.

- The Characters menu contains the commands Upper, Lower, Reverse, First, and Last. The Upper and Lower commands display, in the Result edit box, the uppercase and lowercase versions of the main string, respectively. The Reverse command displays, in the Result edit box, the reversed characters of the main string. The First and Last commands display, in the Result edit box, the first and last characters, respectively, of the main string.

- The Extract menu contains the options Mid, Left, and Right. The Mid command displays, in the Result edit box, a middle portion of the main string. The Left command displays, in the Result edit box, the first half of the main string. The Right command displays, in the Result edit box, the last half of the main string. The static text control that displays the name of the last operation includes the arguments used by the functions tested in the commands Mid, Left, and Right.

■ The Compare menu offers two selections that carry out a case-sensitive and case-insensitive comparison between the strings in the Main String and String Argument edit boxes. Each command displays, in the Result edit box, a string that indicates how the main string compares with the contents of the String Argument edit box.

Listing 14.2 shows the contents of the STRING1.DEF definition file.

Listing 14.2 The STRING1.DEF Definition File

```
NAME          String1
DESCRIPTION   'An MFC Windows Application'
EXETYPE       WINDOWS
CODE          PRELOAD MOVEABLE DISCARDABLE
DATA          PRELOAD MOVEABLE MULTIPLE
HEAPSIZE      1024
```

Listing 14.3 shows the source code for the STRING1.H header file.

Listing 14.3 Source Code for the STRING1.H Header File

```
#define CM_EXIT          100
#define CM_IS            101
#define CM_GETLENGTH     102
#define CM_APPEND        103
#define CM_MAKEUPPER     104
#define CM_MAKELOWER     105
#define CM_MAKEREVERSE   106
#define CM_GETAT_0       107
#define CM_GETAT_N       108
#define CM_MID           109
#define CM_LEFT          110
#define CM_RIGHT         111
#define CM_COMPARE       112
#define CM_COMPARENOCASE 113
```

Listing 14.4 contains the script for the STRING1.RC resource file.

Listing 14.4 Script for the STRING1.RC Resource File

```
#include <windows.h>
#include <afxres.h>
#include "string1.h"
MAINMENU MENU LOADONCALL MOVEABLE PURE DISCARDABLE
```

```
BEGIN
  MENUITEM "E&xit", CM_EXIT
  POPUP "&String"
  BEGIN
    MENUITEM "&Is", CM_IS
    MENUITEM "&Length", CM_GETLENGTH
    MENUITEM "&Append", CM_APPEND
  END
  POPUP "&Characters"
  BEGIN
    MENUITEM "&Upper", CM_MAKEUPPER
    MENUITEM "&Lower", CM_MAKELOWER
    MENUITEM "&Reverse", CM_MAKEREVERSE
    MENUITEM "&First", CM_GETAT_0
    MENUITEM "L&ast", CM_GETAT_N
  END
  POPUP "&Extract"
  BEGIN
    MENUITEM "&Mid", CM_MID
    MENUITEM "&Left", CM_LEFT
    MENUITEM "&Right", CM_RIGHT
  END
  POPUP "&Compare"
  BEGIN
    MENUITEM "Case-&sensitive", CM_COMPARE
    MENUITEM "Case-&insensitive", CM_COMPARENOCASE
  END
END
```

The source code for the STRING1.CPP program file is provided in Listing 14.5.

Listing 14.5 Source Code for the STRING1.CPP Program File

```
/*

   Program to set a selection of the CString member functions.

*/

#include <afxwin.h>
#include <stdio.h>
#include "string1.h"

// declare the constants that represent the sizes of the controls
const Wlbl = 500;
const Hlbl = 18;
const LblVertSpacing = 5;
const LblHorzSpacing = 40;
const Wbox = 500;
const Hbox = 30;
const BoxVertSpacing = 10;
const BoxHorzSpacing = 40;
const MaxStringLen = 255;
```

III

Advanced Programming

(continues)

Listing 14.5 Continued

```
// declare the ID_XXXX constants for the controls
#define ID_STR1_EDIT    101
#define ID_STR2_EDIT    102
#define ID_RESULT_EDIT 103
#define ID_LASTOP_TXT  104


// Define an application class derived from CWinApp
class CStringDemoApp : public CWinApp
{
public:

  virtual BOOL InitInstance();
};

// Define a window class derived from CFrameWnd
class CMainWnd : public CFrameWnd
{
 public:

  CMainWnd()
  {
    Create(NULL, "CString Demo Program", WS_OVERLAPPEDWINDOW,
           rectDefault, NULL, "MAINMENU");
  }

  ~CMainWnd();

 protected:

  // declare CString objects
  CString MainStrObj;
  CString StringArgObj;
  CString ResultStrObj;

  // declare pointers to visual controls
  CStatic* pLastOpTxt;
  CStatic* pStr1Txt;
  CStatic* pStr2Txt;
  CStatic* pResultTxt;
  CEdit* pStr1Box;
  CEdit* pStr2Box;
  CEdit* pResultBox;

  // handle creating the controls
  afx_msg int OnCreate(LPCREATESTRUCT lpCS);

  // handle the menu options
  afx_msg void CmExit();
  afx_msg void CmIs();
  afx_msg void CmGetLength();
  afx_msg void CmAppend();
  afx_msg void CmMakeUpper();
  afx_msg void CmMakeLower();
  afx_msg void CmMakeReverse();
```

```
  afx_msg void CmGetAt0();
  afx_msg void CmGetAtN();
  afx_msg void CmMid();
  afx_msg void CmLeft();
  afx_msg void CmRight();
  afx_msg void CmCompare();
  afx_msg void CmCompareNoCase();

  // return a reference to member r based on individual
  // coordinates and dimensions
  void makerect(int X, int Y, int W, int H, CRect& r)
   { r.SetRect(X, Y, X + W, Y + H); }


  // message map macro
  DECLARE_MESSAGE_MAP()
};


CMainWnd::~CMainWnd()
{
  // delete the controls
  delete pStr1Box;
  delete pStr2Box;
  delete pResultBox;
  delete pStr1Txt;
  delete pStr2Txt;
  delete pResultTxt;
  delete pLastOpTxt;
}

int CMainWnd::OnCreate(LPCREATESTRUCT lpCS)
{
  int x = 70, y = 80;
  CRect r;
  DWORD dwStaticStyle = WS_CHILD | WS_VISIBLE | SS_LEFT;
  DWORD dwBoxStyle = WS_CHILD | WS_VISIBLE | WS_BORDER |
                     ES_LEFT | ES_AUTOHSCROLL;


  makerect(x, y, Wlbl, Hlbl, r);
  pLastOpTxt = new CStatic();
  pLastOpTxt->Create("Last operation: none", dwStaticStyle, r,
                     this, ID_LASTOP_TXT);

  // create the label for the mains tring
  y += Hlbl + LblVertSpacing;
  makerect(x, y, Wlbl, Hlbl, r);
  pStr1Txt = new CStatic();
  pStr1Txt->Create("Main String:", dwStaticStyle, r, this, -1);

  // create the main string edit box
  y += Hlbl + LblVertSpacing;
  makerect(x, y, Wbox, Hbox, r);
  pStr1Box = new CEdit();
  pStr1Box->Create(dwBoxStyle, r, this, ID_STR1_EDIT);
  pStr1Box->LimitText(); // set no limit for text
```

(continues)

Listing 14.5 Continued

```
    // create the Str2 label
    y += Hbox + BoxVertSpacing;
    makerect(x, y, Wlbl, Hlbl, r);
    pStr2Txt = new CStatic();
    pStr2Txt->Create("String Argument:", dwStaticStyle, r, this, -1);

    // create the Str2 edit box
    y += Hlbl + LblVertSpacing;
    makerect(x, y, Wbox, Hbox, r);
    pStr2Box = new CEdit();
    pStr2Box->Create(dwBoxStyle, r, this, ID_STR2_EDIT);
    pStr2Box->LimitText(); // set no limit for text

    // create the Result label
    y += Hbox + BoxVertSpacing;
    makerect(x, y, Wlbl, Hlbl, r);
    pResultTxt = new CStatic();
    pResultTxt->Create("Result:", dwStaticStyle, r, this, -1);

    // create the Result edit box
    y += Hlbl + LblVertSpacing;
    makerect(x, y, Wbox, Hbox, r);
    pResultBox = new CEdit();
    pResultBox->Create(dwBoxStyle, r, this, ID_RESULT_EDIT);
    pResultBox->LimitText(); // set no limit for text

    return CFrameWnd::OnCreate(lpCS);
}


void CMainWnd::CmExit()
{
  // prompt user if he or she want to close the application
  if (MessageBox("Want to close this application", "Query",
                 MB_YESNO | MB_ICONQUESTION) == IDYES)
    SendMessage(WM_CLOSE);
}

void CMainWnd::CmIs()
{
  pStr1Box->GetWindowText(MainStrObj);
  pResultBox->SetWindowText((const char*)MainStrObj);
  pLastOpTxt->SetWindowText("Last operation: operator =");
}

void CMainWnd::CmGetLength()
{
  char szStr[MaxStringLen+1];

  pStr1Box->GetWindowText(MainStrObj);
  sprintf(szStr, "The string '%s' has %d characters",
          (const char*) MainStrObj, MainStrObj.GetLength());
  pResultBox->SetWindowText(szStr);
  pLastOpTxt->SetWindowText("Last operation: function GetLength");
}
```

```
void CMainWnd::CmAppend()
{
  pStr1Box->GetWindowText(MainStrObj);
  pStr2Box->GetWindowText(StringArgObj);
  ResultStrObj = MainStrObj + StringArgObj;
  pResultBox->SetWindowText((const char*)ResultStrObj);
  pLastOpTxt->SetWindowText("Last operation: operator +");
}

void CMainWnd::CmMakeUpper()
{
  pStr1Box->GetWindowText(MainStrObj);
  MainStrObj.MakeUpper();
  pResultBox->SetWindowText((const char*)MainStrObj);
  pLastOpTxt->SetWindowText("Last operation: function MakeUpper");
}

void CMainWnd::CmMakeLower()
{
  pStr1Box->GetWindowText(MainStrObj);
  MainStrObj.MakeLower();
  pResultBox->SetWindowText((const char*)MainStrObj);
  pLastOpTxt->SetWindowText("Last operation: function MakeLower");
}

void CMainWnd::CmMakeReverse()
{
  pStr1Box->GetWindowText(MainStrObj);
  MainStrObj.MakeReverse();
  pResultBox->SetWindowText((const char*)MainStrObj);
  pLastOpTxt->SetWindowText("Last operation: function MakeReverse");
}

void CMainWnd::CmGetAt0()
{
  pStr1Box->GetWindowText(MainStrObj);
  ResultStrObj = MainStrObj[0];
  pResultBox->SetWindowText((const char*)ResultStrObj);
  pLastOpTxt->SetWindowText("Last operation: operator [0]");
}

void CMainWnd::CmGetAtN()
{
  char szStr[MaxStringLen+1];
  int n;

  pStr1Box->GetWindowText(MainStrObj);
  n = MainStrObj.GetLength() - 1;
  ResultStrObj = MainStrObj[n];
  pResultBox->SetWindowText((const char*)ResultStrObj);
  sprintf(szStr, "Last operation: operator [%d]", n);
  pLastOpTxt->SetWindowText(szStr);
}
```

(continues)

Listing 14.5 Continued

```
void CMainWnd::CmMid()
{
  char szStr[MaxStringLen+1];
  int n, m, k;

  pStr1Box->GetWindowText(MainStrObj);
  n = MainStrObj.GetLength();
  // calculate indices and number of characters to extract
  m = ((n / 2) > 1) ? n / 2 : 1;
  k = ((n / 4) > 1) ? n / 4 : 1;
  ResultStrObj = MainStrObj.Mid(m, k);
  pResultBox->SetWindowText((const char*)ResultStrObj);
  sprintf(szStr, "Last operation: function Mid(%d, %d)", m, k);
  pLastOpTxt->SetWindowText(szStr);
}

void CMainWnd::CmLeft()
{
  char szStr[MaxStringLen+1];
  int n;

  pStr1Box->GetWindowText(MainStrObj);
  n = MainStrObj.GetLength();
  ResultStrObj = MainStrObj.Left(n / 2);
  pResultBox->SetWindowText((const char*)ResultStrObj);
  sprintf(szStr, "Last operation: function Left(%d)", n / 2);
  pLastOpTxt->SetWindowText(szStr);
}

void CMainWnd::CmRight()
{
  char szStr[MaxStringLen+1];
  int n;

  pStr1Box->GetWindowText(MainStrObj);
  n = MainStrObj.GetLength();
  ResultStrObj = MainStrObj.Right(n / 2);
  pResultBox->SetWindowText((const char*)ResultStrObj);
  sprintf(szStr, "Last operation: function Right(%d)", n / 2);
  pLastOpTxt->SetWindowText(szStr);
}

void CMainWnd::CmCompare()
{
  int i;

  pStr1Box->GetWindowText(MainStrObj);
  pStr2Box->GetWindowText(StringArgObj);
  i = MainStrObj.Compare(StringArgObj);

  if (i > 0) {
    ResultStrObj = "'" + MainStrObj + "' > '" + StringArgObj + "'";
    pResultBox->SetWindowText((const char*)ResultStrObj);
  }
```

```
  else if (i < 0) {
    ResultStrObj = "'" + MainStrObj + "' < '" + StringArgObj + "'";
    pResultBox->SetWindowText((const char*)ResultStrObj);
  }
  else {
    ResultStrObj = "'" + MainStrObj + "' == '" + StringArgObj + "'";
    pResultBox->SetWindowText((const char*)ResultStrObj);
  }
  pLastOpTxt->SetWindowText("Last operation: function Compare");
}

void CMainWnd::CmCompareNoCase()

{
  int i;

  pStr1Box->GetWindowText(MainStrObj);
  pStr2Box->GetWindowText(StringArgObj);
  i = MainStrObj.CompareNoCase(StringArgObj);

  if (i > 0) {
    ResultStrObj = "'" + MainStrObj + "' > '" + StringArgObj + "'";
    pResultBox->SetWindowText((const char*)ResultStrObj);
  }
  else if (i < 0) {
    ResultStrObj = "'" + MainStrObj + "' < '" + StringArgObj + "'";
    pResultBox->SetWindowText((const char*)ResultStrObj);
  }
  else {
    ResultStrObj = "'" + MainStrObj + "' == '" + StringArgObj + "'";
    pResultBox->SetWindowText((const char*)ResultStrObj);
  }
  pLastOpTxt->SetWindowText("Last operation: function CompareNoCase");
}

BEGIN_MESSAGE_MAP(CMainWnd, CFrameWnd)
    ON_WM_CREATE()
    ON_COMMAND(CM_EXIT, CmExit)
    ON_COMMAND(CM_IS, CmIs)
    ON_COMMAND(CM_GETLENGTH, CmGetLength)
    ON_COMMAND(CM_APPEND, CmAppend)
    ON_COMMAND(CM_MAKEUPPER, CmMakeUpper)
    ON_COMMAND(CM_MAKELOWER, CmMakeLower)
    ON_COMMAND(CM_MAKEREVERSE, CmMakeReverse)
    ON_COMMAND(CM_GETAT_0, CmGetAt0)
    ON_COMMAND(CM_GETAT_N, CmGetAtN)
    ON_COMMAND(CM_MID, CmMid)
    ON_COMMAND(CM_LEFT, CmLeft)
    ON_COMMAND(CM_RIGHT, CmRight)
    ON_COMMAND(CM_COMPARE, CmCompare)
    ON_COMMAND(CM_COMPARENOCASE, CmCompareNoCase)
END_MESSAGE_MAP()
```

III

Advanced Programming

(continues)

Listing 14.5 Continued

```
// Construct the CStringDemoApp's m_pMainWnd data member
BOOL CStringDemoApp::InitInstance()
{
  m_pMainWnd = new CMainWnd();
  m_pMainWnd->ShowWindow(m_nCmdShow);
  m_pMainWnd->UpdateWindow();
  return TRUE;
}

// application's constructor initializes and runs the app
CStringDemoApp WindowApp;
```

The STRING1.H header file in Listing 14.3 defines the various menu commands. The STRING1.RC resource file in Listing 14.4 defines the menu resource MAINMENU. The STRING1.CPP program file contains the source code for the test program. The program declares two sets of constants: The first set specifies the dimensions and spacing of the visual controls. The second set defines the ID of these controls. The program also declares two classes: CMainWnd and CStringDemoApp. The CMainWnd class declares a constructor, three CString-type data members (MainStrObj, StringArgObj, and ResultStrObj), and a set of member functions. Among these functions are the set of CmXXXX functions that respond to the various menu options and selections.

The member function OnCreate creates the edit box and static text controls attached to the main window.

The member function CmIs copies the contents of the Main String edit box to the Result edit box. The function performs the following tasks:

- Obtains the string of the Main String edit box and stores it in member MainStrObj.

- Writes the string in member MainStrObj to the Result edit box.

- Updates the contents of the last operation static text control.

The member function CmGetLength tests the member function GetLength by displaying the number of characters in the Main String edit box. The function performs the following tasks:

- Obtains the string of the Main String edit box and stores it in member MainStrObj.

- Writes a formatted string to the local variable `szStr` that indicates the number of characters in the member `MainStrObj`. This task involves sending the C++ message `GetLength` to the member `MainStrObj`. This task also uses the function `sprintf` to obtain the formatted string.

- Writes the contents of the local variable `szStr` to the Result edit box.

- Updates the contents of the last operation static text control.

The member function `CmAppend` tests the + operator by appending the strings in the Main String and String Argument edit boxes. The function performs the following tasks:

- Obtains the string in the Main String edit box and stores it in member `MainStrObj`.

- Obtains the string in the String Argument edit box and stores it in member `StringArgObj`.

- Concatenates the strings in members `MainStrObj` and `StringArgObj` and stores the result in member `ResultStrObj`. This task involves using the tested + operator.

- Writes the contents of member `ResultStrObj` to the Result edit box.

- Updates the contents of the last operation static text control.

The member function `CmMakeUpper` tests the member function `MakeUpper` by displaying the uppercase version of the main string in the Result edit box. The function performs the following tasks:

- Obtains the string in the Main String edit box and stores it in member `MainStrObj`.

- Converts the characters in member `MainStrObj` to uppercase. This task involves sending the C++ message `MakeUpper` to the object `MainStrObj`.

- Writes the contents of member `MainStrObj` to the Result edit box.

- Updates the contents of the last operation static text control.

The member function `CmMakeLower` is similar to function `CmMakeUpper`. The main difference is that the function `CmMakeLower` sends the C++ message `MakeLower` to the object `MainStrObj`.

III

Advanced Programming

The member function `CmMakeReverse` reverses the characters in object `MainStrObj`. This function is similar to function `CmMakeUpper`. The main difference is that the function `CmMakeReverse` sends the C++ message `MakeReverse` to the member `MainStrObj`.

The member function `CmGetAt0` displays the first character in the main string. The functions use the operator `[ ]` to retrieve the sought characters, using the following tasks:

- Obtains the string in the Main String edit box and stores it in member `MainStrObj`.

- Assigns the character at index 0 of member `MainStrObj` to the member `ResultStrObj`.

- Writes the contents of member `ResultStrObj` to the Result edit box.

- Updates the contents of the last operation static text control.

The member function `CmGetAtN` displays the last character in the main string. The function uses the operator `[ ]` to retrieve the sought character by performing the following tasks:

- Obtains the string in the Main String edit box and stores it in member `MainStrObj`.

- Assigns the index of the last character in member `MainStrObj` to the local variable `n`. This task involves sending the C++ message `GetLength` to the member `MainStrObj`.

- Assigns the character at the index specified by variable `n` of member `MainStrObj` to the member `ResultStrObj`.

- Writes the contents of member `ResultStrObj` to the Result edit box.

- Writes the formatted string for the last operation static text control to the variable `szStr`. This task uses the function `sprintf` to incorporate a string image of the value in variable `n`.

- Updates the contents of the last operation static text control.

The member function `CmMid` extracts the characters from the middle of the main string. The function performs the following tasks:

- Obtains the string in the Main String edit box and stores it in member `MainStrObj`.

- Assigns the number of characters in the member `MainStrObj` to the local variable `n`. This task involves sending the C++ message `GetLength` to the member `MainStrObj`.

- Calculates the index of the median character in the member `MainStrObj` and stores the result in the local variable `m`.

- Calculates one-fourth the number of characters in the member `MainStrObj` and stores the result in variable `k`.

- Assigns the characters in the middle of the member `MainStrObj` to the member `ResultStrObj`. This task involves sending the C++ message `Mid` to the member `MainStrObj`. The arguments for this message are the local variables `m` and `k`.

- Writes the contents of the member `ResultStrObj` to the Result edit box.

- Writes the formatted string for the last operation static text control to the variable `szStr`. This task uses the function `sprintf` to incorporate a string image of the values in variables `m` and `k`.

- Updates the contents of the last operation static text control.

The member function `CmLeft` extracts the first half of the main string. This function is similar to the function `CmMid`. The differences include these:

- Sending the C++ message `Left` (instead of the message `Mid`) to the member `MainStrObj`. The argument for the message `Left` is `n / 2` (`n` is the name of the local variable that stores the size of the string in the member `MainStrObj`).

- The function `CmLeft` updates the last operation static text by including the single argument of the C++ message `Left`.

The member function `CmRight` extracts the second half of the main string. This function is similar to the function `CmLeft`. The main difference between the two functions is that function `CmRight` sends the C++ message `Right` to the member `MainStrObj`.

III

Advanced Programming

The member function `CmCompare` compares the strings in the Main String and String Argument edit boxes and displays an expression that contrasts the two strings. The function performs the following tasks:

- Obtains the string in the Main String edit box and stores it in the member `MainStrObj`.

- Assigns the address of the buffer of the member `StringArgObj` to the local pointer `pszStr`. This task involves sending the C++ message `GetBuffer` to the member `StringArgObj`. The argument for this message is the constant `MaxStringLen`.

- Obtains the string in the String Argument edit box and stores it in member `StringArgObj`.

- Obtains the comparison value by sending the message `Compare` to the member `MainStrObj`. The argument for this message is the member `StringArgObj`. This task assigns the result of the message to the local variable `i`.

- Uses a multiple-decision `if` statement to determine whether the value in variable `i` is positive, negative, or zero (the `else` clause). Each `if` statement clause has two statements: The first builds the string in the member `ResultObjStr` by using the member `MainStrObj`, member `StringArgObj`, and the string image of the appropriate relational operator. The second statement writes the contents of member `ResultStrObj` to the Result edit box.

- Updates the contents of the last operation static text control.

The member function `CmCompareNoCase` is a version of function `CmCompare`, which performs case-insensitive comparisons. The statements in function `CmCompareNoCase` are similar to those of function `CmCompare`. The main difference is that function `CmCompareNoCase` sends the C++ message `CompareNoCase`.

The Array Classes

The MFC library offers seven classes that support popular types of arrays: `CByteArray`, `CWordArray`, `CDWordArray`, `CUIntArray`, `CStringArray`, `CPtrArray`, and `CObArray`. The first four classes support arrays of bytes, words, double words, and unsigned integers, respectively. The `CStringArray` models an array of

CString objects (and the descendants of class CString). The CPtrArray models an array of void pointers. The CObArray models arrays of CObject* (and the pointers of CObject descendants).

The array classes have matching data members and member functions. Listings 14.6 and 14.7 show the declarations of classes CStringArray and CObArray, respectively. The two classes (and the other array classes) have a similar group of member functions and maintain similar operations. The next section discusses the member functions of CStringArray; discussions of the other array classes follow.

Listing 14.6 Declaration of the *CStringArray* Class in the AFXCOLL.H File

```
class CStringArray : public CObject
{
    DECLARE_SERIAL(CStringArray)
public:
// Construction
    CStringArray();
// Attributes
    int GetSize() const;
    int GetUpperBound() const;
    void SetSize(int nNewSize, int nGrowBy = -1);
// Operations
    // Clean up
    void FreeExtra();
    void RemoveAll();
    // Accessing elements
    CString GetAt(int nIndex) const;
    void SetAt(int nIndex, const char* newElement);
    CString& ElementAt(int nIndex);
    // Potentially growing the array
    void SetAtGrow(int nIndex, const char* newElement);
    int Add(const char* newElement);
    // overloaded operator helpers
    CString operator[](int nIndex) const;
    CString& operator[](int nIndex);
    // Operations that move elements around
    void InsertAt(int nIndex, const char* newElement, int nCount = 1);
    void RemoveAt(int nIndex, int nCount = 1);
    void InsertAt(int nStartIndex, CStringArray* pNewArray);
// Implementation
protected:
    CString* m_pData;   // the actual array of data
    int m_nSize;        // # of elements (upperBound - 1)
    int m_nMaxSize;     // max allocated
    int m_nGrowBy;      // grow amount
public:
    ~CStringArray();
    void Serialize(CArchive&);
```

(continues)

III

Advanced Programming

Listing 14.6 Continued

```
#ifdef _DEBUG
    void Dump(CDumpContext&) const;
    void AssertValid() const;
#endif
};
```

Listing 14.7 Declaration of the *CObArray* Class in the AFXCOLL.H File

```
class CObArray : public CObject
{
    DECLARE_SERIAL(CObArray)
public:
// Construction
    CObArray();
// Attributes
    int GetSize() const;
    int GetUpperBound() const;
    void SetSize(int nNewSize, int nGrowBy = -1);
// Operations
    // Clean up
    void FreeExtra();
    void RemoveAll();
    // Accessing elements
    CObject* GetAt(int nIndex) const;
    void SetAt(int nIndex, CObject* newElement);
    CObject*& ElementAt(int nIndex);
    // Potentially growing the array
    void SetAtGrow(int nIndex, CObject* newElement);
    int Add(CObject* newElement);
    // overloaded operator helpers
    CObject* operator[](int nIndex) const;
    CObject*& operator[](int nIndex);
    // Operations that move elements around
    void InsertAt(int nIndex, CObject* newElement, int nCount = 1);
    void RemoveAt(int nIndex, int nCount = 1);
    void InsertAt(int nStartIndex, CObArray* pNewArray);
// Implementation
protected:
    CObject** m_pData;    // the actual array of data
    int m_nSize;          // # of elements (upperBound - 1)
    int m_nMaxSize;       // max allocated
    int m_nGrowBy;        // grow amount
public:
    ~CObArray();
    void Serialize(CArchive&);
#ifdef _DEBUG
    void Dump(CDumpContext&) const;
    void AssertValid() const;
#endif
};
```

The *CStringArray* Class

The class CStringArray declares the default constructor, a destructor, and a set of data members and member functions. The constructor creates an empty array that grows dynamically as you add new string objects. You can also shrink the array by sending it particular C++ messages.

The class CStringArray has the subsequent data members:

- The member m_pData is a pointer to the dynamic array of CString objects.

- The member m_nSize stores the current working size of the array. This is the number of elements occupied by meaningful data.

- The member m_nMaxSize stores the current maximum size of the array.

- The member m_nGrowBy stores the increment in the array size. The member function SetSize alters the value of member m_nGrowBy.

The class CStringArray declares the following member functions to deal with the array bounds and array size:

- The member function GetSize returns the size of the array.

- The member function GetUpperBound returns the index of the last array element. This index is one integer below the result of the function GetSize.

- The member function SetSize sets the new size of the array. This new size can either increase or decrease the array; in other words, you are not limited by increasing the array size. The parameter m_nGrowBy indicates the increments in array size when the array expands. The function SetSize assigns the argument of the parameter nGrowBy to the member m_nGrowBy.

- The member function RemoveAll deletes the array elements but perseveres the targeted instance of class CStringArray.

- The member function FreeExtra deletes the dynamic space utilized by *vacant* array elements.

The class CStringArray declares the following member functions to store and recall string objects in the various array elements:

- The member function ElementAt returns a reference to the CString object at the specified element.

- The member function GetAt yields a CString object at the designated index.

- The member function SetAt stores a string at the designated index.

- The [ ] operator sets and gets an array element. This operator can be replaced by both member functions GetAt and SetAt.

The class CStringArray offers the following member functions to add, insert, and remove elements in the array:

- The member function SetAtGrow stores a CString object at the designated array element and expands the array if necessary. Use this member function when adding new elements to a CStringArray instance.

- The overloaded member function InsertAt inserts a single CString object or a CStringArray object in an array. The first version of the function inserts a string at the designated index the specified number of times. The default number of times is 1. The function moves up the array elements located after the insertion point. The second version of the function inserts a CStringArray object at the specified index and moves up the succeeding array elements.

- The member function Add adds a string to the end of the array. The function expands the array, if necessary, by the value in member m_nGrowBy.

- The member function RemoveAt deletes one or more array elements at the designated index. The parameter nCount (which has a default argument of 1) indicates the number of array elements to delete.

Other Array Classes

The classes CByteArray, CWordArray, CDWordArray, and CUIntArray offer arrays for practical tasks that use sets of integers of various precisions. The class CPtrArray supports storing pointers to homogenous or heterogeneous data. The class CObArray is another versatile class that can support generic arrays of classes that are descendants of CObject—useful in the absence of formal support for C++ templates.

Test of the *CStringArray* Class

This section examines a program that creates a CStringArray object and uses some of the class member functions. Figure 14.2 shows a sample session with the test program CSTRARR1.EXE.

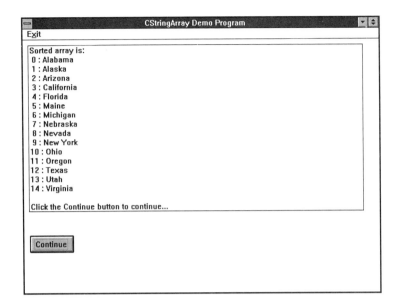

Figure 14.2
A sample session
with the program
CSTRARR1.EXE.

The application's window contains the following controls:

■ *Output list box control*. Displays the output; this control acts as a simple DOS-like screen.

■ *Start pushbutton*. Enables you to step through the various stages of testing. The program alters the caption of this pushbutton from *Start* to *Continue*. After the program finishes the testing, it changes the caption of the button back to *Start*.

The program has a menu with a single selection: Exit.

Initially, the window displays an empty list box, and the pushbutton has the caption *Start*. Click the Start button to begin running the various tests. The caption of the pushbutton becomes *Continue* and program performs the following tests:

1. Displays the unordered array in the output list box.

2. Searches for the elements of the unordered array and displays the result of the search in the output list box. This test uses the linear search algorithm.

3. Sorts the array and displays its ordered elements in the output list box.

4. Searches for the elements of the ordered array and displays the result of the search in the output list box. This test uses the binary search algorithm.

Listing 14.8 shows the contents of the CSTRARR1.DEF file.

Listing 14.8 The CSTRARR1.DEF File

```
NAME         CStrArr1
DESCRIPTION  'An MFC Windows Application'
EXETYPE      WINDOWS
CODE         PRELOAD MOVEABLE DISCARDABLE
DATA         PRELOAD MOVEABLE MULTIPLE
HEAPSIZE     1024
```

Listing 14.9 shows the source code for the CSTRARR1.H header file.

Listing 14.9 Source Code for the CSTRARR1.H Header File

```
#define CM_EXIT         100
#define ID_CONTINUE_BTN 101
#define ID_OUTPUT_LST   102
```

Listing 14.10 contains the script for the CSTRARR1.RC resource file.

Listing 14.10 Script for the CSTRARR1.RC Resource File

```
#include <windows.h>
#include <afxres.h>
#include "cstrarr1.h"
EXITMENU MENU LOADONCALL MOVEABLE PURE DISCARDABLE
BEGIN
  MENUITEM "E&xit", CM_EXIT
END
```

Listing 14.11 contains the source code for the CSTRARR1.CPP program file.

Listing 14.11 Source Code for the CSTRARR1.CPP Program File

```
/*
   Program that sorts and searches CStringArray arrays.
   The program searches for members of unordered and ordered
   arrays using the linear and binary search methods,
   respectively.
*/
#include <stdio.h>
#include <afxwin.h>
#include <string.h>
#include "cstrarr1.h"
// declare constants which dimension the controls
const Hbtn = 30;
const Wbtn = 80;
const BtnHorzSpacing = 60;
const BtnVertSpacing = 20;
```

```
const Hlst = 300;
const Wlst = 600;
const LstHorzSpacing = 30;
const LstVertSpacing = 30;
// declare miscellaneous constants
const MaxStringLen = 255;
const MAX_ARRAY = 15;
const NOT_FOUND = -1;
const MAX_STAGES = 4
char* strArray[MAX_ARRAY] =
    { "Virginia", "California", "Michigan", "Maine",  "Oregon",
      "Florida", "Nevada", "Alaska", "New York", "Ohio",
      "Alabama", "Texas", "Arizona", "Utah", "Nebraska" };
// Define an application class derived from CWinApp
class CWindowApp : public CWinApp
{
 public:
  virtual BOOL InitInstance();
};
class CxButton : public CButton
{
public:
   BOOL Create(const char FAR* lpCaption, const RECT& rect,
        CWnd* pParentWnd, UINT nID, BOOL bIsDefault);

};
// Define a window class derived from CFrameWnd
class CMainWnd : public CFrameWnd
{
public:
  CMainWnd();
  ~CMainWnd();
protected:
  int nArraySize;
  CStringArray StrArr1;
  CStringArray StrArr2;
  CxButton* pContinueBtn;
  CListBox* pOutputLst;
  int nStage;

  // handle button commands
  afx_msg void HandleContinueBtn();
  // handle the menu options
  afx_msg void OnExit();
  // handle creating the controls
  afx_msg int OnCreate(LPCREATESTRUCT lpCS);
  // coordinates and dimensions
  void makerect(int X, int Y, int W, int H, CRect& r)
    { r.SetRect(X, Y, X + W, Y + H); }
  // handle output to list box
  void writeln(const char* szStr)
    { pOutputLst->AddString(szStr); }
  void writeln(CString& StrObj)
    { pOutputLst->AddString((const char*)StrObj); }
  void writeToLastLine(const char* szStr);
  void writeToLastLine(CString& StrObj);
```

III

Advanced Programming

(continues)

Listing 14.11 Continued

```
    // members which manage different test stages
    void progress();
    void ClickContBtn();
    void showArray();
    void sortArray();
    int linearSearch(CString& searchVal);
    int binarySearch(CString& searchVal);
    void searchInUnorderedArray();
    void searchInSortedArray();
    // message map macro
    DECLARE_MESSAGE_MAP()
};

BOOL CxButton::Create(const char FAR* lpCaption, const RECT& rect,
            CWnd* pParentWnd, UINT nID, BOOL bIsDefault)
{
  DWORD dwBtnStyle = (bIsDefault == TRUE) ?
            BS_DEFPUSHBUTTON : BS_PUSHBUTTON;
  return CButton::Create(lpCaption,
    WS_CHILD | WS_VISIBLE | WS_TABSTOP | dwBtnStyle,
    rect, pParentWnd, nID);
}
CMainWnd::CMainWnd()
{
   Create(NULL, "CStringArray Demo Program",
        WS_OVERLAPPEDWINDOW, rectDefault, NULL, "EXITMENU");
   // initialize the progress stage
   nStage = 0;
   // initialize the array size member
   nArraySize = MAX_ARRAY;
}

CMainWnd::~CMainWnd()
{
  delete pOutputLst;
  delete pContinueBtn;
}
int CMainWnd::OnCreate(LPCREATESTRUCT lpCS)
{
  int x = 10;
  int y = 10;
  DWORD dwListBoxStyle = WS_CHILD | WS_VISIBLE | WS_VSCROLL |
                         LBS_STANDARD;
  CRect r;
  // disable sorting of items in the list box
  dwListBoxStyle &= ~LBS_SORT;

  // create the output list box
  makerect(x, y, Wlst, Hlst, r);
  pOutputLst = new CListBox();
  pOutputLst->Create(dwListBoxStyle, r, this, ID_OUTPUT_LST);

  // create the Continue pushbutton
  y += Hlst + LstVertSpacing;
  makerect(x, y, Wbtn, Hbtn, r);
```

```
  pContinueBtn = new CxButton();
  pContinueBtn->Create("Start", r, this, ID_CONTINUE_BTN, TRUE);

  return CFrameWnd::OnCreate(lpCS);
}
void CMainWnd::writeToLastLine(const char* szStr)
{
  char szBuff[MaxStringLen+1];
  int n = pOutputLst->GetCount() - 1;
  pOutputLst->GetText(n, szBuff);
  strcat(szBuff, szStr);
  pOutputLst->DeleteString(n);
  pOutputLst->AddString(szBuff);
}
void CMainWnd::writeToLastLine(CString& StrObj)
{
  char szBuff[MaxStringLen+1];
  int n = pOutputLst->GetCount() - 1;
  pOutputLst->GetText(n, szBuff);
  strcat(szBuff, (const char*)StrObj);
  pOutputLst->DeleteString(n);
  pOutputLst->AddString(szBuff);
}
void CMainWnd::progress()
{
  int i;

  switch (nStage) {
    case 0:
     // assign strings to arrays StrArr1 and StrArr2
     for (i = 0; i < nArraySize; i++) {
       StrArr1.SetAtGrow(i, strArray[i]);
       StrArr2.SetAtGrow(i, strArray[i]);
     }
      break;

    case 1:
      // show array
      writeln("Unordered array is:");
      showArray();
      ClickContBtn();
      break;

    case 2:
      // search in unordered array arr1
      searchInUnorderedArray();
      ClickContBtn();
      break;

    case 3:
      // sort array arr1
      sortArray();
      writeln("Sorted array is:");
      showArray();
      ClickContBtn();
      break;
```

Advanced Programming

(continues)

Listing 14.11 Continued

```
      case 4:
        searchInSortedArray();
        ClickContBtn();
        break;
      default:
        nStage = -1;
        MessageBox("Program has finished testing", "Information",
                 MB_OK | MB_ICONINFORMATION);
        break;
    }
    nStage++;
}
void CMainWnd::ClickContBtn()
{
  writeln("");
  writeln("Click the Continue button to continue...");
}
void CMainWnd::showArray()
{
  char szStr[MaxStringLen+1];

  for (int i = 0; i < nArraySize; i++) {
    sprintf(szStr, "%2d : %s", i, (const char*)StrArr1[i]);
    writeln(szStr);
  }
}
void CMainWnd::sortArray()
// sort the first nArraySize elements of array StrArr1
// using the Comb sort method
{
  int offset, inOrder;
  CString temp;

  offset = nArraySize;
  do {
    offset = (8 * offset) / 11;
    offset = (offset == 0) ? 1 : offset;
    inOrder = TRUE;
    for (int i = 0, j = offset; i < (nArraySize - offset); i++, j++) {
      if (StrArr1[i] > StrArr1[j]) {
        inOrder = FALSE;
        temp = StrArr1[i];
        StrArr1[i] = StrArr1[j];
        StrArr1[j] = temp;
      }
    }
  } while (!(offset = 1 && inOrder == TRUE));
}
int CMainWnd::linearSearch(CString& searchVal)
// perform linear search to locate the first
// element in array StrArr1 that matches the value
// of searchVal
{
  int notFound = TRUE;
  int i = 0;
```

```
  // search through the array elements
  while (i < nArraySize && notFound)
    // no match?
    if (searchVal != StrArr1[i])
      i++; // increment index to compare the next element
    else
      notFound = FALSE; // found a match
  // return search outcome
  return (notFound == FALSE) ? i : NOT_FOUND;
}

int CMainWnd::binarySearch(CString& searchVal)
// perform binary search to locate the first
// element in array StrArr1 that matches the value
// of searchVal
{
  int median, low, high;

  // initialize the search range
  low = 0;
  high = nArraySize - 1;
  // search in array
  do {
    // obtain the median index of the current search range
    median = (low + high) / 2;
    // update search range
    if (searchVal > StrArr1[median])
      low = median + 1;
    else
      high = median - 1;
  } while (!(searchVal == StrArr1[median] || low > high));
  // return search outcome
  return (searchVal == StrArr1[median]) ? median : NOT_FOUND;
}

void CMainWnd::searchInUnorderedArray()
// manage the linear search test
{
  char szStr[MaxStringLen+1];
  int j;
  // perform binary search
  for (int i = nArraySize - 1; i >= 0; i--) {
    j = linearSearch(StrArr2[i]);
    sprintf(szStr, "Searching for %s : ", (const char*)StrArr2[i]);
    writeln(szStr);
    if (j != NOT_FOUND) {
      sprintf(szStr, "found matching element at index %d", j);
      writeToLastLine(szStr);
    }
    else
      writeToLastLine("no match found");
  }
}
void CMainWnd::searchInSortedArray()
// manage the binary search test
{
  char szStr[MaxStringLen+1];
  int j;
```

Listing 14.11 Continued

```
      // perform binary search
      for (int i = nArraySize - 1; i >= 0; i—) {
        j = binarySearch(StrArr2[i]);
        sprintf(szStr, "Searching for %s : ", (const char*)StrArr2[i]);
        writeln(szStr);
        if (j != NOT_FOUND) {
          sprintf(szStr, "found matching element at index %d", j);
          writeToLastLine(szStr);
        }
        else
          writeToLastLine("no match found");
      }
    }

    void CMainWnd::HandleContinueBtn()
    {
      // starting the test?
      if (nStage == 0) {
        progress();
        pContinueBtn->SetWindowText("Continue");
      }
      // clear the list box
      pOutputLst->ResetContent();
      // perform the next testing stage
      progress();
      // finished testing?
      if (nStage > MAX_STAGES) {
        pContinueBtn->SetWindowText("Start");
        nStage = 0;
      }
    }
    void CMainWnd::OnExit()
    {
      // prompt user if he or she wants to close the application
      if (MessageBox("Want to close this application", "Query",
                     MB_YESNO | MB_ICONQUESTION) == IDYES)
        SendMessage(WM_CLOSE);
    }
    BEGIN_MESSAGE_MAP(CMainWnd, CFrameWnd)
      ON_BN_CLICKED(ID_CONTINUE_BTN, HandleContinueBtn)
      ON_COMMAND(CM_EXIT, OnExit)
      ON_WM_CREATE()
    END_MESSAGE_MAP()
    // Construct the CWindowApp's m_pMainWnd data member
    BOOL CWindowApp::InitInstance()
    {
      m_pMainWnd = new CMainWnd();
      m_pMainWnd->ShowWindow(m_nCmdShow);
      m_pMainWnd->UpdateWindow();
      return TRUE;
    }
    // application's constructor initializes and runs the app
    CWindowApp WindowApp;
```

The CSTRARR1.H header file shown in Listing 14.9 declares the IDs for the Exit menu option and the various controls. The CSTRARR1.RC resource file shown in Listing 14.10 declares the EXITMENU menu resource with a single menu selection: Exit. The CSTRARR1.CPP program file shown in Listing 14.11 declares groups of constants and classes. The first set of constants defines the dimensions and spacing of the various controls. The second set of constants defines the maximum string size, maximum array size, the not-found numeric code, the maximum number of testing stages, and the initialized string array, strArray. This array contains a set of unsorted strings. The program also declares three classes: CxButton, CMainWnd, and CWindowApp. The class CxButton, a descendant of the MFC class CButton, models pushbutton controls. The class CMainWnd models the main window. The class CWindowApp models the application.

The class CMainWnd declares a constructor, a destructor, a set of data members, and a group of member functions. The data members are as follows:

- The member nArraySize stores the size of the tested arrays.

- The members StrArr1 and StrArr2 are instances of class CStringArray. The member StrArr1 stores the array whose elements are initially unordered and are later sorted. The member StrArr2 contains the strings in constant strArray. The program uses the elements of member StrArr2 to search for matching elements in elements of member StrArr1.

- The member pContinueBtn is the pointer to the Start/Continue pushbutton.

- The member pOutputLst is the pointer to the output list box.

- The member nStage maintains the current stage of testing.

The constructor for class CMainWnd creates the window and its controls and sets the members nStage and nArraySize to 0 and MAX_ARRAY, respectively.

The class CMainWnd declares the following relevant member functions:

- The member function OnCreate creates the controls attached to the window. The function defines the local variable dwListBoxStyle to define the list box style. I disabled the LBS_SORT style to chronologically store strings in the output list box. The OnCreate function creates the various controls using the control-pointer members.

- The overloaded member function writeln appends an ASCIIZ string and a CString object to the list of items in the output list box.

■ The overloaded member function `writeToLastLine` appends an ASCIIZ string and a `CString` object to the last existing item in the output list box.

■ The member function `ClickContBtn` displays the message `Click the Continue button to continue...` in the output list box. The function uses the member function `writeln` to display a blank line and then the message.

■ The member function `showArray` displays the elements of the member `StrArr1`. The function uses a `for` loop to display each element. The `for` loop contains two statements. The first statement calls function `sprintf` to create, in the local variable `szStr`, the string image of the array index followed by a colon and the array element. This statement recalls the sought element using the `[]` operator. The second loop statement displays the contents of variable `szStr` by using the member function `writeln`.

■ The member function `sortArray` sorts the elements of member `StrArr1` using the Comb sort method. The function uses the `[]` operator on both sides of the assignment statement to recall and store `CString` objects in the elements of member `StrArr1`.

■ The member function `linearSearch` searches for the `CString` object `searchVal` in the member `StrArr1`. The function performs a linear search and uses the `[]` operator on both sides of the assignment statement to recall `CString` objects in the elements of member `StrArr1`. The function returns the index of the matching element or returns `NOT_FOUND` if no match is found.

■ The member function `binarySearch` searches for the `CString` object `searchVal` in the member `StrArr1`. The function performs a binary search and uses the `[]` operator on both sides of the assignment statement to recall `CString` objects in the elements of member `StrArr1`. The function returns the index of the matching element or returns `NOT_FOUND` if no match is found.

■ The member function `searchInUnorderedArray` searches for the elements of member `StrArr2` in the member `StrArr1`. The function uses a downward-counting `for` loop that invokes the function `linearSearch`. The loop iterates from `nArraySize - 1` down to 0. The loop statements compare the search result (stored in the local variable `j`) with the global constant `NOT_FOUND`. If these values differ, the function displays, in the output list box, a message that indicates the index of the matching elements. Otherwise, the function displays the message `no match found` in the output list box. The function uses the member function `writeToLastLine` to append either message to the last item in the output list box.

■ The member function `searchInSortedArray` searches for the elements of member `StrArr2` in the member `StrArr1` (which contains a sorted array). The function uses a downward-counting `for` loop that invokes the function `binarySearch`. The loop iterates from `nArraySize - 1` down to 0. The loop statements compare the search result (stored in the local variable `j`) with the global constant `NOT_FOUND`. If these values differ, the function displays, in the output list box, a message that indicates the index of the matching elements. Otherwise, the function displays the message `no match found` in the output list box. The function uses the member function `writeToLastLine` to append either message to the last item in the output list box.

■ The member function `HandleContinueBtn` responds to the messages sent by the Start/Continue pushbutton control. The function performs the following tasks:

- Determines whether the value of member `nStage` is 0. If this condition is true, the function invokes the function `progress` to initialize the members `StrArr1` and `StrArr2`. Then the function sends the C++ message `SetWindowText` to the pushbutton to change its caption to *Continue*.

- Clears the output list box by sending it the C++ message `ResetContent`. Because the output list box acts as a simple DOS screen, this message is similar to a clear-screen command.

- Executes the next testing stage by invoking the member function `progress`.

- Determines whether the integer in member `nStage` exceeds that of the global `MAX_STAGES`. If this condition is true, the function alters the caption of the pushbutton to *Start* and assigns 0 to the member `nStage`. These actions reset the testing cycle.

- The member function `progress` performs the various tests in various stages by using a `switch` statement. This statement uses the member `nStage` to execute a particular set of statements every time the function stage is invoked. The stages are as follows:

    Stage 0. Initializes the elements of members `StrArr1` and `SrtArr2` by using the global constant `strArray`. This stage uses a `for` loop whose statements send the C++ messages `SetAtGrow` to both members `StrArr1` and `StrArr2`. The arguments for the message are the loop control variable `i` and the string in `strArray[i]`.

Stage 1. Displays the unordered elements in member StrArr1. This task invokes the functions showArray and ClickContBtn.

Stage 2. Displays the results of searching through the unordered elements of member StrArr1. This task invokes the functions searchInUnorderedArray and ClickContBtn.

Stage 3. Displays the results of sorting the elements of member StrArr1. This task invokes the functions sortArray, showArray, and ClickContBtn.

Stage 4. Displays the results of searching through the sorted elements in member StrArr1. This task invokes the functions searchInSortedArray and ClickContBtn.

The last statement in the progress function systematically increments the value in member nStage.

The List Classes

The MFC library offers three classes that support popular types of lists. These classes include CPtrList, CObList, and CStringList. The CStringList models a list of CString objects (and the descendants of class CString). The CPtrList models a list of void pointers. The CObList models lists of CObject* (and the pointers of CObject descendants). The list classes model special kinds of lists that are becoming more popular. The operations that support these lists enable them to do the following:

- Behave as stacks and queues, in addition to doubly linked lists

- Index specific list members

The MFC list classes support indexable doubly linked lists that also work as stacks and queues. Perhaps that is why MFC does not formally declare classes for stacks and queues.

The *CStringList* Class

The three MFC list classes resemble each other and have similar member functions. Listing 14.12 shows the declaration of class CStringList in the AFXCOLL.H header file.

Listing 14.12 Declaration of the *CStringList* Class in the AFXCOLL.H File

```
class CStringList : public CObject
{
    DECLARE_SERIAL(CStringList)
protected:
    struct CNode
    {
        CNode* pNext;
        CNode* pPrev;
        CString data;
    };
public:
// Construction
    CStringList(int nBlockSize=10);
// Attributes (head and tail)
    // count of elements
    int GetCount() const;
    BOOL IsEmpty() const;
    // peek at head or tail
    CString& GetHead();
    CString GetHead() const;
    CString& GetTail();
    CString GetTail() const;
// Operations
    // get head or tail (and remove it) - don't call on empty list !
    CString RemoveHead();
    CString RemoveTail();
    // add before head or after tail
    POSITION AddHead(const char* newElement);
    POSITION AddTail(const char* newElement);
    // add another list of elements before head or after tail
    void AddHead(CStringList* pNewList);
    void AddTail(CStringList* pNewList);
    // remove all elements
    void RemoveAll();
    // iteration
    POSITION GetHeadPosition() const;
    POSITION GetTailPosition() const;
    CString& GetNext(POSITION& rPosition); // return *Position++
    CString GetNext(POSITION& rPosition) const; // return *Position++
    CString& GetPrev(POSITION& rPosition); // return *Position--
    CString GetPrev(POSITION& rPosition) const; // return *Position--
    // getting/modifying an element at a given position
    CString& GetAt(POSITION position);
    CString GetAt(POSITION position) const;
    void SetAt(POSITION pos, const char* newElement);
    void RemoveAt(POSITION position);
    // inserting before or after a given position
    POSITION InsertBefore(POSITION position, const char* newElement);
    POSITION InsertAfter(POSITION position, const char* newElement);
    // helper functions (note: O(n) speed)
```

(continues)

Listing 14.12 Continued

```
        POSITION Find(const char* searchValue, POSITION startAfter = NULL)
                                                                    const;
                                // defaults to starting at the HEAD
                                // return NULL if not found
        POSITION FindIndex(int nIndex) const;
                                // get the 'nIndex'th element
                                // (may return NULL)
// Implementation
protected:
        CNode* m_pNodeHead;
        CNode* m_pNodeTail;
        int m_nCount;
        CNode* m_pNodeFree;
        struct CPlex* m_pBlocks;
        int m_nBlockSize;
        CNode* NewNode(CNode*, CNode*);
        void FreeNode(CNode*);
public:
        ~CStringList();
        void Serialize(CArchive&);
#ifdef _DEBUG
        void Dump(CDumpContext&) const;
        void AssertValid() const;
#endif
};
```

The class CStringList declares a constructor, destructor, and a set of data members and member functions. The constructor creates an empty instance to which you can add and remove data. Many member functions use node-position parameters that have the POSITION type. This type is a special node pointer and should not be equated as an integer index of a list node.

The class declares the following member functions to obtain the status of a list:

■ The Boolean member function IsEmpty returns TRUE if the list is empty. Otherwise, the function returns FALSE.

■ The member function GetCount returns the number of elements in the list.

The class offers the following member functions to support insertion and deletion operations:

■ The overloaded member function AddHead adds a CString object or a CStringList object to the head of the list. The version of the function that adds a CString object makes that object the new head of the list. The version that adds a CStringList object makes the head of the added list the new head of the expanded list.

- The overloaded member function AddTail adds a CString object or a CStringList object to the tail of the list. The version of the function that adds a CString object makes that string the new tail of the list. The version that adds a CStringList object makes the tail of the added list the new tail of the expanded list.

- The member function InsertAfter inserts a CString object after the specified position. The POSITION-type parameter, position, selects the list element after which the new CString object is inserted.

- The member function InsertBefore inserts a CString object before the specified position. The POSITION-type parameter, position, selects the list element before which the new CString object is inserted.

- The member function RemoveAt removes a CString object at the designated position, specified by the POSITION-type parameter. The argument for the position parameter must be valid.

- The member function RemoveHead deletes the head of the list and returns a CString object. Your application should send the C++ message IsEmpty to the CStringList object before sending it the C++ message RemoveHead.

- The member function RemoveTail removes the tail of the list and returns a CString object. Your application should send the C++ message IsEmpty to the CStringList object before sending it the C++ message RemoveTail.

The class declares the following member functions to access the head and tail elements:

- The member function GetHead returns the reference to the CString object stored in the first list element.

- The member function GetTail returns the reference to the CString object stored in the last list element.

The class also offers the following member functions to recall and store strings in a specific list member:

- The member function SetAt stores a new string at the specified position.

- The overloaded member function GetAt retrieves a CString object or a reference to a CString object located at the specified position.

III

Advanced Programming

The class CStringList declares the following member functions to search for and visit the various members of a list:

- The member function Find establishes the position of a CString object in the list. The search starts after the node position specified by the argument of POSITION-type parameter startAfter. This parameter has a default argument of NULL, which makes the search begin at the head of the list. The function returns the position of the matching string or returns NULL if no match is found.

- The member function FindIndex returns the position value of the list member designated by the parameter index.

- The member function GetHeadPosition returns the position value for the head of the list.

- The member function GetTailPosition returns the position value for the tail of the list.

- The member function GetNext returns the string in the list at a specific position and then changes the position value to reference the next element.

- The member function GetPrev returns the string in the list at a specific position and then changes the position value to reference the previous element.

An application can employ the last four member functions to traverse the nodes of a list. Following is an example of forward and backward list traversal:

```
main()
{
  CStringList StrLst;
  CString StrObj
  for (int j = 0; j < 20; j++) {
    StrObj = char(64 + j);
    StrObj += "aaaaa";
    StrLst.AddHead(StrObj);
  }
  cout << "Backward list traversal:\n";
  for (pos = StrLst.GetTailPosition; pos != NULL; ) {
    StrObj = StrLst.GetPrev(pos);
    cout << (const char*)StrObj << "\n";
  }
  cout << "Forward list traversal:\n";
  for (pos = StrLst.GetHeadPosition; pos != NULL; ) {
    StrObj = StrLst.GetNext(pos);
    cout << (const char*)StrObj << "\n";
  }
```

Test of the *CStringList* Class

This section looks at an example that uses a CStringList object. The program
CSTRLST1.EXE employs such an object to work as a stack and later as a
queue. The emulated stack operations include push and pop. The emulated
queue operations include enqueue and dequeue. Figure 14.3 shows a session
with the test program CSTRLST1.EXE.

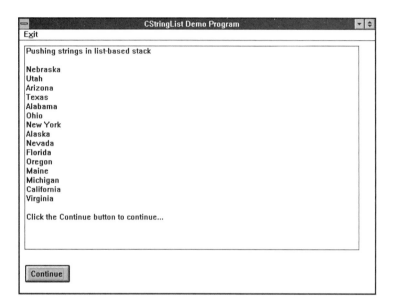

Figure 14.3
A session with the
test program
CSTRLST1.EXE.

The application's window contains the following controls:

- *Output list box control.* Displays the output; this control acts as a simple
  DOS-like screen.

- *Start pushbutton.* Enables you to step through the various stages of testing.
  The program alters the caption of this pushbutton from *Start* to *Continue*.
  After the program finishes testing, it changes the caption of the button
  back to *Start*.

The program has a menu with a single selection: Exit.

Initially, the window displays an empty list box, and the pushbutton has the
caption *Start*. Click the Start button to begin running the various tests. The caption of the pushbutton becomes *Continue* and the program performs the following
tests:

1. Pushes a set of strings in the list-based stack and displays the contents of
the stack in the output list box.

2. Pops the strings off the list-based stack and displays these strings in the output list box.

3. Enqueues a set of strings in the list-based queue and displays the contents of the queue in the output list box.

4. Dequeues the strings from the list-based queue and displays these strings in the output list box.

The program uses short time delays (about half a second per delay) when it displays the inserted and removed strings. This delay results in the visual effect of gradually inserting and removing strings.

Listing 14.13 shows the contents of the CSTRLST1.DEF file.

Listing 14.13 The CSTRLST1.DEF File

```
NAME         CStrLst1
DESCRIPTION  'An MFC Windows Application'
EXETYPE      WINDOWS
CODE         PRELOAD MOVEABLE DISCARDABLE
DATA         PRELOAD MOVEABLE MULTIPLE
HEAPSIZE     1024
```

Listing 14.14 shows the source code for the CSTRLST1.H header file.

Listing 14.14 Source Code for the CSTRLST1.H Header File

```
#define CM_EXIT         100
#define ID_CONTINUE_BTN 101
#define ID_OUTPUT_LST   102
```

Listing 14.15 contains the script for the CSTRLST1.RC resource file.

Listing 14.15 Script for the CSTRLST1.RC Resource File

```
#include <windows.h>
#include <afxres.h>
#include "cstrlst1.h"
EXITMENU MENU LOADONCALL MOVEABLE PURE DISCARDABLE
BEGIN
  MENUITEM "E&xit", CM_EXIT
END
```

The source code for the CSTRLST1.CPP program file is provided in Listing 14.16.

Listing 14.16 Source Code for the CSTRLST1.CPP Program File

```
/*
  Program that uses class CStringList to emulate a stack and
  a queue of names.

*/
#include <stdio.h>
#include <afxwin.h>
#include <string.h>
#include "cstrlst1.h"
// declare constants which dimension the controls
const Hbtn = 30;
const Wbtn = 80;
const BtnHorzSpacing = 60;
const BtnVertSpacing = 20;
const Hlst = 350;
const Wlst = 600;
const LstHorzSpacing = 30;
const LstVertSpacing = 30;
// declare miscellaneous constants
const MaxStringLen = 255;
const MAX_ARRAY = 15;
const MAX_STAGES = 3;
const DWORD DELAY = 500;
char* strArray[MAX_ARRAY] =
     { "Virginia", "California", "Michigan", "Maine",  "Oregon",
       "Florida", "Nevada", "Alaska", "New York", "Ohio",
       "Alabama", "Texas", "Arizona", "Utah", "Nebraska" };
// Define an application class derived from CWinApp
class CWindowApp : public CWinApp
{
 public:
   virtual BOOL InitInstance();
};
class CxButton : public CButton
{
public:
   BOOL Create(const char FAR* lpCaption, const RECT& rect,
         CWnd* pParentWnd, UINT nID, BOOL bIsDefault);

};
// Define a window class derived from CFrameWnd
class CMainWnd : public CFrameWnd
{
public:
  CMainWnd();
  ~CMainWnd();
protected:
  CStringList StrLst;
  CxButton* pContinueBtn;
  CListBox* pOutputLst;
  int nStage;

  // handle button commands
  afx_msg void HandleContinueBtn();
```

III

Advanced Programming

(continues)

Listing 14.16 Continued

```
// handle the menu options
afx_msg void OnExit();
// handle creating the controls
afx_msg int OnCreate(LPCREATESTRUCT lpCS);
// coordinates and dimensions
void makerect(int X, int Y, int W, int H, CRect& r)
  { r.SetRect(X, Y, X + W, Y + H); }
// handle output to list box
void writeln(const char* szStr)
  { pOutputLst->AddString(szStr); }
void writeln(CString& StrObj)
  { pOutputLst->AddString((const char*)StrObj); }
// members which manage different test stages
void progress();
void ClickContBtn();
void showList();
void pushHead(CString& StrObj)
  { StrLst.AddHead(StrObj); }

void pushTail(CString& StrObj)
  { StrLst.AddTail(StrObj); }

BOOL popHead(CString& StrObj);
BOOL popTail(CString& StrObj);
void pushInStack();
void popOffStack();
void enQueue();
void deQueue();
void wait(DWORD delay);
// message map macro
DECLARE_MESSAGE_MAP()
};

BOOL CxButton::Create(const char FAR* lpCaption, const RECT& rect,
              CWnd* pParentWnd, UINT nID, BOOL bIsDefault)
{
  DWORD dwBtnStyle = (bIsDefault == TRUE) ?
              BS_DEFPUSHBUTTON : BS_PUSHBUTTON;
  return CButton::Create(lpCaption,
      WS_CHILD | WS_VISIBLE | WS_TABSTOP | dwBtnStyle,
      rect, pParentWnd, nID);
}
CMainWnd::CMainWnd()
{
  Create(NULL, "CStringList Demo Program",
         WS_OVERLAPPEDWINDOW, rectDefault, NULL, "EXITMENU");
  // initialize the progress stage
  nStage = 0;
}

CMainWnd::~CMainWnd()
{
  delete pOutputLst;
  delete pContinueBtn;
```

```
}
int CMainWnd::OnCreate(LPCREATESTRUCT lpCS)
{
  int x = 10;
  int y = 10;
  DWORD dwListBoxStyle = WS_CHILD | WS_VISIBLE | WS_VSCROLL |
                         LBS_STANDARD;
  CRect r;
  // disable sorting of items in the list box
  dwListBoxStyle &= ~LBS_SORT;

  // create the output list box
  makerect(x, y, Wlst, Hlst, r);
  pOutputLst = new CListBox();
  pOutputLst->Create(dwListBoxStyle, r, this, ID_OUTPUT_LST);

  // create the Continue pushbutton
  y += Hlst + LstVertSpacing;
  makerect(x, y, Wbtn, Hbtn, r);
  pContinueBtn = new CxButton();
  pContinueBtn->Create("Start", r, this, ID_CONTINUE_BTN, TRUE);

  return CFrameWnd::OnCreate(lpCS);
}
void CMainWnd::progress()
{
  switch (nStage) {
    case 0:
      pushInStack();
      break;

    case 1:
      popOffStack();
      break;

    case 2:
      enQueue();
      break;

    case 3:
      deQueue();
      break;

    default:
      nStage = -1;
      MessageBox("Program has finished testing", "Information",
                 MB_OK | MB_ICONINFORMATION);
      break;
  }
  nStage++;
}
void CMainWnd::ClickContBtn()
{
  writeln("");
  writeln("Click the Continue button to continue...");
}
void CMainWnd::showList()
```

(continues)

Advanced Programming

III

Listing 14.16 Continued

```
{
  CString StrObj;

  for (POSITION pos = StrLst.GetHeadPosition(); pos != NULL; ) {
    StrObj = StrLst.GetNext(pos);
    writeln(StrObj);
    wait(DELAY);
    UpdateWindow();
  }
}
BOOL CMainWnd::popHead(CString& StrObj)
{
  if (StrLst.GetCount()) {
    StrObj = StrLst.GetHead();
    StrLst.RemoveHead();
    return TRUE;
  }
  else
    return FALSE;
}
BOOL CMainWnd::popTail(CString& StrObj)
{
  if (StrLst.GetCount()) {
    StrObj = StrLst.GetTail();
    StrLst.RemoveTail();
    return TRUE;
  }
  else
    return FALSE;
}
void CMainWnd::pushInStack()
{
  // push strings in list-based stack
  for (int i = 0; i < MAX_ARRAY; i++)
    pushHead(CString(strArray[i]));
  writeln("Pushing strings in list-based stack");
  writeln("");
  showList();
  ClickContBtn();
}
void CMainWnd::popOffStack()
{
  CString StrObj;

  writeln("Popping strings off list-based stack");
  writeln("");
  // popping strings off list-based stack
  while (popHead(StrObj)) {
    writeln(StrObj);
    wait(DELAY);
    UpdateWindow();
  }
  ClickContBtn();
}
void CMainWnd::enQueue()
{
```

```
  // push strings in list-based queue
  for (int i = 0; i < MAX_ARRAY; i++)
    pushHead(CString(strArray[i]));
  writeln("Pushing strings in list-based queue");
  writeln("");
  showList();
  ClickContBtn();
}
void CMainWnd::deQueue()
{
  CString StrObj;

  writeln("Popping strings off list-based queue");
  writeln("");
  // popping strings off list-based queue
  while (popTail(StrObj)) {
    writeln(StrObj);
    wait(DELAY);
    UpdateWindow();
  }
  ClickContBtn();
}
void CMainWnd::HandleContinueBtn()
{
  // starting the test?
  if (nStage == 0)
    pContinueBtn->SetWindowText("Continue");
  // clear the list box
  pOutputLst->ResetContent();
  // perform the next testing stage
  progress();
  // finished testing?
  if (nStage > MAX_STAGES) {
    pContinueBtn->SetWindowText("Start");
    nStage = 0;
  }
}
void CMainWnd::wait(DWORD delay)
{
  DWORD initTime = GetTickCount();

  while ((GetTickCount() - initTime) < delay)
    // do nothing
    ;
}
void CMainWnd::OnExit()
{
  // prompt user if he or she wants to close the application
  if (MessageBox("Want to close this application", "Query",
                 MB_YESNO | MB_ICONQUESTION) == IDYES)
    SendMessage(WM_CLOSE);
}
BEGIN_MESSAGE_MAP(CMainWnd, CFrameWnd)
  ON_BN_CLICKED(ID_CONTINUE_BTN, HandleContinueBtn)
  ON_COMMAND(CM_EXIT, OnExit)
  ON_WM_CREATE()
END_MESSAGE_MAP()
```

III

Advanced Programming

(continues)

Listing 14.16 Continued

```
// Construct the CWindowApp's m_pMainWnd data member
BOOL CWindowApp::InitInstance()
{
  m_pMainWnd = new CMainWnd();
  m_pMainWnd->ShowWindow(m_nCmdShow);
  m_pMainWnd->UpdateWindow();
  return TRUE;
}
// application's constructor initializes and runs the app
CWindowApp WindowApp;
```

The CSTRLST1.H header file in Listing 14.14 declares the ID for the Windows command message for the single menu option, Exit. The file also declares the IDs for the various controls. The CSTRLST1.RC resource file in Listing 14.15 declares the EXITMENU menu resource. The CSTRLST1.CPP program file in Listing 14.16 declares groups of constants and classes. The first set of constants defines the dimensions and spacing of the various controls. The second set of constants defines the maximum string size, maximum array size, maximum number of testing stages, delay value, and initialized string array strArray. This array contains a set of unsorted strings. The program also declares three classes: CxButton, CMainWnd, and CWindowApp. The class CxButton, a descendant of MFC class CButton, models pushbutton controls. The class CMainWnd models the main window. The class CWindowApp models the application.

The class CMainWnd declares a constructor, a destructor, a set of data members, and a group of member functions. The data members are as follows:

- The member StrLst is an instance of class CStringList.

- The member pContinueBtn is the pointer to the Start/Continue pushbutton.

- The member pOutputLst is the pointer to the output list box.

- The member nStage maintains the current stage of testing.

The constructor for class CMainWnd creates the window and its controls and sets the member nStage to 0.

The class CMainWnd declares the following relevant member functions:

- The member function OnCreate creates the controls attached to the window. The function defines the local variable dwListBoxStyle to define the list box style. The LBS_SORT style was disabled to chronologically store strings in the output list box. The OnCreate function creates the various controls using the control-pointer members.

■ The overloaded member function `writeln` appends an ASCIIZ string and a `CString` object to the list of items in the output list box.

■ The member function `ClickContBtn` displays the message `Click the Continue button to continue...` in the output list box. The function uses the member function `writeln` to display a blank line and then the message.

■ The member function `showList` displays the elements of the member `StrLst`. The function uses a `for` loop to display each list element. The `for` loop uses the POSITION-type control variable `pos` to traverse the member `StrLst`. The loop initializes the variable `pos` with the result of the C++ message `GetHeadPosition`, sent to member `StrLst`. The loop iterates as long as the variable `pos` is not a null pointer. The statements in the loop perform the following tasks:

- Sends the C++ message `GetNext` to the member `StrLst`. The argument for this message is the loop control variable `pos`. This message obtains the next `CString` object in the list and assigns it to the local `CString` object `StrObj`.

- Displays the string of object `StrObj` in the output list box. This task involves the member function `writeln`.

- Waits for `DELAY` milliseconds. This task involves using the member function `delay`.

- Updates the main window and its contents by using the inherited function `UpdateWindow`. Without this function, the program updates the contents of the output list box only when the loop stops iterating.

■ The member function `pushHead` inserts the argument of the `CString` parameter `StrObj` at the head of the member `StrLst`. This function emulates pushing a `CString` object into the list-based stack or queue. The function sends the C++ message `AddHead` to the member `StrLst`. The argument for this message is `StrObj`.

■ The member function `pushTail` inserts the argument of the `CString` parameter `StrObj` at the tail of the member `StrLst`. This function emulates pushing a `CString` object into the list-based queue. The function sends the C++ message `AddTail` to the member `StrLst`. The argument for this message is `StrObj`.

III

Advanced Programming

■ The Boolean member function popHead removes a CString object from the head of the member StrLst. This function emulates popping a string off the list-based stack. The function performs the following tasks:

- Determines whether the member StrLst is an empty list. If this is true, the function returns FALSE and exits. This task involves sending the C++ message GetCount to the member StrLst. If the member StrLst is not an empty list, the function performs the remaining tasks.

- Obtains the CString object at the head of the member StrLst and assigns the object to the reference parameter StrObj. This task involves sending the C++ message GetHead to the member StrLst.

- Removes the head of the member StrLst. This task involves sending the C++ message RemoveHead to the member StrLst.

- Returns TRUE.

■ The Boolean member function popTail removes a CString object from the tail of the member StrLst. This function emulates popping a string off the list-based queue. The function performs the following tasks:

- Determines whether the member StrLst is an empty list. If this is true, the function returns FALSE and exits. This task involves sending the C++ message GetCount to the member StrLst. If the member StrLst is not an empty list, the function performs the remaining tasks.

- Obtains the CString object at the tail of the member StrLst and assigns the object to the reference parameter StrObj. This task involves sending the C++ message GetTail to the member StrLst.

- Removes the tail of the member StrLst. This task involves sending the C++ message RemoveTail to the member StrLst.

- Returns TRUE.

■ The member function pushInStack supports pushing CString objects into the list-based stack. The function uses a for loop to insert the string of the global constant strArray in with the member StrLst. The loop statements invoke the function pushHead and supply it the argument CString(strArray[i]). Then the function displays a heading in the output list box and invokes the function showList to display the contents of the member StrLst in the output list box.

- The member function popOffStack supports popping the CString objects off the list-based stack. The function first displays a heading in the output list box. Next, the function uses a while loop to pop strings off the stack. The loop's condition is the Boolean expression popHead(StrObj). The loop statements display the string of the variable StrObj in the output list box and then invoke the function delay. The last loop statement invokes the inherited function UpdateWindow.

- The member function enQueue is similar to the function pushInStack. The main difference between the two functions is the heading displayed by each one.

- The member function deQueue supports removing the CString objects from the list-based queue. The function first displays a heading in the output list box. Next, the function uses a while loop to dequeue strings. The loop's condition is the Boolean expression popTail(StrObj). The loop statements display the string of the variable StrObj in the output list box and then invoke the function delay. The last loop statement invokes the inherited function UpdateWindow.

- The member function HandleContinueBtn responds to the messages sent by the Start/Continue pushbutton control. The function performs the following tasks:

    - Determines whether the value of member nStage is 0. If this condition is true, the function sends the C++ message SetWindowText to the pushbutton to change its caption to *Continue*.

    - Clears the output list box by sending it the C++ message ResetContent. Because the output list box acts as a simple DOS screen, this message is similar to a clear-screen command.

    - Executes the next testing stage by invoking the member function progress.

    - Determines whether the integer in the member nStage exceeds that of the global MAX_STAGES. If this condition is true, the function alters the caption of the pushbutton to *Start* and assigns 0 to the member nStage. These actions reset the testing cycle.

- The member function progress performs the various tests in various stages by using a switch statement. This statement uses the member nStage to execute a particular set of statements every time the function stage is invoked. The stages are as follows:

Stage 0. Invokes the function `pushInStack` to push strings into the list-based stack (which uses the member `StrLst`).

Stage 1. Invokes the function `popOffStack` to pop strings off the list-based stack.

Stage 2. Invokes the function `enQueue` to enqueue strings into the list-based queue (which uses the member `StrLst`).

Stage 3. Invokes the function `deQueue` to dequeue strings from the list-based queue.

The last statement in the `progress` function systematically increments the value in the member `nStage`.

The Map Classes

Maps are associations built using hash tables. The MFC library offers the map classes `whether`, `CMapPtrToWord`, `CMapPtrToPtr`, `CMapWordToOb`, `CMapStringToPtr`, `CMapStringToOb`, and `CMapStringToString`. Each map class relates one type of data with another. The class `whether` relates 16-bit unsigned integers to pointers. These integers become handles of the pointers. The class `CMapPtrToWord` associates 16-bit unsigned integers to pointers. For example, you can use this class to obtain the window ID number by supplying its pointer. The class `CMapWordToOb` relates unsigned integers to objects. Therefore, these integers turn into numeric IDs for the objects. The classes `CMapStringToPtr` and `CMapStringToOb` associate strings to pointers and string to objects, respectively. You can use these classes to label pointers or objects. The class `CMapStringToString` is used to associate two sets of strings.

The *CMapStringToString* Class

This section presents the class `CMapStringToString`. Listing 14.17 shows the declaration of the class `CMapStringToString` in the AFXCOLL.H header file.

Listing 14.17 Declaration of the *CMapStringToString* Class in the AFXCOLL.H Header File

```
class CMapStringToString : public CObject
{
    DECLARE_SERIAL(CMapStringToString)
protected:
    // Association
    struct CAssoc
```

```
        {
            CAssoc* pNext;
            UINT nHashValue;   // needed for efficient iteration
            CString key;
            CString value;
        };
public:
// Construction
    CMapStringToString(int nBlockSize=10);
// Attributes
    // number of elements
    int GetCount() const;
    BOOL IsEmpty() const;
    // Lookup
    BOOL Lookup(const char* key, CString& rValue) const;
// Operations
    // Lookup and add if not there
    CString& operator[](const char* key);
    // add a new (key, value) pair
    void SetAt(const char* key, const char* newValue);
    // removing existing (key, ?) pair
    BOOL RemoveKey(const char* key);
    void RemoveAll();
    // iterating all (key, value) pairs
    POSITION GetStartPosition() const;
    void GetNextAssoc(POSITION& rNextPosition, CString& rKey,
                      CString& rValue) const;
    // advanced features for derived classes
    UINT GetHashTableSize() const;
    void InitHashTable(UINT hashSize);
// Overridables: special non-virtual (see map implementation for
// details)
    // Routine used to user-provided hash keys
    UINT HashKey(const char* key) const;
// Implementation
protected:
    CAssoc** m_pHashTable;
    UINT m_nHashTableSize;
    int m_nCount;
    CAssoc* m_pFreeList;
    struct CPlex* m_pBlocks;
    int m_nBlockSize;
    CAssoc* NewAssoc();
    void FreeAssoc(CAssoc*);
    CAssoc* GetAssocAt(const char*, UINT&) const;
public:
    ~CMapStringToString();
    void Serialize(CArchive&);
#ifdef _DEBUG
    void Dump(CDumpContext&) const;
    void AssertValid() const;
#endif
};
```

III

Advanced Programming

The class CMapStringToString declares a single constructor, a destructor,
a local structure, and a group of data members and member functions.

The constructor has the single parameter, nBlockSize, with a default argument of 10. This parameter defines the increments in the size of the hash table, which is created using a linked list. Each map entry is made up of a key and a value. The class employs the key part of the entry to access the value associated with that key.

The class declares the following relevant member functions:

- The parameterless member function GetCount obtains the number of entries in the map.

- The Boolean member function IsEmpty returns TRUE if the map is empty.

- The member function SetAt stores an ASCIIZ string at a designated key (which is also an ASCIIZ string). The function translates the string parameter key into the address of a hash-table entry which stores the argument for the parameter newValue.

- The Boolean member function Lookup searches for a value associated with the string-parameter key. The function returns TRUE if the targeted map has an entry that matches the argument of the parameter key. Otherwise, the function returns FALSE. The reference CString parameter rValue returns the value associated with the argument of the parameter key when the search is successful.

- The [] operator is an appropriate alternative for the function SetAt. Employ this operator only on the left side of an assignment statement.

- The Boolean member function RemoveKey deletes the map entry with a key value matching the argument of the parameter key. The function returns TRUE if the map has the sought entry and successfully removes that entry. Otherwise, the function returns FALSE.

- The member function RemoveAll deletes all the entries in the map but retains the map object.

- The member function GetStartPosition returns the position of the first map entry. The function returns a result of the type position.

- The member function GetNextAssoc returns the next key and value. The function has three reference parameters: rNextPosition, rKey, and rValue. The POSITION-type rNextPosition parameter returns the position of the next map entry. The parameters rKey and rValue return the key and value of the visited map entry. Following is a short example of how to use the functions GetStartPosition and GetNextAssoc to traverse a map:

```
CMapStringToString StrMap;
CString KeyStr;
CString ValStr;
ValStr = "Virginia";
StrMap.SetAt("Richmond", ValStr);
ValStr = "New York";
StrMap.SetAt("Albany", ValStr);
ValStr = "Michigan";
StrMap.SetAt("Lansing", ValStr);
ValStr = "California";
StrMap.SetAt("Sacramento", ValStr);
for (POSITION p = StrMap.GetStartPosition(); p != NULL; ) {
  StrMap.GetNextAssoc(p, KeyStr, ValStr);
  cout << "KeyStr: " << (const char*)KeyStr
       << "  ValStr: " << (const char*)ValStr << "\n";
}
```

Test of the *CMapStringToString* Class

This section looks at an example that uses a CMapStringToString object (called *the map* for short). The program CSTRMAP1.EXE employs such an object to relate the names of countries and their capitals. Figure 14.4 shows a session with the test program CSTRMAP1.EXE.

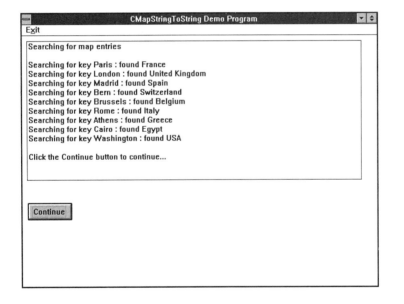

Figure 14.4
A session with the test program CSTRMAP1.EXE.

The application's window contains the following controls:

- *Output list box control.* Displays the output; this control acts as a simple DOS-like screen.

- *Start pushbutton.* Enables you to step through the various stages of testing. The program alters the caption of this pushbutton from *Start* to *Continue*. Ater the program finishes the testing, it changes the caption of the button back to *Start*.

The program has a menu with single selection: Exit.

Initially, the window displays an empty list box, and the pushbutton has the caption *Start*. Click the Start button to begin running the various tests. The caption of the pushbutton becomes *Continue* and the program performs the following tests:

- Builds the map and displays its entries in the output list box.

- Searches for the entries in the map and displays the outcome of the search in the output list box.

- Deletes two entries in the map and repeats the search.

The program uses short time delays (about half a second per delay) when it displays the searched strings.

Listing 14.18 shows the contents of the CSTRMAP1.DEF file.

Listing 14.18 The CSTRMAP1.DEF File

```
NAME         CMapStr1
DESCRIPTION  'An MFC Windows Application'
EXETYPE      WINDOWS
CODE         PRELOAD MOVEABLE DISCARDABLE
DATA         PRELOAD MOVEABLE MULTIPLE
HEAPSIZE     1024
```

Listing 14.19 shows the source code for the CSTRMAP1.H header file.

Listing 14.19 Source Code for the CSTRMAP1.H Header File

```
#define CM_EXIT        100
#define ID_CONTINUE_BTN 101
#define ID_OUTPUT_LST   102
```

Listing 14.20 contains the script for the CSTRMAP1.RC resource file.

Listing 14.20 Script for the CSTRMAP1.RC Resource File

```
#include <windows.h>
#include <afxres.h>
#include "cstrmap1.h"
EXITMENU MENU LOADONCALL MOVEABLE PURE DISCARDABLE
BEGIN
  MENUITEM "E&xit", CM_EXIT
END
```

Listing 14.21 contains the source code for the CSTRMAP1.CPP program file.

Listing 14.21 Source Code for the CSTRMAP1.CPP Program File

```
/*
  Program that uses class CMapStringToString to create
  a table that maps the capital cities to their
  respective countries.
*/
#include <stdio.h>
#include <afxwin.h>
#include <string.h>
#include "cstrmap1.h"
// declare constants which dimension the controls
const Hbtn = 30;
const Wbtn = 80;
const BtnHorzSpacing = 60;
const BtnVertSpacing = 20;
const Hlst = 250;
const Wlst = 600;
const LstHorzSpacing = 30;
const LstVertSpacing = 30;
// declare miscellaneous constants
const MaxStringLen = 255;
const MAX_ARRAY = 15;
const MAX_STAGES = 2;
const DWORD DELAY = 500;
const char* dbKey[] = { "Paris", "London", "Madrid", "Bern",
                "Brussels", "Rome", "Athens", "Cairo",
                "Washington", "EOL" };

const char* dbValue[] = { "France", "United Kingdom", "Spain",
                "Switzerland", "Belgium", "Italy", "Greece",
                "Egypt", "USA", "EOL" };
// Define an application class derived from CWinApp
class CWindowApp : public CWinApp
{
 public:
  virtual BOOL InitInstance();
};
class CxButton : public CButton
{
```

(continues)

Listing 14.21 Continued

```
public:
   BOOL Create(const char FAR* lpCaption, const RECT& rect,
          CWnd* pParentWnd, UINT nID, BOOL bIsDefault);

};
// Define a window class derived from CFrameWnd
class CMainWnd : public CFrameWnd
{
public:
  CMainWnd();
  ~CMainWnd();
protected:
  CMapStringToString StrMap;
  CxButton* pContinueBtn;
  CListBox* pOutputLst;
  POSITION Pos;
  int nStage;

  // handle button commands
  afx_msg void HandleContinueBtn();
  // handle the menu options
  afx_msg void OnExit();
  // handle creating the controls
  afx_msg int OnCreate(LPCREATESTRUCT lpCS);
  // coordinates and dimensions
  void makerect(int X, int Y, int W, int H, CRect& r)
    { r.SetRect(X, Y, X + W, Y + H); }
  // handle output to list box
  void writeln(const char* szStr)
    { pOutputLst->AddString(szStr); }
  void writeln(CString& StrObj)
    { pOutputLst->AddString((const char*)StrObj); }
  void writeToLastLine(const char* szStr);
  void writeToLastLine(CString& StrObj);

  // members which manage different test stages
  void progress();
  void ClickContBtn();
  void putMapEntry(CString& KeyStr, CString& ValueStr);
  BOOL getMapEntry(CString& KeyStr, CString& ValueStr);
  BOOL removeMapEntry(CString& KeyStr);
  BOOL getFirstMapEntry(CString& KeyStr, CString& ValueStr);
  BOOL getNextMapEntry(CString& KeyStr, CString& ValueStr);

  void showMap();
  void buildMap();
  void searchMap();
  void wait(DWORD delay);
  // message map macro
  DECLARE_MESSAGE_MAP()
};

BOOL CxButton::Create(const char FAR* lpCaption, const RECT& rect,
            CWnd* pParentWnd, UINT nID, BOOL bIsDefault)
{
```

```
    DWORD dwBtnStyle = (bIsDefault == TRUE) ?
                BS_DEFPUSHBUTTON : BS_PUSHBUTTON;
  return CButton::Create(lpCaption,
     WS_CHILD ¦ WS_VISIBLE ¦ WS_TABSTOP ¦ dwBtnStyle,
     rect, pParentWnd, nID);
}
CMainWnd::CMainWnd()
{
  Create(NULL, "CMapStringToString Demo Program",
        WS_OVERLAPPEDWINDOW, rectDefault, NULL, "EXITMENU");
  // initialize the progress stage
  nStage = 0;
}

CMainWnd::~CMainWnd()
{
  delete pOutputLst;
  delete pContinueBtn;
}
int CMainWnd::OnCreate(LPCREATESTRUCT lpCS)
{
  int x = 10;
  int y = 10;
  DWORD dwListBoxStyle = WS_CHILD ¦ WS_VISIBLE ¦ WS_VSCROLL ¦
                        LBS_STANDARD;
  CRect r;
  // disable sorting of items in the list box
  dwListBoxStyle &= ~LBS_SORT;

  // create the output list box
  makerect(x, y, Wlst, Hlst, r);
  pOutputLst = new CListBox();
  pOutputLst->Create(dwListBoxStyle, r, this, ID_OUTPUT_LST);

  // create the Continue pushbutton
  y += Hlst + LstVertSpacing;
  makerect(x, y, Wbtn, Hbtn, r);
  pContinueBtn = new CxButton();
  pContinueBtn->Create("Start", r, this, ID_CONTINUE_BTN, TRUE);

  return CFrameWnd::OnCreate(lpCS);
}
void CMainWnd::writeToLastLine(const char* szStr)
{
  char szBuff[MaxStringLen+1];
  int n = pOutputLst->GetCount() - 1;
  pOutputLst->GetText(n, szBuff);
  strcat(szBuff, szStr);
  pOutputLst->DeleteString(n);
  pOutputLst->AddString(szBuff);
}
void CMainWnd::writeToLastLine(CString& StrObj)
{
  char szBuff[MaxStringLen+1];
  int n = pOutputLst->GetCount() - 1;
  pOutputLst->GetText(n, szBuff);
```

(continues)

Listing 14.21 Continued

```
      strcat(szBuff, (const char*)StrObj);
      pOutputLst->DeleteString(n);
      pOutputLst->AddString(szBuff);
  }
  void CMainWnd::progress()
  {
    switch (nStage) {
      case 0:
        buildMap();
        break;

      case 1:
        searchMap();
        break;

      case 2:
        StrMap.RemoveKey(dbKey[0]);
        StrMap.RemoveKey(dbKey[1]);
        searchMap();
        break;

      default:
        nStage = -1;
        MessageBox("Program has finished testing", "Information",
                   MB_OK | MB_ICONINFORMATION);
        break;
    }
    nStage++;
  }
  void CMainWnd::ClickContBtn()
  {
    writeln("");
    writeln("Click the Continue button to continue...");
  }
  void CMainWnd::putMapEntry(CString& KeyStr, CString& ValueStr)
  {
    StrMap.SetAt((const char*)KeyStr, ValueStr);
  }
  BOOL CMainWnd::getMapEntry(CString& KeyStr, CString& ValueStr)
  {
    return StrMap.Lookup((const char*)KeyStr, ValueStr);
  }
  BOOL CMainWnd::removeMapEntry(CString& KeyStr)
  {
    return StrMap.RemoveKey((const char*)KeyStr);
  }
  BOOL CMainWnd::getFirstMapEntry(CString& KeyStr, CString& ValueStr)
  {
    Pos = StrMap.GetStartPosition();
    if (Pos != NULL) {
      StrMap.GetNextAssoc(Pos, KeyStr, ValueStr);
      return TRUE;
    }
    else {
      ValueStr = "";
```

```
      KeyStr = "";
      return FALSE;
    }
  }
BOOL CMainWnd::getNextMapEntry(CString& KeyStr, CString& ValueStr)
{
  if (Pos != NULL) {
    StrMap.GetNextAssoc(Pos, KeyStr, ValueStr);
    return TRUE;
  }
  else {
    ValueStr = "";
    KeyStr = "";
    return FALSE;
  }
}
void CMainWnd::showMap()
{
  CString KeyStr, ValueStr;
  BOOL moreEntries = getFirstMapEntry(KeyStr, ValueStr);
  char szStr[MaxStringLen+1];

  while (moreEntries) {
    sprintf(szStr, "%s is the capital of %s",
                   (const char*)KeyStr, (const char*)ValueStr);
    writeln(szStr);
    moreEntries = getNextMapEntry(KeyStr, ValueStr);
  }
}

void CMainWnd::buildMap()
{
  writeln("Map is:");
  writeln("");
  for (int i = 0; stricmp(dbKey[i], "EOL") != 0; i++)
    putMapEntry(CString(dbKey[i]), CString(dbValue[i]));

  showMap();
  ClickContBtn();
}
void CMainWnd::searchMap()
{
  CString ValueStr;
  char szStr[MaxStringLen+1];

  writeln("Searching for map entries");
  writeln("");
  for (int i = 0; stricmp(dbKey[i], "EOL") != 0; i++) {
    sprintf(szStr, "Searching for key %s : ", dbKey[i]);
    writeln(szStr);
    // search for dbKey[i] in table
    if (getMapEntry(CString(dbKey[i]), ValueStr)) {
      sprintf(szStr, "found %s", (const char*)ValueStr);
      writeToLastLine(szStr);
    }
    else
```

(continues)

Listing 14.21 Continued

```
          writeToLastLine("not found");

    wait(DELAY);
    UpdateWindow();
  }
  ClickContBtn();
}
void CMainWnd::HandleContinueBtn()
{
  // starting the test?
  if (nStage == 0)
    pContinueBtn->SetWindowText("Continue");
  // clear the list box
  pOutputLst->ResetContent();
  // perform the next testing stage
  progress();
  // finished testing?
  if (nStage > MAX_STAGES) {
    pContinueBtn->SetWindowText("Start");
    nStage = 0;
  }
}
void CMainWnd::wait(DWORD delay)
{
  DWORD initTime = GetTickCount();

  while ((GetTickCount() - initTime) < delay)
    // do nothing
    ;
}
void CMainWnd::OnExit()
{
  // prompt user if he or she wants to close the application
  if (MessageBox("Want to close this application", "Query",
                 MB_YESNO | MB_ICONQUESTION) == IDYES)
    SendMessage(WM_CLOSE);
}
BEGIN_MESSAGE_MAP(CMainWnd, CFrameWnd)
  ON_BN_CLICKED(ID_CONTINUE_BTN, HandleContinueBtn)
  ON_COMMAND(CM_EXIT, OnExit)
  ON_WM_CREATE()
END_MESSAGE_MAP()
// Construct the CWindowApp's m_pMainWnd data member
BOOL CWindowApp::InitInstance()
{
  m_pMainWnd = new CMainWnd();
  m_pMainWnd->ShowWindow(m_nCmdShow);
  m_pMainWnd->UpdateWindow();
  return TRUE;
}
// application's constructor initializes and runs the app
CWindowApp WindowApp;
```

The CSTRMAP1.H header file shown in Listing 14.19 defines the Windows command message CM_EXIT sent by the program's single menu item, Exit. The header file also defines the IDs for the various controls. The CSTRMAP1.RC resource file shown in Listing 14.20 defines the Options menu resource with its single menu option. The CSTRMAP1.CPP program file shown in Listing 14.21 defines a group of constants and classes. The first set of constants defines the dimensions and spacing of the various controls. The second set of constants defines the maximum string size, maximum array size, maximum number of testing stages, delay value, and the initialized string arrays dbKey and dbValue. The array dbKey contains the names of the capital cities. The array dbValue contains the names of the corresponding countries. The program also declares three classes: CxButton, CMainWnd, and CWindowApp. The class CxButton, a descendant of MFC class CButton, models pushbutton controls. The class CMainWnd models the main window. The class CWindowApp models the application.

The class CMainWnd declares a constructor, a destructor, a set of data members, and a group of member functions. The data members are as follows:

- The member StrMap is an instance of class CMapStringToString.

- The member pContinueBtn is the pointer to the Start/Continue pushbutton.

- The member pOutputLst is the pointer to the output list box.

- The member Pos has the type POSITION. The class uses this member to track the traversing of the map StrMap.

- The member nStage maintains the current stage of testing.

The constructor for class CMainWnd creates the window and its controls and sets the member nStage to 0.

The class CMainWnd declares the following relevant member functions:

- The member function OnCreate creates the controls attached to the window. The function defines the local variable dwListBoxStyle to define the list box style. The LBS_SORT style was disabled to chronologically store strings in the output list box. The OnCreate function creates the various controls using the control-pointer members.

- The overloaded member function writeln appends an ASCIIZ string and a CString object to the list of items in the output list box.

- The overloaded member function `writeToLastLine` appends an ASCIIZ string and a `CString` object to the last item in the output list box.

- The member function `ClickContBtn` displays the message `Click the Continue button to continue...` in the output list box. The function uses the member function `writeln` to display a blank line and the message.

- The member function `putMapEntry` stores a new entry in the map `StrMap`. The function has the `CString` parameters `KeyStr` (the key) and `ValueStr` (the value associated with the key). The function performs this task by sending the C++ message `SetAt` to the member `StrMap`. The arguments for this message are the parameters `KeyStr` and `ValueStr`.

- The member function `getMapEntry` recalls a value from the map `StrMap`, given a key value. The function has the `CString` parameters `KeyStr` (the key) and `ValueStr` (the value associated with the key). The function performs this task by sending the C++ message `Lookup` to the member `StrMap`. The arguments for this message are the parameters `KeyStr` and `ValueStr`. The reference parameter `ValueStr` reports the obtained value.

- The member function `removeMapEntry` removes a map entry for a given key value. The function has a single parameter, a `CString` object that specifies the removed map entry. The function performs this task by sending the C++ message `RemoveKey` to the member `StrMap`. The argument for this message is the parameter `KeyStr`.

- The Boolean member function `getFirstMapEntry` obtains the key and value for the first map entry. The function returns these values through the reference `CString` parameters `KeyStr` and `ValueStr`. The function `getFirstMapEntry` returns TRUE if the map is not empty. The function performs the following tasks:

  - Assigns the position of the first map entry to the member `Pos`. This task involves sending the C+ message `GetStartPosition` to the member `StrMap`.

  - Determines whether the member `Pos` is not NULL. If this condition is true, the function sends the C++ message `GetNextAssoc` to the member `StrMap`. The arguments for this message are `Pos`, `KeyStr`, and `ValueStr`. The function also returns TRUE. If the member `Pos` is NULL, the function assigns empty strings to the parameters `KeyStr` and `ValueStr` and then returns FALSE.

- The Boolean member function `getNextMapEntry` obtains the key and value for the next map entry. The function returns these values through the reference `CString` parameters `KeyStr` and `ValueStr`. The function `getNextMapEntry` returns TRUE if it did not reach the end of the map `StrMap`. The function determines whether the member `Pos` is not NULL. If this condition is true, the function sends the C++ message `GetNextAssoc` to the member `StrMap`. The arguments for this message are `Pos`, `KeyStr`, and `ValueStr`. The function also returns TRUE. If the member `Pos` is NULL, the function assigns empty strings to the parameters `KeyStr` and `ValueStr` and then returns FALSE.

- The member function `showMap` displays the elements of the member `StrMap`. The function declares a local `CString` object, an ASCIIZ string, and the BOOL variable `moreEntries`. The function initializes the latter variable with the value of member function `getFirstMapEntry`. The arguments for the latter function are the local `CString` objects `KeyStr` and `ValueStr`. Visiting the map entries involves a `while` loop that examines the Boolean value of the variable `moreEntries`. The statements of the loop perform the following tasks:

  - Create a formatted string (using the function `sprintf`) that contains the strings in the variables `KeyStr` and `ValueStr`. This task stores the formatted string in the local variable `szStr`.

  - Display the contents of variable `szStr` in the output list box by invoking the member function `writeln`.

  - Obtain the next map entry. This task involves the function `getNextMapEntry`. The arguments of this member function are the local variables `KeyStr` and `ValueStr`. This task assigns the result of the function `getNextMapEntry` to the local variable `moreEntries`.

- The member function `buildMap` builds the map using the global string constants `dbKey` and `dbValue`. The function uses a `for` loop to process the strings in these constants. The loop has a single statement that invokes the member function `putMapEntry`. The arguments for this function are the `CString` typecast of `dbKey[i]` and `dbValue[i]`. After the loop finishes iterating, the function invokes the function `showMap` to display the contents of the member `StrMap`.

III

Advanced Programming

■ The member function searchMap searches for the map entries using the
key values supplied by the global constant array dbKey. The function
displays a heading and then uses a for loop to search for the map
entries. Each loop iteration performs the following tasks:

- Creates a formatted string (using the function sprintf) that contains the search string dbKey[i]. This task stores the formatted
  string in the local variable szStr.

- Displays the contents of the variable szStr in the output list box
  by invoking the member function writeln.

- Searches for a map entry that matches the key dbKey[i]. This task
  involves calling member function getMapEntry in an if statement.
  If the called function returns TRUE, the function searchMap first
  creates a formatted string that contains the associated value string.
  Then the function displays the formatted string in the output list
  box. If the function getMapEntry returns FALSE, the function
  searchMap displays the message not found in the output list box.

- Delays the program by invoking the member function delay.

- Updates the main window and its controls by invoking the
  inherited function UpdateWindow.

■ The member function HandleContinueBtn responds to the messages sent
by the Start/Continue pushbutton control. The function performs the
following tasks:

- Determines whether the value of member nStage is 0. If this condition is true, the function sends the C++ message SetWindowText
  to the pushbutton to change its caption to *Continue*.

- Clears the output list box by sending it the C++ message
  ResetContent. Because the output list box acts as a simple DOS
  screen, this message is similar to a clear-screen command.

- Executes the next testing stage by invoking the member function
  progress.

- Determines whether the integer in member nStage exceeds that of
  the global MAX_STAGES. If this condition is true, the function alters
  the caption of the pushbutton to *Start* and assigns 0 to the member nStage. These actions reset the testing cycle.

- The member function progress performs the various tests in various stages by using a switch statement. This statement uses the member nStage to execute a particular set of statements every time the function stage is invoked. The stages are as follows:

  Stage 0. Invokes the function buildMap to build the map and displays its entries in the output list box.

  Stage 1. Invokes the function searchMap to search for map entries that match the strings in the global constant dbKey.

  Stage 2. Deletes the map entries that contain keys dbKey[0] and dbKey[1] and then repeats the search.

The last statement in the function progress systematically increments the value in member nStage.

Summary

This chapter presented the class CString and the collection classes that are part of the MFC library. Here's what you learned:

- The CString class models string objects and provides operations to support these objects.

- The array classes include a group of classes that model unordered arrays of various kinds of integers, pointers, strings, and CObject pointers. These classes have similar data members and member functions.

- The list classes include a group of classes that model lists of pointers, strings, and CObject pointers. The lists modeled are indexable doubly linked lists. These kinds of lists can emulate arrays, stacks, and queues.

- The map classes include a group of classes that implement hash-table-based maps that associate integers to pointers, pointers to integers, pointers to pointers, integers to CObject pointers, strings to CObject pointers, and strings to other strings. These classes provide the framework and search speed used to associate various kinds of data types.

III

Advanced Programming

Chapter 15

Using the Exceptions Classes

Programming languages such as BASIC, Pascal, C, C++, and Ada share somewhat similar constructs, such as loops, decision-making statements, and subprograms (functions and procedures). However, in the area of error handling, these languages exhibit more differences than similarities. Microsoft BASIC and Ada, for example, support error handling statements, whereas C and Pascal do not. C and Pascal programs, therefore, must rely on defensive programming techniques to fend off run-time errors. BASIC and Ada programs, on the other hand, don't have to resort to using defensive techniques. What about C++? Initially, C++ followed the path of C in handling errors. In the last few years, however, the primary C++ designer, Bjarne Stroustrup, has proposed a formal exceptions mechanism that is being considered by the ANSI C++ Standards Committee. In the meantime, Microsoft has implemented its own macro-based exceptions mechanism for Visual C++. This exceptions implementation uses special MFC classes and is inspired by Stroustrup's proposal. This chapter presents Microsoft's exceptions mechanism and covers the following topics:

- An introduction to the Visual C++ exceptions

- The CException class

- The CMemoryException class

- The CFileException class

- The CArchiveException class

- The CResourceException class

III

Advanced Programming

- The `CUserException` class

- The `CNotSupportedException` class

- The `COleException` class

The Visual C++ Exceptions

The proposed ANSI C++ exceptions have influenced how Visual C++ implements exceptions. The Visual C++ exceptions use macros to trap and handle various kinds of errors.

The Visual C++ Exception Syntax

In general, the syntax for trapping an error is as follows:

```
TRY
{
  // statements that may raise one or more errors
  .
  .
  .
}
CATCH(exceptionClass1, e)
{
  // statements to handle error of type exceptionClass1
}
[AND_CATCH(exceptionClass2, e)
{
  // statements to handle error of type exceptionClass2
}
AND_CATCH(exceptionClass3, e)
{
  // statements to handle error of type exceptionClass3
}
// other AND_CATCH blocks
AND_CATCH(exceptionClassN, e)
{
  // statements to handle error of type exceptionClassN
}]
END_CATCH
```

The TRY block holds statements that may cause one or more errors. The mandatory CATCH block contains the statements that handle the `exceptionClass1` type of error raised in the TRY block. The identifier e is the pointer to the exception class. This pointer accesses more detailed information about the cause of the error. You can use one or more AND_CATCH blocks to handle various kinds of errors generated by the code in the TRY block. As with the CATCH block, the AND_CATCH block specifies the error class to be handled.

Visual C++ also supports the catch-all exception block AND_CATCH_ALL. If you use this kind of block, you must use the END_CATCH_ALL macro after the end of the block. Following is the general syntax for the multi-exception handlers that use the AND_CATCH_ALL block:

```
TRY
{
  // statements that may raise one or more errors
  .
  .
  .
}
CATCH(exceptionClass1, e)
{
  // statements to handle error of type exceptionClass1
}
[AND_CATCH(exceptionClass2, e)
{
  // statements to handle error of type exceptionClass2
}
AND_CATCH(exceptionClass3, e)
{
  // statements to handle error of type exceptionClass3
}
// other AND_CATCH blocks
AND_CATCH_ALL(e)
{
  // statements to handle other kinds of errors
}
END_CATCH_ALL]
```

Notice that the AND_CATCH_ALL macro takes only one argument—the pointer to the exception.

> **Note**
>
> Visual C++ supports placing a TRY block in CATCH, AND_CATCH, and AND_CATCH_ALL blocks, which means that you can handle a new exception that might be thrown while it is handling an old one.

The MFC Exception Classes

First, let's take an overall look at the MFC classes that model various types of exceptions. Table 15.1 shows these classes, and subsequent sections discuss these classes in greater detail.

III

Advanced Programming

Table 15.1 MFC Library Exception Classes	
Exception Class	**Purpose**
CException	Root of other exception classes
CFileException	File exception
CArchiveException	Archive exception
CResourceException	Resource exception
CMemoryException	Memory exception
CUserException	User exception
CNotSupportedException	Unsupported exception
COleException	OLE exception

The Process of Generating Exceptions

Visual C++ supports two basic mechanisms for *raising* (or *throwing*) exceptions. The first mechanism is automatic: An offending statement throws a specific exception in the TRY block. The second kind of exception has to be thrown explicitly using either the THROW macro or one of the AfxThrowXXXXException functions (these functions and their respective exception classes are discussed later in this chapter). The macro THROW requires a single argument that is a pointer to an exception object. In addition, Visual C++ supports the THROW_LAST macro that throws the last exception. The THROW_LAST macro requires no arguments.

The *CException* Class

The class CException is the root of the class exceptions sub-hierarchy. Following is the declaration of class CException, which is a descendant of CObject:

```
class CException : public CObject
{
  // abstract class for dynamic type checking
  DECLARE_DYNAMIC(CException)
};
```

The class CException serves two purposes: first, it is the root of the exception classes sub-hierarchy; second, it acts as a general kind of exception. You can trap diverse types of errors utilizing this class along with the member function CObject::IsKindOf to support the descendant class that specifies the raised exception.

The *CMemoryException* Class

The class CMemoryException models an out-of-memory error condition.
The declaration of the CMemoryException class follows:

```
class CMemoryException : public CException
{
  DECLARE_DYNAMIC(CMemoryException)
public:
  CMemoryException();
};
```

The operator new automatically throws the memory exception. In contrast,
using the function malloc requires a statement that explicitly throws the
memory exception. Two code fragments follow. The first uses the operator
new, which automatically throws the exception; the second code fragment
uses the function malloc, which requires an explicit call to the function
AfxThrowMemoryException:

```
const MAX_SIZE = 30000;
char *pszStr;
TRY
{
  pszStr = new char[MAX_SIZE]; // create a large string
  // statements to process dynamic string
  .
  .
  .
  delete [] pszStr;
}
CATCH(CMemoryException, e)
{
  cout << "Error allocating string\n";
}
END_CATCH
```

The following version uses the function malloc. Notice that this version
requires an additional if statement in the next TRY block:

```
const MAX_SIZE = 30000;
char *pszStr;
TRY
{
  pszStr = (char*) malloc(MAX_SIZE); // create a large string
  if (!pszStr)
    AfxThrowMemoryException()
  // statements to process dynamic string
  .
  .
  .
  free(pszStr);
```

```
}
CATCH(CMemoryException, e)
{
  cout << "Error allocating string\n";
}
END_CATCH
```

Test of the *CMemoryException* Class

In this section, I present a simple Windows program that uses the class
CMemoryException to handle errors in dynamic memory allocation. The
MEMERR1.EXE program displays a simple window with the two menus: Exit
and Test Memory Error. When you click the Test Memory Error menu, the
program performs these tests:

1. Dynamically allocates an array of integers.

2. Deallocates the dynamic array.

3. Increases the size of the next dynamic array by a factor of 10.

4. Repeats steps 1 through 3 until a memory allocation error occurs. The
   program displays a message dialog box for every array that is successfully created. Using an exception handler, the program detects the
   memory allocation error and displays a message box indicating the
   occurrence of that error and the size of the array to be allocated when
   the error occurs. Figure 15.1 shows the memory allocation error message box in a session with the MEMERR1.EXE program.

Figure 15.1
The memory
allocation error
message box in a
session with the
MEMERR1.EXE
program.

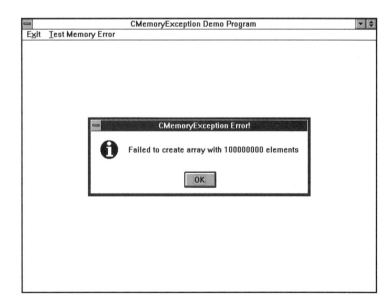

Listing 15.1 contains the contents of the MEMERR1.DEF definition file.

Listing 15.1 The MEMERR1.DEF Definition File

```
NAME         MemErr1
DESCRIPTION  'An MFC Windows Application'
EXETYPE      WINDOWS
CODE         PRELOAD MOVEABLE DISCARDABLE
DATA         PRELOAD MOVEABLE MULTIPLE
HEAPSIZE     1024
```

Listing 15.2 shows the source code for the MEMERR1.H header file.

Listing 15.2 Source Code for the MEMERR1.H Header File

```
#define CM_EXIT           (WM_USER + 100)
#define CM_TEST_MEM_ERROR (WM_USER + 101)
```

Listing 15.3 provides the script for the MEMERR1.RC resource file.

Listing 15.3 Script for the MEMERR1.RC Resource File

```
#include <windows.h>
#include <afxres.h>
#include "memerr1.h"
MAINMENU MENU LOADONCALL MOVEABLE PURE DISCARDABLE
BEGIN
    MENUITEM "E&xit", CM_EXIT
    MENUITEM "&Test Memory Error", CM_TEST_MEM_ERROR
END
```

The source code for the MEMERR1.CPP program file is provided in
Listing 15.4.

III

Listing 15.4 Source Code for the MEMERR1.CPP Program File

```
/*
  Program tests the class CMemoryException by creating a sequence
  of dynamic arrays that increase in size, until the program
  is unable to create the dynamic array.
*/
#include <stdio.h>
#include <afxwin.h>
#include "memerr1.h"
const INIT_SIZE = 1000;
const SCALE_SIZE = 10;
const MaxStringLen = 80;
// declare the custom application class as
class CMemErrApp : public CWinApp
```

Advanced Programming

(continues)

Listing 15.4 Continued

```
{
public:
    virtual BOOL InitInstance();
};
// expand the functionality of CFrameWnd by deriving
// class CMainWnd
class CMainWnd : public CFrameWnd
{
public:
  CMainWnd();
protected:
  // handle the Files menu item
  afx_msg void CMTestMemException();

  // handle exiting the application
  afx_msg void OnExit()
    { SendMessage(WM_CLOSE); }

  // handle closing the window
  afx_msg void OnClose();
  // declare message map macro
  DECLARE_MESSAGE_MAP()
};
CMainWnd::CMainWnd()
{
  // create the window
  Create(NULL, "CMemoryException Demo Program",
         WS_OVERLAPPEDWINDOW, rectDefault, NULL, "MAINMENU");
}
void CMainWnd::CMTestMemException()
{
  int* pIntArr;
  char szStr[MaxStringLen];
  long numElem = INIT_SIZE;
  TRY {
    for (;;) {
      // create dynamic array with numElem elements
      pIntArr = new int[numElem];
      sprintf(szStr, "Created dynamic array with %ld elements",
              numElem);
      MessageBox(szStr, "Success!", MB_OK | MB_ICONINFORMATION);
      delete [] pIntArr;
      // increase the size of the next array
      numElem *= SCALE_SIZE;
    }
  }
  CATCH(CMemoryException, e)
  {
    sprintf(szStr, "Failed to create array with %ld elements",
            numElem);
    MessageBox(szStr, "CMemoryException Error!",
               MB_OK | MB_ICONINFORMATION);
  }
  END_CATCH
}
void CMainWnd::OnClose()
```

```
{
  if (MessageBox("Want to close this application",
                 "Query", MB_YESNO | MB_ICONQUESTION) == IDYES)
    DestroyWindow();

}
BEGIN_MESSAGE_MAP(CMainWnd, CFrameWnd)
  ON_COMMAND(CM_TEST_MEM_ERROR, CMTestMemException)
  ON_COMMAND(CM_EXIT, OnExit)
  ON_WM_CLOSE()
END_MESSAGE_MAP()
// Construct the CMemErrApp'szStr m_pMainWnd data member
BOOL CMemErrApp::InitInstance()
{
  m_pMainWnd = new CMainWnd();
  m_pMainWnd->ShowWindow(m_nCmdShow);
  m_pMainWnd->UpdateWindow();
  return TRUE;
}
// application'szStr constructor initializes and runs the app
CMemErrApp WindowApp;
```

The program shown in Listing 15.4 declares three global constants and two classes. The constant INIT_SCALE defines the initial size of the dynamic array, and the constant SCALE_SIZE defines the scaling factor for that size. The constant MaxStringLen specifies the size of string variables.

The program declares the application class CMemErrApp and the window class CMainWnd. The class CMainWnd declares a constructor and three member functions. The relevant member function is CMTestMemError. This function performs its test in the TRY block, which carries out the following tasks in an open for loop:

■ Allocates the dynamic array of integers using the operator new and the local pointer pIntArr. The local variable numElem (initialized using the global constant INIT_SIZE) specifies the number of elements in the dynamic array. If the operator new fails, it automatically throws a CMemoryException exception. The CATCH block handles this error by displaying a message box to inform you of the error.

■ Creates a formatted string image consisting of a message and the value in the variable numElem. This task uses the function sprintf and stores the formatted string in the local variable szStr.

■ Displays the formatted string in a message dialog box. This message box tells you that the dynamic array was successfully created and also specifies its size.

■ Deletes the dynamic array.

■ Increases the value in the variable numElem by a factor of SCALE_SIZE.

The CATCH clause specifies the class CMemoryException and performs two simple tasks. First, the formatted string image is created that contains the error message and the offending number of array elements. Second, this formatted string is displayed in a message dialog box.

The *CFileException* Class

The class CFileException deals with exceptions thrown by the various MFC library classes that perform file I/O. Following is the declaration of the class CFileException:

```
class CFileException : public CException
{
    DECLARE_DYNAMIC(CFileException)
public:
    enum {
        none,
        generic,
        fileNotFound,
        badPath,
        tooManyOpenFiles,
        accessDenied,
        invalidFile,
        removeCurrentDir,
        directoryFull,
        badSeek,
        hardIO,
        sharingViolation,
        lockViolation,
        diskFull,
        endOfFile
    };
// Constructors
    CFileException(int cause = CFileException::none,
                    LONG lOsError = -1);
// Attributes
    int m_cause;
    LONG m_lOsError;
// Operations
    // convert a OS dependent error code to a Cause
    static int PASCAL OsErrorToException(LONG lOsError);
    static int PASCAL ErrnoToException(int nErrno);
    // helper functions to throw exception after converting
    // to a Cause
    static void PASCAL ThrowOsError(LONG lOsError);
    static void PASCAL ThrowErrno(int nErrno);
```

```
#ifdef _DEBUG
    virtual void Dump(CDumpContext&) const;
#endif
};
```

The class CFileException is not trivial. It declares a constructor, two data members, and a collection of member functions (most of which are static functions). The class declares a nested enumerated type that enumerates the errors related to file I/O operations. Table 15.2 provides the various enumerated values and their meanings. The class instances assign these enumerated values to the data member m_cause. The data member m_1OsError holds the codes related to operating system errors.

The member function OsErrorToException returns a cause code that coincides with an MS-DOS error code. The member function ErrnoToException returns a numeric error-cause code that parallels a run-time error number. The helper function ThrowOsError throws a file exception based on an operating system error number. The helper function ThrowErrno throws a file exception based on a run-time error number.

Table 15.2 Enumerated Values for the Data Member
CFileException::m_cause

Enumerated Value	Meaning
accessDenied	Access denied to file
badPath	Invalid path was supplied
badSeek	Invalid file pointer in a seek
directoryFull	Directory is full
diskFull	Disk is full
endOfFile	End of file reached
fileNotFound	File was not found
generic	General kind of error
hardIO	Hardware error
invalidFile	Filename is not valid

(continues)

III

Advanced Programming

Table 15.2 Continued	
Enumerated Value	**Meaning**
lockViolation	Cannot lock region already locked
none	No error has occurred
removeCurrentDir	Unable to remove current drirectory
sharingViolation	SHARE.EXE needs to be loaded
tooManyOpenFiles	Maximum number of opened file was surpassed

The function AfxThrowFileException lets your program explicitly throw a file exception. The declaration of the function AfxThrowFileException is

```
void AFXAPI AfxThrowFileException(int cause, LONG lOsError = -1);
```

The parameter cause indicates the cause of the exception. The parameter lOsError specifies the error number related to the operating system.

Test of the *CFileException* Class

In this section, the program FILEERR1.EXE is presented as an example of using the file exception class to handle simple file I/O operations. The program is a simple text file viewer and has two menus: Exit and View File. When you invoke the View File menu, the program displays an input dialog box that prompts you for a filename (with an optional path). For the sake of demonstration, I made the program use an input dialog box rather than the standard file dialog box. This approach makes entering filenames more vulnerable to typos, which leads to a request for opening a nonexisting file. In addition, the new program version also guards against opening binary files with popular extensions, such as .EXE, .COM, .OVR, .SYS, .BIN, .OBJ, .RES, .PDB, .VCW. .SBR, and .DLL. If you request to view a file with any one of these extensions, the program raises an exception and displays a message box telling you that you cannot view these binary files. The only exception made is for the CONFIG.SYS file.

The program reads the lines of the text file you specify and displays them in a list box. The title of the main window also incorporates the name of the file you are currently viewing. If the text file is too long, the program reads the part that it can and displays an error message dialog box to inform you of the problem. Figure 15.2 shows a session with the FILEERR1.EXE program.

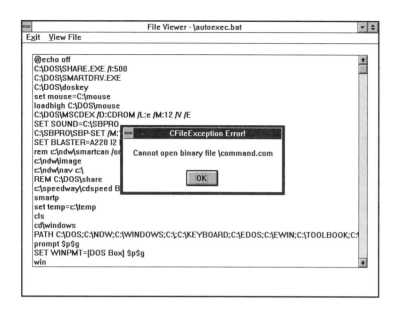

Figure 15.2
A sample
session with the
FILEERR1.EXE
program.

The FILEERR1.EXE program illustrates the following aspects of exception handling:

- Handling the error-cause code CFileException::fileNotFound.

- Handling the error-cause code CFileException::generic.

- In a CFileException error, distinguishing between the two error-cause codes just mentioned.

- Handling multiple exceptions using the AND_CATCH block to trap CMemoryException, which is raised by reading a huge text file.

Listing 15.5 contains the contents of the FILEERR1.DEF definition file.

Listing 15.5 The FILEERR1.DEF Definition File

```
NAME           FileErr1
DESCRIPTION    'An MFC Windows Application'
EXETYPE        WINDOWS
CODE           PRELOAD MOVEABLE DISCARDABLE
DATA           PRELOAD MOVEABLE MULTIPLE
HEAPSIZE       1024
```

III

Advanced Programming

Listing 15.6 shows the source code for the FILEERR1.H header file.

Listing 15.6 Source Code for the FILEERR1.H Header File

```
#define CM_EXIT  (WM_USER + 100)
#define CM_VIEW  (WM_USER + 101)
#define ID_STRING_LST   100
#define ID_FILENAME_TXT 101
```

Listing 15.7 shows the source code for the INPUTDIA.H header file.

Listing 15.7 Source Code for the INPUTDIA.H Header File

```
#define ID_INPUT_FILENAME_TXT   200
#define ID_INPUT_FILENAME_EDIT 201
```

Listing 15.8 shows the script for the FILEERR1.RC resource file.

Listing 15.8 Script for the FILEERR1.RC Resource File

```
#include <windows.h>
#include <afxres.h>
#include "fileerr1.h"
MAINMENU MENU LOADONCALL MOVEABLE PURE DISCARDABLE
BEGIN
    MENUITEM "E&xit", CM_EXIT
    MENUITEM "&View File", CM_VIEW
END
rcinclude inputdia.rc
```

Listing 15.9 shows the script for the INPUTDIA.RC resource file.

Listing 15.9 Script for the INPUTDIA.RC Resource File

```
#include <windows.h>
#include <afxres.h>
#include "inputdia.h"
INPUT_FILENAME DIALOG 44, 34, 200, 80
STYLE DS_MODALFRAME ¦ WS_CAPTION ¦ WS_VISIBLE ¦ WS_SYSMENU
CAPTION "Open File"
BEGIN
   LTEXT "Enter a filename:", ID_INPUT_FILENAME_TXT, 20, 10, 160, 12,
        NOT WS_GROUP
   EDITTEXT ID_INPUT_FILENAME_EDIT, 20, 25, 160, 12, ES_AUTOHSCROLL
   DEFPUSHBUTTON "OK", IDOK, 20, 45, 65, 14, WS_GROUP
   PUSHBUTTON "Cancel", IDCANCEL, 110, 45, 65, 14, WS_GROUP
END
```

The source code for the FILEERR1.CPP program file is provided in
Listing 15.10.

Listing 15.10 Source Code for the FILEERR1.CPP Program File

```
/*
  Program which tests the CFileException to handle file errors.
  The program views a text file and displays error messages
  if it cannot find the file, open a binary file, and
  read the entire file in the list box control.

*/
#include <fstream.h>
#include <afxwin.h>
#include <afxdlgs.h>
#include "fileerr1.h"
#include "inputdia.h"
// define global constants
const MaxStringLen = 80;
const BigStringLen = 255;
const Wlst = 600;
const Hlst = 375;
// declare the custom application class as
class CFileErrApp : public CWinApp
{
public:
    virtual BOOL InitInstance();
};
// expand the functionality of CFrameWnd by deriving
// class CMainWnd
class CMainWnd : public CFrameWnd
{
public:
  CMainWnd()
    {      // create the window
        Create(NULL, "File Viewer",
               WS_OVERLAPPEDWINDOW, rectDefault, NULL, "MAINMENU");
    }

  ~CMainWnd()
    { delete pTextLst; }
protected:

  CListBox* pTextLst;

  // handle creating the controls
  afx_msg int OnCreate(LPCREATESTRUCT lpCS);

  // handle the Files menu item
  afx_msg void CMView();

  // handle exiting the application
  afx_msg void OnExit()
    { SendMessage(WM_CLOSE); }
  // handle closing the window
```

(continues)

Listing 15.10 Continued

```
    afx_msg void OnClose();
    // coordinates and dimensions
    void makerect(int X, int Y, int W, int H, CRect& r)
      { r.SetRect(X, Y, X + W, Y + H); }
    // verify that file is not an executable one
    BOOL IsTextFile(CString& Filename);
    // declare message map macro
    DECLARE_MESSAGE_MAP()
};
// declare a class for the line input dialog box
class CFilenameInputDlg : public CDialog
{
public:
  CFilenameInputDlg(CWnd* pParent) :
    CDialog("INPUT_FILENAME", pParent)
    { InputFilename = ""; }

  // handle initializing the dialog box
  virtual BOOL OnInitDialog();

  // handle the OK button
  virtual void OnOK();

  // access input
  CString& GetInputFilename()
     { return InputFilename; }
protected:
  CString InputFilename;
};
BOOL CFilenameInputDlg::OnInitDialog()
{
  // assign the message a default input to the dialog
  // box static and edit box controls
  SetDlgItemText(ID_INPUT_FILENAME_EDIT, (const char*) InputFilename);
  return TRUE;
}
void CFilenameInputDlg::OnOK()
{
  // obtain the user's input
  GetDlgItemText(ID_INPUT_FILENAME_EDIT,
                 InputFilename.GetBuffer(MaxStringLen),
                 MaxStringLen);
  InputFilename.ReleaseBuffer();
  EndDialog(IDOK);
}
int CMainWnd::OnCreate(LPCREATESTRUCT lpCS)
{
  int x = 20;
  int y = 20;
  DWORD dwListBoxStyle = WS_CHILD | WS_VISIBLE | WS_VSCROLL |
                         LBS_STANDARD;
  CRect r;
   // disable sorting of items in the list box
```

```
      dwListBoxStyle &= ~LBS_SORT;

      makerect(x, y, Wlst, Hlst, r);
      pTextLst = new CListBox();
      pTextLst->Create(dwListBoxStyle, r, this, ID_STRING_LST);
      return CFrameWnd::OnCreate(lpCS);
   }
   void CMainWnd::CMView()
   {
      CString selectedFile;
      CString windowTitle;
      CString StrObj;
      char szStr[BigStringLen+1];
      fstream f;
      CFilenameInputDlg FilenameInputDlg(this);
      if (FilenameInputDlg.DoModal() == IDOK) {
         TRY
         {
            // get the filename
            selectedFile = FilenameInputDlg.GetInputFilename();
            if (!IsTextFile(selectedFile))
               AfxThrowFileException(CFileException::generic);
            // open the file
            f.open(selectedFile, ios::in | ios::nocreate);
            if (!f.good())
               AfxThrowFileException(CFileException::fileNotFound);
            // set the new window title
            windowTitle = "File Viewer - " + selectedFile;
            SetWindowText((const char*)windowTitle);
            // clear the list box first
            pTextLst->ResetContent();
            // inserts the lines from the text file
            while (!f.eof()) {
               f.getline(szStr, BigStringLen);
               pTextLst->AddString(szStr);
            }
         }
         CATCH(CFileException, e)
         {
            switch (e->m_cause) {
               case CFileException::generic:
                  StrObj = "Cannot open binary file " + selectedFile;
                  break;
               case CFileException::fileNotFound:
                  StrObj = "Cannot open file " + selectedFile;
                  break;
               default:
                  StrObj = "Untrapped file error";
            }
            MessageBox(StrObj, "CFileException Error!");
         }
         AND_CATCH(CMemoryException, e)
         {
            StrObj = "Cannot read the entire file" +
                  selectedFile +
                  " in the list box";
```

(continues)

Advanced Programming

III

Listing 15.10 Continued

```
        MessageBox(StrObj, "CMemoryException Error!");
      }
      END_CATCH
      // close file anyway
      f.close();
    }
}
void CMainWnd::OnClose()
{
  if (MessageBox("Want to close this application",
                "Query", MB_YESNO ¦ MB_ICONQUESTION) == IDYES)
    DestroyWindow();
}
BOOL CMainWnd::IsTextFile(CString& Filename)
{
  CStringList StrList;
  CString StrObj(Filename);
  CString FilenameCopy(Filename);
  // deal with the special case of config.sys
  // convert the copy of the filename into uppercase
  FilenameCopy.MakeUpper();
  if (FilenameCopy == "\\CONFIG.SYS" ¦¦
      FilenameCopy == "CONFIG.SYS")
      return TRUE;
  // build the list of binary file extensions
  StrList.AddHead(".EXE");
  StrList.AddHead(".COM");
  StrList.AddHead(".OVR");
  StrList.AddHead(".SYS");
  StrList.AddHead(".BIN");
  StrList.AddHead(".OBJ");
  StrList.AddHead(".RES");
  StrList.AddHead(".PDB");
  StrList.AddHead(".VCW");
  StrList.AddHead(".SBR");
  StrList.AddHead(".DLL");

  // extract the last four characters
  StrObj = StrObj.Right(4);
  // convert them into uppercase
  StrObj.MakeUpper();
  // return the result of searching for STR in string list
  return (StrList.Find(StrObj)) ? FALSE : TRUE;
}
BEGIN_MESSAGE_MAP(CMainWnd, CFrameWnd)
  ON_WM_CREATE()
  ON_COMMAND(CM_VIEW, CMView)
  ON_COMMAND(CM_EXIT, OnExit)
  ON_WM_CLOSE()
END_MESSAGE_MAP()
// Construct the CFileErrApp'szStr m_pMainWnd data member
BOOL CFileErrApp::InitInstance()
{
  m_pMainWnd = new CMainWnd();
```

```
      m_pMainWnd->ShowWindow(m_nCmdShow);
      m_pMainWnd->UpdateWindow();
      return TRUE;
   }
   // application'szStr constructor initializes and runs the app
   CFileErrApp WindowApp;
```

The FILEERR1.EXE program uses the dialog box resource defined in the files INPUTDIA.H and INPUTDIA.RC. The FILEERR1.RC resource file includes the INPUTDIA.RC file using the rcinclude command.

The program shown in Listing 15.10 declares a set of global constants and three classes. The global constants specify small and large string sizes and define the width and height of the list box control attached to the main window. The listing declares the application class, CFileErrApp, the main window class, CMainWnd, and the input dialog box class, CFilenameInputDlg.

The Dialog Box Class

The class CFilenameInputDlg declares a constructor, the protected data member InputFilename, and the member functions OnInitDialog, OnOK, and GetInputFilename. The constructor invokes the constructor of the parent class CDialog and assigns an empty string to the data member InputFilename. The dialog box class defines the following member functions:

- The member function OnInitDialog copies the string in the member InputFilename to the edit control of the dialog box and returns TRUE. The string copy task guarantees that the dialog box displays the last string that appears in the dialog box (before the OK button is clicked).

- The member function OnOK copies the string in the edit control to the data member InputFilename.

- The member function GetInputFilename returns a copy of the value in the member InputFilename.

The Main Window Class

The class CMainWnd declares a constructor, a destructor, the data member pTextLst, and a group of member functions. The relevant member functions are as follows:

- The member function OnCreate creates the list box attached to the main window.

III

Advanced Programming

■ The member function CMView responds to the View File menu by performing the following tasks:

- Creating the instance of CFilenameInputDlg, which is FilenameInputDlg.

- Sending the C++ message DoModal to the object FilenameInputDlg. If the message returns IDOK, the function performs the remaining tasks placed inside a TRY block.

- Sending the C++ message GetInputFilename to the object FilenameInputDlg. The function CMView assigns the result of this message to the local CString instance selectedFile.

- Invoking the member function IsTextFile (with the argument selectedFile) to determine whether the object selectedFile is a possible binary file. If the function IsTextFile returns FALSE, the function CMView calls the function AfxThrowFileException to explicitly throw a file exception with the cause code CFileException::generic.

- Opening the input file stream f for input. This task involves sending the C++ message open to the input stream object f.

- Determining if the stream was opened successfully by sending the C++ message good to the object f. If this message returns a zero, the function CMView calls the function AfxThrowFileException to explicitly raise a file exception with the cause code CFileException::fileNotFound.

- Updating the caption of the main window to include the name of the selected file.

- Clearing the current contents of the list box by sending it the C++ message ResetContent.

- Reading the lines from the input file stream and inserting them in the list box control. This task uses a while loop. The loop sends the C++ message getline to the stream object f in order to read the next text line. The loop also sends the C++ message AddString to the list box control to insert the text line just read.

- Closing the input file stream f by sending it the C++ message close.

  The function CMView has the CATCH and AND_CATCH blocks to trap the CFileException and CMemoryException errors. The CATCH block uses a switch statement to examine the value of the data member CFileException::m_cause. The switch statement has three case labels, including the default clause. Each case label assigns a string to the CString object StrObj. The CATCH block then displays the message in the object StrObj.

■ The Boolean member function IsTextFile determines whether a file *probably* is a text file (although being absolutely certain requires an AI (artificial intelligence) based function that opens the file and examines its character patterns). The IsTextFile function uses a local instance of class CStringList to build the list of popular binary file extensions. The function also creates two local copies, StrObj and FilenameCopy, of the argument Filename. The function performs the following tasks:

  - Converts to uppercase the characters in the object FilenameCopy.

  - Compares the string in the object FilenameCopy with the string literals CONFIG.SYS and \CONFIG.SYS. If the characters in the object FilenameCopy match either literal string, the function returns the value TRUE. Otherwise, the function performs the remaining tasks.

  - Builds a list of binary file extensions by sending a sequence of the C++ message AddHead to the local string-list object StrList.

  - Extracts the last four characters of the object StrObj by sending it the C++ message Right.

  - Converts the characters in the object StrObj to uppercase by sending the object the C++ message MakeUpper.

  - Sends the C++ message Find to the object StrList to determine whether the object StrObj is a member of StrList. The function IsTextFile returns FALSE if the message Find returns TRUE, and vice versa.

III

Advanced Programming

The *CArchiveException* Class

The class CArchiveException deals with exceptions raised while working with instances of the MFC class CArchive. Archives are special streams (that also utilize instances of the MFC class CFile) to write and read predefined data types and instances of CObject and its descendants. The archive operations, which are beyond the scope of this book, are organized as follows:

1. The client program generates an instance of class CFile with the targeted I/O mode.

2. The program creates an instance of class CArchive with the same kind of I/O mode as the CFile instance.

3. The program carries out the required data or object I/O as designated by the I/O mode of the CArchive instance. You can either read or write to an archive, but not both.

4. The program closes the instance of CArchive.

5. The program closes the instance of CFile.

Typically, the archive exception happens in step 3—during the object I/O operations. Consult your Visual C++ *Class Reference Manual* for the member functions of classes CFile and CArchive. Here is the declaration of class CArchiveException:

```
class CArchiveException : public CException
{
    DECLARE_DYNAMIC(CArchiveException)
public:
    enum {
        none,
        generic,
        readOnly,
        endOfFile,
        writeOnly,
        badIndex,
        badClass,
        badSchema
    };
// Constructor
    CArchiveException(int cause = CArchiveException::none);
// Attributes
    int m_cause;
#ifdef _DEBUG
    virtual void Dump(CDumpContext& dc) const;
#endif
};
```

The class `CArchiveException` declares a constructor, a nested enumerated type, the data member `m_cause`, and the member function `Dump`. The nested enumerated type lists the various causes of an `CArchiveException` exception. Table 15.3 lists the various enumerated values for the cause code and briefly states their meanings. You can utilize the data member `m_cause` to conclude the reason for the archive exception.

Table 15.3. Enumerated Values for the Data Member
CArchiveException::m_cause

Enumerated Value	Meaning
badClass	Failed to read object into a new object type
badIndex	Invalid file
badSchema	Cannot read object of different version
endOfFile	Reached end of file
generic	General error
none	No error
readOnly	Attempted to write into a read-only archive
writeOnly	Attempted to read into a write-only archive

The *CResourceException* Class

The exception class `CResourceException` handles the errors raised by resource failure. These errors occur when a resource-loading function fails to locate the targeted resource. The declaration of the class `CResourceException` is

```
class CResourceException : public CException      // resource failure
{
  DECLARE_DYNAMIC(CResourceException)
public:
  CResourceException();
};
```

Most resource loading functions return `BOOL` results or handles. Therefore, your application can inspect these values and call the function `AfxThrowResourceException`. Here is an example:

```
CMenu* pMenu = new CMenu;
CString MenuName("A_LA_CART_MENU");
TRY
{
  if (!pMenu->LoadMenu((const char*)MenuName)
    AfxThrowResourceException();
  SetMenu(pMenu);
  DrawMenuBar();
}
CATCH(CResourceException, e)
{
  CString msgStr = "Cannot load " + MenuName + " menu resource";
  AfxMessageBox((const char*)msgStr);
}
END_CATCH
```

Test of the *CResourceException* Class

In this section, I use the RESERR1.EXE program to illustrate resource exceptions—a nonexistent menu resource to be specific. The program has two sets of minimally functioning menus. The File menu in each menu resource, however, implies three menus: the current menu and two others. The resources for the actual menus are NOVICE_MENU and EXPERT_MENU, whereas the name of the missing menu resource is SPECIAL_MENU. When selected, most of the menu commands simply bring a message dialog box to the screen that says that the feature for that command is not yet implemented.

The initial and default menu is the novice menu. Run the program and click the Expert Menu menu command in the File menu. This action replaces the novice menu with the expert (shorter) version. Click the Novice Menu command, and you're back to the novice (longer) menu. Switch to the expert menu again and then click the Special Menu command. This time, the program displays a resource error message box informing you that it was unable to find the menu resource SPECIAL_MENU. After you click the OK button in the message dialog box, the program brings up the novice menu, which is the default. Figure 15.3 shows a session with the RESERR1.EXE program with the File menu pulled down.

Figure 15.4 shows the same program. In this figure, however, the resource exception message box appears because the Special Menu command was selected. Notice that in this second figure no menu is visible in the background when the error message dialog box pops up. The menu is not visible because the program has already deleted the last menu in preparation for the new one.

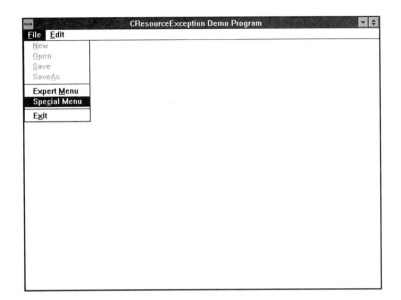

Figure 15.3
The RESERR1.EXE program showing the novice version of the File menu.

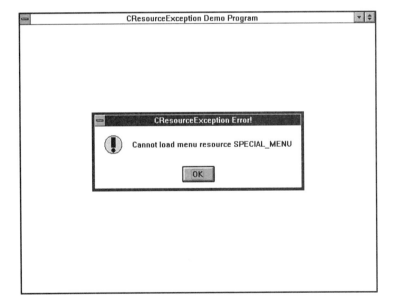

Figure 15.4
The RESERR1.EXE program showing the resource exception message box after the Special Menu command was selected.

Listing 15.11 shows the contents of the RESERR1.DEF definition file.

Listing 15.11 The RESERR1.DEF Definition File

```
NAME         ResErr1
DESCRIPTION  'An MFC Windows Application'
EXETYPE      WINDOWS
CODE         PRELOAD MOVEABLE DISCARDABLE
DATA         PRELOAD MOVEABLE MULTIPLE
HEAPSIZE     1024
```

III

Advanced Programming

Listing 15.12 shows the source code for the RESERR1.H header file.

Listing 15.12 Source Code for the RESERR1.H Header File

```
#define CM_FILENEW          (WM_USER + 100)
#define CM_FILEOPEN         (WM_USER + 101)
#define CM_FILESAVE         (WM_USER + 102)
#define CM_FILESAVEAS       (WM_USER + 103)
#define CM_EXIT             (WM_USER + 104)
#define CM_EDITUNDO         (WM_USER + 105)
#define CM_EDITCUT          (WM_USER + 106)
#define CM_EDITCOPY         (WM_USER + 107)
#define CM_EDITPASTE        (WM_USER + 108)
#define CM_EDITDELETE       (WM_USER + 109)
#define CM_EDITDELETE_BLOCK (WM_USER + 110)
#define CM_EDITCLEAR        (WM_USER + 111)
#define CM_EXPERT_MENU      (WM_USER + 112)
#define CM_NOVICE_MENU      (WM_USER + 113)
#define CM_SPECIAL_MENU     (WM_USER + 114)
```

Listing 15.13 shows the script for the RESERR1.RC resource file.

Listing 15.13 Script for the RESERR1.RC Resource File

```
#include <windows.h>
#include <afxres.h>
#include "reserr1.h"
NOVICE_MENU MENU LOADONCALL MOVEABLE PURE DISCARDABLE
BEGIN
  POPUP "&File"
  BEGIN
    MENUITEM "&New", CM_FILENEW, INACTIVE, GRAYED
    MENUITEM "&Open", CM_FILEOPEN, INACTIVE, GRAYED
    MENUITEM "&Save", CM_FILESAVE, INACTIVE, GRAYED
    MENUITEM "Save&As", CM_FILESAVEAS, INACTIVE, GRAYED
    MENUITEM SEPARATOR
    MENUITEM "Expert &Menu", CM_EXPERT_MENU
    MENUITEM "Spe&cial Menu", CM_SPECIAL_MENU
    MENUITEM SEPARATOR
    MENUITEM "E&xit", CM_EXIT
  END
  POPUP "&Edit"
  BEGIN
    MENUITEM "&Undo", CM_EDITUNDO, INACTIVE, GRAYED
    MENUITEM SEPARATOR
    MENUITEM "C&ut", CM_EDITCUT
    MENUITEM "C&opy", CM_EDITCOPY
    MENUITEM "&Paste", CM_EDITPASTE
    MENUITEM "&Delete", CM_EDITDELETE, INACTIVE, GRAYED
    MENUITEM "&Clear", CM_EDITCLEAR, INACTIVE, GRAYED
  END
END
EXPERT_MENU MENU LOADONCALL MOVEABLE PURE DISCARDABLE
```

```
BEGIN
  POPUP "&File"
  BEGIN
    MENUITEM "&Open", CM_FILEOPEN, INACTIVE, GRAYED
    MENUITEM "Save&As", CM_FILESAVEAS, INACTIVE, GRAYED
    MENUITEM SEPARATOR
    MENUITEM "&Novice Menu", CM_NOVICE_MENU
    MENUITEM "Spe&cial Menu", CM_SPECIAL_MENU
    MENUITEM SEPARATOR
    MENUITEM "E&xit", CM_EXIT
  END
  POPUP "&Edit"
  BEGIN
    MENUITEM "C&ut", CM_EDITCUT
    MENUITEM "C&opy", CM_EDITCOPY
    MENUITEM "&Paste", CM_EDITPASTE
  END
END
```

The source code for the RESERR1.CPP program file is provided in
Listing 15.14.

Listing 15.14 Source Code for the RESERR1.CPP Program Field

```
/*
 Program uses the class CResourceException to trap resource errors.
 The program tests this kind of error by attempting to load a
 nonexistent menu resource.

*/

#include <afxwin.h>
#include "reserr1.h"
// Define an application class derived from CWinApp
class CResErrApp : public CWinApp
{
public:
  virtual BOOL InitInstance();
};
// Define a window class derived from CFrameWnd
class CMainWnd : public CFrameWnd
{
public:
    CMainWnd();
    ~CMainWnd()
      { if (pMenu)
          delete pMenu;
      }
protected:
    // pointer to the current menu
    CMenu* pMenu;
    // handle the left mouse button click
    afx_msg void OnLButtonDown(UINT nFlags, CPoint point)
      {
          MessageBox("You clicked the left button!",
```

Listing 15.14 Continued

```
        "Mouse Click Event!", MB_OK ¦ MB_ICONINFORMATION);
         }

      // handle the right mouse button click
      afx_msg void OnRButtonDown(UINT nFlags, CPoint point)
        { confirmExit(); }

      // load the long menu
      afx_msg void CMNoviceMenu()
       { loadNewMenu("NOVICE_MENU"); }
      // load the special menu
      afx_msg void CMSpecialMenu()
        { loadNewMenu("SPECIAL_MENU"); }
      // load the short menu
      afx_msg void CMExpertMenu()
        { loadNewMenu("EXPERT_MENU"); }
      // exit the application
      afx_msg void CMExit()
        { confirmExit(); }
      // handle the Cut menu option
      afx_msg void CMEditCut()
       { featureNotSupported(); }
      // handle the Copy menu option
      afx_msg void CMEditCopy()
       { featureNotSupported(); }
      // handle the Paste menu option
      afx_msg void CMEditPaste()
       { featureNotSupported(); }
      // display a message "Feature not implemented"
      void featureNotSupported()
        {
          MessageBox("This feature is not implemented",
                     "Information", MB_OK ¦ MB_ICONEXCLAMATION);
        }
      // prompt user to quit the application
      void confirmExit()
        {
          // prompt user if he or she want to close the application
          if (MessageBox("Want to close this application?", "Query",
                     MB_YESNO ¦ MB_ICONQUESTION) == IDYES)
              SendMessage(WM_CLOSE);
        }
      // Assign new menu
      void loadNewMenu(LPCSTR lpszMenuName);
      // message map macro
      DECLARE_MESSAGE_MAP()
  };
CMainWnd::CMainWnd()
{
  BOOL bError = FALSE;

  Create(NULL, "CResourceException Demo Program",
         WS_OVERLAPPEDWINDOW, rectDefault);
```

```
  TRY
  {
    pMenu = new CMenu;
  }
  CATCH(CMemoryException, e)
  {
    AfxMessageBox("Cannot create the menu");
    bError = TRUE;
  }
  END_CATCH

  // exit if can't find NOVICE_MENU resource
  if (bError)
    return;

  TRY
  {
    if (!pMenu->LoadMenu("NOVICE_MENU"))
      AfxThrowResourceException();
    SetMenu(pMenu);
    DrawMenuBar();
  }
  CATCH(CResourceException, e)
  {
    AfxMessageBox("Cannot load NOVICE_MENU menu resource");
  }
  END_CATCH
}
void CMainWnd::loadNewMenu(LPCSTR lpszMenuName)
{
  CString Str;

  SetMenu(NULL);
  pMenu->DestroyMenu();
  TRY
  {
    if (!pMenu->LoadMenu(lpszMenuName))
      AfxThrowResourceException();
  }
  CATCH(CResourceException, e)
  {
    Str = "Cannot load menu resource ";
    Str += lpszMenuName;
    MessageBox(Str, "CResourceException Error!",
               MB_OK | MB_ICONEXCLAMATION);
    pMenu->LoadMenu("NOVICE_MENU");
  }
  END_CATCH
  SetMenu(pMenu);
  DrawMenuBar();
}
BEGIN_MESSAGE_MAP(CMainWnd, CFrameWnd)
    ON_WM_LBUTTONDOWN()
    ON_WM_RBUTTONDOWN()
    ON_COMMAND(CM_NOVICE_MENU, CMNoviceMenu)
    ON_COMMAND(CM_SPECIAL_MENU, CMSpecialMenu)
```

III

Advanced Programming

(continues)

Listing 15.14 Continued

```
        ON_COMMAND(CM_EXPERT_MENU, CMExpertMenu)
        ON_COMMAND(CM_EXIT, CMExit)
        ON_COMMAND(CM_EDITCUT, CMEditCut)
        ON_COMMAND(CM_EDITCOPY, CMEditCopy)
        ON_COMMAND(CM_EDITPASTE, CMEditPaste)
END_MESSAGE_MAP()
// Construct the CResErrApp's m_pMainWnd data member
BOOL CResErrApp::InitInstance()
{
  m_pMainWnd = new CMainWnd();
  m_pMainWnd->ShowWindow(m_nCmdShow);
  m_pMainWnd->UpdateWindow();
  return TRUE;
}
// application's constructor initializes and runs the app
CResErrApp WindowApp;
```

The RESERR1.CPP program shown in Listing 15.14 declares two classes: the application class, CResErrApp, and the main window class, CMainWnd.

The class CMainWnd declares a constructor, a destructor, the data member pMenu, and a set of member functions. The CMainWnd constructor creates the main window by invoking the function Create. Then, using the menu resource NOVICE_MENU defined in the resource file RESERR1.RC, the constructor uses a TRY block to create the default menu. The CATCH block traps the memory exception that might be thrown by the operator new. If this error occurs, the CATCH block displays a message box and assigns TRUE to the local Boolean flag bError. The constructor then exits if the operator new fails. The constructor uses a second TRY block when loading the menu resource NOVICE_MENU. If the C++ message LoadMenu (which is sent to the dynamic CMenu object) returns FALSE, the constructor invokes the function AfxThrowResourceException. The related CATCH block displays an error message dialog box, which states that the program is unable to load the menu resource NOVICE_MENU.

The destructor deletes the object accessed by member pMenu if it exists.

The class CMainWnd contains several members that offer minimal response to the various menu commands. Following are the relevant member functions:

- The member function CMNoviceMenu responds to the command sent by the Novice Menu command. The function calls the member function loadNewMenu and supplies it with the argument NOVICE_MENU. This argument is the name of the novice menu resource defined in file RESERR1.RC.

- The member function CmExpertMenu responds to the command sent by the Expert Menu command. The function calls the member function loadNewMenu and supplies it with the argument EXPERT_MENU. This argument is the name of the expert menu resource defined in the file RESERR1.RC.

- The member function CMSpecialMenu responds to the command sent by the Special Menu command. The function calls the member function loadNewMenu and supplies it with the argument SPECIAL_MENU. This argument is supposed to be the name of an existing menu resource, but it isn't. Consequently, the function loadNewMenu raises a resource exception.

- The member function loadNewMenu loads the menu resource specified by the argument of the parameter lpszMenuName. The function performs the following tasks:

  - Removes the current menu by first sending the C++ message SetMenu to the main window object. Then the loadNewMenu function sends the C++ message DestroyMenu to the dynamic menu object, which is accessed by the member pMenu.

  - Loads into a TRY block the menu resource specified by the parameter lpszMenuName. This task involves sending the C++ message LoadMenu to the dynamic instance of CMenu. If the message returns FALSE, the loadNewMenu function calls the function AfxThrowResourceException to throw a resource exception. The loadNewMenu function handles this exception using the CATCH block, which displays a resource exception message box and then loads the menu resource NOVICE_MENU.

  - Sets and displays the selected (or default) menu.

The *CUserException* Class

The class CUserException deals with application-specific exceptions. Here are just a few examples of such exceptions:

- The user enters a string that is either too long or too short.

- The user types a string with invalid characters.

■ The user enters numbers that are out of range.

■ The user selects a file with the wrong extension.

■ The user selects a file from the wrong directory.

The declaration of class CUserException is

```
class CUserException : public CException
{
  DECLARE_DYNAMIC(CUserException)
public:
  CUserException();
}
```

Use the function AfxThrowUserException to throw a user exception.

Test of the *CUserException* Class

Here I present the USERERR1.EXE program, which employs the class CUserException to manage user exceptions. The program is a special version of FILEERR1.EXE that uses the Open File common dialog box to select files, and it also detects attempts to read a binary file. The files with the extensions .EXE, .COM, .OVR. .SYS, .BIN, .OBJ, .RES, .MAK, .PDB, .VCW, .SBR, and .DLL are considered binary.

Run the program and choose a file to view. Click the View File menu. When the Open File dialog box appears, select an .EXE or one of the other binary files referred to in the preceding paragraph. The program responds by displaying a user exception message box. Click once more on the View File menu, and this time choose the COMMAND.COM file in the root directory. The program displays a special user exception message dialog box reflecting its surprise that you elected to view COMMAND.COM. This message dialog box is the result of the nested TRY block. I'll explain the details following the program listings.

Figure 15.5 displays a session with the USERERR1.EXE program, which shows an ordinary user exception message dialog box.

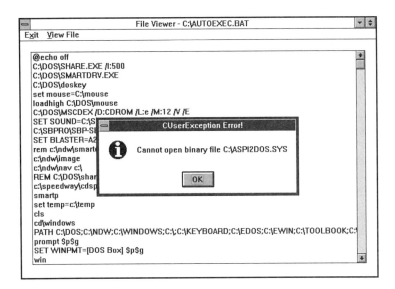

Figure 15.5

The USERERR1. EXE program showing an ordinary user exception message dialog box.

Figure 15.6 displays the USERERR1.EXE program and shows the special user exception message dialog box that appears when you elect to view file COMMAND.COM.

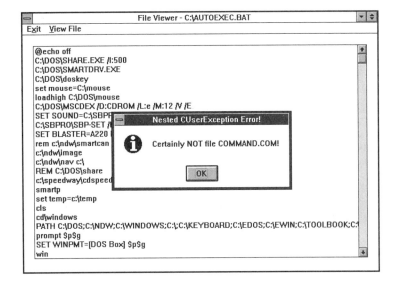

Figure 15.6

The USERERR1.EXE program showing the special user exception message dialog box that appears when you elect to view COMMAND.COM.

III

Advanced Programming

Listing 15.15 contains the contents of the USERERR1.DEF definition file.

Listing 15.15 The USERERR1.DEF Definition File

```
NAME         UserErr1
DESCRIPTION  'An MFC Windows Application'
EXETYPE      WINDOWS
CODE         PRELOAD MOVEABLE DISCARDABLE
DATA         PRELOAD MOVEABLE MULTIPLE
HEAPSIZE     1024
```

Listing 15.16 shows the source code for the USERERR1.H header file.

Listing 15.16 Source Code for the USERERR1.H Header File

```
#define CM_EXIT  (WM_USER + 100)
#define CM_VIEW  (WM_USER + 101)
#define ID_TEXT_LST   100
```

Listing 15.17 shows the script for the USERERR1.RC resource file.

Listing 15.17 The USERERR1.RC Resource File

```
#include <windows.h>
#include <afxres.h>
#include "usererr1.h"
MAINMENU MENU LOADONCALL MOVEABLE PURE DISCARDABLE
BEGIN
    MENUITEM "E&xit", CM_EXIT
    MENUITEM "&View File", CM_VIEW
END
```

The source code for the USERERR1.CPP program file is provided in
Listing 15.18.

Listing 15.18 Source Code for the USERERR1.CPP Program File

```
/*
  Program which tests the CUserException, CFileException,
  and CMemoryException to handle errors in selecting and
  reading text files. The program views a text file and
  displays error messages if it cannot find the file,
  open a binary file, and read the entire file in
  the list box control.

*/
#include <fstream.h>
#include <afxwin.h>
```

```
#include <afxdlgs.h>
#include "usererr1.h"
const MaxStringLen = 255;
const Wlst = 600;
const Hlst = 375;
// declare the custom application class as
class CUserErrApp : public CWinApp
{
public:
    virtual BOOL InitInstance();
};
// expand the functionality of CFrameWnd by deriving
// class CMainWnd
class CMainWnd : public CFrameWnd
{
 public:
  CMainWnd()
    {
      // create the window
      Create(NULL, "File Viewer",
             WS_OVERLAPPEDWINDOW, rectDefault, NULL, "MAINMENU");
    }

  ~CMainWnd()
    { delete pTextLst; }
 protected:

  CListBox* pTextLst;

  // handle creating the controls
  afx_msg int OnCreate(LPCREATESTRUCT lpCS);

  // handle the Files menu item
  afx_msg void CMView();

  // handle exiting the application
  afx_msg void OnExit()
    { SendMessage(WM_CLOSE); }

  // handle closing the window
  afx_msg void OnClose();

  // coordinates and dimensions
  void makerect(int X, int Y, int W, int H, CRect& r)
    { r.SetRect(X, Y, X + W, Y + H); }

  // verify that file is not an executable one
  BOOL IsTextFile(CString& Filename);
  // declare message map macro
  DECLARE_MESSAGE_MAP()
};

int CMainWnd::OnCreate(LPCREATESTRUCT lpCS)
{
  int x = 20;
  int y = 20;
  DWORD dwStaticStyle = WS_CHILD | WS_VISIBLE | SS_LEFT;
```

III

Advanced Programming

(continues)

Listing 15.18 Continued

```
        DWORD dwListBoxStyle = WS_CHILD ¦ WS_VISIBLE ¦ WS_VSCROLL ¦
                               LBS_STANDARD;
      CRect r;
// disable sorting of items in the list box
      dwListBoxStyle &= ~LBS_SORT;

      makerect(x, y, Wlst, Hlst, r);
      pTextLst = new CListBox();
      pTextLst->Create(dwListBoxStyle, r, this, ID_TEXT_LST);
      return CFrameWnd::OnCreate(lpCS);
}
void CMainWnd::CMView()
{
      CString selectedFile;
      CString selFileCopy;
      CString windowTitle;
      CString StrObj;
      CString Filter;
      char szStr[MaxStringLen+1];
      fstream f;

      Filter =  "All Files (*.*)¦*.*¦";
      Filter += "Text files (*.txt)¦*.txt¦";
      Filter += "Doc files (*.doc)¦*.doc¦";
      Filter += "Header files (*.h*)¦*.h*¦";
      Filter += "C++ Programs (*.cpp)¦*.cpp¦";
      Filter += "¦";

      CFileDialog FileDialog(
         TRUE,  // use file open dialog
         NULL, // ".* is the default extension"
         "*.*",
         OFN_HIDEREADONLY,
         Filter,
         this);
      if (FileDialog.DoModal() == IDOK) {
        // get the filename
        selectedFile = FileDialog.GetPathName();
        f.open(selectedFile, ios::in);
        TRY
        {
          if (!IsTextFile(selectedFile))
            AfxThrowUserException();
          // set the new window title to include the input filename
          windowTitle = "File Viewer - " + selectedFile;
          SetWindowText((const char*)windowTitle);
          // clear the list box first
          pTextLst->ResetContent();
          // inserts the lines from the text file
          while (!f.eof()) {
            f.getline(szStr, MaxStringLen);
            pTextLst->AddString(szStr);
          }
        }
        CATCH(CUserException, e)
        {
```

```
    TRY
    {
      selFileCopy = selectedFile.Mid(3);
      if (selFileCopy == "COMMAND.COM")
        AfxThrowUserException();
      StrObj = "Cannot open binary file " + selectedFile;
      MessageBox(StrObj, "CUserException Error!",
                 MB_OK | MB_ICONINFORMATION);
    }
    CATCH(CUserException, e)
    {
      MessageBox("Certainly NOT file COMMAND.COM!",
                 "Nested CUserException Error!",
                 MB_OK | MB_ICONINFORMATION);
    }
    END_CATCH
  }
  AND_CATCH(CMemoryException, e)
  {
    StrObj = "Cannot read the entire file " +
          selectedFile +
          " in the list box";
    MessageBox(StrObj, "CMemoryException Error!",
               MB_OK | MB_ICONINFORMATION);
  }
  AND_CATCH_ALL(e)
  {
    MessageBox("Unanticipated error",
               "General Exception Error!",
               MB_OK | MB_ICONINFORMATION);
  }
  END_CATCH_ALL
  // close input stream anyway
  f.close();
  }
}
void CMainWnd::OnClose()
{
  if (MessageBox("Want to close this application",
                  "Query", MB_YESNO | MB_ICONQUESTION) == IDYES)
    DestroyWindow();
}
BOOL CMainWnd::IsTextFile(CString& Filename)
{
  CStringList StrList;
  CString StrObj(Filename);
  CString FilenameCopy;
  // deal with the special case of config.sys
  // convert the copy of the filename into uppercase
  FilenameCopy = Filename.Mid(3); // delete first two characters
  FilenameCopy.MakeUpper();
  if (FilenameCopy == "CONFIG.SYS")
      return TRUE;
  // build the list of binary file extensions
  StrList.AddHead(".EXE");
  StrList.AddHead(".COM");
  StrList.AddHead(".OVR");
  StrList.AddHead(".SYS");
```

III

Advanced Programming

(continues)

Listing 15.18 Continued

```
        StrList.AddHead(".BIN");
        StrList.AddHead(".OBJ");
        StrList.AddHead(".RES");
        StrList.AddHead(".PDB");
        StrList.AddHead(".VCW");
        StrList.AddHead(".SBR");
        StrList.AddHead(".DLL");

        // extract the last four characters
        StrObj = StrObj.Right(4);
        // convert them into uppercase
        StrObj.MakeUpper();
        // return the result of searching for STR in string list
        return (StrList.Find(StrObj)) ? FALSE : TRUE;
}
BEGIN_MESSAGE_MAP(CMainWnd, CFrameWnd)
    ON_WM_CREATE()
    ON_COMMAND(CM_VIEW, CMView)
    ON_COMMAND(CM_EXIT, OnExit)
    ON_WM_CLOSE()
END_MESSAGE_MAP()
// Construct the CUserErrApp's m_pMainWnd data member
BOOL CUserErrApp::InitInstance()
{
    m_pMainWnd = new CMainWnd();
    m_pMainWnd->ShowWindow(m_nCmdShow);
    m_pMainWnd->UpdateWindow();
    return TRUE;
}
// application's constructor initializes and runs the app
CUserErrApp WindowApp;
```

The USERERR1.CPP program shown in Listing 15.18 declares a set of global constants and two classes. The constants define the size of the program's strings and the width and height of the list box control. The program also declares the application class, CUserErrApp, and the window class, CMainWnd.

The class CMainWnd declares a constructor, destructor, two data members, and a group of member functions. The data member pTextLst is the pointer to the list box control created by the program.

The CMainWnd constructor creates the main window, whereas the destructor removed the dynamic instances of the static text and list box controls.

The class CMainWnd declares the following relevant member functions:

- The member function OnCreate creates the controls attached to the main window. The function uses the member pTextLst to create and access the list box control.

■ The member function `CMView` responds to the `CM_VIEW` message command generated by the View File menu. The function performs the following tasks:

- Builds the file selection filter using the local `CString` instance, `Filter`. The function appends the various strings that define the set of file wild cards that are available in the dialog box.

- Creates the instance of `CFileDialog`—`FileDialog`—and sends it the C++ message `DoModal`. If the message yields `IDOK`, the function performs the remaining tasks.

- Sends the C++ message `GetPathName` to the object FileDialog. The function `CMView` assigns the result of this message to the local `CString` instance `selectedFile`.

- Opens the input file stream f for input by sending the C++ message `open`.

- Uses a `TRY` block to detect user allocation errors. The statements in the `TRY` block perform the following subtasks:

  > Ensures that the object `selectedFile` does not represent a possible binary file. This task involves the member function `IsTextFile`. If this function yields FALSE, the function `CMView` calls the function `AfxThrowUserException` to throw a user exception.

  > Updates the caption of the main window to include the name of the selected file.

  > Clears the current contents of the list box by sending it the C++ message `ResetContent`.

  > Reads the lines from the input file stream and inserts them in the list box control. This task uses a `while` loop. The loop sends the C++ message `getline` to the stream object f in order to read the next text line. The loop also sends the C++ message `AddString` to the list box control to insert the text line just read.

III

Advanced Programming

- Uses the CATCH block to handle any user exception by performing the following tasks:

    Determining whether or not the string in the object selectedFile contains the name of the COMMAND.COM file. If this condition is true, the function throws yet another user exception. A nested CATCH block handles the nested user exception and displays the special user exception message dialog box.

    Displays the user exception message dialog box.

    Uses an AND_CATCH block to handle memory exceptions generated by the attempt to read a huge text file.

    Uses an AND_CATCH_ALL block to handle other unanticipated exceptions.

    Closes the input file stream f by sending it the C++ message close.

The *CNotSupportedException* Class

The class CNotSupportedException manages exceptions generated by a request for unsupported features. The declaration of class CNotSupportedException is

```
class CNotSupportedException : public CException
{
  DECLARE_DYNAMIC(CNotSupportedException)
public:
  CNotSupportedException();
};
```

You can throw the unsupported feature exception using the function AfxThrowNotSupportedException.

The *COleException* Class

The class COleException handles the exceptions generated by OLE errors. The declaration of class COleException is as follows:

```
class COleException : public CException
{
    DECLARE_DYNAMIC(COleException)
public:
    SCODE m_sc;
```

```
        static SCODE PASCAL Process(const CException* pAnyException);
// Implementation (use AfxThrowOleException to create)
        COleException();
};
```

The class COleException uses the enumerated type SCODE to distinguish between the various kinds of OLE-related errors. The class declares the public data member m_sc to report the OLE status. The enumerated type SCODE defines the OLE status code. You can throw an OLE exception using the function AfxThrowOleException. This function has one parameter with the SCODE type.

Summary

This chapter introduced you to the new C++ error-handling features. Here's what you learned:

- Visual C++ exceptions. Visual C++ uses the TRY block to trap exceptions and offers the CATCH, AND_CATCH, and AND_CATCH_ALL blocks to handle one or more exceptions. The general syntax for the TRY, CATCH, and AND_CATCH blocks is as follows:

```
TRY
{
  // statements that may raise one or more errors
  .
  .
  .
}
CATCH(exceptionClass1, e)
{
  // statements to handle error of type exceptionClass1
}
[AND_CATCH(exceptionClass2, e)
{
  // statements to handle error of type exceptionClass2
}
AND_CATCH(exceptionClass3, e)
{
  // statements to handle error of type exceptionClass3
}
// other AND_CATCH blocks
AND_CATCH(exceptionClassN, e)
{
  // statements to handle error of type exceptionClassN
}]
END_CATCH
```

- The class CException is the root of the exception classes sub-hierarchy in the MFC library. This class also models general purpose exceptions.

- The class CMemoryException models dynamic allocation errors. The new operator automatically throws a memory exception when it fails. You can explicitly throw a memory exception by calling the function AfxThrowMemoryException.

- The class CFileException models file I/O errors related to the operation of CFile objects. This class contains the public data member m_cause, which stores enumerated values that describe the kind of error. You can explicitly throw a memory exception by calling the function AfxThrowFileException.

- The class CArchiveException models archive I/O errors related to the operations of CArchive objects. This class contains the public data member m_cause, which stores enumerated values that describe the kind of error. You can explicitly throw a memory exception by calling the function AfxThrowArchiveException.

- The class CResourceException models errors related to resource failure. Typically, you call the function AfxThrowResourceException when a resource loading function returns a Boolean FALSE or a NULL handle.

- The class CUserException models application-specific errors. To throw a user exception, your program calls the function AfxThrowUserException when illegal values or offending conditions occur.

- The class CNotSupportedException models errors related to unsupported features. You throw an unsupported feature exception by calling the function AfxThrowNotSupportedException when a requested feature is not available.

- The class COleException models errors related to OLE classes. The class declares the public data member m_sc to report the OLE status. The type SCODE defines the OLE status values.

Chapter 16

Using the Workbench Browse Window

The sophisticated programming aspects of Windows applications offer a formidable challenge to programmers who must handle a maze of information. Determining the location of definitions and of the references of certain data types, variables, functions, and classes becomes frustrating when you use *manual* search methods. The Visual Workbench offers the Browse menu to automate the process of studying the various components of your programs. This chapter introduces you to browsing and covers the following topics:

- Examining the Browse menu
- Browsing through macros
- Browsing through data types
- Browsing through variables
- Browsing through functions
- Using the Call Graph feature
- Using the Caller Graph feature
- Using the Base Class Graph feature
- Using the Derived Class Graph feature

III

Advanced Programming

Examining the Browse Menu

The Browse menu offers a versatile set of commands that enables you to browse through symbols (data types, variables, constants, functions, and so on), create new classes, and manage the Windows messages to which these classes respond. Table 16.1 summarizes the Browse menu commands.

Table 16.1 Browse Menu Commands		
Command	**Shortcut Key**	**Purpose**
Go to Definition	F11	Jumps to the start of the symbol definition.
Go to Reference	Shift+F11	Jumps to the first location where the symbol is referenced.
Next	Ctrl+NumPad+	Jumps to the next location where the symbol is referenced.
Previous	Ctrl+NumPad–	Jumps to the previous location where the symbol is referenced.
Pop Context	Ctrl+NumPad*	Jumps to the location of the selected symbol.
Open PRJ.BSC		Opens the Browse window.
ClassWizard...	Ctrl+W	Generates a new class or maps a Windows message to a member function.

Note: The NumPad *designation that precedes the characters +, –, and * in the second column indicates that you must access these characters by using the numeric keypad.*

Chapter 1 discussed the function of each Browse command. This chapter focuses on how you can use these commands with the various programs I presented earlier in this book.

When you build a program, the Visual Workbench generates a database of the various symbols. The database contains sophisticated information that tracks where a symbol is defined and referenced—valuable information for studying and debugging complex applications.

Figure 16.1 shows a sample Browse window.

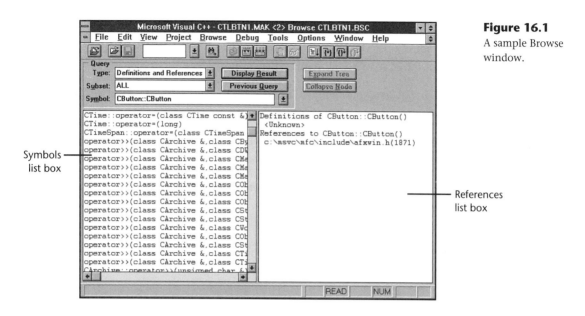

Figure 16.1
A sample Browse window.

The Browse window has the following controls:

- *Type drop-down combo box.* Enables you to select the kind of symbol you want from the following list:

    Definitions and References

    Call Graph

    Caller Graph

    Derived Class Graph

    Base Class Graph

- *Subset drop-down combo box.* Enables you to select the subset symbols you want to focus on from the following list:

    ALL

    Functions

    Variables

    Types

    Macros

    Classes

III

Advanced Programming

- *Symbol drop-down combo box*. Acts as a history list box. The initial content of this control is the asterisk character (*), which represents a wild card that matches all items.

- *Display Result pushbutton*. Enables you to execute a query and display its results in the symbols list box.

- *Previous Query pushbutton*. Retrieves the symbols for the previous symbol query.

- *Expand Tree and Collapse Node pushbuttons*. Manipulate the class hierarchy diagrams that appear in the symbols list box when you are viewing classes.

- *Symbols list box*. Contains the names of the symbols that match the current query.

- *References list box*. Lists the definitions and references of the currently selected symbol.

Browsing through Macros

Take advantage of the Browse window to find the definitions for some of the globally predefined macros, as well as for the macros of the CTLBTN1.EXE program (originally introduced in Chapter 6). Select the following items: the Definitions and References item in the Type combo box, the Macros item in the Subset combo box, and the * item in the Symbol combo box. Click the Display Result pushbutton. The Browse window displays what you see in Figure 16.2 (after you have maximized the Browse window). The symbols list box indicates (with qualifiers in parentheses following the macro names) which items are constants and which items are members of enumerated data types. The following sections examine a few of the macros more closely.

The *afx_msg* Macro

The initial list of macros shows the afx_msg macro. You typically place the afx_msg macro before the declaration of message-handling member functions. Select the afx_msg macro. The references list box shows that the macro is defined in line 173 of the AFXWIN.H header file. When you double-click the macro afx_msg, the Visual Workbench loads the header file AFXWIN.H and selects the macro name. Listing 16.1 shows the portion of the header file AFXWIN.H that appears in a maximized window (because the Browse

window was maximized) when you choose to view the definition of the
macro afx_msg.

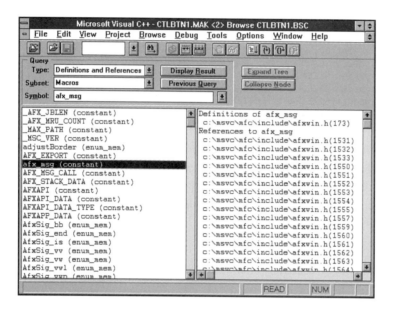

Figure 16.2
The Browse window showing the
list of macros.

**Listing 16.1 Portion of the AFXWIN.H Header File Displayed
in a Maximized Window When You View the
Definition of the *afx_msg* Macro**

```
#ifdef _INC_WINDOWSX
// The following names from WINDOWSX.H collide with names in
// this header
#undef SubclassWindow
#undef CopyRgn
#endif

// Type modifier for message handlers
#ifndef afx_msg

#define afx_msg          // intentional placeholder
#endif

// AFXDLL support
#undef AFXAPP_DATA
#define AFXAPP_DATA      AFXAPI_DATA

//////////////////////////////////////////////////////////////////
// Win 3.1 types provided for Win3.0 as well
```

(continues)

III

Advanced Programming

Listing 16.1 Continued

```
#if (WINVER < 0x030a)
typedef struct tagSIZE
{
    int cx;
    int cy;
} SIZE;
typedef SIZE*       PSIZE;
typedef SIZE NEAR* NPSIZE;
typedef SIZE FAR*  LPSIZE;
```

The definition of the afx_msg macro reveals that it does not expand to anything. My guess is that the compiler uses the macro to track the declarations of member functions in a class. The technical reviewer for this book noted that you can omit this macro without affecting the program. I commented out the afx_msg in one of the programs and still managed to compile and run the program!

After you have finished browsing the AFXWIN.H file, close it by pressing Ctrl+F4.

The *BEGIN_MESSAGE_MAP* Macro

Scroll through the list of macros and double-click the BEGIN_MESSAGE_MAP macro. The references list box shows that this macro is defined in line 991 of the AFXWIN.H header file. Double-click the macro name to load AFXWIN.H. Listing 16.2 shows the portion of the header file AFXWIN.H that appears in a maximized window when you choose to view the definition of the macro BEGIN_MESSAGE_MAP. The definition spans lines 984 to 991. The Browse window specifies line 991 because that is the location where the macro is *completely* defined. The definition of macro BEGIN_MESSAGE_MAP involves the member functions messageMap of the target class and its base class. The listing also shows the definition of the END_MESSAGE_MAP macro. After you have finished viewing the header file, close its window.

Listing 16.2 Portion of the AFXWIN.H Header File Displayed in a Maximized Window When You View the Definition of the BEGIN_MESSAGE_MAP Macro

```
struct AFXAPI_DATA_TYPE AFX_MSGMAP
{
    AFX_MSGMAP* pBaseMessageMap;
    AFX_MSGMAP_ENTRY FAR* lpEntries;
};
```

```
#define DECLARE_MESSAGE_MAP() \
private: \
    static AFX_MSGMAP_ENTRY BASED_CODE _messageEntries[]; \
protected: \
    static AFX_MSGMAP AFXAPP_DATA messageMap; \
    virtual AFX_MSGMAP* GetMessageMap() const;

#define BEGIN_MESSAGE_MAP(theClass, baseClass) \
    AFX_MSGMAP* theClass::GetMessageMap() const \
        { return &theClass::messageMap; } \
    AFX_MSGMAP AFXAPP_DATA theClass::messageMap = \
    { &(baseClass::messageMap), \
        (AFX_MSGMAP_ENTRY FAR*) &(theClass::_messageEntries) }; \
    AFX_MSGMAP_ENTRY BASED_CODE theClass::_messageEntries[] = \
    {

#define END_MESSAGE_MAP() \
    { 0, 0, AfxSig_end, (AFX_PMSG)0 } \
    };

// Message map signature values and macros in separate header
#include <afxmsg_.h>
```

The *CM_EXIT* Macro

As you scroll through the symbols list box, you can see the macro CM_EXIT defined by the header file CTLBTN1.H. Double-click this macro to load the host header file. Listing 16.3 shows the contents of the header file CTLBTN1.H. Close this file when you have finished browsing it.

Listing 16.3 CTLBTN1.H Header File Displayed When You View the Definition of the CM_EXIT Macro

```
#define CM_EXIT    (WM_USER + 200)
#define CM_DECIMAL (WM_USER + 201)
#define CM_HEX     (WM_USER + 202)
#define CM_BINARY  (WM_USER + 203)

#define ID_CALC_BTN  100
#define ID_STORE_BTN 101
#define ID_EXIT_BTN  102
```

The *MB_OK* Macro

Scroll down the symbols list again until you see the macro MB_OK and select this macro. The references list box indicates that the header file WINDOWS.H defines the macro MB_OK in line 4092. Double-click MB_OK to load the WINDOWS.H file. Listing 16.4 contains the portion of WINDOWS.H that appears in a maximized window when you choose to view the definition of the macro MB_OK. The listing shows the long integer values associated with the MB_OK macro and the other MB_*XXXX* macros.

Listing 16.4 Portion of the WINDOWS.H Header File Displayed in a Maximized Window When You View the Definition of the *MB_OK* Macro

```
#endif  /* NOICONS */

/****** Message Box support ***************************************/

#ifndef NOMB

int     WINAPI MessageBox(HWND, LPCSTR, LPCSTR, UINT);
void    WINAPI MessageBeep(UINT);

#define MB_OK                 0x0000
#define MB_OKCANCEL           0x0001
#define MB_ABORTRETRYIGNORE   0x0002
#define MB_YESNOCANCEL        0x0003
#define MB_YESNO              0x0004
#define MB_RETRYCANCEL        0x0005
#define MB_TYPEMASK           0x000F

#define MB_ICONHAND           0x0010
#define MB_ICONQUESTION       0x0020
#define MB_ICONEXCLAMATION    0x0030
#define MB_ICONASTERISK       0x0040
#define MB_ICONMASK           0x00F0

#define MB_ICONINFORMATION    MB_ICONASTERISK
#define MB_ICONSTOP           MB_ICONHAND

#define MB_DEFBUTTON1         0x0000
#define MB_DEFBUTTON2         0x0100
#define MB_DEFBUTTON3         0x0200
```

The *NULL* Macro

Continue to scroll through the symbols list until you reach the familiar NULL macro. The references list box shows that the header files STDLIB.H and AFX.H both define this macro. To view the STDLIB.H file, double-click the line in the references list box that contains STDLIB.H. Listing 16.5 shows the portion of the STDLIB.H header file that appears in a maximized window when you choose to view the definition of the macro NULL. The listing uses the #ifdef and #ifndef compiler directives to define NULL as 0 for C++

programs and as `((void*)0)` for C programs. You should keep this difference in mind if you also program in C and convert source code between the two languages. Close the STDLIB.H window to return to the Browse window. Double-click the line containing the AFX.H header file in order to view that file (which simply defines NULL as 0). The file uses no `#ifdef` or `#ifndef` macros because it is intended to be used by C++ programs only.

Listing 16.5 Portion of the STDLIB.H Header File Displayed in a Maximized Window When You View the Definition of the *NULL* Macro

```
#ifndef _WCHAR_T_DEFINED
typedef unsigned short wchar_t;
#define _WCHAR_T_DEFINED
#endif

/* define NULL pointer value */

#ifndef NULL
#ifdef __cplusplus

#define NULL    0

#else
#define NULL    ((void *)0)
#endif
#endif

/* exit() arg values */

#define EXIT_SUCCESS    0
#define EXIT_FAILURE    1

#ifndef _ONEXIT_T_DEFINED
typedef int (__cdecl * _onexit_t)();
typedef int (__far __cdecl * _fonexit_t)();
#ifndef __STDC__
/* Non-ANSI name for compatibility */
typedef int (__cdecl * onexit_t)();
#endif
#define _ONEXIT_T_DEFINED
#endif
```

Browsing through Data Types

Select the Types item in the Browse window's Subset combo box and select the * symbol to query all the data types. Click the Display Result pushbutton to view the list of matching data types. The symbols list box displays that list and indicates which items are structures or typedefs. The following sections examine the definitions of two sets of data types.

The *BOOL* Data Type

Scroll through the symbols list box and select the type BOOL. The references list box indicates that it is defined in both the AFX.H and WINDOWS.H header files. Double-click the BOOL type to open the AFX.H file. Listing 16.6 shows the portion of the AFX.H header file that appears in a maximized window when you choose to view the definition of the macros BOOL. The listing also shows the definitions of other simple types such as BYTE, WORD, UINT, LONG, and DWORD. Close the AFX.H window when you finish browsing the definitions.

Listing 16.6 Portion of the Header File AFX.H Displayed in a Maximized Window When You View the Definitions of the Macros *BYTE*, *WORD*, *UINT*, *LONG*, *DWORD*, and *BOOL*

```
///////////////////////////////////////////////////////////////////
// Basic types (from Windows)

typedef unsigned char  BYTE;    // 8-bit unsigned entity
typedef unsigned short WORD;    // 16-bit unsigned number
typedef unsigned int   UINT;    // machine sized unsigned number
                                // (preferred)
typedef long           LONG;    // 32-bit signed number
typedef unsigned long  DWORD;   // 32-bit unsigned number
typedef int            BOOL;    // BOOLean (0 or !=0)
typedef char FAR*      LPSTR;   // far pointer to a string
typedef const char FAR* LPCSTR; // far pointer to a read-only
                                // string

typedef void*          POSITION; // abstract iteration position

// Standard constants
#undef FALSE
#undef TRUE
#undef NULL

#define FALSE   0
#define TRUE    1
#define NULL    0

///////////////////////////////////////////////////////////////////
// Diagnostic support
#ifdef _DEBUG
extern "C"
{
```

The *RECT* Data Type

Scroll towards the end of the symbols list box and select the RECT data type (which is a typedef). The references list box indicates that the header file WINDOWS.H defines the RECT type. Double-click the type RECT to load the WINDOWS.H file. Listing 16.7 shows the portion of the WINDOWS.H header file that appears in a maximized window when you choose to view the definition of the data types RECT, POINT, and SIZE. The listing indicates that these types are typedefs for the formal structures tagRECT, tagPOINT, and tagSIZE, respectively.

Listing 16.7 Portion of the WINDOWS.H Header File Displayed in a Maximized Window When You View the Definitions of the Data Types *RECT*, *POINT*, and *SIZE*

```
DECLARE_HANDLE(HPALETTE);
DECLARE_HANDLE(HFONT);

typedef struct tagRECT
{
    int left;
    int top;
    int right;
    int bottom;

} RECT;
typedef RECT*      PRECT;
typedef RECT NEAR* NPRECT;
typedef RECT FAR*  LPRECT;

typedef struct tagPOINT
{
    int x;
    int y;
} POINT;
typedef POINT*      PPOINT;
typedef POINT NEAR* NPPOINT;
typedef POINT FAR*  LPPOINT;

#if (WINVER >= 0x030a)
typedef struct tagSIZE
{
    int cx;
    int cy;
} SIZE;
typedef SIZE*      PSIZE;
```

Browsing through Variables

The Browse window lets you view some or all of the variables in your program. Let's examine the data members of the main window class, CMainWnd. Select the Definitions and References item in the Type combo box, the Variables item in the Subset combo box, and then type **CMainWnd::** in the Symbol combo box. Click the Display Result pushbutton to obtain the list of data members of class CMainWnd. Figure 16.3 shows the information obtained by the Browse window.

Figure 16.3

The list of data members of class CMainWnd.

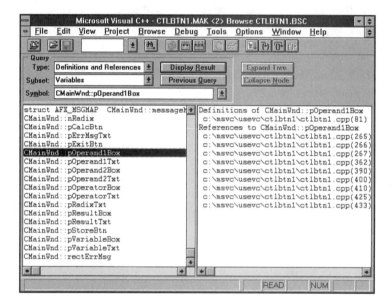

Select the data member pOperand1Box to reveal the lines that define it and reference it (Figure 16.3 also contains this information). Double-click the member pOperand1Box to load the file CTLBTN1.CPP, which defines and uses this data member. Listing 16.8 shows the portion of the header file CTLBTN1.CPP that appears in a maximized window when you choose to view the definition of the variable pOperand1Box. The listing also shows the definitions of the various data members of class CMainWnd.

Listing 16.8 Portion of the CTLBTN1.CPP Header File Displayed in a Maximized Window When You View the Definition of the Variable *pOperand1Box*

```
    CMainWnd();

    ~CMainWnd();

    protected:

    // declare the pointers to the various controls
    // first, the edit box controls

    CEdit* pOperand1Box;
    CEdit* pOperatorBox;
    CEdit* pOperand2Box;
    CEdit* pResultBox;
    CxEdit* pVariableBox;
    // then the static text controls
    CStatic* pRadixTxt;
    CStatic* pOperand1Txt;
    CStatic* pOperatorTxt;
    CStatic* pOperand2Txt;
    CStatic* pResultTxt;
    CStatic* pErrMsgTxt;
    CStatic* pVariableTxt;
    // pushbuttons
    CxButton* pCalcBtn;
    CxButton* pStoreBtn;
    CxButton* pExitBtn;
    // math mode
    int nRadix;
```

Using the Call Graph Feature

The Browse window enables you to select a function or a member function and list all the functions and member functions called by that function. This characteristic uses the Call Graph feature that appears in the symbols list box. The Call Graph has bitmapped nodes with the image of either an empty document box or a document box with horizontally stacked papers. The empty-box bitmap indicates that the function does not call any other function (within the scope of the current project). The box-with-papers bitmap, on the other hand, indicates that the function at that node calls other functions. You can use the Expand Tree and Collapse Node pushbuttons to expand and collapse the nodes of the Call Graph. The Expand Tree pushbutton offers additional details about nested functions that are called, whereas the Collapse Tree pushbutton hides such details and shows the main nodes.

III

Advanced Programming

The following section presents examples of using the Call Graph feature with the member functions CMCalc, setDecimal, and getVar, which are all part of the main window class CMainWnd.

The Member Function *CMCalc*

To view a list of the functions called by the member function CMainWnd::CMCalc, select or type the following information in the Browse window's controls:

1. Select the Call Graph item in the Type combo box.

2. Type the member function name **CMainWnd::CMCalc** in the Symbols combo box. If you enter a wild card or incomplete specification, you are prompted with a dialog box.

Click the Display Result pushbutton to view the results shown in Figure 16.4. The symbols list box displays the Call Graph, which reveals that the member function CMCalc invokes the following functions:

■ The member functions GetWindowText and SetWindowText of class CWnd.

■ The member functions getVar, EnableButton, and DisableButton of class CMainWnd.

■ The functions _ltoa, strtol, and strcmp.

The graph also shows the functions called by the member functions getVar, EnableButton, and DisableButton. The Call Graph in Figure 16.4 is not fully expanded. The nodes for the member functions CxEdit::GetLineLength and CxEdit::GetLine contain nested nodes. If you select these nodes and click the Expand Tree pushbutton, you can see the functions called by the cxEdit::GetLineLength and CxEdit::GetLine member functions. You get the same effect if you double-click the nodes.

The references list box shows where the member function CMCalc is defined and where it is referenced. You can obtain the same information for any function called by CMCalc simply by selecting that function. The Browse window automatically updates the references list box to show the information for the currently selected function.

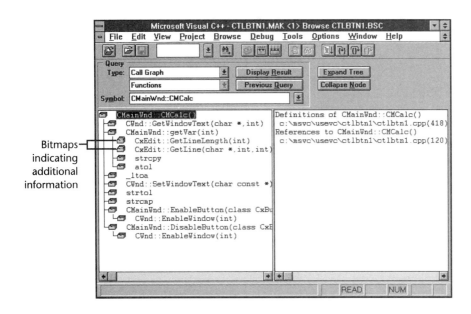

Figure 16.4
The Call Graph
for the member
function CMCalc.

The Member Function *setDecimal*

To view a list of the functions called by the CMainWnd::setDecimal member function, type the member function name **CMainWnd::setDecimal** and then click the Display Result pushbutton. The Browse window displays the results shown in Figure 16.5. The symbols list box displays the Call Graph, which reveals that the member function setDecimal invokes the following functions:

- The member functions GetWindowText and SetWindowText of class CWnd.

- The functions strtol and _ltoa.

The Member Function *getVar*

To view a list of the functions called by the CMainWnd::getVar member function, type the member function name **CMainWnd::getVar** and then click the Display Result pushbutton. The Browse window displays the results shown in Figure 16.6. The symbols list box displays the Call Graph, which reveals that the member function getVar invokes the following functions:

- The member functions GetLineLength and GetLine of class CxEdit.

- The functions strcpy and atol.

III

Advanced Programming

Figure 16.5

The Call Graph
for the member
function
setDecimal.

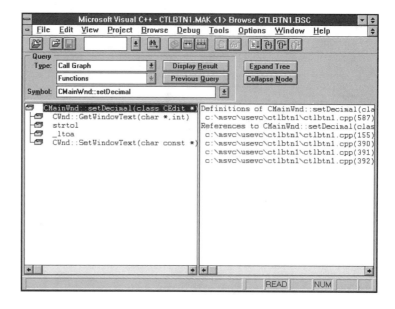

Figure 16.6

The Call Graph for
the member func-
tion getVar.

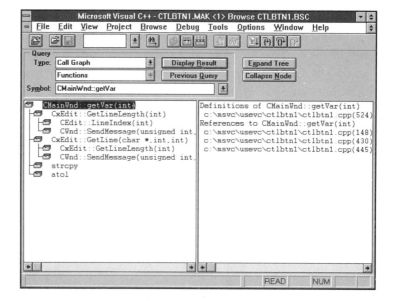

The Call Graph feature provides you with a powerful tool to study the call
tree of a function and also to resolve nasty bugs—especially ones that are
caused by a function coded by other programmers.

Using the Caller Graph Feature

In addition to producing the Call Graph, the Browse window lets you view the Caller Graph—a feature that tells you which functions are calling a specific function in your program. The following sections apply the Caller Graph feature to the same three member functions (CMCalc, setDecimal, and getVar) of class CMainWnd that we just examined with the Call Graph feature.

The Member Function *CMCalc*

To view a list of the functions that call the CMainWnd::CMCalc member function, select or type the following information in the Browse window's controls:

1. Select the Caller Graph item in the Type combo box.

2. Select the Functions item in the Subset combo box.

3. Type the member function name **CMainWnd::CMCalc**.

Click the Display Result pushbutton to view the results. In this case, the results are not so impressive—function CMCalc has no caller because its main task is to respond to the Window command message CM_CALC.

The Member Function *setDecimal*

To view a list of the functions that call the member function CMainWnd::setDecimal, type the **CMainWnd::setDecimal** member function name and then click the Display Result pushbutton. The Browse window displays the results shown in Figure 16.7. The results indicate that the function setDecimal is called by the member function CMDecimal, which, in turn, responds to the Windows command message CM_DECIMAL.

The Member Function *getVar*

To view a list of the functions that call by the member function CMainWnd::getVar, type the member function name **CMainWnd::getVar** and then click the Display Result pushbutton. The Browse window displays the results shown in Figure 16.8. The results indicate that the function getVar is called by the member function CMCalc.

The Caller Graph feature provides you with a powerful tool to study the caller tree of a function. This tree can help you determine whether a function is the culprit in causing a nasty bug.

III

Advanced Programming

Figure 16.7

The Caller Graph
for the member
function
setDecimal.

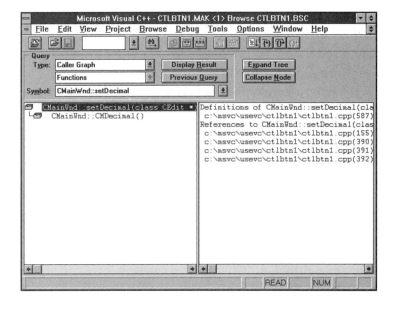

Figure 16.8

The Caller Graph
for the member
function getVar.

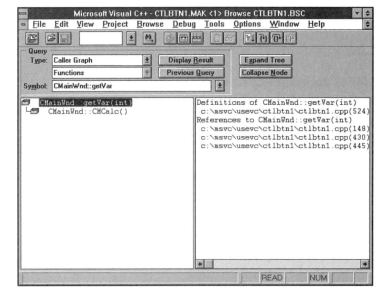

Using the Base Class Graph Feature

The Browse window supports the Base Class Graph feature, which lets you
view the hierarchy of classes involved in creating a class. You can use the
Expand Tree and Collapse Tree pushbuttons to expand and collapse the
nodes of the Base Class Graph. In this section, the Base Class Graph feature

is applied to the classes `CMainWnd`, `CxEdit`, and `CxButton`, which are part of the CTNBTN1.EXE program.

The *CMainWnd* Class

To view the base classes of `CMainWnd`, select or type the following information:

1. Select the Base Class Graph item in the Type combo box.

2. Select the Classes item in the Subset combo box.

3. Type the class name **CMainWnd** in the Symbol combo box.

Click the Display Result pushbutton to view the ancestor classes of `CMainWnd`. Figure 16.9 shows the lineage of class `CMainWnd`, which goes all the way to classes `CObject` and `CObjectRoot`. The Browse window display contains two additional panes: one for the list of class members and one for the list of lines containing the definitions and references for the class. You can scroll through the information in these two panes. The list of members includes the constructor, destructor, data members, and member functions.

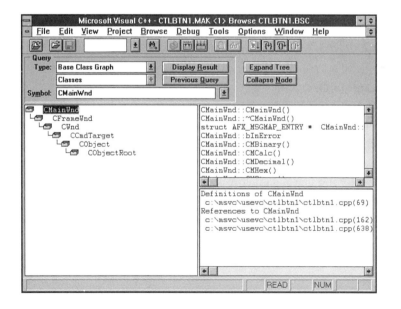

Figure 16.9
The Base Class Graph for class *CMainWnd*.

The *CxEdit* Class

To view the base classes of `CxEdit`, either select it from the Symbol combo box or type the class name **CxEdit** in the box. Then click the Display Result pushbutton to view the ancestor classes of `CxEdit`. Figure 16.10 shows the lineage of class `CxEdit`, which also goes all the way to the classes `CObject` and

III

Advanced Programming

CObjectRoot. The class member pane shows that class CxEdit declares the
member functions GetLine and GetLineLength. There are no new data members declared by class CxEdit. In addition, the graph reminds you that class
CxEdit inherits its constructor.

Figure 16.10

The Base Class
Graph for class
CxEdit.

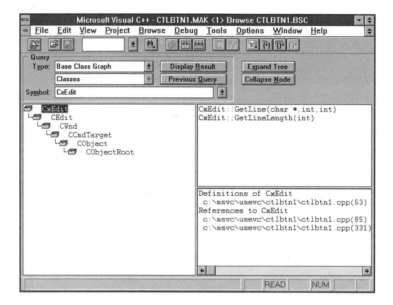

The *CxButton* Class

To view the base classes of CxButton, select or type the class name CxButton in
the Symbol combo box and then click the Display Result pushbutton to view
the ancestor classes of CxButton. Figure 16.11 shows the complete lineage of
class CxButton. The class member pane shows that class CxButton only declares
a constructor; no new data members or member functions are declared by
class CxButton.

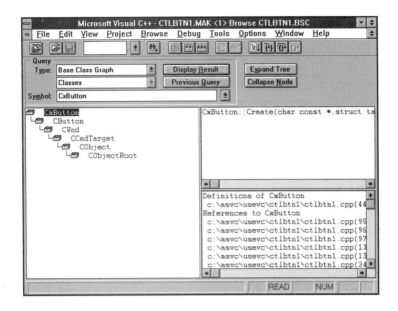

Figure 16.11
The Base Class
Graph for class
CxButton.

Using the Derived Class Graph Feature

The reverse of the Base Class Graph feature is the Derived Class Graph feature. This feature enables you to view how a class is refined by deriving other classes from it. A good example is the class CWnd from which the MFC library and your program derive many classes. To view the classes derived from CWnd, select or type the following information:

1. Select the Derived Class Graph item in the Type combo box.

2. Select the Classes item in the Subset combo box.

3. Type the class name **CWnd** in the Symbol combo box.

Click the Display Result pushbutton to view the ancestor classes of CMainWnd. Figure 16.12 shows the offspring classes of class CWnd, which include the program's own classes: CMainWnd, CxEdit, and CxButton. The Browse window display contains two additional panes: one for the list of class members and one for the list of lines containing the definitions and references for the class. You can scroll through the information in these two panes. The list of members include the constructor, destructor, data members, and member functions.

Figure 16.12

The Derived Class
Graph for class
CWnd.

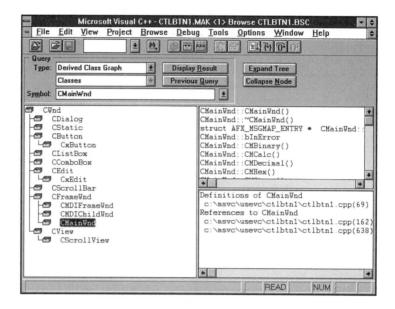

Summary

The Browse window is a powerful tool built into the Visual Workbench.
The Browse window lets you track the use of macros, data types, variables,
functions, classes, and class members across a project's files. In this chapter,
you learned about the following topics:

■ The commands in the Browse menu.

■ How to browse through both predefined macros and macros you define.

■ How to browse through both predefined data types and data types you
defined in your projects.

■ How to browse through variables and data members in your project's
classes.

■ How to browse through both general functions and member functions.

■ How to use the Call Graph feature to determine which functions are
called by a specific function.

■ How to use the Caller Graph feature to determine which functions call
a specific function.

- How to use the Base Class Graph feature to view the parent and ancestor classes of a specific class.

- How to use the Derived Class Graph feature to view the classes derived from a specific class.

In addition, the information presented in this chapter shows how the Browse window represents a versatile hand-holding tool that helps the Visual Workbench guide you through a maze of information.

III

Advanced Programming

Chapter 17

Using the Workbench Debugger

Building a Windows program can generate a number of bugs—a number that is likely to increase as the complexity of your programs increases. Visual C++ offers two debuggers for Windows applications: CodeView for Windows and the Workbench debugger. This chapter introduces the Workbench debugger, shows you how to apply its various features, and includes the following topics:

- Reviewing the Debug menu commands

- Examining the hard and soft debugging modes

- Setting various kinds of breakpoints

- Using the Watch window to monitor variables and data members

- Using the Locals window to monitor local variables

- Using the Call Stack

- Viewing mixed source and assembly code

- Managing the Watch window

Reviewing the Debug Menu Commands

This section provides a quick refresher of the Debug menu commands, first introduced in Chapter 1 and summarized in Table 17.1. You may want to review the section in Chapter 1 that discusses the Debug menu before continuing in this chapter.

Table 17.1 Debug Menu Commands		
Command	**Shortcut Key**	**Purpose**
Go	F5	Runs the program associated with the current project.
Restart	Shift+F5	Reloads the program and starts again.
Stop Debugging	Alt+F5	Ends the debugging session.
Step Into	F8	Single-steps through each program line.
Step Over	F10	Single-steps through each program line, but executes functions without entering them.
Step Out	Shift+F7	Runs the program to the first statement after the current function call.
Step to Cursor	F7	Runs the program until it reaches the place of the insertion point.
Show Call Stack...		Displays the call stack.
Breakpoints...		Clears and sets a breakpoint.
QuickWatch	Shift+F9	Opens the QuickWatch window to add, view the value of, or alter the value of a watched variable.

Examining the Hard and Soft Debugging Modes

The Workbench debugger supports two debugging modes: hard and soft. In short, hard mode is a *task exclusive* approach in which the Windows application being debugged directs all input from the mouse or the keyboard to that application. Hard mode has the potential to cause the debugger to destabilize the Windows system by interacting with it. While in hard mode, you can't invoke the on-line help, print, run App Studio, or use any programming tools in the Tools menu.

The soft debugging mode, which is the default mode, is not as task exclusive as the hard mode. Microsoft recommends that you work with the soft debugging mode unless it is necessary to use the hard mode. Use the hard mode when you want to monitor all mouse and keyboard input to determine why your application is experiencing an error. You can select either mode by invoking the Debug command from the Options menu. When you choose the Debug command, a simple dialog box appears in which you can select the debugging mode, specify program arguments, specify additional DLLs, and request hexadecimal display.

Setting Breakpoints

The Workbench debugger supports various kinds of breakpoints, which range from simple to sophisticated. To set any kind of breakpoint, you have to choose the Breakpoints command from the Debug menu. The Breakpoints command then invokes the Breakpoints dialog box shown in Figure 17.1.

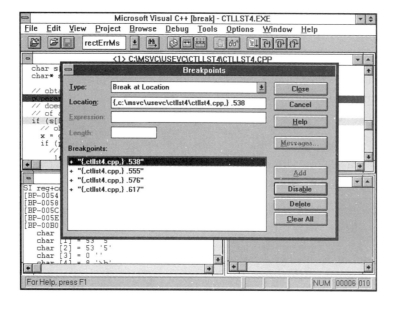

Figure 17.1
The Breakpoints dialog box.

This Breakpoints dialog box contains the following controls:

- *Type drop-down combo box*. Lists the various kinds of breakpoints (more about these breakpoints later in this section).

- *Location edit box*. Enables you to specify the location of the breakpoint if one is used.

■ *Expression edit box.* Supports typing the name of the expression used in the breakpoint. The expression can be a simple variable or can include variables, constants, and operators.

■ *Length edit box.* Enables you to enter the number of bytes for the type size to use with pointers.

■ *Breakpoints list box.* Lists the current breakpoints. The dialog box places a + or - character to the left of an enabled or disabled breakpoint, respectively.

■ *Close pushbutton.* Closes the Breakpoints dialog box.

■ *Cancel pushbutton.* Cancels any new changes you made since you opened the Breakpoints dialog box.

■ *Help pushbutton.* Offers on-line help.

■ *Messages... pushbutton.* Disabled by default and enabled when you use breakpoints that involve Windows messages.

■ *Add pushbutton.* Takes the information in the Type, Location, Expression, and Length controls and uses the information to add a new breakpoint.

■ *Disable pushbutton.* Disables the breakpoint that is currently selected in the Breakpoints list box. If you select a disabled breakpoint, the dialog box automatically changes the caption of the pushbutton to *Enable*.

■ *Delete pushbutton.* Deletes the breakpoint that is currently selected in the Breakpoints list box.

■ *Clear All pushbutton.* Clears all breakpoints.

Understanding the Various Breakpoints

The Workbench debugger supports the following kinds of breakpoints:

Break at location. This type of unconditional breakpoint is the most common one and is the default breakpoint type. When the program reaches this kind of breakpoint, it simply pauses. You can then inspect variables in the Watch and Local windows, and you can resume execution either by single-stepping through subsequent statements (to track bugs) or by full-speed program execution.

Break at location if expression is true. This is a simple kind of conditional breakpoint: at the breakpoint location it examines the expression you entered in the Expression edit box. If the expression is true, the program pauses so that you can inspect variables.

Break at location if expression has changed. This kind of location-bound breakpoint examines the contents of a variable or uses the address of a pointer to examine a memory location. If the value of any byte in the examined memory location has changed, the program pauses.

Break when expression is true. This kind of conditional breakpoint is not bound by a specific program location. Consequently, the program examines the tested expression after every line or every instruction. The program pauses when the expression is true. This kind of breakpoint incurs a high overhead and causes the debugged program to slow down.

Break when expression has changed. This kind of conditional breakpoint is not bound by a specific program location. Consequently, the program examines the targeted memory location (which belongs to a variable or is accessed by a pointer) after every line or every instruction. The program pauses when at least one byte in the examined memory location has changed. This kind of breakpoint also incurs a high overhead and causes the debugged program to slow down.

Break at `WndProc` *if message is received.* This kind of breakpoint is very specific to Windows. You specify either a single message or one or more classes of messages on which to break. When the anticipated message or messages are received, the program pauses at the specified Windows callback function.

Examining the Breakpoint Location Formats

The Workbench debugger supports various formats that are used to specify breakpoint locations. Table 17.2 presents these formats and offers an example of each.

Table 17.2 Breakpoint Location Formats		
Format	**Example**	**Comments**
`.lineNumber`	.125	Line 125 of the active source file
`Filename!lineNumber`	CTL.CPP!90	Line 90 in file CTL.CPP

III

Advanced Programming

Table 17.2 Continued		
Format	**Example**	**Comments**
Offset	0x1A34	Offset 0x1A34 in code segment
Offset	IP	Instruction pointer offset to code segment CS
Segment:Offset	0xA100:0x1A34	Offset 0x1A34 to segment 0xA100
Segment:Offset	CS:0x1A34	Offset 0x1A34 to code segment CS
Segment:Offset	CS:IP	Instruction pointer offset to code segment CS

Debugging the CTLLST4.EXE Program

The CTLLST4.EXE program was presented in Chapter 8. The program is one version of the Programmer's Calculator that uses the list box and combo box controls to store the information for the operands, operator, result, and variables. The CTLLST4.EXE program is used again in this chapter—this time to illustrate particular debugging features. Listing 17.1 presents the line-numbered source code for the CTLLST4.CPP implementation file. The line numbers make it easy to refer to a source code line when you are inserting a breakpoint or when the program pauses at a breakpoint.

Listing 17.1 Line-Numbered Source Code for the CTLLST4.CPP Implementation File

```
 1:  /*
 2:
 3:              Programmer's Calculator version 4.0 11/8/93
 4:              -------------------------------------------
 5:
 6:    Program illustrates the combo box and list box.
 7:    These controls support history list and pick lists.
 8:    The program uses a list box to store and recall the
 9:    single-letter variables.
10:
11:  */
12:
13:  #include <stdlib.h>
14:  #include <ctype.h>
15:  #include <stdio.h>
16:  #include <string.h>
17:  #include <afxwin.h>
18:  #include "ctllst4.h"
19:
```

```
20:  // declare the constants that represent the sizes of the
     // controls
21:  const WErrMsglbl = 150;
22:  const Wlbl = 100;
23:  const Hlbl = 20;
24:  const LblVertSpacing = 5;
25:  const LblHorzSpacing = 40;
26:  const Wlst = 200;
27:  const Hlst = 150;
28:  const LstVertSpacing = 10;
29:  const LstHorzSpacing = 40;
30:  const Hbtn = 30;
31:  const Wbtn = 80;
32:  const BtnHorzSpacing = 30;
33:  const BtnVertSpacing = 10;
34:  const Wcmb = 100;
35:  const Hcmb = 150;
36:  const CmbVertSpacing = 10;
37:  const CmbHorzSpacing = 40;
38:  const Hgrp = 150;
39:  const Wgrp = 180;
40:  const GrpHorzSpacing = 30;
41:  const GrpVertSpacing = 10;
42:  const Hchk = 30;
43:  const Wchk = 250;
44:  const ChkHorzSpacing = 30;
45:  const ChkVertSpacing = 10;
46:  const Hrbt = 30;
47:  const Wrbt = 120;
48:  const RbtHorzSpacing = 30;
49:  const RbtVertSpacing = 30;
50:  const RbtLeftMargin = 20;
51:
52:  const MaxStringLen = 80;
53:  const MAX_MEMREG = 26;
54:  // maximum number of items in a combo box that doubles up as
55:  // history list box
56:  const MaxHistory = 25;
57:
58:  // declare the ID_XXXX constants for the edit boxes
59:  #define ID_OPERAND1_CMB   101
60:  #define ID_OPERATOR_CMB   102
61:  #define ID_OPERAND2_CMB   103
62:  #define ID_RESULT_CMB     104
63:  #define ID_ERRMSG_TXT     105
64:  #define ID_VARIABLE_LST   106
65:  #define ID_AUTOSUBST_CHK 107
66:  #define ID_RADIX_GRP      108
67:  #define ID_DECIMAL_RBT    109
68:  #define ID_HEX_RBT        110
69:  #define ID_BINARY_RBT     111
70:
71:  // declare constants for the check box and radio button states
72:  const BF_CHECKED = 1;
```

(continues)

III

Advanced Programming

Listing 17.1 Continued

```
 73:   const BF_UNCHECKED = 0;
 74:
 75:   class CxButton : public CButton
 76:   {
 77:   public:
 78:
 79:      BOOL Create(const char FAR* lpCaption, const RECT& rect,
 80:               CWnd* pParentWnd, UINT nID, BOOL bIsDefault);
 81:
 82:   };
 83:
 84:   // declare check box class
 85:   class CCheckBox : public CButton
 86:   {
 87:   public:
 88:      BOOL Create(const char FAR* lpCaption, const RECT& rect,
 89:                  CWnd* pParentWnd, UINT nID)
 90:      {
 91:          return CButton::Create(lpCaption,
 92:                                 WS_CHILD | WS_VISIBLE |
 93:                                 WS_TABSTOP | BS_AUTOCHECKBOX,
 94:                                 rect, pParentWnd, nID);
 95:      }
 96:
 97:      void Check()
 98:         { SetCheck(BF_CHECKED); }
 99:
100:      void UnCheck()
101:         { SetCheck(BF_UNCHECKED); }
102:   };
103:
104:   // declare radio button class
105:   class CRadioButton : public CButton
106:   {
107:   public:
108:      BOOL Create(const char FAR* lpCaption, const RECT& rect,
109:                  CWnd* pParentWnd, UINT nID)
110:      {
111:          return CButton::Create(lpCaption,
112:                                 WS_CHILD | WS_VISIBLE |
113:                                 WS_TABSTOP |
114:                                 BS_AUTORADIOBUTTON,
115:                                 rect, pParentWnd, nID);
116:      }
117:
118:      void Check()
119:         { SetCheck(BF_CHECKED); }
120:
121:      void UnCheck()
122:         { SetCheck(BF_UNCHECKED); }
123:   };
124:
125:   // declare group box class
126:   class CGroupBox : public CButton
```

```
127:  {
128:  public:
129:      BOOL Create(const char FAR* lpCaption, const RECT& rect,
130:                  CWnd* pParentWnd, UINT nID)
131:      {
132:          return CButton::Create(lpCaption,
133:                                  WS_CHILD | WS_VISIBLE |
134:                                  WS_TABSTOP | BS_GROUPBOX,
135:                                  rect, pParentWnd, nID);
136:      }
137:  };
138:
139:  class CComboListApp : public CWinApp
140:  {
141:  public:
142:      virtual BOOL InitInstance();
143:  };
144:
145:  // expand the functionality of CFrameWnd by deriving class
      // CMainWnd
146:  class CMainWnd : public CFrameWnd
147:  {
148:   public:
149:
150:    CMainWnd();
151:
152:    ~CMainWnd();
153:
154:   protected:
155:
156:    // declare the pointers to the various controls
157:    // first, the combo box controls
158:    CComboBox* pOperand1Cmb;
159:    CComboBox* pOperatorCmb;
160:    CComboBox* pOperand2Cmb;
161:    CComboBox* pResultCmb;
162:    // then the list box control
163:    CListBox* pVariableLst;
164:    // then the static text controls
165:    CStatic* pOperand1Txt;
166:    CStatic* pOperatorTxt;
167:    CStatic* pOperand2Txt;
168:    CStatic* pResultTxt;
169:    CStatic* pErrMsgTxt;
170:    CStatic* pVariableTxt;
171:    // pushbuttons
172:    CxButton* pCalcBtn;
173:    CxButton* pStoreBtn;
174:    CxButton* pExitBtn;
175:    // group box
176:    CGroupBox* pRadixGrp;
177:    // radio buttons
178:    CRadioButton* pDecimalRbt;
179:    CRadioButton* pHexRbt;
180:    CRadioButton* pBinaryRbt;
181:    // check box
```

III

Advanced Programming

(continues)

Listing 17.1 Continued

```
182:    CCheckBox* pAutoSubstChk;
183:
184:    // math mode
185:    int nRadix;
186:
187:    // math error flag
188:    BOOL bInError;
189:
190:    // coordinates for the Error Message static text area
191:    CRect rectErrMsg;
192:
193:    // handle the notification messages from the Operator combo box
194:    afx_msg void HandleOperatorCmb();
195:
196:    // handle the Variables list box when it gets the focus
197:    afx_msg void HandleVariableLst();
198:
199:    // initialize the instances of CAppWindow
200:    void InitAppWindow();
201:
202:    // update the combo box with the text in the
203:    // accompanying edit box, assuming that the text
204:    // is not already in the box
205:    void updateComboBox(CComboBox* pComboBox);
206:
207:    // handle clicking the left mouse button
208:    afx_msg void OnLButtonDown(UINT nFlags, CPoint point);
209:
210:    // handle selecting the decimal mode
211:    afx_msg void HandleDecimalRbt();
212:
213:    // handle selecting the hexadecimal mode
214:    afx_msg void HandleHexRbt();
215:
216:    // handle selecting the binary mode
217:    afx_msg void HandleBinaryRbt();
218:
219:    // handle the calculation
220:    afx_msg void CMCalc();
221:
222:    // handle storing the result in a variable
223:    afx_msg void CMStore();
224:
225:    // handle exiting the application
226:    afx_msg void OnExit();
227:
228:    // handle creating the controls
229:    afx_msg int OnCreate(LPCREATESTRUCT lpCS);
230:
231:    // handle closing the window
232:    afx_msg void OnClose();
233:
234:    // enable a pushbutton control
```

```
235:    virtual void EnableButton(CxButton* pBtn)
236:      { pBtn->EnableWindow( TRUE); }
237:
238:    // disable a pushbutton control
239:    virtual void DisableButton(CxButton* pBtn)
240:      { pBtn->EnableWindow(FALSE); }
241:
242:    // return a reference to member r based on individual
243:    // coordinates and dimensions
244:    void makerect(int X, int Y, int W, int H, CRect& r)
245:     { r.SetRect(X, Y, X + W, Y + H); }
246:
247:    // obtain a number of a Variable edit box line
248:    long getVar(int lineNum);
249:
250:    // store a number in the selected text of
251:    // the Variable edit box line
252:    void putVar(long x);
253:
254:    // set contents of edit controls to integers in various bases
255:    void setDecimal(CComboBox* pEdit);
256:    void setHexaDecimal(CComboBox* pEdit);
257:    void setBinary(CComboBox* pEdit);
258:
259:    // declare message map macro
260:    DECLARE_MESSAGE_MAP();
261:
262:  };
263:
264:  BOOL CxButton::Create(const char FAR* lpCaption, const RECT& rect,
265:                CWnd* pParentWnd, UINT nID, BOOL bIsDefault)
266:
267:  {
268:    DWORD dwBtnStyle = (bIsDefault == TRUE) ?
269:                BS_DEFPUSHBUTTON : BS_PUSHBUTTON;
270:
271:      return CButton::Create(lpCaption,
272:                WS_CHILD ¦ WS_VISIBLE ¦
273:                WS_TABSTOP ¦ dwBtnStyle,
274:                rect, pParentWnd, nID);
275:  }
276:
277:  CMainWnd::CMainWnd()
278:  {
279:
280:    // load the main accelerator table to handle
281:    // keystroke input
282:    LoadAccelTable("BUTTONS");
283:    // create the window
284:    Create(NULL,
285:      "Programmer's Calculator Version 4",
286:      WS_OVERLAPPEDWINDOW,
287:      rectDefault, NULL, "EXITMENU");
288:
```

III

Advanced Programming

(continues)

Listing 17.1 Continued

```
289:    // initialize application
290:    InitAppWindow();
291:  }
292:
293:  int CMainWnd::OnCreate(LPCREATESTRUCT lpCS)
294:  {
295:
296:    int x0 = 20;
297:    int y0 = 10;
298:    int x = x0, y = y0;
299:    int x1, y1;
300:    DWORD dwStaticStyle = WS_CHILD | WS_VISIBLE | SS_LEFT;
301:    DWORD dwEditStyle = WS_CHILD | WS_VISIBLE | WS_BORDER |
302:               ES_LEFT | ES_AUTOHSCROLL | ES_UPPERCASE;
303:    DWORD dwComboStyle = WS_CHILD | WS_VISIBLE | WS_VSCROLL;
304:    DWORD dwListStyle = WS_CHILD | WS_VISIBLE | WS_VSCROLL |
305:               WS_HSCROLL | LBS_STANDARD;
306:    CRect r;
307:
308:    // create the first set of labels for the edit boxes
309:    makerect(x, y, Wlbl, Hlbl, r);
310:    pOperand1Txt = new CStatic();
311:    pOperand1Txt->Create("Operand1", dwStaticStyle, r, this);
312:    x += Wlbl + LblHorzSpacing;
313:    makerect(x, y, Wlbl, Hlbl, r);
314:    pOperatorTxt = new CStatic();
315:    pOperatorTxt->Create("Operator", dwStaticStyle, r, this);
316:    x += Wlbl + LblHorzSpacing;
317:    makerect(x, y, Wlbl, Hlbl, r);
318:    pOperand2Txt = new CStatic();
319:    pOperand2Txt->Create("Operand2", dwStaticStyle, r, this);
320:    x += Wlbl + LblHorzSpacing;
321:    makerect(x, y, Wlbl, Hlbl, r);
322:    pResultTxt = new CStatic();
323:    pResultTxt->Create("Result", dwStaticStyle, r, this);
324:
325:    // create the Operand1, Operator, Operand2, and Result
326:    // combo list boxes
327:    x = x0;
328:    y += Hlbl + LblVertSpacing;
329:    makerect(x, y, Wcmb, Hcmb, r);
330:    pOperand1Cmb = new CComboBox();
331:    pOperand1Cmb->Create(dwComboStyle | CBS_DROPDOWN, r,
332:                this, ID_OPERAND1_CMB);
333:    // create the Operator combo box
334:    x += Wcmb + CmbHorzSpacing;
335:    makerect(x, y, Wcmb, Hcmb, r);
336:    pOperatorCmb = new CComboBox();
337:    pOperatorCmb->Create(dwComboStyle | CBS_SIMPLE, r,
338:                this, ID_OPERATOR_CMB);
339:    x += Wcmb + CmbHorzSpacing;
340:    makerect(x, y, Wcmb, Hcmb, r);
341:    pOperand2Cmb = new CComboBox();
342:    pOperand2Cmb->Create(dwComboStyle | CBS_DROPDOWN, r,
343:                this, ID_OPERAND2_CMB);
```

```
344:    x += Wcmb + CmbHorzSpacing;
345:    makerect(x, y, Wcmb, Hcmb, r);
346:    pResultCmb = new CComboBox();
347:    pResultCmb->Create(dwComboStyle ¦ CBS_DROPDOWN, r,
348:                       this, ID_RESULT_CMB);
349:    // create the static text and edit box for the error message
350:    x = x0;
351:    y += Hcmb + CmbVertSpacing;
352:    // store coordinates for the button controls
353:    x1 = x + WErrMsglbl + LblHorzSpacing;
354:    y1 = y;
355:    makerect(x, y, WErrMsglbl, Hlbl, r);
356:    pErrMsgTxt = new CStatic();
357:    pErrMsgTxt->Create("Error: none", dwStaticStyle, r, this);
358:    rectErrMsg = r;
359:    // create the static text and list box for the single-letter
360:    // variable selection
361:    y += Hlbl + LblVertSpacing;
362:    makerect(x, y, Wlbl, Hlbl, r);
363:    pVariableTxt = new CStatic();
364:    pVariableTxt->Create("Variables", dwStaticStyle, r, this);
365:    y += Hlbl + LblVertSpacing;
366:    makerect(x, y, Wlst, Hlst, r);
367:    pVariableLst = new CListBox();
368:    pVariableLst->Create(dwListStyle, r, this, ID_VARIABLE_LST);
369:    // create the Calc pushbutton
370:    x = x1;
371:    y = y1;
372:    makerect(x, y, Wbtn, Hbtn, r);
373:    pCalcBtn = new CxButton();
374:    pCalcBtn->Create("&Calc", r, this, ID_CALC_BTN, TRUE);
375:
376:    // create the Store Btn
377:    x += Wbtn + BtnHorzSpacing;
378:    makerect(x, y, Wbtn, Hbtn, r);
379:    pStoreBtn = new CxButton();
380:    pStoreBtn->Create("&Store", r, this, ID_STORE_BTN, FALSE);
381:
382:    // Create the Exit Btn
383:    x += Wbtn + BtnHorzSpacing;
384:    makerect(x, y, Wbtn, Hbtn, r);
385:    pExitBtn = new CxButton();
386:    pExitBtn->Create("&Exit", r, this, ID_EXIT_BTN, FALSE);
387:
388:    // create the group box
389:    x = x1 + Wbtn + BtnHorzSpacing;
390:    y = y1 + Hbtn + BtnVertSpacing;
391:    makerect(x, y, Wgrp, Hgrp, r);
392:    pRadixGrp = new CGroupBox();
393:    pRadixGrp->Create(" Radix ", r, this, ID_RADIX_GRP);
394:    y1 = y;
395:    x1 = x;
396:
397:    // create the Decimal radio button
```

(continues)

Listing 17.1 Continued

```
398:    y += RbtVertSpacing;
399:    makerect(RbtLeftMargin + x, y, Wrbt, Hrbt, r);
400:    pDecimalRbt = new CRadioButton();
401:    pDecimalRbt->Create("Decimal", r, this, ID_DECIMAL_RBT);
402:
403:    // create the Hexadecimal radio button
404:    y += RbtVertSpacing;
405:    makerect(RbtLeftMargin + x, y, Wrbt, Hrbt, r);
406:    pHexRbt = new CRadioButton();
407:    pHexRbt->Create("Hexadecimal", r, this, ID_HEX_RBT);
408:
409:    // create the Binary radio button
410:    y += RbtVertSpacing;
411:    makerect(RbtLeftMargin + x, y, Wrbt, Hrbt, r);
412:    pBinaryRbt = new CRadioButton();
413:    pBinaryRbt->Create("Binary", r, this, ID_BINARY_RBT);
414:
415:    // create auto substitute check box
416:    x = x1;
417:    y = y1 + Hgrp + GrpVertSpacing;
418:    makerect(x, y, Wrbt, Hrbt, r);
419:    pAutoSubstChk = new CCheckBox();
420:    pAutoSubstChk->Create("Substitute Vars", r,
421:                          this, ID_AUTOSUBST_CHK);
422:
423:    // check the decimal radix
424:    pDecimalRbt->SetCheck(BF_CHECKED);
425:
426:    return CFrameWnd::OnCreate(lpCS);
427:  }
428:
429:  CMainWnd::~CMainWnd()
430:  {
431:    // delete the controls
432:    delete pOperand1Cmb;
433:    delete pOperatorCmb;
434:    delete pOperand2Cmb;
435:    delete pResultCmb;
436:    delete pVariableLst;
437:    delete pOperand1Txt;
438:    delete pOperatorTxt;
439:    delete pOperand2Txt;
440:    delete pResultTxt;
441:    delete pErrMsgTxt;
442:    delete pVariableTxt;
443:    delete pCalcBtn;
444:    delete pStoreBtn;
445:    delete pExitBtn;
446:    delete pDecimalRbt;
447:    delete pHexRbt;
448:    delete pBinaryRbt;
449:    delete pRadixGrp;
```

```
450:     delete pAutoSubstChk;
451:   }
452:
453:   void CMainWnd::InitAppWindow()
454:   {
455:     char s[MaxStringLen];
456:
457:     // disable the Store button
458:     DisableButton(pStoreBtn);
459:     // build the initial contents of the Variable list box
460:     for (char c = 'Z'; c >= 'A'; c—) {
461:       sprintf(s, "%c: 0", c);
462:       pVariableLst->AddString(s);
463:     }
464:     // select the first item
465:     pVariableLst->SetCurSel(0);
466:
467:     // add the operators in the Operator combo box
468:     pOperatorCmb->AddString("+");
469:     pOperatorCmb->AddString("-");
470:     pOperatorCmb->AddString("*");
471:     pOperatorCmb->AddString("/");
472:     pOperatorCmb->AddString("!");
473:     pOperatorCmb->AddString("&");
474:     pOperatorCmb->AddString("~");
475:     pOperatorCmb->AddString("<<");
476:     pOperatorCmb->AddString(">>");
477:
478:     // clear the bInError flag
479:     bInError = FALSE;
480:
481:     // set the default math mode
482:     nRadix = 10;
483:   }
484:
485:   void CMainWnd::HandleOperatorCmb()
486:   {
487:     char s[MaxStringLen+1];
488:
489:     // get the text in the Operator combo box edit area
490:     pOperatorCmb->GetWindowText(s, MaxStringLen);
491:     // use it to search for a matching list item
492:     pOperatorCmb->SelectString(-1, s);
493:   }
494:
495:
496:   void CMainWnd::OnLButtonDown(UINT nFlags, CPoint point)
497:   {
498:     // did you click the mouse over the Error Message static text?
499:     if (rectErrMsg.PtInRect(point)) {
500:         pErrMsgTxt->SetWindowText("Error: none");
501:         EnableButton(pStoreBtn);
502:     }
503:   }
504:
```

(continues)

Listing 17.1 Continued

```
505: void CMainWnd::HandleDecimalRbt()
506: {
507:   setDecimal(pOperand1Cmb);
508:   setDecimal(pOperand2Cmb);
509:   setDecimal(pResultCmb);
510:   nRadix = 10;
511: }
512:
513:   // handle selecting the hexadecimal mode
514: void CMainWnd::HandleHexRbt()
515: {
516:   setHexaDecimal(pOperand1Cmb);
517:   setHexaDecimal(pOperand2Cmb);
518:   setHexaDecimal(pResultCmb);
519:   nRadix = 16;
520: }
521:
522:   // handle selecting the binary mode
523: void CMainWnd::HandleBinaryRbt()
524: {
525:   setBinary(pOperand1Cmb);
526:   setBinary(pOperand2Cmb);
527:   setBinary(pResultCmb);
528:   nRadix = 2;
529: }
530:
531: void CMainWnd::CMCalc()
532: {
533:   long x, y, z;
534:   char opStr[MaxStringLen+1];
535:   char s[MaxStringLen+1];
536:   char* ss;
537:
538:   // obtain the string in the Operand1 edit box
539:   pOperand1Cmb->GetWindowText(s, MaxStringLen);
540:   // does the pOperand1Cmb contain the name
541:   // of a single-letter variable which begins with @?
542:   if (s[0] == '@') {
543:     // obtain value from the Variable edit control
544:     x = getVar(s[1] - 'A');
545:     if (pAutoSubstChk->GetCheck() == BF_CHECKED) {
546:       // substitute variable name with its value
547:       _ltoa(x, s, nRadix);
548:       pOperand1Cmb->SetWindowText(s);
549:     }
550:   }
551:   else
552:     // convert the string in the edit box
553:     x = strtol(s, &ss, nRadix);
554:
555:   // obtain the string in the Operand2 edit box
556:   pOperand2Cmb->GetWindowText(s, MaxStringLen);
557:   // does the pOperand2Cmb contain the name
558:   // of a single-letter variable which begins with @?
```

```
559:    if (s[0] == '@') {
560:      // obtain value from the Variable edit control
561:      y = getVar(s[1] - 'A');
562:      if (pAutoSubstChk->GetCheck() == BF_CHECKED) {
563:        // substitute variable name with its value
564:        _ltoa(y, s, nRadix);
565:        pOperand2Cmb->SetWindowText(s);
566:      }
567:    }
568:    else
569:      // convert the string in the edit box
570:      y = strtol(s, &ss, nRadix);
571:
572:    // obtain the string in the Operator edit box
573:    pOperatorCmb->GetWindowText(opStr, MaxStringLen);
574:
575:    // clear the error message box
576:    pErrMsgTxt->SetWindowText("Error: none");
577:    bInError = FALSE;
578:
579:    // determine the requested operation
580:    if (opStr[0] == '+')
581:      z = x + y;
582:    else if (opStr[0] == '-')
583:      z = x - y;
584:    else if (opStr[0] == '*') {
585:      if (x == 0 || y < (2147483647L / x))
586:        z = x * y;
587:      else {
588:        z = 0;
589:        bInError = TRUE;
590:        pErrMsgTxt->SetWindowText("Error: overflow error");
591:      }
592:    }
593:    else if (opStr[0] == '/') {
594:      if (y != 0)
595:        z = x / y;
596:      else {
597:        z = 0;
598:        bInError = TRUE;
599:        pErrMsgTxt->SetWindowText("Error: Division-by-zero error");
600:      }
601:    }
602:    else if (opStr[0] == '|')
603:      z = x | y;
604:    else if (opStr[0] == '&')
605:      z = x & y;
606:    else if (opStr[0] == '!')
607:      z = !x;
608:    else if (opStr[0] == '~')
609:      z = ~x;
610:    else if (strcmp(opStr, "<<") == 0)
611:      z = x << y;
612:    else if (strcmp(opStr, ">>") == 0)
613:      z = x >> y;
```

(continues)

Listing 17.1 Continued

```
614:    else {
615:      bInError = TRUE;
616:      pErrMsgTxt->SetWindowText("Error: Invalid operator");
617:    }
618:    // display the result if no error has occurred
619:    if (!bInError) {
620:      _ltoa(z, s, nRadix);
621:      pResultCmb->SetWindowText(s);
622:      // update the Result comb box
623:      updateComboBox(pResultCmb);
624:      EnableButton(pStoreBtn);
625:    }
626:    else
627:      DisableButton(pStoreBtn);
628:
629:    // update the operand combo boxes
630:    updateComboBox(pOperand1Cmb);
631:    updateComboBox(pOperand2Cmb);
632:  }
633:
634:  void CMainWnd::CMStore()
635:  {
636:    char s[MaxStringLen+1];
637:    char* ss;
638:    long z;
639:
640:    // get the string in the Result edit box
641:    pResultCmb->GetWindowText(s, MaxStringLen);
642:
643:    // store the result in the selected text of
644:    // the Variable edit box
645:    z = strtol(s, &ss, nRadix);
646:    putVar(z);
647:  }
648:
649:  void CMainWnd::HandleVariableLst()
650:  {
651:    char s[MaxStringLen+1];
652:    char operandText[MaxStringLen];
653:
654:    pVariableLst->GetText(pVariableLst->GetCurSel(), s);
655:    strcpy(s, (s+3));
656:    // get the text in the Operand1 combo box
657:    pOperand1Cmb->GetWindowText(operandText, MaxStringLen);
658:    // is the first character in the Operand1 combo box a #?
659:    if (operandText[0] == '#')
660:      pOperand1Cmb->SetWindowText(s);
661:    // get the text in the Operand2 edit box
662:    pOperand2Cmb->GetWindowText(operandText, MaxStringLen);
663:    // is the first character in the Operand2 combo box a #?
664:    if (operandText[0] == '#')
665:      pOperand2Cmb->SetWindowText(s);
666:  }
667:
```

```
668:  long CMainWnd::getVar(int lineNum)
669:  {
670:    char s[MaxStringLen+1];
671:
672:    if (lineNum >= pVariableLst->GetCount())
673:      return 0;
674:    pVariableLst->GetText(lineNum, s);
675:    strcpy(s, (s+3));
676:
677:    // return the number stored in the target line
678:    return atol(s);
679:  }
680:
681:  void CMainWnd::putVar(long x)
682:  {
683:    char s[MaxStringLen+1];
684:    char c;
685:    int selectIndex = pVariableLst->GetCurSel();
686:
687:    pVariableLst->DeleteString(selectIndex);
688:    strcpy(s, "A:");
689:    c = selectIndex + 'A';
690:    // locate the character position of the cursor
691:    sprintf(s, "%c: %ld", c, x);
692:    // insert it
693:    pVariableLst->InsertString(selectIndex, s);
694:    pVariableLst->SetCurSel(selectIndex);
695:  }
696:
697:  void CMainWnd::updateComboBox(CComboBox* pComboBox)
698:  {
699:    char s[MaxStringLen+1];
700:    int i;
701:
702:    pComboBox->GetWindowText(s, MaxStringLen);
703:    // is string s in the combo list
704:    i = pComboBox->FindString(-1, s);
705:    if (i == 0) return;
706:    else if (i < 0) {
707:      pComboBox->InsertString(0, s);
708:      // delete extra history list members?
709:      while (pComboBox->GetCount() >= MaxHistory)
710:        pComboBox->DeleteString(pComboBox->GetCount()-1);
711:    }
712:    else {
713:      // delete the current selection
714:      pComboBox->DeleteString(i);
715:      // insert the string s at the first position
716:      pComboBox->InsertString(0, s);
717:      // select the first combo box item
718:      pComboBox->SetCurSel(0);
719:    }
720:  }
721:
722:  void CMainWnd::OnExit()
723:  {
```

Advanced Programming

(continues)

Listing 17.1 Continued

```
724:     SendMessage(WM_CLOSE);
725:   }
726:
727:   void CMainWnd::OnClose()
728:   {
729:     if (MessageBox("Want to close this application",
730:                       "Query", MB_YESNO ¦ MB_ICONQUESTION) == IDYES)
731:       DestroyWindow();
732:   }
733:
734:   void CMainWnd::setDecimal(CComboBox* pEdit)
735:   {
736:     char s[MaxStringLen+1];
737:     char* ss;
738:     long n;
739:
740:     pEdit->GetWindowText(s, MaxStringLen);
741:     n = strtol(s, &ss, nRadix);
742:     _ltoa(n, s, 10);
743:     pEdit->SetWindowText(s);
744:   }
745:
746:   void CMainWnd::setHexaDecimal(CComboBox* pEdit)
747:   {
748:     char s[MaxStringLen+1];
749:     char *ss;
750:     long n;
751:
752:     pEdit->GetWindowText(s, MaxStringLen);
753:     n = strtol(s, &ss, nRadix);
754:     _ltoa(n, s, 16);
755:     pEdit->SetWindowText(s);
756:   }
757:
758:   void CMainWnd::setBinary(CComboBox* pEdit)
759:   {
760:     char s[MaxStringLen+1];
761:     char* ss;
762:     long n;
763:
764:     pEdit->GetWindowText(s, MaxStringLen);
765:     n = strtol(s, &ss, nRadix);
766:     _ltoa(n, s, 2);
767:     pEdit->SetWindowText(s);
768:   }
769:
770:   BEGIN_MESSAGE_MAP(CMainWnd, CFrameWnd)
771:       ON_CBN_EDITUPDATE(ID_OPERATOR_CMB, HandleOperatorCmb)
772:       ON_LBN_DBLCLK(ID_VARIABLE_LST, HandleVariableLst)
773:       ON_WM_LBUTTONDOWN()
774:       ON_COMMAND(ID_CALC_BTN, CMCalc)
775:       ON_COMMAND(ID_STORE_BTN, CMStore)
776:       ON_COMMAND(ID_EXIT_BTN, OnExit)
```

```
777:        ON_COMMAND(CM_EXIT, OnExit)
778:        ON_BN_CLICKED(ID_DECIMAL_RBT, HandleDecimalRbt)
779:        ON_BN_CLICKED(ID_HEX_RBT, HandleHexRbt)
780:        ON_BN_CLICKED(ID_BINARY_RBT, HandleBinaryRbt)
781:        ON_WM_CREATE()
782:        ON_WM_CLOSE()
783:    END_MESSAGE_MAP()
784:
785:    // Construct the CComboListApp's m_pMainWnd data member
786:    BOOL CComboListApp::InitInstance()
787:    {
788:      m_pMainWnd = new CMainWnd();
789:      m_pMainWnd->ShowWindow(m_nCmdShow);
790:      m_pMainWnd->UpdateWindow();
791:      return TRUE;
792:    }
793:
794:    // application's constructor initializes and runs the app
795:    CComboListApp WindowApp;
```

Using Unconditional Breakpoints

In this section, I use simple, unconditional breakpoints to monitor local variables and data members while executing the member function CMCalc. Load the project CTLLST4, and make sure that it is built in debug mode. Rebuild it if necessary. Open the window to view the file CTLLST4.CPP and use the Breakpoints command to set the following breakpoints:

1. Move the cursor to line 539 and invoke the Breakpoints command. Click the Add pushbutton and then click the Close pushbutton.

2. Move the cursor to line 556 and invoke the Breakpoints command. Click the Add pushbutton and then click the Close pushbutton.

3. Move the cursor to line 577 and invoke the Breakpoints command. Click the Add pushbutton and then click the Close pushbutton.

4. Move the cursor to line 620 and invoke the Breakpoints command. Click the Add pushbutton and then click the Close pushbutton. The program reaches this breakpoint if the math operation is successful.

Open the Watch window and type the names of the data members **bInError** and **nRadix**, on separate lines. Open the Locals window and resize the three windows to an arrangement that resembles the one in Figure 17.2. Press F5 to load the symbols and run the program. When the program's window appears, type **335** in the Operand1 combo box, select the / operator from the Operator combo box, and enter **113** in the Operand2 combo box. Click the Calc pushbutton to send the Windows command message `CM_CALC`, which is handled by the member function `CMCalc`. The program stops at the breakpoint in line 539, and the screen looks like Figure 17.2. The Watch window shows that data members `bInError` and `nRadix` contain the integers 0 and 10, respectively. The Locals window shows the local variables. Notice that the debugger shows the address of a string variable. When you click a string variable, the debugger expands that variable by showing you the contents of each element (both the character and its ASCII code). Figure 17.2 shows the leading elements of the local string variable s when the program single-steps to reach line 542. At this stage, the local variables x, y, z, and `opStr` contain meaningless values.

Figure 17.2

The source code, Watch, and Locals windows during the debugging of the CTLLST4.EXE program.

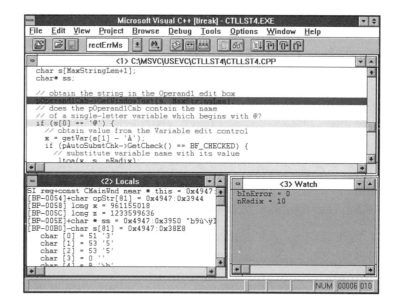

Next, press F5 to reach the second breakpoint, located at line 556. The Locals window shows the value 355 assigned to the variable x. Press F5 again to reach the third breakpoint at line 577. The Locals window shows the value 113 and 355 assigned to the local variables y and x, respectively. In addition, if you expand the local string variable `opStr`, you see that the elements `opStr[0]` and `opStr[1]` store the characters / and null, respectively. This means that the variable `opStr` stores the string "/". Press F5 to reach the last breakpoint at line 620. The Watch window confirms that the data member bInError still contains 0 (a condition necessary for the program execution to reach line 620). The Locals watch shows that the local variables x, y, and z store the integers 355, 113, and 3, respectively. Press F5 to resume program execution. Click the Exit pushbutton to close the program.

Using Breakpoints with Expressions

In this section, I use a conditional breakpoint to pause the program when an expression is true. Consider the code of the member function CMCalc, which uses an if statement to guard against dividing by zero. Let's take the bull by the horns, however, and use the debugger to intercept the condition y == 0 at an earlier statement in order to assign a nonzero value to the variable y.

First, move the insertion cursor to line 573. The statement on line 573 comes after the if statement that obtains the value for the local variable y. Next, choose the Breakpoints command, and the Breakpoints dialog box appears. Click the Clear All pushbutton to clear all the breakpoints from the previous test. In the Type combo box, select the item Break at Location if Expression is True. Then type the expression **y==0** in the Expression edit box. Click the Add pushbutton to add this breakpoint and then click the Close pushbutton to close the dialog box.

Press F5 to run the program in debug mode. When the program's window appears, type **100** in the Operand1 combo box, select the / item from the Operator combo box, type **0** in the Operand2 combo box, and click the Calc pushbutton. The program pauses and displays a message dialog box informing you that the condition of the breakpoint at line 573 is true. You succeeded in trapping the error! Now, let's fix it.

Single-step through the statements in lines 576 and 577. When you reach line 580, you will notice that the next line contains a statement that uses the local variable y. Move the insertion cursor to the left of the variable y, on line 581, and choose the QuickWatch command. The QuickWatch command displays the QuickWatch dialog box (see Figure 17.3) in which you can add, modify, and zoom in on a variable. The dialog box shows the name of the variable y. Click the Modify pushbutton to display the Modify Variable dialog box (see Figure 17.4).

III

Advanced Programming

Figure 17.3

The QuickWatch dialog box.

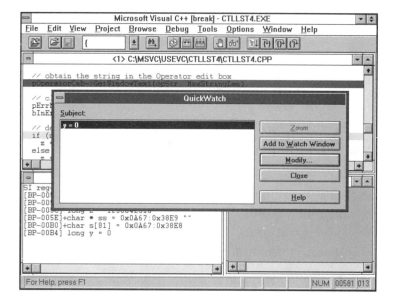

Figure 17.4

The Modify Variable dialog box.

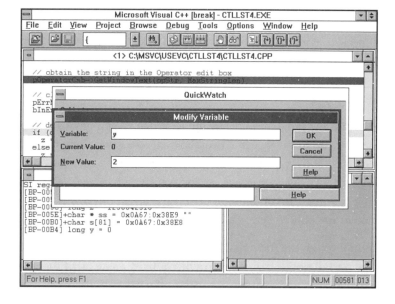

The Modify Variable dialog box shows the name of the variable in an edit box, shows its current value in a static text control, and provides an edit box in which you can type the new value. Type **2**, close the Modify Variable dialog box, and then close the QuickWatch dialog box. Watch the value of the variable y in the Locals window: it is now 2 and not 0. Next, single-step through the rest of the statements in the member function CMCalc. When you reach the end, press F5. The debugger responds by halting the program instead of executing at full speed. The designers of Visual C++ apparently chose to disable full-speed execution in the presence of what they consider to be a serious bug. You must press Alt+F5 to stop the debugging session.

Viewing the Call Stack

The Workbench debugger offers a command in the Debug menu with which you can view the call stack. For example, to view the call stack for the member function setHexadecimal, move the insertion cursor to line 752. Invoke the Breakpoints dialog box and clear all current breakpoints. Insert an unconditional breakpoint and close the dialog box. Press F5 to run the program in debug mode. Next, click the Hexadecimal radio button. The debugger hides the program window and displays the Visual Workbench and the breakpoint. Choose the Call Stack command, and the debugger shows the Call Stack dialog box (see Figure 17.5). The Call Stack dialog box lists the functions that have been called to reach the member function setHexadecimal. The top of the list shows the function setHexadecimal, and right below it is listed the member function HandleHexRbt. The remaining functions in the call stack are defined in the libraries incorporated in the project. The Call Stack dialog box contains the Show Function Parameters check box. If you check this control, the dialog box shows the values or addresses of its arguments.

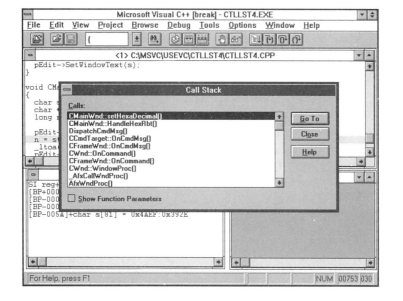

Figure 17.5
The Call Stack dialog box.

III

Advanced Programming

Viewing Mixed Source/ Assembly Code

With the Workbench debugger, you can view both C++ statements and their equivalent assembly language instructions. The Mixed Source/Asm command in the View menu toggles between viewing C++ statements only and showing both C++ statements and assembly language instructions. The shortcut key combination for the Mixed Source/Asm menu option is Ctrl+F7. Figure 17.6 shows a sample debugging session in which the source code window of the CTLLST4.EXE program shows both C++ statements and assembly language instructions. Figure 17.6 shows the C++ statement z = x + y; followed by its equivalent assembly language instructions. If you program in assembler, this kind of information offers valuable insight on the low-level instructions being executed. In addition, the assembly code can tell you whether Visual C++ is compiling your code the way it is supposed to. Even if you are not an assembly language programmer, these instructions can help you gain insight into how C++ statements translate into assembly language instructions.

Figure 17.6

A debugging session showing the source code window of the CTLLST4.EXE program, which displays both C++ statements and assembly language instructions.

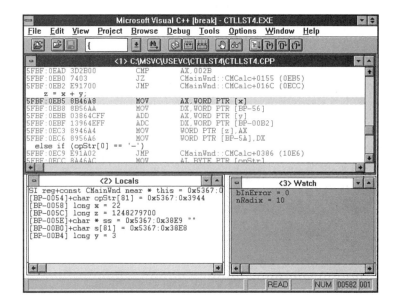

Managing the Watched Window

The Watch window lets you add, delete, and edit expressions. These expressions can include variables, operators, and constants, or they can consist only of the name of a variable or data member. The Workbench debugger evaluates the expression in the Watch window and displays its value.

Adding Expressions

Adding an expression is as easy as typing it. You can insert an expression before you begin a debugging session, while the session is paused between steps, or at a breakpoint. Just type the expression and press Enter—that's all there is to it. If you enter an expression during a debug session, the debugger evaluates the expression.

You also can use the QuickWatch dialog box to add a variable to the Watch window. Place the cursor to the left or within the name of the targeted variable and invoke the QuickWatch dialog box. Then choose the Add to Watch Window pushbutton to insert the targeted variable in the Watch window.

Deleting Expressions

To delete an expression from the Watch window, you first must end the current debug session. After you end the session, simply select the entire line containing the expression you want to remove and press the Delete key.

Expanding and Collapsing Variables

The Watch and Locals windows often include strings, arrays, and structured variables and data members. These windows display the names of such variables and show their addresses. In addition, the Watch and Locals windows display a + character to the left of the variable names. The + character indicates that the variable's information is collapsed. The - character indicates that the variable's information is expanded. To toggle between expanding and collapsing the information, click the variable or move the insertion point to that variable and press Enter. In an earlier section, I showed you how to expand and collapse information to view the contents of a local string variable.

III

Advanced Programming

Summary

This chapter presented the Workbench debugger and focused on techniques for using breakpoints. Here's what this chapter covered:

- The Debug menu commands were reviewed. You can use these commands for versatile single-stepping, as well as for managing breakpoints and viewing the function call stack.

- The hard and soft debugging modes were discussed. The hard mode is task exclusive and should be used only when you have to control the Windows system; otherwise, use the soft mode.

- The various kinds of breakpoints were explained. They include: simple, unconditional breakpoints; breakpoints associated with tested expressions; breakpoints that use tested expressions only; and message-based breakpoints.

- Examples of using the Locals and Watch windows were provided. You can use the Locals window to monitor local variables and the Watch window to monitor global variables. The text illustrated how to use different breakpoints and how to view the targeted variables using the Locals and Watch windows.

- The chapter discussed how to use the function call stack feature to view the stack of function calls that lead to a specific function.

- The Workbench debugger offers the capability to view mixed source and assembly code in the source code window. This feature enables readers who also work with assembly language to gain more insight into the low-level instructions being executed.

- Managing Watch window expressions was discussed. This feature includes adding and deleting expressions, as well as expanding and collapsing the information of string, array, and structured variables.

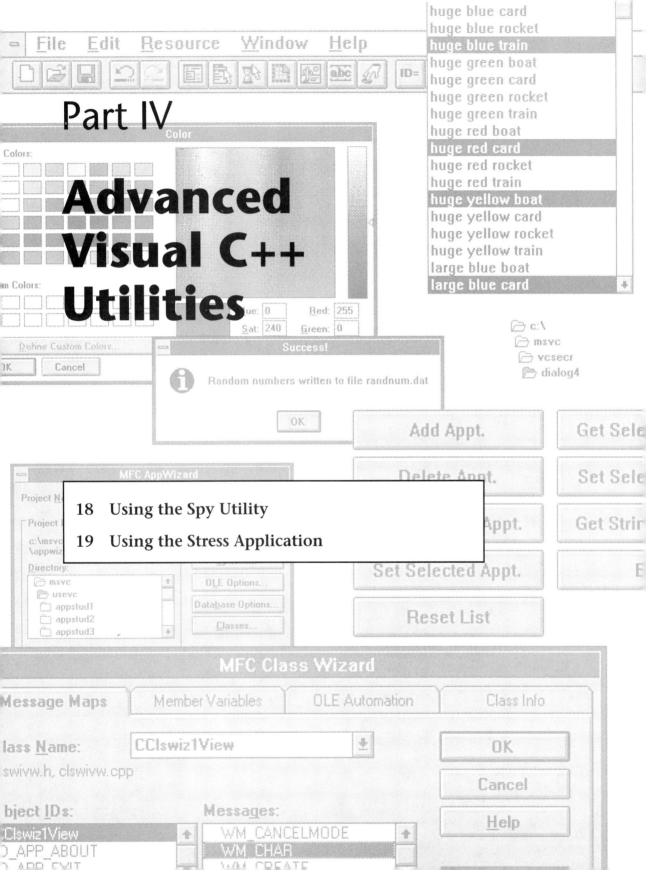

Part IV

Advanced Visual C++ Utilities

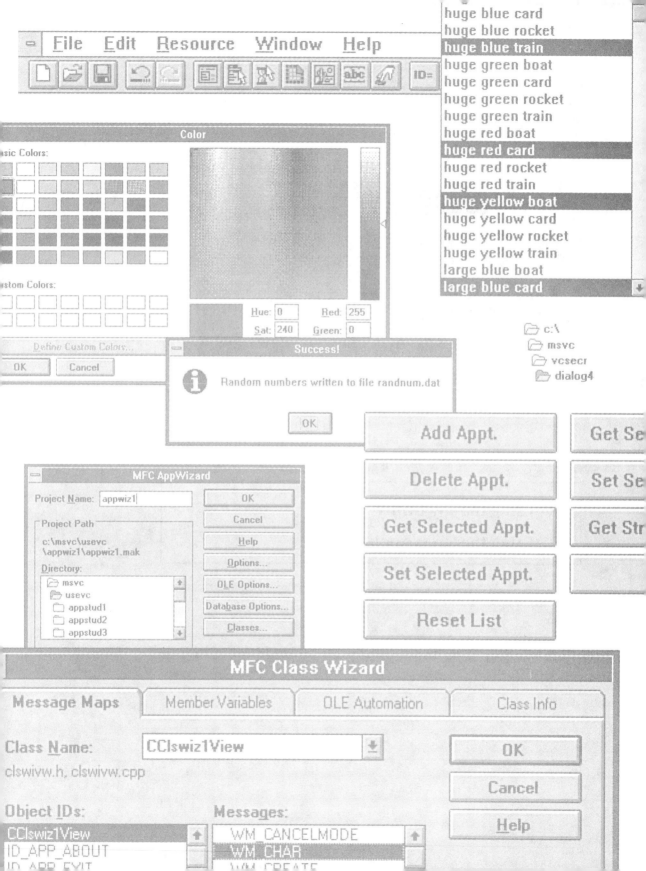

Chapter 18

Using the Spy Utility

Among the programming utilities included with Visual C++ is the Spy message-monitoring utility. This utility lets you monitor some or all of the messages flowing in one or more of the windows on your desktop. This chapter presents the Spy utility and covers the following topics:

- An overview of the Spy utility

- The Spy menu

- The Window menu

- The Options! menu

- Examples of using the Spy utility

This chapter presents examples for monitoring various kinds of messages and discusses the methods that enable you to enhance message monitoring.

Introducing the Spy Utility

Windows relies on sending, receiving, and handling messages to breathe life into its applications. In this sense, Windows resembles an office in which employees who perform various duties communicate with each other and with the outside world. These employees use memos, letters, faxes, proposals, and so on, as a means of communication. Likewise, Windows utilizes a wide variety of messages to support a diverse number of operations. The Spy utility is a transparent tool that inspects, but *does not interfere with*, the flow of messages. There are two dimensions to these messages: type and scope. The Spy utility enables you to limit the category of messages and the windows that you monitor. At one extreme, the Spy utility reports all messages between all windows; at the other extreme, the Spy utility reports one kind of message (such as mouse-related messages) in only one window.

You can invoke the Spy utility from within the Visual Workshop by accessing the Spy command from the Tools menu (if you have added the Spy utility to the list of tools). You also can invoke the Spy utility by clicking the Spy icon (the suspicious-looking fella with the Pierre Cardin hat) in the Visual C++ folder. A third way to launch the Spy utility is from the File Manager. Simply double-click the SPY.EXE file in the \MSVC\BIN directory.

The Spy utility displays a menu-driven window with these menus: Spy, Window, and Options!. Figure 18.1 shows a sample invocation of the Spy utility.

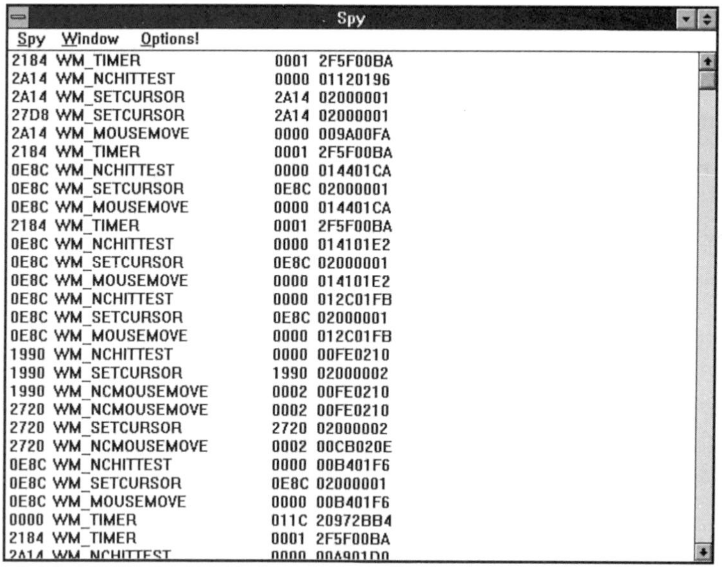

Figure 18.1

Sample invocation of the Spy utility.

Examining the Spy Menu

The Spy menu offers the following commands:

- *Spy On/Off.* Enables you to turn on or off message monitoring.

- *Exit.* Closes the Spy utility.

- *About Spy.* Invokes the About dialog box, which provides the version number of the Spy utility.

Examining the Window Menu

The Window menu offers the following commands, which permit you to select some or all of the windows for monitoring:

- *Window.* Invokes the Spy Window dialog box, which enables you to select a specific window to monitor. The Spy Window dialog box displays the following items:

  Window. The window handle.

  Class. The window class.

  Module. The name of the program that created the window.

  Parent. The handle of the parent window and the name of the program that generated the parent window.

  Rect. The upper-right and lower-left coordinates of the window and the window size in screen coordinates.

  Style. The style bits for the windows over which the cursor is positioned, the principal style of the window, and an identifier (if the window is a child window). The principal style may be WS_POPUP, WS_ICONIC, WS_OVERLAPPED, or WS_CHILD.

- *All Windows.* Selects all windows to monitor.

- *Clear Window.* Clears the Spy utility window.

Figure 18.2 shows a Spy Window dialog box without a selected window.

Figure 18.2

The Spy Window
dialog box
without a selected
window.

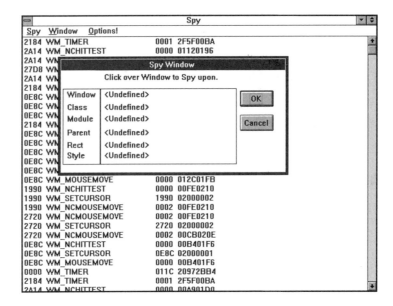

As you move the mouse over a window, the Spy Window dialog box is
udpated to reflect the information for that window. Click OK to lock on the
currently selected window. Figure 18.3 shows the Spy Window dialog box
after locking on a window.

Figure 18.3

The Spy Window
dialog box after
locking on a
window.

Examining the Options! Menu

Unlike the Spy and Window menus, the Options! menu does not pull down to display additional commands. When you choose the Options! menu, a captionless dialog box is invoked (shown in 18.4) that offers many ways to fine tune the operation of the Spy utility.

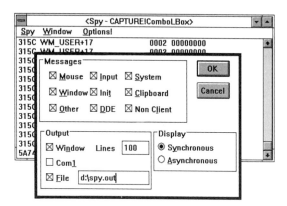

Figure 18.4
This captionless dialog box is displayed when you select the Options! menu.

The dialog box that appears when you invoke the Options! menu contains the following options:

- *Message types.* The dialog box lets you select some or all of the following message categories:

  Mouse: Monitors mouse messages, such as WM_LBUTTONDOWN and WM_MOUSEMOVE.

  Input: Monitors input messages, such as WM_TIMER, WM_COMMAND, and WM_CHAR.

  System: Monitors system-wide messages, such as WM_ENDSESSION and WM_TIMECHANGE.

  Window: Monitors window manager messages, such as WM_MOVE and WM_PAINT.

  Init: Monitors initialization messages, such as WM_INITMENU and WM_INITDIALOG.

Clipboard: Monitors Clipboard messages, such as WM_COPY, WM_CUT, and WM_PASTE.

DDE: Monitors dynamic data exchange (DDE) messages, such as WM_DDE_INIT, WM_DDE_POKE, and WM_DDE_DATA.

Non Client: Monitors windows nonclient messages, such as WM_NCACTIVATE, WM_NCCALCSIZE, and WM_NCCREATE.

Each of these options includes a check box. The initial setting of the Spy utility selects all the preceding message categories.

- *Output devices.* The Spy utility enables you to send the monitored messages to any or all of the following output devices:

Window: The Spy utility window stores the lines of monitored messages in an internal buffer. You can use the corresponding edit box to specify the maximum number of lines to retain. The default setting is 100 lines.

Com1: The Spy utility sends the list of monitored messages to the COM1 port.

File: The Spy utility sends the list of monitored messages to the file you specify in the corresponding edit box. The default name of the output is SPY.OUT.

- *Output frequency.* The Spy utility offers two radio buttons so that you can select between synchronous and asynchronous output. Synchronous output, which is the default output, causes the Spy utility to send messages as it receives them. Asynchronous output makes the Spy utility queue the messages for display.

Spying on the APPSTUD2.EXE Program

In this section, you use the Spy utility to monitor various kinds of messages sent in the main window of the APPSTUD2.EXE, a program originally presented in Chapter 5. The application displays the mouse location in the upper-left corner of the view, echoes keyboard input, and responds to the mouse clicks by displaying custom message dialog boxes. These boxes show the date and time, along with the elapsed time of a simple timer.

Monitoring Mouse Messages

Load the Spy utility and choose the Options! menu. Clear all the Messages check boxes, except the one labeled Mouse. This configuration enables you to focus on monitoring the mouse messages. Specify Window and the file MOUSE.OUT as the output devices. Now, invoke the APPSTUD2.EXE program (do not maximize it) and choose the Window command from the Window menu. Move the mouse over the window of APPSTUD2.EXE and click the mouse two times. Move the mouse into the viewing area of APPSTUD2.EXE and perform the following steps:

1. Move the mouse around in the view.

2. Click the left mouse button to display the custom message dialog box. This dialog box tells you that the timer is now on. To close the dialog box, click the OK pushbutton.

3. Move the mouse around in the view.

4. Click the right mouse button to display the custom message dialog box. This dialog box displays the current system date and time. To close the dialog box, click the OK pushbutton.

5. Move the mouse around in the view.

6. Click the Exit menu.

Listing 18.1 shows the partial contents of the MOUSE.OUT file. The file contains numerous WM_SETCURSOR messages that are generated to redraw the mouse as it moves. The listing contains the two WM_MOUSEACTIVATE messages generated when the left mouse button is clicked. Each message is followed by the values of the wParam and lParam parameters. You have to look at the Software Developer's Kit (SDK) reference (use the on-line help) to determine the exact meaning of these parameters for each message. Look at Listing 18.1; notice that the two WM_MOUSEACTIVATE messages have different lParam values because they are associated with different mouse buttons.

Listing 18.1 Partial Contents of the MOUSE.OUT File

```
3CE4    WM_SETCURSOR          3CE4    02000001
3CE4    WM_SETCURSOR          3CE4    02020001
3CE4    WM_SETCURSOR          3CE4    02000001
3CE4    WM_SETCURSOR          3CE4    02000001
  .
  .
  .
3CE4    WM_SETCURSOR          3CE4    02000001
3CE4    WM_SETCURSOR          3CE4    02000001
3CE4    WM_SETCURSOR          3CE4    02000001
3CE4    WM_MOUSEACTIVATE      3CA4    02010001
3CE4    WM_SETCURSOR          3CE4    02010001
3CE4    WM_SETCURSOR          3CE4    02000001
  .
  .
  .
3CE4    WM_SETCURSOR          3CE4    02000001
3CE4    WM_SETCURSOR          3CE4    02000001
3CE4    WM_SETCURSOR          3CE4    02000001
3CE4    WM_SETCURSOR          3CE4    02000001
3CE4    WM_MOUSEACTIVATE      3CA4    02040001
3CE4    WM_SETCURSOR          3CE4    02040001
3CE4    WM_SETCURSOR          3CE4    02000001
3CE4    WM_SETCURSOR          3CE4    02000001
3CE4    WM_SETCURSOR          3CE4    02000001
3CE4    WM_SETCURSOR          3CE4    02000001
  .
  .
  .
3CE4    WM_SETCURSOR          3CE4    02000001
3CE4    WM_SETCURSOR          3CE4    02000001
3CE4    WM_SETCURSOR          3CE4    02000001
```

Monitoring Input Messages

In this section, you monitor the input messages generated while the word *Input* is typed in the APPSTUD2.EXE program. Select the Options! menu in the Spy utility. Clear the Mouse check box and click the Input check box. Type the output filename **INPUT.OUT**. Close the dialog box and select the APPSTUD2.EXE window. Click the window with the mouse. The program displays the custom message dialog box. Close the dialog box and then type the word **Input**. Click the Exit menu and then turn off the Spy mode. Listing 18.2 shows the contents of the INPUT.OUT file. Your version of the output may show more leading WM_KEYDOWN messages, which are generated by holding down the Shift key a few extra seconds.

Listing 18.2 The INPUT.OUT File

```
3880    WM_KEYDOWN    0010    402A0001
3880    WM_KEYDOWN    0049    00170001
3880    WM_CHAR       0049    00170001
3880    WM_KEYUP      0049    C0170001
3880    WM_KEYUP      0010    C02A0001
3880    WM_KEYDOWN    004E    00310001
3880    WM_CHAR       006E    00310001
3880    WM_KEYUP      004E    C0310001
3880    WM_KEYDOWN    0050    00190001
3880    WM_CHAR       0070    00190001
3880    WM_KEYDOWN    0055    00160001
3880    WM_CHAR       0075    00160001
3880    WM_KEYUP      0050    C0190001
3880    WM_KEYDOWN    0054    00140001
3880    WM_CHAR       0074    00140001
3880    WM_KEYUP      0055    C0160001
3880    WM_KEYUP      0054    C0140001
```

Notice the wParam values for the various WM_CHAR instances. The hexadecimal values are 49 (73 decimal), 63 (decimal 110), 70 (decimal 112), 75 (decimal 117), and 74 (decimal 117). These integers correspond to the ASCII codes for the characters *I, n, p, u,* and *t,* which are, of course, the characters in *input.*

Now, expand monitoring of input messages to all windows and select the INPUT2.OUT file for the output device. The purpose of this variation is to track the menu messages and the commands they generate. Run the APPSTUD2.EXE program and choose the Date/Time, Start Timer, and Stop Timer commands, in that order. Listing 18.3 shows the contents of the INPUT2.OUT file.

Listing 18.3 The INPUT2.OUT File

```
265C    WM_TIMER        0001    2DCF00BA
265C    WM_TIMER        0001    2DCF00BA
265C    WM_TIMER        0001    2DCF00BA
265C    WM_TIMER        0001    2DCF00BA
1F6C    WM_TIMER        0001    00000000
265C    WM_TIMER        0001    2DCF00BA
265C    WM_TIMER        0001    2DCF00BA
265C    WM_TIMER        0001    2DCF00BA
3014    WM_MENUSELECT   00BC    00848090
3014    WM_MENUSELECT   8003    00BC8080
```

(continues)

Listing 18.3 Continued

```
265C    WM_TIMER         0001    2DCF00BA
0000    WM_TIMER         012C    2EF72BB4
265C    WM_TIMER         0001    2DCF00BA
265C    WM_TIMER         0001    2DCF00BA
265C    WM_TIMER         0001    2DCF00BA
265C    WM_TIMER         0001    2DCF00BA
265C    WM_TIMER         0001    2DCF00BA
3014    WM_MENUSELECT    0000    0000FFFF
3014    WM_COMMAND       8003    00000000
3014    WM_COMMAND       8003    00000000
265C    WM_TIMER         0001    2DCF00BA
265C    WM_TIMER         0001    2DCF00BA
0000    WM_TIMER         012C    2EF72BB4
265C    WM_TIMER         0001    2DCF00BA
265C    WM_TIMER         0001    2DCF00BA
265C    WM_TIMER         0001    2DCF00BA
265C    WM_TIMER         0001    2DCF00BA
265C    WM_TIMER         0001    2DCF00BA
265C    WM_TIMER         0001    2DCF00BA
265C    WM_TIMER         0001    2DCF00BA
3240    WM_KEYDOWN       000D    081C0001
32A4    WM_COMMAND       0001    00003240
3054    WM_KEYUP         000D    C01C0001
3054    WM_KEYUP         000D    C01C0001
265C    WM_TIMER         0001    2DCF00BA
0000    WM_TIMER         012C    2EF72BB4
265C    WM_TIMER         0001    2DCF00BA
265C    WM_TIMER         0001    2DCF00BA
3014    WM_MENUSELECT    00BC    00848090
3014    WM_MENUSELECT    8003    00BC8080
265C    WM_TIMER         0001    2DCF00BA
265C    WM_TIMER         0001    2DCF00BA
265C    WM_TIMER         0001    2DCF00BA
265C    WM_TIMER         0001    2DCF00BA
265C    WM_TIMER         0001    2DCF00BA
265C    WM_TIMER         0001    2DCF00BA
3014    WM_MENUSELECT    8004    00BC8080
0000    WM_TIMER         012C    2EF72BB4
265C    WM_TIMER         0001    2DCF00BA
3014    WM_MENUSELECT    0000    0000FFFF
3014    WM_COMMAND       8004    00000000
3014    WM_COMMAND       8004    00000000
265C    WM_TIMER         0001    2DCF00BA
265C    WM_TIMER         0001    2DCF00BA
3240    WM_KEYDOWN       000D    081C0001
32A4    WM_COMMAND       0001    00003240
3054    WM_KEYUP         000D    C01C0001
3054    WM_KEYUP         000D    C01C0001
265C    WM_TIMER         0001    2DCF00BA
265C    WM_TIMER         0001    2DCF00BA
265C    WM_TIMER         0001    2DCF00BA
0000    WM_TIMER         012C    2EF72BB4
265C    WM_TIMER         0001    2DCF00BA
```

265C	WM_TIMER	0001	2DCF00BA
3014	WM_MENUSELECT	00BC	00848090
3014	WM_MENUSELECT	8003	00BC8080
265C	WM_TIMER	0001	2DCF00BA
265C	WM_TIMER	0001	2DCF00BA
265C	WM_TIMER	0001	2DCF00BA
265C	WM_TIMER	0001	2DCF00BA
265C	WM_TIMER	0001	2DCF00BA
265C	WM_TIMER	0001	2DCF00BA
1F6C	WM_TIMER	0001	00000000
3014	WM_MENUSELECT	8005	00BC8080
265C	WM_TIMER	0001	2DCF00BA
3014	WM_MENUSELECT	0000	0000FFFF
3014	WM_COMMAND	8005	00000000
3014	WM_COMMAND	8005	00000000
0000	WM_TIMER	012C	2EF72BB4
265C	WM_TIMER	0001	2DCF00BA
265C	WM_TIMER	0001	2DCF00BA
3240	WM_KEYDOWN	000D	081C0001
32A4	WM_COMMAND	0001	00003240
3054	WM_KEYUP	000D	C01C0001
3054	WM_KEYUP	000D	C01C0001
265C	WM_TIMER	0001	2DCF00BA
265C	WM_TIMER	0001	2DCF00BA
265C	WM_TIMER	0001	2DCF00BA
265C	WM_TIMER	0001	2DCF00BA
0000	WM_TIMER	012C	2EF72BB4
3014	WM_MENUSELECT	E141	00848080
265C	WM_TIMER	0001	2DCF00BA
3014	WM_MENUSELECT	0000	0000FFFF
3014	WM_COMMAND	E141	00000000
3014	WM_COMMAND	E141	00000000
265C	WM_TIMER	0001	2DCF00BA
265C	WM_TIMER	0001	2DCF00BA
265C	WM_TIMER	0001	2DCF00BA
0000	WM_TIMER	012C	2EF72BB4
265C	WM_TIMER	0001	2DCF00BA
265C	WM_TIMER	0001	2DCF00BA
265C	WM_TIMER	0001	2DCF00BA

In Listing 18.3, notice the following:

- The numerous WM_TIMER input messages. These messages are generated by the Windows internal timer.

- The first and second WM_MENUSELECT messages appear immediately after one another. The first of these two messages corresponds to choosing the Timer command. The second message corresponds to the Date/Time command. The value of the wParam is the hexadecimal number 8003, which corresponds to the decimal 32271—the value of the identifier CM_DATE_TIME. The Date/Time command invokes the CM_DATE_TIME Windows command message.

- The third WM_MENUSELECT message has 0 for the wParam value. This argument indicates that the selection of menu commands is finished.

- The first WM_COMMAND message appears immediatedly after the third WM_MENUSELECT and has the same wParam value as the second WM_MENUSELECT message. This WM_COMMAND message is the one that triggers the CmInsertDateTime member function of the view class in the APPSTUD2.EXE program.

- The first WM_KEYDOWN message appears in response to the Enter key being pressed to close the custom message dialog box.

- The INPUT2.OUT file replicates the WM_COMMAND, WM_MENUSELECT, and WM_KEYDOWN message patterns for the Start Timer and Stop Timer menu commands, which have the hexadecimal message IDs of 8004 and 8005. These are the same values (albeit in hexadecimal numbers) that appear in the RESOURCE.H file of the APPSTUD2 project.

- The last set of WM_MENUSELECT and WM_COMMAND belong to the Exit menu, which closes the APPSTUD2.EXE program.

Monitoring Window Messages

In this section, you use the Spy utility to monitor window messages. Invoke the Options! menu and make sure that all the Messages check boxes are clear, except the Window box. Specify the Spy window and the WINDOW.OUT file as output devices. Load the APPSTUD2.EXE program, select that window to monitor, and then, using the APPSTUD2.EXE window, perform the following steps:

1. Resize the window.

2. Minimize the window.

3. Restore the window.

When you are done, close the APPSTUD2.EXE program. Listing 18.4 contains the contents of the WINDOW.OUT file. The listing contains a relatively short list of messages. Most of these messages paint, erase the background, refocus, lose focus, and track the changing window position. The last message, WM_DESTROY, deals with closing the program. None of the messages in Listing 18.4 are *directly* generated by the source code of the APPSTUD2 project; they are *indirectly* generated by the included MFC source files. These messages are sent to APPSTUD2 by Windows and handled in the default code.

Listing 18.4 The WINDOW.OUT File

```
31C4    WM_PAINT                0000    00000000
31C4    WM_ERASEBKGND           0B96    00000000
31C4    WM_SETFOCUS             3014    00000000
31C4    WM_KILLFOCUS            3184    00000000
31C4    WM_SETFOCUS             3184    00000000
31C4    WM_PAINT                0000    00000000
31C4    WM_ERASEBKGND           0B9E    00000000
31C4    WM_WINDOWPOSCHANGING    0000    3A3739D2
31C4    WM_WINDOWPOSCHANGED     0000    3A3739EA
31C4    WM_SIZE                 0000    00CD0163
31C4    WM_PAINT                0000    00000000
31C4    WM_ERASEBKGND           0B9E    00000000
31C4    WM_KILLFOCUS            0000    00000000
31C4    WM_SETFOCUS             3184    00000000
31C4    WM_KILLFOCUS            3184    00000000
31C4    WM_SETFOCUS             3184    00000000
31C4    WM_PAINT                0000    00000000
31C4    WM_ERASEBKGND           0B9E    00000000
31C4    WM_KILLFOCUS            3014    00000000
31C4    WM_DESTROY              0000    00000000
```

Monitoring Pushbutton Input Messages

Now let's look at the APPSTUD3 program, which was originally presented in Chapter 5. The basic features of this program are similar to APPSTUD2.EXE. Program APPSTUD3.EXE, however, uses a form that includes pushbuttons to display the date and time and to start and stop the simple timer.

Load program APPSTUD3.EXE and load the Spy utility. Invoke the Options! menu and clear all the Messages check boxes, except the Input box. Specify the Spy window and the INPUT3.OUT file as output devices. Select the APPSTUD3.EXE window to monitor. Click the Start pushbutton, which changes the caption to *Stop*. Then click the Date/Time pushbutton. The current system date and time is displayed in a read-only edit box located to the right of the Date/Time pushbutton. Next, click the Stop pushbutton (which changes its caption back to *Start*). The elapsed time is displayed in a read-only edit box located to the right of the Start pushbutton. Click the Exit menu to close the program. Listing 18.5 shows the contents of the INPUT3.OUT file.

Listing 18.5 The INPUT3.OUT File

```
3760    WM_COMMAND        03EE    04003848
3760    WM_COMMAND        03EE    03003848
3760    WM_COMMAND        03EE    04003848
3760    WM_COMMAND        03EE    03003848
. . .
3760    WM_COMMAND        03EE    04003848
3760    WM_COMMAND        03EE    03003848
3760    WM_COMMAND        03EA    00003804
3760    WM_COMMAND        03EE    04003848
3760    WM_COMMAND        03EE    03003848
3760    WM_COMMAND        03EE    04003848
3760    WM_COMMAND        03EE    03003848
. . .
3760    WM_COMMAND        03EE    04003848
3760    WM_COMMAND        03EE    03003848
3760    WM_COMMAND        03E9    000037C0
3760    WM_COMMAND        03EF    04003890
3760    WM_COMMAND        03EF    03003890
3760    WM_COMMAND        03EE    04003848
3760    WM_COMMAND        03EE    03003848
3760    WM_COMMAND        03EA    00003804
3760    WM_COMMAND        03EA    00003804
3760    WM_COMMAND        03F0    040038D8
3760    WM_COMMAND        03F0    030038D8
```

In Listing 18.5, notice the following messages:

- The WM_COMMAND messages with the wParam value of 3EE update the mouse coordinates in the read-only mouse-coordinates edit box. The ID of this edit box is 1006 (which is the hexadecimal 3EE).

- The two WM_COMMAND messages with the wParam value of 3EA are commands generated when the Timer pushbutton is clicked. The hexadecimal number 3EA corresponds to the decimal 1002—the value of the constant IDC_TIMER_BTN.

- The WM_COMMAND message with the wParam value of 3E9 is generated by the Date/Time pushbutton. The hexadecimal number 3E9 corresponds to the decimal 1001—the value of the constant IDC_DATE_TIME.

- The WM_COMMAND messages with the wParam value of 3F0 are generated by the Exit menu.

Summary

This chapter presented the Spy utility, which transparently monitors various messages and reports these messages. You learned about the following topics:

- The Spy utility is able to monitor the following messages: all messages sent to all windows, all messages sent to a specific window, some messages sent to all windows, and some messages sent to a single window.

- The Spy menu is used primarily to turn on or off the Spy utility and to exit the Spy utility.

- The Window menu enables you to choose between monitoring a specific window or monitoring all windows.

- The Options! menu invokes a dialog box that enables you to select one or more kinds of messages to monitor, to specify output devices, and to select the output frequency.

In addition, this chapter illustrated how you can use the Spy utility to monitor mouse and input messages for the previously introduced APPSTUD2.EXE and APPSTUD3.EXE programs.

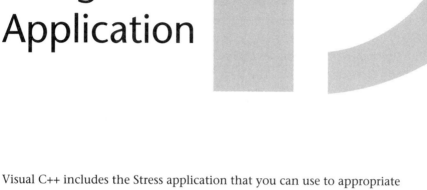

Chapter 19

Using the Stress Application

Visual C++ includes the Stress application that you can use to appropriate system resources to test for low resource stress in your applications. The appropriated resources include the global heap, user heap, GDI heap, disk space, and file handles. In addition, the Stress application supports random and message-dependent allocations of these resources. In this chapter, you learn about the following topics:

- Invoking the Stress application

- Using the Settings menu

- Using the Options menu

- Testing stress in the APPSTUD2.EXE program

How to Invoke the Stress Application

You can invoke the Stress application from the Visual C++ folder by double-clicking the StressApp icon (an image of an elephant walking a tightrope). You also can invoke the Stress application from the Visual Workbench (after you add it to the list of tools). Finally, you can run the Stress application by double-clicking the file STRESS.EXE (in the directory \MSVC\BIN) from the File Manager or any equivalent shell.

The Stress application displays a simple window, as shown in Figure 19.1. The client area displays the current global heap (in kilobytes), user heap (as a percentage), GDI heap (as a percentage), disk space (in megabytes), and file handles.

Figure 19.1

A sample client area for the Stress application.

The Stress application includes a menu system with the following menus: Settings, Options, and Help. The Help menu offers on-line documentation for the Stress application. You might want to use the help system and print all or some of its information on the Stress application.

The Settings Menu

The Settings menu offers three commands you can use to fine-tune the settings of the Stress application. The following sections discuss these commands.

The Fixed Settings Command

When you choose the Fixed Settings command, the Fixed Settings dialog box appears (see Figure 19.2). The Fixed Settings dialog box contains edit boxes for the global heap, user heap, GDI heap, disk space, and file handles. The default setting for all these resources is –1, a value indicating that the Stress application should free the resource allocation. To reset all the resources to –1, click the Free All pushbutton. In contrast, if you enter 0 for a resource, the Stress application appropriates the entire resource. You can, of course, enter positive values in the various resource edit boxes to specify the amount of resource to retain. When you are finished, click the Set pushbutton. To abort the current settings, simply click the Close pushbutton.

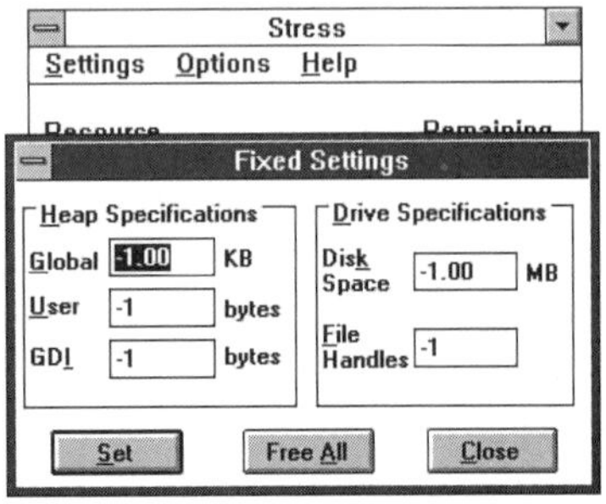

Figure 19.2

The Fixed Settings dialog box.

The Executer Command

When you choose the Executer command, the Executer Options dialog box appears (see Figure 19.3). In the Executor Options dialog box you can determine which resources to test and how to test them.

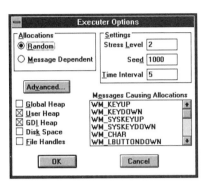

Figure 19.3
The Executer Options dialog box.

The Executor Options dialog box contains the following controls:

- *Allocations frame box.* Contains the Random and Message Dependent radio buttons. The random mode makes the Stress application test resources during the time interval, which can range from 1 to 120 seconds. The time interval is set in the Settings frame box. The message-dependent mode enables you to specify Windows messages in the Messages Causing Allocations list box. The Stress application allocates the specified resources when it detects specified messages.

- *Resources check boxes.* The dialog box offers a check box for the global heap, user heap, GDI heap, disk space, and file handles. Check the boxes of the resources you want tested.

- *Settings frame box.* Contains edit boxes for the stress level, random-number seed, and random-mode time interval.

- *Advanced... pushbutton.* Displays the Stress Level Ranges dialog box, shown in Figure 19.4, which offers four sets of stress levels. Each set contains edit boxes that enable you to specify the range of each resource for each stress level.

- *Messages Causing Allocations list box.* Enables you to select the Windows message that triggers resource allocations by the Stress application. You can click as many messages as you want.

- *OK and Cancel pushbuttons.*

Figure 19.4

The Stress Level
Ranges dialog box.

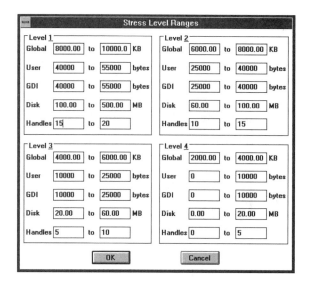

The Log Settings Command

When you choose the Log Settings command, the Log Options dialog box appears (see Figure 19.5). The Log Options dialog box enables you to fine tune how the Stress application information is logged.

Figure 19.5

The Log Options
dialog box.

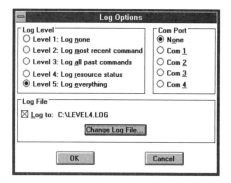

The Log Options dialog box contains the following controls:

- *Log Level frame box.* Contains five radio buttons (Level 1 through Level 5) that offer you logging choices. The choices range from logging nothing to logging everything.

- *Com Port frame box.* Contains five radio buttons you can use to direct the output to communication ports COM1 through COM4, or you can choose no COM port output.

- *Log File frame box.* Contains the Log to: check box control, which indicates whether you are using a log file, and the Change Log File... pushbutton, which enables you to open a file dialog box.

- *OK and Cancel pushbuttons.*

The Options Menu

Using the Options menu, you can start and stop the executer, free resources, move the Stress application display, and repaint the entire screen. The following sections discuss the Options menu commands.

The Begin Executer Command

The Begin Executer command supports the testing of a Windows application while the Stress application dynamically allocates resources in the background to induce the stress of the targeted resource. The work of the executer is based on the information you provide the Stress application in the Executer dialog box. The shortcut key combination for this option is Ctrl+Home.

The End Executer Command

The End Executer command stops the dynamic allocations of resources by the Stress application, but it does not release these allocations. To release the allocations, you have to use the Free All command. The shortcut key combination for this option is Ctrl+End.

The Free All Command

The Free All command frees the dynamic resource allocations of the Stress application. If the executer is still running, the Stress application allocates further resources; in this case, this option acts as a form of run-time reset. If the executer is not running, however, this option simply recoups the dynamic allocations. The shortcut key combination for this option is Ctrl+Del.

The Move to Corner Command

The Move to Corner command moves the Stress window to the lower-right corner of the screen and minimizes its client area. The shortcut key combination for this option is Ctrl+PgDn.

The Put Back Command

The Put Back command restores the Stress window to its location and size before the last time the Move to Corner option was invoked. The shortcut key combination for this option is Ctrl+PgUp.

The Repaint Screen Command

The Repaint Screen command repaints the screen—a step that may be necessary to recover from stressing the GDI heap. The shortcut key combination for this option is Ctrl+Ins.

Stress Testing the APPSTUD2.EXE Program

In this section, you stress test the APPSTUD2.EXE program, which was originally presented in Chapter 5. The first test uses the Windows messages WM_CHAR, WM_LBUTTONDOWN, and WM_RBUTTONDOWN. In addition, make sure that the Global, User, and GDI check boxes in the Executer dialog box are checked. Also, check the Message Dependent radio button. Invoke the Log Options dialog box to select the Log Level 5 radio button and to specify the log file TEST1.LOG.

Invoke the APPSTUD2.EXE program and then start the executer. Click the left and right mouse buttons a few times and then type some text that appears in the view window. When you are finished, stop the executer, free all dynamic allocations, close the Stress application, and then close the APPSTUD2.EXE program.

Listing 19.1 shows the contents of the TEST1.LOG file.

Listing 19.1 The TEST1.LOG File

```
******* Stress Log: Begin Header ***********************
Date: 11/22/93   Time: 21:10:59

Initial State of Resources
. . . . . . . . . . . . . . . . . . . . . . . . . . .
Global Memory     :   30129.06 KB
User Heap         :         60 %
GDI Heap          :         72 %
Disk Space        :     105.61 MB
File Handles      :        109

************* Stress Log: End Header ***************

TIME       LOCATION         TYPE OF ACTION   SPECIFIC DESCRIPTION

21:11:00  Global : 30129.06 KB  User    :     63 %   GDI  :    72 %
          Handles:      109     Disk    :  105.61 MB
21:11:03  Stress            Menu Item       Begin Executer
21:11:06  Global : 7363.81 KB   User    :     42 %   GDI  :    49 %
          Handles:      109     Disk    :  105.61 MB
```

```
21:11:20   Global :  6056.00 KB    User   :     55 %    GDI   :     44 %
           Handles:       109      Disk   :  105.61 MB
21:11:26   Global :  6305.00 KB    User   :     40 %    GDI   :     39 %
           Handles:       109      Disk   :  105.61 MB
21:11:31   Global :  6507.00 KB    User   :     49 %    GDI   :     57 %
           Handles:       109      Disk   :  105.61 MB
21:11:36   Global :  6507.00 KB    User   :     49 %    GDI   :     57 %
           Handles:       109      Disk   :  105.61 MB
21:11:42   Global :  7765.00 KB    User   :     49 %    GDI   :     40 %
           Handles:       109      Disk   :  105.61 MB
21:11:48   Stress          Menu Item        End Executer
21:11:48   Global :  6577.00 KB    User   :     47 %    GDI   :     49 %
           Handles:       110      Disk   :  105.61 MB
21:11:51   Stress          Menu Item        Free All
21:11:54   Global : 30201.56 KB    User   :     63 %    GDI   :     72 %
           Handles:       110      Disk   :  105.61 MB
21:11:55   Stress          Menu Item        Exit

******************** Stress Log: Begin Footer ********************
Date: 11/22/93   Time: 21:11:55

Final State of Resources
- - - - - - - - - - - - - - - - - - - - - - - - - -
Global Memory        :  30201.56 KB
User Heap            :       63 %
GDI Heap             :       72 %
Disk Space           :   105.61 MB
File Handles         :      110

******************** Stress Log: End Footer ********************
```

The log file contains the following sections:

- The date and time at which the logging of information began.

- A table for the initial state resources. This table shows the information as it relates to my own system. The percentages of user and GDI heaps are 62 and 73 percent, respectively.

- Entries indicating your invocations of the various Stress application menu options, such as Begin Executer, End Executer, and Free All.

- Entries indicating the current level of resources taken at the default interval of five seconds. The entries include the time the levels were logged and typically reflect a change in the global, user, and GDI heaps. Table 19.1 shows the statistics for the file TEST1.LOG. These statistics include the minimum, maximum, average, and standard deviation values for the global, user, and GDI heaps.

Table 19.1 Statistics for the TEST1.LOG File				
Item	**Minimum**	**Maximum**	**Average**	**Standard Deviation**
Global (KB)	6056	7765	6750.5	663.89
User (%)	40	55	47.3	8
GDI (%)	39	57	47.7	8

■ The table showing the final state of resources.

Now let's stress test the APPSTUD2.EXE program using random dynamic allocations for the global, user, and GDI heaps. Specify the appropriate settings in the Executer dialog box and then designate the file TEST2.LOG as the log file that logs everything. Work with the APPSTUD2.EXE the same way you did in the message dependent test. Listing 19.2 shows the contents of the TEST2.LOG file.

Listing 19.2 The TEST2.LOG File

```
******************** Stress Log: Begin Header ********************
Date: 11/22/93   Time: 20:33:44

Initial State of Resources
--------------------------
Global Memory      :  30138.50 KB
User Heap          :        62 %
GDI Heap           :        72 %
Disk Space         :    105.64 MB
File Handles       :       109

******************** Stress Log: End Header ********************

TIME        LOCATION          TYPE OF ACTION   SPECIFIC DESCRIPTION

20:33:45    Global : 30138.50 KB  User   :     65 %   GDI   :    73 %
            Handles:       109    Disk   :  105.64 MB
20:33:47    Stress              Menu Item      Executer
20:33:50    Executer Dialog Check Box          Global
20:33:51    Global : 30137.13 KB  User   :     62 %   GDI   :    72 %
            Handles:       109    Disk   :  105.64 MB
20:33:52    Executer Dialog Push Button        OK
20:33:55    Stress              Menu Item      Begin Executer
20:33:56    Global :  6322.00 KB  User   :     52 %   GDI   :    57 %
            Handles:       109    Disk   :  105.64 MB
20:34:01    Global :  7364.06 KB  User   :     40 %   GDI   :    49 %
            Handles:       109    Disk   :  105.64 MB
20:34:06    Global :  6767.00 KB  User   :     49 %   GDI   :    50 %
            Handles:       109    Disk   :  105.64 MB
20:34:12    Global :  6992.00 KB  User   :     50 %   GDI   :    49 %
            Handles:       109    Disk   :  105.64 MB
```

```
20:34:17  Global :  6111.00 KB  User  :    40 %   GDI  :   60 %
          Handles:      109     Disk  :  105.64 MB
20:34:23  Global :  7927.00 KB  User  :    50 %   GDI  :   44 %
          Handles:      109     Disk  :  105.64 MB
20:34:28  Global :  7070.94 KB  User  :    59 %   GDI  :   39 %
          Handles:      109     Disk  :  105.64 MB
20:34:34  Global :  7324.00 KB  User  :    60 %   GDI  :   60 %
          Handles:      109     Disk  :  105.64 MB
20:34:40  Global :  6674.00 KB  User  :    42 %   GDI  :   47 %
          Handles:      109     Disk  :  105.64 MB
20:34:45  Global :  6772.00 KB  User  :    52 %   GDI  :   44 %
          Handles:      109     Disk  :  105.64 MB
20:34:50  Global :  6099.00 KB  User  :    42 %   GDI  :   47 %
          Handles:      109     Disk  :  105.64 MB
20:34:56  Global :  7446.00 KB  User  :    45 %   GDI  :   50 %
          Handles:      109     Disk  :  105.64 MB
20:35:02  Global :  7462.00 KB  User  :    62 %   GDI  :   45 %
          Handles:      109     Disk  :  105.64 MB
20:35:04  Stress         Menu Item      End Executer
20:35:06  Stress         Menu Item      Free All
20:35:07  Global : 30130.50 KB  User  :    65 %   GDI  :   73 %
          Handles:      109     Disk  :  105.64 MB
20:35:10  Stress         Menu Item      Exit

******************** Stress Log: Begin Footer ********************

Date: 11/22/93   Time: 20:35:11

Final State of Resources
------------------------
Global Memory     :   30130.50 KB
User Heap         :        65 %
GDI Heap          :        72 %
Disk Space        :    105.64 MB
File Handles      :       109

******************** Stress Log: End Footer ********************
```

Table 19.2 shows the statistics for the TEST2.LOG file.

Table 19.2 Statistics for the TEST2.LOG File				
Item	Minimum	Maximum	Average	Standard Deviation
Global (KB)	6099	7927	6948.5	559.3
User (%)	40	62	49.5	7.5
GDI (%)	39	60	49.3	6.3

The average values for the resources in TEST2.LOG are slightly higher than their counterparts in TEST1.LOG. The standard deviation values for the resources in TEST2.LOG are slightly less than their counterparts in TEST1.LOG. Thus, the random test made more resources available than the message dependent test. In addition, the random test caused the fluctuation in these resources to be less than in the message dependent test. The test on your system may lead to a different comparison.

To apply a stress level 3 to the APPSTUD2.EXE program, choose the same settings for the Stress application, except specify stress level 3 in the Executer dialog box and designate the TEST3.LOG file as the output log file. Load the APPSTUD2.EXE program and then start the executer. Experiment with the program by clicking the left and right mouse buttons a few times and typing a short string. When you are finished, end the executer, free all dynamic allocations, exit the Stress application, and then close the APPSTUD2.EXE program. Listing 19.3 shows the contents of the TEST3.LOG file.

Listing 19.3 The TEST3.LOG File

```
****************** Stress Log: Begin Header ******************
Date: 11/22/93   Time: 21:54:58

Initial State of Resources
--------------------------
Global Memory      :  30130.00 KB
User Heap          :        60 %
GDI Heap           :        70 %
Disk Space         :    105.61 MB
File Handles       :       112

****************** Stress Log: End Header ******************

TIME       LOCATION         TYPE OF ACTION   SPECIFIC DESCRIPTION

21:55:02   Stress          Menu Item        Begin Executer
21:55:06   Global : 4308.59 KB  User  :     27 %   GDI  :   34 %
           Handles:      109    Disk  :  105.61 MB
21:55:11   Global : 5363.81 KB  User  :     18 %   GDI  :   26 %
           Handles:      109    Disk  :  105.61 MB
21:55:17   Global : 4767.00 KB  User  :     24 %   GDI  :   26 %
           Handles:      109    Disk  :  105.61 MB
21:55:22   Global : 4992.00 KB  User  :     26 %   GDI  :   26 %
           Handles:      109    Disk  :  105.61 MB
21:55:28   Global : 4109.97 KB  User  :     18 %   GDI  :   37 %
           Handles:      109    Disk  :  105.61 MB
21:55:33   Global : 5927.00 KB  User  :     27 %   GDI  :   19 %
           Handles:      109    Disk  :  105.61 MB
21:55:39   Global : 5073.00 KB  User  :     34 %   GDI  :   16 %
           Handles:      109    Disk  :  105.61 MB
```

```
21:55:41   Stress          Menu Item      End Executer
21:55:44   Stress          Menu Item      Free All
21:55:45   Global : 30109.38 KB  User  :    63 %   GDI  :    72 %
           Handles:     109   Disk  :   105.61 MB
21:55:48   Stress          Menu Item      Exit

******************** Stress Log: Begin Footer ********************
Date: 11/22/93   Time: 21:55:49

Final State of Resources
- - - - - - - - - - - - - - - - - - - - - - - - -
Global Memory       :   30109.38 KB
User Heap           :        63 %
GDI Heap            :        70 %
Disk Space          :    105.61 MB
File Handles        :       109

******************** Stress Log: End Footer ********************
```

Table 19.3 contains the statistics for the TEST3.LOG file.

Table 19.3 Statistics for the TEST3.LOG File			
Item	**Minimum**	**Maximum**	**Average**	**Standard Deviation**
Global (KB)	4109.97	5927.00	5071.9	547.43
User (%)	18	34	24.9	5.6
GDI (%)	16	37	26.3	7.45

If you compare the statistics from Tables 19.2 and 19.3, you notice that there are fewer resources in Table 19.3—the minimum, maximum, and average values in Table 19.3 are significantly less than their counterparts in Table 19.2. The standard deviations are roughly the same. Using a higher stress level causes the APPSTUD2.EXE to slow down. The extent of slowing down depends on the system's configuration.

Now increase the stress up to level 4. Set the Stress application to stress level 4 and specify the output log file as TEST4.LOG. Load the APPSTUD2.EXE program and start the executer. Experiment with the program by clicking the left and right mouse buttons a few times and typing a short string. When you are finished, end the executer, free all dynamic allocations, exit the Stress application, and close the APPSTUD2.EXE program. Listing 19.4 shows the contents of the TEST4.LOG file.

Listing 19.4 The TEST4.LOG File

```
******************** Stress Log: Begin Header ********************
Date: 11/22/93   Time: 21:56:43

Initial State of Resources
--------------------------
Global Memory      :  30134.22 KB
User Heap          :     60 %
GDI Heap           :     72 %
Disk Space         :  105.61 MB
File Handles       :    109


******************** Stress Log: End Header *********************

TIME        LOCATION          TYPE OF ACTION  SPECIFIC DESCRIPTION

21:56:44  Global : 30134.22 KB  User  :    63 %   GDI  :   72 %
          Handles:      109    Disk  :  105.61 MB
21:56:46  Stress            Menu Item     Begin Executer
21:56:49  Global :  2293.13 KB  User  :    11 %   GDI  :    9 %
          Handles:      109    Disk  :  105.61 MB
21:56:54  Global :  3363.81 KB  User  :     1 %   GDI  :    9 %
          Handles:      109    Disk  :  105.61 MB
21:57:00  Global :  2767.00 KB  User  :     1 %   GDI  :    9 %
          Handles:      109    Disk  :  105.61 MB
21:57:05  Global :  2992.00 KB  User  :     1 %   GDI  :    9 %
          Handles:      109    Disk  :  105.61 MB
21:57:11  Global :  2111.00 KB  User  :     1 %   GDI  :   13 %
          Handles:      109    Disk  :  105.61 MB
21:57:16  Global :  3922.88 KB  User  :     3 %   GDI  :    4 %
          Handles:      109    Disk  :  105.61 MB
21:57:22  Global :  3071.66 KB  User  :     1 %   GDI  :    0 %
          Handles:      109    Disk  :  105.61 MB
21:57:27  Global :  3324.00 KB  User  :    13 %   GDI  :   11 %
          Handles:      109    Disk  :  105.61 MB
21:57:34  Global :  2649.28 KB  User  :     9 %   GDI  :    8 %
          Handles:      109    Disk  :  105.61 MB
21:57:39  Global :  2772.25 KB  User  :    13 %   GDI  :    4 %
          Handles:      109    Disk  :  105.61 MB
21:57:45  Global :  2099.00 KB  User  :     1 %   GDI  :    8 %
          Handles:      109    Disk  :  105.61 MB
21:57:50  Global :  3446.00 KB  User  :    14 %   GDI  :   11 %
          Handles:      109    Disk  :  105.61 MB
21:57:51  Stress            Menu Item     End Executer
21:57:53  Stress            Menu Item     Free All
21:57:56  Global : 30174.31 KB  User  :    63 %   GDI   : 72 %
          Handles:      109    Disk  :  105.61 MB
21:57:58  Stress            Windows Selection Destroy

******************** Stress Log: Begin Footer ********************
Date: 11/22/93   Time: 21:57:59
```

```
Final State of Resources
-------------------------
Global Memory       :   30174.31 KB
User Heap           :         63 %
GDI Heap            :         72 %
Disk Space          :     105.61 MB
File Handles        :        109

******************** Stress Log: End Footer ********************
```

Table 19.4 contains the statistics for the TEST4.LOG file.

Table 19.4 Statistics for the TEST4.LOG File				
Item	**Minimum**	**Maximum**	**Average**	**Standard Deviation**
Global (KB)	2099.00	3922.88	2901.00	564.6
User (%)	1	14	5.75	5.7
GDI (%)	0	11	7.9	3.6

Table 19.4 shows a significant drop in resources. In fact, my system was very sluggish, although the APPSTUD2.EXE program was able to dynamically create the custom message dialog boxes. In addition, when I closed APPSTUD2.EXE and tried to reload it, Windows gave me an insufficient memory error. Listing 19.4 has an entry at 21:57:50 that shows a jump in resources due to closing the APPSTUD2.EXE application.

Summary

This chapter presented the Stress application, which enables you to test your programs under more limited resources. Here's what you learned:

- You invoke the Stress application from the Visual Workshop, the Visual C++ folder, or the File Manager. The Stress application displays a small dialog box window with a menu system that includes the following menus: Settings, Options, and Help. The Help menu offers on-line documentation.

■ You can use the Settings menu commands to set fixed resources, specify tested resources, and specify log information. The Executer command enables you to select the resources to be limited under the stress testing and then to select the stress testing scheme. You can involve the global heap, user heap, GDI heap, disk space, and file handles in the stress testing. You also can choose between random or message dependent testing modes. When you choose the message dependent testing mode, you can select the Windows messages that trigger the dynamic allocations of resources by the Stress application. The Log Settings command lets you select the output log devices.

■ You can use the Options menu to start the executer, end the executer, free all dynamic allocations, and manage the Stress application display.

In addition, this chapter stress tested the APPSTUD2.EXE program using the message dependent and random modes. This chapter also used levels 2 through 4 to stress test the APPSTUD2.EXE program. For each test, the text included a table showing the minimum, maximum, average, and standard deviation statistics for global, user, and GDI heaps.

Appendix A

ASCII and Extended ASCII Codes

ASCII (American Standard Code for Information Interchange) is a widely used standard that defines numeric values for a common set of alphabetic characters. The first 32 characters are reserved for formatting and hardware control codes. Following these codes are 96 "printable" characters. IBM defined symbols for the final 128 ASCII values when it released the IBM PC, and referred to the additional characters as *Extended ASCII codes*.

Dec X_{10}	Hex X_{16}	Binary X_2	ASCII Character	Ctrl	Key
000	00	0000 0000	null	NUL	^@
001	01	0000 0001	☺	SOH	^A
002	02	0000 0010	☻	STX	^B
003	03	0000 0011	♥	ETX	^C
004	04	0000 0100	♦	EOT	^D
005	05	0000 0101	♣	ENQ	^E
006	06	0000 0110	♠	ACK	^F
007	07	0000 0111	●	BEL	^G
008	08	0000 1000	■	BS	^H
009	09	0000 1001	○	HT	^I

Dec X_{10}	Hex X_{16}	Binary X_2	ASCII Character	Ctrl	Key
010	0A	0000 1010	■	LF	^J
011	0B	0000 1011	♂	VT	^K
012	0C	0000 1100	♀	FF	^L
013	0D	0000 1101	♪	CR	^M
014	0E	0000 1110	♪♪	SO	^N
015	0F	0000 1111	☼	SI	^O
016	10	0001 0000	►	DLE	^P
017	11	0001 0001	◄	DC1	^Q
018	12	0001 0010	↕	DC2	^R
019	13	0001 0011	‼	DC3	^S
020	14	0001 0100	¶	DC4	^T
021	15	0001 0101	§	NAK	^U
022	16	0001 0110	–	SYN	^V
023	17	0001 0111	↨	ETB	^W
024	18	0001 1000	↑	CAN	^X
025	19	0001 1001	↓	EM	^Y
026	1A	0001 1010	→	SUB	^Z
027	1B	0001 1011	←	ESC	^[
028	1C	0001 1100	∟	FS	^\
029	1D	0001 1101	↔	GS	^]
030	1E	0001 1110	▲	RS	^^
031	1F	0001 1111	▼	US	^_
032	20	0010 0000	Space		
033	21	0010 0001	!		
034	22	0010 0010	"		
035	23	0010 0011	#		
036	24	0010 0100	$		
037	25	0010 0101	%		
038	26	0010 0110	&		
039	27	0010 0111	'		
040	28	0010 1000	(		

Dec X_{10}	Hex X_{16}	Binary X_2	ASCII Character
041	29	0010 1001	)
042	2A	0010 1010	*
043	2B	0010 1011	+
044	2C	0010 1100	,
045	2D	0010 1101	-
046	2E	0010 1110	.
047	2F	0010 1111	/
048	30	0011 0000	0
049	31	0011 0001	1
050	32	0011 0010	2
051	33	0011 0011	3
052	34	0011 0100	4
053	35	0011 0101	5
054	36	0011 0110	6
055	37	0011 0111	7
056	38	0011 1000	8
057	39	0011 1001	9
058	3A	0011 1010	:
059	3B	0011 1011	;
060	3C	0011 1100	<
061	3D	0011 1101	=
062	3E	0011 1110	>
063	3F	0011 1111	?
064	40	0100 0000	@
065	41	0100 0001	A
066	42	0100 0010	B
067	43	0100 0011	C
068	44	0100 0100	D
069	45	0100 0101	E
070	46	0100 0110	F
071	47	0100 0111	G
072	48	0100 1000	H
073	49	0100 1001	I

Appendixes

Dec X_{10}	Hex X_{16}	Binary X_2	ASCII Character
074	4A	0100 1010	J
075	4B	0100 1011	K
076	4C	0100 1100	L
077	4D	0100 1101	M
078	4E	0100 1110	N
079	4F	0100 1111	O
080	50	0101 0000	P
081	51	0101 0001	Q
082	52	0101 0010	R
083	53	0101 0011	S
084	54	0101 0100	T
085	55	0101 0101	U
086	56	0101 0110	V
087	57	0101 0111	W
088	58	0101 1000	X
089	59	0101 1001	Y
090	5A	0101 1010	Z
091	5B	0101 1011	[
092	5C	0101 1100	\
093	5D	0101 1101	]
094	5E	0101 1110	^
095	5F	0101 1111	–
096	60	0110 0000	`
097	61	0110 0001	a
098	62	0110 0010	b
099	63	0110 0011	c
100	64	0110 0100	d
101	65	0110 0101	e
102	66	0110 0110	f
103	67	0110 0111	g
104	68	0110 1000	h
105	69	0110 1001	i

Dec X_{10}	Hex X_{16}	Binary X_2	ASCII Character
106	6A	0110 1010	j
107	6B	0110 1011	k
108	6C	0110 1100	l
109	6D	0110 1101	m
110	6E	0110 1110	n
111	6F	0110 1111	o
112	70	0111 0000	p
113	71	0111 0001	q
114	72	0111 0010	r
115	73	0111 0011	s
116	74	0111 0100	t
117	75	0111 0101	u
118	76	0111 0110	v
119	77	0111 0111	w
120	78	0111 1000	x
121	79	0111 1001	y
122	7A	0111 1010	z
123	7B	0111 1011	{
124	7C	0111 1100	¦
125	7D	0111 1101	}
126	7E	0111 1110	~
127	7F	0111 1111	Delete
128	80	1000 0000	Ç
129	81	1000 0001	ü
130	82	1000 0010	é
131	83	1000 0011	â
132	84	1000 0100	ä
133	85	1000 0101	à
134	86	1000 0110	å
135	87	1000 0111	ç
136	88	1000 1000	ê
137	89	1000 1001	ë

Appendixes

Dec X_{10}	Hex X_{16}	Binary X_2	ASCII Character
138	8A	1000 1010	è
139	8B	1000 1011	ï
140	8C	1000 1100	î
141	8D	1000 1101	ì
142	8E	1000 1110	Ä
143	8F	1000 1111	Å
144	90	1001 0000	É
145	91	1001 0001	æ
146	92	1001 0010	Æ
147	93	1001 0011	ô
148	94	1001 0100	ö
149	95	1001 0101	ò
150	96	1001 0110	û
151	97	1001 0111	ù
152	98	1001 1000	ÿ
153	99	1001 1001	Ö
154	9A	1001 1010	Ü
155	9B	1001 1011	¢
156	9C	1001 1100	£
157	9D	1001 1101	¥
158	9E	1001 1110	P$_t$
159	9F	1001 1111	f
160	A0	1010 0000	á
161	A1	1010 0001	í
162	A2	1010 0010	ó
163	A3	1010 0011	ú
164	A4	1010 0100	ñ
165	A5	1010 0101	Ñ
166	A6	1010 0110	a̲
167	A7	1010 0111	o̲
168	A8	1010 1000	¿
169	A9	1010 1001	⌐

Dec X_{10}	Hex X_{16}	Binary X_2	ASCII Character
170	AA	1010 1010	¬
171	AB	1010 1011	½
172	AC	1010 1100	¼
173	AD	1010 1101	¡
174	AE	1010 1110	«
175	AF	1010 1111	»
176	B0	1011 0000	░
177	B1	1011 0001	▒
178	B2	1011 0010	▓
179	B3	1011 0011	│
180	B4	1011 0100	┤
181	B5	1011 0101	╡
182	B6	1011 0110	╢
183	B7	1011 0111	╖
184	B8	1011 1000	╕
185	B9	1011 1001	╣
186	BA	1011 1010	║
187	BB	1011 1011	╗
188	BC	1011 1100	╝
189	BD	1011 1101	╜
190	BE	1011 1110	╛
191	BF	1011 1111	┐
192	C0	1100 0000	└
193	C1	1100 0001	┴
194	C2	1100 0010	┬
195	C3	1100 0011	├
196	C4	1100 0100	─
197	C5	1100 0101	┼
198	C6	1100 0110	╞
199	C7	1100 0111	╟
200	C8	1100 1000	╚
201	C9	1100 1001	╔

Dec X_{10}	Hex X_{16}	Binary X_2	ASCII Character
202	CA	1100 1010	⊥
203	CB	1100 1011	⊤
204	CC	1100 1100	⊢
205	CD	1100 1101	=
206	CE	1100 1110	╬
207	CF	1100 1111	⊥
208	D0	1101 0000	⊥
209	D1	1101 0001	⊤
210	D2	1101 0010	π
211	D3	1101 0011	⊔
212	D4	1101 0100	⊢
213	D5	1101 0101	⊢
214	D6	1101 0110	π
215	D7	1101 0111	╫
216	D8	1101 1000	╪
217	D9	1101 1001	⌐
218	DA	1101 1010	⌐
219	DB	1101 1011	█
220	DC	1101 1100	▄
221	DD	1101 1101	▌
222	DE	1101 1110	▐
223	DF	1101 1111	▀
224	E0	1110 0000	α
225	E1	1110 0001	β
226	E2	1110 0010	Γ
227	E3	1110 0011	π
228	E4	1110 0100	Σ
229	E5	1110 0101	σ
230	E6	1110 0110	μ

Dec X_{10}	Hex X_{16}	Binary X_2	ASCII Character
231	E7	1110 0111	τ
232	E8	1110 1000	Φ
233	E9	1110 1001	θ
234	EA	1110 1010	Ω
235	EB	1110 1011	δ
236	EC	1110 1100	∞
237	ED	1110 1101	$\varnothing$
238	EE	1110 1110	$\in$
239	EF	1110 1111	$\cap$
240	F0	1111 0000	$\equiv$
241	F1	1111 0001	$\pm$
242	F2	1111 0010	$\geq$
243	F3	1111 0011	$\leq$
244	F4	1111 0100	$\lceil$
245	F5	1111 0101	$\rfloor$
246	F6	1111 0110	$\div$
247	F7	1111 0111	$\approx$
248	F8	1111 1000	$\circ$
249	F9	1111 1001	$\bullet$
250	FA	1111 1010	$\cdot$
251	FB	1111 1011	$\sqrt{}$
252	FC	1111 1100	η
253	FD	1111 1101	^{2}
254	FE	1111 1110	$\blacksquare$
255	FF	1111 1111	

Appendixes

Appendix B

Controls Resource Script

This appendix presents the syntax for the menu resource and the controls resource script. The resource script itself was defined by Microsoft long before the MFC class hierarchy was created. However, as you saw in Chapter 8, dialog box instances are created using resources. This appendix describes the following resources:

■ Menu resources

■ Dialog box resource

■ DIALOG option statements

■ General control resources

■ Resources for the default controls

Building Menu Resources

The menu resource file (usually stored in a file with the extension RC) may contain the following statements:

■ The MENU statement defines the contents of a menu resource. The general syntax for the MENU statement is as follows:

```
menuID MENU [load options] [mem options]
BEGIN
        item definitions
END
```

The menuID is the unique name or integer ID of the menu resource. The keywords associated with resource files appear in uppercase (although case is optional—keywords are not case-sensitive—keywords appear in uppercase letters in this book to make it easier to distinguish between resource keywords and non-keywords). The load options are as follows:

PRELOAD loads the resource immediately.

LOADONCALL loads the resource as needed (the default option).

The mem options are as follows:

FIXED keeps the resource in a fixed memory location.

MOVABLE moves the resource when needed for the sake of memory compaction (selected by default).

DISCARDABLE discards the resource when it is no longer needed (also selected by default).

■ The MENUITEM statement defines the name and attributes of an actual menu item. The general syntax for the MENUITEM statement is as follows:

```
MENUITEM text, result [, option list]
```

The text field accepts a string literal (enclosed in double quotation marks) that designates the name of the menu item. To define a hot key for a menu item, place the ampersand (&) character in front of the letter you want to designate as the hot key (the selection is case-insensitive). To display the ampersand as part of the menu name, use two ampersand characters (&&). Use the \t sequence to insert a tab in the menu item name. Use the \a sequence to right-align all text that follows.

The result field contains an integer, usually a CM_*XXXX* constant, that represents the command sent by the menu item.

The option list may contain the following items:

CHECKED displays a check mark next to the menu item.

GRAYED displays the menu item in a gray color to indicate that the menu item is not active.

HELP puts a vertical separator bar (|) to the left of the menu item.

INACTIVE displays the menu item but prevents its selection. This option is usually combined with the GRAYED option to give a better visual indication that the menu item is inactive.

MENUBARBREAK places the menu item on a new line for static menu-bar items. In the case of pop-up menu items, this option separates the new and old columns with a vertical line.

MENUBREAK places the menu item on a new line for static menu-bar items. For pop-up menus, this option places the menu item in a new column, without any dividing line between the columns.

■ The POPUP statement defines the beginning of a pop-up menu. The general syntax for the POPUP statement is as follows:

```
POPUP text [,option list]
BEGIN
    item definitions
END
```

The text and option list fields are similar to their counterparts in the MENUITEM statement. The item definitions are made up of MENUITEM or other POPUP statements. The latter statements let you create nested menus.

■ The MENUITEM SEPARATOR statement is a special form of the MENUITEM statement that creates an inactive menu item and displays a dividing bar between two active menu items.

■ The ACCELERATORS statement defines one or more accelerators for your MFC application. An *accelerator* is a keystroke defined to give the application user a quick way to select a menu item and carry out a specific task. The general syntax for the ACCELERATOR statement is as follows:

```
accTableName ACCELERATORS
BEGIN
    event, idValue, [type] [NOINVERT] [ALT] [SHIFT] [CONTROL]
END
```

The accTableName field defines a unique name or integer ID that distinguishes an accelerator resource from any other type of resource. The event field specifies the keystroke used as an accelerator and can be one of the following:

• A single ASCII character enclosed in double quotation marks. You can place a caret symbol (^) before the character to signal that it is a control character. In this case, the type field is not required.

Appendixes

- An integer value that designates the ASCII code of a character. In this case, the type field must be the keyword ASCII.

- An integer value that represents a virtual key. In this case, the type field must be the keyword VIRTKEY.

  The idValue field is an integer that identifies the accelerator. The type field is required only when the event field is an ASCII character code or a virtual key.

  The NOINVERT option prevents a top-level menu item from being highlighted when the accelerator is used. The ALT, SHIFT, and CONTROL options activate the accelerator when the Alt, Shift, and Control keys, respectively, are pressed.

Following is an example of an accelerators resource:

```
"EditKeys" ACCELERATORS
BEGIN
      "h",          IDDHEADING                      ; the H key
      "H",          IDDHOLD                         ; the Shift+H keys
      "^B", IDDBOLD                                 ; the Control+B keys
      64,           IDDADD                          ; The Shift+A keys
      97,           IDDAPPEND                       ; The A key
      "s",          IDDSEARCH, ALT                  ; The Alt+S keys
      VK_F7,        IDDSAVE, VIRTKEY                ; The F7 function key
      VK_F2,        IDDLOAD, SHIFT, VIRTKEY         ; The Shift+F2 keys
      VK_F3,        IDDSAVEAS, CONTROL, VIRTKEY ; The Control+F3 keys
      VK_F1,    IDDNEW, ALT, SHIFT, VIRTKEY         ; The Alt+Shift+F1 keys
END
```

Examining the Dialog Box Resource

The DIALOG statement defines the resource that can be used in a Windows program to build dialog boxes. The general syntax for the DIALOG statement is as follows:

```
nameID DIALOG [load options][mem options] x, y, width, height
[option-statements]
BEGIN
      control-statements
END
```

The nameID is the unique name or integer ID of the dialog box resource. The keywords associated with resource files appear in uppercase (although case is optional—keywords are not case-sensitive—keywords appear in uppercase letters in this book to make it easier to distinguish between resource keywords and non-keywords).

The load options are as follows:

- PRELOAD loads the resource immediately.

- LOADONCALL loads the resource as needed (the default option).

The mem options are as follows:

- FIXED keeps the resource in a fixed memory location.

- MOVABLE moves the resource when needed for the sake of memory compaction (selected by default).

- DISCARDABLE discards the resource when it is no longer needed (also selected by default).

The x and y parameters specify the location of the upper-left corner of the dialog box. The width and height parameters define the dimensions of the dialog box in pixels.

Following is an example of a dialog-box resource definition (taken from the DIALOG1.RC file):

```
#include <windows.h>
#include <afxres.h>
NEW DIALOG DISCARDABLE LOADONCALL PURE MOVEABLE 30, 50, 200, 100
STYLE WS_POPUP ¦ DS_MODALFRAME
CAPTION "Message"
BEGIN
  CTEXT "Exit the application?", 1, 10, 10, 170, 15
  CONTROL "OK", IDOK, "BUTTON", WS_CHILD ¦ WS_VISIBLE ¦
    WS_TABSTOP ¦ BS_DEFPUSHBUTTON, 20, 50, 70, 15
  CONTROL "Cancel", IDCANCEL, "BUTTON", WS_CHILD ¦ WS_VISIBLE ¦
    WS_TABSTOP ¦ BS_PUSHBUTTON, 110, 50, 70, 15
END
```

Examining the *DIALOG* Option Statements

The DIALOG option statements designate the special attributes of the dialog box, such as style, caption, and menu. These statements are optional. If you do not incorporate any option statements in your dialog box resource definition, you end up with a dialog box that has default attributes. The DIALOG option statements include the following items:

- STYLE

- CAPTION

- MENU

- CLASS

- FONT

The following sections explain each of these dialog box attributes.

The *STYLE* Statement

The STYLE statement specifies the window style of the dialog box. This attribute indicates whether the dialog box is a child window or a pop-up window. The default style for the dialog box has the WS_POPUP, WS_BORDER, and WS_SYSMENU styles. The general syntax for the STYLE statement is as follows:

```
STYLE style
```

The style parameter takes an integer value made up of bitwise ORed style attributes. Here is an example of the STYLE option statement:

```
STYLE WS_POPUP | DS_MODALFRAME
```

The *CAPTION* Statement

The CAPTION statement defines the title for the dialog box. This title appears in the caption bar of the dialog box—if the box has that bar. By default, the title is an empty string. The general syntax for the CAPTION statement is as follows:

```
CAPTION title
```

The title parameter is a string literal. Here is an example of the CAPTION statement:

```
CAPTION "Replace Text"
```

The *MENU* Statement

The MENU statement specifies the menu attached to the dialog box. By default, the dialog box has no menu. The general syntax for the MENU statement is as follows:

```
MENU menuName
```

The `menuName` parameter is the name or number of the menu resource. Here is an example of the MENU statement:

```
#include <windows.h>
#include <owl\windows.h>
YesNo MENU LOADONCALL MOVEABLE PURE DISCARDABLE
BEGIN
    MENUITEM "&Ok", IDOK
    MENUITEM "&Cancel", IDCANCEL
END
NEW DIALOG DISCARDABLE LOADONCALL PURE MOVEABLE 30, 50, 200, 100
STYLE WS_POPUP ¦ DS_MODALFRAME
CAPTION "Message"
MENU YesNo
BEGIN
  CTEXT "Exit the application?", 1, 10, 10, 170, 15
  CONTROL "OK", IDOK, "BUTTON", WS_CHILD ¦ WS_VISIBLE ¦
    WS_TABSTOP ¦ BS_DEFPUSHBUTTON, 20, 50, 70, 15
  CONTROL "Cancel", IDCANCEL, "BUTTON", WS_CHILD ¦ WS_VISIBLE ¦
    WS_TABSTOP ¦ BS_PUSHBUTTON, 110, 50, 70, 15
END
```

The *CLASS* Statement

The CLASS statement specifies the Windows registration class (not the MFC library class) of the dialog box. The general syntax for the CLASS statement is as follows:

```
CLASS className
```

The `className` parameter defines the integer or string name of the registration class. Here is an example of the CLASS statement:

```
CLASS "ChitChat"
```

The *FONT* Statement

The FONT statement specifies the font used by Windows to draw text in the dialog box. The specified font must be already loaded, either from WIN.INI or by invoking the LoadFont API function. The general syntax for the FONT statement is as follows:

```
FONT pointSize, typeface
```

The `pointSize` parameter is an integer that specifies the size of the font in points. The `typeface` parameter is a string that indicates the name of the font. Here is an example of the FONT statement:

```
FONT 10, "Helv"
```

Appendixes

Examining the Dialog Box Control Resources

The resource script supports two types of controls resource. The first is the CONTROL statement, which provides a general way to declare the resource of a control. The other types of resource controls are the modifiable default control resources. These resources use statements with keywords descriptive of the control they define. For example, the RADIOBUTTON statement defines the resource for a radio button. The next section presents the CONTROL statement; subsequent sections present the statements that define the resources for specific controls.

The General *CONTROL* Resource

The CONTROL statement enables you to define the resource for any standard or user-defined control owned by a dialog box. The general syntax for the CONTROL statement is as follows:

```
CONTROL text, id, class, style, x, y, width, height
```

The text parameter specifies a string literal for the text that appears in the control.

The id parameter declares the control's unique ID.

> **Note**
>
> The *class* parameter is a string that indicates the name of the Windows registration class for the control. Table B.1 shows the Windows registration class names for the various standard controls. Notice that the pushbutton, check box, radio button, and group box all share the same registration class name. How are they distinguished from each other? The answer lies with the *style* parameter.

The style parameter is usually a bitwise ORed expression and sets all the styles associated with the control. *There are no default style values!*

The x, y, width, and height parameters specify the location and dimensions of the control in pixels. These parameters are typically integer constants. You also can use the addition operator to build simple expressions.

Table B.1 Windows Registration Class Names for Standard Controls	
Control	**Registration Class Name**
Check Box	BUTTON
Combo Box	COMBOBOX
Edit Box	EDIT
Group Box	BUTTON
List Box	LISTBOX
Pushbutton	BUTTON
Radio Button	BUTTON
Scroll Bar	SCROLLBAR
Static Text	STATIC

Following are some examples of how to use the CONTROL statement to create dialog box controls. The examples are taken from the DIALOG6.RC resource file.

```
ID_DIALOG DIALOG DISCARDABLE LOADONCALL PURE MOVEABLE 10, 10, 200, 150
STYLE WS_POPUP ¦ WS_CLIPSIBLINGS ¦ WS_CAPTION ¦ WS_SYSMENU ¦
  DS_MODALFRAME
CAPTION "Controls Demo"
BEGIN
  CONTROL "Find", ID_FIND_TXT, "STATIC", WS_CHILD ¦ WS_VISIBLE ¦
    SS_LEFT, 20, 10, 100, 15
  CONTROL "", ID_FIND_CMB, "COMBOBOX", WS_CHILD ¦ WS_VISIBLE ¦
    WS_BORDER ¦ WS_TABSTOP ¦ CBS_DROPDOWN, 20, 25, 100, 50
  CONTROL "Replace", ID_REPLACE_TXT, "STATIC", WS_CHILD ¦ WS_VISIBLE ¦
    SS_LEFT, 20, 45, 100, 15
  CONTROL "", ID_REPLACE_CMB, "COMBOBOX", WS_CHILD ¦ WS_VISIBLE ¦
    WS_BORDER ¦ WS_TABSTOP ¦ CBS_DROPDOWN, 20, 60, 100, 50
  CONTROL " Scope ", ID_SCOPE_GRP, "BUTTON", WS_CHILD ¦ WS_VISIBLE
    ¦ WS_GROUP ¦ BS_GROUPBOX, 20, 80, 90, 50
  CONTROL "Global", ID_GLOBAL_RBT, "BUTTON", WS_CHILD ¦ WS_VISIBLE
    ¦ WS_TABSTOP ¦ BS_AUTORADIOBUTTON, 30, 90, 50, 15
  CONTROL "Selected Text", ID_SELTEXT_RBT, "BUTTON", WS_CHILD ¦
    WS_VISIBLE ¦ WS_TABSTOP ¦ BS_AUTORADIOBUTTON, 30, 105, 60, 15
  CONTROL "Case Sensitive", ID_CASE_CHK, "BUTTON", WS_CHILD ¦
    WS_VISIBLE ¦ WS_TABSTOP ¦ BS_AUTOCHECKBOX, 20, 130, 80, 15
  CONTROL "Whole Word", ID_WHOLEWORD_CHK, "BUTTON", WS_CHILD ¦
    WS_VISIBLE ¦ WS_TABSTOP ¦ BS_AUTOCHECKBOX, 100, 130, 80, 15
  CONTROL, "&OK", IDOK, "BUTTON", WS_CHILD ¦ WS_VISIBLE ¦ WS_TABSTOP
    ¦ BS_DEFPUSHBUTTON, 120, 90, 30, 20
  CONTROL "&Cancel", IDCANCEL, "BUTTON", WS_CHILD ¦ WS_VISIBLE ¦
    WS_TABSTOP, 160, 90, 30, 20
END
```

The *LTEXT* Statement

The LTEXT statement defines the resource of a static text control whose text is flush left. The general syntax for the LTEXT statement is as follows:

```
LTEXT text, id, x, y, width, height [, style]
```

The text parameter specifies the static control text. This text may include an & character to underline a hot key character. The id parameter defines the ID of the static control. The x, y, width, and height parameters specify the location and dimensions of the control. The optional style parameter specifies the additional styles for the resource. The default style is SS_LEFT and WS_GROUP. The style parameter can be the WS_TABSTOP style, the WS_GROUP style, or both.

The characters of the text parameter are displayed left-justified. If the entire text does not fit in the specified width, the additional characters are wrapped to the beginning of the next line.

Here are two examples of the LTEXT statement:

```
LTEXT "Current Drive:", ID_DRIVE_TXT, 10, 10, 50, 10
LTEXT "Current Dir:", ID_DIR_TXT, 10, 50, 50, 10, WS_TABSTOP
      ¦ WS_GROUP
```

The *RTEXT* Statement

The RTEXT statement defines the resource of a static text control whose text is flush right. The general syntax for the RTEXT statement is as follows:

```
RTEXT text, id, x, y, width, height [, style]
```

The text parameter specifies the static control text. This text may include an & character to underline a hot key character. The id parameter defines the ID of the static control. The x, y, width, and height parameters specify the location and dimensions of the control. The optional style parameter specifies the additional styles for the resource. The default style is SS_RIGHT and WS_GROUP. The style parameter can be the WS_TABSTOP style, the WS_GROUP style, or both.

The characters of the text parameter are displayed right-justified. If the entire text does not fit in the specified width, the additional characters are wrapped to the next line and also appear right-justified.

Here is an example of the RTEXT statement:

```
RTEXT "Current Drive:", ID_DRIVE_TXT, 70, 10, 50, 10
```

The *CTEXT* Statement

The CTEXT statement defines the resource of a static text control whose text is centered. The general syntax for the CTEXT statement is as follows:

```
CTEXT text, id, x, y, width, height [, style]
```

The text parameter specifies the static control text. This text can include an & character to underline a hot key character. The id parameter defines the ID of the static control. The x, y, width, and height parameters specify the location and dimensions of the control. The optional style parameter specifies the additional styles for the resource. The default style is SS_CENTER and WS_GROUP. The style parameter can be the WS_TABSTOP style, the WS_GROUP style, or both.

The characters of the text parameter are displayed centered. If the entire text does not fit in the specified width, the additional characters are wrapped to the next line and also appear centered.

Here is an example of the CTEXT statement:

```
CTEXT "Current Drive:", ID_DRIVE_TXT, 10, 10, 50, 10
```

The *CHECKBOX* Statement

The CHECKBOX statement defines a check box control resource that has the BUTTON registration class. The general syntax for the CHECKBOX statement is as follows:

```
CHECKBOX text, id, x, y, width, height [, style]
```

The text parameter specifies the caption of the control. This text can include an & character to underline a hot key character. The id parameter defines the ID of the check box control. The x, y, width, and height parameters specify the location and dimensions of the control. The optional style parameter specifies the additional styles for the resource. The default style is BS_CHECKBOX and WS_TABSTOP. The style parameter can be the WS_DISABLED style, the WS_TABSTOP style, or both.

Following is an example of the CHECKBOX statement:

```
CHECKBOX "Case-Sensitive", ID_CASE_CHK, 10, 10, 100, 10
```

Appendixes

The *PUSHBUTTON* Statement

The PUSHBUTTON statement defines a pushbutton control resource that has the BUTTON registration class. The general syntax for the PUSHBUTTON statement is as follows:

```
PUSHBUTTON text, id, x, y, width, height [, style]
```

The text parameter specifies the caption of the control. This text can include an & character to underline a hot key character. The id parameter defines the ID of the pushbutton control. The x, y, width, and height parameters specify the location and dimensions of the control. The optional style parameter specifies the additional styles for the resource. The default style is BS_PUSHBUTTON and WS_TABSTOP. The style parameter can be the WS_TABSTOP style, the WS_DISABLED style, the WS_GROUP style, or any bitwise ORed combination of these styles.

Here is an example of the PUSHBUTTON statement:

```
PUSHBUTTON "Calculate", ID_CALC_BTN, 10, 10, 100, 10, WS_DISABLED
```

The *DEFPUSHBUTTON* Statement

The DEFPUSHBUTTON statement defines a default pushbutton control resource that has the BUTTON registration class. The general syntax for the DEFPUSHBUTTON statement is as follows:

```
DEFPUSHBUTTON text, id, x, y, width, height [, style]
```

The text parameter specifies the caption of the control. This text can include an & character to underline a hot key character. The id parameter defines the ID of the default pushbutton control. The x, y, width, and height parameters specify the location and dimensions of the control. The optional style parameter specifies the additional styles for the resource. The default style is BS_DEFPUSHBUTTON and WS_TABSTOP. The style parameter can be the WS_TABSTOP style, the WS_DISABLED style, the WS_GROUP style, or any bitwise ORed combination of these styles.

Here is an example of the DEFPUSHBUTTON statement:

```
DEFPUSHBUTTON "Calculate", ID_CALC_BTN, 10, 10, 100, 10
```

The *LISTBOX* Statement

The LISTBOX statement defines a list box control resource that has the LISTBOX registration class. The general syntax for the LISTBOX statement is as follows:

```
LISTBOX id, x, y, width, height [, style]
```

The `id` parameter defines the ID of the list box control. The `x`, `y`, `width`, and `height` parameters specify the location and dimensions of the control. The optional `style` parameter specifies the additional styles for the resource. The default `style` is `LBS_NOTIFY`, `WS_VSCROLL`, and `WS_BORDER`. The `style` parameter can be the `WS_BORDER` style, the `WS_VSCROLL` style, or both.

Here is an example of the `LISTBOX` statement:

```
LISTBOX ID_OPERAND_LST, 10, 10, 100, 100
```

The *GROUPBOX* Statement

The `GROUPBOX` statement defines a group box control resource that has the `BUTTON` registration class. The general syntax for the `GROUPBOX` statement is as follows:

```
GROUPBOX text, id, x, y, width, height [, style]
```

The `text` parameter specifies the caption of the control. This text can include an & character to underline a hot key character. The `id` parameter defines the ID of the group box control. The `x`, `y`, `width`, and `height` parameters specify the location and dimensions of the control. The optional `style` parameter specifies the additional styles for the resource. The default `style` is `BS_GROUPBOX` and `WS_TABSTOP`. The `style` parameter can be the `WS_TABSTOP` style, the `WS_DISABLED` style, or both.

Following is an example of the `GROUPBOX` statement:

```
GROUPBOX "Angle", ID_ANGLE_GRP, 10, 10, 200, 200
```

The *RADIOBUTTON* Statement

The `RADIOBUTTON` statement defines a radio button control resource that has the `BUTTON` registration class. The general syntax for the `RADIOBUTTON` statement is as follows:

```
RADIOBUTTON text, id, x, y, width, height [, style]
```

The `text` parameter specifies the caption of the control. This text can include an & character to underline a hot key character. The `id` parameter defines the ID of the radio button control. The `x`, `y`, `width`, and `height` parameters specify the location and dimensions of the control. The optional `style` parameter specifies the additional styles for the resource. The default `style` is `BS_RADIOBUTTON` and `WS_TABSTOP`. The `style` parameter can be the `WS_TABSTOP` style, the `WS_GROUP` style, the `WS_DISABLED` style, or any bitwise ORed combination of these styles.

Appendixes

Following is an example of the RADIOBUTTON statement:

```
RADIOBUTTON "Degrees", ID_DEGREES_RBT, 10, 10, 100, 10
```

The *EDITTEXT* Statement

The EDITTEXT statement defines an edit box control resource that has the EDIT registration class. The general syntax for the EDITTEXT statement is as follows:

```
EDITTEXT id, x, y, width, height [, style]
```

The id parameter defines the ID of the edit box control. The x, y, width, and height parameters specify the location and dimensions of the control. The optional style parameter specifies the additional styles for the resource. The default style is WS_TABSTOP, ES_EDIT, and WS_BORDER. The style parameter can be the WS_TABSTOP style, the WS_GROUP style, the WS_VSCROLL style, the WS_HSCROLL style, the WS_DISABLED style, or any bitwise ORed combination of these styles.

Here is an example of the EDITTEXT statement:

```
EDITTEXT ID_INPUT_BOX, 10, 10, 200, 200
```

The *COMBOBOX* Statement

The COMBOBOX statement defines a combo box control resource that has the COMBOBOX registration class. The general syntax for the COMBOBOX statement is as follows:

```
COMBOBOX id, x, y, width, height [, style]
```

The id parameter defines the ID of the combo box control. The x, y, width, and height parameters specify the location and dimensions of the control. The optional style parameter specifies the additional styles for the resource. The default style is WS_TABSTOP and CBS_SIMPLE. The style parameter can be the WS_TABSTOP style, the WS_GROUP style, the WS_VSCROLL style, the WS_DISABLED style, or any bitwise ORed combination of these styles.

Here is an example of the COMBOBOX statement:

```
COMBOBOX ID_INPUT_BOX, 10, 10, 200, 200
```

The *SCROLLBAR* Statement

The SCROLLBAR statement defines a scroll bar control resource that has the SCROLLBAR registration class. The general syntax for the SCROLLBAR statement is as follows:

```
SCROLLBAR id, x, y, width, height [, style]
```

The id parameter defines the ID of the scroll bar control. The x, y, width, and height parameters specify the location and dimensions of the control. The optional style parameter specifies the additional styles for the resource. The default style is SBS_HORZ. The style parameter can be the WS_TABSTOP style, the WS_GROUP style, the WS_GROUP style, the WS_DISABLED style, or any bitwise ORed combination of these styles.

Here is an example of the SCROLLBAR statement:

```
SCROLLBAR ID_INDEX_SCR, 10, 10, 20, 200
```

Appendixes

Appendix C

Advanced MFC Classes

This appendix supplements Chapter 2 by presenting an overview of the more advanced classes in the MFC library. These classes include:

- The dialog box classes

- The views classes

- The control bar classes

- The collections classes

The Dialog Box Classes

The MFC library provides the dialog box classes to support both custom and common dialog boxes. Common dialog boxes are the standard dialog boxes available in Windows 3.1 and later. The following outline shows the subhierarchy of the dialog box classes:

```
+ CDialog
    - CFileDialog
    - CColorDialog
    - CFontDialog
    - CPrintDialog
    - CFindReplaceDialog
```

Dialog boxes are either *modal* or *modeless*. A modal dialog box requires that you first close it before you can switch to another window in that same program (you can switch to windows of other programs). By contrast, a modeless dialog box lets you select other windows in the same program (or another program) without first closing the dialog box. The difference in behavior depends on whether the dialog box requires critical data—modal dialog boxes do; modeless dialog boxes do not.

The preceding descendants of class CDialog support modal dialog boxes, except for class CFindReplaceDialog.

The *CDialog* Class

The class CDialog models custom modal and modeless dialog boxes. The class relies on compiled resource files (with the extension .RES) to load the dialog box resource and its controls. Following is the declaration of class CDialog:

```
class CDialog : public CWnd
{
    DECLARE_DYNAMIC(CDialog)
    // Modeless construct
    // (protected since you must subclass to implement a modeless
    // Dialog)
protected:
    CDialog();
    BOOL Create(LPCSTR lpszTemplateName, CWnd* pParentWnd = NULL);
    BOOL Create(UINT nIDTemplate, CWnd* pParentWnd = NULL);
    BOOL CreateIndirect(const void FAR* lpDialogTemplate,
        CWnd* pParentWnd = NULL);
    // Modal construct
public:
    CDialog(LPCSTR lpszTemplateName, CWnd* pParentWnd = NULL);
    CDialog(UINT nIDTemplate, CWnd* pParentWnd = NULL);
    BOOL InitModalIndirect(HGLOBAL hDialogTemplate);
                                    // was CModalDialog::Create()
// Attributes
public:
    void MapDialogRect(LPRECT lpRect) const;
    void SetHelpID(UINT nIDR);
// Operations
public:
    // modal processing
    virtual int DoModal();
    // message processing for modeless
    BOOL IsDialogMessage(LPMSG lpMsg);
    // support for passing on tab control - use 'PostMessage' if
    // needed
    void NextDlgCtrl() const;
    void PrevDlgCtrl() const;
    void GotoDlgCtrl(CWnd* pWndCtrl);
    // default button access
    void SetDefID(UINT nID);
    DWORD GetDefID() const;
    // termination
    void EndDialog(int nResult);
// Overridables (special message map entries)
    virtual BOOL OnInitDialog();
    virtual void OnSetFont(CFont* pFont);
protected:
    virtual void OnOK();
    virtual void OnCancel();
// Implementation
public:
    virtual ~CDialog();
```

```
        virtual BOOL PreTranslateMessage(MSG* pMsg);
        virtual WNDPROC* GetSuperWndProcAddr();
        virtual BOOL OnCmdMsg(UINT nID, int nCode, void* pExtra,
            AFX_CMDHANDLERINFO* pHandlerInfo);
    protected:
        UINT m_nIDHelp; // Help ID (0 for none, see HID_BASE_RESOURCE)
        // parameters for 'DoModal'
        LPCSTR m_lpDialogTemplate;  // name or MAKEINTRESOURCE
        HGLOBAL m_hDialogTemplate;  // Indirect if (lpDialogTemplate ==
                                    //                  NULL)
        CWnd* m_pParentWnd;
    protected:
        //{{AFX_MSG(CDialog)
        afx_msg HBRUSH OnCtlColor(CDC* pDC, CWnd* pWnd, UINT nCtlColor);
        afx_msg LRESULT OnCommandHelp(WPARAM wParam, LPARAM lParam);
        afx_msg LRESULT OnHelpHitTest(WPARAM wParam, LPARAM lParam);
        //}}AFX_MSG
        DECLARE_MESSAGE_MAP()
    };
```

The class CDialog builds dialog boxes using one of three sets of constructors.
Two of these constructors create a dialog box by specifying a resource, either
by name or by integer ID. The third constructor is the default constructor,
which works with one of two versions of the overloaded member function
Create. These functions enable you to create a dialog by specifying a resource
(by name or by integer ID), just like the first two constructors. These two
constructors, and the overloaded versions of function Create, also require the
pointer to the parent window. The default argument of NULL indicates that
the dialog boxes are usually stand-alone windows. The class CDialog also
offers a set of member functions that enable you to set, query, and select the
controls it owns. Moreover, the class offers overridable member functions
that let you customize the initialization of your dialog boxes and their
responses to the OK and Cancel buttons being clicked.

The *CFileDialog* Class

The class CFileDialog models the Open File and Save As common dialog
boxes, which enable you to select a file to open and save. The Visual Workbench uses the Open File and Save As dialog boxes when the Open and Save
As commands, respectively, are chosen from the File menu. Including a class
in the MFC library to model these file I/O dialog boxes enables you to use
them in your own application and to maintain an interface that is consistent
with other Windows applications. The declaration of class CFileDialog is
shown in the following code:

```
class CFileDialog : public CDialog
{
    DECLARE_DYNAMIC(CFileDialog)
```

```
public:
// Attributes
    // open file parameter block
    OPENFILENAME m_ofn;
// Constructors
    CFileDialog(BOOL bOpenFileDialog, // TRUE for FileOpen, FALSE for
                                      //  FileSaveAs
            LPCSTR lpszDefExt = NULL,
            LPCSTR lpszFileName = NULL,
            DWORD dwFlags = OFN_HIDEREADONLY ¦ OFN_OVERWRITEPROMPT,
            LPCSTR lpszFilter = NULL,
            CWnd* pParentWnd = NULL);
// Operations
    virtual int DoModal();
    // Helpers for parsing file name after successful return
    CString GetPathName() const;  // return full path name
    CString GetFileName() const;  // return only filename
    CString GetFileExt() const;   // return only ext
    CString GetFileTitle() const; // return file title
    BOOL GetReadOnlyPref() const; // return TRUE if read only checked
// Overridable callbacks
protected:
    friend UINT CALLBACK AFX_EXPORT _AfxCommDlgProc(HWND, UINT,
                                        WPARAM, LPARAM);
    virtual UINT OnShareViolation(LPCSTR lpszPathName);
    virtual BOOL OnFileNameOK();
    virtual void OnLBSelChangedNotify(UINT nIDBox, UINT iCurSel,
                                UINT nCode);
// Implementation
protected:
    virtual void OnOK();
    virtual void OnCancel();
    BOOL m_bOpenFileDialog; // TRUE for file open, FALSE for file save
    CString m_strFilter;    // filter string
                        // separate fields with '¦', terminate
                        // with '¦¦\0'
    char m_szFileTitle[64];       // contains file title after return
    char m_szFileName[_MAX_PATH]; // contains full path name after
                                // return
};
```

The class CFileDialog creates the file I/O dialog boxes using the constructor.
The parameters of this constructor enable you to specify the following aspects
of either file I/O dialog box:

- The choice between the Open File and Save As dialog boxes

- The default filename extension

- The initial filename, which appears in the File Name edit box

- The set of substring pairs that indicates the file filters appearing in the
  Files list box

■ Other aspects that fine-tune the operations of the dialog box, such as showing the read-only check box and prompting the user to confirm writing new data to an existing file

The CFileDialog class offers a set of helper functions that enable you to query the selection made by the dialog box user. These helper functions return the full path name, filename, file extension, title, and the read-only status of the selected file.

The *CColorDialog* Class

The class CColorDialog supports the color selection dialog box. The declaration of class CColorDialog follows:

```
class CColorDialog : public CDialog
{
    DECLARE_DYNAMIC(CColorDialog)
public:
// Attributes
    // color chooser parameter block
    CHOOSECOLOR m_cc;
// Constructors
    CColorDialog(COLORREF clrInit = 0, DWORD dwFlags = 0,
             CWnd* pParentWnd = NULL);
// Operations
    virtual int DoModal();
    // Set the current color while dialog is displayed
    void SetCurrentColor(COLORREF clr);
    // Helpers for parsing information after successful return
    COLORREF GetColor() const;
    // Custom colors are held here and saved between calls
    static COLORREF AFXAPI_DATA clrSavedCustom[16];
// Overridable callbacks
protected:
    friend UINT CALLBACK AFX_EXPORT _AfxCommDlgProc(HWND, UINT,
                                      WPARAM, LPARAM);
    virtual BOOL OnColorOK();        // validate color
// Implementation
protected:
    virtual void OnOK();
    virtual void OnCancel();
    //{{AFX_MSG(CColorDialog)
    afx_msg HBRUSH OnCtlColor(CDC* pDC, CWnd* pWnd, UINT nCtlColor);
    //}}AFX_MSG
    DECLARE_MESSAGE_MAP()
};
```

The class CColorDialog creates the color selection dialog box using the constructor. The parameters of this constructor enable you to indicate the default color selection, customize the appearance and operation of the dialog box, and specify the parent window. The class provides the helper member function GetColor to return a COLORREF value (which is a 32-bit integer code for the color) representing the selected color.

The *CFontDialog* Class

The class CFontDialog models the font selection dialog box. This dialog box lets you choose the font type name, style, color, and size. The dialog box also includes a view that displays sample text for the currently selected font. The declaration of class CFontDialog is shown in the following code:

```
class CFontDialog : public CDialog
{
    DECLARE_DYNAMIC(CFontDialog)
public:
// Attributes
    // font choosing parameter block
    CHOOSEFONT m_cf;
// Constructors
    CFontDialog(LPLOGFONT lplfInitial = NULL,
        DWORD dwFlags = CF_EFFECTS | CF_SCREENFONTS,
        CDC* pdcPrinter = NULL,
        CWnd* pParentWnd = NULL);
// Operations
    virtual int DoModal();
    // Retrieve the currently selected font while dialog is displayed
    void GetCurrentFont(LPLOGFONT lplf);
    // Helpers for parsing information after successful return
    CString GetFaceName() const;   // return the face name of the font
    CString GetStyleName() const;  // return the style name of the font
    int GetSize() const;           // return the pt size of the font
    COLORREF GetColor() const;     // return the color of the font
    int GetWeight() const;         // return the chosen font weight
    BOOL IsStrikeOut() const;      // return TRUE if strikeout
    BOOL IsUnderline() const;      // return TRUE if underline
    BOOL IsBold() const;           // return TRUE if bold font
    BOOL IsItalic() const;         // return TRUE if italic font
// Implementation
    LOGFONT m_lf; // default LOGFONT to store the info
protected:
    virtual void OnOK();
    virtual void OnCancel();
    char m_szStyleName[64]; // contains style name after return
};
```

The class CFontDialog uses the constructor to create the font selection dialog boxes. The parameters of this constructor enable you to select the initial font, specify the choose-font flags, optionally point to a printer-device context, and specify the parent window. The class offers a set of helper member functions that return the name, face name, style name, point size, color, and weight of the selected font. In addition, some of these helper functions return Boolean values, which indicate whether the selected font is displayed with strikeout, underlining, bold, or italics.

The *CPrintDialog* Class

The class CPrintDialog supports the Print and Print Setup dialog boxes. The class offers a convenient way for your Windows application to be consistent with other Windows applications in prompting the end user to print or to set up to print. Here is the declaration of the class CPrintDialog:

```
class CPrintDialog : public CDialog
{
    DECLARE_DYNAMIC(CPrintDialog)
public:
// Attributes
    // print dialog parameter block (note this is a reference)
#ifdef AFX_CLASS_MODEL
    PRINTDLG FAR& m_pd;
#else
    PRINTDLG& m_pd;
#endif
// Constructors
    CPrintDialog(BOOL bPrintSetupOnly,
        // TRUE for Print Setup, FALSE for Print Dialog
        DWORD dwFlags = PD_ALLPAGES | PD_USEDEVMODECOPIES |
            PD_NOPAGENUMS | PD_HIDEPRINTTOFILE | PD_NOSELECTION,
        CWnd* pParentWnd = NULL);
// Operations
    virtual int DoModal();
    // GetDefaults will not display a dialog but will get
    // device defaults
    BOOL GetDefaults();
    // Helpers for parsing information after successful return
    int GetCopies() const;          // num. copies requested
    BOOL PrintCollate() const;      // TRUE if collate checked
    BOOL PrintSelection() const;    // TRUE if printing selection
    BOOL PrintAll() const;          // TRUE if printing all pages
    BOOL PrintRange() const;        // TRUE if printing page range
    int GetFromPage() const;        // starting page if valid
    int GetToPage() const;          // starting page if valid
    LPDEVMODE GetDevMode() const;   // return DEVMODE
    CString GetDriverName() const;  // return driver name
    CString GetDeviceName() const;  // return device name
    CString GetPortName() const;    // return output port name
    HDC GetPrinterDC() const;       // return HDC (caller must delete)
    // This helper creates a DC based on the DEVNAMES and DEVMODE
    // structures. This DC is returned, but also stored in m_pd.hDC as
    // though it had been returned by CommDlg. It is assumed that any
    // previously obtained DC has been/will be deleted by the user.
    // This may be used without ever invoking the print/print setup
    // dialogs.
    HDC CreatePrinterDC();
// Implementation
private:
    PRINTDLG m_pdActual; // the Print/Print Setup need to share this
protected:
    virtual void OnOK();
    virtual void OnCancel();
    // The following handle the case of print setup... from the print
```

```
                // dialog
#ifdef AFX_CLASS_MODEL
     CPrintDialog(PRINTDLG FAR& pdInit);
#else
     CPrintDialog(PRINTDLG& pdInit);
#endif
     virtual CPrintDialog* AttachOnSetup();
     //{{AFX_MSG(CPrintDialog)
     afx_msg void OnPrintSetup();
     //}}AFX_MSG
     DECLARE_MESSAGE_MAP()
};
```

The class CPrintDialog creates its dialog boxes using the constructor. The parameters of this constructor enable you to specify the following:

- Whether to select the Print or Print Setup dialog box

- Whether to print all pages, only selected text, or a range of pages

- Whether to show or hide the print-to-file check box

The class offers a set of helper member functions that return the number of copies requested, the name of the currently selected printer device, the DEVMODE structure, the name of the currently selected printer driver, the starting page, the ending page, the name of the selected printer port, and the handle to the printer device context.

The *CFindReplaceDialog* Class

The class CFindReplaceDialog supports the Find and Replace dialog boxes. These dialog boxes are modeless and remain in view while text search and replacement takes place. The declaration of class CFindReplaceDialog is shown in the following code:

```
class CFindReplaceDialog : public CDialog
{
     DECLARE_DYNAMIC(CFindReplaceDialog)
public:
// Attributes
     FINDREPLACE m_fr;
// Constructors
     CFindReplaceDialog();
     // NOTE: you must allocate these on the heap.
     // If you do not, you must derive and override PostNcDestroy()
     BOOL Create(BOOL bFindDialogOnly, // TRUE for Find, FALSE for
                                       // FindReplace
             LPCSTR lpszFindWhat,
             LPCSTR lpszReplaceWith = NULL,
             DWORD dwFlags = FR_DOWN,
             CWnd* pParentWnd = NULL);
     // find/replace parameter block
```

```
        static CFindReplaceDialog* PASCAL GetNotifier(LPARAM lParam);
// Operations
        // Helpers for parsing information after successful return
        CString GetReplaceString() const;// get replacement string
        CString GetFindString() const;   // get find string
        BOOL SearchDown() const;         // TRUE if search down, FALSE is up
        BOOL FindNext() const;         // TRUE if command is find next
        BOOL MatchCase() const;        // TRUE if matching case
        BOOL MatchWholeWord() const; // TRUE if matching whole words only
        BOOL ReplaceCurrent() const; // TRUE if replacing current string
        BOOL ReplaceAll() const;       // TRUE if replacing all occurrences
        BOOL IsTerminating() const;  // TRUE if terminating dialog
// Implementation
protected:
        virtual void OnOK();
        virtual void OnCancel();
        virtual void PostNcDestroy();
protected:
        char m_szFindWhat[128];
        char m_szReplaceWith[128];
};
```

The class CFindReplaceDialog creates the Find and Replace dialog boxes using the constructor and the member function Create. The parameters of this function specify various aspects of the dialog box, including:

- Whether to create the Find or Replace dialog box

- The text search string

- The text replacement string

- Whether to set or clear the various check boxes and radio buttons (case sensitivity, whole word, search/replacement direction) that fine-tune the text processing operation

The class provides a set of helper member functions that return the current search string, the current replacement string, the match-case state, the match-whole-word state, and the downward search state. In addition, the class offers member functions that enable you to determine the progress and the modes of finding and replacing text.

The Views Classes

The views classes are descendants of class CWnd and offer a sophisticated interface between the end user and the Windows application. Views enable end users to view and print data, in addition to accepting keyboard or mouse input from the user. The various classes in this group provide different levels of sophistication in data input and output. Views are attached to documents that store the views' data. A document can have multiple views, but a view can only belong to one document. The views in a document can display similar or different kinds of data. For example, one set of views may let you browse through a group of text files; another set of views may let you browse through both text and graphics files.

The following outline shows the subhierarchy of the views classes:

```
+ CView
     + CScrollView
          - CFormView
     - CEditView
```

Typically, you derive your own views classes from the CView, CScrollView, and CFormView classes.

The *CView* Class

The class CView, the root of the views classes, supports the basic view window. The most noted operation supported by a view is printing (including print preview). The declaration of class CView is shown in the following code:

```
class CView : public CWnd
{
    DECLARE_DYNAMIC(CView)
// Constructors
protected:
    CView();
// Attributes
public:
    CDocument* GetDocument() const;
// Operations
public:
    // for standard printing setup (override OnPreparePrinting)
    BOOL DoPreparePrinting(CPrintInfo* pInfo);
// Overridables
public:
    // support for OLE
    virtual BOOL IsSelected(const CObject* pDocItem) const;
protected:
    // Activation
    virtual void OnActivateView(BOOL bActivate, CView* pActivateView,
                    CView* pDeactiveView);
    // General drawing/updating
    virtual void OnInitialUpdate();    // first time after construct
    virtual void OnUpdate(CView* pSender, LPARAM lHint,
                    CObject* pHint);
    virtual void OnDraw(CDC* pDC) = 0;
    virtual void OnPrepareDC(CDC* pDC, CPrintInfo* pInfo = NULL);
    // Printing support
    virtual BOOL OnPreparePrinting(CPrintInfo* pInfo);
            // must override to enable printing and print preview
```

```
            virtual void OnBeginPrinting(CDC* pDC, CPrintInfo* pInfo);
            virtual void OnPrint(CDC* pDC, CPrintInfo* pInfo);
            virtual void OnEndPrinting(CDC* pDC, CPrintInfo* pInfo);
            // Advanced: end print preview mode, move to point
            virtual void OnEndPrintPreview(CDC* pDC, CPrintInfo* pInfo,
                                 POINT point, CPreviewView* pView);
    // Implementation
    public:
            virtual ~CView();
            // Advanced: for implementing custom print preview
            BOOL DoPrintPreview(UINT nIDResource, CView* pPrintView,
                    CRuntimeClass* pPreviewViewClass,
                    CPrintPreviewState* pState);
    protected:
            CDocument* m_pDocument;
            virtual BOOL OnCmdMsg(UINT nID, int nCode, void* pExtra,
                AFX_CMDHANDLERINFO* pHandlerInfo);
            virtual BOOL PreCreateWindow(CREATESTRUCT& cs);
            virtual void PostNcDestroy();
            virtual CScrollBar* GetScrollBarCtrl(int nBar) const;
            // friend classes that call protected CView overridables
            friend class CDocument;
            friend class CPreviewView;
            friend class CFrameWnd;
            friend class CMDIFrameWnd;
            friend class CMDIChildWnd;
            friend class CSplitterWnd;
            //{{AFX_MSG(CView)
            afx_msg int OnCreate(LPCREATESTRUCT lpcs);
            afx_msg void OnDestroy();
            afx_msg void OnPaint();
            afx_msg int OnMouseActivate(CWnd* pDesktopWnd, UINT nHitTest,
                                 UINT message);
            // commands
            afx_msg void OnUpdateSplitCmd(CCmdUI* pCmdUI);
            afx_msg BOOL OnSplitCmd(UINT nID);
            afx_msg void OnUpdateNextPaneMenu(CCmdUI* pCmdUI);
            afx_msg BOOL OnNextPaneCmd(UINT nID);
            // not mapped commands - must be mapped in derived class
            afx_msg void OnFilePrint();
            afx_msg void OnFilePrintPreview();
            //}}AFX_MSG
            DECLARE_MESSAGE_MAP()
    };
```

The class CView (and its descendants) creates a view using the constructor.
The class then uses the member function OnInitialUpdate to complete the
creation of the view. The class offers the member function OnDraw and
OnUpdate to redraw and update the view. The class also offers a number of
message-handling member functions to deal with preparing to print or
preview a document, starting and ending document printing, and ending the
print preview of a document. The class CView declares the classes CDocument,
CPreviewView, CFrameWnd, CMDIFrameWnd, CMDIChildWnd, CSplitterWnd to be

friends. This friendship allows these classes to manipulate the nonpublic members of class CView.

The *CScrollView* Class

The class CScrollView, a descendant of class CView, supports scrollable views. This class conveniently manages the data and operations required to support scrolling a view. Here is the declaration of class CScrollView:

```
class CScrollView : public CView
{
    DECLARE_DYNAMIC(CScrollView)
// Constructors
protected:
    CScrollView();
public:
    static const SIZE AFXAPI_DATA sizeDefault;
        // used to specify default calculated page and line sizes
    // in logical units - call one of the following Set routines
    void SetScaleToFitSize(SIZE sizeTotal);
    void SetScrollSizes(int nMapMode, SIZE sizeTotal,
                const SIZE& sizePage = sizeDefault,
                const SIZE& sizeLine = sizeDefault);
// Attributes
public:
    CPoint GetScrollPosition() const;  // upper corner of scrolling
    CSize GetTotalSize() const;        // logical size
    // for device units
    CPoint GetDeviceScrollPosition() const;
    void GetDeviceScrollSizes(int& nMapMode, SIZE& sizeTotal,
            SIZE& sizePage, SIZE& sizeLine) const;
// Operations
public:
    void ScrollToPosition(POINT pt);     // set upper left position
    void FillOutsideRect(CDC* pDC, CBrush* pBrush);
    void ResizeParentToFit(BOOL bShrinkOnly = TRUE);
// Implementation
protected:
    int m_nMapMode;
    CSize m_totalLog; // total size in logical units (no rounding)
    CSize m_totalDev; // total size in device units
    CSize m_pageDev;  // per page scroll size in device units
    CSize m_lineDev;  // per line scroll size in device units
    BOOL m_bCenter;   // Center output if larger than total size
    BOOL m_bInsideUpdate;  // internal state for OnSize callback
    void CenterOnPoint(CPoint ptCenter);
    void ScrollToDevicePosition(POINT ptDev); // explicit scrolling no
                                              // checking
protected:
    virtual void OnDraw(CDC* pDC) = 0;       // pass on pure virtual
    virtual void OnPrepareDC(CDC* pDC, CPrintInfo* pInfo = NULL);
    void UpdateBars(); // adjust scrollbars etc
    // size with no bars
    BOOL GetTrueClientSize(CSize& size, CSize& sizeSb);
public:
```

```
        virtual ~CScrollView();
        void OnScroll(int nBar, UINT nSBCode, UINT nPos);
        //{{AFX_MSG(CScrollView)
        afx_msg void OnSize(UINT nType, int cx, int cy);
        afx_msg void OnHScroll(UINT nSBCode, UINT nPos,
                        CScrollBar* pScrollBar);
        afx_msg void OnVScroll(UINT nSBCode, UINT nPos,
                        CScrollBar* pScrollBar);
        //}}AFX_MSG
        DECLARE_MESSAGE_MAP()
    };
```

The class CScrollView (and its descendants) creates scrollable views using the constructor, followed by calling the member function SetScrollSizes or SetScaleToFitSize. The class offers member functions to manage assigning and obtaining scrolling-related data and Windows messages (such as OnHScroll and OnVScroll). The functions that manage the scrolling-related data enable you to scroll to a given position, obtain the current scroll position, resize the view to fit in its parent window, obtain the total size of the scroll view, obtain the current scroll position in device units, and obtain the current device-related scroll data.

The *CFormView* Class

The CFormView class supports a view that contains controls. The instances of class CFormView are similar to modeless dialog boxes. The declaration of class CFormView is as follows:

```
    class CFormView : public CScrollView
    {
        DECLARE_DYNAMIC(CFormView)
    // Construction
    protected:      // must derive your own class
        CFormView(LPCSTR lpszTemplateName);
        CFormView(UINT nIDTemplate);
    // Implementation
    protected:
        LPCSTR m_lpszTemplateName;
        CCreateContext* m_pCreateContext;
        virtual void OnDraw(CDC* pDC);       // default does nothing
        virtual void OnInitialUpdate();
        // special case override of child window creation
        virtual BOOL Create(LPCSTR, LPCSTR, DWORD,
            const RECT&, CWnd*, UINT, CCreateContext*);
        virtual BOOL PreTranslateMessage(MSG* pMsg);
        virtual WNDPROC* GetSuperWndProcAddr();
        //{{AFX_MSG(CFormView)
        afx_msg int OnCreate(LPCREATESTRUCT lpcs);
        //}}AFX_MSG
        DECLARE_MESSAGE_MAP()
    };
```

The descendants of class CFormView create form views using either one of the two CFormView constructors. The first constructor has a single parameter that specifies the name of the dialog-template resource used to create the form view. Similarly, the second constructor has a single parameter that identifies the integer code of the dialog-template resource used to create the form view. The descendants of class CFormView also have to override member functions OnDraw, OnUpdate, and OnInitUpdate to accommodate the specific operations of the custom form view.

The *CEditView* Class

The class CEditView, a descendant of class CView, supports the operations of a Windows edit control and adds the ability to print, search for text, replace text, and edit text (using the cut, copy, paste, clear, and undo operations). The declaration of class CEditView is shown in the following code:

```
class CEditView : public CView
{
    DECLARE_DYNCREATE(CEditView)
// Construction
public:
    CEditView();
    static const DWORD dwStyleDefault;
// Attributes
public:
    // CEdit control access
    CEdit& GetEditCtrl() const;
    // presentation attributes
    CFont* GetPrinterFont() const;
    void SetPrinterFont(CFont* pFont);
    void SetTabStops(int nTabStops);
    // other attributes
    void GetSelectedText(CString& strResult) const;
// Operations
public:
    BOOL FindText(LPCSTR lpszFind, BOOL bNext = TRUE,
                    BOOL bCase = TRUE);
    void SerializeRaw(CArchive& ar);
    UINT PrintInsideRect(CDC* pDC, RECT& rectLayout, UINT nIndexStart,
                    UINT nIndexStop);
// Overrideables
protected:
    virtual void OnFindNext(LPCSTR lpszFind, BOOL bNext, BOOL bCase);
    virtual void OnReplaceSel(LPCSTR lpszFind, BOOL bNext, BOOL bCase,
                    LPCSTR lpszReplace);
    virtual void OnReplaceAll(LPCSTR lpszFind, LPCSTR lpszReplace,
                    BOOL bCase);
    virtual void OnTextNotFound(LPCSTR lpszFind);
// Implementation
public:
    virtual ~CEditView();
```

```
        virtual void OnDraw(CDC* pDC);
        virtual void Serialize(CArchive& ar);
        virtual void DeleteContents();
        void ReadFromArchive(CArchive& ar, UINT nLen);
        void WriteToArchive(CArchive& ar);
        static const UINT nMaxSize;    // maximum number of characters
                                       // supported
protected:
        UINT m_segText;                // global segment for edit control data
        int m_nTabStops;               // tab stops in dialog units
        CUIntArray m_aPageStart;       // array of starting pages
        HFONT m_hPrinterFont;          // if NULL, mirror display font
        HFONT m_hMirrorFont;           // font object used when mirroring
        // construction
        WNDPROC* GetSuperWndProcAddr();
        virtual BOOL PreCreateWindow(CREATESTRUCT& cs);
        virtual void CalcWindowRect(LPRECT lpClientRect);
        // printing support
        virtual BOOL OnPreparePrinting(CPrintInfo* pInfo);
        virtual void OnBeginPrinting(CDC* pDC, CPrintInfo* pInfo);
        virtual void OnPrepareDC(CDC* pDC, CPrintInfo* pInfo);
        virtual void OnPrint(CDC* pDC, CPrintInfo* pInfo);
        virtual void OnEndPrinting(CDC* pDC, CPrintInfo* pInfo = NULL);
        BOOL PaginateTo(CDC* pDC, CPrintInfo* pInfo);
        // find & replace support
        void OnEditFindReplace(BOOL bFindOnly);
        BOOL InitializeReplace();
        BOOL SameAsSelected(LPCSTR lpszCompare, BOOL bCase);
        // buffer access
        LPCSTR LockBuffer() const;
        void UnlockBuffer() const;
        UINT GetBufferLength() const;
        //{{AFX_MSG(CEditView)
        afx_msg int OnCreate(LPCREATESTRUCT lpCreateStruct);
        afx_msg void OnPaint();
        afx_msg LRESULT OnSetFont(WPARAM wParam, LPARAM lParam);
        afx_msg void OnUpdateNeedSel(CCmdUI* pCmdUI);
        afx_msg void OnUpdateNeedClip(CCmdUI* pCmdUI);
        afx_msg void OnUpdateNeedText(CCmdUI* pCmdUI);
        afx_msg void OnUpdateNeedFind(CCmdUI* pCmdUI);
        afx_msg void OnUpdateEditUndo(CCmdUI* pCmdUI);
        afx_msg void OnEditChange();
        afx_msg void OnEditCut();
        afx_msg void OnEditCopy();
        afx_msg void OnEditPaste();
        afx_msg void OnEditClear();
        afx_msg void OnEditUndo();
        afx_msg void OnEditSelectAll();
        afx_msg void OnEditFind();
        afx_msg void OnEditReplace();
        afx_msg void OnEditRepeat();
        afx_msg LRESULT OnFindReplaceCmd(WPARAM wParam, LPARAM lParam);
        //}}AFX_MSG
        DECLARE_MESSAGE_MAP()
};
```

Appendixes

The class CEditView creates an edit view by using the default constructor and the inherited member function Create. The class offers several groups of member functions to support operations, including the following:

- Printing-related operations, such as font manipulation, printing, and print-previewing

- Text search and replacement

- Support for cut, copy, paste, clear, and undo text editing operations

The Control Bar Classes

The control bar classes support a special category of controls that mostly appear as bars either at the top or bottom of a window. These bars let you quickly select operations or view the status of a window without using the menus. The following outline shows the subhierarchy of the control bar classes, which are derived from class CWnd:

```
+ CControlBar
     - CToolBar
     - CStatusBar
     - CDialogBar
- CSplitterWnd
```

Typically, control bar windows are child windows of a parent frame window. The control bars usually are siblings either to the client window or to the MDI client of a frame window.

The *CControlBar* Class

The class CControlBar is the base class for the classes CToolBar, CStatusBar, and CDialogBar. The main purpose of class CControlBar is to offer common operations to its descendant classes. The following code shows the declaration of class CControlBar:

```
class CControlBar : public CWnd
{
     DECLARE_DYNAMIC(CControlBar)
// Construction
protected:
     CControlBar();
// Attributes
public:
     int GetCount() const;
     BOOL m_bAutoDelete;
// Implementation
public:
```

```
        virtual ~CControlBar();
protected:
        // info about bar (for status bar and toolbar)
        int m_cxLeftBorder;
        int m_cyTopBorder, m_cyBottomBorder;
        int m_cxDefaultGap;      // default gap value
        CSize m_sizeFixedLayout; // fixed layout size
        // array of elements
        int m_nCount;
        void* m_pData;// m_nCount elements - type depends on derived class
        virtual BOOL PreTranslateMessage(MSG* pMsg);
        virtual void DoPaint(CDC* pDC);
        virtual void OnUpdateCmdUI(CFrameWnd* pTarget,
                            BOOL bDisableIfNoHndler) = 0;
        virtual void PostNcDestroy();
        BOOL AllocElements(int nElements, int cbElement);// one time only
        LRESULT WindowProc(UINT nMsg, WPARAM wParam, LPARAM lParam);
        void CalcInsideRect(CRect& rect) const; // adjusts borders, etc.
        //{{AFX_MSG(CControlBar)
        afx_msg void OnPaint();
        afx_msg HBRUSH OnCtlColor(CDC* pDC, CWnd* pWnd, UINT nCtlColor);
        afx_msg LRESULT OnSizeParent(WPARAM wParam, LPARAM lParam);
        afx_msg int OnCreate(LPCREATESTRUCT lpcs);
        afx_msg LRESULT OnHelpHitTest(WPARAM wParam, LPARAM lParam);
        afx_msg void OnInitialUpdate();
        afx_msg LRESULT OnIdleUpdateCmdUI(WPARAM wParam, LPARAM lParam);
        //}}AFX_MSG
        DECLARE_MESSAGE_MAP()
};
```

The class CControlBar declares a protected constructor, thus preventing a
client application from creating an instance of class CControlBar. Most of
its member functions also are protected and support operations available
through the descendants of class CControlBar. The class declares the public
member function GetCount, which returns the number of non-HWND items on
the control bar object.

The *CToolBar* Class

The class CToolBar supports the toolbar that typically contains bitmapped
buttons that offer shortcuts to various operations. Using the toolbars has
become more popular in recent years. The declaration of class CToolBar is
shown in the following code:

```
class CToolBar : public CControlBar
{
        DECLARE_DYNAMIC(CToolBar)
// Construction.
public:
        CToolBar();
        BOOL Create(CWnd* pParentWnd,
                    DWORD dwStyle = WS_CHILD | WS_VISIBLE | CBRS_TOP,
                    UINT nID = AFX_IDW_TOOLBAR);
        void SetSizes(SIZE sizeButton, SIZE sizeImage);
```

```
                                // button size should be bigger than image
            void SetHeight(int cyHeight);
                        // call after SetSizes, height overrides bitmap size
            BOOL LoadBitmap(LPCSTR lpszResourceName);
            BOOL LoadBitmap(UINT nIDResource);
            BOOL SetButtons(const UINT FAR* lpIDArray, int nIDCount);
                        // lpIDArray can be NULL to allocate empty buttons
// Attributes
public: // standard control bar things
        int CommandToIndex(UINT nIDFind) const;
        UINT GetItemID(int nIndex) const;
        virtual void GetItemRect(int nIndex, LPRECT lpRect) const;
public:
        // for changing button info
        void GetButtonInfo(int nIndex, UINT& nID, UINT& nStyle,
                        int& iImage) const;
        void SetButtonInfo(int nIndex, UINT nID, UINT nStyle, int iImage);
// Implementation
public:
        virtual ~CToolBar();
        inline UINT _GetButtonStyle(int nIndex) const;
        void _SetButtonStyle(int nIndex, UINT nStyle);
protected:
        inline AFX_TBBUTTON* _GetButtonPtr(int nIndex) const;
        void InvalidateButton(int nIndex);
        void CreateMask(int iImage, CPoint offset,
                        BOOL bHilite, BOOL bHiliteShadow);
        // for custom drawing
        struct DrawState
        {
            HBITMAP hbmMono;
            HBITMAP hbmMonoOld;
            HBITMAP hbmOldGlyphs;
        };
        BOOL PrepareDrawButton(DrawState& ds);
        BOOL DrawButton(HDC hdC, int x, int y, int iImage, UINT nStyle);
        void EndDrawButton(DrawState& ds);
protected:
        CSize m_sizeButton;         // size of button
        CSize m_sizeImage;          // size of glyph
        HBITMAP m_hbmImageWell;     // glyphs only
        int m_iButtonCapture;       // index of button with capture (-1 =>
                                    // none)
        HRSRC m_hRsrcImageWell;     // handle to loaded resource for image
                                    // well
        HINSTANCE m_hInstImageWell; // instance handle to load image well
                                    // from
        virtual void DoPaint(CDC* pDC);
        virtual void OnUpdateCmdUI(CFrameWnd* pTarget,
                            BOOL bDisableIfNoHndler);
        virtual int HitTest(CPoint point);
        //{{AFX_MSG(CToolBar)
        afx_msg void OnLButtonDown(UINT nFlags, CPoint point);
        afx_msg void OnMouseMove(UINT nFlags, CPoint point);
        afx_msg void OnLButtonUp(UINT nFlags, CPoint point);
        afx_msg void OnCancelMode();
        afx_msg LRESULT OnHelpHitTest(WPARAM wParam, LPARAM lParam);
```

```
        afx_msg void OnSysColorChange();
        //}}AFX_MSG
        DECLARE_MESSAGE_MAP()
};
```

The class CToolBar creates a toolbar in several steps. These steps begin with
the default constructor and continue with the member functions Create,
LoadBitmap, and SetButtons. The member function Create has parameters that
specify the parent window, style, and ID of the toolbar. The style parameter
enables you to specify whether the toolbar is at the top or the bottom of the
frame window. In addition, the style specifies whether to reposition the
toolbar when you resize the frame window. The function LoadBitmap loads
the bitmap resource, which contains the images for each toolbar button.
The function SetButtons sets the ID and value for each toolbar button.

The class CToolBar also offers member functions to perform tasks such as the
following:

■ Setting the height of the toolbar

■ Setting the sizes and the images of the buttons

■ Setting and getting the button's value, style, and image

■ Setting and getting the commands to specific buttons

The *CStatusBar* Class

The class CStatusBar supports the status bar that appears at the bottom of a
frame window to indicate the state of specific values, such as Insert/Overwrite
mode, page number, line number, the state of the Scroll Lock, Num Lock, and
Caps Lock keys, and so on. In addition, status lines also display short help
message lines explaining the current menu selection. Here is the declaration
of class CStatusBar:

```
class CStatusBar : public CControlBar
{
    DECLARE_DYNAMIC(CStatusBar)
// Construction
public:
    CStatusBar();
    BOOL Create(CWnd* pParentWnd,
            DWORD dwStyle = WS_CHILD | WS_VISIBLE | CBRS_BOTTOM,
            UINT nID = AFX_IDW_STATUS_BAR);
    BOOL SetIndicators(const UINT FAR* lpIDArray, int nIDCount);
// Attributes
public: // standard control bar things
    int CommandToIndex(UINT nIDFind) const;
    UINT GetItemID(int nIndex) const;
```

```
            void GetItemRect(int nIndex, LPRECT lpRect) const;
    public:
            void GetPaneText(int nIndex, CString& s) const;
            BOOL SetPaneText(int nIndex, LPCSTR lpszNewText,
                            BOOL bUpdate = TRUE);
            void GetPaneInfo(int nIndex, UINT& nID, UINT& nStyle,
                            int& cxWidth) const;
            void SetPaneInfo(int nIndex, UINT nID, UINT nStyle, int cxWidth);
    // Implementation
    public:
            virtual ~CStatusBar();
            inline UINT _GetPaneStyle(int nIndex) const;
            void _SetPaneStyle(int nIndex, UINT nStyle);
    protected:
            HFONT m_hFont;
            int m_cxRightBorder;    // right borders (panes get clipped)
            inline AFX_STATUSPANE* _GetPanePtr(int nIndex) const;
            static void PASCAL DrawStatusText(HDC hDC, CRect const& rect,
                    LPCSTR lpszText, UINT nStyle);
            virtual void DoPaint(CDC* pDC);
            virtual void OnUpdateCmdUI(CFrameWnd* pTarget,
                                    BOOL bDisableIfNoHndler);
            //{{AFX_MSG(CStatusBar)
            afx_msg void OnSize(UINT nType, int cx, int cy);
            afx_msg LRESULT OnSetFont(WPARAM wParam, LPARAM lParam);
            afx_msg LRESULT OnGetFont(WPARAM wParam, LPARAM lParam);
            afx_msg LRESULT OnSetText(WPARAM wParam, LPARAM lParam);
            afx_msg LRESULT OnGetText(WPARAM wParam, LPARAM lParam);
            afx_msg LRESULT OnGetTextLength(WPARAM wParam, LPARAM lParam);
            //}}AFX_MSG
            DECLARE_MESSAGE_MAP()
    };
```

The class CStatusBar creates a status bar in three steps. These steps involve the default constructor, the member function Create, and the member function SetIndicators. The function Create has parameters that specify the parent window, style, and ID of the status bar. The style enables you to indicate whether the status bar appears at the top or bottom of the frame window. The function SetIndicators stores the indices of the indicators, which store the information for the panes in the status bar. The CStatusBar class offers member functions which support operations that set and query the text in the panes, set and query the pane information, obtain the display area for a given pane, and obtain the index of a given indicator ID.

The *CDialogBar* Class

The class CDialogBar supplies the operations of a modeless dialog box. Some applications replace a regular modeless dialog box with a dialog bar while the application processes data. The dialog bar maintains only the relevant controls appearing in the initial modeless dialog box. This approach enables the applications to prevent the end user from altering the state or value of critical dialog box controls. The declaration of class `CDialogBar` is shown in the following code:

```
class CDialogBar : public CControlBar
{
    DECLARE_DYNAMIC(CDialogBar)
// Construction
public:
    CDialogBar();
    BOOL Create(CWnd* pParentWnd, LPCSTR lpszTemplateName,
            UINT nStyle, UINT nID);
    BOOL Create(CWnd* pParentWnd, UINT nIDTemplate,
            UINT nStyle, UINT nID);
// Implementation
public:
    virtual ~CDialogBar();
protected:
    virtual void OnUpdateCmdUI(CFrameWnd* pTarget,
                            BOOL bDisableIfNoHndler);
    virtual WNDPROC* GetSuperWndProcAddr();
};
```

The class `CDialogBar` creates the dialog bar using the default constructor and either one of the overloaded versions of member function `Create`. These functions let you specify the parent window, the name of the dialog box resource template (by name or by integer ID number), the style, and the ID of the dialog box. The style parameter enables you to place the dialog bar at the bottom, left, or right side of the frame window. In addition, the style parameter enables you to indicate whether the control bar is repositioned when you resize the parent window.

The *CSplitterWnd* Class

The class `CSplitterWnd`, a descendant of class `CWnd`, supports splitter windows that contain multiple panes. The class `CView` and its descendants support the panes in a splitter window. Often, multiple panes display related data. For example, you can have one pane display text in ASCII characters, while another pane displays the same text in hexadecimal integers. The declaration of class `CSplitterWnd` is as follows:

```
class CSplitterWnd : public CWnd
{
    DECLARE_DYNAMIC(CSplitterWnd)
// Construction
public:
    CSplitterWnd();
    // Create a single view type splitter with multiple splits
    BOOL Create(CWnd* pParentWnd,
            int nMaxRows, int nMaxCols, SIZE sizeMin,
            CCreateContext* pContext,
            DWORD dwStyle = WS_CHILD | WS_VISIBLE |
```

```
                              WS_HSCROLL | WS_VSCROLL | SPLS_DYNAMIC_SPLIT,
                    UINT nID = AFX_IDW_PANE_FIRST);
        // Create a multiple view type splitter with static layout
        BOOL CreateStatic(CWnd* pParentWnd,
                          int nRows, int nCols,
                          DWORD dwStyle = WS_CHILD | WS_VISIBLE,
                          UINT nID = AFX_IDW_PANE_FIRST);
        virtual BOOL CreateView(int row, int col,
            CRuntimeClass* pViewClass, SIZE sizeInit,
            CCreateContext* pContext);
// Attributes
public:
        int GetRowCount() const;
        int GetColumnCount() const;
        // information about a specific row or column
        void GetRowInfo(int row, int& cyCur, int& cyMin) const;
        void SetRowInfo(int row, int cyIdeal, int cyMin);
        void GetColumnInfo(int col, int& cxCur, int& cxMin) const;
        void SetColumnInfo(int col, int cxIdeal, int cxMin);
        // views inside the splitter
        CWnd* GetPane(int row, int col) const;
        BOOL IsChildPane(CWnd* pWnd, int& row, int& col);
        int IdFromRowCol(int row, int col) const;
// Operations
public:
        void RecalcLayout();     // call after changing sizes
// Implementation Overridables
protected:
        // to customize the drawing
        enum ESplitType { splitBox, splitBar, splitIntersection };
        virtual void OnDrawSplitter(CDC* pDC, ESplitType nType,
                                    const CRect& rect);
        virtual void OnInvertTracker(const CRect& rect);
        // for customizing scrollbar regions
        virtual BOOL CreateScrollBarCtrl(DWORD dwStyle, UINT nID);
        // for customizing DYNAMIC_SPLIT behavior
        virtual void DeleteView(int row, int col);
        virtual BOOL SplitRow(int cyBefore);
        virtual BOOL SplitColumn(int cxBefore);
        virtual void DeleteRow(int row);
        virtual void DeleteColumn(int row);
// Implementation
public:
        virtual ~CSplitterWnd();
        // high level command operations - called by default view
        // implementation
        virtual BOOL CanActivateNext(BOOL bPrev = FALSE);
        virtual void ActivateNext(BOOL bPrev = FALSE);
        virtual BOOL DoKeyboardSplit();
        // implementation structure
        struct CRowColInfo
        {
            int nMinSize;       // below that try not to show
            int nIdealSize;     // user set size
            // variable depending on the available size layout
            int nCurSize;       // 0 => invisible, -1 => nonexistant
        };
```

```
protected:
    // customizable implementation attributes (set by constructor or
    // Create)
    CRuntimeClass* m_pDynamicViewClass;
    int m_nMaxRows, m_nMaxCols;
    int m_cxSplitter, m_cySplitter; // size of box or splitter bar
    // current state information
    int m_nRows, m_nCols;
    BOOL m_bHasHScroll, m_bHasVScroll;
    CRowColInfo* m_pColInfo;
    CRowColInfo* m_pRowInfo;
    // Tracking info - only valid when 'm_bTracking' is set
    BOOL m_bTracking, m_bTracking2;
    CPoint m_ptTrackOffset;
    CRect m_rectLimit;
    CRect m_rectTracker, m_rectTracker2;
    int m_htTrack;
    // implementation routines
    BOOL CreateCommon(CWnd* pParentWnd, SIZE sizeMin, DWORD dwStyle,
                      UINT nID);
    void StartTracking(int ht);
    void StopTracking(BOOL bAccept);
    int HitTest(CPoint pt) const;
    void GetInsideRect(CRect& rect) const;
    void GetHitRect(int ht, CRect& rect);
    void TrackRowSize(int y, int row);
    void TrackColumnSize(int x, int col);
    void DrawAllSplitBars(CDC* pDC, int cxInside, int cyInside);
    //{{AFX_MSG(CSplitterWnd)
    afx_msg BOOL OnSetCursor(CWnd* pWnd, UINT nHitTest, UINT message);
    afx_msg void OnMouseMove(UINT nFlags, CPoint pt);
    afx_msg int OnCreate(LPCREATESTRUCT lpcs);
    afx_msg void OnPaint();
    afx_msg void OnLButtonDown(UINT nFlags, CPoint pt);
    afx_msg void OnLButtonDblClk(UINT nFlags, CPoint pt);
    afx_msg void OnLButtonUp(UINT nFlags, CPoint pt);
    afx_msg void OnCancelMode();
    afx_msg void OnKeyDown(UINT nChar, UINT nRepCnt, UINT nFlags);
    afx_msg void OnSize(UINT nType, int cx, int cy);
    afx_msg void OnHScroll(UINT nSBCode, UINT nPos,
                           CScrollBar* pScrollBar);
    afx_msg void OnVScroll(UINT nSBCode, UINT nPos,
                           CScrollBar* pScrollBar);
    //}}AFX_MSG
    DECLARE_MESSAGE_MAP()
};
```

The class CSplitterWnd creates splitter windows using the default constructor
and the member function Create. The parameters of this function specify
the parent window, maximum rows, maximum columns, minimum size,
context-creation data, style, and the unique ID of the splitter window. The
CSplitterWnd class offers the member functions CreateStatic and CreateView
to create a static splitter and a pane in the splitter window, respectively.
The function CreateStatic has parameters that specify the parent window,

number of columns, number of rows, style, and unique ID of the static splitter window. The function `CreateView` has parameters that specify the number of columns, the number of rows, the run-time class information about the new view, the initial view size, and the creation-context data. The class `SplitterWnd` offers member functions to obtain the number of rows and columns, to set and query the row/column information, and to obtain the pane and the pane ID at a specific row/column location.

The Collections Classes

The MFC library is a software tool with the caliber of a commercial third-party package. You cannot build such an extensive library without the support of fundamental data structures, such as arrays, lists, and hash tables. The collections classes offer these structures to be used by the other classes in the MFC library and directly in your applications (including MS-DOS programs). The following outline shows the collections classes:

- CByteArray
- CWordArray
- CDWordArray
- CPtrArray
- CObArray
- CStringArray
- CUIntArray
- CPtrList
- CObList
- CStringList
- CMapWordToPtr
- CMapPtrToWord
- CMapPtrToPtr
- CMapWordToOb
- CMapStringToPtr
- CMapStringToOb
- CMapStringToString

The Arrays Classes

The arrays classes support arrays of bytes, words, double words, unsigned integers, pointers, instances of `CObject` (and their descendants), and `CString` instances. The various integer-type arrays provide a convenient way to store integers, commonly used in numerous Windows API functions and MFC class member functions. The array of pointers offers a valuable structure that stores pointers to different kinds of objects and data items. The array of `CObject` enables you to store instances of `CObject` and its descendants. This array is the closest thing to C++ templates without actually using them. The array of `CString` instances offers a convenient way to store text.

The various kinds of array classes are similar in the way they are declared and operate. As a sample, here is the declaration of the class CStringArray:

```
class CStringArray : public CObject
{
        DECLARE_SERIAL(CStringArray)
public:
// Construction
        CStringArray();
// Attributes
        int GetSize() const;
        int GetUpperBound() const;
        void SetSize(int nNewSize, int nGrowBy = -1);
// Operations
        // Clean up
        void FreeExtra();
        void RemoveAll();
        // Accessing elements
        CString GetAt(int nIndex) const;
        void SetAt(int nIndex, const char* newElement);
        CString& ElementAt(int nIndex);
        // Potentially growing the array
        void SetAtGrow(int nIndex, const char* newElement);
        int Add(const char* newElement);
        // overloaded operator helpers
        CString operator[](int nIndex) const;
        CString& operator[](int nIndex);
        // Operations that move elements around
        void InsertAt(int nIndex, const char* newElement, int nCount = 1);
        void RemoveAt(int nIndex, int nCount = 1);
        void InsertAt(int nStartIndex, CStringArray* pNewArray);
// Implementation
protected:
        CString* m_pData;   // the actual array of data
        int m_nSize;        // # of elements (upperBound - 1)
        int m_nMaxSize;     // max allocated
        int m_nGrowBy;      // grow amount
public:
        ~CStringArray();
        void Serialize(CArchive&);
};
```

The class CStringArray dynamically grows by m_nGrowBy elements and consequently may contain vacant array elements. The class CStringArray offers member functions to remove these vacant elements, to clear the array, to insert new elements, to insert another CStringArray array, to remove elements, to store strings (with the option to expand the array if needed), to recall strings, to obtain the number of occupied elements, and to obtain the upper array bound.

The other array classes have similar operations. The difference between these classes and the class CStringArray is the type of the individual array element.

Appendixes

The List Classes

The collections classes include classes for pointer lists, lists of the instances of CObject (and their descendants), and lists of the instances of CString. The lists of pointers provide a powerful structure to handle a set of dynamic data or a set of objects whose numbers are not known ahead of time. The class CObList manages MFC classes and your own classes which are derived from CObject. The collections classes come close to modeling generic lists. The class CStringList provides a convenient way to manage a list of strings. The three list classes have similar declarations and member functions. As a sample, here is the declaration of class CStringList:

```
class CStringList : public CObject
{
    DECLARE_SERIAL(CStringList)
protected:
    struct CNode
    {
        CNode* pNext;
        CNode* pPrev;
        CString data;
    };
public:
// Construction
    CStringList(int nBlockSize=10);
// Attributes (head and tail)
    // count of elements
    int GetCount() const;
    BOOL IsEmpty() const;
    // peek at head or tail
    CString& GetHead();
    CString GetHead() const;
    CString& GetTail();
    CString GetTail() const;
// Operations
    // get head or tail (and remove it) - don't call on empty list !
    CString RemoveHead();
    CString RemoveTail();
    // add before head or after tail
    POSITION AddHead(const char* newElement);
    POSITION AddTail(const char* newElement);
    // add another list of elements before head or after tail
    void AddHead(CStringList* pNewList);
    void AddTail(CStringList* pNewList);
    // remove all elements
    void RemoveAll();
    // iteration
    POSITION GetHeadPosition() const;
    POSITION GetTailPosition() const;
    CString& GetNext(POSITION& rPosition); // return *Position++
    CString GetNext(POSITION& rPosition) const; // return *Position++
    CString& GetPrev(POSITION& rPosition); // return *Position--
    CString GetPrev(POSITION& rPosition) const; // return *Position--
    // getting/modifying an element at a given position
```

```
        CString& GetAt(POSITION position);
        CString GetAt(POSITION position) const;
        void SetAt(POSITION pos, const char* newElement);
        void RemoveAt(POSITION position);
        // inserting before or after a given position
        POSITION InsertBefore(POSITION position, const char* newElement);
        POSITION InsertAfter(POSITION position, const char* newElement);
        // helper functions (note: O(n) speed)
        POSITION Find(const char* searchValue, POSITION startAfter = NULL)
                                                       const;
                            // defaults to starting at the HEAD
                            // return NULL if not found
        POSITION FindIndex(int nIndex) const;
                        // get the 'nIndex'th element (may return NULL)
// Implementation
protected:
        CNode* m_pNodeHead;
        CNode* m_pNodeTail;
        int m_nCount;
        CNode* m_pNodeFree;
        struct CPlex* m_pBlocks;
        int m_nBlockSize;
        CNode* NewNode(CNode*, CNode*);
        void FreeNode(CNode*);
public:
        ~CStringList();
        void Serialize(CArchive&);
    };
```

The declaration of class CStringList indicates that the list classes implement
lists with indices (which are hybrids between pure lists and arrays). Moreover,
the class offers member functions that enable you to insert and remove data
from the end and tail of the lists. Consequently, the list classes are able to
behave like arrays, stacks, and queues. The class also offers functions to insert
items before or after specific nodes, to remove nodes, to traverse the lists in
either direction, and to search for data items in the list.

The Map Classes

The map classes provide convenient forms of hash tables that use integers,
pointers, and strings as indices. The map classes enable you to map pointers
using WORD-type indices, WORD-type integers using pointer indices, pointers
using pointer indices, CObject instances using WORD-type indices, pointers
using CString instances, CObject instances using CString instances, and
CString instances using other CString instances. The last three kinds of maps
represent more typical hash tables that use strings as indices. The last kind
of map is commonly called a *table*. The declaration and operation of the
three map classes are similar. As a sample, here is the declaration of the class
CMapStringToString:

```
class CMapStringToString : public CObject
{
    DECLARE_SERIAL(CMapStringToString)
protected:
    // Association
    struct CAssoc
    {
        CAssoc* pNext;
        UINT nHashValue;   // needed for efficient iteration
        CString key;
        CString value;
    };
public:
// Construction
    CMapStringToString(int nBlockSize=10);
// Attributes
    // number of elements
    int GetCount() const;
    BOOL IsEmpty() const;
    // Lookup
    BOOL Lookup(const char* key, CString& rValue) const;
// Operations
    // Lookup and add if not there
    CString& operator[](const char* key);
    // add a new (key, value) pair
    void SetAt(const char* key, const char* newValue);
    // removing existing (key, ?) pair
    BOOL RemoveKey(const char* key);
    void RemoveAll();
    // iterating all (key, value) pairs
    POSITION GetStartPosition() const;
    void GetNextAssoc(POSITION& rNextPosition, CString& rKey,
                    CString& rValue) const;
    // advanced features for derived classes
    UINT GetHashTableSize() const;
    void InitHashTable(UINT hashSize);
// Overridables: special non-virtual (see map implementation for
// details)
    // Routine used to user-provided hash keys
    UINT HashKey(const char* key) const;
// Implementation
protected:
    CAssoc** m_pHashTable;
    UINT m_nHashTableSize;
    int m_nCount;
    CAssoc* m_pFreeList;
    struct CPlex* m_pBlocks;
    int m_nBlockSize;
    CAssoc* NewAssoc();
    void FreeAssoc(CAssoc*);
    CAssoc* GetAssocAt(const char*, UINT&) const;
public:
    ~CMapStringToString();
    void Serialize(CArchive&);
};
```

The class `CMapStringToString` provides member functions to support operations such as storing, removing, and searching data in hash tables. In addition, the class offers the functions `GetStartPosition` and `GetNextAssoc` for traversing the hash tables.

Moving from OWL2 to MFC2

Programmers often port Windows programs from one C++ implementation to another. This appendix introduces you to moving Borland C++ 4.0 code (which uses OWL version 2) to Visual C++ 1.x (which uses MFC 2.x). A discussion of all aspects of this kind of conversion could fill an entire book; this appendix introduces you to the conversion process using a hands-on approach. You learn about the following topics:

- General comments about translating Windows applications into MFC programs using OWL

- General guidelines for translating OWL classes into MFC classes

- General guidelines for translating message map macros

- An example of translating a minimal Windows program

- An example of translating a nontrivial Windows program

General Translation Comments

The Borland C++ 4.0 package supports a redesigned and expanded version of OWL that is more similar to MFC than the first version of OWL. The earlier version of OWL was limited and relied on extending the syntax of C++ to map the messages with their associated member functions. Although this language extension made the mapping mechanism simple for the programmer, it did not comply with the proposed C++ standard. In contrast, the various versions of the MFC classes rely on macros to perform the mapping between various Windows messages and their associated member functions. The C++ compiler in Borland C++ 4.0 no longer supports this language extension. Consequently, Borland redesigned the OWL library to use message response macros in a manner similar to Visual C++. OWL2-based programs are generally similar to MFC2-based programs.

Translating Classes

The designers of both the OWL and MFC libraries performed the similar tasks of creating C++ classes that represent intelligent wrappers to the numerous API Windows functions. This process dictated the creation of classes that support general windows, frame windows, MDI windows, controls, dialog boxes, and so on. Certain aspects of encapsulating API Windows functions resulted in the creation of OWL and MFC classes that are very similar to one another. Other aspects offered the class-library designers more freedom and resulted in greater differences between OWL and MFC classes.

It is worth pointing out that the MFC library does not use multiple inheritance (this perhaps shows the attitude of Microsoft programmers toward multiple inheritance)—although the OWL library does use multiple inheritance. The root of most of the classes in the MFC library is class CObject. The root of most classes in the OWL library are classes TEventHandler and TStreamable.

Table D.1 shows a partial list of OWL classes and their MFC counterpart classes. The table shows a general one-to-one correspondence between the OWL and MFC classes. There are exceptions, of course. For example, OWL supports the distinct classes TButton, TCheckBox, and TRadioButton for the pushbutton, check box, radio button, and group (or frame) box controls, respectively. In contrast, the MFC library uses the class CButton to model all these controls—the arguments of the constructor determine the exact kind of control. Another example of the slight differences in class hierarchy are the common dialog box classes. The MFC library uses the class CFileDialog to support the open and save file dialog boxes. The OWL library splits the operations of these dialog boxes among three classes: TOpenSaveDialog, TFileOpenDialog, and TFileSaveDialog. The first class is the parent of the last two. Borland uses the same approach in implementing the classes that support the find and replace dialog boxes.

Table D.1 Comparison of Some Classes in the OWL and MFC Libraries

Class Category	OWL Class	MFC Class
Application	TApplication	CWinApp
General window	TWindow	Cwnd
Frame window	TFrameWindow	CFrameWnd
	TMDIChild	CMDIChild
	TMDIFrame	CMDIFrame
Control	TStatic	CStatic
	TEdit	CEdit
	TButton	CButton
	TCheckBox	CButton
	TRadioButton	CButton
	TGroupBox	CButton
	TListBox	CListBox
	TComboBox	CComboBox
	TScrollBar	CScrollBar
	TSlider	none
	THSlider	none
	TVSlider	none
	TEditSearch	none
	TEditFile	none
	none	CHEdit
	none	CVEdit
	TVbxControl	CVBControl
Dialog box	TDialog	CDialog
	TInputDialog	none
	TFileOpenDialog	CFileDialog
	TFileSaveDialog	CFileDialog
	TChooseColorDialog	CColorDialog
	TChooseFontDialog	CFontDialog
	TPrintDialog	CPrintDialog
	TFindDialog	CFindReplaceDialog
	TReplaceDialog	CFindReplaceDialog
Document/view	TView	CView
	TDocument	CDocument
	TEditView	CEditView
	TListView	CScrollView
	TWindowView	CFormView

Appendixes

Translating Message Map Macros

Both Borland C++ 4.0 and Visual C++ 1.x use macros to map the various
Windows messages to their associated member functions. Both products define a list of standard message macros (called *shorthand message map macros*).

Such macros define, in one swoop, both the handled message and the pre-assigned name of the handler member function. For example, the Visual C++ message macro ON_WM_CLOSE specifies that the member function OnClose handles the Windows message WM_CLOSE. Similarly, Borland C++ uses the macro EV_WM_CLOSE to specify that the member function EvClose handles the Windows message WM_CLOSE. The following general rules apply to shorthand message map macros:

- *Borland C++ 4.0:* Macro EV_WM_*XXXX* specifies that member function Ev*XXXX* handles Windows message WM_*XXXX*

- *Visual C++:* Macro ON_WM_*XXXX* specifies that member function On*XXXX* handles Windows message WM_*XXXX*

Borland C++ classes declare a message map table using the following macro:

```
DECLARE_RESPONSE_TABLE(className);
```

Visual C++ uses the following argument-less macro:

```
DECLARE_MESSAGE_MAP()
```

Borland C++ defines the message map table as follows:

```
DEFINE_RESPONSE_TABLE1(className, parentClassName)
  EV_XXXX,
  ⋮
  EV_YYYY,
END_RESPONSE_TABLE;
```

Notice that the name of the DEFINE_REPONSE_TABLE1 macro ends with the digit 1. This digit indicates that the mapped class has one parent class. In the case of a class with two parent classes, the macro would be named DEFINE_RESPONSE_TABLE2, and so on. Visual C++ defines the message map table as follows:

```
BEGIN_MESSAGE_MAP(className, parentClassName)
  ON_XXXX()
  ⋮
  ON_YYYY()
END_MESSAGE_MAP()
```

The Borland C++ and Visual C++ message maps are similar (taking into account the difference in syntax).

A good number of message map macros in both implementations either bear different names (for example, the Borland C++ EV_REGISTERED and the Visual C++ ON_REGISTERED_MESSAGE macros) or have no equivalent (for example, the Borland C++ macro EV_CHILD_NOTIFY_ALL_CODES).

The next two sections present two programs and offer the listing for the OWL and MFC versions of the programs. The first program is a minimal application whose code enables you to see the differences between the basic OWL and MFC code.

> **Note**
>
> If you declare an OWL-based class using multiple inheritance, you have your work cut out for you. You must redesign the equivalent MFC class using single inheritance. Although this is a rather uncommon case, it can create a lot of work for you.

A Minimal Program Example

This section looks at the source code of a minimal OWL-based Windows program. The program supports the following features:

- Clicking the left mouse button displays a simple message in a message dialog box.

- Clicking the right mouse button causes the program to prompt you to close the application.

- Invoking the Close command from the system menu causes the program to prompt you to close the application.

Listing D.1 shows the source code for the OWL version of the CNVRT1.CPP file, and Listing D.2 shows the source code for the MFC version of the CNVRT1.CPP file. First examine the two listings, and then read the comments that follow.

Listing D.1 Source Code for the OWL Version of the CNVRT1.CPP File

```
/*
  Simple Borland C++ 4.0 program that responds to
  the left and right mouse button clicks
*/

#include <owl\applicat.h>
#include <owl\framewin.h>
```

(continues)

Appendixes

Listing D.1 Continued

```
// declare the custom application class as
// a subclass of TApplication
class TWindowApp : public TApplication
{
public:
  TWindowApp() : TApplication() {}

protected:
  virtual void InitMainWindow();
};

class TMainWindow : public TWindow
{
 public:
    TMainWindow() : TWindow(0, 0, 0) {}

 protected:
    // handle clicking the left mouse button
    void EvLButtonDown(UINT, TPoint&);

    // handle clicking the right mouse button
    void EvRButtonDown(UINT, TPoint&);

    // handle confirming closing the window
    virtual BOOL CanClose();

   // declare the response table
   DECLARE_RESPONSE_TABLE(TMainWindow);

};

DEFINE_RESPONSE_TABLE1(TMainWindow, TWindow)
  EV_WM_LBUTTONDOWN,
  EV_WM_RBUTTONDOWN,
END_RESPONSE_TABLE;

void TMainWindow::EvLButtonDown(UINT, TPoint&)
{
  MessageBox("You clicked the left button!", "Mouse Click Event!",
        MB_OK | MB_ICONEXCLAMATION);
}

void TMainWindow::EvRButtonDown(UINT, TPoint&)
{
  Parent->SendMessage(WM_CLOSE);
}

BOOL TMainWindow::CanClose()
{
  return MessageBox("Want to close this application?",
            "Query", MB_YESNO | MB_ICONQUESTION) == IDYES;
}

void TWindowApp::InitMainWindow()
{
```

```
    MainWindow = new TFrameWindow(0, "Simple Windows Program (BC++ 4.0)",
                    new TMainWindow);
}

int OwlMain(int /* argc */, char** /*argv[] */)
{
  TWindowApp app;
  return app.Run();
}
```

Listing D.2 Source Code for the MFC Version of the CNVRT1.CPP File

```
/*
  Simple Visual C++ 1.5 program that responds to
  the left and right mouse button clicks
*/

#include <afxwin.h>

// Define an application class derived from CWinApp
class CWindowApp : public CWinApp
{
public:
  CWindowApp() : CWinApp() {}

protected:
  virtual BOOL InitInstance();
};

// Define a window class derived from CFrameWnd
class CMainWindow : public CFrameWnd
{
public:
  CMainWindow()
  { Create(NULL, "Simple Windows Program (Visual C++ 1.5)",
                  WS_OVERLAPPEDWINDOW, rectDefault); }

protected:
  // handle the left mouse button click
  afx_msg void OnLButtonDown(UINT nFlags, CPoint point);

  // handle the right mouse button click
  afx_msg void OnRButtonDown(UINT nFlags, CPoint point);

  // handle Closing the window
  afx_msg void OnClose();

  // message map macro
  DECLARE_MESSAGE_MAP()
};
```

(continues)

Listing D.2 Continued

```
void CMainWindow::OnLButtonDown(UINT nFlags, CPoint point)
{
  MessageBox("You clicked the left button!",
             "Mouse Click Event!", MB_OK | MB_ICONEXCLAMATION);
}

void CMainWindow::OnRButtonDown(UINT nFlags, CPoint point)
{
  SendMessage(WM_CLOSE);
}

void CMainWindow::OnClose()
{ if (MessageBox("Want to close this application?",
             "Query", MB_YESNO | MB_ICONQUESTION) == IDYES)
    DestroyWindow();
}

BEGIN_MESSAGE_MAP(CMainWindow, CFrameWnd)
    ON_WM_LBUTTONDOWN()
    ON_WM_RBUTTONDOWN()
    ON_WM_CLOSE()
END_MESSAGE_MAP()

// Construct the CWindowApp's m_pMainWnd data member
BOOL CWindowApp::InitInstance()
{
  m_pMainWnd = new CMainWindow();
  m_pMainWnd->ShowWindow(m_nCmdShow);
  m_pMainWnd->UpdateWindow();
  return TRUE;
}

// application's constructor initializes and runs the app
CWindowApp WindowApp;
```

After comparing the two listings, observe the following aspects in the code:

- Both the OWL and MFC versions declare an application class and a main window class. Both classes have a minimally coded constructor and the member function InitInstance.

- Both programs declare the main window class to have constructors and member functions to handle the confirmation of closing the window and to handle the clicking of the left and right mouse buttons. The OWL functions EvLButtonDown, EvRButtonDown, and CanClose parallel the MFC functions OnLButtonDown, OnRButtonDown, and OnClose, respectively. Notice that the OWL function CanClose does not have a message map macro; the MFC function OnClose does.

■ The OWL version of the program defines the message map macros as follows:

```
DEFINE_RESPONSE_TABLE1(TMainWindow, TWindow)
  EV_WM_LBUTTONDOWN,
  EV_WM_RBUTTONDOWN,
END_RESPONSE_TABLE;
```

The MFC version of the program defines the message map macros as follows:

```
BEGIN_MESSAGE_MAP(CMainWindow, CFrameWnd)
    ON_WM_LBUTTONDOWN()
    ON_WM_RBUTTONDOWN()
    ON_WM_CLOSE()
END_MESSAGE_MAP()
```

■ The statements defining the member functions of the main window in both versions are similar. Notice that the function EvRButtonDown sends the C++ message SendMessage to the parent window and not to itself as is the case for function OnRButtonDown. The difference exists because the OWL application class creates a TFrameWindow instance and inserts in it a dynamic instance of class TMainWindow. The MFC code uses a more direct approach that involves the main window class CMainWindow.

■ The code for the member function InitWindow differs in both versions. The MFC version uses steps that create the main window, show the window, and then update the window.

■ The two program versions differ in triggering the programs. The OWL version uses the function OwlMain, which declares an application instance and then sends it the C++ message Run. The MFC version simply creates an instance of the application class; creation suffices to start the program.

A Working Program Example

This section presents a working program that performs simple floating-point calculations. This program is similar to the DIALOG2.EXE program presented in Chapter 9. The program's window contains the following controls:

■ The Operand1 edit box accepts floating-point numbers or the name of a single-letter variable. In this program, the name of a single-letter variable does not have to begin with the character @.

Appendixes

- The Operator edit box accepts the operators +, –, /, *, or ^ (raising to power).

- The Operand2 edit box accepts floating-point numbers or the name of a single-letter variable.

- The Result edit box displays the result of an operation.

- The Error Message edit box displays any error messages.

- The Variables multi-line edit box displays the contents of the single-letter variables. These variables store floating-point numbers.

- The Calc pushbutton executes the operation that appears in the Operator edit box by using the operands in the Operand1 and Operand2 edit boxes.

- The Store pushbutton stores the value of the Result edit box in the current line of the Variables edit box.

- The Exit pushbutton exits the application.

Now examine the header, resource, and implementation files for both the OWL and MFC versions. Listing D.3 shows the source code for the OWL version of the header file.

Listing D.3 Source Code for the OWL Version of the CNVRT2.H Header File

```
#define ID_CALC_BTN   100
#define ID_STORE_BTN  101
#define ID_EXIT_BTN   102
#define CM_CALC_BTN   103
#define CM_STORE_BTN  104
#define CM_EXIT_BTN   105
#define IDR_BUTTONS   200
#define IDM_EXITMENU  201
```

Listing D.4 shows the MFC version of the header file.

Listing D.4 Source Code for the MFC Version of the CNVRT2.H Header File

```
#define CM_EXIT (WM_USER + 100)
#define ID_CALC_BTN   100
#define ID_STORE_BTN  101
#define ID_EXIT_BTN   102
```

The MFC version of the header file declares the command identifier CM_EXIT and contains fewer ID_*xxxx* constants than the OWL version. The reason for the lack of CM_*xxxx*_BTN constants in the MFC version is that the MFC version can map Windows commands and button-click commands using different macros; the OWL version can't and therefore requires the extra identifiers.

Listing D.5 shows the script for the OWL version of the resource file.

Listing D.5 Script for the OWL Version of the CNVRT2.RC Resource File

```
#include <windows.h>
#include <owl\window.rh>
#include "cnvrt2.h"

IDR_BUTTONS ACCELERATORS
BEGIN
  "c", ID_CALC_BTN, ALT
  "s", ID_STORE_BTN, ALT
  "e", ID_EXIT_BTN, ALT
END

IDM_EXITMENU MENU LOADONCALL MOVEABLE PURE DISCARDABLE
BEGIN
    MENUITEM "E&xit", CM_EXIT
END
```

Listing D.6 shows the script for the MFC version of the resource file.

Listing D.6 Script for the MFC Version of the CNVRT2.RC Resource File

```
#include <windows.h>
#include <afxres.h>
#include "cnvrt2.h"

BUTTONS ACCELERATORS
BEGIN
  "c", ID_CALC_BTN, ALT
  "s", ID_STORE_BTN, ALT
  "e", ID_EXIT_BTN, ALT
END

EXITMENU MENU LOADONCALL MOVEABLE PURE DISCARDABLE
BEGIN
    MENUITEM "E&xit", CM_EXIT
END
```

The resource files in Listings D.5 and D.6 are similar—both declare accelerators and menu resources. The OWL version includes the file OWL\WINDOW.RH to access the predefined constant CM_EXIT. In contrast, the MFC version includes the AFXRES.H header file. The other difference is that the OWL version uses resource names, while the MFC version has integer-constant identifiers for the resources.

Listing D.7 shows the OWL version of the implementation file.

Listing D.7 Source Code for the OWL Version of the CNVRT2.CPP Implementation File

```
/*
  Borland C++ 4.0 program to test the static text, edit box,
  and pushbutton controls. The program uses these controls
  to implement a command-line-oriented calculator application (COCA)
*/

#include <owl\applicat.h>
#include <owl\framewin.h>
#include <owl\static.h>
#include <owl\edit.h>
#include <owl\button.h>
#include <owl\window.rh>
#include "cnvrt2.h"
#include <stdlib.h>
#include <ctype.h>
#include <stdio.h>
#include <math.h>
#include <string.h>

// declare the constants that represent the sizes of the controls
const Wlbl = 100;
const Hlbl = 20;
const LblVertSpacing = 2;
const LblHorzSpacing = 40;
const Wbox = 100;
const Hbox = 30;
const BoxVertSpacing = 30;
const BoxHorzSpacing = 40;
const WLongbox = 4 * (Wbox + BoxHorzSpacing);
const Wvarbox = 2 * Wbox;
const Hvarbox = 3 * Hbox + 20;
const Hbtn = 30;
const Wbtn = 80;
const BtnHorzSpacing = 30;
const MaxEditLen = 30;
const MAX_MEMREG = 26;

// declare the ID_XXXX constants for the edit boxes
#define ID_OPERAND1_EDIT 101
#define ID_OPERATOR_EDIT 102
```

```
#define ID_OPERAND2_EDIT 103
#define ID_RESULT_EDIT    104
#define ID_ERRMSG_EDIT    105
#define ID_VARIABLE_EDIT 106

// declare the custom application class as
// a subclass of TApplication
class TWindowApp : public TApplication
{
public:
  TWindowApp() : TApplication() {}

protected:
  virtual void InitMainWindow();
};

// expand the functionality of TWindow by
// deriving class TMainWindow
class TMainWindow : public TWindow
{
public:

  TMainWindow();

protected:
  // pointers to the controls
  TEdit* Operand1Box;
  TEdit* OperatorBox;
  TEdit* Operand2Box;
  TEdit* ResultBox;
  TEdit* ErrMsgBox;
  TEdit* VariableBox;
  TButton* CalcBtn;
  TButton* StoreBtn;
  TButton* ExitBtn;

  // math error flag
  BOOL InError;

  // coordinates for the Error Message static text area
  int MSG_xulc, MSG_yulc, MSG_xlrc, MSG_ylrc;

  //-------------- member functions -----------------

  // handle clicking the left mouse button
  void EvLButtonDown(UINT, TPoint&);

  // handle the calculation
  void HandleCalcBtn();

  // handle the accelerator key for the Calculate button
  void CMCalcBtn();

  // handle storing the result in a variable
  void HandleStoreBtn();
```

(continues)

Appendixes

Listing D.7 Continued

```
// handle the accelerator key for the Store button
void CMStoreBtn();

// handle exiting the application
void HandleExitBtn();

// handle the accelerator key for the Exit button
void CMExitBtn();

// enable a pushbutton control
void EnableButton(TButton* pBtn)
  { pBtn->EnableWindow(TRUE); }

// disable a pushbutton control
void DisableButton(TButton* pBtn)
  { pBtn->EnableWindow(FALSE); }

// handle closing the window
virtual BOOL CanClose();

// obtain a number of a Variable edit box line
double getVar(int lineNum);

// store a number in the selected text of
// the Variable edit box line
void putVar(double x);

// declare the message map macro
DECLARE_RESPONSE_TABLE(TMainWindow);
};

DEFINE_RESPONSE_TABLE1(TMainWindow, TWindow)
  EV_WM_LBUTTONDOWN,
  EV_COMMAND(ID_CALC_BTN, HandleCalcBtn),
  EV_COMMAND(CM_CALC_BTN, CMCalcBtn),
  EV_COMMAND(ID_STORE_BTN, HandleStoreBtn),
  EV_COMMAND(CM_STORE_BTN, CMStoreBtn),
  EV_COMMAND(ID_EXIT_BTN, HandleExitBtn),
  EV_COMMAND(CM_EXIT_BTN, CMExitBtn),
END_RESPONSE_TABLE;

TMainWindow::TMainWindow() :
        TWindow(0, 0, 0)
{
  char s[81];
  char bigStr[6 * MAX_MEMREG + 1];
  char c;
  int x0 = 20;
  int y0 = 30;
  int x = x0, y = y0;

  // create the first set of labels for the edit boxes
  strcpy(s, "Operand1");
  new TStatic(this, -1, s, x, y, Wlbl, Hlbl, strlen(s));
```

```
strcpy(s, "Operator");
x += Wlbl + LblHorzSpacing;
new TStatic(this, -1, s, x, y, Wlbl, Hlbl, strlen(s));
strcpy(s, "Operand2");
x += Wlbl + LblHorzSpacing;
new TStatic(this, -1, s, x, y, Wlbl, Hlbl, strlen(s));
x += Wlbl + LblHorzSpacing;
strcpy(s, "Result");
new TStatic(this, -1, s, x, y, Wlbl, Hlbl, strlen(s));

// create the operand1, operator, operand2, and result
// edit boxes
x = x0;
y += Hlbl + LblVertSpacing;
Operand1Box = new TEdit(this, ID_OPERAND1_EDIT, "", x, y,
            Wbox, Hbox, 0, FALSE);

// force conversion of letters to uppercase
Operand1Box->Attr.Style |= ES_UPPERCASE;
x += Wbox + BoxHorzSpacing;
OperatorBox = new TEdit(this, ID_OPERATOR_EDIT, "", x, y,
            Wbox, Hbox, 0, FALSE);
x += Wbox + BoxHorzSpacing;
Operand2Box = new TEdit(this, ID_OPERAND2_EDIT, "", x, y,
            Wbox, Hbox, 0, FALSE);
// force conversion of letters to uppercase
Operand2Box->Attr.Style |= ES_UPPERCASE;
x += Wbox + BoxHorzSpacing;
ResultBox = new TEdit(this, ID_RESULT_EDIT, "", x, y, Wbox, Hbox,
            0, FALSE);

// create the static text and edit box for the error message
x = x0;
y += Hbox + BoxVertSpacing;
// store the coordinates for the static text area
MSG_xulc = x;
MSG_yulc = y;
MSG_xlrc = x + Wlbl;
MSG_ylrc = y + Hlbl;
strcpy(s, "Error Message");
new TStatic(this, -1, s, x, y, Wlbl, Hlbl, strlen(s));
y += Hlbl + LblVertSpacing;
ErrMsgBox = new TEdit(this, ID_ERRMSG_EDIT, "", x, y,
          WLongbox, Hbox, 0, FALSE);
// create the static text and edit box for the single-letter
// variable selection
y += Hbox + BoxVertSpacing;
strcpy(s, "Variables");
new TStatic(this, -1, s, x, y, Wlbl, Hlbl, strlen(s));
y += Hlbl + LblVertSpacing;
bigStr[0] = '\0';
// build the initial contents of the Variable edit box
for (c = 'A'; c <= 'Z'; c++) {
  sprintf(s, "%c: 0\r\n", c);
  strcat(bigStr, s);
}
```

(continues)

Listing D.7 Continued

```
        VariableBox = new TEdit(this, ID_VARIABLE_EDIT, bigStr, x, y,
                  Wvarbox, Hvarbox, 0, TRUE);
        // force conversion of letters to uppercase
        VariableBox->Attr.Style |= ES_UPPERCASE;

        // create the Calc pushbutton
        x += Wvarbox + BtnHorzSpacing;
        CalcBtn = new TButton(this, ID_CALC_BTN, "&Calc",
                  x, y, Wbtn, Hbtn, FALSE);

        // create the Store button
        x += Wbtn + BtnHorzSpacing;
        StoreBtn = new TButton(this, ID_STORE_BTN, "&Store",
                    x, y, Wbtn, Hbtn, FALSE);

        // Create the Exit button
        x += Wbtn + BtnHorzSpacing;
        ExitBtn = new TButton(this, ID_EXIT_BTN, "&Exit",
                    x, y, Wbtn, Hbtn, FALSE);

        // clear the InError flag
        InError = FALSE;

        UpdateWindow();
    }

    void TMainWindow::EvLButtonDown(UINT, TPoint& point)
    {
      if (point.x >= MSG_xulc && point.x <= MSG_xlrc &&
          point.y >= MSG_yulc && point.y <= MSG_ylrc) {
          ErrMsgBox->Clear();
          // enable the Store button
          EnableButton(StoreBtn);
      }
    }

    void TMainWindow::HandleCalcBtn()
    {
      double x, y, z;
      char opStr[MaxEditLen+1];
      char s[MaxEditLen+1];

      // obtain the string in the Operand1 edit box
      Operand1Box->GetText(s, MaxEditLen);
      // does the Operand1Box contain the name
      // of a single-letter variable?
      if (isalpha(s[0]))
        // obtain value from the Variable edit control
        x = getVar(s[0] - 'A');
      else
        // convert the string in the edit box
        x = atof(s);

      // obtain the string in the Operand2 edit box
      Operand2Box->GetText(s, MaxEditLen);
```

```
// does the Operand2Box contain the name
// of a single-letter variable?
if (isalpha(s[0]))
  // obtain value from the Variable edit control
    y = getVar(s[0] - 'A');
else
    // convert the string in the edit box
  y = atof(s);

// obtain the string in the Operator edit box
OperatorBox->GetText(opStr, MaxEditLen);

// clear the error message box
ErrMsgBox->Clear();
InError = FALSE;

// determine the requested operation
if (strcmp(opStr, "+") == 0)
  z = x + y;
else if (strcmp(opStr, "-") == 0)
  z = x - y;
else if (strcmp(opStr, "*") == 0)
  z = x * y;
else if (strcmp(opStr, "/") == 0) {
  if (y != 0)
      z = x / y;
  else {
    z = 0;
    InError = TRUE;
    ErrMsgBox->SetText("Division-by-zero error");
  }
}
else if (strcmp(opStr, "^") == 0) {
  if (x > 0)
    z = exp(y * log(x));
  else {
    InError = TRUE;
      ErrMsgBox->SetText(
    "Cannot raise the power of a negative number");
    }
}
else {
  InError = TRUE;
  ErrMsgBox->SetText("Invalid operator");
}
// display the result if no error has occurred
if (!InError) {
  sprintf(s, "%g", z);
  ResultBox->SetText(s);
  // enable the Store button
  EnableButton(StoreBtn);
}
else
  // disable the Store button
  DisableButton(StoreBtn);
}
```

Appendixes

(continues)

Listing D.7 Continued

```
void TMainWindow::CMCalcBtn()
{
  HandleCalcBtn();
}

void TMainWindow::HandleStoreBtn()
{
  char result[MaxEditLen+1];

  // get the string in the Result edit box
  ResultBox->GetText(result, MaxEditLen);

  // store the result in the selected text of
  // the Variable edit box
  putVar(atof(result));
}

void TMainWindow::CMStoreBtn()
{
  HandleStoreBtn();
}

void TMainWindow::HandleExitBtn()
{
  // send a WM_CLOSE message to the parent window
  Parent->SendMessage(WM_CLOSE);
}

void TMainWindow::CMExitBtn()
{
  // send a WM_CLOSE message to the parent window
  Parent->SendMessage(WM_CLOSE);
}

double TMainWindow::getVar(int lineNum)
{
  int lineSize;
  char s[MaxEditLen+1];

  if (lineNum >= MAX_MEMREG) return 0;
  // get the size of the target line
  lineSize = VariableBox->GetLineLength(lineNum);
  // get the line
  VariableBox->GetLine(s, lineSize+1, lineNum);
  // delete the first three characters
  strcpy(s, (s+3));
  // return the number stored in the target line
  return atof(s);
}

void TMainWindow::putVar(double x)
{
```

```
      UINT startPos, endPos;
      int lineNum;
      int lineSize;
      char s[MaxEditLen+1];

      // locate the character position of the cursor
      VariableBox->GetSelection(startPos, endPos);
      // turn off the selected text
      if (startPos != endPos)
        VariableBox->SetSelection(startPos, startPos);
      // get the line number where the cursor is located
      lineNum = VariableBox->GetLineFromPos(startPos);
      // get the line size of line lineNum
      lineSize = VariableBox->GetLineLength(lineNum);
      // obtain the text of line lineNum
      VariableBox->GetLine(s, lineSize+1, lineNum);
      // delete line lineNum
      VariableBox->DeleteLine(lineNum);
      // build the new text line
      sprintf(s, "%c: %g\r\n", s[0], x);
      // insert it
      VariableBox->Insert(s);
    }

    BOOL TMainWindow::CanClose()
    {
      return MessageBox("Want to close this application?",
                "Query", MB_YESNO | MB_ICONQUESTION) == IDYES;
    }

    void TWindowApp::InitMainWindow()
    {
      MainWindow = new TFrameWindow(0,
            "Command-Oriented Calculator Application (COCA)",
            new TMainWindow);
      // load the keystroke resources
      MainWindow->Attr.AccelTable = IDR_BUTTONS;
      // load the menu resource
      MainWindow->AssignMenu(TResID(IDM_EXITMENU));
      // enable the keyboard handler
      MainWindow->EnableKBHandler();
    }

    int OwlMain(int /* argc */, char** /*argv[] */)
    {
      TWindowApp app;
      return app.Run();
    }
```

Listing D.8 shows the MFC version of this file.

Listing D.8 Source Code for the MFC Version of the CNVRT2.CPP Implementation File

```
/*
  Visual C++ 1.5 program to test the static text, edit box,
  and pushbutton controls. The program uses these controls
  to implement a command-line-oriented calculator application (COCA)
*/

#include <stdlib.h>
#include <ctype.h>
#include <stdio.h>
#include <math.h>
#include <string.h>
#include <afxwin.h>
#include "cnvrt2.h"

// declare the constants that represent the sizes of the controls
const Wlbl = 100;
const Hlbl = 20;
const LblVertSpacing = 5;
const LblHorzSpacing = 40;
const Wbox = 100;
const Hbox = 30;
const BoxVertSpacing = 40;
const BoxHorzSpacing = 40;
const WLongbox = 4 * (Wbox + BoxHorzSpacing);
const Wvarbox = 2 * Wbox;
const Hvarbox = 3 * Hbox;
const Hbtn = 30;
const Wbtn = 80;
const BtnHorzSpacing = 30;
const MaxEditLen = 30;
const MAX_MEMREG = 26;

// declare the ID_XXXX constants for the edit boxes
#define ID_OPERAND1_EDIT 101
#define ID_OPERATOR_EDIT 102
#define ID_OPERAND2_EDIT 103
#define ID_RESULT_EDIT 104
#define ID_ERRMSG_EDIT 105
#define ID_VARIABLE_EDIT 106

class CxButton : public CButton
{
public:
    BOOL Create(const char FAR* lpCaption, const RECT& rect,
            CWnd* pParentWnd, UINT nID, BOOL bIsDefault);

};

class CxEdit : public CEdit
{
public:
```

```
  // get an ASCIIZ string from a line
  BOOL GetLine(LPSTR lpString, int nStrSize, int nLineNumber);
  // get the line length given a line number
  int GetLineLength(int nLineNumber);

};

class CWindowApp : public CWinApp
{
public:
  CWindowApp() : CWinApp() {}

protected:
    virtual BOOL InitInstance();
};

// expand the functionality of CFrameWnd by deriving
// class CMainWindow
class CMainWindow : public CFrameWnd
{
public:

  CMainWindow();

  ~CMainWindow();

protected:
  // declare the pointers to the various controls
  // first, the edit box controls
  CEdit* Operand1Box;
  CEdit* OperatorBox;
  CEdit* Operand2Box;
  CEdit* ResultBox;
  CEdit* ErrMsgBox;
  CxEdit* VariableBox;
  // then the static text controls
  CStatic* Operand1Txt;
  CStatic* OperatorTxt;
  CStatic* Operand2Txt;
  CStatic* ResultTxt;
  CStatic* ErrMsgTxt;
  CStatic* VariableTxt;
  // then the pushbuttons
  CxButton* CalcBtn;
  CxButton* StoreBtn;
  CxButton* ExitBtn;
  // math error flag
  BOOL bInError;
  // coordinates for the Error Message static text area
  int nXulc, nYulc, nXlrc, nYlrc;

  // handle clicking the left mouse button
  afx_msg void OnLButtonDown(UINT nFlags, CPoint point);
  // handle the calculation
  afx_msg void HandleCalcBtn();
```

(continues)

Appendixes

Listing D.8 Continued

```
    // handle the calculation
    afx_msg void CMCalc() { HandleCalcBtn(); }
    // handle storing the result in a variable
    afx_msg void HandleStoreBtn();
    // handle storing the result in a variable
    afx_msg void CMStore() { HandleStoreBtn(); }
    // handle exiting the application
    afx_msg void HandleExitBtn()
      { SendMessage(WM_CLOSE); }
    // handle exiting the application
    afx_msg void CMExit() { SendMessage(WM_CLOSE); }
    // handle exiting the application
    afx_msg void OnExit() { SendMessage(WM_CLOSE); }
    // enable a pushbutton control
    virtual void EnableButton(CxButton* pBtn)
      { pBtn->EnableWindow( TRUE); }
    // disable a pushbutton control
    virtual void DisableButton(CxButton* pBtn)
      { pBtn->EnableWindow(FALSE); }
    // handle creating the controls
    afx_msg int OnCreate(LPCREATESTRUCT lpCS);
    // handle closing the window
    afx_msg void OnClose();
    // return a reference to member r based on individual
    // coordinates and dimensions
    void makeRect(int X, int Y, int W, int H, CRect& r);
    // obtain a number of a Variable edit box line
    double getVar(int lineNum);
    // store a number in the selected text of
    // the Variable edit box line
    void putVar(double x);

    // declare message map macro
    DECLARE_MESSAGE_MAP();
};

BOOL CxButton::Create(const char FAR* lpCaption, const RECT& rect,
            CWnd* pParentWnd, UINT nID, BOOL bIsDefault)

{
  DWORD dwBtnStyle = (bIsDefault == TRUE) ?
            BS_DEFPUSHBUTTON : BS_PUSHBUTTON;

  return CButton::Create(lpCaption, WS_CHILD | WS_VISIBLE |
            WS_TABSTOP | dwBtnStyle, rect, pParentWnd, nID);
}

BOOL CxEdit::GetLine(LPSTR lpString, int nStrSize,
                    int nLineNumber)
{
  int nCopyCount;
  BOOL bResult;

  if (nStrSize <= 0)
    return FALSE;
```

```
    bResult = (nStrSize >= GetLineLength(nLineNumber) + 1) ? TRUE
                                                           : FALSE;
    if (nStrSize == 1)
    {
      lpString[0] = '\0';
      return bResult;
    }
    ((WORD FAR *)lpString)[0] = nStrSize;
    nCopyCount = (WORD)(SendMessage(EM_GETLINE, nLineNumber,
                                    long(lpString)));
    if (nCopyCount)
    {
      // Windows returns non-null-terminated string
      lpString[nCopyCount] = '\0';
      return bResult;
    }
    return FALSE;
}

int CxEdit::GetLineLength(int nLineNumber)
{
  int nStartPos = -1;

  if (nLineNumber > -1)
    nStartPos = LineIndex(nLineNumber);
  return (WORD) SendMessage(EM_LINELENGTH, nStartPos);
}

CMainWindow::CMainWindow()
{
  // load accelerator resources
  LoadAccelTable("BUTTONS");
  // create the window
  Create(NULL,
    "Command-Oriented Calculator Application (COCA)",
    WS_OVERLAPPEDWINDOW | WS_MAXIMIZE,
        rectDefault, NULL, "EXITMENU");
  // clear the bInError flag
  bInError = FALSE;
}

int CMainWindow::OnCreate(LPCREATESTRUCT lpCS)
{
  char s[81];
  char bigStr[6 * MAX_MEMREG + 1];
  char chC;
  int x0 = 20;
  int y0 = 30;
  int x = x0, y = y0;
  CRect r;
  DWORD dwStaticStyle = WS_CHILD | WS_VISIBLE | SS_LEFT;
  DWORD dwBoxStyle = WS_CHILD | WS_VISIBLE | WS_TABSTOP |
                     WS_BORDER | ES_LEFT | ES_AUTOHSCROLL |
                     ES_UPPERCASE;
  // create the first set of labels for the edit boxes
  makeRect(x, y, Wlbl, Hlbl, r);
```

Appendixes

(continues)

Listing D.8 Continued

```
Operand1Txt = new CStatic();
Operand1Txt->Create("Operand1", dwStaticStyle, r, this);
strcpy(s, "Operator");
x += Wlbl + LblHorzSpacing;
makeRect(x, y, Wlbl, Hlbl, r);
OperatorTxt = new CStatic();
OperatorTxt->Create(s, dwStaticStyle, r, this);
x += Wlbl + LblHorzSpacing;
makeRect(x, y, Wlbl, Hlbl, r);
Operand2Txt = new CStatic();
Operand2Txt->Create("Operand2", dwStaticStyle, r, this);
x += Wlbl + LblHorzSpacing;
makeRect(x, y, Wlbl, Hlbl, r);
ResultTxt = new CStatic();
ResultTxt->Create("Result", dwStaticStyle, r, this);
// create the operand1, operator, operand2, and result
// edit boxes
x = x0;
y += Hlbl + LblVertSpacing;
makeRect(x, y, Wbox, Hbox, r);
Operand1Box = new CEdit();
Operand1Box->Create(dwBoxStyle, r, this, ID_OPERAND1_EDIT);
Operand1Box->LimitText(); // set no limit for text
x += Wbox + BoxHorzSpacing;
makeRect(x, y, Wbox, Hbox, r);
OperatorBox = new CEdit();
OperatorBox->Create(dwBoxStyle, r, this, ID_OPERATOR_EDIT);
OperatorBox->LimitText(); // set no limit for text
x += Wbox + BoxHorzSpacing;
makeRect(x, y, Wbox, Hbox, r);
Operand2Box = new CEdit();
Operand2Box->Create(dwBoxStyle, r, this, ID_OPERAND2_EDIT);
Operand2Box->LimitText(); // set no limit for text
x += Wbox + BoxHorzSpacing;
makeRect(x, y, Wbox, Hbox, r);
ResultBox = new CEdit();
ResultBox->Create(dwBoxStyle, r, this, ID_RESULT_EDIT);
ResultBox->LimitText(); // set no limit for text
// create the static text and edit box for the error message
x = x0;
y += Hbox + BoxVertSpacing;
// store the coordinates for the static text area
nXulc = x;
nYulc = y;
nXlrc = x + Wlbl;
nYlrc = y + Hlbl;
makeRect(x, y, Wlbl, Hlbl, r);
ErrMsgTxt = new CStatic();
ErrMsgTxt->Create("Error Message", dwStaticStyle, r, this);
y += Hlbl + LblVertSpacing;
makeRect(x, y, WLongbox, Hbox, r);
ErrMsgBox = new CEdit();
ErrMsgBox->Create(dwBoxStyle, r, this, ID_ERRMSG_EDIT);
ErrMsgBox->LimitText(); // set no limit for text
```

```
  // create the static text and edit box for the single-letter
  // variable selection
  y += Hbox + BoxVertSpacing;
  makeRect(x, y, Wlbl, Hlbl, r);
  VariableTxt = new CStatic();
  VariableTxt->Create("Variables", dwStaticStyle, r, this);
  y += Hlbl + LblVertSpacing;
  bigStr[0] = '\0';
  // build the initial contents of the Variable edit box
  for (chC = 'A'; chC <= 'Z'; chC++) {
    sprintf(s, "%c: 0\r\n", chC);
    strcat(bigStr, s);
  }
  makeRect(x, y, Wvarbox, Hvarbox, r);
  VariableBox = new CxEdit();
  VariableBox->Create(dwBoxStyle | ES_MULTI-LINE | WS_HSCROLL
              | WS_VSCROLL | ES_AUTOVSCROLL,
                      r, this, ID_VARIABLE_EDIT);
  VariableBox->LimitText(); // set no limit for text
  VariableBox->SetWindowText(bigStr);
  // create the Calc pushbutton
  x += Wvarbox + BtnHorzSpacing;
  CalcBtn = new CxButton();
  makeRect(x, y, Wbtn, Hbtn, r);
  CalcBtn->Create("&Calc", r, this, ID_CALC_BTN, TRUE);
  // create the Store button
  x += Wbtn + BtnHorzSpacing;
  makeRect(x, y, Wbtn, Hbtn, r);
  StoreBtn = new CxButton();
  StoreBtn->Create("&Store", r, this, ID_STORE_BTN, FALSE);
  // Create the Exit button
  x += Wbtn + BtnHorzSpacing;
  makeRect(x, y, Wbtn, Hbtn, r);
  ExitBtn = new CxButton();
  ExitBtn->Create("&Exit", r, this, ID_EXIT_BTN, FALSE);
  return CFrameWnd::OnCreate(lpCS);
}

CMainWindow::~CMainWindow()
{
  // delete the controls
  delete Operand1Box;
  delete OperatorBox;
  delete Operand2Box;
  delete ResultBox;
  delete ErrMsgBox;
  delete VariableBox;
  delete Operand1Txt;
  delete OperatorTxt;
  delete Operand2Txt;
  delete ResultTxt;
  delete ErrMsgTxt;
  delete VariableTxt;
  delete CalcBtn;
  delete StoreBtn;
  delete ExitBtn;
}
```

(continues)

Listing D.8 Continued

```cpp
void CMainWindow::OnLButtonDown(UINT nFlags, CPoint point)
{
  int x = point.x;
  int y = point.y;

  if (x >= nXulc && x <= nXlrc &&
      y >= nYulc && y <= nYlrc) {
      ErrMsgBox->SetWindowText("");
      EnableButton(StoreBtn);
  }
}

void CMainWindow::HandleCalcBtn()
{
  double x, y, z;
  char opStr[MaxEditLen+1];
  char s[MaxEditLen+1];

  // obtain the string in the Operand1 edit box
  Operand1Box->GetWindowText(s, MaxEditLen);
  // does the Operand1Box contain the name
  // of a single-letter variable?
  if (isalpha(s[0]))
    // obtain value from the Variable edit control
    x = getVar(s[0] - 'A');
  else
    // convert the string in the edit box
    x = atof(s);

  // obtain the string in the Operand2 edit box
  Operand2Box->GetWindowText(s, MaxEditLen);
  // does the Operand2Box contain the name
  // of a single-letter variable?
  if (isalpha(s[0]))
    // obtain value from the Variable edit control
    y = getVar(s[0] - 'A');
  else
    // convert the string in the edit box
    y = atof(s);

  // obtain the string in the Operator edit box
  OperatorBox->GetWindowText(opStr, MaxEditLen);
  // clear the error message box
  ErrMsgBox->SetWindowText("");
  bInError = FALSE;
  // determine the requested operation
  if (strcmp(opStr, "+") == 0)
    z = x + y;
  else if (strcmp(opStr, "-") == 0)
    z = x - y;
  else if (strcmp(opStr, "*") == 0)
    z = x * y;
  else if (strcmp(opStr, "/") == 0) {
    if (y != 0)
```

```
      z = x / y;
    else {
      z = 0;
      bInError = TRUE;
      ErrMsgBox->SetWindowText("Division-by-zero error");
    }
  }
  else if (strcmp(opStr, "^") == 0) {
    if (x > 0)
      z = exp(y * log(x));
    else {
      bInError = TRUE;
      ErrMsgBox->SetWindowText(
        "Cannot raise the power of a negative number");
    }
  }
  else {
    bInError = TRUE;
    ErrMsgBox->SetWindowText("Invalid operator");
  }
  // display the result if no error has occurred
  if (!bInError) {
    sprintf(s, "%g", z);
    ResultBox->SetWindowText(s);
    // enable the Store button
    EnableButton(StoreBtn);
  }
  else
    // disable the Store button
    DisableButton(StoreBtn);
}

void CMainWindow::HandleStoreBtn()
{
  char result[MaxEditLen+1];

  // get the string in the Result edit box
  ResultBox->GetWindowText(result, MaxEditLen);
  // store the result in the selected text of
  // the Variable edit box
  putVar(atof(result));
}

void CMainWindow::makeRect(int x, int y, int nW,
                           int nH, CRect& r)
{
  r.top = y;
  r.left = x;
  r.bottom = y + nH;
  r.right = x + nW;
}

double CMainWindow::getVar(int nLineNum)
{
  int nLineSize;
  char s[MaxEditLen+1];
```

(continues)

Listing D.8 Continued

```
    if (nLineNum >= MAX_MEMREG) return 0;
    // get the size of the target line
    nLineSize = VariableBox->GetLineLength(nLineNum);
    // get the line
    VariableBox->GetLine(s, nLineSize, nLineNum);
    // delete the first three characters
    strcpy(s, (s+3));
    // return the number stored in the target line
    return atof(s);
}

void CMainWindow::putVar(double x)
{
    DWORD dwSelPos;
    WORD wStartPos, wEndPos;
    int nLineNum;
    int nLineSize;
    char s[MaxEditLen+1];

    // locate the character position of the cursor
    dwSelPos = VariableBox->GetSel();
    wStartPos = LOWORD(dwSelPos);
    wEndPos = HIWORD(dwSelPos);
    // turn off the selected text
    if (wStartPos != wEndPos) {
        dwSelPos = MAKELONG(wStartPos, wStartPos);
        VariableBox->SetSel(dwSelPos);
    }
    // get the line number where the cursor is located
    nLineNum = VariableBox->LineFromChar(-1);
    // get the line size of line lineNum
    nLineSize = VariableBox->GetLineLength(nLineNum);
    // obtain the text of line lineNum
    VariableBox->GetLine(s, nLineSize, nLineNum);
    // build the new text line
    sprintf(s, "%c: %g", s[0], x);
    // get the character positions for the deleted line
    wStartPos = (WORD) (VariableBox->LineIndex(-1));
    wEndPos = (WORD) (wStartPos + VariableBox->LineLength(-1));
    // select the current line
    dwSelPos = MAKELONG(wStartPos, wEndPos);
    VariableBox->SetSel(dwSelPos);
    // replace the current line with the new line
    VariableBox->ReplaceSel(s);
}

void CMainWindow::OnClose()
{
    if (MessageBox("Want to close this application",
                   "Query", MB_YESNO | MB_ICONQUESTION) == IDYES)
        DestroyWindow();
}
```

```
BEGIN_MESSAGE_MAP(CMainWindow, CFrameWnd)
    ON_WM_LBUTTONDOWN()
    ON_BN_CLICKED(ID_CALC_BTN, HandleCalcBtn)
    ON_COMMAND(ID_CALC_BTN, CMCalc)
    ON_BN_CLICKED(ID_STORE_BTN, HandleStoreBtn)
    ON_COMMAND(ID_STORE_BTN, CMStore)
    ON_BN_CLICKED(ID_EXIT_BTN, HandleExitBtn)
    ON_COMMAND(ID_EXIT_BTN, CMExit)
    ON_COMMAND(CM_EXIT, OnExit)
    ON_WM_CREATE()
    ON_WM_CLOSE()
END_MESSAGE_MAP()

// Construct the CWindowApp's m_pMainWnd data member
BOOL CWindowApp::InitInstance()
{
  m_pMainWnd = new CMainWindow();
  m_pMainWnd->ShowWindow(m_nCmdShow);
  m_pMainWnd->UpdateWindow();
  return TRUE;
}

// application's constructor initializes and runs the app
CWindowApp WindowApp;
```

In comparing the implementation files for the OWL and MFC versions, notice the following aspects:

■ The OWL version has a longer list of #include directives than the MFC version. The MFC version can include the declarations of the various control classes by including just the AFXWIN.H header file.

■ The two listings declare similar sets of global constants.

■ The MFC version contains the declaration of classes CxButton and CxEdit. The class CxButton supports the specialized creation of pushbuttons. The class CxEdit supports important multi-line edit operations not available in the MFC class CEdit.

■ Both versions declare an application class with a minimally coded constructor and the member function InitInstance.

■ Both versions declare a main window class. The MFC version declares a constructor and more data members to access the static text controls.

■ The MFC version uses the destructor to remove the dynamic instances of all the controls. The OWL version performs this task automatically (that's why the OWL class TMainWindow declares members only to access the static text and pushbutton controls).

■ The two versions declare a similar set of member functions for the main window class. Notice that the OWL version has separate functions to handle the accelerators' commands and their counterpart pushbutton commands. This is because the OWL message map macros for resource commands and pushbutton-click commands both use EV_COMMAND. In contrast, the MFC version uses EV_COMMAND and EV_BN_CLICKED for the resource commands and pushbutton-click commands, respectively. These macros allow MFC to use the same message ID and member function in the EV_COMMAND and EV_BN_CLICKED macros.

■ The OWL version creates each dynamic control using a single statement involving the operator new and the constructor for the control. The MFC version first creates an empty dynamic instance and then sends the C++ message Create to that instance to define it.

■ The OWL and MFC versions start the program in the same manners presented for the preceding program. The OWL version uses separate statements to specify the accelerators and menu resources. The MFC version performs these tasks by supplying the inherited member function Create with the name of the accelerators and menu resources.

Index

Symbols

C

M

GO AHEAD. PLUG YOURSELF INTO
PRENTICE HALL COMPUTER PUBLISHING.
Introducing the PHCP Forum on CompuServe®

Yes, it's true. Now, you can have CompuServe access to the same professional, friendly folks who have made computers easier for years. On the PHCP Forum, you'll find additional information on the topics covered by every PHCP imprint—including Que, Sams Publishing, New Riders Publishing, Alpha Books, Brady Books, Hayden Books, and Adobe Press. In addition, you'll be able to receive technical support and disk updates for the software produced by Que Software and Paramount Interactive, a division of the Paramount Technology Group. It's a great way to supplement the best information in the business.

WHAT CAN YOU DO ON THE PHCP FORUM?

Play an important role in the publishing process—and make our books better while you make your work easier:

- Leave messages and ask questions about PHCP books and software—you're guaranteed a response within 24 hours
- Download helpful tips and software to help you get the most out of your computer
- Contact authors of your favorite PHCP books through electronic mail
- Present your own book ideas
- Keep up to date on all the latest books available from each of PHCP's exciting imprints

JOIN NOW AND GET A FREE COMPUSERVE STARTER KIT!

To receive your free CompuServe Introductory Membership, call toll-free, **1-800-848-8199** and ask for representative **#597**. The Starter Kit Includes:

- Personal ID number and password
- $15 credit on the system
- Subscription to CompuServe Magazine

HERE'S HOW TO PLUG INTO PHCP:

Once on the CompuServe System, type any of these phrases to access the PHCP Forum:

GO PHCP	**GO BRADY**
GO QUEBOOKS	**GO HAYDEN**
GO SAMS	**GO QUESOFT**
GO NEWRIDERS	**GO PARAMOUNTINTER**
GO ALPHA	

Once you're on the CompuServe Information Service, be sure to take advantage of all of CompuServe's resources. CompuServe is home to more than 1,700 products and services—plus it has over 1.5 million members worldwide. You'll find valuable online reference materials, travel and investor services, electronic mail, weather updates, leisure-time games and hassle-free shopping (no jam-packed parking lots or crowded stores).

Seek out the hundreds of other forums that populate CompuServe. Covering diverse topics such as pet care, rock music, cooking, and political issues, you're sure to find others with the sames concerns as you—and expand your knowledge at the same time.

Complete Computer Coverage

Que's 1994 Computer Hardware Buyer's Guide

Que Development Group

This absolute must-have guide packed with comparisons, recommendations, and tips for asking all the right questions familiarizes the reader with terms they will need to know. This book offers a complete analysis of both hardware and software products, and it's loaded with charts and tables of product comparisons.

IBM-compatibles, Apple, & Macintosh

$16.95 USA

1-56529-281-2, 480 pp., 8 x 10

Que's Computer User's Dictionary, 4th Edition

Bryan Pfaffenberger

This compact, practical reference contains hundreds of definitions, explanations, examples, and illustrations on topics from programming to desktop publishing. You can master the "language" of computers and learn how to make your personal computer more efficient and more powerful. Filled with tips and cautions, *Que's Computer User's Dictionary* is the perfect resource for anyone who uses a computer.

IBM, Macintosh, Apple, & Programming

$12.95 USA

1-56529-604-4, 650 pp., 4³/₄ x 8

Only Que gives you the most comprehensive programming guides!

DOS Programmer's Reference, 3rd Edition
Through DOS 5.0

$29.95 USA
0-88022-790-7, 1,000 pp., 7³/₈ x 9¹/₈

Borland C++ 3.1Programmer's Reference2nd Edition
Latest Versions of Borland C++ and Turbo C++

$29.95 USA
1-56529-082-8, 900 pp., 7³/₈ x 9¹/₈

FoxPro 2.5 Programmer's Reference
Version 2.5

$35.00 USA
1-56529-210-3, 1,258 pp., 7³/₈ x 9¹/₈

Paradox 4 Developer's Guide
Latest Version

$44.95 USA
0-88022-705-2, 800 pp., 7³/₈ x 9¹/₈

Using Visual Basic 3
Version 3

$34.95 USA
0-88022-763-x, 650 pp., 7³/₈ x 9¹/₈

 To Order, Call: (800) 428-5331 OR (317) 581-3500